Using Microsoft Works

Ron Mansfield

Que™ Corporation
Carmel, Indiana

Using Microsoft® Works.

Library of Congress Catalog No.: 87-060814
ISBN 0-88022-296-4

91 90 89 88 8 7 6 5 4 3

Interpretation of the printing code: the rightmost double-digit number is the year of the book's printing; the rightmost single-digit number, the number of the book's printing. For example, a printing code of 87-1 shows that the first printing of the book occurred in 1987.

Using Microsoft Works is based on Microsoft Works Versions 1.0 and 1.1.

Dedication

To my best friend and wonderful wife

Nancy

Product Director
David Paul Ewing

Acquisitions Editor
Pegg Kennedy

Editors
Jeannine Freudenberger, M.A.
Pamela Fullerton
Betty White

Technical Editor
Terry Rector

Book Design and Production
Dan Armstrong
Jennifer Matthews
Joe Ramon
Dennis Sheehan
Peter Tocco

Composed in Garamond and Que Digital
by Que Corporation

Cover designed by
Listenberger Design Associates

About the Author

Ron Mansfield

Ron Mansfield is president of Mansfield and Associates, a California-based consulting firm that helps businesses select, install, and learn how to use microcomputer sytems. Mansfield and Associates also prepares technical documentation. Ron writes monthly computer columns and feature articles for a number of national magazines. He also is the author of the *1987 Computer Buying Guide*.

Trademark Acknowledgments

Que Corporation has made every effort to supply trademark information about company names, products, and services mentioned in this book. Trademarks indicated below were derived from various sources. Que Corporation cannot attest to the accuracy of this information.

Apple, Apple II, Apple Font/DA Mover Utility, AppleTalk, ImageWriter, LaserWriter, MacDraw, MacPaint, MacTerminal, and MacWrite are registered trademarks and AppleNet, AppleShare, Macintosh, MultiFinder, and Switcher are trademarks of Apple Computer, Inc.

Art ala Mac is a trademark of Springboard Software, Inc.

ClickArt is a registered trademark of T/Maker Company.

CompuServe is a registered trademark of CompuServe Incorporated and H&R Block, Inc.

DIALOG is a registered trademark of Dialog Information Services, Inc.

Easy3D is a registered trademark of Enabling Technologies, Inc.

Fluent Fonts is a trademark of CasadyWare Inc.

FONTagenix and LASERgenix are trademarks of Devonian International Software Co.

FullPaint is a trademark of Ann Arbor Softworks, Inc.

GLUE and SuperGlue are trademarks of Solutions, Inc.

Graphic Accents is a trademark of Kensington Microware.

Hayes Smartcom II is a registered trademark of Hayes Microcomputer Products, Inc.

Housebuilder is a trademark of Alternative Enterprises.

IBM is a registered trademark of International Business Machines Corporation.

LaserServe is a trademark of Infosphere, Inc.

Mac3D is a registered trademark of Challenger Software Corp.

Mac-Art Library is a trademark of CompuCraft.

MacAtlas is a trademark of MicroMaps.

MacPerspective is a trademark of B. Knick Drafting.

McPic! is a trademark of Magnum Software.

Microsoft, MS-DOS, and Multiplan are registered trademarks of Microsoft Corporation.

Omnis is a registered trademark of Blyth Holding Ltd.

PageMaker is a registered trademark of Aldus Corporation.

Radio Shack is a registered trademark of Radio Shack.

SuperLaserSpool is a trademark of Super Mac Software, a Division of Scientific Micro Systems, Inc.

SuperPaint is a trademark of Silicon Beach Software, Inc.

The Source is a service mark of Source Telecomputing Corporation, a subsidiary of the Reader's Digest Association, Inc.

Telenet is a registered trademark of GTE Telenet Communications Corporation.

Tempo is a trademark of Affinity Microsystems, Ltd.

ThunderScan is a registered trademark of Thunderware®, Inc.

TOPS is a registered trademark of Centram Systems West, Inc.

Tymnet is a registered trademark of Tymnet, Inc.

WorksPlus Spell is a trademark of Lundeen & Associates.

Table of Contents

Part I Learning About and Starting Works

Part II Word Processing

2 Entering, Editing, Saving, and Printing Text

Part III Spreadsheets and Graphs

Part IV Databases

8 Databases

9 Database Reports 359

Part V Communications

Part VI Integrating Applications

11 Tying It All Together 431

12 Using Works with Other Products 465

Preface

I distrust long book prefaces and seldom read them, so I'll keep this one brief. After all, if information is both introductory and important, it should be in the first chapter, right?

As a working member of the computer press, I review software. In addition, the people in my consulting firm deal with both new and experienced computer users daily. We help people select, install, and learn how to use business micros. Obviously, we use computers in our own business, too. As a result of my experience with computers over the past ten years, I have seen many ugly software programs and frustrated users, so I'm skeptical of new software.

In my experience, software is rarely as good as the brochures describe it. I brought that skepticism to my first tour of the Microsoft® Works program. How could something that costs so little do so much? Where's the catch? Anything this big with so many features must have bugs. Where are they?

The Works program was already a best-seller when I started writing *Using Microsoft Works*. After living with the evolving manuscript night and day for about eight months, I know why Works is a best-seller. Works is good software. It "feels" right. Programs work as you'd expect. You don't need to master a host of new skills for each different function. Once you've learned how to insert and delete text, for example, you can use those same skills when creating database and spreadsheet entries. You are not distracted by dozens of illogical rules, so you are free to concentrate on the creative aspects of computing. The program has enough power to help you effectively communicate, file, and compute, but it does not have scores of "Hey lookit" features that do little but complicate and confuse you.

Yes, I did find compromises and even a few bugs—they're described in this book—but my skepticism is gone. You can easily work around the few problems and shortcomings, and many of them have been eliminated altogether in the recently released Works Version 1.1. The power and easy use of the Works program far outweigh its shortcomings. It is a reliable "Swiss army knife" for business and family computing. Works may be the only application software you'll ever need for your Mac, with the exception of a paint program.

Many of the examples you will see in this book are from actual business and home applications. I wrote *Using Microsoft Works* while using Works Versions 1.0 and 1.1 on a Macintosh Plus, a Macintosh SE, and a Macintosh II.

It's a rare piece of software that stays on my computer after a project is completed. Works is a "keeper." Once you've read this book and used Works for a while, I think you'll agree.

Acknowledgments

Thanks to everyone at Microsoft, including Sarah Charf, Coby Kressy, Doug Rosencrans, Mike Slade, and, of course, Jody Snodgrass.

The folks at Apple were a big help, too—they alway are. Hats off to Doedy Hunter, Ric Jones, and Keri Walker.

Speaking of vendors, thanks are due to everyone at Affinity Microsystems, Inc.; Centram; The Laser Connection; Solutions, Inc.; and SuperMac Software.

Finally, because a book without a publisher is like a ship without a crew, you wouldn't be reading any of this without the sung and unsung heroes at Que, including—but by no means limited to—Pegg Kennedy, Dave Ewing, Betty White, Jeannine Freudenberger, Pamela Fullerton, Tim Stanley, and Bill Nolan.

Conventions Used in This Book

The conventions used in this book have been established to help you learn to use the program quickly and easily. As much as possible, the conventions correspond with those used in the Microsoft Works documentation.

Commands and options are written with initial capital letters, as they appear on the screen: New command, Create New Document command. Menus are written with initial capitals, as seen on-screen: File menu.

Dialog boxes are called by the name that appears in the dialog box. If no name is given, the box is given the name of the command used to display that box. The Open command displays the Open dialog box; the Page Setup command displays the Page Setup dialog box (although you don't see that on-screen).

Buttons in dialog boxes are written as they appear on-screen: Yes button, Open button, OK button.

File names are also written with initial capitals: the Resume Works file, for instance. Keys use all lowercase italic: *backspace, control, return, options*. Key combinations are hyphenated: *command*-O.

At times you are instructed to type a word or press a specific key. Only what you are told to type or press is written in boldface. For example, type **1**, press **command-A**, and choose Open from the menu.

Part I

LEARNING ABOUT AND STARTING WORKS

Introduction

Overview of Microsoft Works

This introduction, which contains examples of projects that have been created with Works, is designed to give you an overall understanding of Works' features. After you finish reading the introduction, you probably will know whether Works is the program for you. And you will understand why Works is a best-selling software package.

How To Use This Book

If Works is one of the first Macintosh™ programs you've used, read this Introduction and Chapter 1 carefully. You really do need to know how to cut and paste, click and drag, open and close, and so forth. Never mind what the computer salesperson told you: you need to know things about your Macintosh before you can get the most out of it. You'll learn the basics quickly, and in no time you'll be off to the chapters about word processing, spreadsheets, graphs, databases, and communications.

When you get to Chapter 2, you'll probably want to continue to take things in the order they appear in the book. Feel free, however, to skip a chapter that doesn't interest you. For example, the communications section (Chapter 10) is of little value unless you have a modem or want to hard-wire your computer to another for data exchange.

Some skills you learn in one section apply to others, however. For instance, you learn things about spreadsheets that will be helpful when you are using Works list window for databases; and "Database Reports" won't make sense until you learn about databases.

If you're an experienced Macintosh user and want to get started in a hurry, you may want to read this introduction quickly to get an overview of Works and then move on to Chapter 1 for help with installation of the software.

Chapters 2, 5, 7, 8, and 9 end with Quick Start sections. By working through the Quick Starts, you have the opportunity to create sample documents and practice the important features presented in the chapters. If you decide to do a Quick Start section before reading the rest of the chapter, remember that Quick Starts cover only the basics. At some future time, you'll probably want to read—or at least skim—the remainder of the chapter to pick up the more advanced features and shortcuts that make Works so powerful.

What Is Microsoft Works?

Microsoft Works is designed specifically for the Apple® Macintosh. Works takes full advantage of the Mac's power and uses much of the standard Macintosh interface. If you've used programs like MacWrite® or MacPaint®, you'll feel right at home with Works.

A key difference between the Works package and stand-alone software programs you may have used is that Works performs four major functions: word processing, database management, spreadsheet and graph creation, and data communications. You can perform all these functions with stand-alone programs, such as MacWrite, Excel, Omnis 3, and MacTerminal®; but Works ties the functions together, or *integrates* them. For example, you can create spreadsheets with related pie graphs and include them in a word-processing document. You then can personalize the resulting document for selected people on your computerized mailing list and send the document to them either on paper or through your modem.

Although the chapters of this book contain detailed descriptions of Works' capabilities, a few moments spent exploring Works as a whole may be helpful. As you'll see from the examples, Works is designed to make you look good on paper. The program also can help you organize information and exchange information with others.

Word Processor

Works includes a full-featured, word-processing module that enables you to create simple correspondence or complex multipage reports and proposals. For example, you can create a letterhead for your correspondence (see fig. I.1), business cards (see fig. I.2), and memos (see fig. I.3). A typical word-processing screen appears in figure I.4.

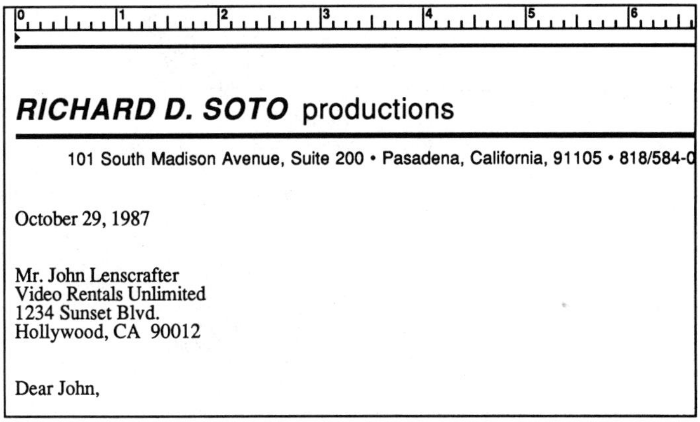

RICHARD D. SOTO productions

101 South Madison Avenue, Suite 200 • Pasadena, California, 91105 • 818/584-0

October 29, 1987

Mr. John Lenscrafter
Video Rentals Unlimited
1234 Sunset Blvd.
Hollywood, CA 90012

Dear John,

Fig. I.1

Letterhead created in Works.

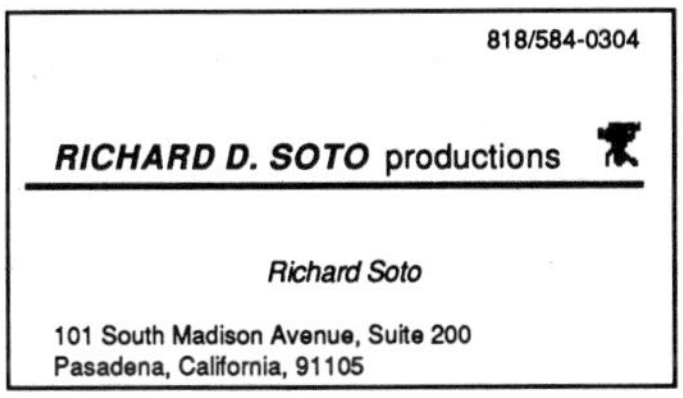

818/584-0304

RICHARD D. SOTO productions

Richard Soto

101 South Madison Avenue, Suite 200
Pasadena, California, 91105

Fig. I.2

Sample business card done in Works.

Fig. I.3

Sample memo from Works.

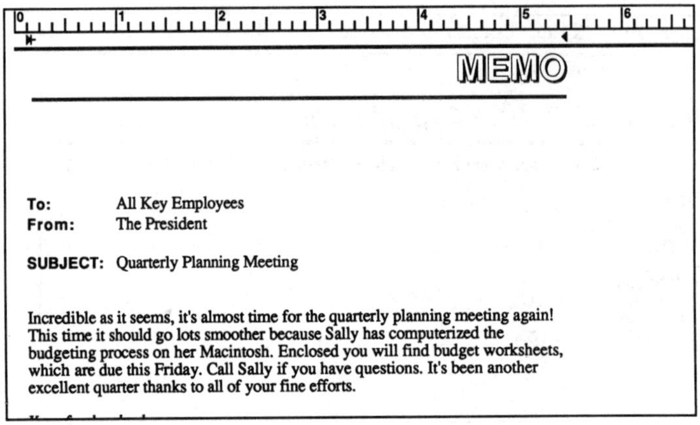

MEMO

To: All Key Employees
From: The President

SUBJECT: Quarterly Planning Meeting

Incredible as it seems, it's almost time for the quarterly planning meeting again! This time it should go lots smoother because Sally has computerized the budgeting process on her Macintosh. Enclosed you will find budget worksheets, which are due this Friday. Call Sally if you have questions. It's been another excellent quarter thanks to all of your fine efforts.

Fig. I.4

Typical Works word-processing window.

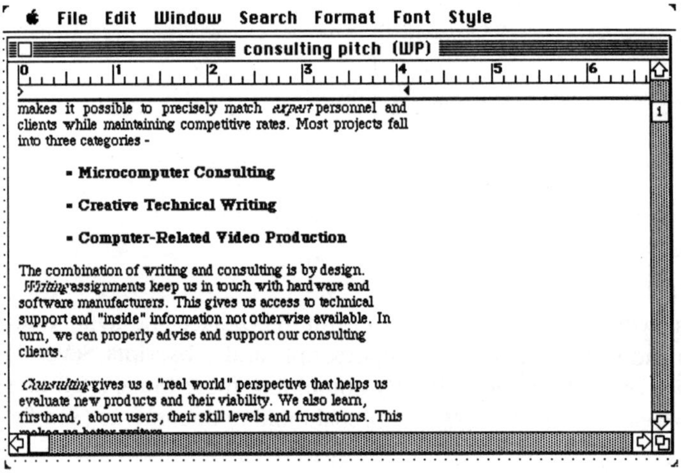

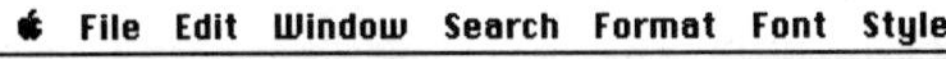

consulting pitch (WP)

makes it possible to precisely match *expert* personnel and clients while maintaining competitive rates. Most projects fall into three categories -

- **Microcomputer Consulting**

- **Creative Technical Writing**

- **Computer-Related Video Production**

The combination of writing and consulting is by design. *Writing* assignments keep us in touch with hardware and software manufacturers. This gives us access to technical support and "inside" information not otherwise available. In turn, we can properly advise and support our consulting clients.

Consulting gives us a "real world" perspective that helps us evaluate new products and their viability. We also learn, firsthand, about users, their skill levels and frustrations. This

Works provides the features you'd expect from any good Macintosh word-processing program. It has an insert mode (the default) and a strikeover mode. With the Clipboard and Scrapbook, you can move, duplicate, and store text temporarily. You can place up to 14 documents in windows simultaneously (memory permitting), and you can easily move text from one window to another. A search-and-replace feature is provided, as well as a way to move quickly to any page in your document.

To be edited, documents must fit in memory. The maximum size of a document varies, but you can expect to be able to work with 60 to 80 pages at a time on a 512K Macintosh and up to about 240 pages on a standard Macintosh Plus or 1MB Macintosh SE. (For more information, see Chapter 1.) Documents too large to fit in memory can be broken into smaller "chapters" and combined after they have been printed.

Rulers and page setup facilities enable you to control the format of word-processing documents (see fig. I.5). You can define margins, page size, indentation, standard tabs, decimal tabs, line spacing, justification, and more for individual paragraphs or for a whole document. Up to one line of header information can be added to each page, along with one line of footer information. Headers and footers can include automatic date and time insertions and automatic page numbers. You also can define title pages, control starting page numbers, and force page breaks (which appear on the screen).

Unlike many other word-processing programs, Works has a drawing feature that quickly creates lines, boxes, and circles in a variety of line widths (see fig. I.6). You also can import graphics (through the Clipboard and Scrapbook) from MacPaint-compatible programs and from the Works Chart feature, which is described in Chapter 7, "Graphs."

Works comes with five fonts: Boston, Athens, Monaco, Geneva, and Chicago. By using the Apple Font/DA Mover Utility®, you can use other fonts as well. In each font, you can print in boldface and italic, underline words and sentences, and use superscripts and subscripts. Several point sizes are offered for each font. By combining these fonts, attributes, and point sizes, you can create professional-looking documents (see fig. I.7).

Works also provides a merge capability. You can combine database information with word-processing documents to create personalized form letters, forms, mailing labels, and more.

The Works word-processing module is *not* a replacement for desktop publishing software. The module does not easily support multiple columns per page. The current version of Works does not take full advantage

Fig. I.5

A Works document with complex formats.

July 14, 1987

Fees and Terms

RATES: Projects are usually quoted on an hourly-rate basis. In some cases, we will be able to quote a fixed-fee or not-to-exceed price. Hourly rates range from a high of $95.00 per-hour for "senior" time to a low of $25.00 per-hour for less technical tasks.

TRAVEL TIME: Normally, *one-half* of all travel time is billable. Usually, this means that you will be billed for our time spent getting from our office or another client's office to your location. We make every effort to schedule other meetings in your proximity to minimize travel costs. Feel free to ask about travel time and ways to save money through alternative scheduling when you request services. If you are more than *fifty* miles from Long Beach, you will be charged for travel time in *both directions.*

MILEAGE: There is no automobile *mileage* charge for travel within fifty miles of Long Beach. Automobile travel outside of the fifty mile radius is billed at $ 0.25 per-mile for all miles travelled. Air travel will be used instead when cost-effective, with your prior authorization.

SUPPLIES: Hourly rates *include* normal office items like incidental photocopies, diskettes, local phone charges, etc. You will not be billed for these items.

MISC. COSTS: Major copying jobs, long distance phone charges, etc. *will* be billed at our actual cost. You will be asked to authorize such expenses if we think they might exceed $50.00 in any one month.

PAYMENT TERMS: Bills are mailed monthly, and are *due when received.* Normally we will require a small deposit from new clients.

DISCOUNTS: It is possible to obtain discounted rates by pre-paying. Ask about these discounts if you are interested.

For More Information

For additional information, please contact:

Ferd Berfel
Berfel and Associates,
1101 N. Madison Ave., suite 2200
Long Beach, CA 91101

Phone 714/555-0684.

Thank you for your interest in Berfel and Associates.

Mouse Replacement
Part Price List

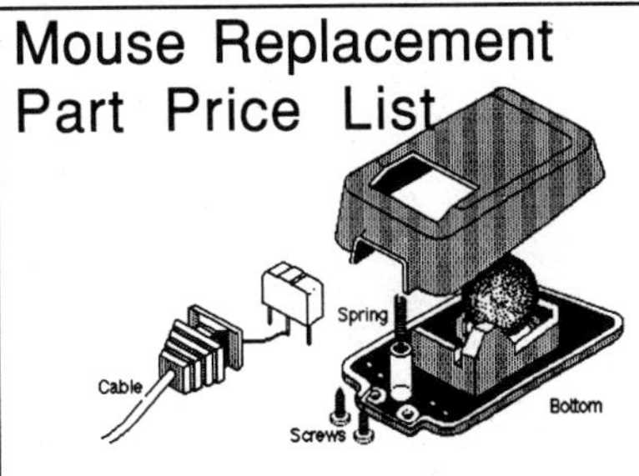

Item	Single	2-5	6+
Cable	$ 4.50	$4.00	$3.95
Spring	.50	.25	.20
Screw set	.50	.25	.20
Switch	1.95	1.75	1.85
Bottom	1.95	1.75	1.85
Top	4.50	4.00	3.95

Contact factory for other parts

Fig. I.6

Using graphics imported from paint programs to improve the appearance of documents.

Anybody's Guess
123 Side Street
Harm's Way PA 56433

No Postage
Necessary if
Mailed in USA

BUSINESS REPLY MAIL PERMIT 12345

Name
Address
City State Zip

Fig. I.7

When used with a laser printer, Works can often produce near-typeset quality.

of the refined character-spacing features of newer Macintosh hardware, and no built-in automatic hyphenation feature is provided. Text and graphics from Works, however, can be exported to desktop publishers, such as Aldus' PageMaker® so that you can use these advanced formatting features.

Works has no spelling checker, although many companies sell spelling checkers that are compatible with Works. As mentioned, Works does handle superscripts and subscripts, but it does not produce automatic footnotes (students, take note.)

Database Manager

Databases are simply organized collections of information. A phone book is a database. So are recipe collections, inventory records, mailing lists, and shoe boxes filled with receipts for tax-deductible expenses.

Works can help you organize many kinds of information into useful computerized databases. Once you've designed a Works database, you can enter information and quickly organize it for easy retrieval and report generation. Think of a Works database as the electronic equivalent of a box of file cards. Each record in your computerized database is the computer's equivalent of a card in a file box or a rotary card file. The number of records permitted in a Works database varies from 2,000 to 6,000 or more, based on factors described in Chapter 8. The individual entries in a record are placed in *fields*. A field contains one item of data—the ZIP code, for instance. Basic database concepts are explored in more detail at the beginning of Chapter 8.

When you first set up a database, Works helps you create a form on the computer screen containing blanks and labels for each blank (see fig. I.8). If you design your form properly, Works tries (to some extent) to prevent you from entering the wrong type of information in a blank.

After designing a database and entering the information (an employee list, for example), you can use Works to get organized. For example, you can scroll through all employee records, sorted by hire date; you can display a list of managers making more than $20,000 a year; and so on.

You also can have calculated fields in a Works database. For example, the EARNINGS 12 MO field in figure I.8 is computed by Works based on the RATE entry and some assumptions about hours worked. When-

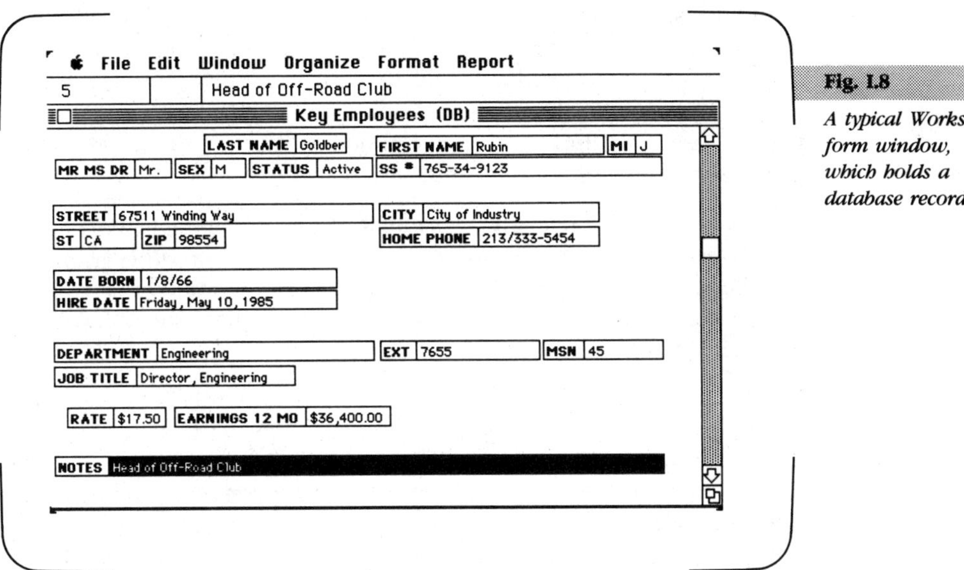

Fig. I.8

A typical Works form window, which holds a database record.

ever the employee's rate changes for a record, Works automatically computes a new annual earnings amount and places that number in the EARNINGS 12 MO field.

Works can display single records or lists of records. The list window, illustrated in figure I.9, makes viewing multiple records easy.

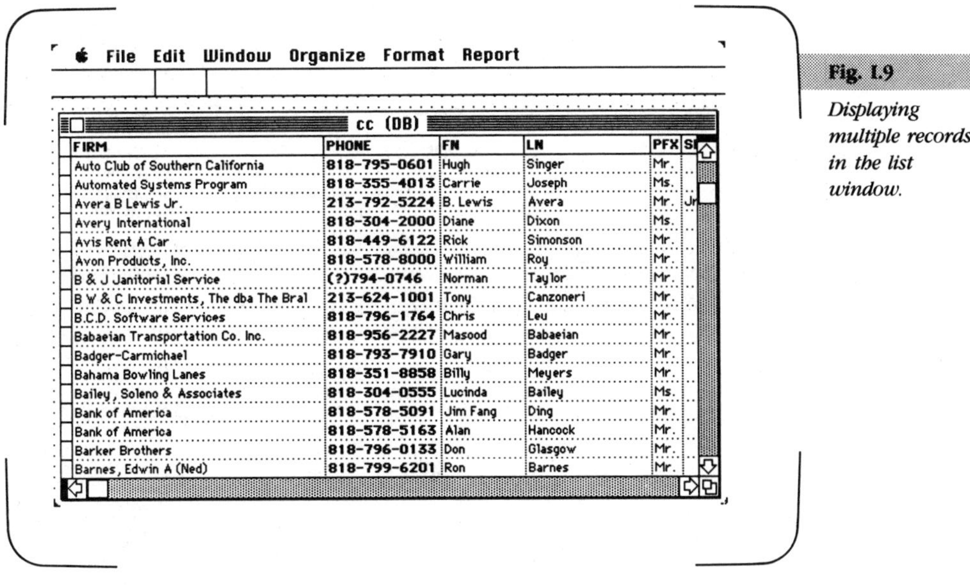

Fig. I.9

Displaying multiple records in the list window.

With Works, you can easily redesign databases (something that isn't even possible with some competitive products). You can quickly add, delete, resize, or move fields; and inserting, deleting, and editing records is just as easy. Because Works sticks closely to most Macintosh conventions, you can use the Clipboard and Scrapbook as you would expect in the process of maintaining your databases.

Search and selection features (similar to those found in the word-processing module) enable you to find quickly records containing specific items. The search criteria can be simple (find Smith) or complex (find Smith or Smyth or Smythe with a salary greater than $20,000 but less than $40,000).

In addition to displaying the results of these requests, you can print them. You can control page layout, report titles, type styles, headers, footers, margins, and so on (see fig. I.10). And you can pass selected data to a spreadsheet for further analysis and graphing. Using database information with the word-processing module, you can create personalized documents such as form letters or mailing labels (see fig. I.11).

Fig. I.10

Printed report from a Works database.

KEY EMPLOYEE PAY BY DEPARTMENT July 14, 1987

LAST NAME	FIRST NAME	JOB TITLE	DEPARTMENT	EARNINGS 12 M
Baxter	James	Director Personnel	Personnel	$41,600.00
Baxter	Tammy	Assistant Director	Personnel	$37,440.00
				$79,040.00
Berfel	Ferd	Pull Tab Inspector	Test Lab	$18,470.40
				$18,470.40
Flusher	Johnathon	Cleaning Associate	Maintenance	$10,400.00
				$10,400.00
Goldberg	Rubin	Director, Engineering	Engineering	$36,400.00
				$36,400.00
Goldsmith	Ray	President	Corporate	$83,200.00
Goldsmith	Nancy Rae	Assistant to the President	Corporate	$81,120.00
				$164,320.00
Makit	Willie	Production Supervisor	Production	$26,520.00
				$26,520.00
Mi	Sue	New Product Development	Engineering	$58,240.00
				$58,240.00
West	George	Sales	Sales	$62,400.00
Quickcloser	John	Inside Sales	Sales	$52,000.00
So	Mi	Inside Sales	Sales	$52,000.00
				$166,400.00
Winston	Doc	Sr. Sardine Eye Closer	Production	$16,536.00
				$16,536.00
				$576,326.40

Mansfield and Associates
101 South Madison Avenue
Suite 200
Pasadena, CA 91101

A & D Building Maintenance Co.
Mr. Andre Chambers
2120 E. Foothill Blvd. #1
Pasadena CA 91107

First Class Mail

Fig. I.11

Sample mailing labels created from a Works database.

The Works database feature is nonrelational, or "flat"; that is, you can work with only one database at a time. You can't have one database containing names, addresses, and client numbers and another database containing only client numbers and expenses, and use both databases to create invoices containing the names and addresses from the first database and the expense details from the second. For most applications, this restriction can be overcome with some careful planning.

The Works database has uses at home, too. For example, figure I.12 shows how you might use Works to aid and help control your shopping. The Works database module can meet the needs of most business and home computer users, particularly when combined with Works' other modules.

QTY	DESCRIPTION	NOTES	CATEGORY	AISLE
	Baby Wipes		BABY	7
	Bacon - Thin Sliced		MEAT	2
	Bagels	Water	BAKERY	2
3	Bananas		PRODUCE	3
	Bandaids		HEALTH CARE	6
	Bath Soap - Bars, Irish Spring	3-Pack	SOAP	5
	Batteries 9 Volt		HARDWARE	7
	Batteries, AA		HARDWARE	7
	BBQ Sauce		GARNISH	7
	Beef Stew Dry Mix Kits		DRY GOODS	3
	Beef, Stewing		MEAT	3
3	Beer		LIQUOR	10
	Bologna - Turkey		MEAT	4
	Bread - Non-Deli		BAKERY	1
1	Bread - Wheat		BAKERY	1
	Bread Crums, Seasoned		SPICE	1
	Bread, Egg, Sliced		BAKERY	1
	Brillo Pads		SOAP	5

Fig. I.12

Home application of a Works database.

Spreadsheets with Graphs

Spreadsheets consist of cells containing labels, numbers, and equations (see fig. I.13). (If you've ever made a budget, you know what a simple spreadsheet is.) The equations are used to perform the computations on the numbers in the columns and rows and so produce statistical reports. For the calculations, a wide range of math, statistical, trigonometric, logarithmic, and financial functions is provided. (Chapter 6 describes these functions in detail.)

Fig. I.13

A typical Works spreadsheet window.

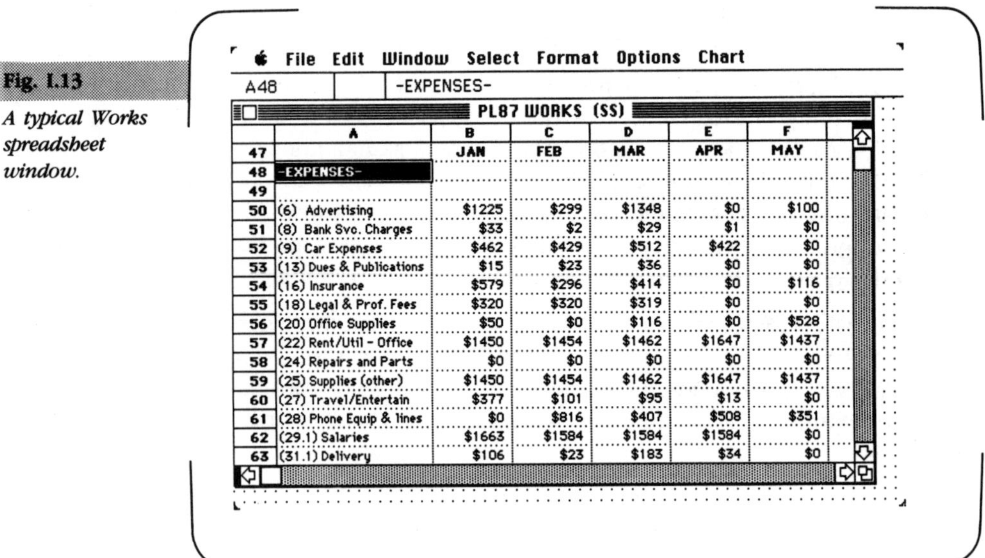

	A	B	C	D	E	F
47		JAN	FEB	MAR	APR	MAY
48	-EXPENSES-					
49						
50	(6) Advertising	$1225	$299	$1348	$0	$100
51	(8) Bank Svc. Charges	$33	$2	$29	$1	$0
52	(9) Car Expenses	$462	$429	$512	$422	$0
53	(13) Dues & Publications	$15	$23	$36	$0	$0
54	(16) Insurance	$579	$296	$414	$0	$116
55	(18) Legal & Prof. Fees	$320	$320	$319	$0	$0
56	(20) Office Supplies	$50	$0	$116	$0	$528
57	(22) Rent/Util - Office	$1450	$1454	$1462	$1647	$1437
58	(24) Repairs and Parts	$0	$0	$0	$0	$0
59	(25) Supplies (other)	$1450	$1454	$1462	$1647	$1437
60	(27) Travel/Entertain	$377	$101	$95	$13	$0
61	(28) Phone Equip & lines	$0	$816	$407	$508	$351
62	(29.1) Salaries	$1663	$1584	$1584	$1584	$0
63	(31.1) Delivery	$106	$23	$183	$34	$0

The Works spreadsheet module enables you to set up simple or complex spreadsheets and see the results of changes in your assumptions. Practically anything you can work out with a pencil and a calculator can be placed in a Works spreadsheet. Once you've designed and tested your spreadsheets, you can perform "what if" calculations quickly and accurately. Recalculation can occur automatically or only when requested. To prevent important parts of the spreadsheet from being changed accidentally, you can protect cells.

A 512K Macintosh can hold spreadsheets containing up to about 7,500 cells. Theoretically, Macintosh Plus and other 1MB systems can hold spreadsheets with as many as 22,500 cells. In either case, plenty of room is available for most applications.

You can think of spreadsheets as chess games. In a short time, you can get good enough at chess to have fun and win a game or two with players at your skill level. *Mastering* chess, on the other hand, can take a lifetime. Such is the case with spreadsheets. Even relatively easy-to-use spreadsheet packages like the one in Works have hundreds of features and offer many ways to accomplish similar tasks.

Works enables you to set up professional-looking spreadsheets with a limited but useful variety of type styles and formats. You can display and print numbers and labels in boldface, with or without underscores to add emphasis; center or align cell contents to the left or the right; turn grid lines on or off; display numbers with dollar signs and commas; and define the number of places to the right of the decimal point.

To copy and move things around, you use the Clipboard and Scrapbook. You quickly locate cells and edit them, using features that will be familiar to you if you have used other Works modules. New rows and columns can be inserted easily, and the information in rows or columns can be sorted. Suppose, for example, that you have a list of customers and the amounts they have spent this year. Works helps you quickly rearrange their order of appearance on the spreadsheet, based on their expenditures.

You can print spreadsheets vertically (portrait mode) or horizontally (landscape mode), and you can reduce them to fit your page. You also can display and print the results graphically by using Works Charting feature (see fig. I.14). These graphs, with or without their corresponding spreadsheets, can be pasted into word-processing documents or transferred to other Works users through the data communications module.

Some compatibility exists between Works spreadsheets and others such as Excel and Multiplan® (see Chapter 12 for details). Not all Excel functions are supported, however; for example, Excel has macros that automate certain operations, but Works does not. Considering that the Works spreadsheet is only one part of a fully integrated package, the spreadsheet is surprisingly powerful and feature-packed.

Data Communications Tool

Rounding out Works is a data communications capability that enables you to connect with other computers worlds away. Works, an Apple-compatible modem, and your normal telephone lines are your keys to paid services such as CompuServe®, The Source™, and DIALOG® (see fig. I.15). You also can dial free bulletin boards (BBS) and exchange files of all types with others.

Fig. I.14

The types of graphs that Works can produce.

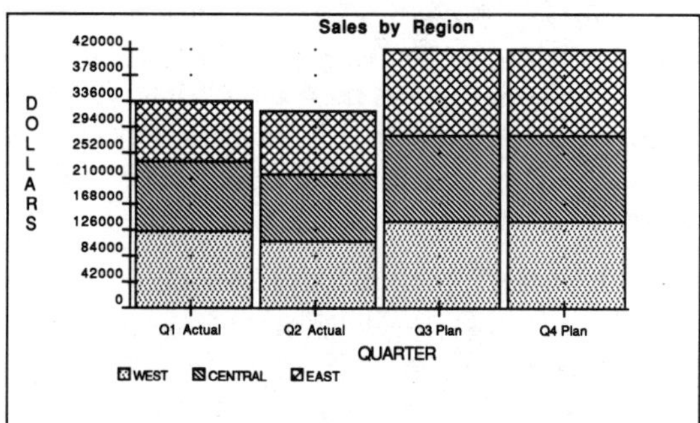

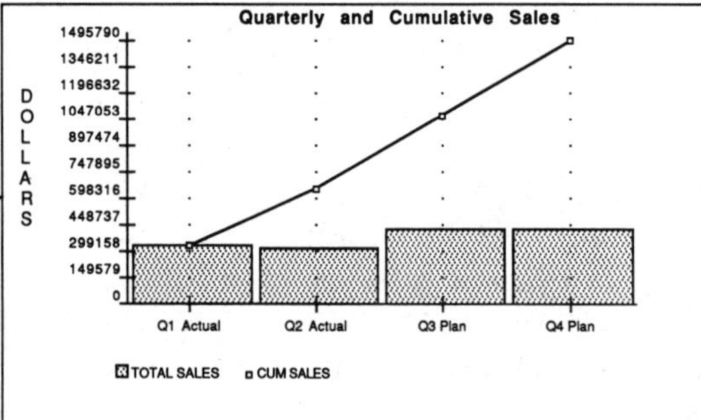

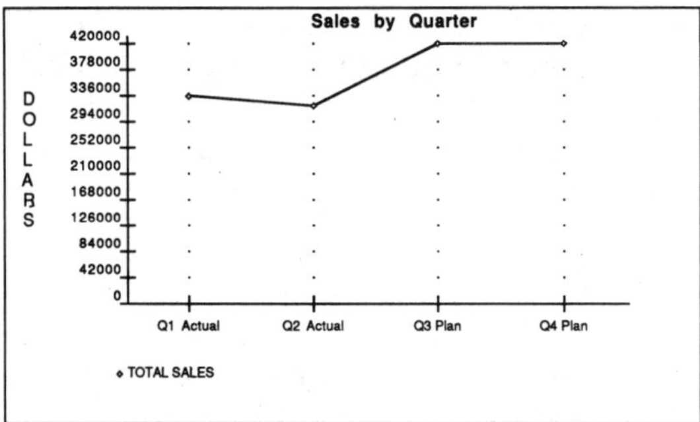

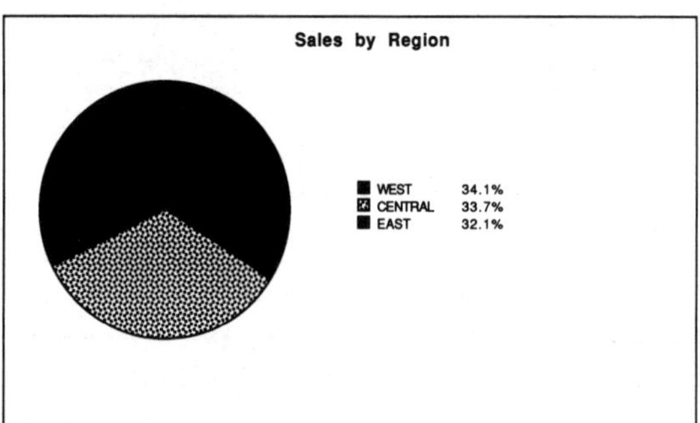

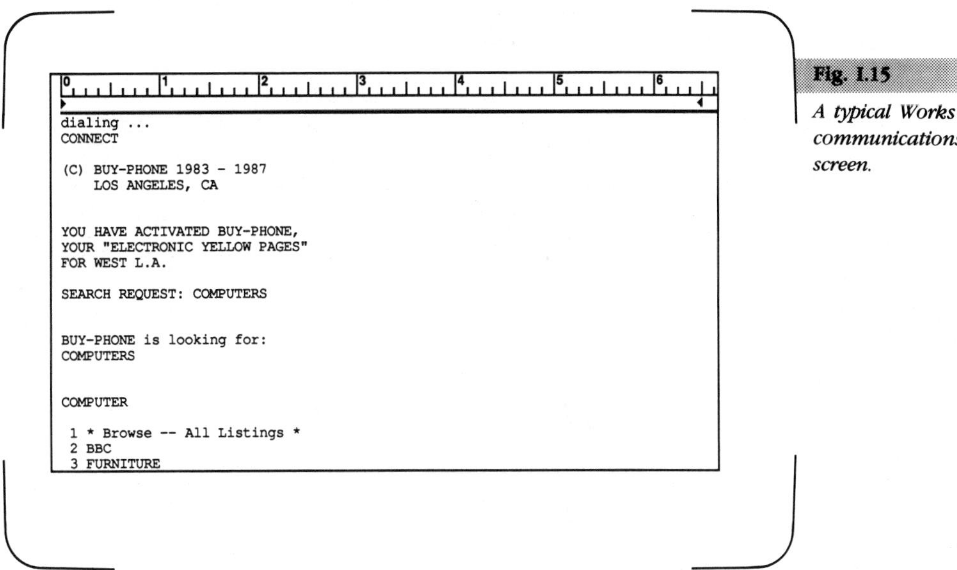

Fig. I.15
A typical Works communications screen.

Works captures incoming data on disk for later review and printing. You also can send files from your disk or converse with another user by using the keyboard. Works supports a wide range of data communications speeds and protocols (communication methods). A simple but effective "phone book" is provided, in which you can store ten phone numbers for quick automatic dialing. The current Works communications module, however, provides no automatic log-on or script feature. Through a modem, Works can answer the phone unattended, and send and receive data in the background while you're doing other things such as working on a word-processing document.

You can use the communications feature without a modem to exchange data with another computer located nearby. This direct-connection capability makes possible the exchange of information with dissimilar computers, such as Apple II®s, IBM® PCs, Radio Shack (Tandy®) portables, and so forth. Chapter 10 shows you how.

Now that you know what Works can do, you are ready to learn how to use the program. You'll be pleasantly surprised at how easy it is.

Target Users

Microsoft Works was designed for both personal and business use. It's an excellent first program for beginners, and many people will find that it's the only program they will ever need for their Macintosh. Running a multimillion-dollar business with Works is possible.

Some "power" users, however, may outgrow Works, particularly if their applications are very demanding. For example, the spreadsheet portion of Works is not as full-featured as Excel, Microsoft's stand-alone spreadsheet. Usually, this limitation won't be a problem unless you need features like macros or functions like date math to compute the number of days between two dates. In many cases, you can work around missing features by using the techniques described in this book or by adding compatible software to your system.

Who Should Use This Book?

Using Microsoft Works is for beginners and pros alike. If you already own Microsoft Works, you will find that this book is a helpful supplement to your Works owner's manual.

This book contains a great deal of information that you won't find in your Microsoft manual or in other books on the subject. For instance, heretofore unpublished warnings about Works bugs are provided, as well as shortcuts and ways to use Works with other programs. This book contains information about Version 1.1, the latest release of Works.

If you're trying to decide whether to purchase Works, this book can help you, too. *Using Microsoft Works* will help you discover Works' strengths and weaknesses and show you how to get the most from one of today's best integrated software packages for the Apple Macintosh.

You'll learn both basic operating skills and advanced techniques. You'll even see how to use other software to add features not found in Works, such as a spelling checker, automatic hyphenation, spreadsheet macros, templates, purchased databases, true desktop-publishing capabilities, and automated computer log-on files.

You'll discover sources of low-cost templates, public-domain utilities, and databases that will make you more productive without having to reinvent the wheel or spend a fortune. Even a list of Macintosh-related electronic bulletin boards is included so that you can try using Works communications feature without running up a big bill with CompuServe or The Source.

How This Book Is Organized

After the overview of Works' capabilities provided in this Introduction, Chapter 1 offers a brief review of Macintosh basics for those of you who need to brush up on concepts such as clicking, dragging, and so on. Chapter 1 also shows you how to make backup copies and configure Works for your system.

The book then moves on to describe the power of Works itself. Chapters 2 through 10 deal with word processing, spreadsheets, graphs, databases, database reporting, and data communications. Each chapter contains at least four elements:

- An overview of concepts and steps
- Illustrations of the concepts at work
- Tips for advanced users, often accompanied by examples
- Information about common beginners' mistakes

Once you've learned as little or as much as you care to about the separate modules, turn to Chapter 11 to learn how to tie everything together. You'll learn how to move graphics into word-processing documents. Also explored is the process of merging name-and-address files with text to create personalized correspondence. You see how and why to move spreadsheet data into a database and back.

Chapter 12 discusses how to augment Microsoft Works by using software packages such as MacPaint, MacDraw®, MultiFinder, GLUE™, Camera, WorksPlus Spell™, Switcher™, PageMaker, and others.

Those of you who have created files using other software such as MacWrite, Excel, and so on, can see how Works imports and exports word-processing documents, spreadsheets, and databases.

The appendixes provide additional resources: lists of free and low-cost electronic bulletin boards and the names and addresses of hardware and software makers.

Finally, this book contains a complete index, designed to help you find whatever you need quickly. The index turns *Using Microsoft Works* into a powerful reference tool after you've used it as a tutorial.

How Works Was Used To Prepare This Book

To produce this book, I used a Macintosh Plus and an Apple 20MB hard disk, along with a PS Jet laser printer from The Laser Connection and an Apple modem. The text of the book was written using Microsoft Works' word-processing features. Obviously, I created the sample spreadsheets, databases, and so on, with Works itself. Because Works allows up to 14 windows to be open simultaneously, I could easily switch back and forth between the examples and the manuscript.

Most illustrations in the book showing computer screens were captured by using the Mac's capability to save screen images as MacPaint (picture) files. When this method was not possible, I used a public-domain program called Camera to capture the screen images (see Chapter 12 for details).

I modified some of the illustrations in the book by using MacPaint and SuperPaint. In some of the word-processing examples, I used special fonts from Educomp to illustrate Works' capability to use something other than its standard font complement.

Works does not include a spelling checker, so I chose WorksPlus Spell to help with that (sizable) task.

Because the publisher needed IBM-compatible (MS-DOS®) text files for final editing and phototypesetting, I exported the text from Works to an IBM Personal Computer AT by using the TOPS® network, which is described in more detail in Chapter 12.

Appendix A contains the names, addresses, and telephone numbers of the companies offering these and other Works-compatible products. Your Apple dealer can help you locate additional products for use with the best-seller Works.

1

Getting Started

The first part of this chapter is geared toward new Mac users and those who need to brush up on the basics. To get the most from your investment in Microsoft Works, you need to know the techniques and terms described here. This information is not meant to replace that provided in your Apple Macintosh manuals, so you may want to reread them as well.

The second part of the chapter focuses on Works itself. You learn the minimum requirements, start-up procedures, and backup techniques. New users should read this material carefully. The importance of making a backup copy of your original Works disk can't be overstated.

If you're an experienced Macintosh user and know how to click, drag, use the *command* key, and so on, you may want to skim or skip the first section and read the installation procedures and "Hints for Experienced Macintosh Users."

Review of Basic Macintosh Techniques

The developers of the Macintosh created a series of simple techniques and standards often referred to as the Macintosh interface. This interface provides standardized ways to do things. For instance, the use of pull-down menus is a part of the interface. So is the mouse and what you do with it—clicking, double-clicking, dragging, and so on.

Apple has provided these tools and rules to software developers like Microsoft. For the most part, Microsoft Works adheres to the Macintosh interface. Therefore, if you've used other Mac programs, many of the techniques described in this section will seem familiar.

At places, however, Works differs from the basic Apple procedures, and the interface does evolve over time. So even if you're an experienced Macintosh user, you'll want at least to skim the paragraphs that follow.

New users should realize that an understanding of the information contained here is critical to understanding Works and most other Macintosh software. This chapter uses examples from Works and gives you a sufficient understanding of the Macintosh interface for successful Works operation. For additional information, consult your Apple manuals and any of the many books on the subject.

Understanding the Macintosh Desktop and Icons

Everything you do takes place on the Macintosh desktop. It's where you keep your documents and tools, such as Microsoft Works. You can arrange things on a Macintosh desktop in much the same way you arrange things on a wooden desk. Figure 1.1 shows what a simple, uncluttered desktop might look like.

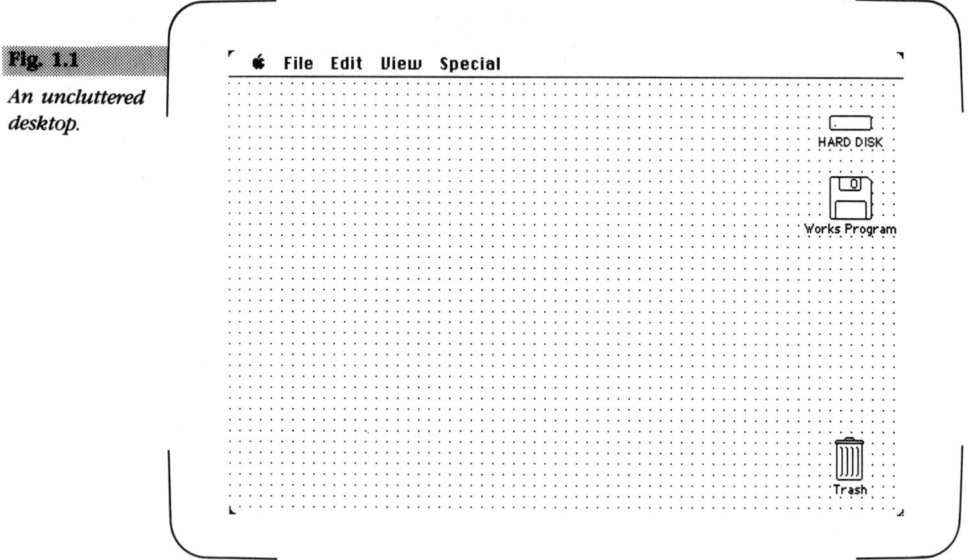

Fig. 1.1
An uncluttered desktop.

The little pictures on the screen are called *icons* (see fig. 1.2). Microsoft Works icons usually represent specific kinds of files such as word-processing documents, specific devices such as printers and disk drives, or specific functions such as the deletion of unwanted files. Frequently, although not always, the icons are self-explanatory. Throughout the book, pictures of the Works (and other Macintosh) icons are presented and explained in context.

Fig. 1.2

The Works icons.

Using the Mouse

You use the mouse in a variety of ways. With the mouse, you tell your programs to perform specific functions, such as select text or data that you want to move, delete, or modify. You can use the mouse to rearrange things (for example, icons) on your desktop. You also can choose from a variety of options by using the mouse with pull-down menus and dialog boxes, which are explained in following sections.

When you move the mouse across a clean, flat surface, a pointer on the screen moves a corresponding distance in the same direction as the mouse. The pointer's size and shape is under software control and changes from time to time (see fig. 1.3). These changes frequently give you additional information about the operation you're performing.

Fig. 1.3

Some of the shapes and sizes of Works pointers.

You use the button on the top of the mouse to select things. The process of pressing and quickly releasing the mouse button is called *clicking*. Clicking usually initiates an action or tells Works what you want to do.

Sometimes Works asks you to ***double-click*** the mouse button, which is the process of pressing and releasing the mouse button twice in rapid succession. Frequently, double-clicking is a shortcut for commonly used procedures or for choices that would otherwise require many more steps.

Double-clicking requires some practice. If you wait too long between clicks, your Macintosh "thinks" that you made two regular clicks rather than one double-click. Your Macintosh manual tells you how to adjust the double-click time delay on your Control Panel.

Moving the mouse while holding down the mouse button is called *dragging*. As you'll see, dragging comes in handy. This technique enables you to move things (icons, for example), highlight text for later editing, or pull down menus from the menu bar. Sometimes, dragging is done while pressing another key. For example, dragging while holding down the *shift* key sometimes produces different results than regular dragging does.

Working with Menus and Menu Shortcuts

Most Macintosh programs, including Works, have a menu bar at the top of the screen (see fig. 1.4). The menu bar lists categories of things that can be done with the program. Frequently, items appear and disappear indicating their availability, based on what you are doing or "where you are" in the program.

Computer menus offer choices. For instance, the Works Font menu shows a list of type styles. You tell the computer what you want by selecting the appropriate choice on the menu.

You usually pull down a menu by dragging the pointer over the menu title in the menu bar. As the pointer passes over the available choices in the menu, Works highlights them. (The letters turn white, and the background becomes black.) Normally, if you release the mouse button on a highlighted choice, Works executes your request. If you change your mind, you can slide the pointer off the choice before releasing the mouse button. The menu then disappears without any choice being activated.

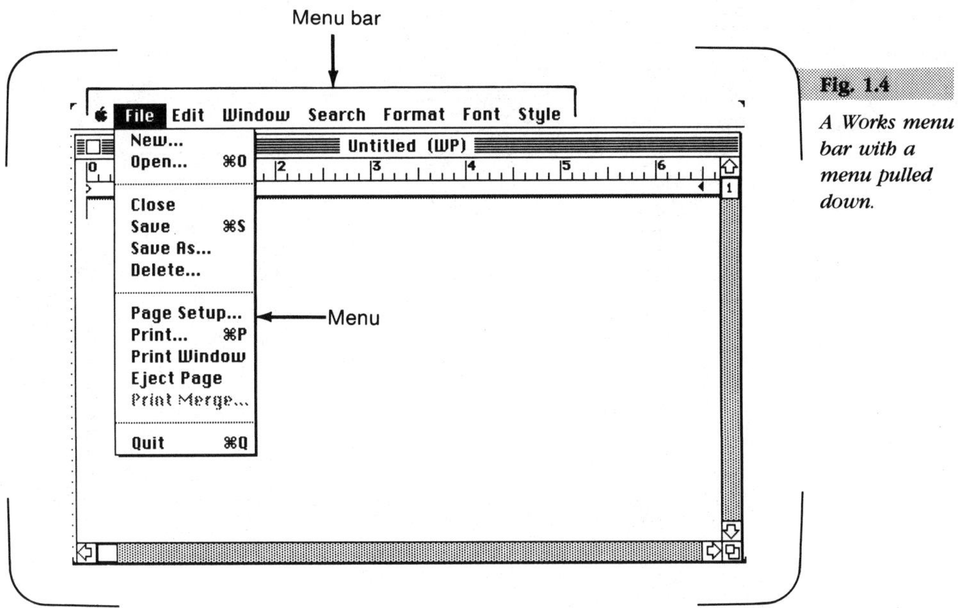

Fig. 1.4

A Works menu bar with a menu pulled down.

Frequently, some of the choices on a menu are dimmed, which indicates that they aren't available at that moment—probably because you need to do something else first (see fig. 1.5). You can evoke some frequently used Works menu items without pulling down the menu. You do so by holding down the *command* key (it looks like a clover leaf) and pressing a letter key. For example, the shortcut for accessing the Print dialog box involves holding down the *command* key and pressing the P. The menu item tells you whether it has a shortcut.

NOTE: Apple has recently renamed the *command* key and restyled it. New Apple manuals refer to the *command* key as the Apple key. New Apple keyboards have two icons on their *command* (or Apple) key caps: the familiar cloverleaf and a new apple that looks like the Apple logo. This book uses the traditional term *command* key.

Menu options followed by three dots have accompanying dialog boxes. That is, Works displays a dialog box if you choose that option; and you then must make more choices. For instance, in figure 1.6, the three dots after Save As indicate that you must answer additional questions about saving before it actually occurs. The dialog box for Save As is also shown in figure 1.6.

Fig. 1.5

The dimmed choices on this typical pull-down menu are unavailable for now.

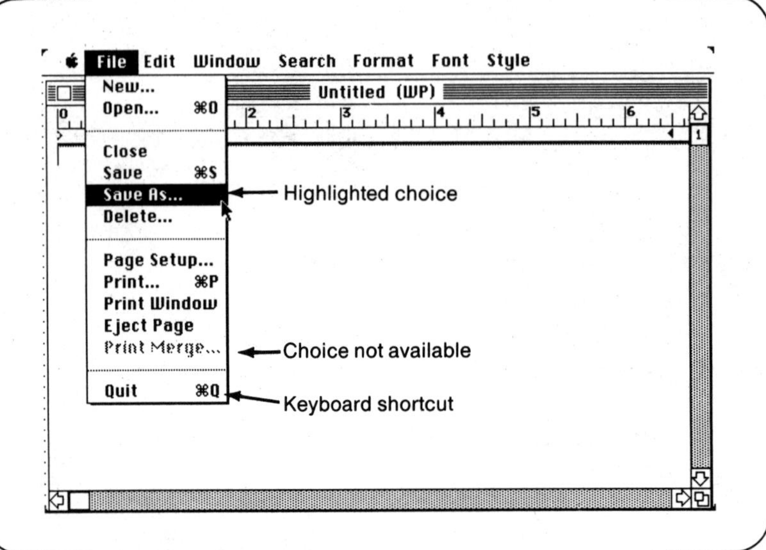

Fig. 1.6

The Save As command and accompanying dialog box.

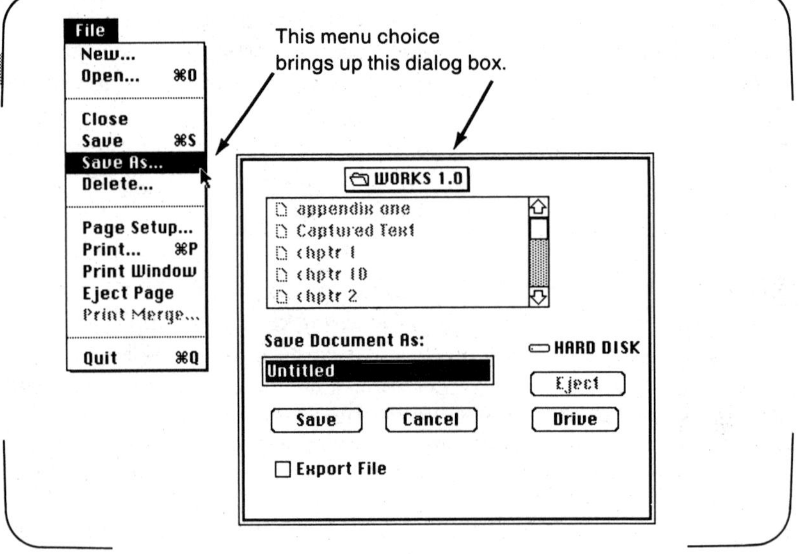

Moving, Activating, and Changing Sizes of Windows

Just like a regular desktop, your Mac's desktop can contain several things at once. For example, at one time you can have open two word-processing documents, a spreadsheet, and a database. Each project occupies its own window. Microsoft Works Version 1.0 supports up to 10 windows; Version 1.1, up to 14 windows (see fig. 1.7).

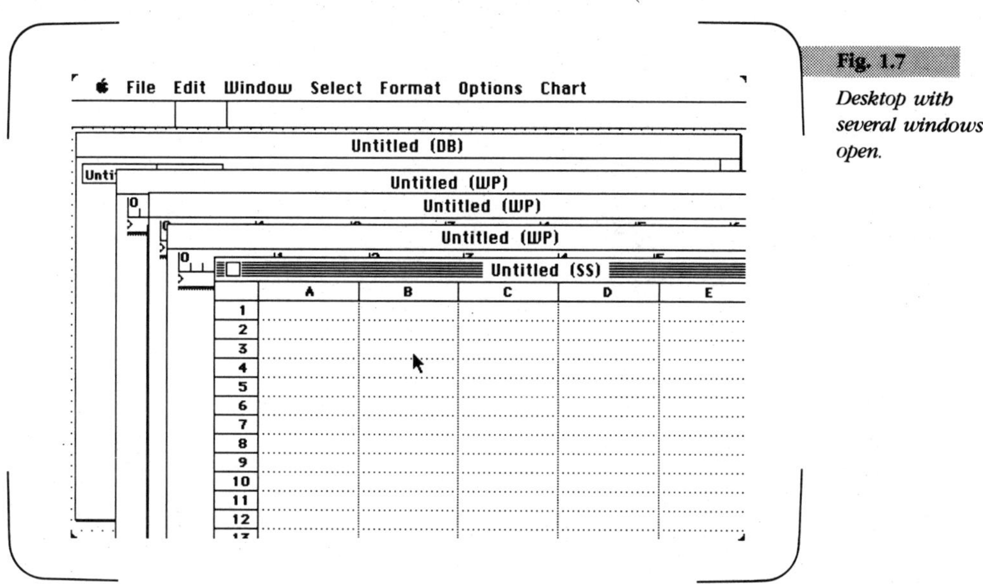

Fig. 1.7

Desktop with several windows open.

Available memory and document size may reduce the actual number of windows you can have open at once. Works notifies you when a problem occurs (see fig. 1.8).

You can move windows by positioning the cursor on the window's title bar and dragging the window. When moving a window, be careful that you don't completely cover another, or else using (or even finding) the covered window will be difficult. Dragging a window too far off the screen can prevent you from using size boxes, scroll bars, and close boxes (see fig. 1.9).

You can have as many as fourteen windows *open* at one time, but you can have only one *active* window at a time. To activate a window, you click on any part of the window or its title bar. The active window

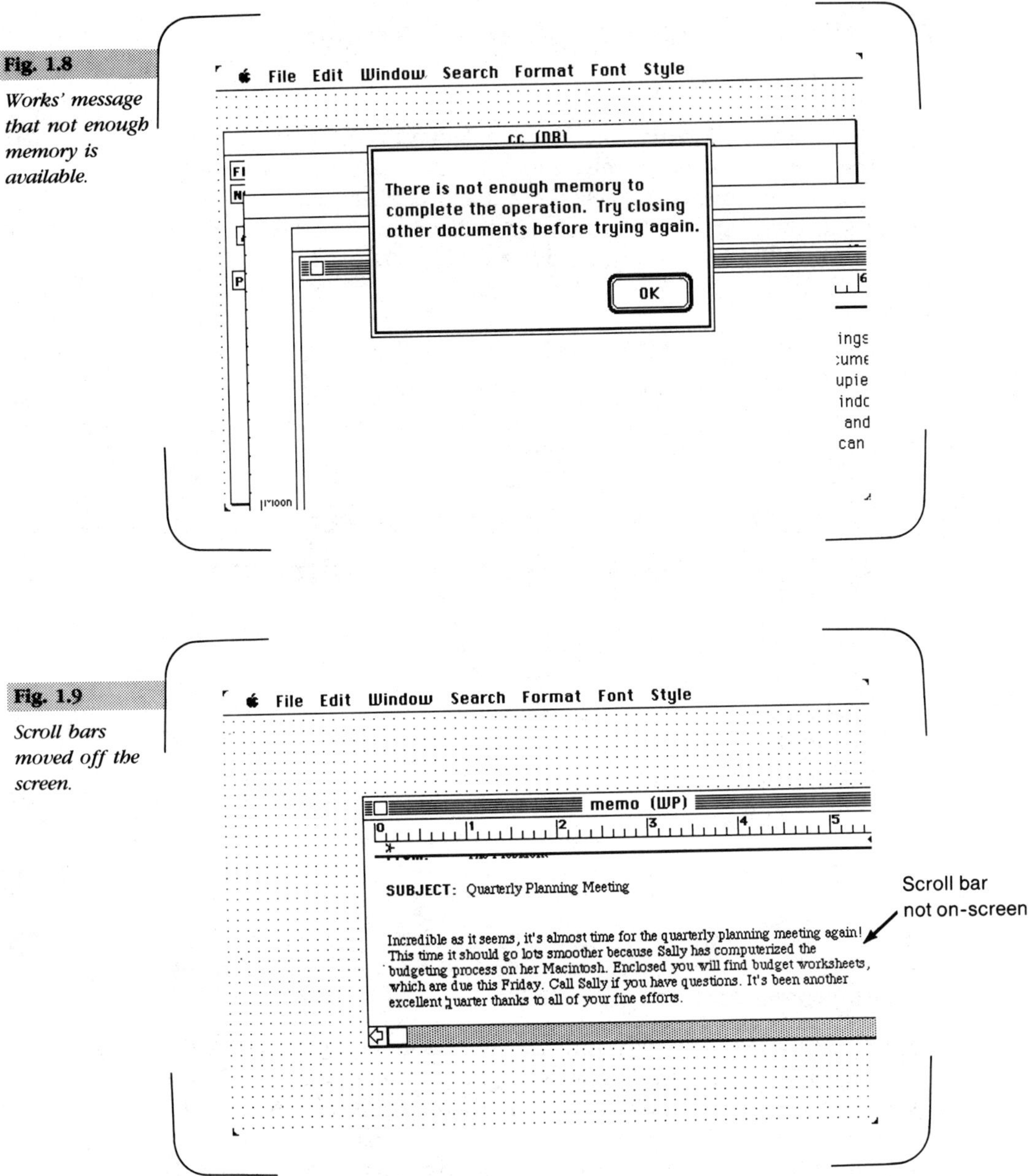
File Edit Window Search Format Font Style
There is not enough memory to complete the operation. Try closing other documents before trying again.
OK
File Edit Window Search Format Font Style
memo (WP)
SUBJECT: Quarterly Planning Meeting
Incredible as it seems, it's almost time for the quarterly planning meeting again! This time it should go lots smoother because Sally has computerized the budgeting process on her Macintosh. Enclosed you will find budget worksheets, which are due this Friday. Call Sally if you have questions. It's been another excellent quarter thanks to all of your fine efforts.
Scroll bar not on-screen

Fig. 1.8 *Works' message that not enough memory is available.*

Fig. 1.9 *Scroll bars moved off the screen.*

"comes forward," and the title bar changes, indicating that that window is now active (see fig. 1.10).

You can resize a window in two ways (see fig. 1.11). One method involves placing the pointer on the size box in the lower right corner of

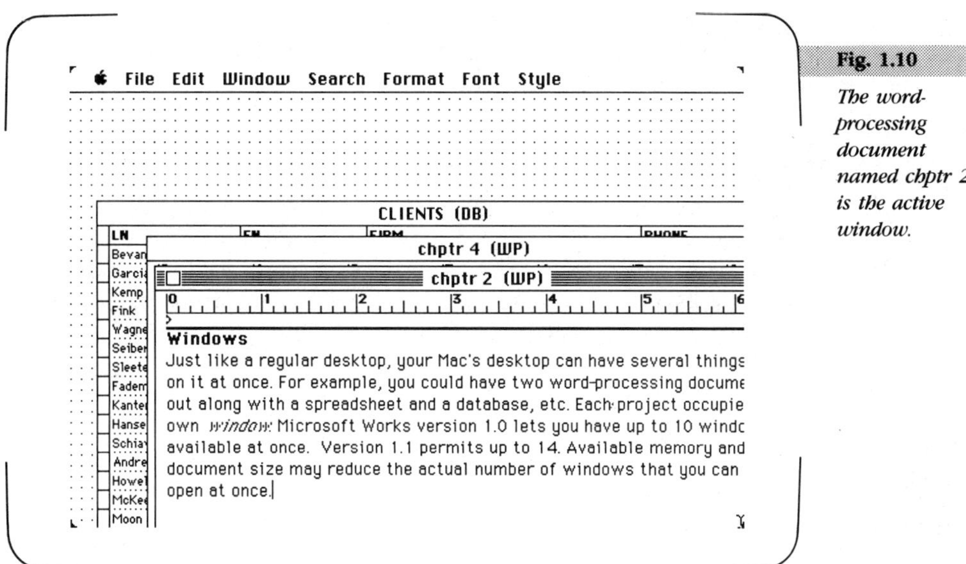

Fig. 1.10

The word-processing document named chptr 2 is the active window.

a window and dragging the window to the size you want. With the other method, you point at the zoom box (if there is one) in the upper right corner of the window and click. The window will fill nearly the entire screen. Click a second time on the zoom box, and the window returns to its former size. Works Version 1.0 doesn't have zoom boxes on all windows; Version 1.1 does.

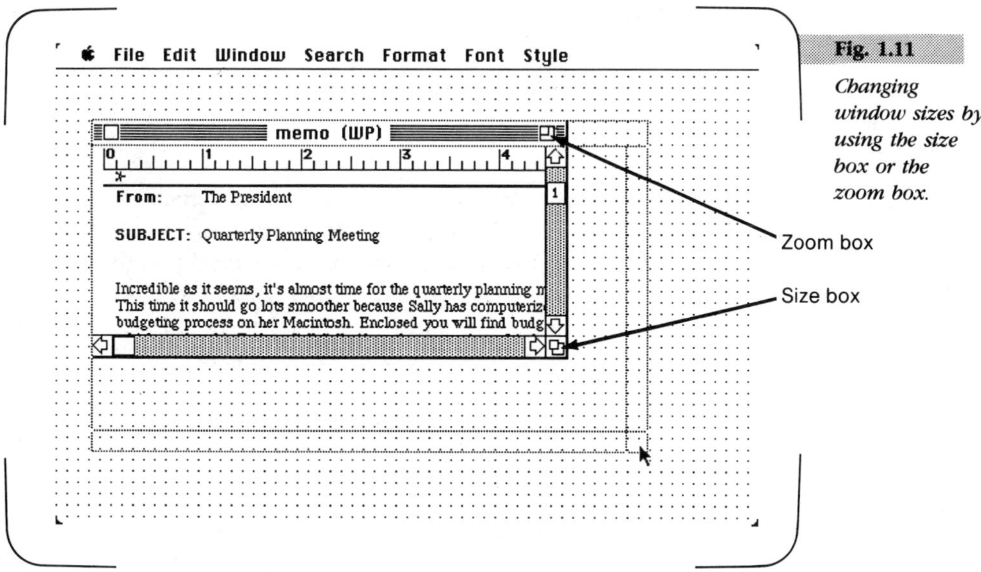

Fig. 1.11

Changing window sizes by using the size box or the zoom box.

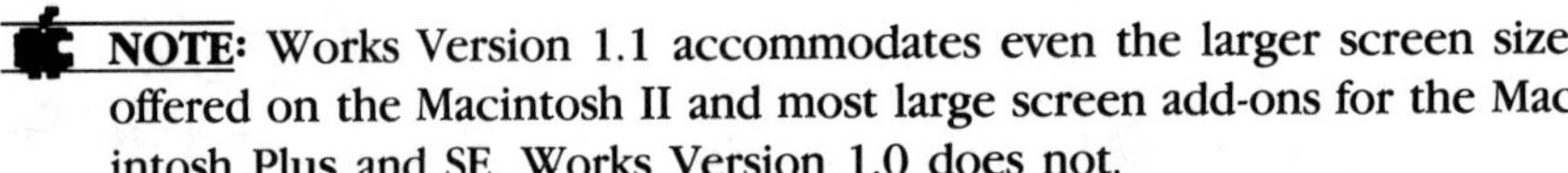

NOTE: Works Version 1.1 accommodates even the larger screen sizes offered on the Macintosh II and most large screen add-ons for the Macintosh Plus and SE. Works Version 1.0 does not.

Using Scroll Bars and Scroll Boxes

Some Macintosh windows, including most Works windows, have horizontal and vertical scroll bars. They're used to display things that won't otherwise fit in a window. Because most word-processing and spreadsheet documents are too big to fit on the screen all at once, scroll bars are quite useful (see fig. 1.12).

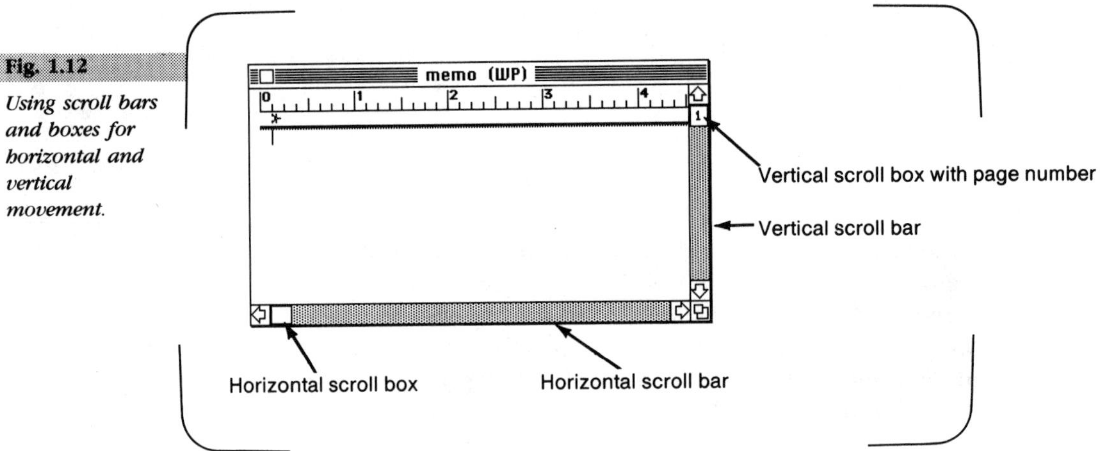

Fig. 1.12

Using scroll bars and boxes for horizontal and vertical movement.

The horizontal scroll bar is located along the bottom of the screen and moves things left or right. The vertical bar is on the right side of the screen and is used to display things that have scrolled off the top or bottom of the screen.

Clicking on the arrows in the scroll bars moves the screen contents in small increments. If you hold down the mouse button while pointing at a scroll arrow, the screen movement continues until you release the mouse button. For faster moves, point at either scroll box and, with the button held down, drag the box in the desired direction. Later chapters explain the finer points of working with the scroll bars.

Using the Boxes and Buttons

From time to time, your Mac needs information from you or requires that you make a decision. In such cases, Works displays a dialog box (see fig. 1.13). You also may hear a beep to get your attention.

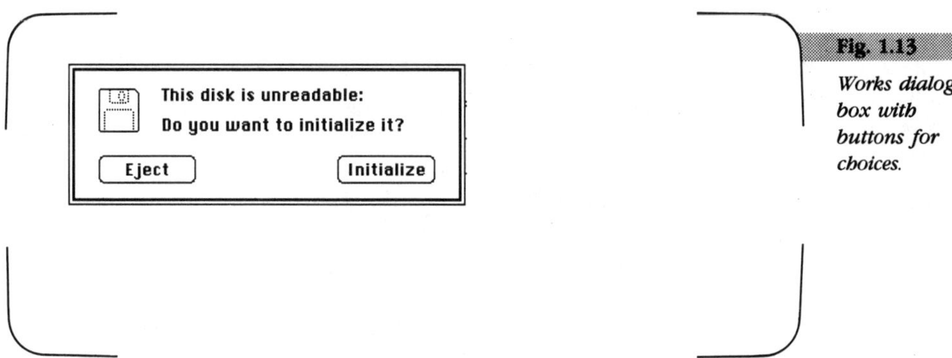

Fig. 1.13

Works dialog box with buttons for choices.

Most dialog boxes contain one or more buttons and check boxes; some also contain edit boxes (see fig. 1.14). Buttons come in two styles: push buttons and radio buttons. Push buttons contain words or command choices. To indicate your choice, you can point and then click anywhere inside the button. Sometimes one of the buttons on the screen is darker than the rest, indicating that the option is the default. Usually, you can press the *return* key to accept the default choice.

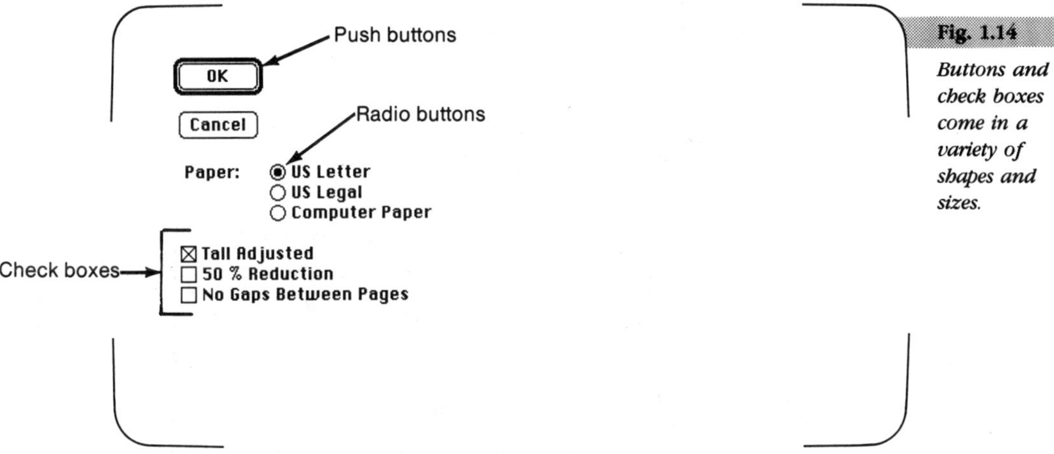

Fig. 1.14

Buttons and check boxes come in a variety of shapes and sizes.

Radio buttons are circles next to choices on the screen. To select or deselect a choice, you point and click in the circle. When a choice is selected, the center of the radio button is black. Check boxes are what you'd expect and are selected and deselected like radio buttons.

Edit boxes appear when you need to enter or modify information through the keyboard (see fig. 1.15). For example, the Works word-processing module presents edit boxes for entering header and footer information. Frequently, Works suggests an entry for you.

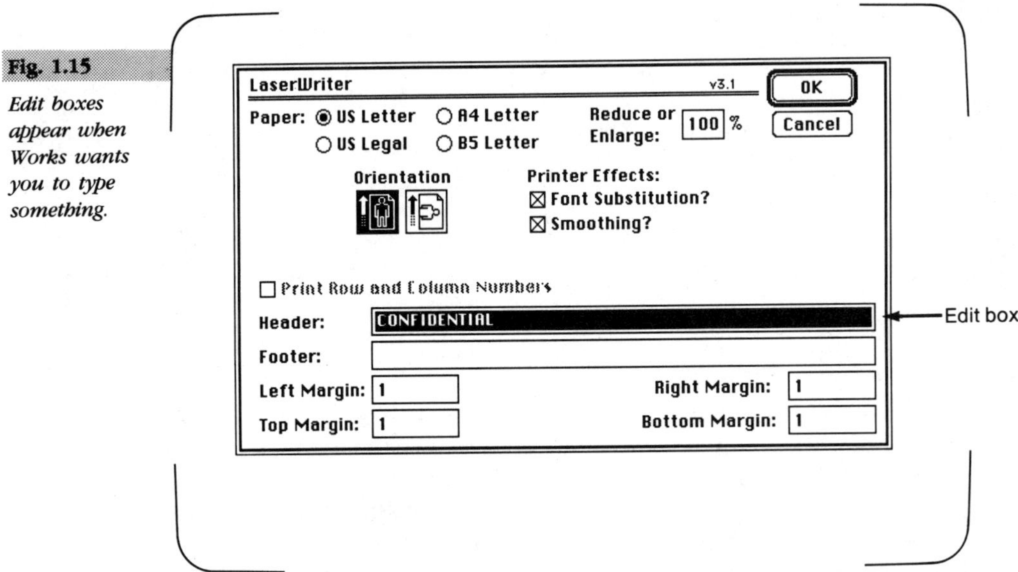

Fig. 1.15

Edit boxes appear when Works wants you to type something.

Alert boxes usually contain warnings or bad news (see fig. 1.16). You need to acknowledge the alert by clicking the OK button; sometimes you can press the *return* key instead.

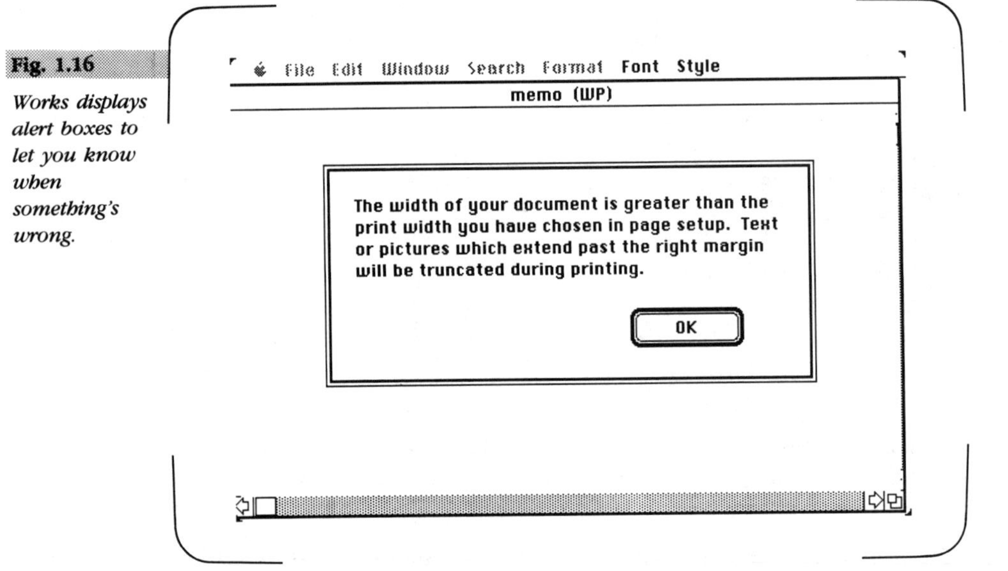

Fig. 1.16

Works displays alert boxes to let you know when something's wrong.

Working with the Clipboard

The Clipboard is found on the Edit menu in Works and most other programs. The Clipboard does what you might expect: It's where you store text and graphics temporarily to facilitate copying and movement (see fig. 1.17). For example, in the Works word-processing module, to move a paragraph from one location in the document to another, you move the paragraph temporarily to the Clipboard first.

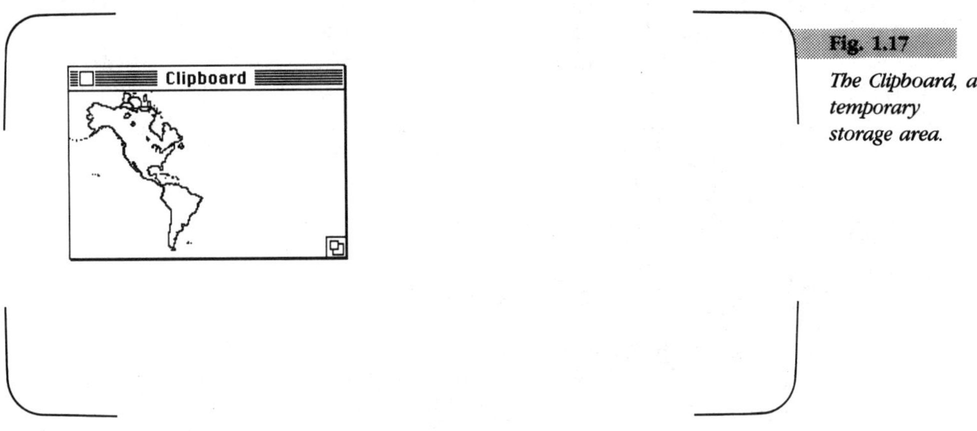

Fig. 1.17

The Clipboard, a temporary storage area.

You can also use the Clipboard to move things from one document or Works module to another. As you'll see, this method is one way to move graphs created in the spreadsheet module into word-processing documents.

Under the right conditions, you can even use the Clipboard to move things to and from other programs. For example, if you have both Microsoft Works and MacPaint loaded with the Apple Switcher or new MultiFinder, you can use the Clipboard to transfer graphics and text quickly from your MacPaint screen to the Works word processor.

Cutting and Copying to and Pasting from the Clipboard

Usually, you highlight (select) whatever interests you (text, a drawing, and so on) and then either cut or copy that item to the Clipboard. Cutting removes whatever you've selected from the screen and places that item on the Clipboard. Copying leaves the original undisturbed and makes a duplicate on the Clipboard.

Once you have something useful on the Clipboard, you can place the pointer wherever you want in the currently active window and paste a copy of the Clipboard's contents wherever the pointer is pointing. The Clipboard's contents remain unchanged after you issue the Paste command, so you can paste additional copies elsewhere.

Remember, though, that the Clipboard is a temporary storage area in your computer's RAM. The Clipboard can hold only one item at a time—and only while the computer is turned on. If a power failure occurs, if you turn off the computer's power, or if you copy something new to the Clipboard, you lose its prior contents (usually forever). This loss can be particularly frustrating if you cut something of value, then accidentally cut away unwanted things (thus altering the Clipboard contents) before pasting "the good stuff." That possibility is why the Macintosh also has a Scrapbook, which is a better place to store things of value. Using the Copy command instead of cutting also reduces the chance of your losing items before you paste them.

Viewing the Clipboard

To see what (if anything) is currently on your Clipboard, select Show Clipboard from the Works Window menu. A window like the one in figure 1.17 appears, containing the Clipboard's contents. When you've finished looking at the Clipboard, either click the close box or click anywhere on another window to deactivate the Clipboard window.

Working with the Scrapbook

Because you need a permanent way to store things that you would like to paste from time to time, the Macintosh offers a disk-based Scrapbook (see fig. 1.18). You can have one Scrapbook on each start-up disk. (Hard disk users usually have only one Scrapbook.) To access the Scrapbook, you pull down the Apple menu.

Adding to and Viewing the Scrapbook

You add to the Scrapbook by pasting from the Clipboard. Copy or cut to the Clipboard as usual; then pull down the Apple menu, open the Scrapbook, and paste from the Clipboard to the Scrapbook. That's all there is to it.

The Scrapbook has scroll bars and arrows, which you can use to "flip" through it. Holding down the mouse button while pointing at an arrow

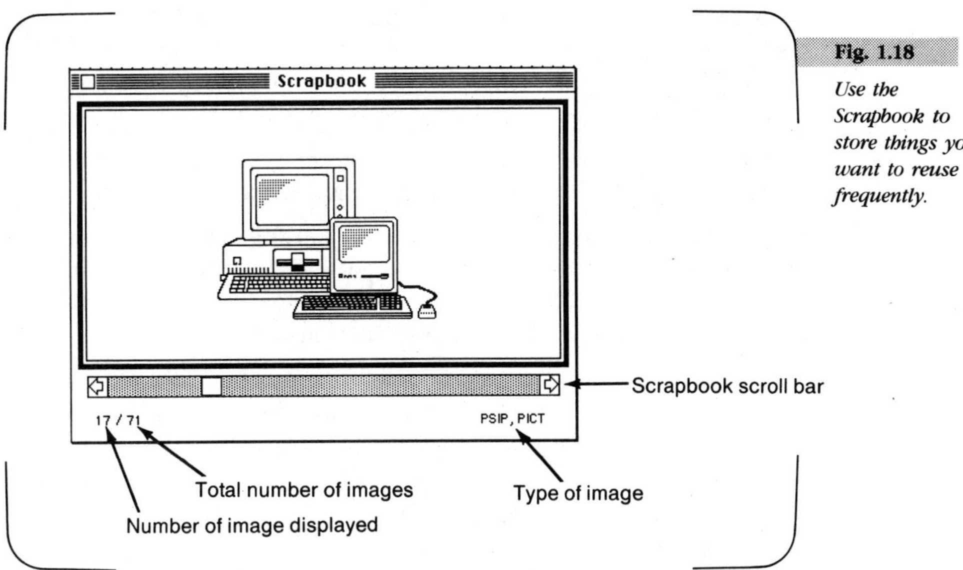

Fig. 1.18

Use the Scrapbook to store things you want to reuse frequently.

scrolls through the Scrapbook. You'll probably need to practice a little before you can click quickly enough to move from image to image without missing any.

Pasting and Removing from the Scrapbook

Once you have something useful in the Scrapbook, you can place the pointer wherever you want on the screen, call up the Scrapbook, find the image you want, and paste it to the Clipboard. Then, close the Scrapbook and paste from the Clipboard. Because the Clipboard's contents remain unchanged after you issue the Paste command, you can paste other copies elsewhere.

To remove an item from the Scrapbook, open the Scrapbook, display the item, and then use the Cut option on the Edit menu. The Clear command works here, too.

Using the Option *and* Command *(or Apple) Keys and Alternative Key Caps*

For the most part, Macintosh keyboards resemble typewriter keyboards. Some important additions, however, are located to the left of the space bar. The first is the *option* key; and the second, to its right, is the *command* (or Apple) key. (The *command* key's legend looks like a cloverleaf.)

You use these two keys either by themselves or together, but always with one of the other regular typewriter keys. For example, in Works, if you hold down the *command* key while pressing **S**, you evoke the Save command without having to use a pull-down menu.

Similarly, you can use the *option* key with other keys. For example, Works uses the *option* key for selected database and communications functions.

The *option* and *command* keys can be held down simultaneously as well. You'll see an example of this keystroke sequence when you learn about Works spreadsheets. The shortcut sections of chapters in this book describe *option-* and *command*-key combinations.

The *command* and *option* keys enable you to access the special characters or alternative key caps on your Mac. Did you know that in most Macintosh fonts, special characters are available besides the usual letters, numbers, and punctuation shown on your Mac's keycaps? You can access these special characters by using the *option* key or the *option* and *shift* keys together. You can see the available alternative keyboards by selecting the Key Caps option on the Apple menu (see fig.1.19). You even can type short entries in the entry bar of the Key Caps window; then you can select that text and copy it to your other Words windows.

Fig. 1.19

An alternative keyboard display.

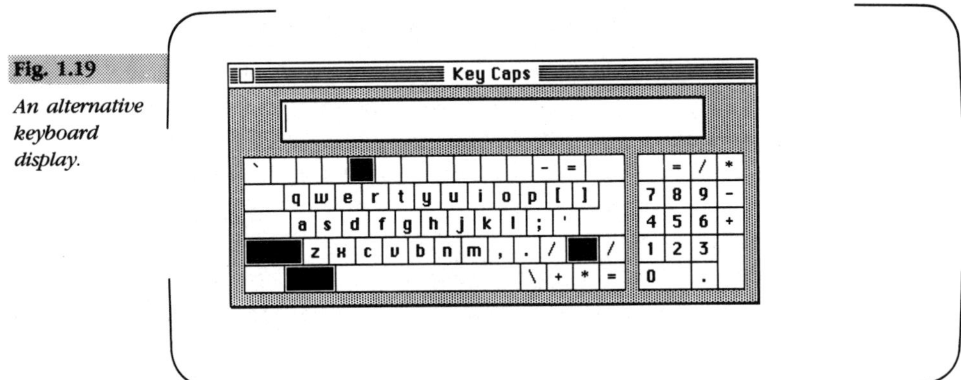

Using the Apple Menu and Desk Accessories

From time to time, this book refers to the Apple menu and desk accessories. All programs that follow the Macintosh convention, including Works, have an Apple menu choice at the left of the menu bar (see fig. 1.20).

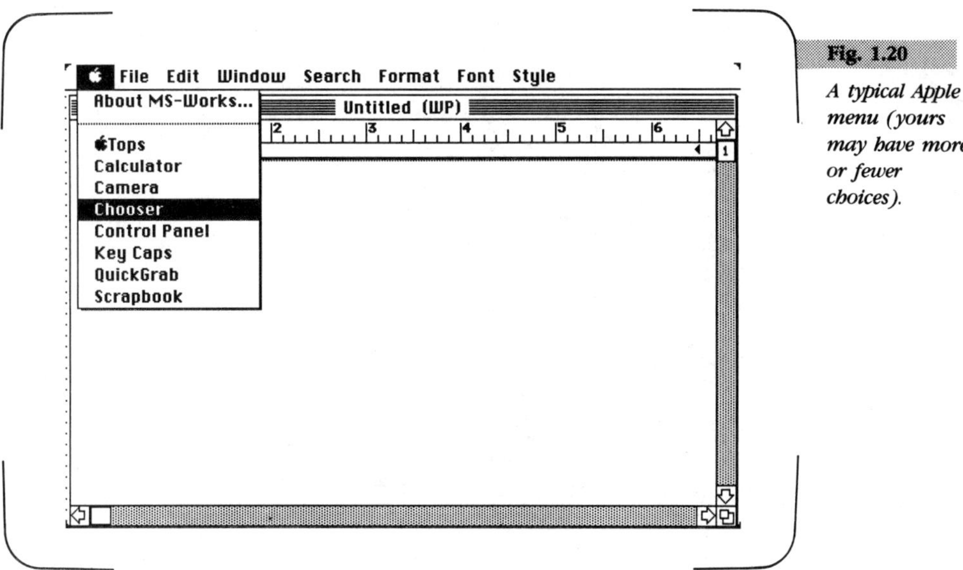

Fig. 1.20

A typical Apple menu (yours may have more or fewer choices).

The contents of this Apple menu vary depending on the program you're using. Decisions that you've made when setting up your Macintosh also affect the contents of the Apple menu. At a minimum, the menu contains five choices, some of which you've already learned about: About MS-Works (or other program being run), Chooser, Control Panel, Key Caps, and Scrapbook.

The About MS-Works Screen

The About MS-Works choice tells you which version of the program you are using and how much memory is available, and provides information about the author and copyrights. If you're using memory-resident software such as WorksPlus Spell, you may see information about the software as well. Version 1.1 and later show your name and company name as you entered them when you first installed the program. Figure 1.21 shows the About MS-Works screen for a beta-test version of Works 1.1.

The Chooser Option

Chooser is another Apple menu choice. The Chooser's dialog box varies based on the software you are using, the hardware you own, and the setup choices you have made previously (see fig. 1.22). With the Chooser dialog box, you decide which printer to use if you have more than one. You also use this box to tell the Macintosh which external devices (such

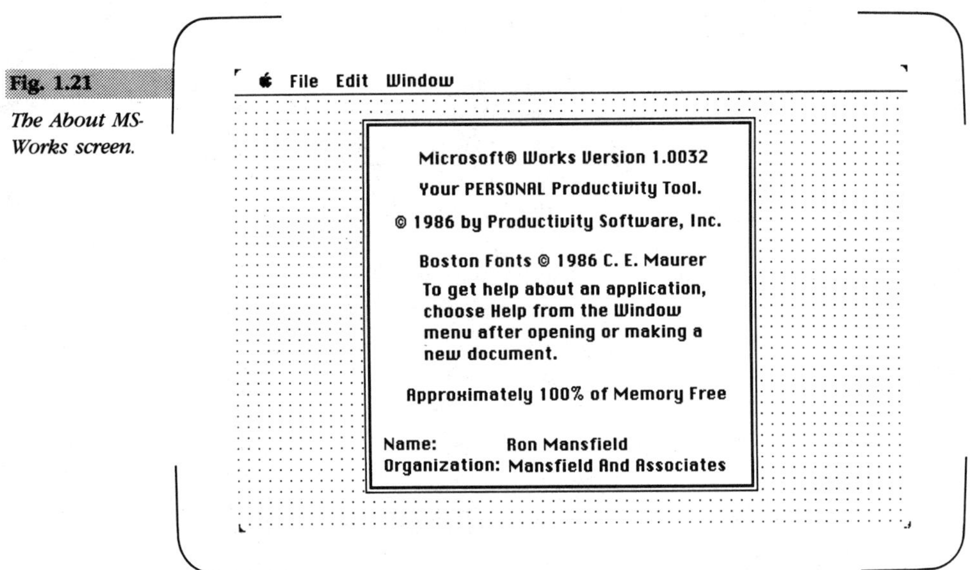

Fig. 1.21

The About MS-Works screen.

as printers, modems, scanners, and networks) are hooked to which connector on the back of your computer. For more information about the Chooser option, see your Macintosh manual.

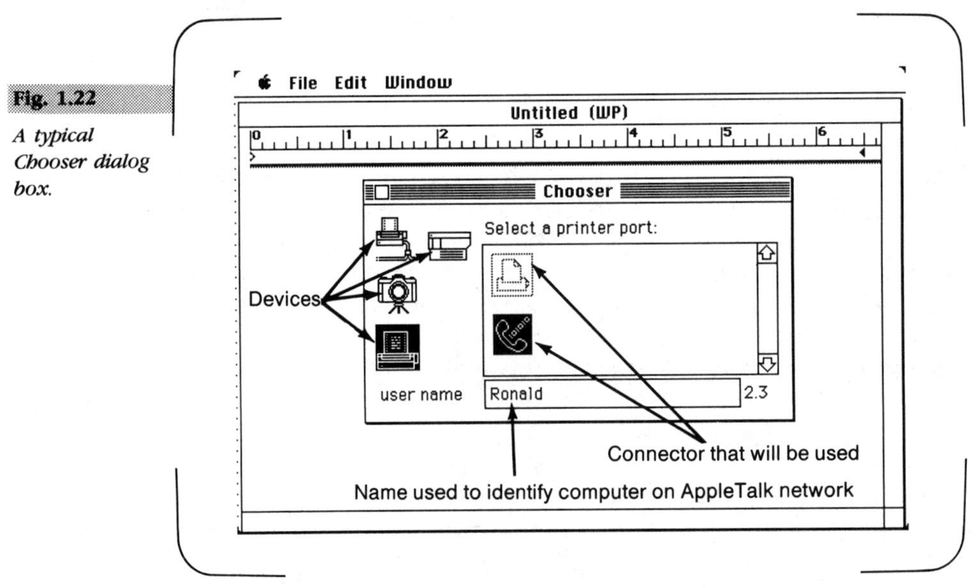

Fig. 1.22

A typical Chooser dialog box.

The Control Panel

You also access the Control Panel from the Apple menu (see fig. 1.23). The Control Panel gives you some control over the "look and feel" of your system; and you use the Control Panel to connect or disconnect your Mac from an AppleTalk® network, if you have one. You can change the pattern on your desktop, adjust the speaker volume, fine-tune keyboard repeat and mouse-clicking times, and so forth. You also use the Control Panel to increase or decrease the amount of RAM used for the cache. See your Macintosh manual for more information about the Control Panel and RAM cache. Your control panel may look quite different from figure 1.23.

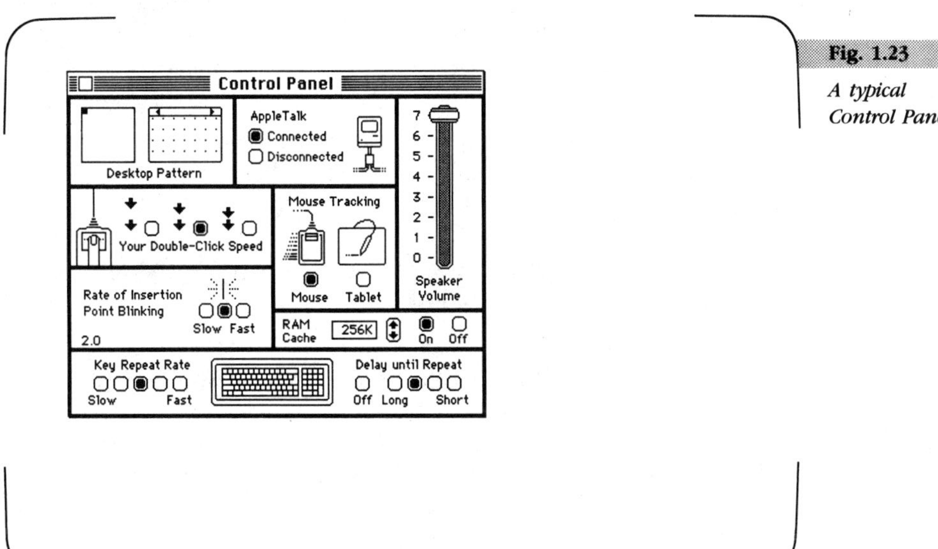

Fig. 1.23 *A typical Control Panel.*

Other Desk Accessories

Most Apple menus have desk accessories installed besides the Chooser and Control Panel. For example, if you plan to adjust your Mac's internal clock and calendar, you need to have the alarm clock desk accessory installed. The calculator is another popular desk accessory. Many useful public domain utilities such as time-delayed screen grabbers and print spoolers are installed as desk accessories.

Minimum Requirements for Running Works

Works was designed to function with all of today's most popular Macintosh configurations. Version 1.1 even supports over-sized display screens and networks like AppleShare™. But what if you have a simple system? What are the minimum requirements for running Works?

Hardware Requirements

Hardware requirements are concerned with memory, disk drives, keyboards, printers, modems, and cables. Some of these elements must be used with Works; others are optional.

Random-access memory (RAM) is the part of the computer where programs and documents reside while you're using them. Microsoft Works Version 1.0 requires a minimum of 512K RAM. If you have a 256K Macintosh, you need to have a reputable Apple dealer add RAM to your computer. Works runs just fine on any Macintosh Plus or Macintosh SE because these computers come from the factory with a minimum of 1MB (about a million bytes) of RAM.

For most applications, 512K of RAM is plenty, but there are exceptions. Obviously, if you plan to use other memory-resident software with Works, you may need more than 512K or even more than 1MB. For example, even with 1MB of RAM, you can't use Works with both the Apple Switcher and SuperPaint. Works does function in 512K of RAM with the Switcher and MacPaint, however, because MacPaint requires less memory than SuperPaint does.

Other elements reduce the amount of RAM available to Works. The number of fonts you've loaded, the size of the RAM cache (set on your Control Panel), and the version of the Finder you use all reduce the amount available for word-processing documents and databases. A 1MB Macintosh with only Works loaded should be capable of handling word-processing documents of 180 to 240 pages. Adding other memory-resident software, large font collections, and big RAM caches considerably reduces the size of the documents you can edit. If you include graphics in your word-processing documents or frequently change fonts, you may find the maximum page count reduced.

Likewise, maximum database capacity is affected by the contents of the records. And spreadsheet size limits vary with the complexity of the spreadsheet.

Disk drives read information to and obtain information from disks. Disks are used to store programs and projects while the computer is turned off. If you've never used a Macintosh disk before, read your Macintosh manuals before continuing or get help from an experienced user.

The copy of Works you purchase in the store is delivered on one 800K, double-sided disk. If you have a Macintosh with only one or two single-sided (400K) drives, you need to order single-sided disks. Your manual contains an order form for this purpose. You need to send the completed form to Microsoft, along with proof of purchase and a completed registration card.

Adding a second, external drive improves performance and makes Works more convenient to use. A hard disk really makes things fly. Hard disks eliminate the need for frequent disk swapping. They also transfer data to and from your Macintosh memory more quickly than minidisks.

Works is compatible with all current Macintosh keyboards. The more advanced keyboards have some keys that aren't on the earlier, simpler keyboards. Usually, Works ignores these new keys. Sometimes the extra keys simply duplicate functions. For instance, the Macintosh Plus keyboard has a period (.) key in the alphabetic portion of the keyboard and a decimal key on the numeric keypad; Works treats them both as the same key.

Works supports the ImageWriter™ and LaserWriter® printer families. If your ImageWriter is equipped with the AppleTalk option, you can connect either standard or wide ImageWriters directly to the computer's printer port or the AppleTalk network. The ImageWriter sheet-feeder family is supported.

LaserWriters are always used with AppleTalk. The LaserWriter (or other compatible laser printer) driver must be installed and available in your Chooser dialog box. For help with laser printer installation, see the instructions that came with your printer or ask a dealer. The Apple LaserWriter offers no custom paper-size option. If using a laser printer, you may want to add or replace fonts; again, consult your printer manual for details.

Using more than one printer is easy. You simply connect them all to your Macintosh and select the printer you want from the Chooser dialog box. Works even shows you the effect of printer choices on page layout.

Hayes and truly Hayes-compatible modems work with the auto-dialing and auto-answer features of Works' data communications module. All Apple modems designed to work with the Macintosh are compatible with Works. Some non-Hayes-compatible modems, and even acoustically coupled modems, can be used to exchange data through Works, although you will give up Works' auto-dialing and, possibly, auto-answer capabilities.

Your cables must be compatible with your computer, printer(s), and modem. You should obtain these cables with the assistance of a knowledgeable dealer; many cables look alike, and the wrong cable can damage your equipment.

Software Requirements

Regardless of whether you are using Microsoft Works, MacWrite, or a game, you also need some software called the *system files.* These programs, which are provided by Apple, must be available to your Macintosh when it runs Microsoft Works.

You should always use the most recently available system files. Works is shipped with a system folder. Among others, the Works system folder contains a system file and a finder file, which you must have. You don't have to copy these files to your hard disk unless they're newer than the versions on your hard disk. Your Macintosh and hard disk manuals contain information on this subject.

You need a printer driver for each printer you intend to use with Works. Works comes with an ImageWriter driver in the system folder. If you plan to use Works with a LaserWriter or other printer, use the instructions that come with the printer to install the driver(s) in your Works system folder(s).

Networks

Works files can be passed around most local area networks, including AppleTalk, AppleShare, and Centram's TOPS. Each network user is required to purchase his or her own copy of Works.

Backup and Start-up Procedures

It's human nature to want to get up and running quickly. Therefore, you may be tempted to skim the following sections or pop the original Works program disk into your computer without making a backup of your original Works disk. I advise you, however, to take a few minutes to read and understand these sections because those few minutes may save you hours of frustration. The investment in time could also keep you from irreparably damaging that original disk.

The original Works program disk includes the following (see fig. 1.24):

- The Works application (program) itself
- A Works help file
- Sample files
- A system folder (Your system file icon may look different.)

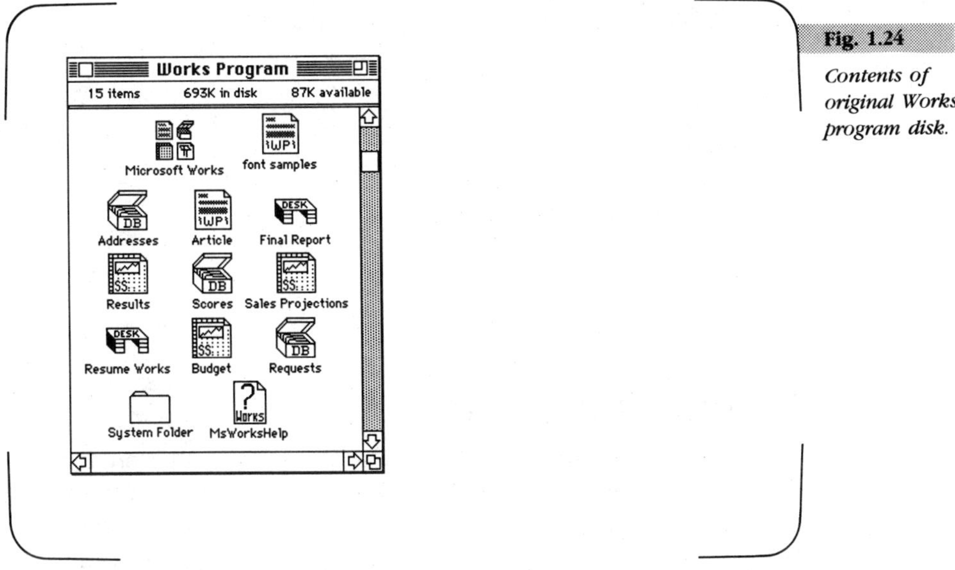

Fig. 1.24

Contents of original Works program disk.

The system folder contains files that the Macintosh needs for operation. You already have similar files on your other disks. However, the files that come with Works may not be the most current ones; check with your Apple dealer to find out.

If you're copying Works to a hard disk, you probably won't want to copy the system files from the Works distribution disk to the hard disk unless the system files on the Works disk are newer than the ones on your hard disk. You may want to get help from your dealer before copying system folders to hard disks. Never simply drag an entire disk icon to the hard disk. Read the rest of this chapter before attempting to copy works to your hard disk.

The system folder on your Works disk (see fig. 1.25) contains:

- The system itself
- The Finder
- An ImageWriter printer driver
- An empty Clipboard
- An empty Scrapbook

Fig. 1.25

The five files in the system folder.

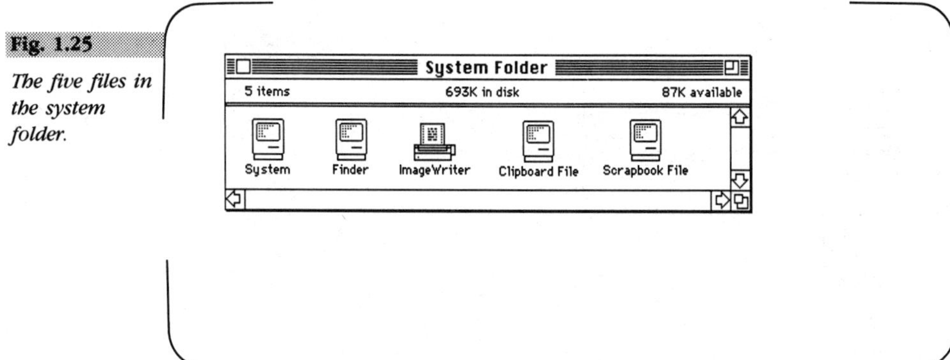

Personalizing Version 1.1

The first time you insert the original copy of Works Version 1.1 into your Macintosh, the personalization screen appears. You must enter your name and organization name before Works will let you continue (see fig. 1.26). From then on, your name and organization appear on the screen whenever you use the original disk or any copies made from it. Version 1.0 of Works doesn't prompt you this way.

Making a Working Copy (Backup)

Despite what your Microsoft Version 1.0 manual may say, copies of Microsoft Works were never copy protected. Ignore the suggestion about contacting your dealer for a non-copy-protected version; you already have it.

You should always use a working copy, not the original disk. Store the original in a safe place, away from your computer. You may make a working copy for yourself, but making copies for other people is against the law.

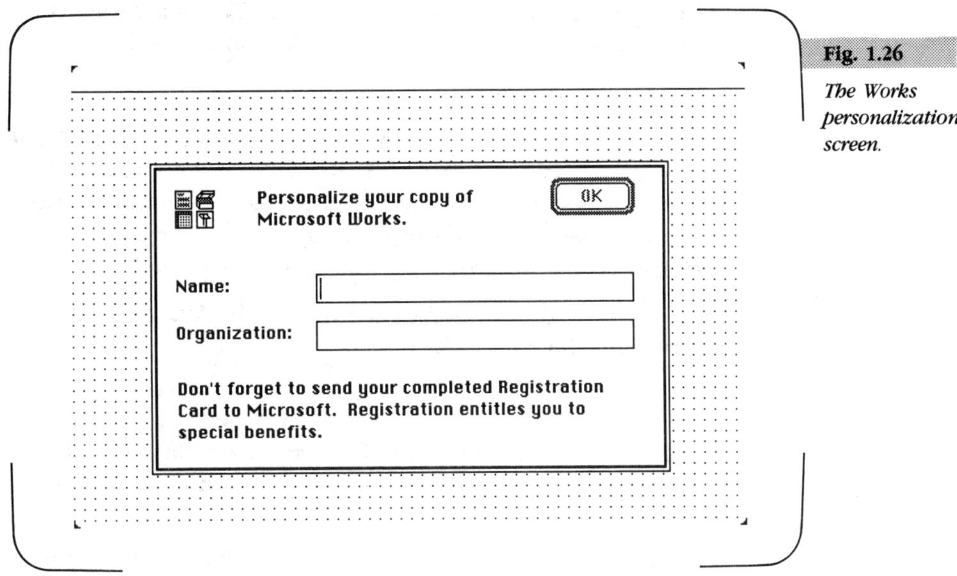

Fig. 1.26

The Works personalization screen.

To make a working disk, you need to copy the appropriate files from your original Microsoft Works program disk onto a different disk. You may or may not need to copy all the files supplied on the Works disk, depending on your system and your needs. Obviously, disk copying requires two disks. The first is called the original, or *source disk*; the other is the *destination disk*. You can copy if you have only one disk drive, but copying with two drives is easier and quicker.

Unless you're copying Works to your hard disk, you'll need an empty initialized disk to use as the destination disk. This disk needs to be unlocked; to unlock it, slide the plastic tab away from the outer edge of the disk.

If you're unfamiliar with the disk initialization or locking procedures, see your Macintosh manual or ask someone for help before continuing. The Works files take up quite a bit of space, so the initialized destination disk should be empty before you start the copying process. If you're reusing an old disk, drag any old unwanted files to the trash can.

Copying Works with One Disk Drive

If you have only one disk drive, follow the procedure described in this section. (If you have more than one drive or if you have a hard disk, skip ahead to the appropriate instructions.)

1. Eject any other disk you have been using. The quick way to eject is to hold down the **command** key and press **E**.
2. Turn off your Macintosh.
3. If you've already personalized your original disk, be certain that the original Works disk is locked so that you don't alter its contents accidentally. To lock the disk, slide the small plastic tab toward the outside edge of the disk. If you have not personalized the original, leave the disk unprotected.
4. Place the original Works Program disk in the Macintosh drive and turn on the computer.

   Works loads itself automatically (you may be asked to personalize your disk if it's brand new). When you see the Works greeting screen shown in figure 1.27, either pull down the File menu and select Quit or use the **command-Q** shortcut.

   You are returned to the desktop, and the Works disk icon is visible.
5. Eject the original Works disk by pressing **command-E**. This disk is your source disk.
6. Insert and then eject the unlocked initialized destination disk. It soon will become your working copy.
7. Reinsert the original Works disk. Your desktop should look something like figure 1.28.
8. Select the original Works disk with the mouse, by pointing and clicking. Then drag the dashed outline of the source icon to the destination icon (see fig. 1.28). Don't confuse the two disks.

You'll be prompted to insert and remove the disks, and you'll be notified of the operation's progress. If the destination disk contains files, you may be asked whether you want to replace them. When you're finished, put the original program disk in a safe place.

Copying Works with Two Disk Drives

If you have external and internal disk drives for your Macintosh, use the procedure described in this section to make a working copy. Skip this procedure if you want to install Works on your hard disk.

1. Eject any other disk(s) you have been using and turn off your Macintosh.

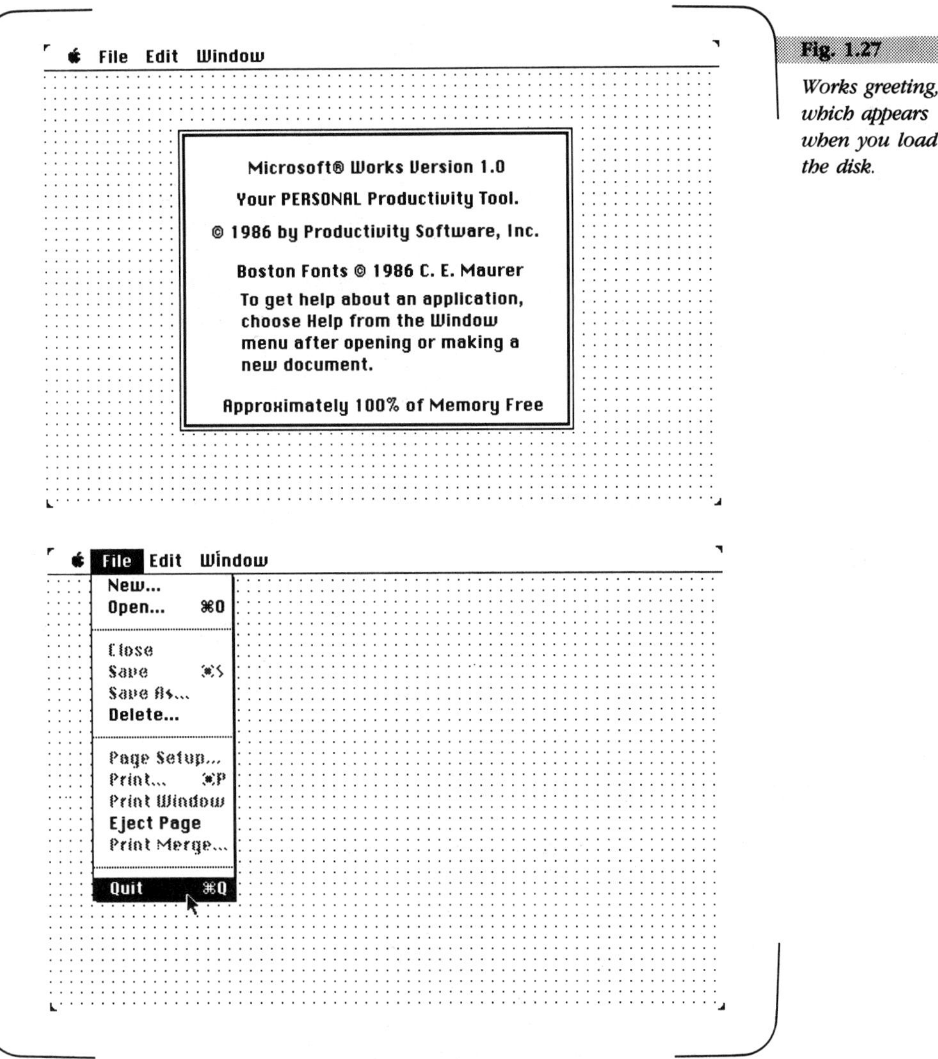

Fig. 1.27

Works greeting, which appears when you load the disk.

2. Be certain that the original Works disk is locked so that you don't accidentally alter its contents. To lock the disk, slide the small plastic tab toward the outside edge of the disk.

3. Place the original, protected Works disk in the internal drive, (or the top drive if you have a two-drive Macintosh SE). Place the destination disk in the external Macintosh drive (or bottom SE drive) and turn on the computer.

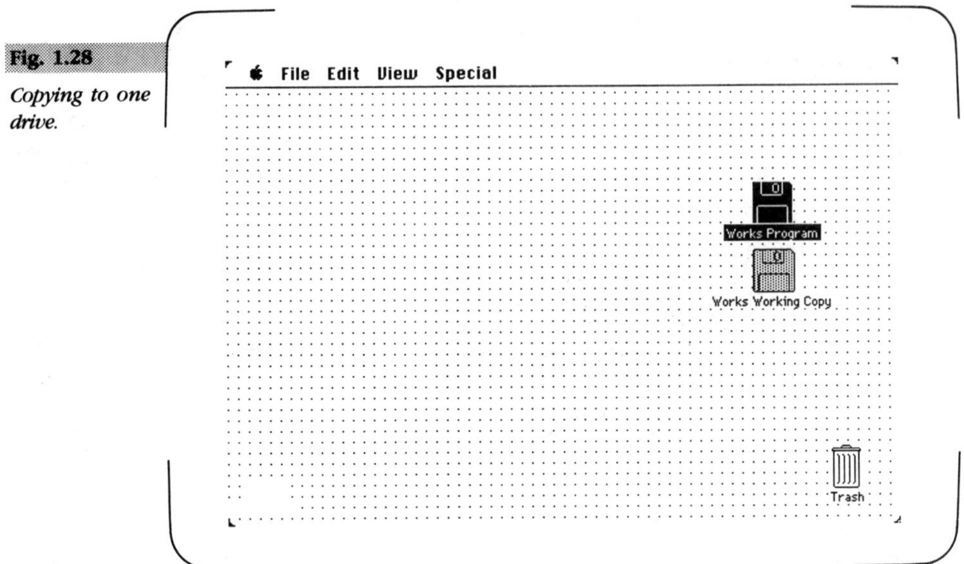

Fig. 1.28

Copying to one drive.

4. When you see the Works greeting screen, either select Quit on the File menu or use the **command-Q** shortcut (see again fig. 1.27).

   You are returned to the desktop, and both the original and destination disk icons are visible. Your desktop should look something like figure 1.28.

5. Select (point to) the original Works disk with the mouse button held down, and drag the outline of the original disk icon to the destination disk icon. Don't confuse the two disks.

You'll be notified of the operation's progress. When you're finished, put the original disk in a safe place.

Installing Works on Your Hard Disk

WARNING: The procedure for copying to a hard disk differs slightly from other disk-copying procedures. If you have a hard disk, read the complete hard disk procedure before trying to copy Works. The following explanation assumes that you or your dealer have already installed a current version of the system folder and fonts on your hard disk.

You can't simply drag the whole Microsoft Works disk onto the hard disk. Instead, you must drag selected files and folders. Dragging the whole Works disk might replace the entire contents of the hard disk with only the files on the Works disk. Moreover, your Microsoft Works original program disk contains a system folder, which should not be copied onto the hard disk. Your hard disk already has a system folder, and two system folders on a hard disk is one too many.

To keep things organized, you should copy all the required Works files into a single new folder on the hard disk.

1. From the desktop, open the hard disk by double-clicking on its icon.
2. Pull down the File menu and create a new folder. You can name it immediately by typing **Works** or whatever pleases you.
3. Insert the protected Microsoft Works original disk into the internal drive, and open the disk by double-clicking on its icon. Your desk should look something like figure 1.29.

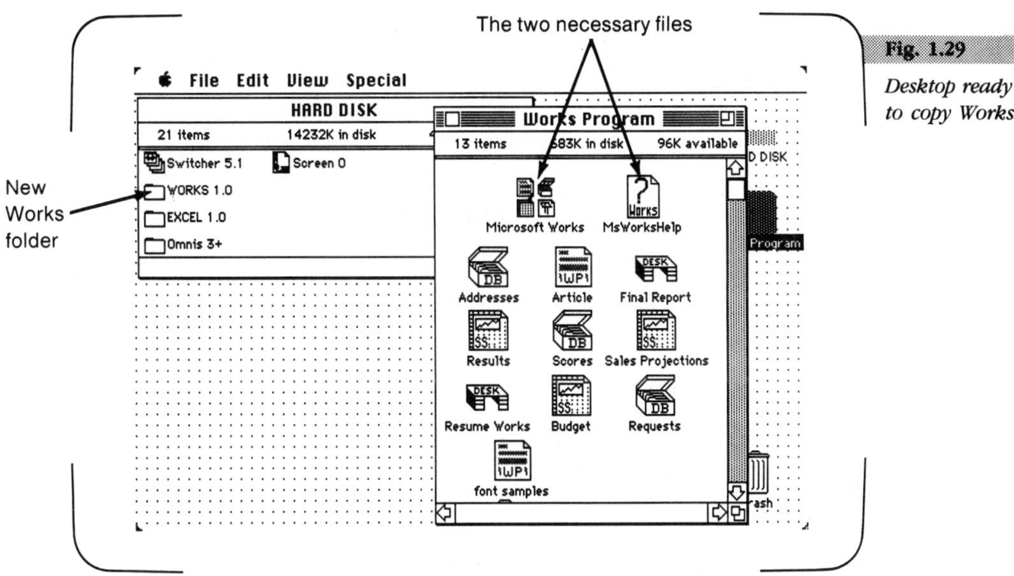

Fig. 1.29

Desktop ready to copy Works.

4. If necessary, move the Works disk window around so that you can see the new Works folder you've just created.

   Look at the Works-disk window; you should see at least 12 icons. One is the unneeded system folder; most of the rest are sample files, which you don't need in order to complete the exercises in this book. The only two files you really need are the Microsoft Works file and the MsWorksHelp file (see fig. 1.30).

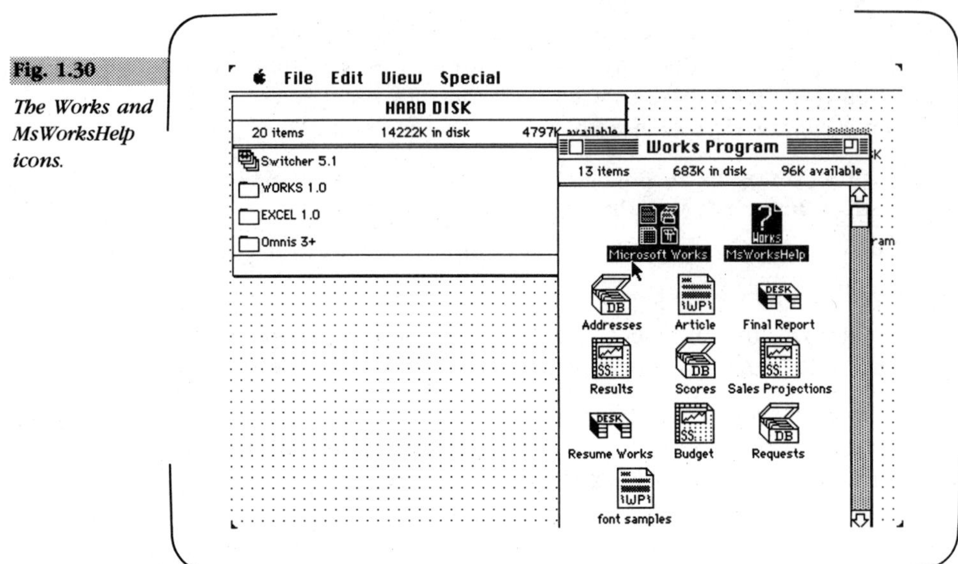

Fig. 1.30

The Works and MsWorksHelp icons.

5. Drag the two necessary files to the new Works folder on your hard disk. Feel free to drag along all the rest except the system folder. Here's a short cut. If you click on one icon and then press the **shift** key when clicking on the second icon, you can drag both files to the hard disk at once.
6. Close the Works-disk window to close Works.
7. Eject the original disk either by pressing **command-E** or by dragging the disk icon to the trash can.
8. Store the original in a safe place.

Starting Works

Works starts automatically when you turn on your computer with the Works disk in a drive. If you have a hard disk on which Works has been installed, you don't need to place the Works disk in a drive before starting your system. You start Works from the hard disk itself.

To start Works from the hard disk, you double-click on the Works icon. Obviously, if you have Works in its own folder, you must open the folder by double-clicking on it first.

NOTE: You can start works by double-clicking on any Works document icon instead of on the Works icon itself. For example, in figure 1.31, you can double-click on the Memo icon instead of the Microsoft Works icon. This step starts Works and then loads and activates the Memo—a word-processing document.

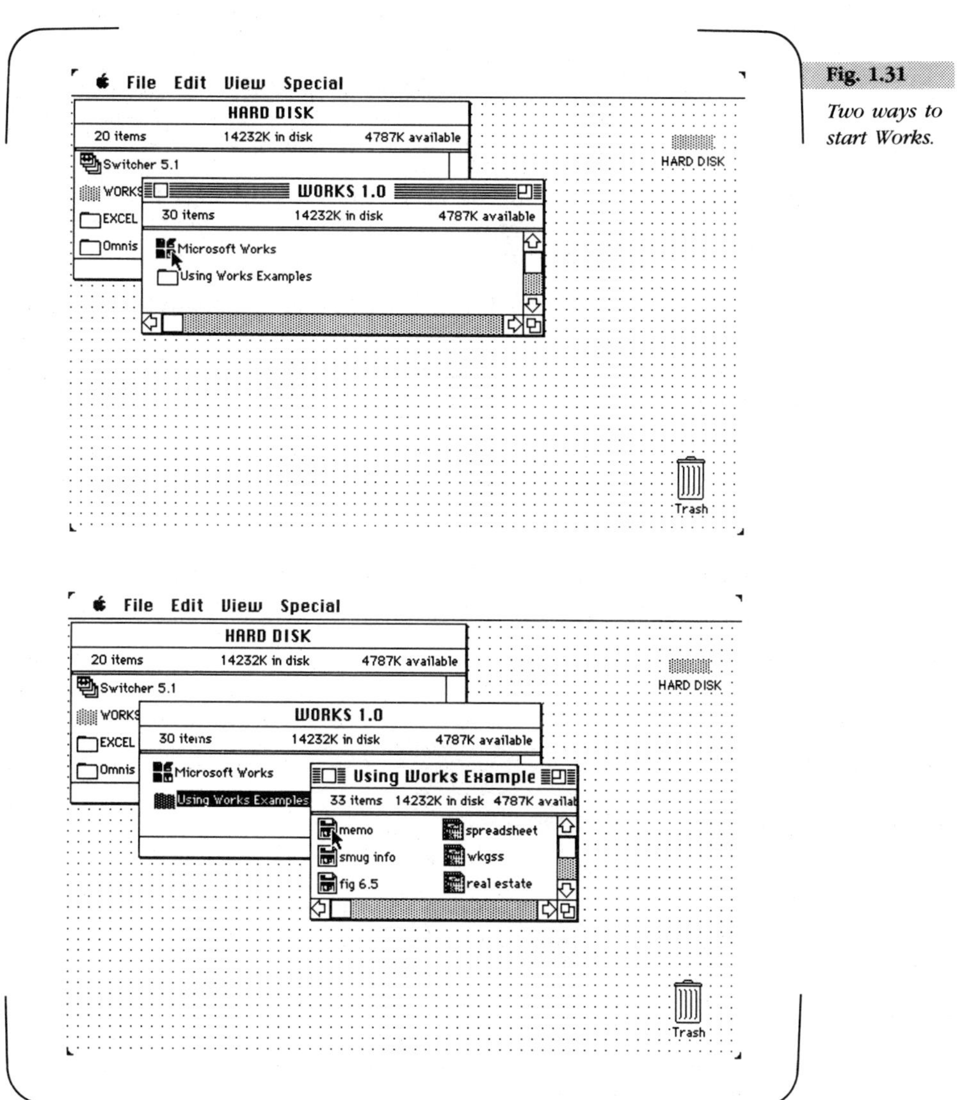

Fig. 1.31

Two ways to start Works.

Hints for Experienced Macintosh Users

Most people will want to use Works just as it is shipped from Microsoft. Sometimes, certain tips and techniques can help advanced users better match Works to their particular needs. If you require extra space on your disk for storing documents, for instance, or if you want to stop at the Macintosh Finder rather than launching Works automatically, you can find ways to do either. The "Hints for Experienced Users" sections of this and other chapters contain advice that may be helpful.

As I've mentioned before, this book is not meant to be a replacement for your Apple Macintosh manuals, nor is it a replacement for the help you'll receive from local users groups, your dealer, and others.

Advanced hints are meant to give you new areas to explore. Don't be afraid to seek additional help if the hints don't make sense at first. No one is born knowing everything about computers, and we all learn something new about them each day.

Saving Space on Crowded Disks

You actually need only one or two files on your working disk: the Works Application itself and the MsWorksHelp file (see fig. 1.32). You can even eliminate MsWorksHelp if you don't need the (somewhat limited) on-line help feature.

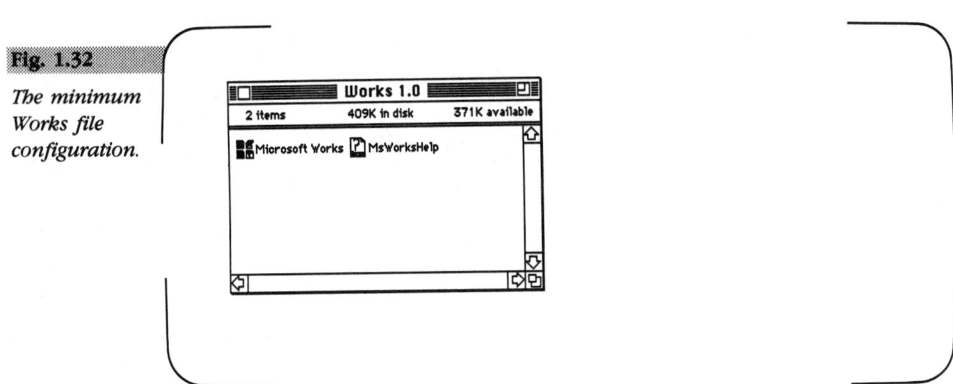

Fig. 1.32

The minimum Works file configuration.

Using this minimal configuration, you can start your Macintosh from another disk containing the system folder, fonts, printer drivers, and so forth. You then have extra room for word-processing documents, spreadsheets, and so on.

Disabling the Auto-Start Feature

Here is what you do to make the Mac stop at the Finder rather than go automatically to the Works greeting screen when you insert the Works disk (see fig. 1.33):

1. Open the system folder on the Works disk.
2. Select the Finder icon.
3. Choose Start Setup from the Special menu.
4. Close the system folder.

The next time you start your Macintosh from your Works disk, you will see the Works desktop.

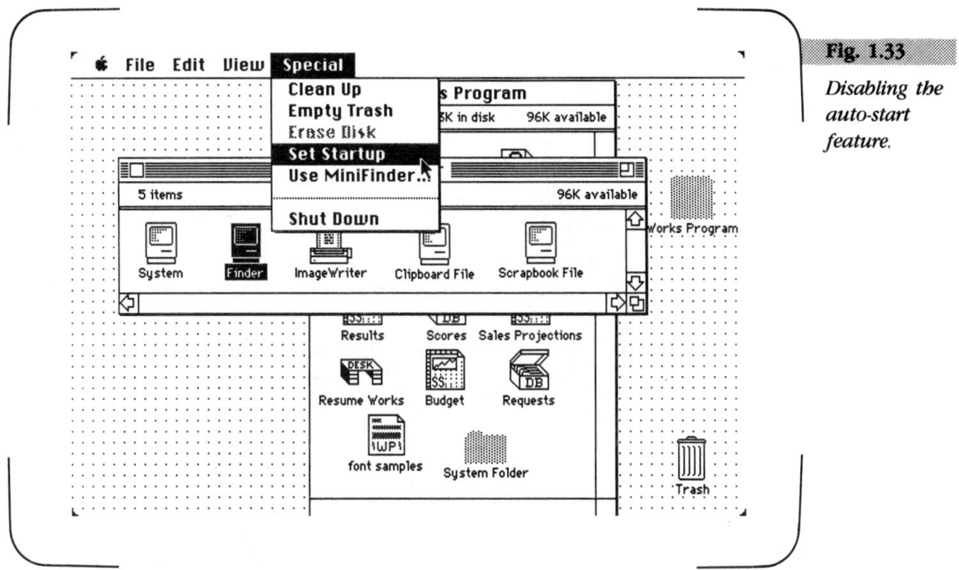

Fig. 1.33

Disabling the auto-start feature.

Now that you have Works installed, you are ready to start using the program. The next chapter introduces you to the Works word processor.

NOTE: If you want to launch a resident program first, (like SuperLaser Spool) highlight that icon instead of the finder before performing steps 3 and 4.

Part II

WORD PROCESSING

2

Entering, Editing, Saving, and Printing Text

How many times have you been ready to send an important letter, only to find a typo at the last minute? In many cases, a single typing error results in five, ten, or even more minutes spent retyping the entire letter or article. A word processor eliminates tedious retyping to make corrections.

With Works' word-processing features, you can enter and change (edit) text, save it on disk, and retrieve it later. And you can print your documents on a variety of printers. In this chapter, you learn how to accomplish these tasks.

Specifically, you learn how to open a word-processing window, type text, do some simple corrections, move things around, save your work to disk, and print your document. Much of this chapter describes text-selection shortcuts and other useful techniques. It will be worth your while to understand these techniques fully before you move on. After you've learned the basics outlined in this chapter, the next chapter (Chapter 3) shows you how to make Works documents come alive with different typestyles and advanced formatting features.

Entering and Editing Text

The first step in any new Works word-processing project is to open a new (untitled) document and enter some text. Even if you've never used a typewriter before, Works makes you look like a pro. The beauty of word processing is that it lets you type along as quickly as you wish because, at first, your mistakes happen on the screen rather than on paper. You make corrections on the screen either as you go or after you've entered the entire rough draft. Thus, only you (or the person looking over your shoulder) will see your typos. You also can save your document as a file on a disk for later revision.

In this section you learn the basics for opening a word-processing document, typing text, and correcting as you type. You also learn shortcuts for editing and "undoing" your mistakes. Selection is a basic technique in working with text. In the following paragraphs, you learn how to select and manipulate text in amounts ranging from a single word to an entire document.

Opening a Word-Processing Window

The quickest way to begin a new typing project is either to double-click on the word-processor icon in the Open File dialog box or to click the word-processor icon once and then click the Open button (see fig. 2.1). (You can accomplish the same thing by selecting the New option on the pull-down File menu.) If you are new to the Mac, you can practice this procedure in the Quick Start at the end of this chapter. (See Chapter 1 for detailed instructions.)

Fig. 2.1

Selecting the word-processor icon.

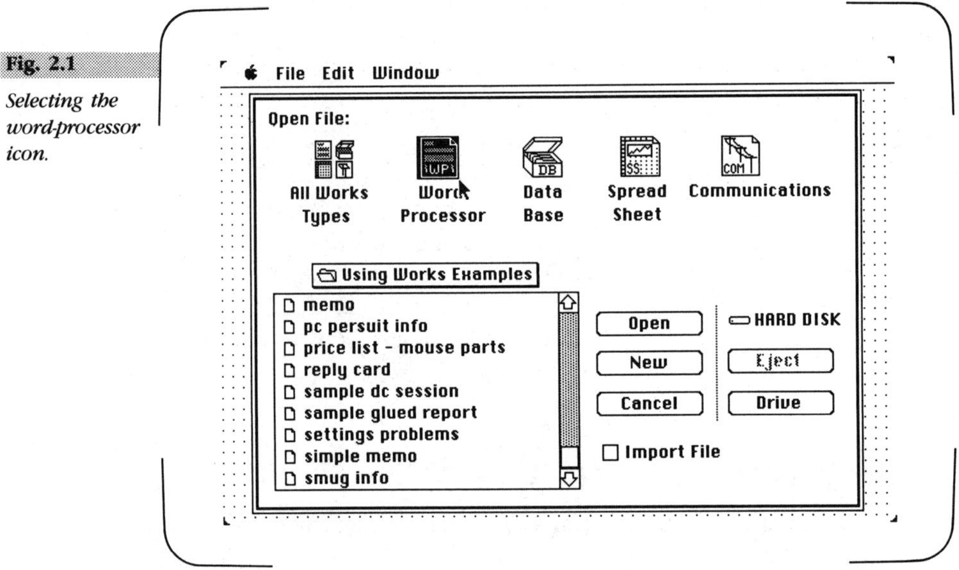

A word-processing screen then appears, as shown in figure 2.2. The window's title is Untitled; the letters *(WP)* indicate that you're working with a word-processing window. A cursor bar blinks at the top left corner of the page displayed below the ruler. When you start typing, the first character is positioned at this point. Some people call this point the insertion point.

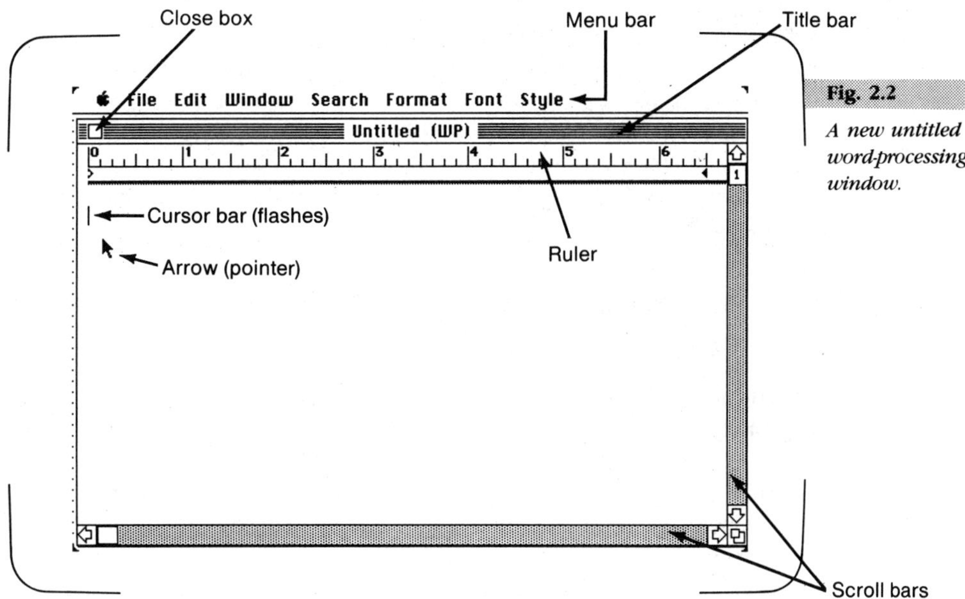

Fig. 2.2

A new untitled word-processing window.

Like other Works windows, the word-processing window has a title bar, scroll bars, a menu bar, a close box, and so on. The window ruler, which shows the document's approximate width in inches, contains markers for margins, indents, and tabs; you learn more about these markers in Chapter 3.

Typing Text

You enter text as you would type it using a typewriter—with one exception. When you near the end of a line, you don't press the *return* key. Like most word processors, Works takes care of that task for you by "wrapping" words automatically.

Automatic Wordwrap and Forced Line Endings

Because of Works' *automatic wordwrap* feature, words that don't fit entirely on a line are moved to the line below. This feature makes adding or deleting text anywhere in your document easy. Whenever you make a change to a document—insert a word or line, for example—Works immediately adjusts the remaining text to accommodate your changes. If your changes affect the page breaks, a process called *automatic repagination* also adjusts the page breaks for you. The whole process happens without your intervention. (See Chapter 3 for more information about controlling page breaks in a document.)

Wordwrap is automatic, so you press *return* only if you want to force a line ending—for example, when typing an inside address in a letter or when formatting poetry. You also press *return* to end a paragraph or to insert a blank line. If you accidentally press *return*, you can remove the return character the way you remove any other typed character: by backspacing or by using the other deletion techniques explained in this chapter.

Using the Backspace *(or* Delete*) Key To Correct as You Type*

If you make a mistake and notice it immediately, you can correct your error right away by using the *backspace* key. Newer Macintosh keyboards label the key *delete*, rather than *backspace*. It's in the upper right corner of the main keyboard on your Macintosh. Some people call this backspace "destructive" because it erases characters as it moves the cursor to the left.

Like most of the rest of the keys on your Mac, the *backspace* key is a repeating key. If you hold down the *backspace* key for more than a second or two, the key "marches" to the left devouring characters until you release it.

Editing Your Entered Text

Once text is on the screen, you can add more text to it, correct errors, rearrange the text, remove portions of it, or copy parts of it to other documents. Most, but not all, of these processes require that you select the text before you manipulate it. For that reason, Works provides a number of selection tools, which you'll learn about in the following sections. Dragging is the only selection technique you really need to know, but you'll find the shortcuts quite helpful. Before examining selection techniques, however, look at inserting, an important editing technique that is used with or without selection techniques. Then, you see how to strike over existing text, a special kind of insertion technique that requires you to select the text first.

Inserting Text

Suppose that you want to add an entire paragraph or page of information somewhere in a document. Or, to take a simpler case, you want to add Sally's last name after her first name in the memo in figure 2.3.

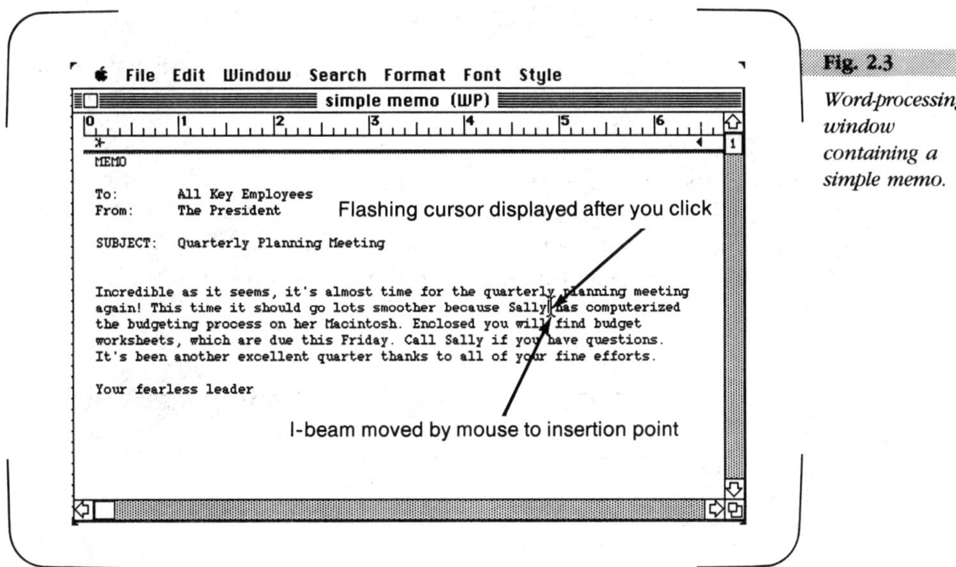
File Edit Window Search Format Font Style
simple memo (WP)
MEMO
To: All Key Employees
From: The President
SUBJECT: Quarterly Planning Meeting
Incredible as it seems, it's almost time for the quarterly planning meeting again! This time it should go lots smoother because Sally has computerized the budgeting process on her Macintosh. Enclosed you will find budget worksheets, which are due this Friday. Call Sally if you have questions. It's been another excellent quarter thanks to all of your fine efforts.
Your fearless leader
Flashing cursor displayed after you click
I-beam moved by mouse to insertion point

Fig. 2.3

Word-processing window containing a simple memo.

First, you need to tell Works where you want to insert text. You do so with the mouse. When you move the mouse, the pointer follows. Notice that a flashing cursor (bar) stays where you last entered text, but the mouse pointer moves.

After you position the I-beam to the left of the place where you want to insert text, click once. The flashing cursor then moves to the position you've selected; that spot is where the new characters will be inserted. As you type, everything to the right and below the insertion point moves to the right, then down. This movement is the wordwrap feature at work.

In large documents, you may notice that the I-beam bulges in the center from time to time. Works is telling you that it is reformatting (wrapping) the information. It's okay to keep typing while Works does this.

Striking Over Text

Usually, Works is in insert mode. When Works is in this mode, the new text inserted pushes old text to the right without deleting it. But what if you want to replace something? One way to accomplish this task is to select the text that you want removed. Whenever text is selected, it is replaced by whatever is typed next.

CAUTION: Beginners frequently lose text by accidentally typing something (anything) while valuable text is highlighted. If you spot your error immediately, you can undo it; see "Undoing Mistakes."

Selecting Text by Dragging

Selection is the first step in many operations, including striking over old text. One way to select text is to drag the mouse over the area to be affected.

Point to the first letter in something you want to select—for example, the letter *S* in Sally's name in figure 2.4. One way to select her name is to drag across her whole name (hold down the mouse button as you move the mouse) and then release the mouse button.

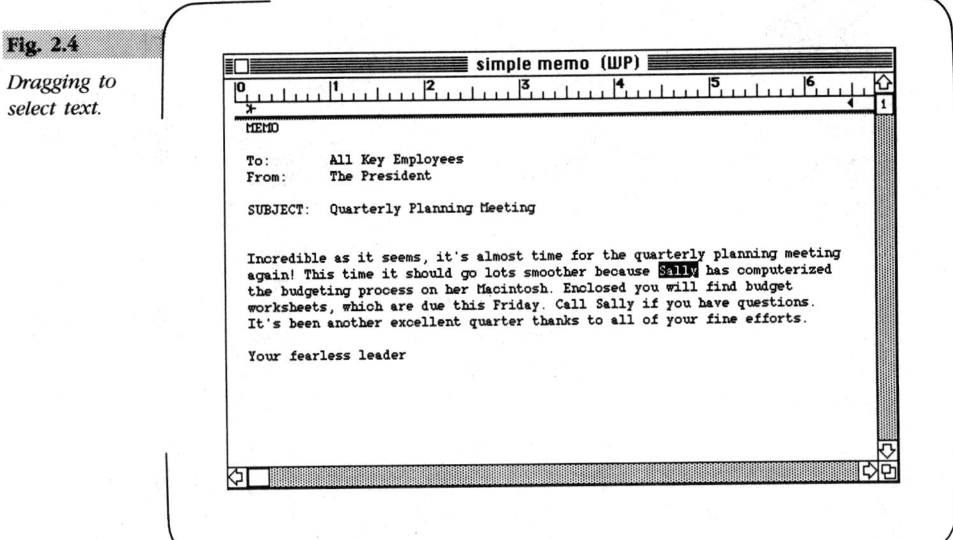
simple memo (WP)
MEMO
To: All Key Employees
From: The President
SUBJECT: Quarterly Planning Meeting
Incredible as it seems, it's almost time for the quarterly planning meeting again! This time it should go lots smoother because Sally has computerized the budgeting process on her Macintosh. Enclosed you will find budget worksheets, which are due this Friday. Call Sally if you have questions. It's been another excellent quarter thanks to all of your fine efforts.
Your fearless leader

Fig. 2.4

Dragging to select text.

Works then highlights, or selects, *Sally* (the word appears in white letters on a black background). If you select too many or not enough letters, click again on the selected area to deselect and try again. Mastering dragging as a way to select single letters, words, and lines takes some practice.

As you may imagine, you can use dragging to select just the letter *S* or an entire paragraph. Some selection shortcuts, however, are often faster than dragging; you'll learn about them in the following paragraphs.

Reminder: After you select text, anything you type replaces all the selected text. For example, if you select the entire memo in figure 2.4 and press K, that single letter replaces the entire memo. Usually, you'll want to do something less dramatic—for example, highlight *Sally* and type **Joan**.

Undoing Mistakes

What if you have a change of heart and wish that you hadn't replaced *Sally*? You can retype her name, of course, but you may be able to undo the strikeover instead.

Pull down the Edit menu and select Undo. Sally's name should then reappear right where it was. The Undo command, however, remembers only the last thing you've done, and the command can't replace characters if you've erased them by backspacing. Undo is still a handy feature, and you'll probably use it frequently. Works has an undo shortcut, too. You hold down the *command* (Apple) key and press Z.

Using Selection Shortcuts

Because so many Works features require that you select text first, the system provides quick methods to select words, lines, or an entire document. Because these techniques are worth learning, they are described in the following sections.

Selecting a Single Word, Line, or Paragraph

To select a word, you place the pointer on the word and double-click (see fig. 2.5). Punctuation enclosing words, however, can't be selected this way (for example, quotation marks or parentheses). Nor can you select numbers containing dollar signs or decimal points this way. If you double-click on *$20.00*, for example, Works highlights only the *20*. To deselect a selected word, you click once anywhere in the document.

To select a single line, you place the pointer (which should look like an arrow) to the left of the line and click once (see fig. 2.6). The entire line is highlighted.

To select a paragraph, you double-click in the left margin next to that paragraph (see fig. 2.7). You may need to move the pointer around until it looks like an arrow, not an I-beam.

Dragging To Select Multiple Lines and Irregular Areas

Works enables you to select several lines at once. Place the pointer, which should look like an I-beam, in the space to the left of any line in your document, but not past the left edge of the window. (If the pointer changes from an I-beam to a pointer, you've gone too far "west.") When you drag down slowly, Works highlights the first line. Keep dragging to select additional lines.

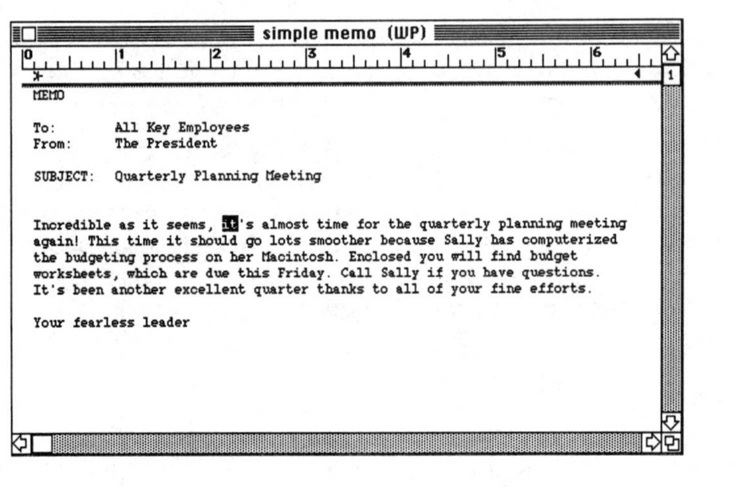
simple memo (WP)
MEMO
To: All Key Employees
From: The President
SUBJECT: Quarterly Planning Meeting
Incredible as it seems, it's almost time for the quarterly planning meeting
again! This time it should go lots smoother because Sally has computerized
the budgeting process on her Macintosh. Enclosed you will find budget
worksheets, which are due this Friday. Call Sally if you have questions.
It's been another excellent quarter thanks to all of your fine efforts.
Your fearless leader

Fig. 2.5

Selecting the word it.

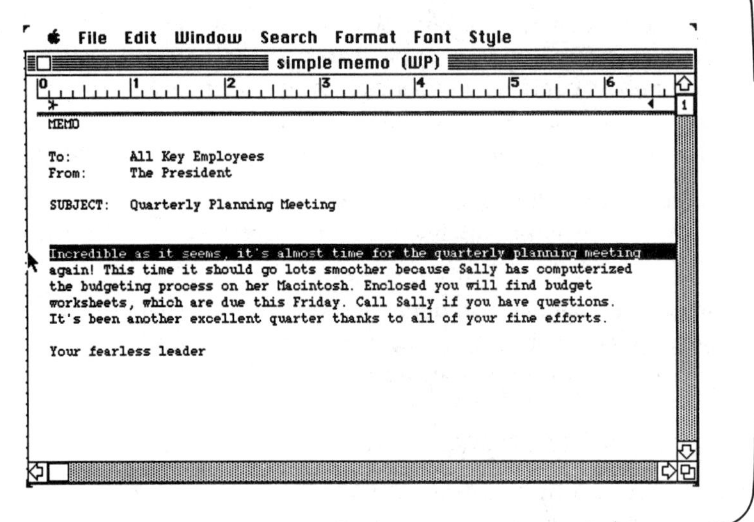
File Edit Window Search Format Font Style
simple memo (WP)
MEMO
To: All Key Employees
From: The President
SUBJECT: Quarterly Planning Meeting
Incredible as it seems, it's almost time for the quarterly planning meeting
again! This time it should go lots smoother because Sally has computerized
the budgeting process on her Macintosh. Enclosed you will find budget
worksheets, which are due this Friday. Call Sally if you have questions.
It's been another excellent quarter thanks to all of your fine efforts.
Your fearless leader

Fig. 2.6

Selecting a line.

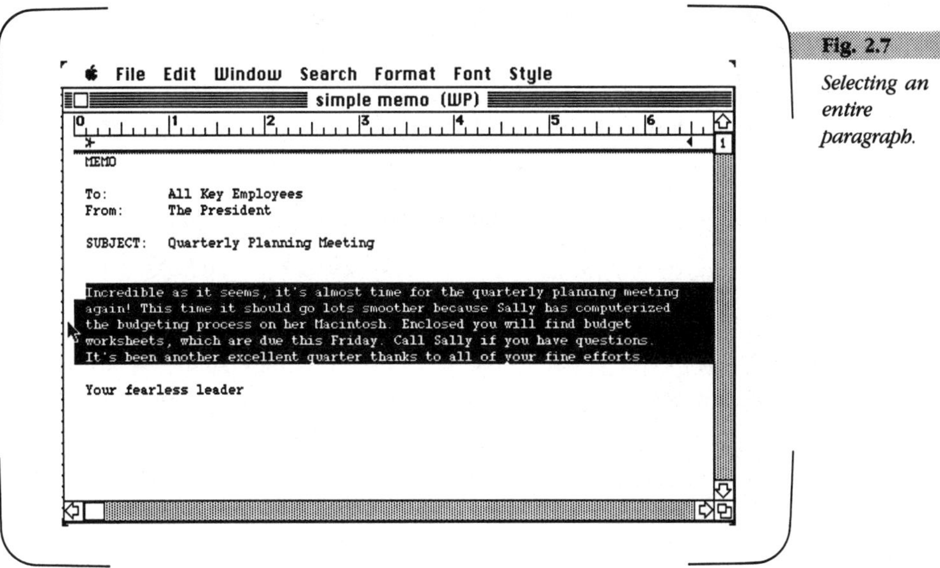
File Edit Window Search Format Font Style
simple memo (WP)
MEMO
To: All Key Employees
From: The President
SUBJECT: Quarterly Planning Meeting
Incredible as it seems, it's almost time for the quarterly planning meeting again! This time it should go lots smoother because Sally has computerized the budgeting process on her Macintosh. Enclosed you will find budget worksheets, which are due this Friday. Call Sally if you have questions. It's been another excellent quarter thanks to all of your fine efforts.
Your fearless leader

Fig. 2.7

Selecting an entire paragraph.

You also can select irregular areas by dragging. For example, suppose that you want to select the last part of one line and the beginning of the next (see fig. 2.8). You simply start dragging where you want to begin highlighting and stop dragging where you want to end highlighting.

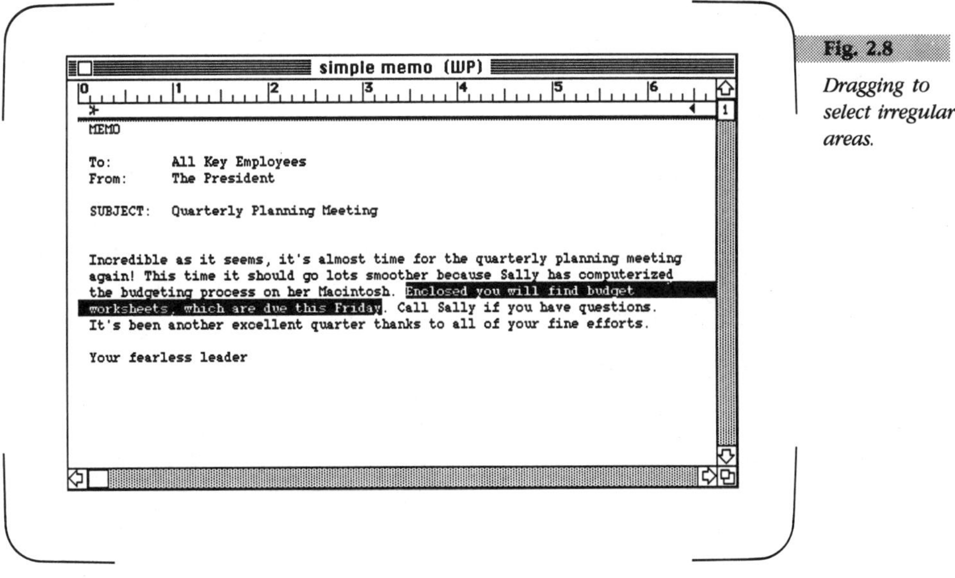
simple memo (WP)
MEMO
To: All Key Employees
From: The President
SUBJECT: Quarterly Planning Meeting
Incredible as it seems, it's almost time for the quarterly planning meeting again! This time it should go lots smoother because Sally has computerized the budgeting process on her Macintosh. Enclosed you will find budget worksheets, which are due this Friday. Call Sally if you have questions. It's been another excellent quarter thanks to all of your fine efforts.
Your fearless leader

Fig. 2.8

Dragging to select irregular areas.

Dragging To Increase or Decrease Selected Areas

Dragging selects multiple words, too. Place the pointer on a word in the middle of the memo, and drag to the left or right. To select multiple lines or characters, you place the pointer where you want to begin selecting and drag up and down or left and right.

Shift-Dragging for Fine-Tuning or Selecting Quickly

Occasionally when dragging, you may select too much or too little text and notice the error only after you've released the mouse button. Rather than starting the selection process over, you can fine-tune the selection. Point to the place where you want to begin the change. Hold down the *shift* key and move the mouse to increase or decrease the selected area.

NOTE: Here's some useful Mactrivia. If you double-click to select a word and then hold down the *shift* key while dragging, you select whole words rather than single characters. This technique is a quick way to select several words.

Selecting Large Areas and Entire Documents

Another way to select portions of a document is to click once at the beginning of a specific area and then move the pointer to the other end of that area. Hold down the *shift* key and click again. Voila! This method is a fast way to select areas larger than the window.

From time to time, you'll want to select an entire document (see fig. 2.9). You pull down the Edit menu and specify Select All. Works highlights the whole document. To deselect, click anywhere in the document.

Selecting Pictures

You can include pictures in your word-processing documents. The pictures can come from other programs, or you can draw pictures with Works Draw command. Pictures are selected by a technique different from the techniques you use for selecting words.

To select pictures, either choose the Select Picture option on the Edit menu or use the *command*-A shortcut. If more than one picture is on the screen, you may need to repeat the selection process while Works moves around the window, alternately selecting each picture.

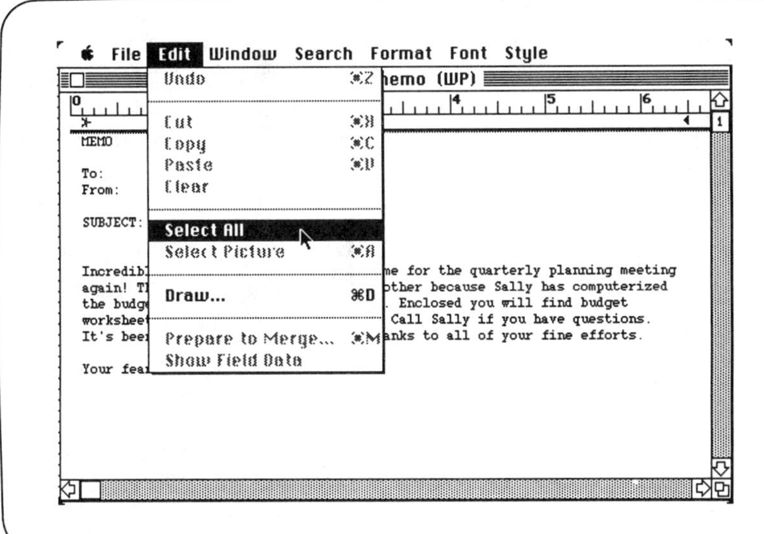

Fig. 2.9

Selecting an entire document.

Copying, Cutting, and Pasting

After selecting text or pictures, you can copy the item to the Clipboard by choosing Copy on the Edit menu. A shortcut is also available: Hold down the *command* key and press C.

When you use Copy, Works duplicates selected items without altering the document. The Clipboard can hold only one thing at a time, however, so when you copy something to the Clipboard, that item replaces the Clipboard's previous contents.

Selected text and drawings can be cut rather than copied. Cut items are removed from the document and placed on the Clipboard. You can return accidentally cut items to the document by using the Undo key if you catch your mistake soon enough.

Once copied or cut, items can be pasted elsewhere in the document you're working on or in another document. You can move things to the Scrapbook this way, too.

Pasting is a method of inserting copies of the Clipboard's contents at specific spots in your document. Place the pointer where you want to paste the item. Then either select Paste on the Edit menu or hold down the *command* key and press V.

Viewing the Clipboard's Contents

If you forget what's on the Clipboard and want to display its contents, select Show Clipboard on the Window menu (see fig. 2.10). The Clipboard immediately appears on-screen (see fig. 2.11). When you're finished looking at the Clipboard, click anywhere in the document.

Fig. 2.10

Selecting the Show Clipboard option.

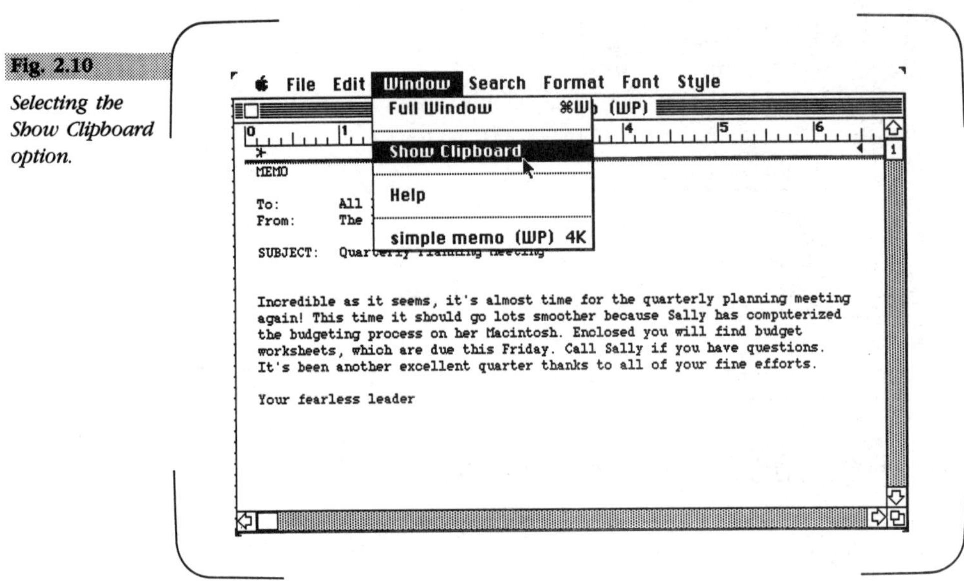
File Edit Window Search Format Font Style
Full Window ⌘W
Show Clipboard
Help
simple memo (WP) 4K
(WP)
MEMO
To: All
From: The
SUBJECT: Quar
Incredible as it seems, it's almost time for the quarterly planning meeting
again! This time it should go lots smoother because Sally has computerized
the budgeting process on her Macintosh. Enclosed you will find budget
worksheets, which are due this Friday. Call Sally if you have questions.
It's been another excellent quarter thanks to all of your fine efforts.
Your fearless leader

Fig. 2.11

Viewing the Clipboard's contents.

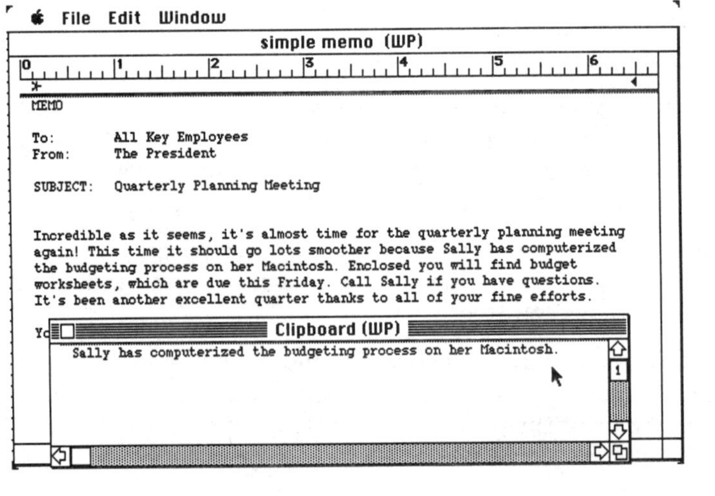
File Edit Window
simple memo (WP)
MEMO
To: All Key Employees
From: The President
SUBJECT: Quarterly Planning Meeting
Incredible as it seems, it's almost time for the quarterly planning meeting
again! This time it should go lots smoother because Sally has computerized
the budgeting process on her Macintosh. Enclosed you will find budget
worksheets, which are due this Friday. Call Sally if you have questions.
It's been another excellent quarter thanks to all of your fine efforts.
Clipboard (WP)
Sally has computerized the budgeting process on her Macintosh.

Moving Text or Pictures

To move text or pictures, you use the Cut or Copy option and then paste the item where you please. You can move items around in the same document, or you can move things from one document to another by opening more than one window.

Here's the safest way to move text or graphics within the same document:

1. Copy the selected item to the Clipboard (rather than cutting it).
2. Point to the desired destination.
3. Click to position the pointer at the insert point.
4. Paste immediately. Press **command-V** or select Paste from the Edit menu.
5. Go back to delete the original item.

Cutting and pasting is faster than copying, but you may lose cut items if you get interrupted or forget to paste them before using the Clipboard for something else.

You can use the Scrapbook as a more secure home for items in transit, although this process is more time-consuming (see Chapter 1). Remember that if you make a big mistake, you may be able to recover by using the Undo command. In the worst case, you can always reload a copy of the document from the disk (if you've been saving your work as you go).

Saving Your Work

Whenever you create a new document, it resides in your computer's random-access memory; the document isn't stored on disk until you tell Works to do so. If you turn off the computer without saving, or if a power failure or computer malfunction occurs, your work is lost forever. For these reasons, you should save your work regularly. In fact, many experienced computer users issue the Save command about every 15 minutes and whenever they are interrupted, such as by a telephone call or a visitor. This habit is a good one.

You start the Save procedure by choosing Save or Save Document As on the File menu. Works displays a dialog box with several options (see fig. 2.12).

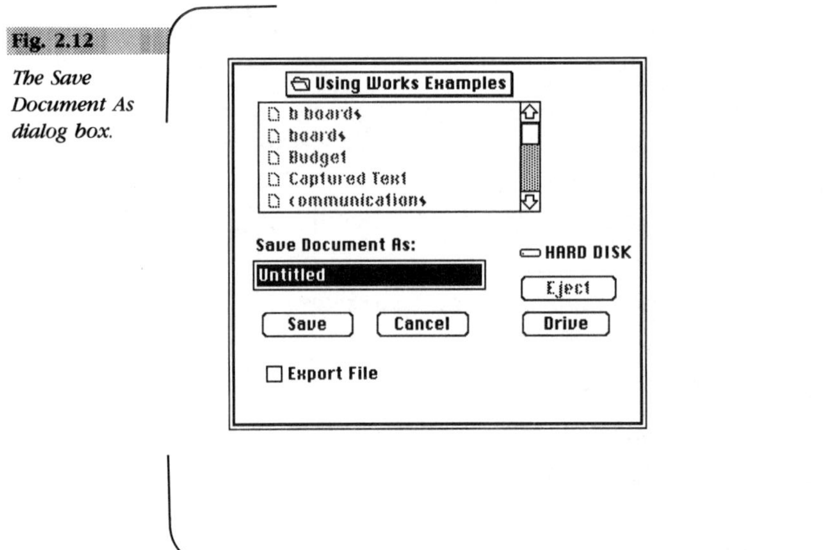

Fig. 2.12

The Save Document As dialog box.

Before you can save a document, you must decide where to store it. If you have disks in more than one disk drive, you have a choice of drives. Regardless of how many drives you have, you can always swap disks by ejecting and inserting them. If you have a hard disk or have placed folders on your disk, you can select the destination folder as well.

After deciding where you want to save your work, you need to pick a file name. Notice that the title bar in figure 2.2 shows that the document is untitled—because it is a new document and has never been saved before.

Now, look at figure 2.12. The top of the dialog box tells you which disk (or folder) will receive the document when you save it. The style of icon displayed tells you whether you're about to save to a diskette or a hard disk, if you have a hard disk (see fig. 2.13). Diskette icons look like diskettes; hard disk icons look like hard disk (they are rectangular). In the example, the memo will be saved in the M&A folder on the M&A backup diskette.

You also see a list of other files (if any exist) on the current disk. The scroll bars on the list box enable you to view long lists. If you have more than one disk drive, you use the Drive button to switch from one to another. If you have diskettes in your internal or external drive, you can swap them by using the Eject button.

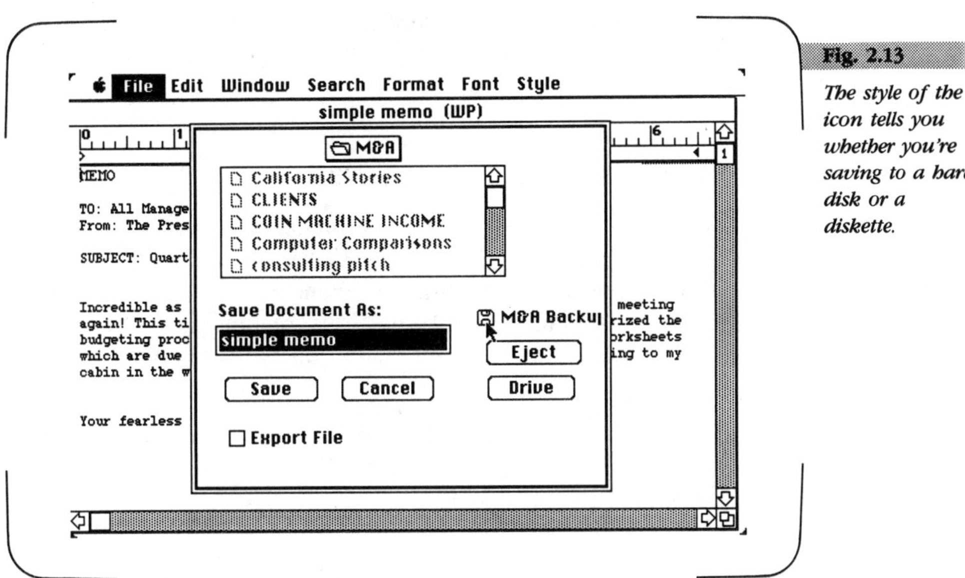

Fig. 2.13

The style of the icon tells you whether you're saving to a hard disk or a diskette.

If your disk contains several folders, you can select different folders by dragging down choices from the box above the file-name list (see fig. 2.14). The Quick Start at the end of this chapter gives you an opportunity to practice saving a file.

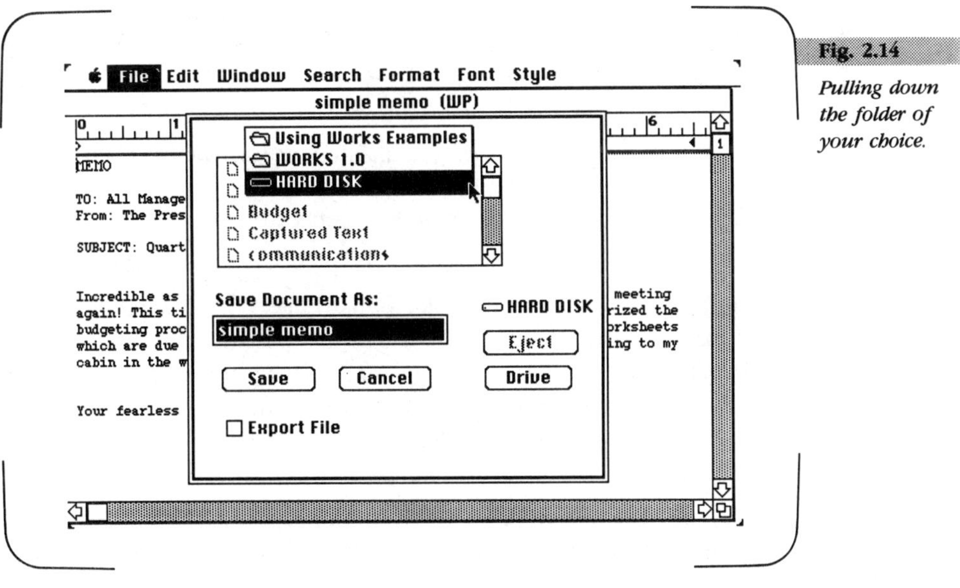

Fig. 2.14

Pulling down the folder of your choice.

If you decide not to save your work, press the Cancel button. Works takes you back to the word-processing document without saving anything.

Naming a New Document

When you save a document, Works highlights the Save Document As box, which contains the last name used to save the document you were working on when you executed the Save command. In the case of a new document, like the memo example, this box contains the word *Untitled* (see fig. 2.12). A sequential number follows the word if you have opened more than one untitled document.

Because the Save Document As box is highlighted, you can simply type the new file name of your choosing. File names can be up to 32 characters long and can contain any keyboard character except the colon (:).

After you have entered the file name, click the Save button. The disk drive runs for a moment, and the word-processing window reappears. Notice that the title bar now displays the new document name.

Saving a Previously Named Document

Once you've named a document, you can save it periodically without retyping the file name. Either choose the Save command from the File menu or—quicker yet—hold down the *command* key and press S. The pointer turns into a watch while the document is being saved.

If you accidentally try to save an untitled document by using either version of the Save command (instead of the Save As command), Works displays the Save As dialog box, where you can name the file.

Printing

Works offers a variety of printing features, which are an integral part of the word-processing process. You can print entire documents, selected pages, or even single windows. Works supports a wide variety of printers as well.

NOTE: The designers of Works really understand the impact of different printer models on the relationship between what you see on-screen and what is printed. For example, some printers require half-inch margins around all four edges of the pages. Some printers can take large paper sizes. When creating documents, you should consider the capabilities and restrictions of your printer. Works provides a Page Setup feature. Before you even start typing a new document, you can use Page Setup to tell the program about the paper size, margins, and other printing decisions you plan to make.

Advanced Works users can take advantage of the Page Setup feature. For new users, the default Page Setup used by Works is fine for most standard typing jobs on all Apple printers.

Preparing Your Printer

Before you start, your printer must be properly connected and loaded with supplies. If you have an ImageWriter, be sure that the power is on and that the select light is on. If you have a loaded sheet feeder, Works automatically feeds a clean sheet when you issue the Print command. If you are hand-feeding paper or have a forms tractor, advance your ImageWriter to the beginning of a new sheet.

LaserWriter owners, make sure that your printer has paper and is warmed up and that the ready light is on. The AppleTalk feature needs to be enabled on your Control Panel because laser printers are connected by means of AppleTalk. See your Apple manuals or dealer for details.

Works offers quite a bit of printing flexibility. If more than one printer is attached to your Macintosh, select the Chooser option from your Apple menu. Works displays dialog boxes in which you specify where your printer is connected and choose the printer you want to use (see figs. 2.15 and 2.16). If this is the first time you've used the Chooser, consult your Apple manuals or get help.

Works may remind you to check your page setup specifications when you pick a new printer (see fig. 2.17). This reminder comes because different printers use different paper widths, support different printing margins, and so on. Works reminds you that it will help you take these differences into consideration if you include them in the page setup information for the document you're working on.

Fig. 2.15

A sample Chooser screen.

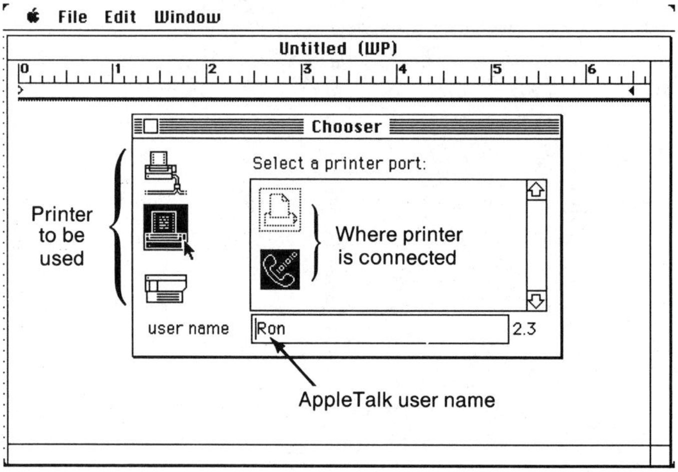

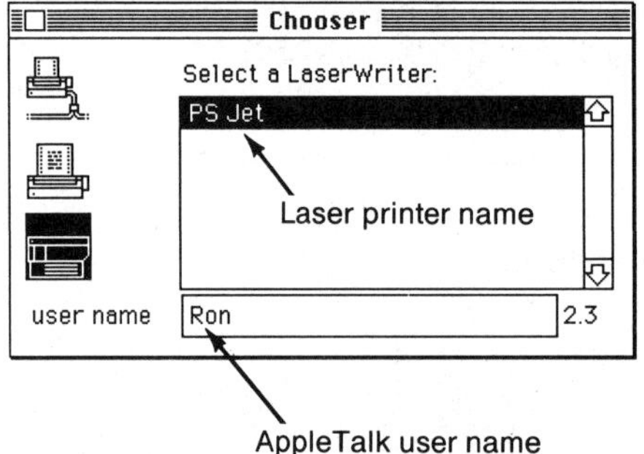

Fig. 2.16

Specifying a printer.

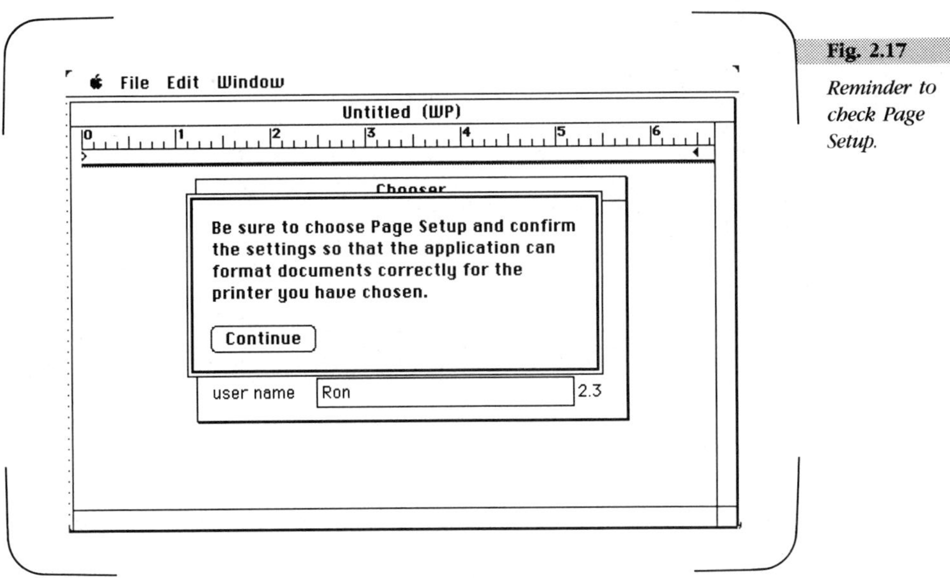
File Edit Window
Untitled (WP)
Chooser
Be sure to choose Page Setup and confirm the settings so that the application can format documents correctly for the printer you have chosen.
Continue
user name
Ron
2.3

Fig. 2.17

Reminder to check Page Setup.

After choosing a printer and setting it up, you're ready to print. Select the Print command on the File menu. The Print dialog box, two examples of which are shown in figures 2.18 and 2.19, appears.

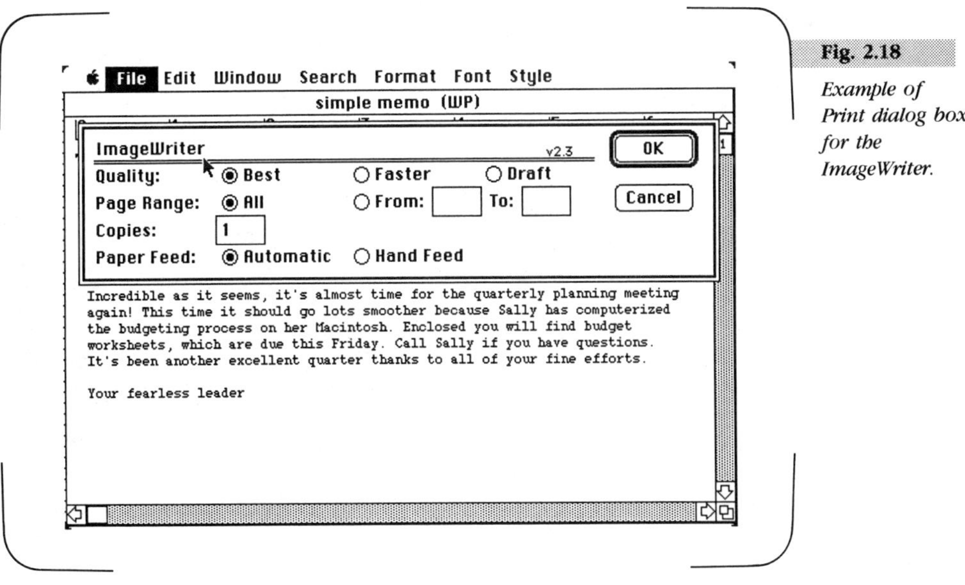
File Edit Window Search Format Font Style
simple memo (WP)
ImageWriter
v2.3
OK
Quality:
Best
Faster
Draft
Page Range:
All
From:
To:
Cancel
Copies:
1
Paper Feed:
Automatic
Hand Feed
Incredible as it seems, it's almost time for the quarterly planning meeting again! This time it should go lots smoother because Sally has computerized the budgeting process on her Macintosh. Enclosed you will find budget worksheets, which are due this Friday. Call Sally if you have questions. It's been another excellent quarter thanks to all of your fine efforts.
Your fearless leader

Fig. 2.18

Example of Print dialog box for the ImageWriter.

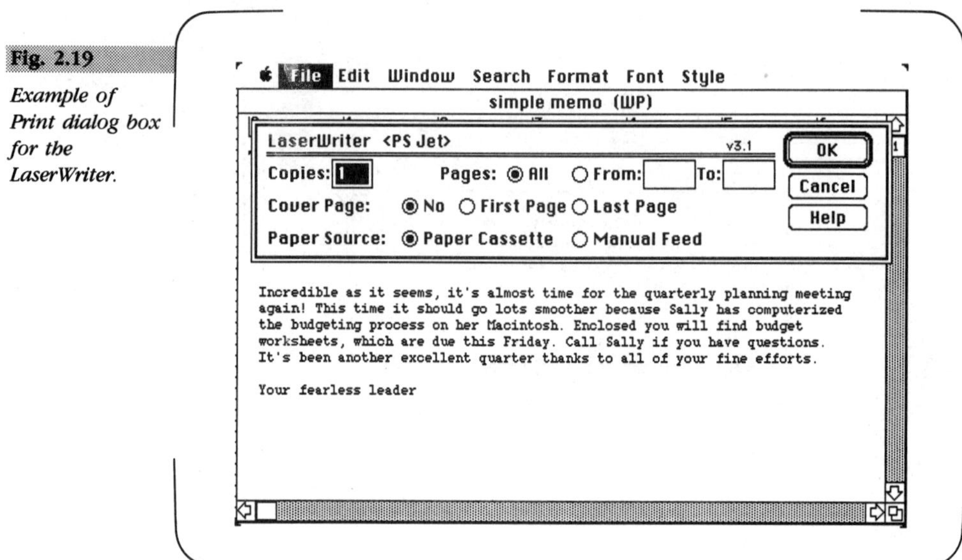
File Edit Window Search Format Font Style
simple memo (WP)
LaserWriter <PS Jet>
v3.1
OK
Copies: 1
Pages: All From: To:
Cancel
Cover Page: No First Page Last Page
Help
Paper Source: Paper Cassette Manual Feed
Incredible as it seems, it's almost time for the quarterly planning meeting
again! This time it should go lots smoother because Sally has computerized
the budgeting process on her Macintosh. Enclosed you will find budget
worksheets, which are due this Friday. Call Sally if you have questions.
It's been another excellent quarter thanks to all of your fine efforts.
Your fearless leader

Fig. 2.19

Example of Print dialog box for the LaserWriter.

The exact appearance of the Print dialog box is determined by the printer model. The upper left corner of the Print dialog box tells you which printer you selected earlier with the Chooser.

This dialog box offers you several options for printing. For either printer, you can choose to print all or only selected pages and the number of copies to be printed. Other options determine the quality of the printing and indicate the size and source of paper you are using.

Printing Your Document

To start the printing process after you have specified all the options, you either click on the OK button or press *return*. A new dialog box appears to report printing progress. After the Mac spends a short time getting ready, the printer starts to print. In the case of a laser printer, the status lights may blink. When the document has been printed, the Print dialog box disappears.

If you need to abort the printing process, hold down the *command* key and press either the period or decimal key. Your printer may run for a moment after printing has been aborted; this procedure is normal.

Printing Selected Pages

You don't have to print an entire document. Suppose, for example, that you want to print the third, fourth, and fifth pages of document. In the Print dialog box, tab to the From box and enter **3**; then tab to the To box and enter **5**, as shown in figure 2.20. You can't, however, cause reverse printing by entering the last page as the From entry and the first page as the To choice.

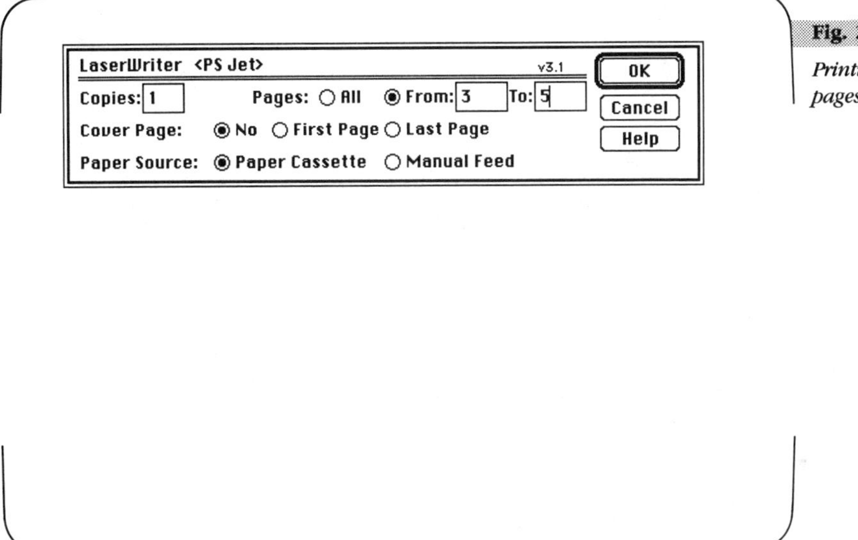

Fig. 2.20

Printing specific pages.

Printing Word-Processing Windows

To print a single window of a document, use the Print Window option on the Edit menu (see fig. 2.21). Works prints the contents of the window and the ruler but doesn't print scroll bars or the cursor. Laser printer owners get laser rather than screen fonts on the paper output (see fig. 2.22).

Don't confuse this procedure with the Apple Print Screen feature, which you invoke by holding down the *shift* and *command* keys while pressing 4. The Works Print Window command works with laser printers; the Apple command doesn't. Moreover, the appearance of the output differs. The Print Window option eliminates scroll bars, menus, and other clutter. When the command is used with a laser printer, text is printed using cleaner, clearer laser fonts rather than the fuzzier screen fonts. Experiment to find the feature you prefer.

Fig. 2.21

Choosing the Print Window option.

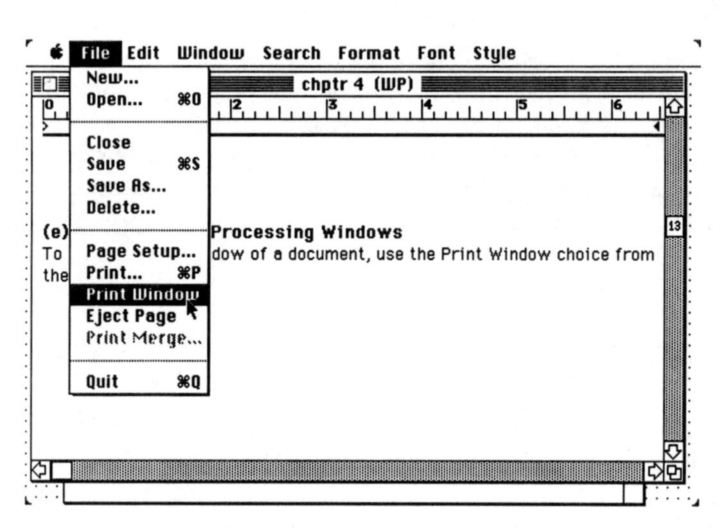

Fig. 2.22

One window printed in laser fonts rather than screen fonts.

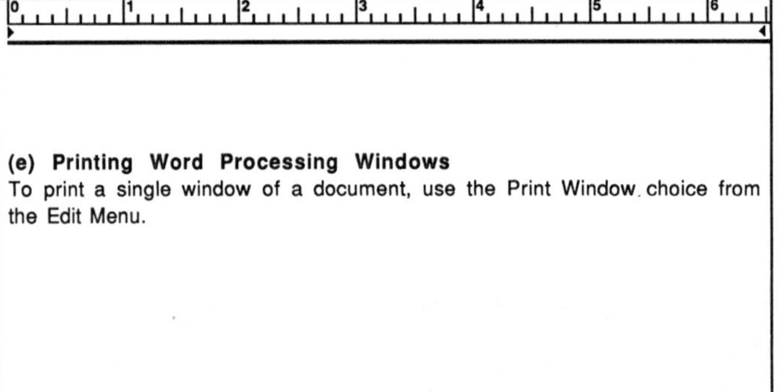

Quick Start: Creating a Word-Processing Document

As explained in the Introduction, Quick Starts are designed to take you through the essential procedures covered in the chapter. In this Quick Start, you learn how to start Works; open a word-processing window; create a document; use the Copy, Cut, and Paste commands; edit your text; save the document; and print it. You learn about automatic repagination, dragging to select text, and the Undo command.

Opening a Word-Processing Window

When you start Works, the Open File menu appears on the screen. Not only can you open previously created files from this screen; you also can create new documents.

Create a new word-processing document by performing the following steps:

1. Using the mouse, move the arrow to the Word Processor icon, and click the mouse button. The Word Processor icon is selected.
2. Point (move the arrow) to the New button, and click once. You see on the screen a blank word-processing window named Untitled.

Creating a Document in the Window

The beauty of using a word processor is the capability to correct text either while it is being typed or after the document is completed. As you type the following memo, do not correct the errors until you are instructed to do so.

Wordwrap and Forced Line Endings

When you want to force a line ending, you press the *return* key. When you type regular text that extends past the right margin, however, you do not need to press *return*. The word processor automatically causes the line to wrap to the following line. To see the contrast, work through the following steps:

1. With the cursor on the first line, press the **tab** key five times; then type **MEMO** and press **return** twice.
2. Type **To:** and press **tab** two times.
3. Type **All Key Employees** and press **return** once.
4. Type **From:** and press **tab** once.
5. Type **The President** and press **return**.
6. Type **Subject:** and press **tab**.
7. Type **Quarterly Planning Meeting** and press **return** three times.

Your document so far should look as follows:

MEMO

To: **All Key Employees**
From: **The President**
Subject: **Quarterly Planning Meeting**

What you have typed so far is text with forced line endings. That is to say, you pressed *return* at the end of every line just as you do when you use a typewriter. Now, let's contrast the forced line endings with automatic wordwrap.

1. Type the following paragraph. Pay particular attention to your screen when typing the phrase *been another*

Incredible as it seems, it's time for the Meeting again! It's been another excellent quarter htakns to all of your fine efforts.

You should have noticed that as you were typing the word *another*, that word moved to the next line, and you continued the sentence. This movement is the effect of wordwrap.

The Backspace Key

The *backspace* key can be used to correct errors you make while you are typing. Follow the next steps to understand its use.

1. As a second sentence in the paragraph, type the following, beginning after the last word of the preceding sentence:

Incredible as it seems, it's time for the meeting again! It's been another excellent quarter htakns to all of your fine efforts. **This time it should go lots smooo**

2. The word that you are now typing is *smoother*. To delete the extra *o*, press the **backspace** key one time. The extra *o* is done away with.

3. Finish typing the rest of the paragraph and press *return*.

Incredible as it seems, it's time for the meeting again! It's been another excellent quarter htakns to all of your fine efforts. This time it should go lots smoo**ther because Sally has computerized the budgeting process on her Macintosh. Enclosed you will find budget worksheets, which are due this Friday. Call Sally if you have questions.**

Your fearless leader,

The memo should look like figure 2.23. However, other things are yet to be done.

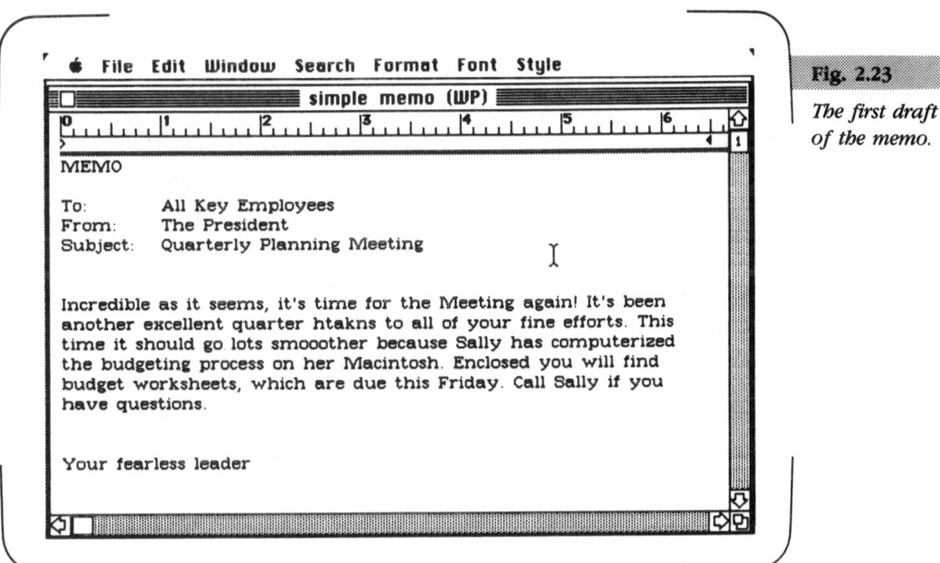
File Edit Window Search Format Font Style
simple memo (WP)
MEMO
To: All Key Employees
From: The President
Subject: Quarterly Planning Meeting
Incredible as it seems, it's time for the Meeting again! It's been another excellent quarter htakns to all of your fine efforts. This time it should go lots smooother because Sally has computerized the budgeting process on her Macintosh. Enclosed you will find budget worksheets, which are due this Friday. Call Sally if you have questions.
Your fearless leader

Fig. 2.23

The first draft of the memo.

Editing the Memo

No doubt, after you type a first draft of a document, you have additions and corrections to make. You need to make additions and corrections in this memo. This section takes you through the most commonly used editing procedures.

Inserting Text

Suppose that you want to insert a word in the middle of a sentence. Follow these steps to insert the word *almost* into the paragraph:

1. Move the mouse so that the pointer is in the typing area. Notice that the pointer becomes an I-beam.
2. Move the mouse so that the vertical line of the I-beam is positioned directly before the *t* in the word *time* in the first line of the paragraph.
3. Click the mouse button once. The insertion point has now repositioned before the *t* by the click of the mouse button.
4. Type the word **almost** and press the **space bar** once.

Notice that the word *almost* has been inserted into the sentence. The paragraph has been adjusted automatically because of wordwrap.

Selecting Text

Not only can you position the insertion point at desired locations to insert text; text already typed can be selected and copied or moved to other areas in the memo. Three necessary operations while editing a document are to copy text, move text, and correct misspellings. However, before you make these editing changes, you must select the appropriate text by the dragging technique.

1. Move the mouse to position the I-beam directly to the left of the phrase *Quarterly Planning Meeting*.
2. Press and hold the mouse button.
3. Move the mouse slowly to the right. Notice that as the mouse moves, the I-beam also moves, and the text the I-beam crosses becomes highlighted, or selected.
4. Following the technique in step 3, select the words *Quarterly Planning* and one space after the *g*.
5. When *Quarterly Planning* is selected, release the mouse button.

The text remains selected. Selecting is the fundamental operation for any cut-and-paste maneuvers, as well as for changing misspellings.

Copying Selected Text

Copying text from one area of the document to another is basically a three-step process: select, copy, and paste. You have previously selected two words, *Quarterly Planning*. Now, perform the other steps as follows:

1. Move the mouse until the arrow points to Edit in the menu.
2. Press and hold the mouse button; drag the mouse until the Copy command is selected and release the button.

The selected text is copied to the Clipboard. The same text remains selected.

3. Move the mouse so the I-beam is positioned to the left of the word *meeting* in the first line of the paragraph.
4. Click the mouse button to establish the insertion point.
5. Move the mouse so that the arrow points to the Edit menu.
6. Press and hold the mouse button, drag the mouse until Paste is selected, and release the button.

The copied text is inserted at the insertion point. The previously selected text is no longer selected. Just as when you type to insert text, the paragraph is repaginated because of the wordwrap.

Moving Selected Text

Moving text from one area of the document to another, as with copying, is a three-step process: select, cut, and paste.

Suppose that on a second reading, you decide that the second sentence of the paragraph should be the last sentence in the paragraph. The following steps move the sentence:

1. Move the mouse until the I-beam is directly to the left of the second sentence in the paragraph.
2. Press and hold the mouse button, and drag the mouse until the I-beam moves down one line. Notice that the entire sentence is selected.
3. Select the entire sentence, including one space after the sentence, and release the mouse button.
4. Move the mouse to the Edit menu.
5. Press and hold the mouse button; drag the mouse until Cut is selected, and release the button.

At this point, the selected text disappears from the screen. The text, though, is simply moved to the Clipboard.

6. Move the mouse to position the I-beam to the right of *questions.* at the end of the paragraph.
7. Click the mouse button to position the insertion point, and press the **space bar** once.
8. Point the arrow to the Edit menu and select Paste from the menu.

The previously cut text is now placed at the end of the paragraph.

Using the Undo Command

You sometimes make mistakes even in correcting text. Works provides a way to undo your mistakes. You now learn how valuable the Undo option can be. Remember, however, that Undo is good only until the next change to the document. Undo remembers only the latest change.

1. Drag to select the word *quarter* in the last sentence of the paragraph.
2. Select Cut from the Edit menu.

The word *quarter*, in effect, has been deleted from the sentence.

3. With the mouse, move the arrow to the Edit menu and press the mouse button.
4. Select Undo from the menu.

The word *quarter* has been placed back in its proper position in the sentence. You can select Undo from the menu only if you truly have something to undo. Otherwise, the selection is dimmed on the menu.

Correcting Misspellings

Just as copying and moving text is easy with Works, so too is correcting misspellings.

1. Move the I-beam to the word *htakns* in the second from the last sentence in the paragraph.
2. Select the word *htakns* by dragging.

As you know, *htakns* is not a word; it should be *thanks*.

3. While *htakns* is selected, type **thanks**.

The misspelled *htakns* is replaced by *thanks*. The memo looks like the one in figure 2.24.

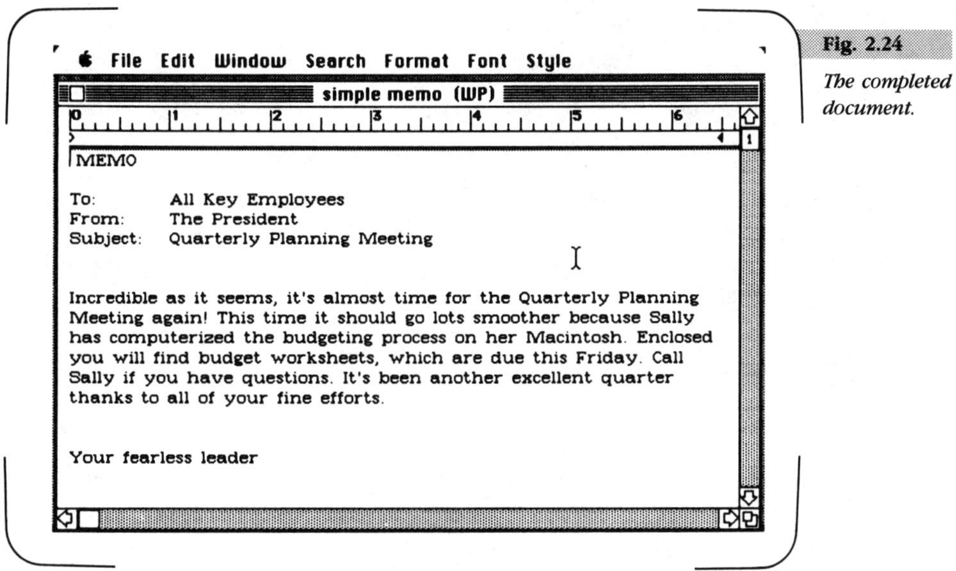
File Edit Window Search Format Font Style
simple memo (WP)
MEMO
To: All Key Employees
From: The President
Subject: Quarterly Planning Meeting
Incredible as it seems, it's almost time for the Quarterly Planning Meeting again! This time it should go lots smoother because Sally has computerized the budgeting process on her Macintosh. Enclosed you will find budget worksheets, which are due this Friday. Call Sally if you have questions. It's been another excellent quarter thanks to all of your fine efforts.
Your fearless leader

Fig. 2.24
The completed document.

Saving Your Work

Now, you need to save your work before printing. In fact, you should save your work regularly. The following steps take you through this essential process:

1. Point to File in the menu.
2. Press and hold the mouse button; select Save As and release the mouse button.

A dialog box appears on the screen. The box has several options so that you can select another name, eject the current disk, or select another drive. The name Untitled is selected now because no other name has been given to the document.

3. Type **Simple Memo**, point to the Save button, and click the mouse button.

The file is saved on the current disk with the new name Simple Memo. Also, the name in the title bar of the word-processing window has changed from Untitled to Simple Memo.

Printing the Memo

After all corrections have been made and the document has been saved, you are ready to print the memo for distribution. Printing, like all other operations on the Macintosh, is an easy process. The following steps take you through this process:

1. Point to File on the menu bar and press the mouse button.
2. Select Print and release the mouse button.

A print window appears on the screen. As with saving, you are offered several options. The options determine print quality, page range, number of copies to print, and type of paper feed. For now, keep the default settings.

3. Make sure that your printer is connected, turned on, and the select light is on.
4. Point to the OK button in the box and click the mouse button.

In the matter of minutes, the memo comes out on the printer.

Closing the Document

Before you end your work session or go on to other documents, you need to close the Simple Memo. The following steps help you through this:

1. Point to File in the menu, using the mouse.
2. Select Close from the File menu.

If you had made any other changes to the document, a box would have appeared on the screen asking you to save the document. You could answer by clicking Yes, No, or Cancel. Cancel, as a choice, keeps the document on the screen.

You are returned to the Open File screen, from where you started.

3

Opening Stored Files and Formatting and Adding Style to Your Documents

After you have entered and edited your text, you are ready to move into more advanced formatting techniques. For instance, you can create documents with indented paragraphs, and you can change margins easily, too, either before or after you type the document. By selecting from a variety of type styles and point sizes, you can alter the style of the document. Other type attributes are available, such as boldface, italic, and underlining.

In this chapter, you learn how to find and open a previously created document. Then you learn ways to format your document pages: setting margins, indenting, tabbing, changing page breaks. After the basic formatting information, the discussion moves into stylistic considerations. You learn how to work with type sizes and styles, choose fonts, use italic and boldface, use special characters. You learn to center your text or print it flush right, flush left, or justified. With the techniques you learn in this chapter, you can produce attractive, professional-quality word-processing documents.

Opening a File

One advantage of computers is that you can store documents on disk and reuse them. Before you can work on a document that has been stored on your disk, however, you need to open the document. You can accomplish this task in more than one way.

In every case, you start by telling Works that you want to open a word-processing document. You use the Open File dialog box (see fig. 3.1). When you select the word-processing icon, Works displays a list of word-processing documents. You can open any Works document by double-clicking on the file name in the Open File dialog box.

The steps to open a file are the following:

1. Start Works either by inserting your Works diskette or by double-clicking on the Works icon.
2. The Open File dialog box is displayed.
3. Click on the word processor or other icon if you want to limit the search to only one type of file.
4. Double-click on the name of the desired file or click on the file name and then click on the Open button.

Fig. 3.1

Opening a word-processing document.

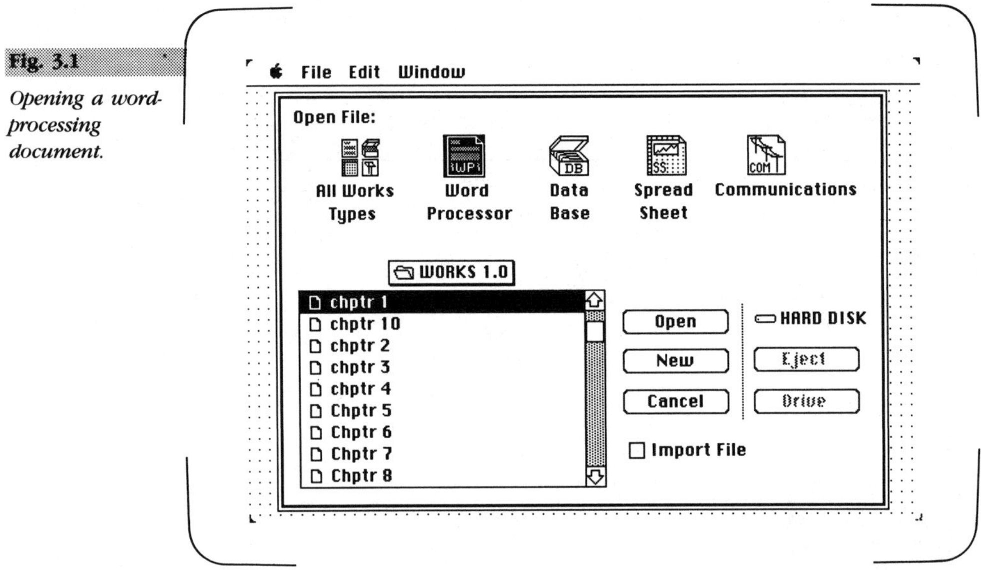

Speeding the Search for a Document

In addition to narrowing the field by clicking on the word-processing icon, you can enter the first one or two letters of a document name immediately after you click the icon. The file list scrolls to the part of the list containing documents that start with the letters you've entered.

Opening Several Documents at Once

Version 1.0 of Works supports up to 10 open windows; Version 1.1, up to 14. To open a document while working on others, you either select Open from the File menu or press *command*-O to access the Open File dialog box. You can move from document to document by choosing the desired document from the Window menu or by scrolling through open windows with the *command*-, (comma) shortcut (see fig. 3.2). You can have only one active window at a time, but each time you press *command*-, (comma), a different window becomes active. That is, the window comes to the top of the pile on your desktop. This capability comes in handy when you are transferring information from one document to another.

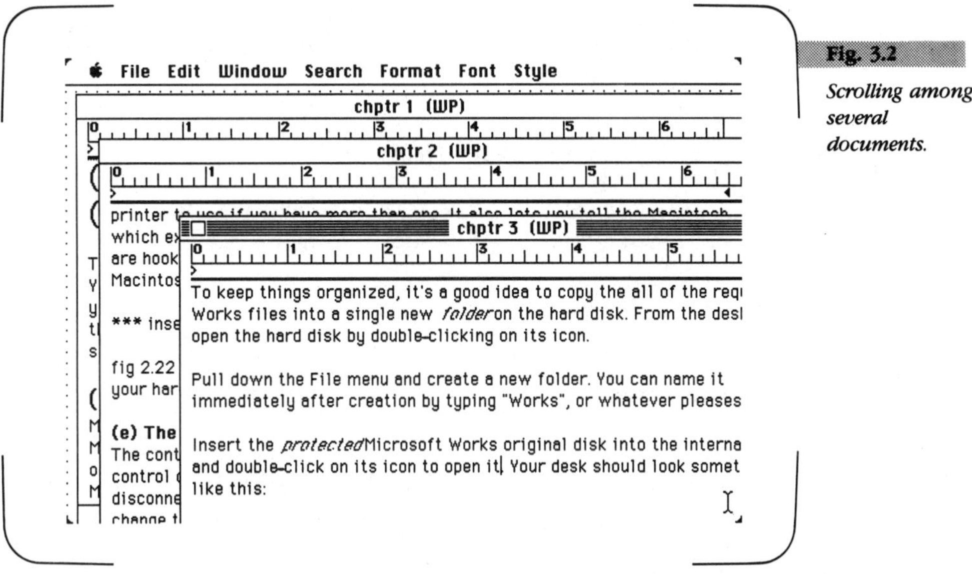

Fig. 3.2

Scrolling among several documents.

Loading Works and a Word-Processing Document Simultaneously

You can load Works and a word-processing document at the same time by double-clicking on any word-processing document.

Formatting Your Document Pages

One advantage of Works is the ease with which you can change the appearance of your document pages. With no additional typing, you can change the margins. You can add or delete indents or change the amount of indents. You can even change page breaks. Without a word processor, any of these changes requires retyping the entire document.

Setting Margins

New Works users frequently confuse margins and indents. *Margins* are the white spaces at the left, right, top, and bottom of the text and pictures on your printed page. These white spaces don't appear on the screen when you're entering and editing text. Rather, you see what's going on between the margins. *Indents* are the amount by which text is pulled inside the margin. Every page has margins, but text can be completely without indents.

The Page Setup Dialog Box

Margins are set in inches and decimal fractions of an inch. You use the Page Setup dialog box, which is shown in figure 3.3:

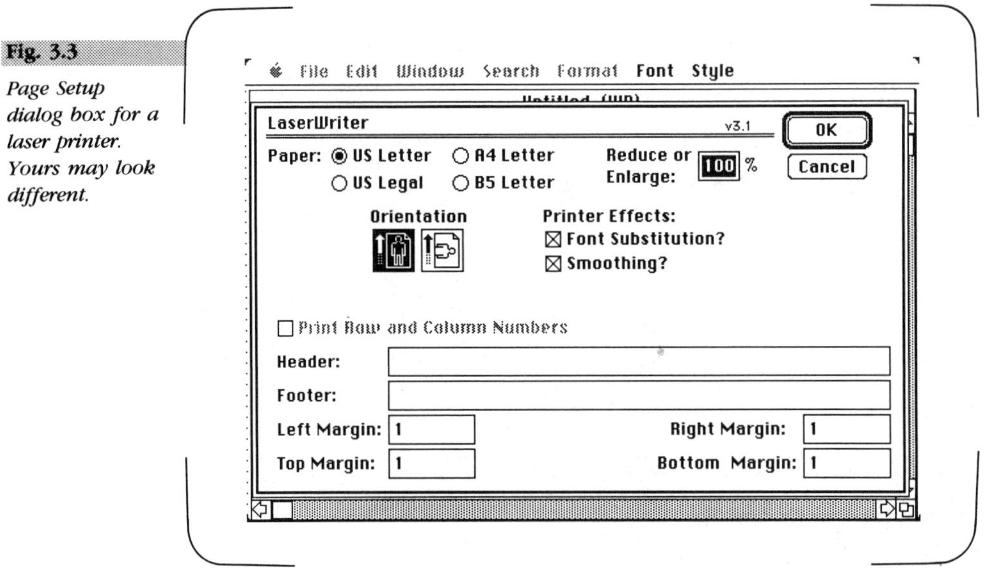

Fig. 3.3

Page Setup dialog box for a laser printer. Yours may look different.

When setting margins, you should remember a few simple rules. The most important is pretty obvious when you think about it: The combination of the left and right margins, when added to the length of the longest text line or largest picture in a document, can't exceed the width of the paper.

For example, if you're using 8 1/2-inch paper and want a 1-inch left margin and a 1-inch right margin, you can't make text lines or pictures longer than 6 1/2 inches. If you select combinations that break this rule, Works warns you and truncates (does not print) portions of images that fall outside the available area (see fig. 3.4).

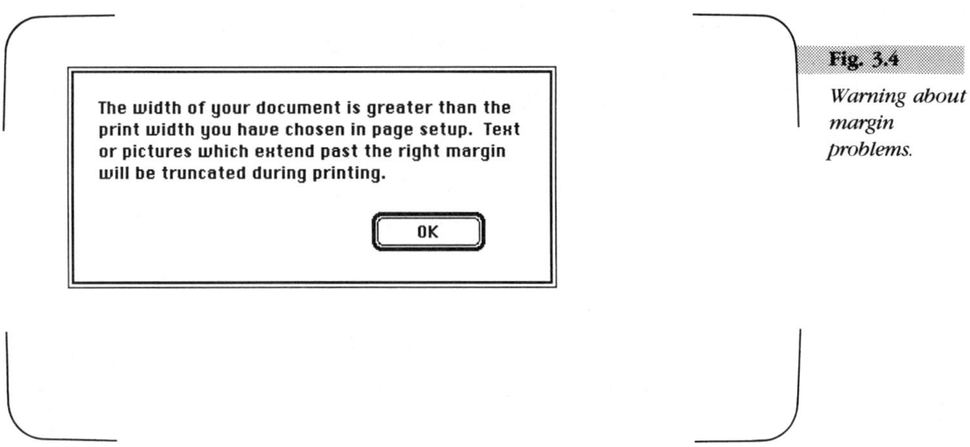

The width of your document is greater than the print width you have chosen in page setup. Text or pictures which extend past the right margin will be truncated during printing.
OK

Fig. 3.4

Warning about margin problems.

Remember, too, that not all printers can print at the outer edges of paper. Many laser printers, including the Apple LaserWriter®, require a minimum of 1/2 inch at the top, bottom, left, and right sides of the page. Take this requirement into consideration when setting margins for the page setup.

When defining margins in the Page Setup dialog box, enter fractional inches as decimals. For example, you enter 1 1/2 inches as 1.5; 2 1/4 inches, as 2.25; and so on.

The margin settings you define in the Page Setup dialog box are used for the entire document. Works uses what are called indent markers to set "temporary margins" within a document (see "Using the Indent Markers—An Overview").

The Screen Ruler

At the top of the Works word-processing window is displayed a ruler that shows the position (in inches) of text and images relative to the left margin. Zero on the ruler is not the edge of the paper but the left edge of the image area.

You can remove the ruler from the screen by using the Hide Ruler option on the Format menu (see fig. 3.5). While the ruler is hidden, the Show Ruler option replaces Hide Ruler on the menu. To restore the ruler, you choose the Show Ruler option (see fig. 3.6).

Using the Indent Markers—An Overview

Among other things, the bottom portion of the ruler contains markers that indicate the paragraph formatting choices you've made (see fig. 3.7). Each paragraph can have its own set of indents. The markers are

- Left indent
- Right indent
- First-line indent

When you open a new document, Works assumes that you don't want indents of any kind. You can, however, easily tell Works otherwise.

Fig. 3.5

The Hide Ruler option.

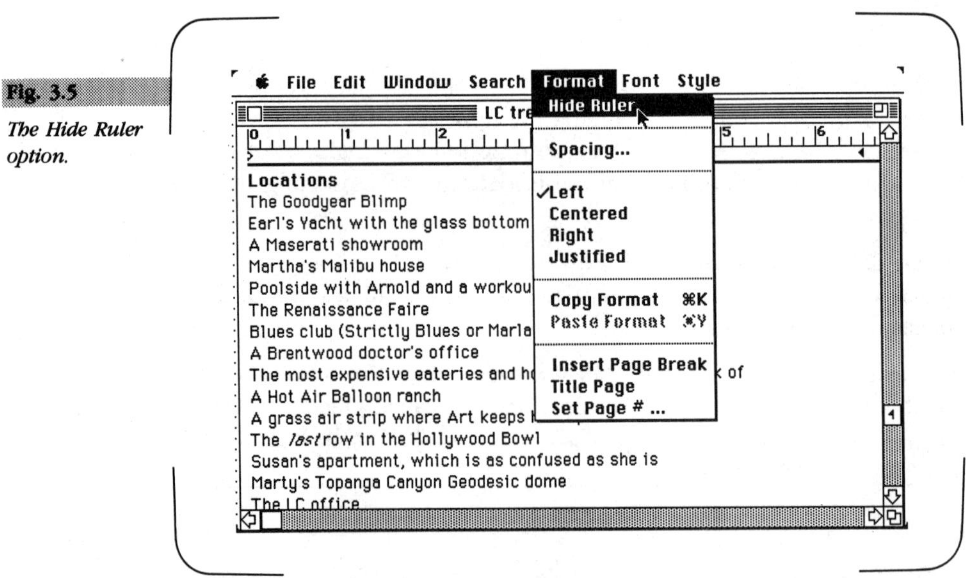

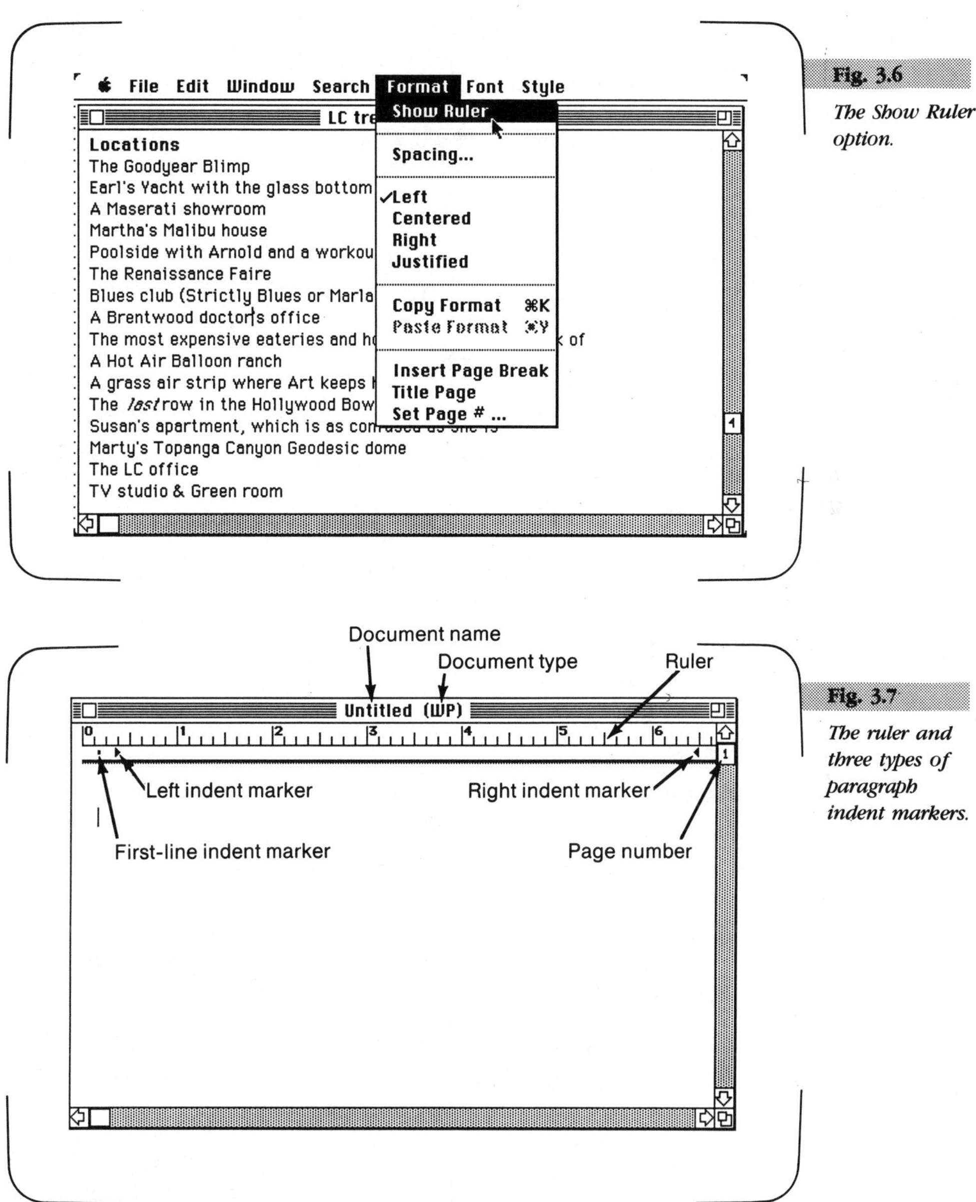

Fig. 3.6 *The Show Ruler option.*

Fig. 3.7 *The ruler and three types of paragraph indent markers.*

Right Indent Marker

The right indent marker usually is a solid black triangle located inside the ruler near the right edge of the screen. The triangle's long side defines the point on the ruler where wordwrap will occur.

When you open a new document, the right indent marker appears 6 1/2 inches from the left margin. You can move the marker before you start typing; this change affects all the text you type thereafter.

To affect selected paragraphs in a document, you select the desired area and then move the marker. This way, Works alters only the selected text.

Experiment with moving the right indent marker. Pointing directly at the marker requires a little practice. To practice using the right indent marker, do the following:

1. Select an entire paragraph.
2. Point to the right indent marker and drag it to the left.
3. Release the mouse button and watch Works reformat the text.

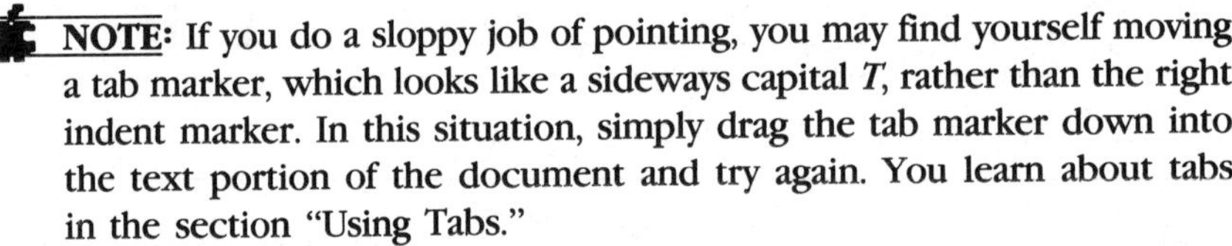

NOTE: If you do a sloppy job of pointing, you may find yourself moving a tab marker, which looks like a sideways capital *T*, rather than the right indent marker. In this situation, simply drag the tab marker down into the text portion of the document and try again. You learn about tabs in the section "Using Tabs."

You can move the right indent marker to the right as well as to the left. Works then makes the lines of text longer rather than shorter. The screen scrolls when necessary.

NOTE: If you move the marker so far to the right that a conflict occurs with the right margin, or so far that your text won't fit on the page size you've chosen, the marker changes from solid black to a hollow triangle, as a warning. If you ignore the subtle warning, Works truncates your work when you print it.

First-Line Indent

Works provides a first-line indent marker that makes indenting the first lines of paragraphs easy (see fig. 3.8). The marker is a small box that appears on top of the left indent marker when you open a new document.

To indent the first line of a paragraph, drag the little square marker (not the triangle) along the ruler to the position you choose. The first line in the current paragraph moves a corresponding amount, and each paragraph you type thereafter starts with a similarly indented line. To indent only certain paragraphs, you must select those paragraphs before you move the marker.

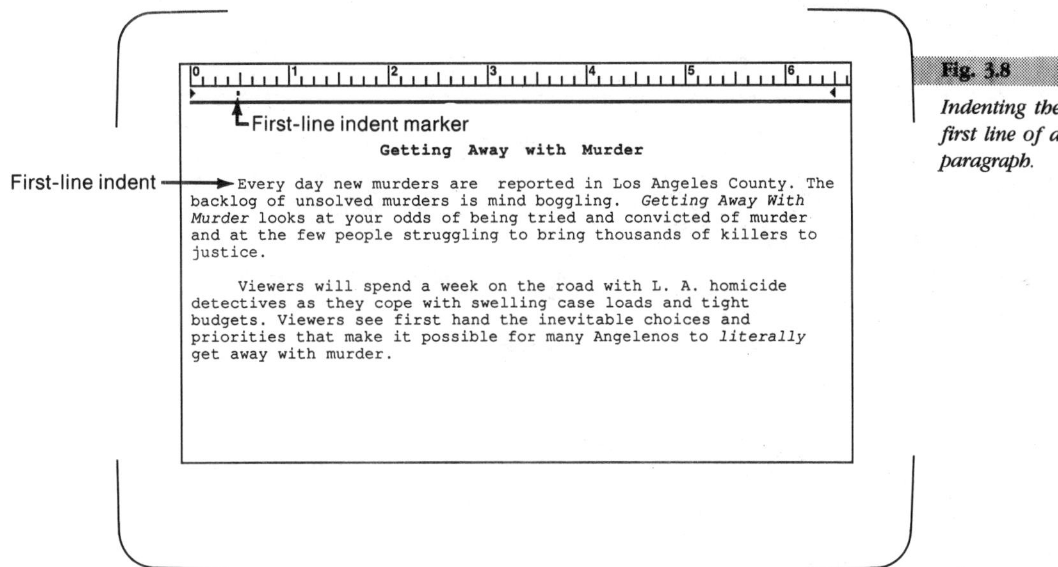

Fig. 3.8

Indenting the first line of a paragraph.

Left Indent

Using Works' left indent capability, you can force entire paragraphs to move to the right of a document's regular left margin. Some people call these left indents "temporary left margins." You can set left indents while you are typing or after the document is finished.

The left indent marker, which is usually a solid black triangle, may be partially covered by the first-line indent marker. You may need to move the small box slightly to the right temporarily in order to point properly at the left indent marker.

The long (left) edge of the triangle defines the left edge of indented paragraphs (see fig. 3.9). To move the left marker, drag it, just as you drag the right indent marker. Selected text follows the marker's movements. If you set up indent markers before typing a paragraph, that paragraph and any that you type after it are indented. You also can select one or more previously typed paragraphs and indent them by moving the marker while the paragraphs are selected.

Hanging Left Indents

Using hanging left indents is a great way to add emphasis to a paragraph (see fig. 3.10). To produce hanging indents, you use the first-line indent and left indent markers together:

Fig. 3.9

Left indentations.

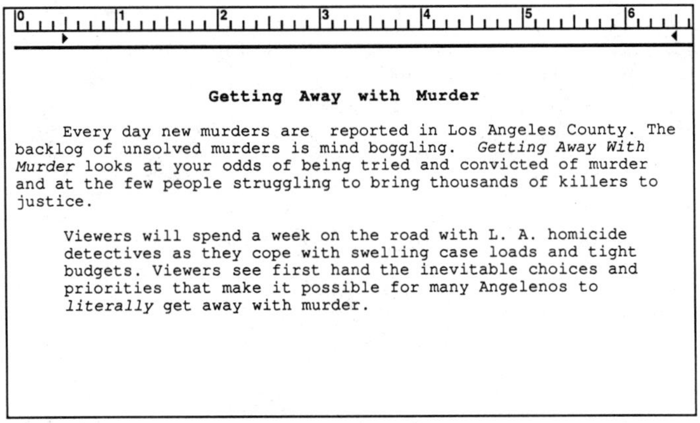

Getting Away with Murder

Every day new murders are reported in Los Angeles County. The backlog of unsolved murders is mind boggling. *Getting Away With Murder* looks at your odds of being tried and convicted of murder and at the few people struggling to bring thousands of killers to justice.

Viewers will spend a week on the road with L. A. homicide detectives as they cope with swelling case loads and tight budgets. Viewers see first hand the inevitable choices and priorities that make it possible for many Angelenos to *literally* get away with murder.

1. Place the left indent marker to the right of the left margin.
2. Move the first-line indent marker to the left of the left indent.

As a result, the first line of the paragraph is flush with the left margins, and all following lines are indented. This technique is a great way to insert numbers or bullets to the left of indented paragraphs.

Fig. 3.10

Hanging left indentations.

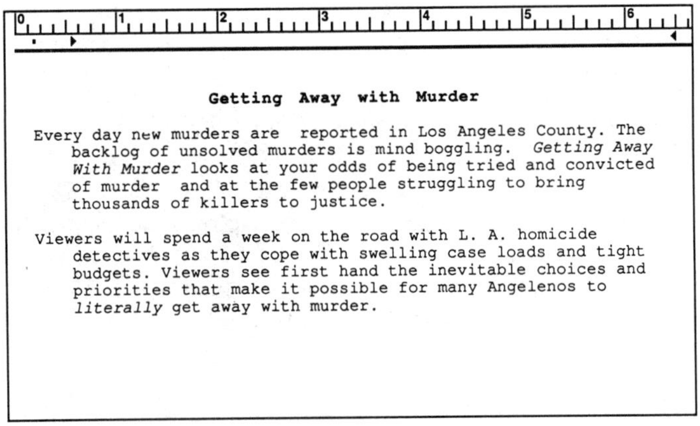

Getting Away with Murder

Every day new murders are reported in Los Angeles County. The backlog of unsolved murders is mind boggling. *Getting Away With Murder* looks at your odds of being tried and convicted of murder and at the few people struggling to bring thousands of killers to justice.

Viewers will spend a week on the road with L. A. homicide detectives as they cope with swelling case loads and tight budgets. Viewers see first hand the inevitable choices and priorities that make it possible for many Angelenos to *literally* get away with murder.

Using Tabs

Tabs enable you to move the cursor specified distances on the screen without using the space bar. Tabs are particularly useful for typing tables. Works offers three types of tabs: preset left tabs, custom left tabs, and right tabs. They all have different uses.

Using Preset Left Tabs for Text

Using left tabs, you can easily move to a specific point on a line without typing a number of spaces. Left tabs frequently are used for typing text in tables. When you open a new document, Works provides preset left tabs every half-inch. Pressing the *tab* key causes Works to move the cursor to the next available tab.

To experiment with preset tabs, open a new document and press the *tab* key. Notice that the cursor moves about one-half inch each time you press *tab*. Pressing the *backspace* key tells Works to move the cursor back one tab stop.

Setting Custom Left Tabs

You can use Work's preset left tabs, or you can replace them with your own. Work's standard tabs don't show up on the ruler; your custom tabs do.

To set a custom left tab, make sure that the ruler is visible, and then click once at the desired position on the bottom half of the ruler. A left tab marker appears. Click wherever and as often as you like, but click only once per tab. In figure 3.11, for example, two left tabs are set—one on either side of the ruler's one-inch marker.

NOTE: When you set your own tabs, all preset tabs to the left of the new tab disappear.

Using Right Tabs for Columns of Numbers

Works' right tabs make typing columns of numbers simple (see fig. 3.12). A right tab aligns columns at the right edge—as with columns of numbers. To set right tabs, you double-click on the ruler. The markers for right tabs point in the opposite direction from left tab markers.

When you press the *tab* key, tab to a right tab stop, and then begin typing, everything you type moves left. Aligning numbers on subsequent lines containing identical formats (right tab settings) is therefore easy.

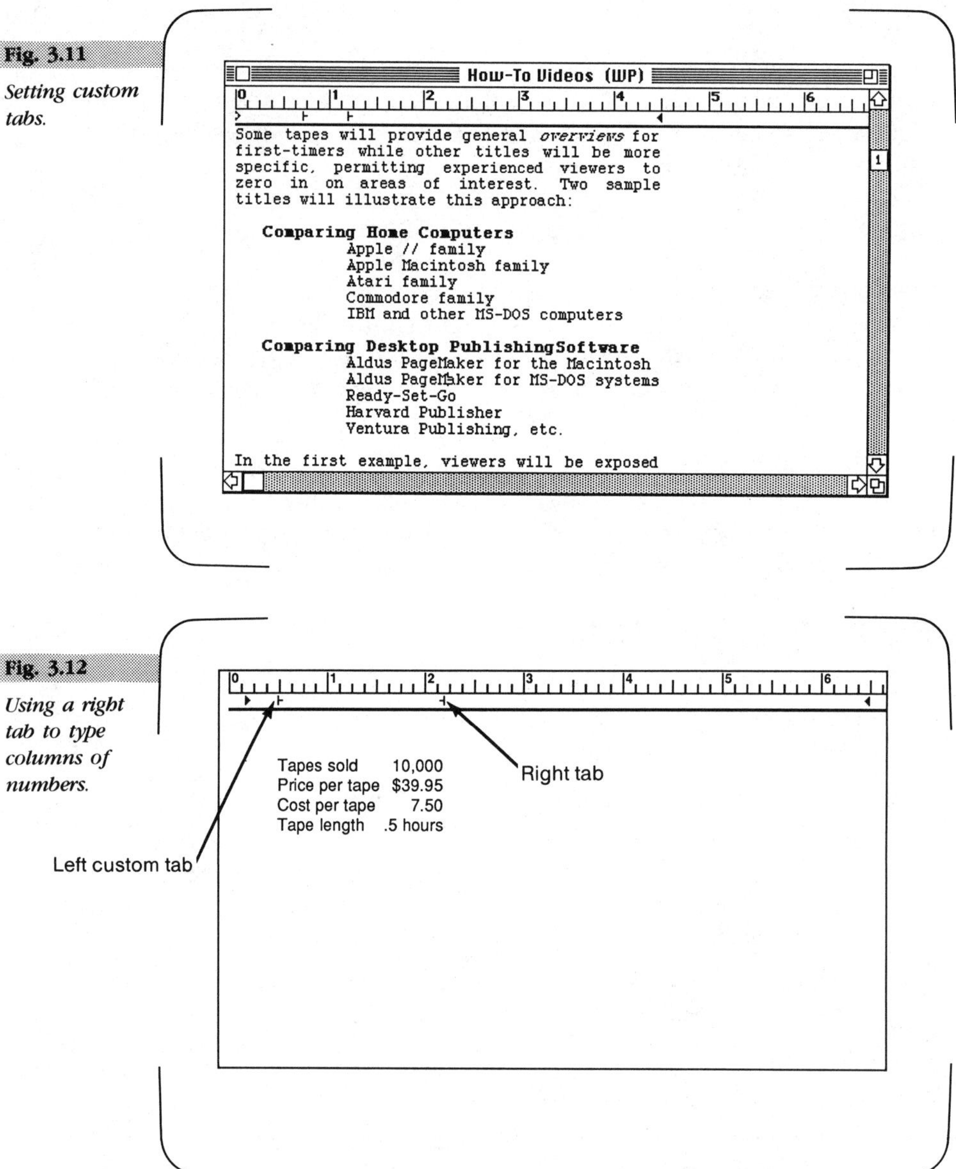

Fig. 3.11 *Setting custom tabs.*

Fig. 3.12 *Using a right tab to type columns of numbers.*

Moving and Deleting Tabs

To move a tab, drag its marker along the ruler to any place you choose between the left margin and the right indent marker. Dragging a tab marker elsewhere causes Works to move the tab to the place where you stop dragging. To delete tabs, you drag them off the ruler and then release the mouse button.

Working with Paragraph Formats

A collection of tabs, indent markers, line-spacing specifications, type styles, and so forth, is called a *format*; and formats can change from paragraph to paragraph. That is, you can have one format for a whole document or as many different formats as the document has paragraphs. Remember, too, that with Works, a single line can be a paragraph. The script in figure 3.13, for example, contains varied indented sections.

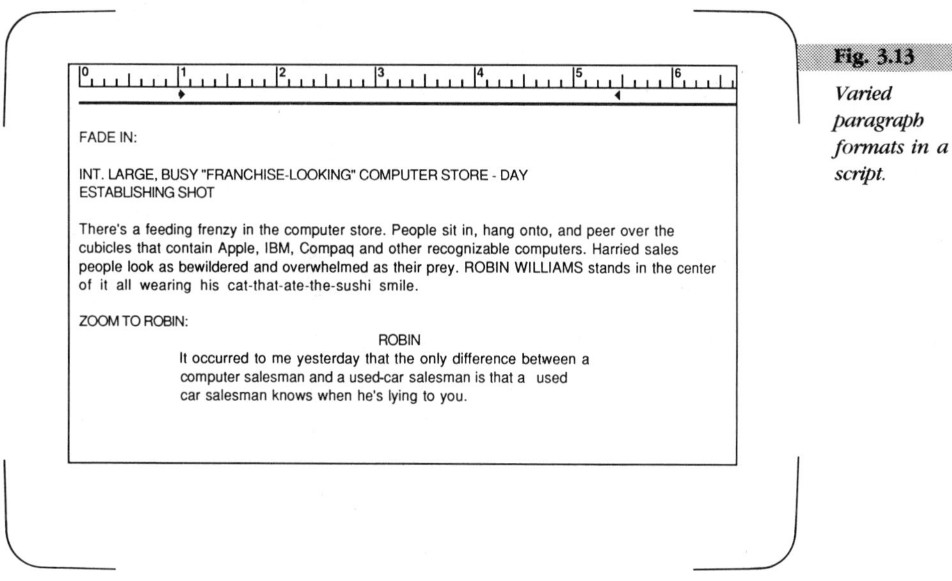

Fig. 3.13 *Varied paragraph formats in a script.*

To avoid having to re-create formats repeatedly—in scripts, for example—you can copy formats within the same document. Follow these steps:

1. Click anywhere in a paragraph with a format you want to copy.
2. Select the Copy Format option on the Format menu.
3. Point to the destination paragraph (click in it anywhere).
4. Choose Paste Format on the Format menu.

If you copy formats a great deal, the *command*-key shortcuts come in handy. Hold down the *command* key and press **K** to copy or **Y** to paste.

You can repeat the format-pasting function for multiple paragraphs scattered throughout your document. To paste a common format to several adjacent paragraphs, select the destination paragraphs before you paste.

The only way to copy formats from one document to another is to copy a paragraph containing the desired format to the new document. Then, you can modify or eliminate the old text while maintaining the format.

Changing Page Breaks

Using the page size you choose in the Page Setup box, Works displays automatic page breaks, which appear as dashed lines on the screen. Works considers the size of the paper, the margins you've set, the size of the type and type styles you've used, and so on.

Forcing Early Page Breaks

You can force Works to break the page early. Forced page breaks help you keep together similar portions of text, such as tables. Some people refer to this process as "defining the place where a new page will begin."

1. Click anywhere on the first line of text that belongs on the new page.
2. Select Insert Page Break from the Format menu.
3. A new dashed line appears above the line on which you clicked. That line is the first line on a new page when you print.

You can use a keyboard shortcut. If you hold down the *shift* key and then press the *enter* key (not the *return* key), Works inserts a page break above the pointer.

NOTE: The lines on-screen showing forced page breaks look just like standard page breaks in Works Version 1.0. Forced page-break lines have bigger dots in Version 1.1. Figure 3.14 shows forced page breaks in Works Version 1.1.

Removing Page Breaks

Sometimes a forced page break becomes unnecessary. For example, if you insert text above the forced page break, it may no longer be needed. When this change occurs, often you'll see two page breaks on the screen: the automatic page break and the forced page break (see fig. 3.14).

When you print the text, Works prints a blank page between the two page breaks.

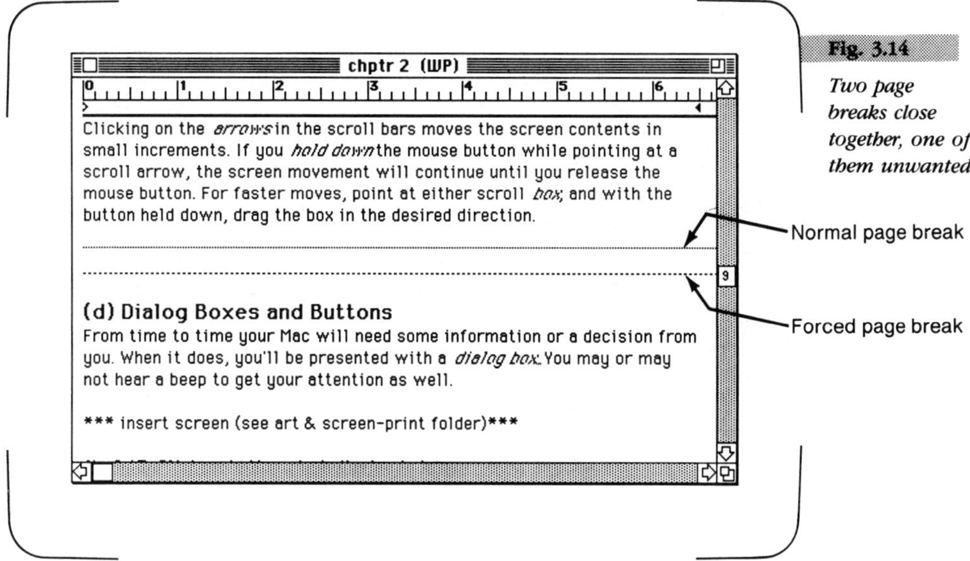

Fig. 3.14

Two page breaks close together, one of them unwanted.

To remove an unwanted forced page break, you do the following:

1. Click anywhere on the first line below the forced page break.
2. Choose Remove Page Break from the Format menu.
3. The forced page break disappears.

Adding Style to Your Documents

Anybody can type a simple word-processing document. In fact, the procedures described in Chapter 2 and the first part of this chapter may be all you'll need for everyday typing projects. But to make full use of the Macintosh and its graphics capabilities, read about the following stylistic techniques—either now or after you've had a chance to practice the basics.

Type Sizes and Styles

Works takes full advantage of the Mac's capability to display and print a variety of typefaces and styles. You can select from many fonts (character designs) and point sizes. In addition, the following attributes are available:

- Bold
- Italic
- Underline
- Outline
- Shadow
- Superscripts and subscripts

Figure 3.15 shows examples of all these attributes, which are usually available for any font. You can mix and match type styles, point sizes, and attributes. And you can make these choices either before or after you type something.

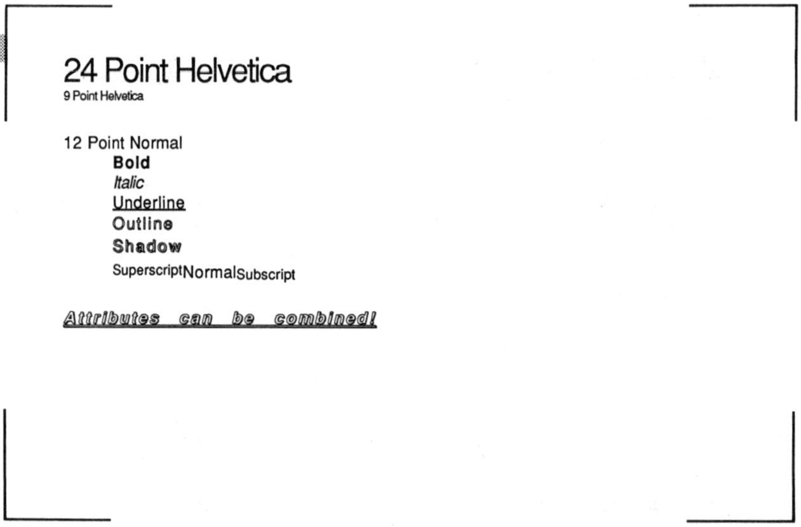

Fig. 3.15

Examples of Macintosh typestyles and attributes on a laser printer.

24 Point Helvetica
9 Point Helvetica

12 Point Normal
Bold
Italic
Underline
Outline
Shadow
SuperscriptNormalSubscript

Attributes can be combined!

Choosing Fonts and Point Sizes

Works comes with a system folder containing five fonts: Boston, Athens, Monaco, Geneva, and Chicago. The preset (also called the default) choice for Works word-processing documents is 10-point Boston.

You can use fonts other than the five shipped with Works if they reside in the system folder. And you can add fonts to your system folder; many fonts are available from computer dealers or are in the public domain.

Regardless of which fonts you use, remember that the appearance of your printed text will be somewhat different from its appearance on the screen. Line endings and page breaks do not change; but overall sharpness, smoothness, character spacing, and other design elements do change. The kind of printer you use and its physical condition also affect the quality of the printed piece.

LaserWriter owners can use the Font Mover (Apple® Font/DA Mover Utility) program (which comes on the Macintosh System disk) to add Helvetica, Times, and other fonts. Follow the instructions that came with your fonts and printer. When adding laser fonts, remember that you need to add both screen and printer fonts.

Type is available in a number of sizes, measured in points (see fig. 3.16). Generally, the lower the number, the smaller the type. For example, 10-point Geneva is smaller than 24-point Geneva. Because typeface designers are the ones who define point sizes, however, one 10-point typeface may be slightly larger or smaller than another 10-point typeface.

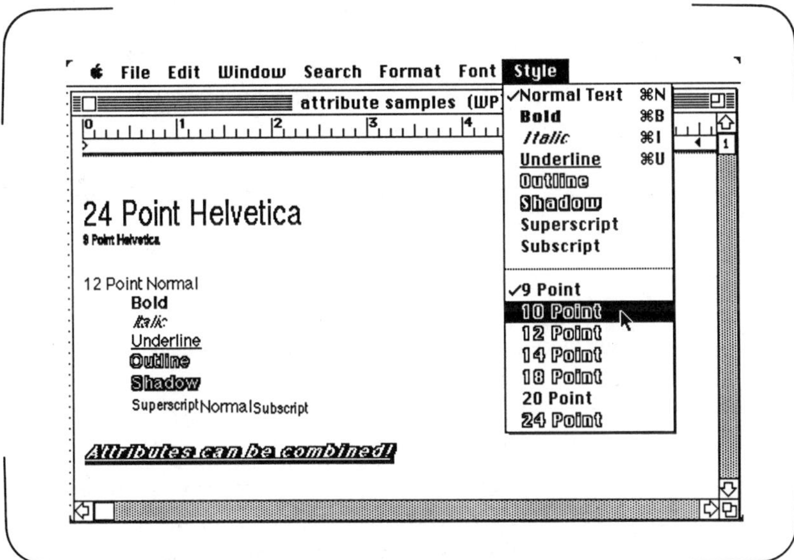

Fig. 3.16
The Style menu, displaying the sizes available for the chosen font. Check marks indicate selected options.

Not all point sizes in every font look good when displayed. Works recommends the best sizes for each font. In figure 3.16, the recommended fonts appear on the Style menu in outlined type. The point sizes displayed in normal type can be used but may be harder to read on-screen; 9 point and 20 point are examples.

Changing Type Sizes and Attributes (Styles)

Select the text that you want to change. (You can use any of the selection methods explained in Chapter 2.) You can select single words, paragraphs, or an entire document. Then, pull down the Font or Style menu (see fig. 3.17). After you make your choices, Works simulates the results on the screen. In figure 3.17, the heading *MEMO* has been selected. It will be printed in 24-point boldface outline type.

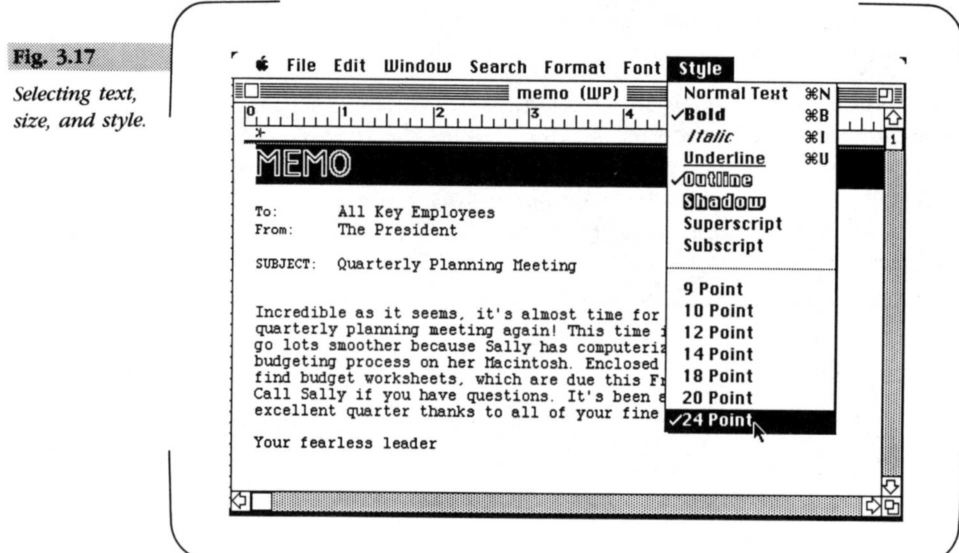
File Edit Window Search Format Font Style
memo (WP)
MEMO
To: All Key Employees
From: The President
SUBJECT: Quarterly Planning Meeting
Incredible as it seems, it's almost time for
quarterly planning meeting again! This time
go lots smoother because Sally has computeri
budgeting process on her Macintosh. Enclosed
find budget worksheets, which are due this F
Call Sally if you have questions. It's been
excellent quarter thanks to all of your fine
Your fearless leader
Normal Text ⌘N
✓Bold ⌘B
Italic ⌘I
Underline ⌘U
✓Outline
Shadow
Superscript
Subscript
9 Point
10 Point
12 Point
14 Point
18 Point
20 Point
✓24 Point

Fig. 3.17
Selecting text, size, and style.

To see how your printer interprets the choices you've made, print the document (or just the window). The document may look slightly different in print than it does on-screen, but aspects such as line endings shouldn't change.

Reverting to Normal Text

If you select text and then choose the Normal Text option on the Style menu, Works eliminates such attributes as boldface, italic, underline, and so forth. However, Works doesn't change point size or fonts. To change these features, you must select text and choose a new point size from the Style menu. You make other changes from the Font menu.

Changing Attributes as You Type

Works shortcuts let you use popular attributes without pulling down the Style menu. To change attributes while typing, hold down the *com-*

mand key and press **B** for bold, **I** for italic, **U** for underline, or **N** for normal.

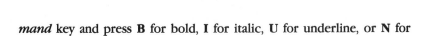

To stop bold, italic, or underlined attributes from appearing as you type, hold down the *command* key and press **N** (for Normal). You can combine attributes—for example, pressing *command*-N immediately followed by *command*-I produces bold italic. No shortcuts are available for outline, shadow, superscript, or subscript attributes.

Changing Type Styles and Attributes for an Entire Document

You can change the typestyle for an entire document by using the Select All option on the Edit menu and then choosing a different font (see figs. 3.18, 3.19, and 3.20). You can change the point size throughout a document this way, too. If you select the whole document and then choose the Normal attribute, all bold, underline, italic, and other attributes disappear.

Different typefaces take up different space on a page, so you may need to adjust margins and page endings after changing fonts.

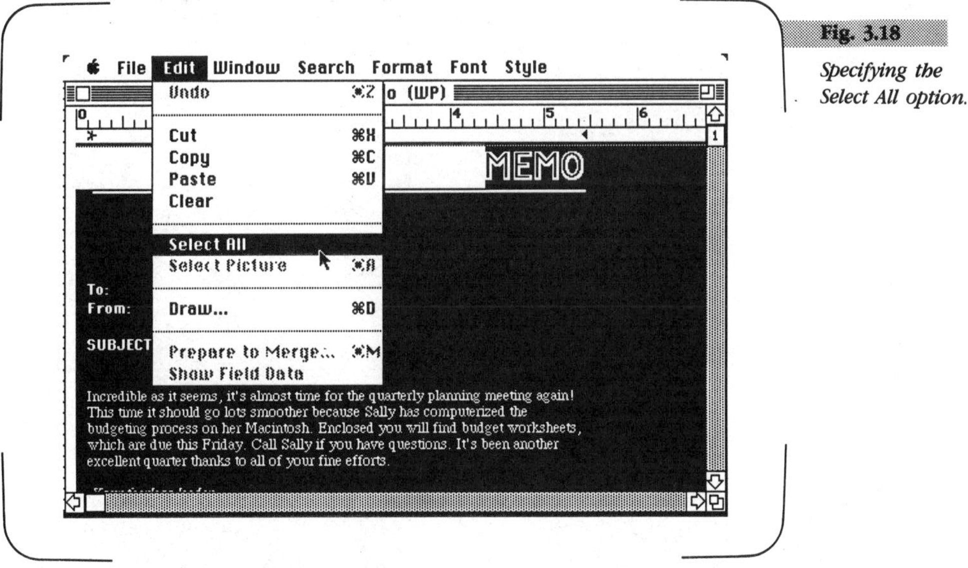
File Edit Window Search Format Font Style
Undo ⌘Z
Cut ⌘X
Copy ⌘C
Paste ⌘V
Clear
Select All
Select Picture ⌘A
Draw... ⌘D
Prepare to Merge... ⌘M
Show Field Data
MEMO
To:
From:
SUBJECT
Incredible as it seems, it's almost time for the quarterly planning meeting again! This time it should go lots smoother because Sally has computerized the budgeting process on her Macintosh. Enclosed you will find budget worksheets, which are due this Friday. Call Sally if you have questions. It's been another excellent quarter thanks to all of your fine efforts.

Fig. 3.18

Specifying the Select All option.

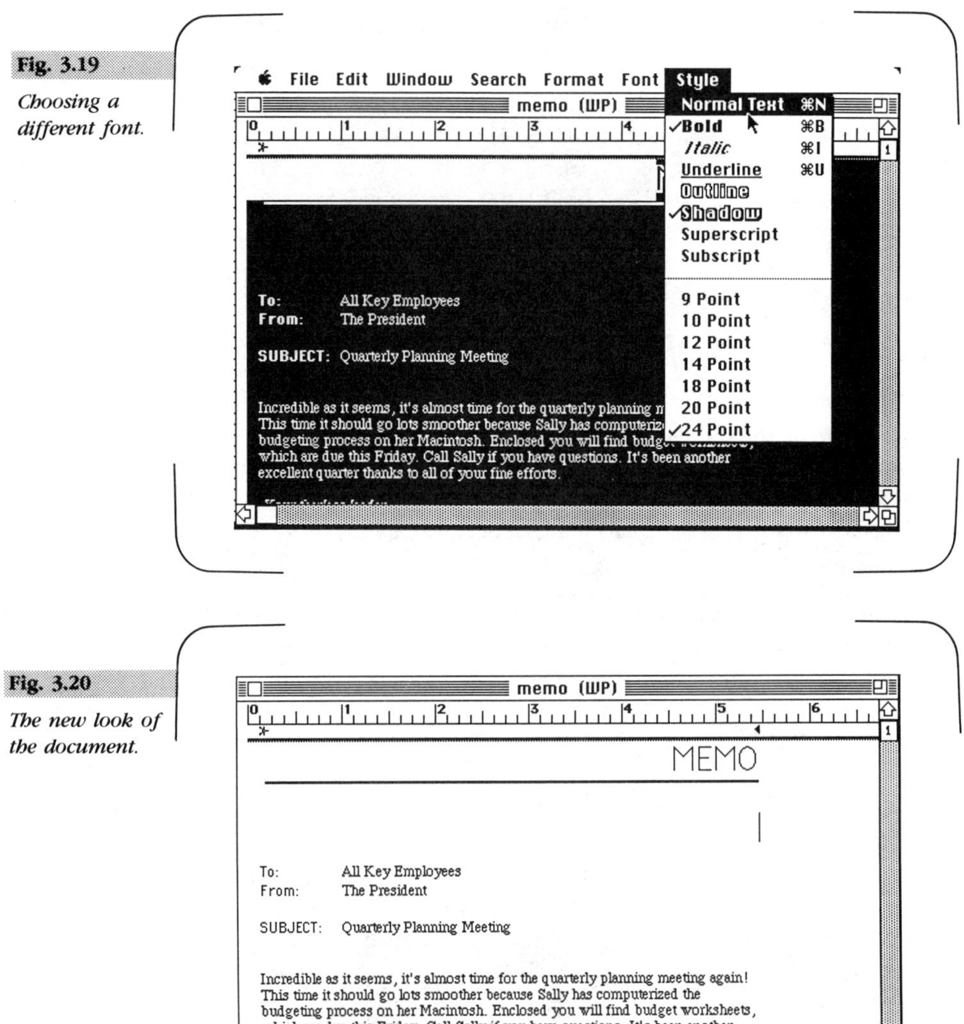
File Edit Window Search Format Font Style
memo (WP)
Normal Text ⌘N
✓Bold ⌘B
Italic ⌘I
Underline ⌘U
Outline
✓Shadow
Superscript
Subscript
9 Point
10 Point
12 Point
14 Point
18 Point
20 Point
✓24 Point
To: All Key Employees
From: The President
SUBJECT: Quarterly Planning Meeting
memo (WP)
MEMO
To: All Key Employees
From: The President
SUBJECT: Quarterly Planning Meeting
Incredible as it seems, it's almost time for the quarterly planning meeting again!
This time it should go lots smoother because Sally has computerized the
budgeting process on her Macintosh. Enclosed you will find budget worksheets,
which are due this Friday. Call Sally if you have questions. It's been another
excellent quarter thanks to all of your fine efforts.
Your fearless leader

Fig. 3.19

Choosing a different font.

Fig. 3.20

The new look of the document.

Other Stylistic Options

Works offers still other stylistic variations. For example, you can use special characters for foreign languages. You can adjust line spacing to achieve the appearance you want. Works also has the capability of printing text centered, flush left or flush right on the line, or justified. As you use the word processor, you will discover many occasions for these options.

Special Characters

The special characters on your Mac's keyboard can be entered and displayed as you would expect. To see which special keys are available for the font you're using, select Key Caps on the Apple menu. Then choose the desired font from the Key Caps menu. Watch the display as you press the *shift*, *option*, and *command* keys. Figure 3.21 shows a typical Key Caps window. Notice that a new menu item (Key Caps) appears on the menu bar. You use it to inspect the various typefaces installed on your system.

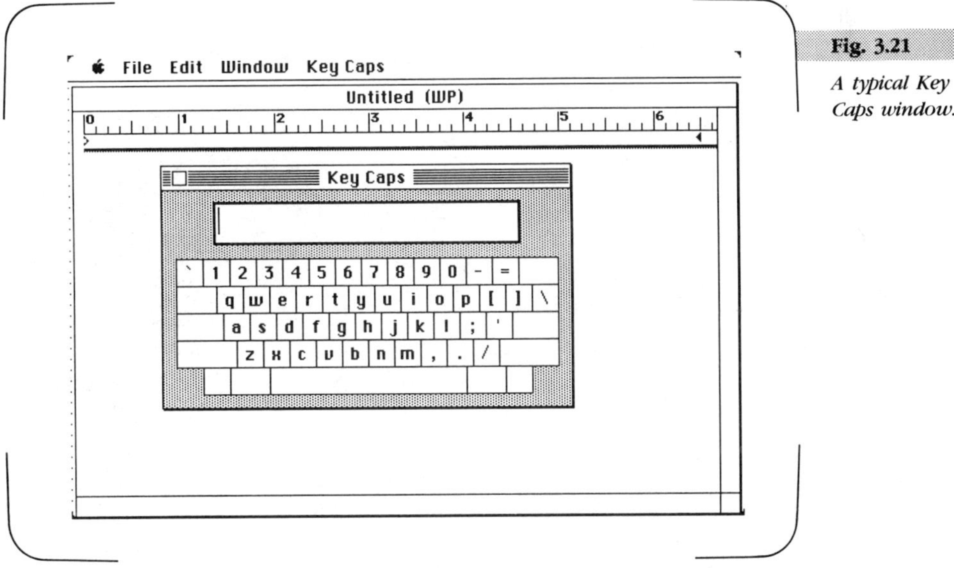

Fig. 3.21

A typical Key Caps window.

For example, to put an umlaut on the *o* in the German word *schön*, you hold down the *option* key, press **U**, and release both keys together before typing the letter **o**. An umlauted letter *ö* then appears.

To place a tilde over the *n* in the Spanish word *La Cañada*, hold down the *option* key and then press and release the **N** key before typing the **n**.

Remember that different fonts offer different special characters. If a word contains special characters and you change its font, Works may display or print the wrong special character.

You can copy text typed in the Key Caps window to the Clipboard and then paste your work where you want it.

Line Spacing and Font Sizes

To change line spacing, choose Spacing on the Format menu. Works then displays the Select Spacing dialog box, which offers line-and-a-half and double-line spacing (see fig. 3.22). You can change the spacing for an entire document or selected areas, such as paragraphs. Spacing can be selected before typing begins or after the text has been entered.

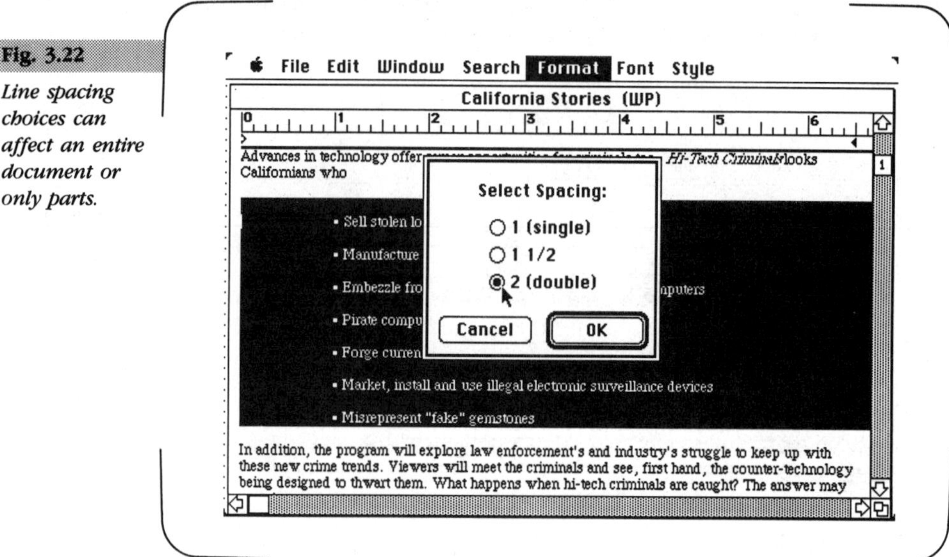

Fig. 3.22 *Line spacing choices can affect an entire document or only parts.*

Blank lines vary in height, just as lines containing text vary in height. Usually, blank lines are as high as the type in the font used for text lines that precede them. You can control blank-line height (and even paragraph spacing) by first selecting a blank line and then changing the font or type size for the blank line in order to create the desired effect. For example, to create a larger-than-normal space, pick a bigger size. To squeeze paragraphs, make the blank lines a smaller size than that used for text. Figure 3.23 shows two 12-point paragraphs separated by an 18-point blank line.

Centered Text

To center text between margins, select the text and then choose Centered on the Format menu. You can center single lines, paragraphs, or entire documents this way. Remember that if you select leading or trailing spaces, Works includes them in the centering process. Usually, you'll

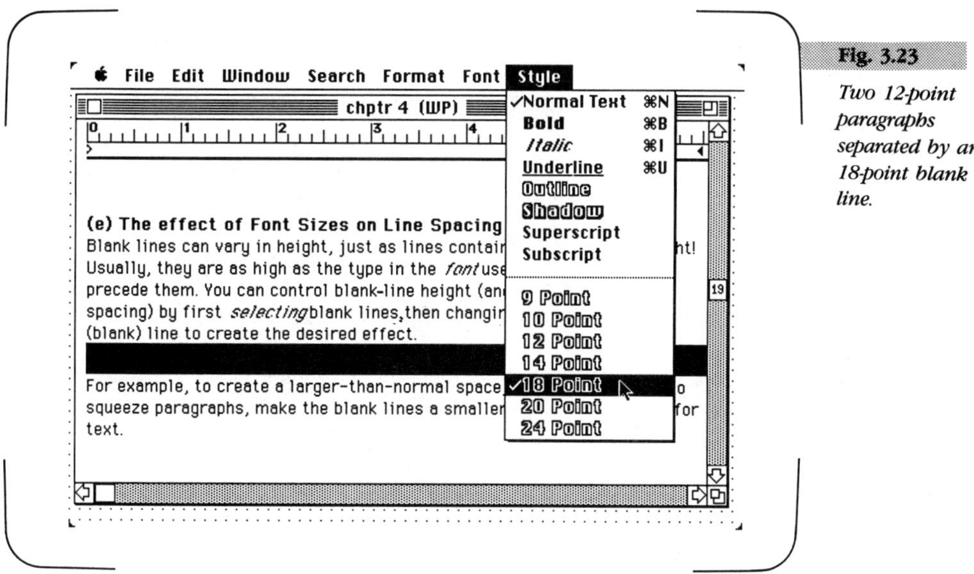

Fig. 3.23 *Two 12-point paragraphs separated by an 18-point blank line.*

want to select text and not leading or trailing spaces when you are preparing to center.

Flush-Left and Flush-Right Text

Usually, Works text is flush left; that is, Works places the first word of every line at the left margin. You may, however, format lines, paragraphs, or even entire documents so that text is flush right instead. Flush-right text has an even right margin.

You can set text flush right while you enter it. If no text is selected when you choose the Right option, newly typed text is all flush right until you select Left again. Figure 3.24 provides examples of lines that have been centered, set flush left, and set flush right.

Justified Text

If you choose the Justified option on the Format menu, Works tries to create both flush right and flush left margins (see fig. 3.25). The system justifies by adding random spaces between words to fill out each line (see fig. 3.26).

If you choose the Justified option *before* typing text, Works justifies the text as you type it. To justify *existing* text, you select it and then choose the Justified option on the Format menu.

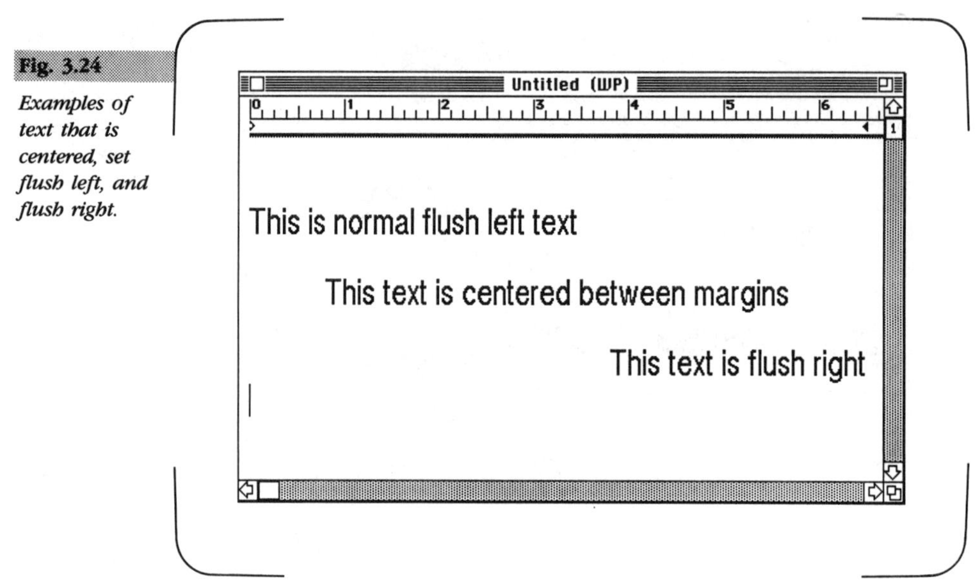

Fig. 3.24

Examples of text that is centered, set flush left, and flush right.

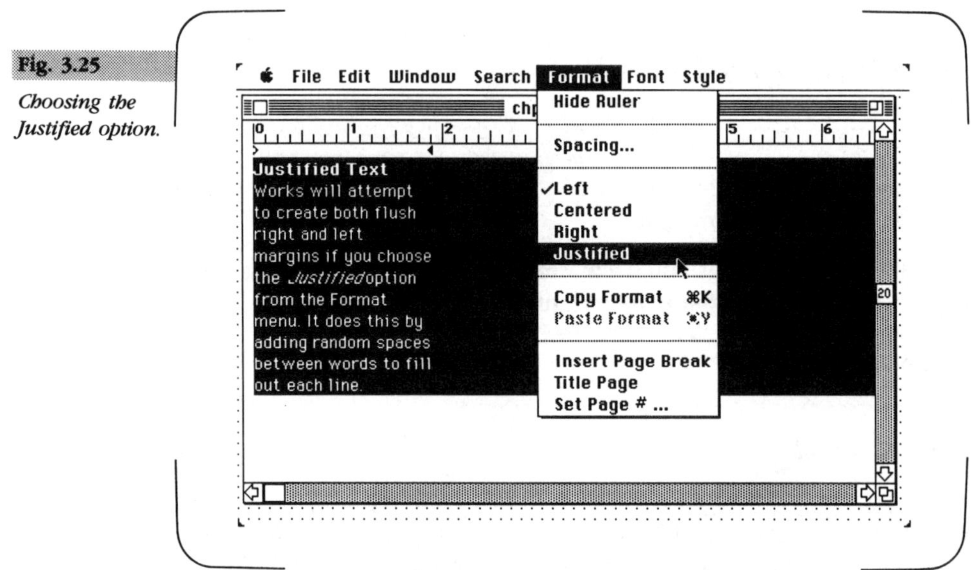

Fig. 3.25

Choosing the Justified option.

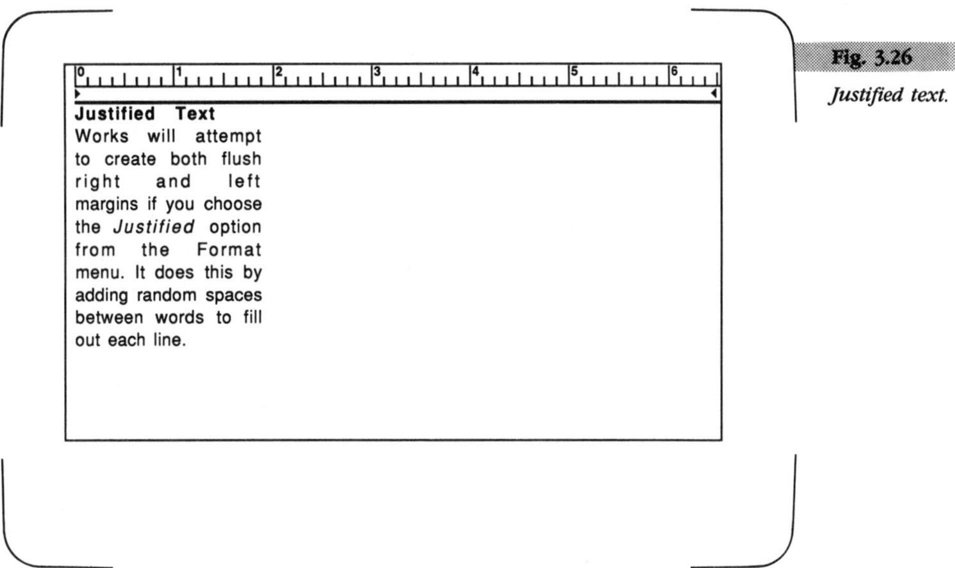

Fig. 3.26

Justified text.

Works does not automatically hyphenate words, so you'll find that it occasionally must insert quite a bit of space on a particular line to create flush left and right margins. If you find this process annoying, either hyphenate words manually or purchase additional software such as WorksPlus Spell, which performs automatic hyphenation.

Conclusion

This chapter covers the basic formatting options that you will use most frequently. With the capability of changing margins, indents, fonts, type styles, and type sizes, you can create attractive professional documents. Chapter 4 moves you into more complicated and advanced formatting features, such as using the drawing feature, including headers and footers, and using the search features.

4

More Advanced Word-Processing Techniques

This chapter includes advanced word-processing techniques that you can use to create unique and attractive documents. First, you learn how to use Works' Draw command to add circles, boxes, and lines to labels, letterheads, organizational charts, and other documents. As you'll see, you can include pictures from other Macintosh programs, such as MacPaint, as well as graphs from the Works spreadsheet module, in your word-processing documents, too.

You also learn how to include headers and footers both with and without page numbers and dates. You see how to use the search features to search for specific pages or specific text. Finally, the last section of this chapter presents a number of tips for using Works more effectively.

The Drawing Feature

Although Works' drawing feature is no substitute for a complete paint program, with the drawing feature you can add lines, boxes, circles, and ellipses to your documents in order to make them more professional looking. These lines, boxes, circles, and ellipses are called *pictures* and can be treated just like any other picture (see "Working with Pictures" for details). You can add text to these graphics elements, move them, and change their size.

Starting the Drawing Process

The Works word processor has two modes: text editing mode and drawing mode. You can use only one at a time, not both at once. To toggle between the two modes, select Draw or Draw Off on the Edit menu (see fig. 4.1). You also can use the shortcut, *command*-D, to toggle between drawing and text editing. Don't try to enter text while Works is in drawing mode.

As you can see in figure 4.1, Works provides a number of drawing tools. Some make lines; others, boxes and circles. Different line thicknesses also are available. You can choose to make circles, for example, with thin lines or thicker lines.

Fig. 4.1

Selecting Draw on the Edit menu.

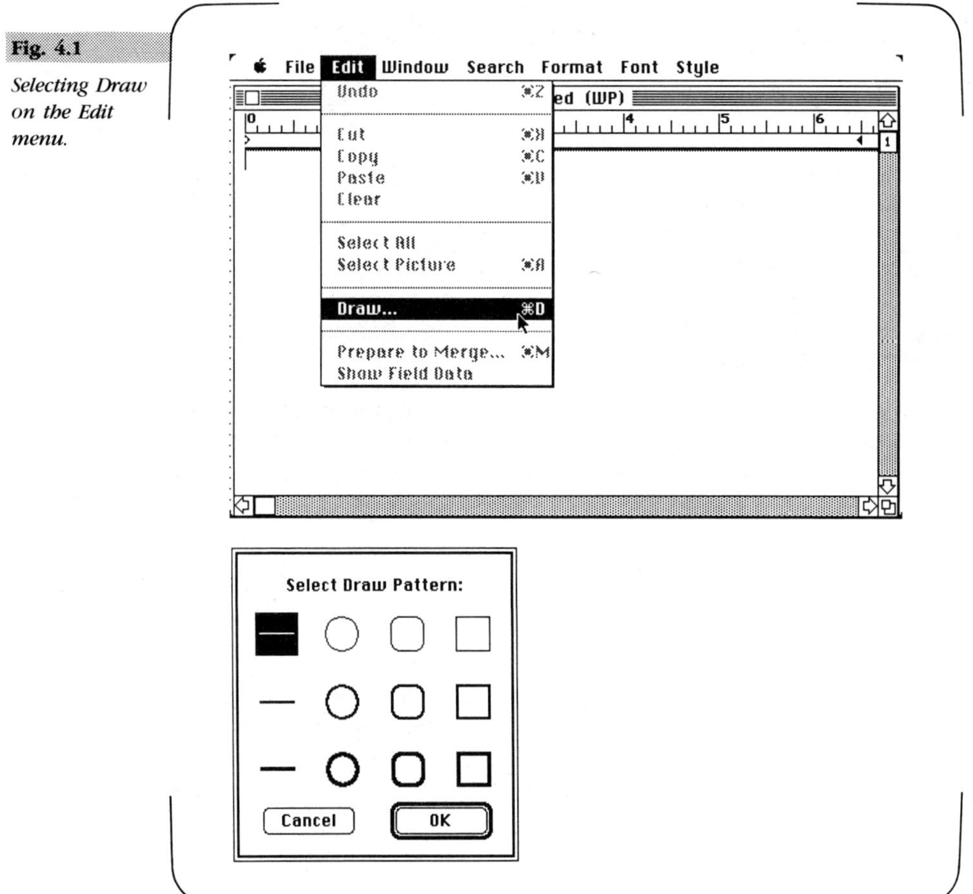

Drawing Lines

You can use lines to add your personal style to your work, as illustrated in the sample memo in Chapter 3. You can draw lines when you are creating organizational charts or forms. You even can make simple maps.

As you become comfortable with the Draw commands, you will think of many ways to use these lines.

To draw a line, you do the following:

1. In the Select Draw Pattern dialog box, click on the line thickness you want.
2. Click the OK button. The cursor becomes cross hairs.
3. Point to the spot in your document where you want the line to begin.
4. Hold down the mouse button and drag to the point where you want the line to end (see fig. 4.2).
5. Release the mouse button.
6. Either select Draw Off on the Edit menu or press **command-D**.

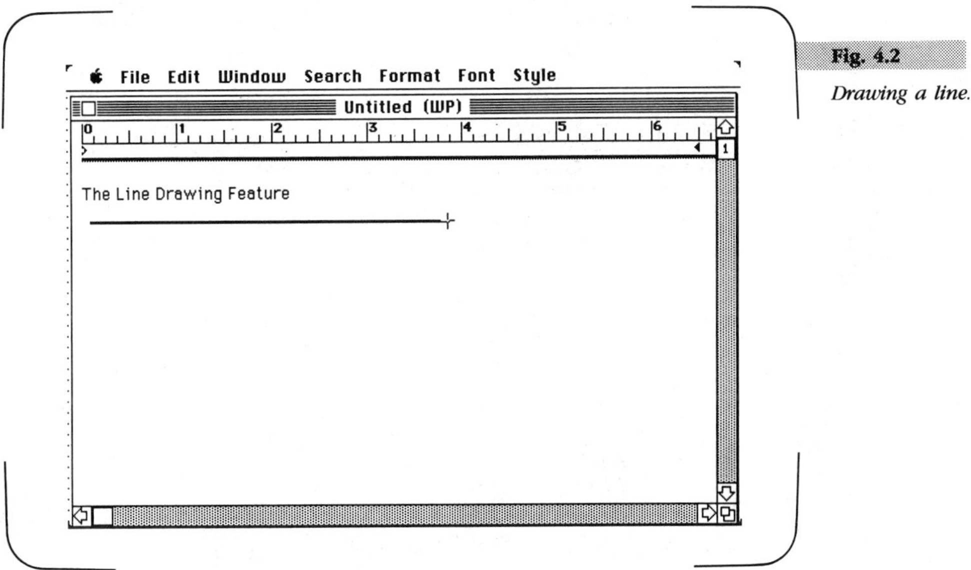

Fig. 4.2
Drawing a line.

Drawing Circles and Ellipses

You also can draw circles and ellipses by using the tool that looks like a circle. Either select Draw on the Edit menu or use the *command*-D shortcut. You can choose from several shapes and line thicknesses (see again fig. 4.1).

The procedure for drawing circles or ellipses is the following:

1. Click on the circle with the line thickness you want.
2. Click the OK button. The cursor becomes cross hairs.
3. Point to the general area where you want the circle to appear.
4. Drag to produce the correct size and shape. You may need to experiment with dragging techniques. Dragging from the center toward the lower right corner of the screen makes a circle. If you drag more toward the right than the bottom of the screen, you elongate the drawing and create an ellipse (see fig. 4.3).
5. Release the mouse button. If you release the mouse button before you get the shape you want, choose Undo from the Edit menu and try again.
6. Either select Draw Off on the Edit menu or press **command-D**.
7. Move (drag) the circle to its correct location, if necessary.

Fig. 4.3

Drawing a circle or an ellipse.

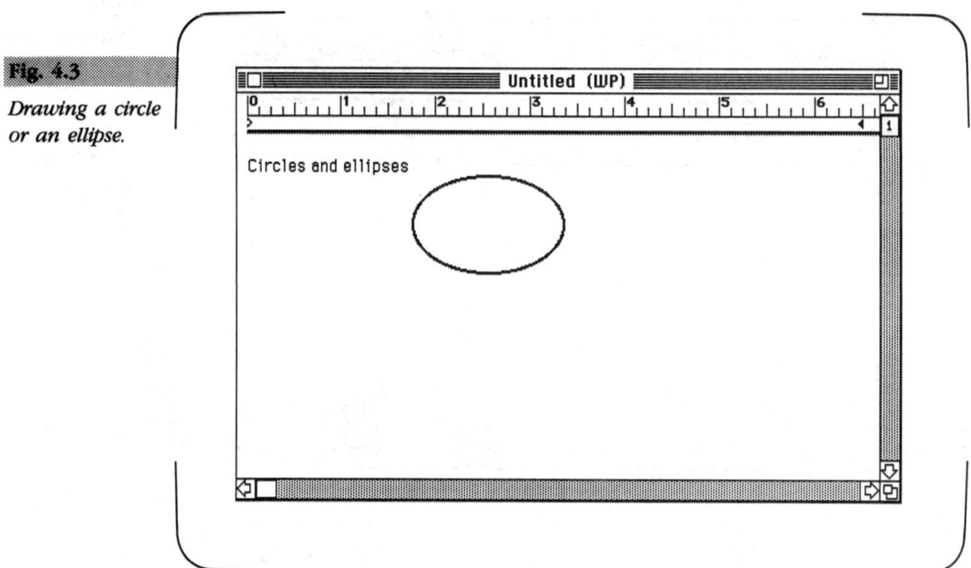

Drawing Boxes

To draw a box, you either select Draw on the Edit menu or use the *command*-D shortcut. In the Draw dialog box, you see a variety of shapes and line thicknesses. You can draw boxes with square or rounded corners in three different line thicknesses.

Here's how to draw square or rectangular boxes:

1. Click on the square with the line thickness and corners that please you.
2. Click the OK button. The cursor becomes cross hairs.
3. Point to where the square or rectangle will be located.
4. Drag to produce the correct size and shape. Dragging toward the lower right creates squares. If you drag more to the right or toward the bottom, the square becomes a rectangle (see fig. 4.4). You may need to experiment to learn to create different shapes and sizes.
5. Release the mouse button.
6. Either select Draw Off on the Edit menu or press **command-D**.
7. Drag the box to a new location if you want.

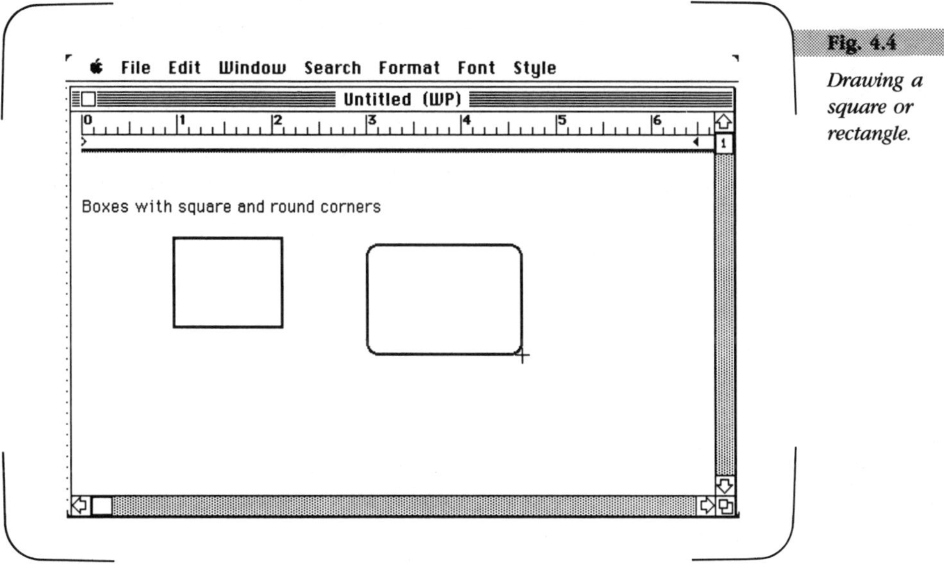

Fig. 4.4
Drawing a square or rectangle.

Working with Pictures

Works drawings are pictures; so are Works graphs if you paste them from the Clipboard. Your Scrapbook may contain pictures from paint programs, scanners—you name it. You work with all these images in the same way.

Importing and Selecting Pictures

You can paste any Scrapbook or Clipboard image into a Works word-processing document. If you can get the image to the Scrapbook or Clipboard, you probably can paste the image to a Works word-processing document. This capability means that you can create images with MacPaint, SuperPaint, MacDraw™, Easy3D®—any program which can create "paint" images—and use the images in your documents. Follow these steps:

1. Place the cursor where you want the picture to be pasted.
2. Choose the Scrapbook from the Apple menu and scroll through the images with the scroll bar.
3. Copy the desired image to the Clipboard (press **command-C** or use the Edit menu).
4. Paste the image from the Clipboard to the word-processing document (press **command-V** or use the Edit menu).
5. The image is already selected, so you can move or resize it if you need to.
6. Click elsewhere in the document to deselect the picture.

The process for selecting pictures in your word-processing document is the same whether you've drawn them with the Works Draw feature or imported them from your Scrapbook or paint program:

1. Click on or next to the picture.
2. Either select Picture on the Edit menu or press **command-A**. Works then outlines the picture with "marching ants," a blinking dashed line.

Once selected, a picture can be moved, cut, copied, or resized.

NOTE: If several pictures are closely spaced or overlapping, you may need to keep pressing **command-A** until the marching ants find the right picture.

Moving Pictures

After a picture is selected, it can be moved by several techniques. For example, you can drag it. The cursor changes to a hand when it encounters a selected picture. When this change happens, hold down the mouse button; you can move the picture anywhere you like. Naturally, you can cut and paste or copy pictures just as you do text. Pictures move down when you insert text above them.

Notice that when you drag a selected picture, any text within the picture stays behind. To move the text, you use regular text-cutting and text-pasting techniques.

If you cut or copy a selected picture, selected text and text attributes go along with the picture. Simply paste the combination wherever you want it.

Resizing Pictures

Selected pictures can be resized completely or just vertically or horizontally. The pointer changes shape depending on where it is in relation to the selected picture. Watch the shape of the pointer as you move it outside the selected image. Generally, the pointer becomes a plus sign (+) when it is near any edge of a picture, an X when it is at a corner, and a hand when it covers part of the inside of the picture. The pointer's shape tells you whether you're about to resize an image proportionally in all directions or distort it. If the pointer looks like the letter X, you will resize the entire image in both directions (see fig. 4.5). A pointer that looks like a plus sign (+) indicates that you will be resizing on only one axis and so distort the image's final shape (see fig. 4.6).

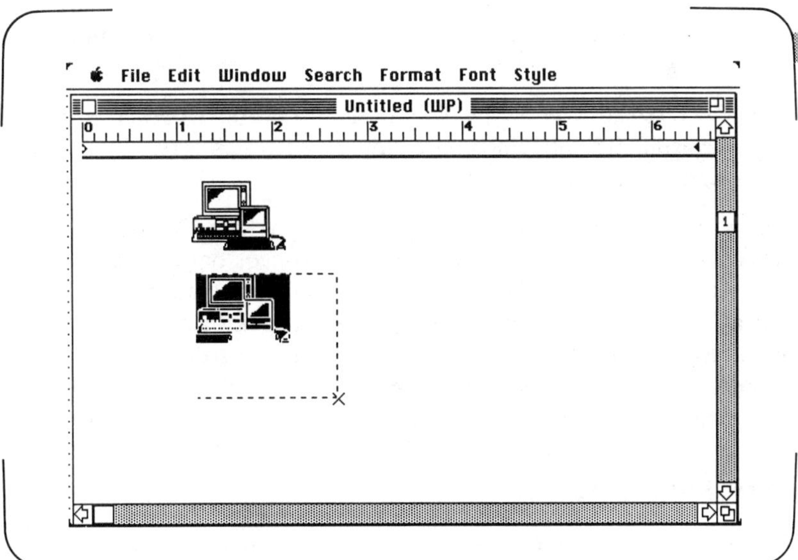

Fig. 4.5

Using the mouse to change the size and shape of a picture in proportion.

Fig. 4.6

Resizing that distorts the image.

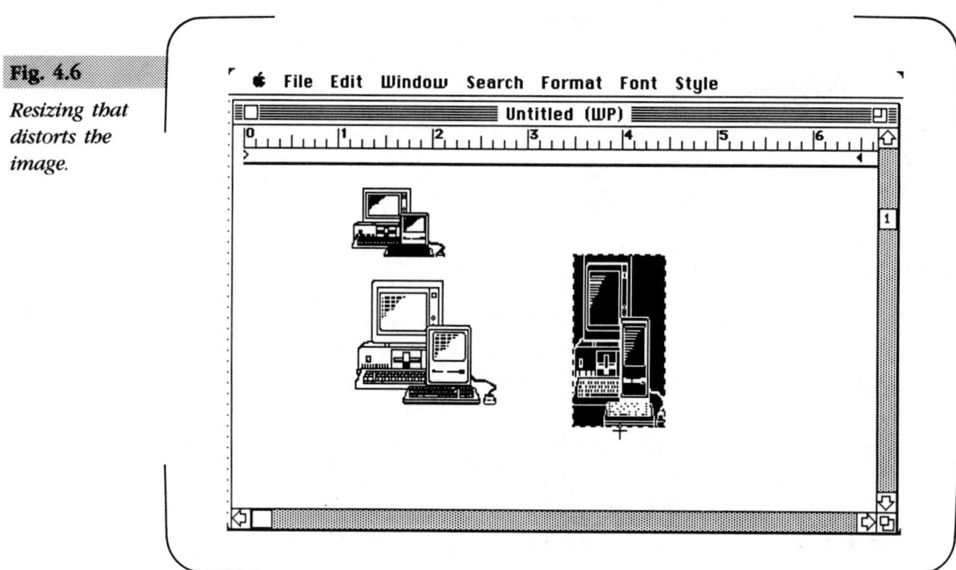

The resizing procedure is as follows:

1. Select the picture. (Marching ants surround selected rectangle.)
2. Move the cursor outside the picture. The cursor becomes an arrow.
3. To resize the whole picture, push or pull on a corner; to resize horizontally only, push on a side; or to resize vertically only, push on the top or bottom.

Works does not resize text that you've typed with the Works word-processing feature, even if the text is on top of or surrounded by a picture. If you want to resize text with a picture, you can select the text as a separate step and choose a different point size from the Style menu. Another method is to create the text in a paint program. Text imported as part of a picture (from a Works graph, for example) can be resized with the picture.

Fixing Torn Drawings

Works Version 1.0 sometimes has a problem displaying text and pictures together. Occasionally, the screen images look torn, or the portions of the text and pictures seem to move without relation to each other (see fig. 4.7). These problems can occur at any time, but they usually arise immediately after a document has been printed. Microsoft is aware of these problems and suggests scrolling the offending section of the document off the screen and back. A click or two in the scroll bars above and below the page number box ought to do the trick. The problem seems to have been eliminated—or at least minimized—in Works Version 1.1.

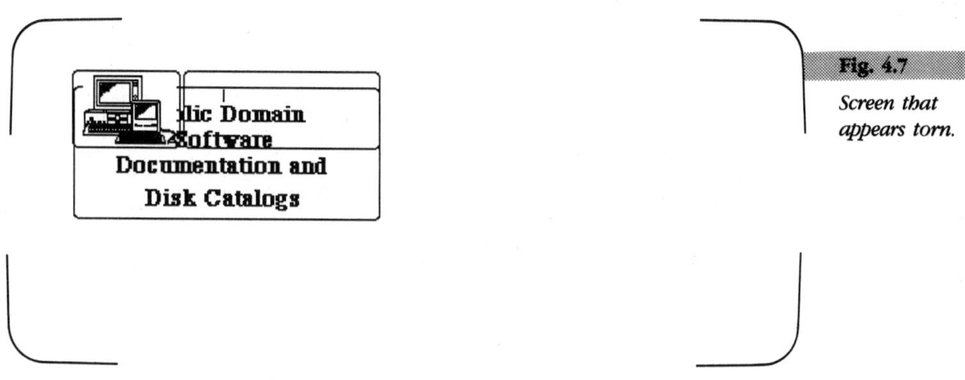

Fig. 4.7

Screen that appears torn.

Headers and Footers

You use *headers*, lines at the top of pages, to identify documents or number and date pages automatically. *Footers* do the same thing at the bottom of printed pages.

Headers and footers don't appear on-screen, only in printed documents. You can control their appearance to a large extent. For example, you can center or left- or right-justify the headers; you can print them in boldface or italic, and so on. Moreover, when printing, Works consults your system clock if you like and inserts the current date and time in headers and footers. You control all these capabilities through the Page Setup menu, using a kind of shorthand (see fig. 4.8). The header information in the figure prints *PRELIMINARY REPORT* centered at the top of each page. The current date is printed flush right on the same line. A page number is centered at the bottom of each page. The following sections explain the Works shorthand.

Typing Text-Only Headers and Footers

In the simplest case, you type text in the Header and Footer boxes, and that text appears on each printed page in your document. The procedure is the following:

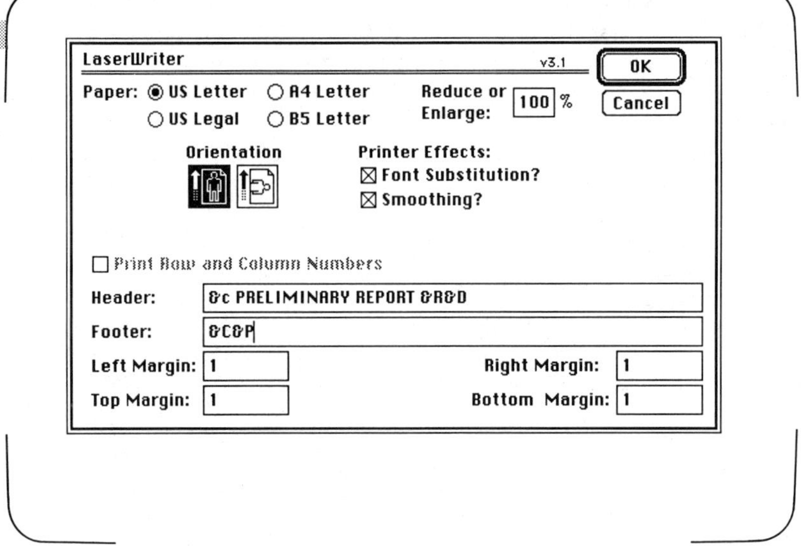

Fig. 4.8

Entering headers and footers in the LaserWriter Page Setup dialog box.

1. Choose Page Setup on the File menu.
2. Type the text in the Header or Footer boxes.
3. Click the OK button.
4. Print your document.

Works, however, has additional header and footer features that are worth learning about. They're described in the following sections.

Using Different Type Styles in Headers and Footers

With some exceptions, the type style and size in Works word-processing documents is the same in headers and footers as in the active paragraph you left when you chose the Page Setup menu. You can, however, change the type style and size. While the Page Setup dialog box is on the screen, choose a new type style and size or both before you begin typing headers or footers. To pick a font, you pull down the Font menu; to pick a style, choose the Style menu. If you want to change the size or style after typing headers and footers, select the desired header or footer text and then choose a new style.

To see what type style options Works "plans" to use on your headers and footers, select the text and look at the Style menu to see which options are checked. This habit is a good one to develop.

Using Header and Footer Format Commands

Works offers a number of powerful shorthand commands for use in headers and footers. The commands begin with the ampersand (&) and are followed by a letter that tells Works what to do; you can use either upper- or lowercase letters.

For example, you can center or justify text by preceding it with the following shorthand commands:

- To center text, enter **&c**.
- To right-justify text, enter **&r**.
- To left-justify text, enter **&l**.

Figure 4.9 shows an example; the word *Confidential* will be centered in the printed header.

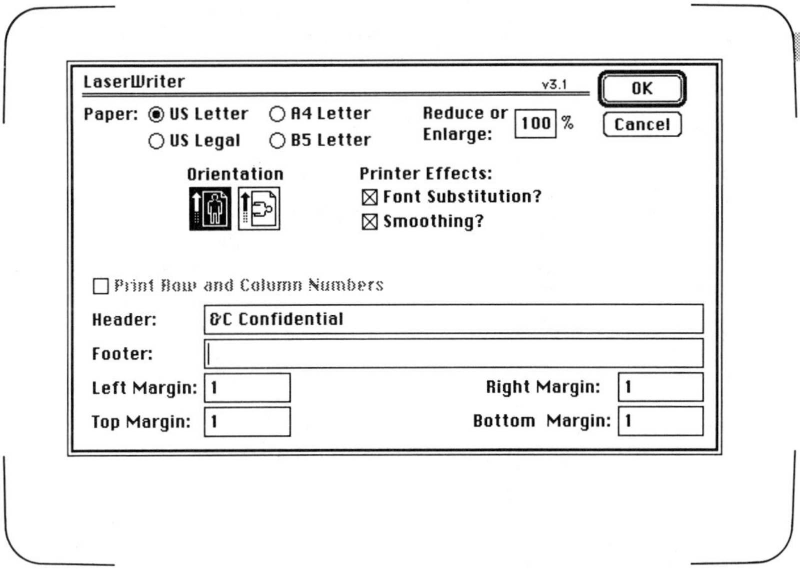

LaserWriter v3.1 OK
Paper: ◉ US Letter ○ A4 Letter Reduce or Enlarge: 100 % Cancel
○ US Legal ○ B5 Letter
Orientation
Printer Effects:
☒ Font Substitution?
☒ Smoothing?
☐ Print Row and Column Numbers
Header: &C Confidential
Footer:
Left Margin: 1 Right Margin: 1
Top Margin: 1 Bottom Margin: 1

Fig. 4.9

Centering the word Confidential *at the top of the page.*

Using Date and Time in Headers and Footers

To print the date in a header or footer, you enter **&d**. To print the current time, enter **&t**. You can combine these commands with others to place the date and time where you want them. For example, **&l&d &r&t** prints the date on the left and the time on the right. You don't need to separate these commands with spaces, but you can in order to make your screen easier to read.

Numbering Pages

To place a page number in a header or footer automatically, you use the &p command. It makes Works print consecutive page numbers, starting with the number 1. To place the page number where you want, you combine &p with other commands such as &c.

You can add text as well. For example, *&rPage &p* causes Works to print right-justified page numbers preceded by the word *Page* and a space (see fig. 4.10).

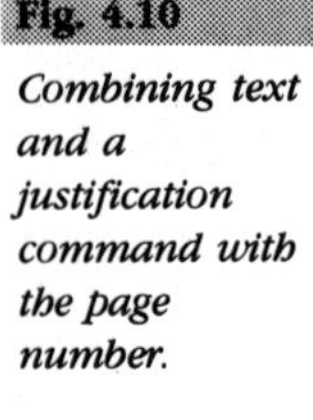

Fig. 4.10

Combining text and a justification command with the page number.

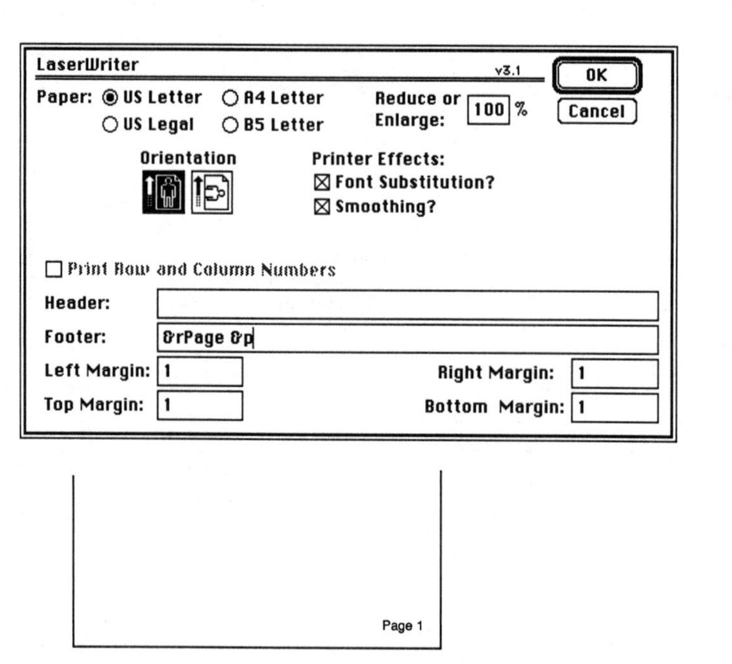

Eliminating Headers and Footers from Title Pages

If you don't want headers and footers to appear on your title page, choose Title Page on the Format menu (see fig. 4.11). This option prevents Works from printing headers and footers on the first page.

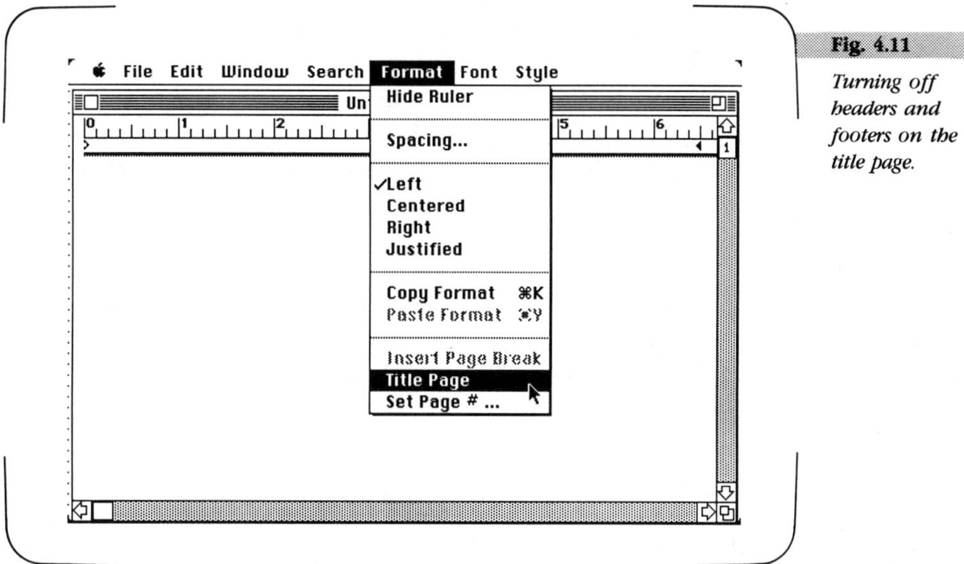

Fig. 4.11
Turning off headers and footers on the title page.

Setting Starting Page Numbers

To start automatic page numbering with a number other than 1, you can define the starting number by using the Set Page # option on the Format menu. This method is useful for numbering pages consecutively in large documents that you have broken up into chapters and stored in separate files. For example, suppose that you are working on a project so big that you can't fit it all in memory at one time. You enter, edit, and save the first 30 pages in a file. Then you close that document. Your computer's memory is cleared, so you start a new file to continue the project. Because your first chapter (file) has 30 pages, you set the starting page number at 31 for the second chapter (file).

NOTE: If you have typed a title or table of contents page and don't want it to have a page number but do want the page following to be page number 1, you type a **0** in the Set Starting Page # box. This trick works only if you choose All Pages in the Print dialog box. You cannot specify page 0 as the first page to print when you are using the From and To boxes.

Search and Replace Features

Works' search features are powerful tools that enable you to move quickly to specific parts of a document with only a few keystrokes. This capability can save laborious scrolling through large documents and is particularly helpful when a draft is being turned into final copy.

In addition, Works can replace text that meets specific criteria, either automatically or with your approval. For example, suppose that you have typed a contract for Mr. Jones and want to create a similar one for Ms. Smith. You can have Works locate each occurrence of *Mr. Jones* and replace it with *Ms. Smith*.

You can search for specific pages or specific text. Works starts its search at the position of the cursor, searches to the end of the document, and then goes to the top of the document and continues searching. The search stops when Works finds a match or has searched the entire document.

Searching for Specific Pages

You can tell Works to scroll quickly to the top of any page in a document. Here's what you do:

1. Either choose Go to Page # on the Search menu or press **command-G**.
2. Enter any valid page number in the blank in the Go To Page # dialog box.
3. Press **enter** or click the OK box.

Works displays the page you have specified (see fig. 4.12).

Finding Specific Text

With the Find command on the Search menu, you can quickly locate specific text. You can find words, groups of words, parts of words, numbers—you name it. The procedure is the following:

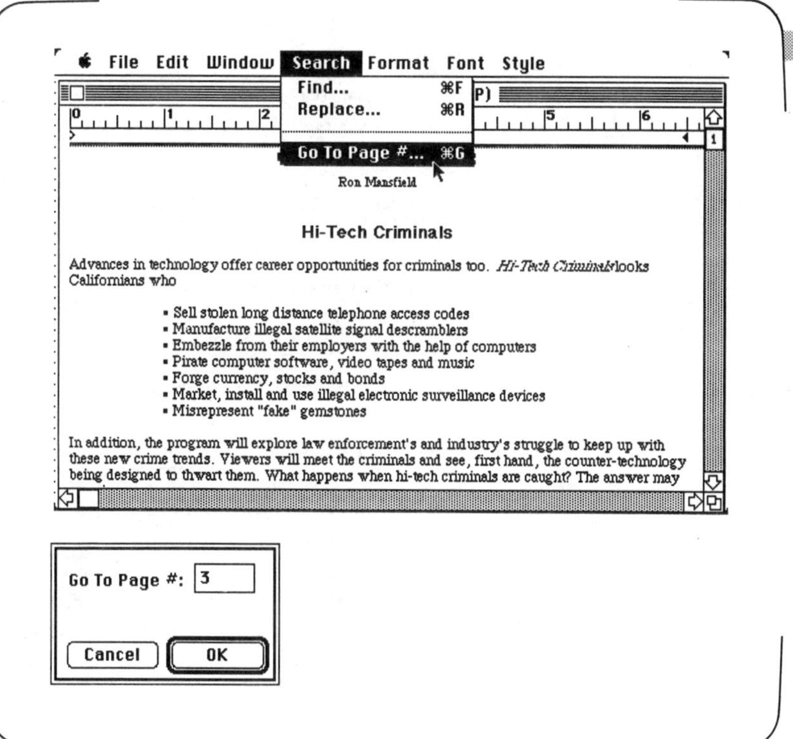

Fig. 4.12

Specifying a specific page.

1. Choose Find on the Search menu or press **command-F**. Works displays the Find What dialog box.
2. Enter the text you're looking for in the Find What box (see fig. 4.13).
3. Press **enter** or **return**.

The search begins immediately. Works finds and highlights the first occurrence. The dialog box remains on-screen. To find the next occurrence, either press *enter* or click Find Next in the dialog box.

Works ignore upper- and lowercase in the search method described in the preceding steps. Therefore, Works frequently finds words that contain the searched-for text. For example, if you specify *man*, Works finds *manual* and *Mansfield*, too.

Sometimes, however, you want to be more selective. Two options in the Find What dialog box help restrict searches: Check Upper/Lower Case and Match Whole Words Only. Suppose that you search for *man* and

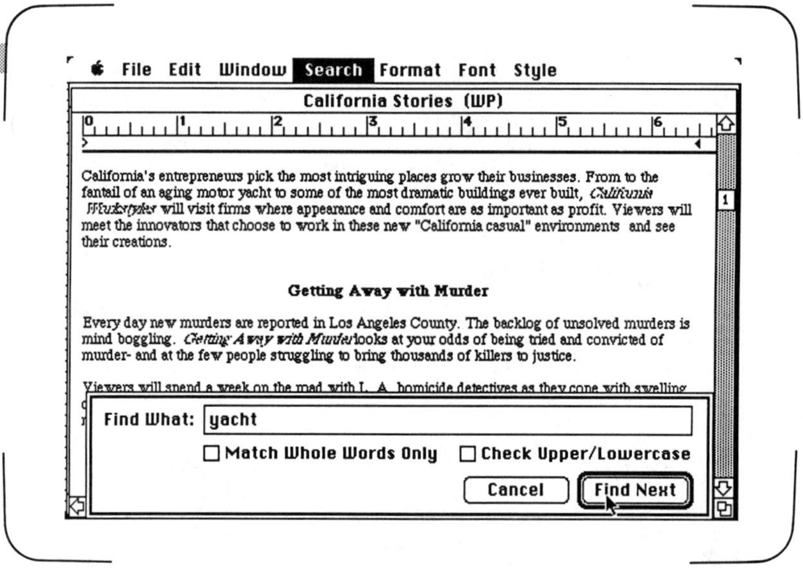

Fig. 4.13

Using Find on the Search menu to locate specific text.

check only the Check Upper/Lower Case option. Works ignores *Mansfield* but not *manual.* The Match Whole Words Only box does what it says. If you check this box, Works ignores both *Mansfield* and *manual* in a search for *man.*

You need to know a few more things about finding. For example, spaces count, so if you put a space before *man* in the Find dialog box, Works won't find *Goodman.*

If you want to find words containing special characters, you must enter them. Searching for *LaCanada*, Works won't find *La Cañada.* Required, or so-called hard spaces, are special characters too. (See "Notes on Spaces" in this chapter.)

If you manually hyphenate words to "pretty up" line endings, search for portions of those words rather than the whole words. Otherwise, you risk missing hyphenated versions of those words. Good automatic hyphenation features like the one found in WorksPlus/Spell won't confuse the Find feature.

Replacing Text

With Works' Replace feature, you can find whole words or parts of words and then change all or only some occurrences of those strings. Works gives you two methods to use this feature. The basic steps are outlined first. Here's what you do:

1. Either choose Replace on the Search menu or press **command-R** (see fig. 4.14).
2. Enter up to 80 characters in the Find What box (see fig. 4.15).
3. Check the Match Whole Words Only and the Check Upper/LowerCase boxes if appropriate.
4. Tab to move to the Replace With box.
5. Enter the replacement string in the Replace With box.
6. If you want to replace all occurrences, click Replace All (fig. 4.15). Works performs all replacements and displays an information box; you click OK to proceed.

   or

   Click Find Next or press *enter* if you don't know whether you want to change all occurrences of the string (see fig. 4.16). The first occurrence of the string is found. You have the following options:

   - Click Replace to perform that single replacement (see fig. 4.17)
   - Click Replace, then Find to replace the string and find the next occurrence
   - Click Find Next to leave the present occurrence unchanged and move to the next
   - Click Replace All to replace all subsequent occurrences

   You also can click Cancel to stop.

7. Click Replace to replace the currently highlighted string, or click Replace, then Find to replace that occurrence and find the next. If the Find What string is not found, an information box tells you so; you click OK to proceed.

The following shortcut method for searching and replacing text strings gets the procedure going faster. Some of the steps are identical. The shortcut steps are as follows:

1. Either choose Replace on the Search menu or press **command-R**.
2. Enter up to 80 characters in the Find What box (see fig. 4.15).

3. Check the Match Whole Words Only and the Check Upper/LowerCase boxes if appropriate. (The steps vary after this step.)
4. Press **enter**. Works moves to and highlights the first occurrence of the Find What text.
5. Put the I-beam in the Replace With box and type the replacement string.
6. You can click Replace to replace that one occurrence (fig. 4.14); Replace, then Find to replace that occurrence and find the next; or Replace All to replace all occurrences.

Using the Replace, then Find or the Find Next option is a quick way to move through a document manually. It lets you look at a potential replacement, decide whether or not to make the replacement, then takes you to the next occurrence.

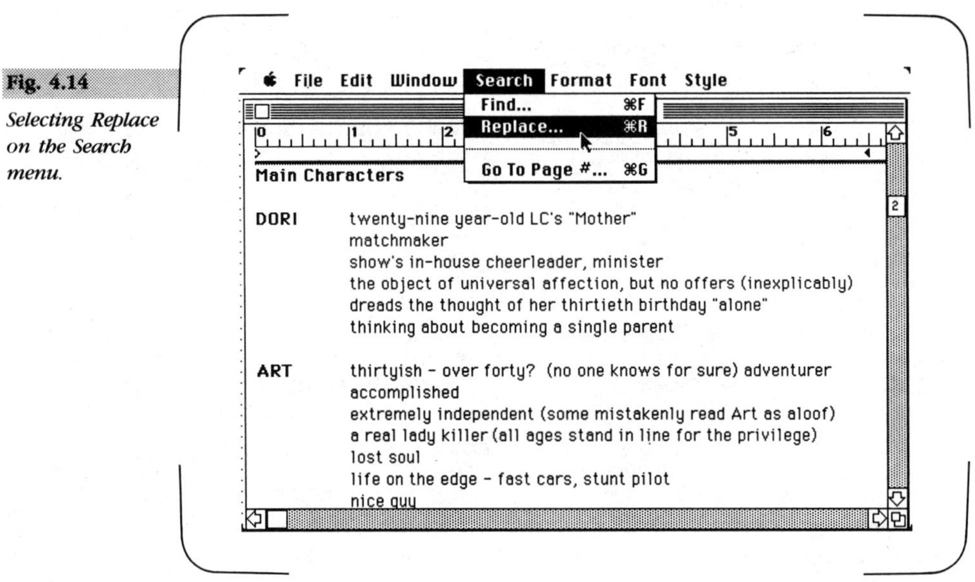

Fig. 4.14

Selecting Replace on the Search menu.

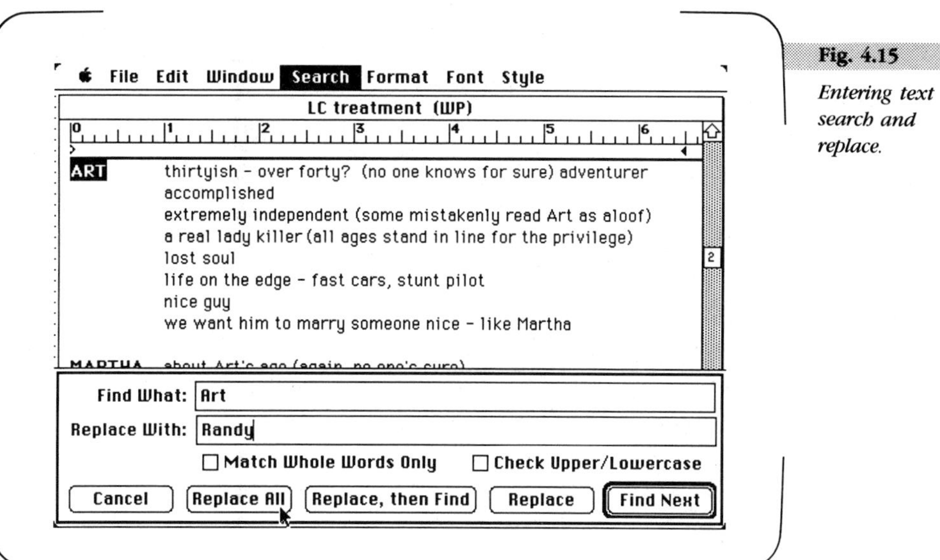

Fig. 4.15

Entering text to search and replace.

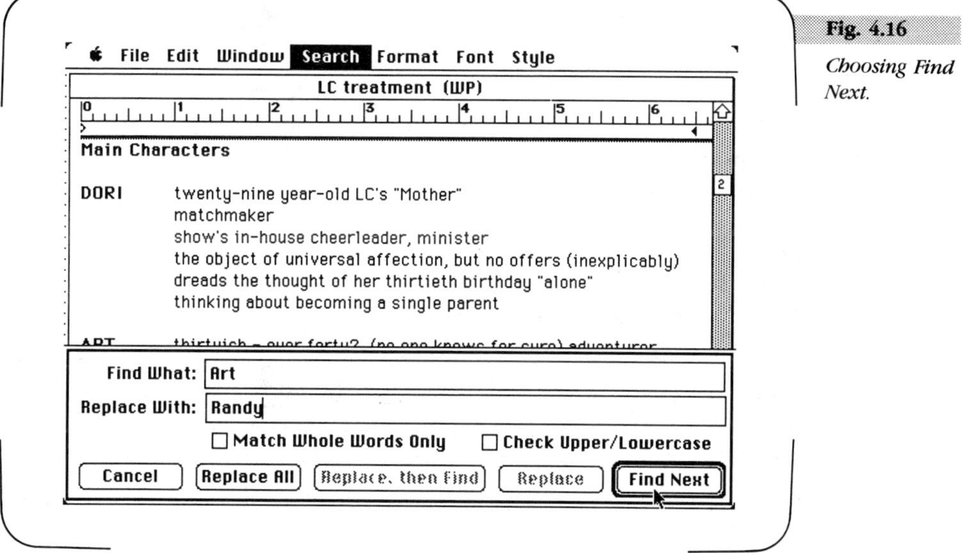

Fig. 4.16

Choosing Find Next.

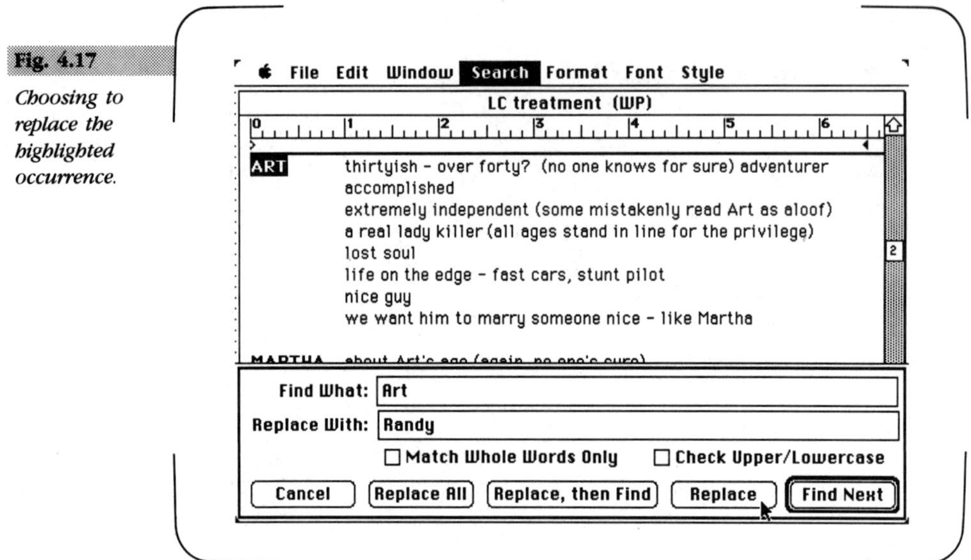

Fig. 4.17

Choosing to replace the highlighted occurrence.

Advanced Word-Processing Tips

Once you've spent an hour or two getting used to Works' basic word-processing features, you'll probably want to learn some timesaving tips and techniques that professionals use to make their documents stand out in a crowd. This section gives you shortcuts for both new and experienced Works users.

Summary of Command-*Key Shortcuts*

In these word-processing chapters, you have been given the keyboard shortcuts for the commands. Table 4.1 lists the Works *command*-key shortcuts. You may find the shortcuts so useful that you'll want to keep table 4.1 near your Macintosh until the commands become second nature. They will save you many "trips to the mouse"—a real plus for fast typists.

Table 4.1
Works' *Command*-Key Shortcuts

Keystroke	*Action*
command-A	Selects picture
command-B	Turns Bold on/off
command-C	Copies selected item to Clipboard
command-F	Finds (invokes Find menu)
command-G	Goes to Page # menu
command-I	Turns Italic on/off
command-K	Copies paragraph format
command-M	Prepares to merge (see Chapter 10)
command-N	Turns on Normal text (turns off Bold, Italic, Superscript, Subscript, and so on)
command-O	Opens file (invokes Open File dialog box)
command-P	Prints (invokes Print menu)
command-Q	Quits (asks about saving and exits Works)
command-R	Invokes Replace menu
command-S	Saves (using last-used file name unless untitled)
command-U	Turns Underline on/off
command-V	Pastes from Clipboard
command-W	Changes window size
command-X	Cuts selected item to Clipboard
command-Y	Pastes paragraph format
command-Z	Undoes (attempts to undo last action)
command-, (comma)	Activates window shown at bottom of Window menu
command-. (period)	Stops printing

Notes on Spaces

When you're assigning file names and requesting files by name from the keyboard, capitalization is not important, but spaces count.

If you don't want Works' wordwrap feature to break up words that are separated by spaces, you can enter hard, or required, spaces. This capability is useful in names, titles, telephone numbers, part numbers, addresses, and so on. Hard spaces keep words on the same line no matter what. To create a hard space, you hold down the *option* key and press the space bar.

NOTE: On the screen, hard spaces look bigger than normal spaces. You enter hard spaces with the *option* key when you are using the Find feature to locate them.

Em and En Dashes

Many people prefer the appearance of the dashes created by holding the *shift* or *option* key while pressing the hyphen key. These dashes are called em and en dashes. The em dash is called that because it's as wide as the font's letter *m*. An en dash is approximately half the width of an em dash. Both are wider than the hyphen.

To create an em dash, you hold down the *shift* and *option* keys, and press the hyphen key. To create an en dash, you press the *option* and hyphen keys together.

To summarize, you create each by the following keys:

hyphen (-)	Press - (hyphen)
em dash (—)	Press *shift-option*-[hyphen]
en dash (–)	Press *option*-[hyphen]

NOTE: On the screen, em dashes look bigger and en dashes look smaller than normal dashes. When you are finding en and em dashes with search features, enter them the same way you entered them originally.

Curly Quotation Marks

Regular Works quotation marks look like typewriter quotation marks. For a typeset look, try creating single or double curly quotation marks by pressing the *shift*, *option*, and bracket key together. You can experiment with these by using your Keycap desk accessory.

Regular quotation marks: "
option-]: '
shift-option-]: '

Ellipses and Ligatures

To generate the three dots that make up an ellipsis (. . .), you hold down the *option* key while pressing the semicolon key (;). If you type an ellipsis in text this way, enter the search request the same way.

The Macintosh and Works support ligatures such as œ and æ. Just press the *option* key and the appropriate letter key. Consult the Key Caps window to see where the ligatures are located and what they look like when displayed. Press the *shift* key too if you need uppercase ligatures such as Œ and Æ.

Eye-Saving Tip

For the early drafts of your documents, use a font that's easy to read on the screen—for example, Boston or Geneva. Helvetica and other fonts look nice in print but are hard to read on the screen. The same goes for italic because accurately positioning the cursor is difficult. When the document's content, grammar, and spelling are in order, select the entire document and choose the font you want to use for the final printing.

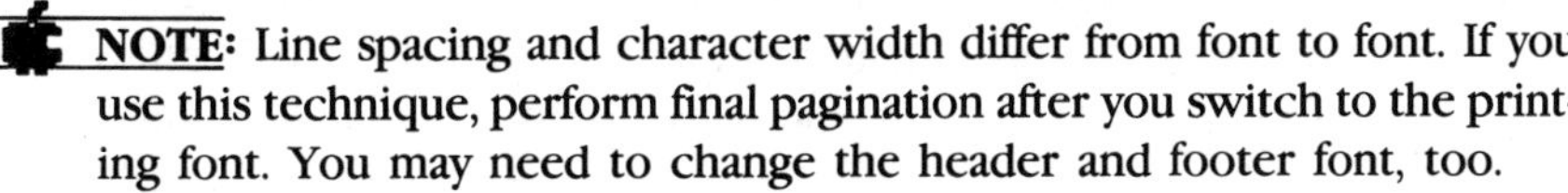

NOTE: Line spacing and character width differ from font to font. If you use this technique, perform final pagination after you switch to the printing font. You may need to change the header and footer font, too.

Italic On-Screen

Getting the cursor between the last character in an italicized word and the first character in the next normal word is hard. One way to get around this problem is to insert two spaces: a required space (hold down the *option* key and press the space bar) and then a regular space after italicized words. Delete the unneeded hard spaces before printing.

When To Cut and When To Backspace

You can cause selected text to disappear by pressing the *backspace* key. This approach leaves the contents of your Clipboard intact. Undo still recovers text or pictures if you select them before you backspace. Frequently, this method is a better way to delete than cutting if you keep important things on your Clipboard.

Scrolling

If you click in the shaded area of the vertical scroll bar, Works scrolls up or down one screen at a time. This technique is a fast way to move a predictable distance. Clicking in the shaded area of the horizontal scroll bar causes the screen to make big jumps to the left or right.

Usually, clicking a scroll arrow moves you about an inch at a time. To move shorter distances (micro scrolling), hold down the *shift* key and click on the scroll arrows. Works scrolls a shorter distance with each click.

Keeping the Key Caps and Scrapbook Windows on Your Desktop

If you're doing a great deal of work with the Scrapbook or special characters, keep the Key Caps window or the Scrapbook under your documents. Or move the document down so that you can see a portion of the Key Caps window.

Bring the Key Caps window forward as needed for quick reference. You may need to shrink the document window slightly so that everything fits and so that you can still use the scroll arrows on the document window. Or you can just have the Keycaps window on the desktop and scroll around to it with the *command-*, (comma) shortcut. You can use the same technique with the Scrapbook window (see fig. 4.18). If you have a big screen, you may be able to keep the windows in full view.

Printing on Preprinted Forms

Most preprinted forms require six-lines-per-inch spacing, but not all Mac fonts space this way. Fonts that do use this spacing include Apple's versions of 9-point ImageWriter fonts. Not all third-party, 9-point fonts print six lines per inch. You may need to experiment. The screen ruler can help with text positioning.

Eliminating Extra Spaces and Blank Pages

Spaces sometimes pile up at the end of Works documents. (You usually can't see spaces, but Works knows they're there and prints them.) Frequently, the result is an extra page that is completely blank except, possibly, for headers and footers.

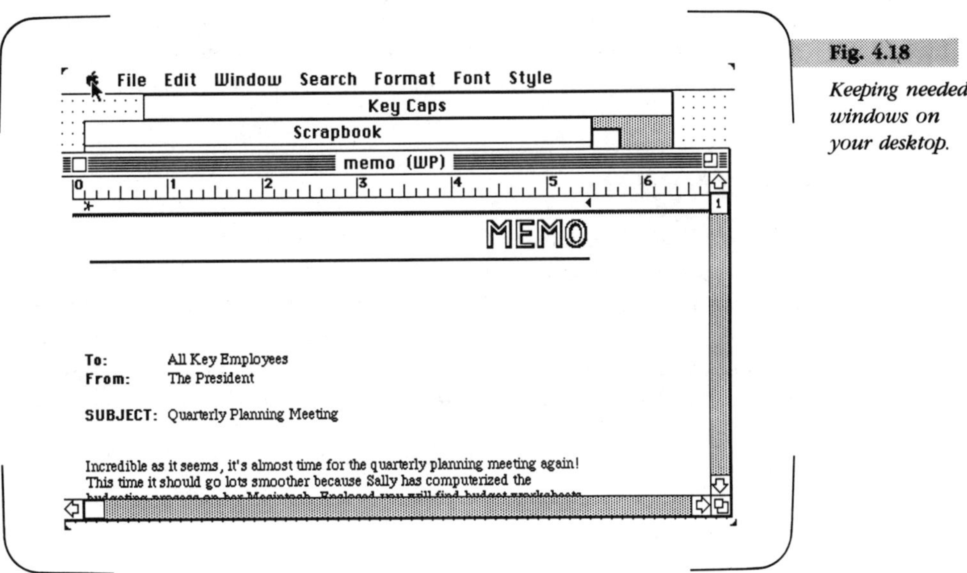

File Edit Window Search Format Font Style
Key Caps
Scrapbook
memo (WP)
MEMO
To: All Key Employees
From: The President
SUBJECT: Quarterly Planning Meeting
Incredible as it seems, it's almost time for the quarterly planning meeting again!
This time it should go lots smoother because Sally has computerized the

Fig. 4.18

Keeping needed windows on your desktop.

To find spaces, select them. You drag the mouse down from the last "good" character. If you can select white space, chances are that you've found unwanted spaces, which turn black (see fig. 4.19). To delete the spaces, press the *backspace* key.

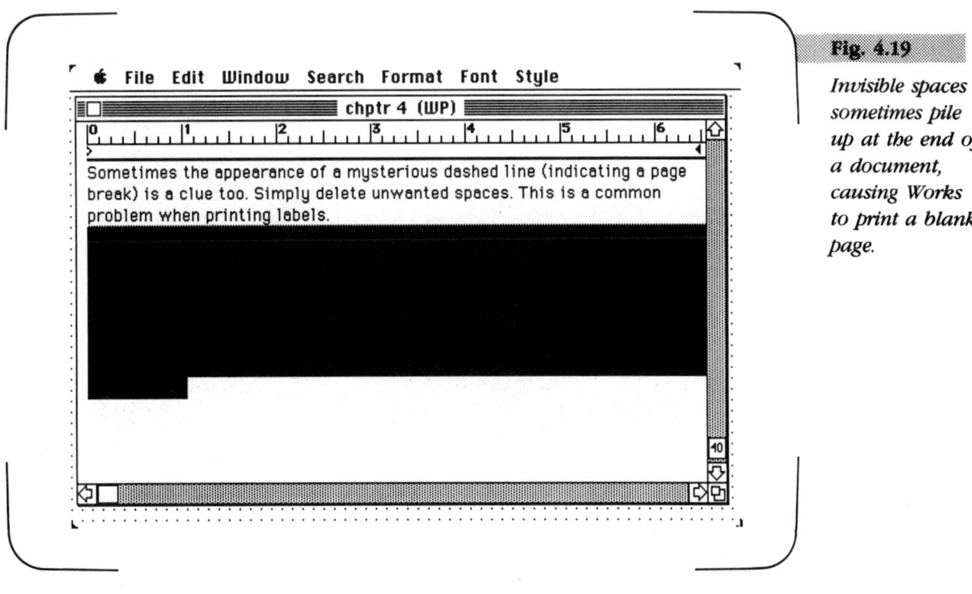

File Edit Window Search Format Font Style
chptr 4 (WP)
Sometimes the appearance of a mysterious dashed line (indicating a page
break) is a clue too. Simply delete unwanted spaces. This is a common
problem when printing labels.

Fig. 4.19

Invisible spaces sometimes pile up at the end of a document, causing Works to print a blank page.

Sometimes, the appearance of a dashed line (representing a page break) indicates unwanted spaces. This problem occurs frequently when labels are being printed. Again, simply delete the unwanted spaces.

Conclusion

The Works word processor has most of the capabilities of a stand-alone word-processing program. You easily enter, edit, and print text in many different formats. Many of the entry and editing techniques you have learned in these chapters are the same ones you use in other Works modules. The following chapter introduces the Works spreadsheet. Having mastered the word processor, you will find the transition to the spreadsheet a simple one.

Part III

SPREADSHEETS AND GRAPHS

5

Spreadsheets—the Basics

The Works spreadsheet module is a popular and useful part of the package. A Works spreadsheet window is like an accountant's paper pad, except that when you change an entry on a Works spreadsheet, the effects of the change appear almost instantly. Works takes care of all recalculations and eliminates the need for a pencil, an eraser, and a calculator. Before you can use a Works spreadsheet, however, you need to design and test it. You learn how in this chapter.

Spreadsheet Concepts

Certain concepts are basic to all spreadsheet programs. You work in a spreadsheet window. The spreadsheet consists of cells, which are organized into rows and columns (see fig. 5.1). You make entries into these cells, and the programs calculates the answers that you need according to the formulas and functions you choose.

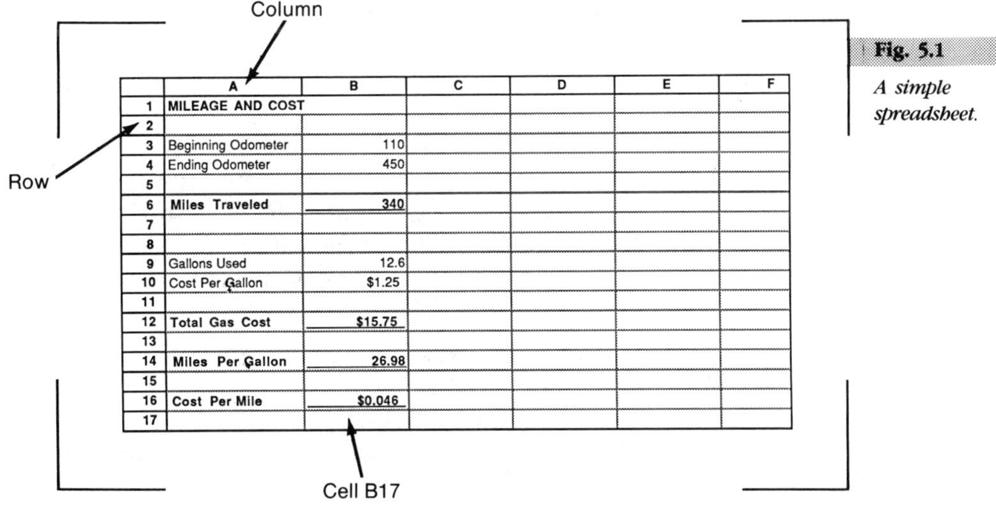

	A	B	C	D	E	F
1	MILEAGE AND COST					
2						
3	Beginning Odometer	110				
4	Ending Odometer	450				
5						
6	Miles Traveled	340				
7						
8						
9	Gallons Used	12.6				
10	Cost Per Gallon	$1.25				
11						
12	Total Gas Cost	$15.75				
13						
14	Miles Per Gallon	26.98				
15						
16	Cost Per Mile	$0.046				
17						

Fig. 5.1

A simple spreadsheet.

The Spreadsheet Window

A typical spreadsheet window is slightly more complex than a word-processing window. Figure 5.2 provides an example of a spreadsheet window. Take a moment to familiarize yourself with it and the related terms used in this chapter.

Fig. 5.2

The entry bar, enter box, cancel box, and other spreadsheet elements.

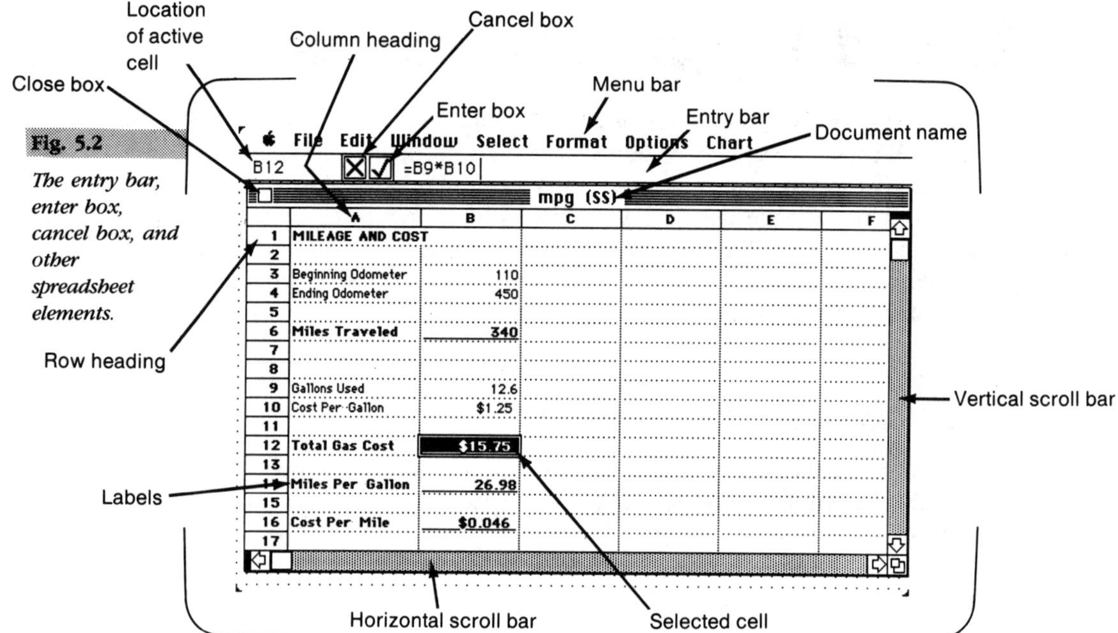

Spreadsheet Cells, Rows, and Columns

Spreadsheets consist of boxes, called *cells*, which are arranged in rows and columns. Works spreadsheet cells help keep things neat and organized the way printed boxes do on an accountant's worksheet. Each cell has an identity or address, sometimes referred to as its *location*.

Horizontal rows have numbers, and vertical columns have letters. Theoretically, Works spreadsheets can contain up to 9,999 rows, numbered 1 through 9,999. Columns are identified with letters. The first 26 columns are A through Z; the rest are labeled AA, AB, AC, and so on, through IV. Usable maximums, however, vary according to memory and other considerations.

To refer to a cell's location, you use its corresponding row number and and column letter. For example, the cell in the extreme upper left corner of a spreadsheet is A1. The cell to its right is B1; the cell immediately beneath A1 is A2; and so on.

When you want to do something to a cell—such as enter or edit a value or an equation—you first must make the cell active. You do so by clicking on the cell. You can always spot the active cell; it's black with a small white border, as illustrated in cell B12 in figure 5.2. Only one cell can be active at a time. Works displays the location of the active cell (B12, for instance) to the left of the cancel box (the box containing an X) at the top of the window.

The Entry Bar and Enter and Cancel Boxes

The entry bar is the long white rectangle between the menu bar and the spreadsheet to the right of the box containing the check mark. There, you enter and edit the contents of the active cell. As you type something, it appears in the entry bar. If you select a cell containing a value, that value appears in the entry bar. If the selected cell contains an equation, the equation, not the resulting answer, appears in the entry bar.

To the left of the entry bar is the enter box, which contains a check mark. Clicking on this box is like pressing the *enter* key on the keyboard. If you change your mind about something that you have done to the contents of the entry bar, you can click the cancel box, which is to the left of the enter box. The cancel box contains an X. As mentioned, the location of the active cell is displayed to the left of the cancel box.

Labels, Values, Equations, and Arithmetic Operators

The Works spreadsheet contains four types of entries: labels, values, equations, and arithmetic operators. *Labels* are text entries used to describe or explain things in the spreadsheet. In figure 5.2, for example, column A contains labels.

Values are the numbers used in spreadsheet calculations. The numbers can be positive or negative and written with or without decimal points. You can use scientific notation if necessary. In figure 5.2, cells B3, B4, B9, and B10 contain values.

You create *equations*, or formulas, to tell Works what to do with the values you've entered. For example, in figure 5.3, to compute miles traveled, you subtract the beginning odometer reading (cell B3) from the ending odometer reading (cell B4). To do this, you enter the equation =B4–B3 in the cell for miles traveled (B6). Equations always start with an equal sign, as you can see in cells B6, B12, B14, and B16.

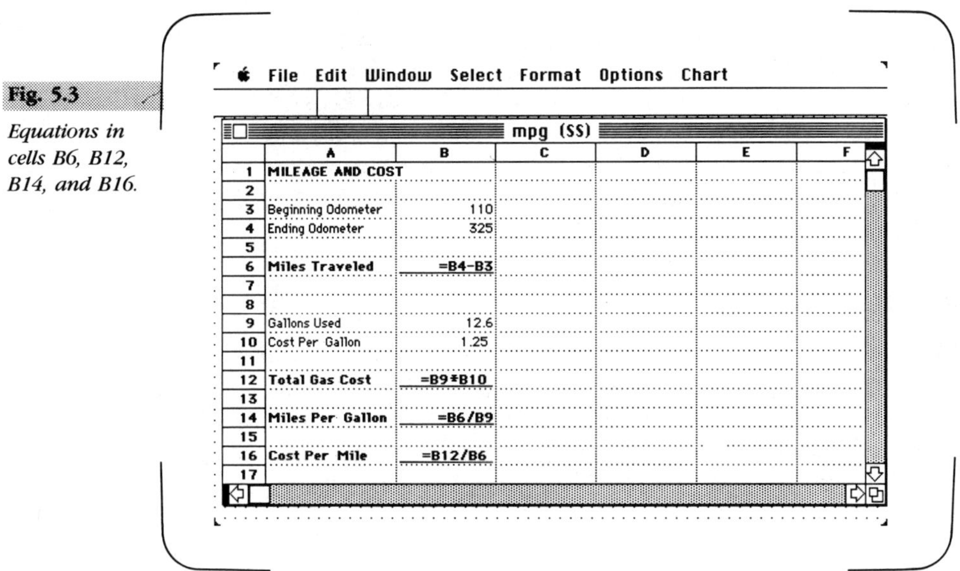

Fig. 5.3

Equations in cells B6, B12, B14, and B16.

Works displays the results of an equation in the cell in which you type the equation. If you enter the equation in cell B6, that's where the answer appears. Equations can be simple, like the ones in this example, or quite complex and powerful, as you'll see in later sections.

Operators are used in equations to tell Works what you want done with values. Works operators, which are similar to calculator functions, are the following:

+	Addition
–	Subtraction
*	Multiplication
/	Division
^	Exponentiation (raises to a power)
–	Negation (makes a number negative)

Works' Recognition of Cell Types

Works decides whether you're entering a label, a value, or an equation according to the first character you type in the entry bar and what else you type.

Labels

If the first keystroke in an entry is a letter or one of most punctuation marks, Works treats the entry as a label. For example, the following are labels:

Sales
%
-1-
.1 Solution
04/10/87
Q4
4th. Quarter
"1984"

The third item, -1-, is a label, not a negative number 1. If a minus sign were to the left of the 1 but none to the right, Works would treat the number as a negative 1.

Works treats the date 04/10/87 as a label even though other makers of spreadsheets (such as Lotus) treat the date as an equation because of the two division operators. Works treats this date as a label because equations must always start with an equal sign.

The number 1984 is a label because 1984 has leading quotation marks. The quotation marks are visible in the entry bar but not in the cell. To display quotation marks in a cell, you enclose them with another pair of double quotation marks. For example, to create a cell with the label "4", you enter ""4"".

Numbers

Works treats the following entries as numbers:

1	
-1	
12	
0.12	
.12	(converts to 0.12)
12,000	(ignores commas)
$1200	(ignores entered dollar signs)
12%	(converts to 0.12)
12E3	(displays 12000)
12e3	(displays 12000)

NOTE: If you place a space between the 12 and E3 in the next-to-last entry, Works treats the entry as a label (see "Controlling Precision, Number of Decimals, and Dollar Signs" for other details). In cases where Works converts what you've entered into something else, your original entry appears in the entry bar whenever you select the cell.

Equations

Works treats the entry =04/10/87 as an equation. It's the same as dividing 4 by 10 and the results by 87. Works tries to treat any entry that starts with an equal sign as an equation. If Works discovers a potential problem with your equation, a dialog box appears asking for help.

Spreadsheet Editing Tools

Equations and labels can be edited, moved, copied, and deleted, by features that resemble those found in the Works word-processing window. These tools enable you to create large, complex spreadsheets with a minimum of retyping. For instance, you can insert and delete in the entry bar just as you do on a line of word-processing text. The pointer even resembles a word-processing pointer when it's in the entry bar.

Other spreadsheet editing tools are also available. For example, special Copy and Move commands enable you to create large spreadsheets without unnecessary retyping. You can change individual or all column widths, create equations, and set up the page for printing your spreadsheet. You also can format the display of numbers and work with single cells or entire ranges of cells.

Basic Spreadsheet Skills

If you've never created a spreadsheet before, you need to study the mileage spreadsheet in figure 5.1. Experienced spreadsheet users will want at least to read this section because Works behaves a little differently than other spreadsheet packages you have used.

Opening a New Document

The quickest way to begin a new spreadsheet project is to double-click on the spreadsheet icon in the Works Open File dialog box (see fig. 5.4).

NOTE: You can accomplish the same thing by selecting the Open option from the pull-down File menu. Either way, you see a spreadsheet screen with the title *Untitled* and the letters *(SS)*, indicating your success.

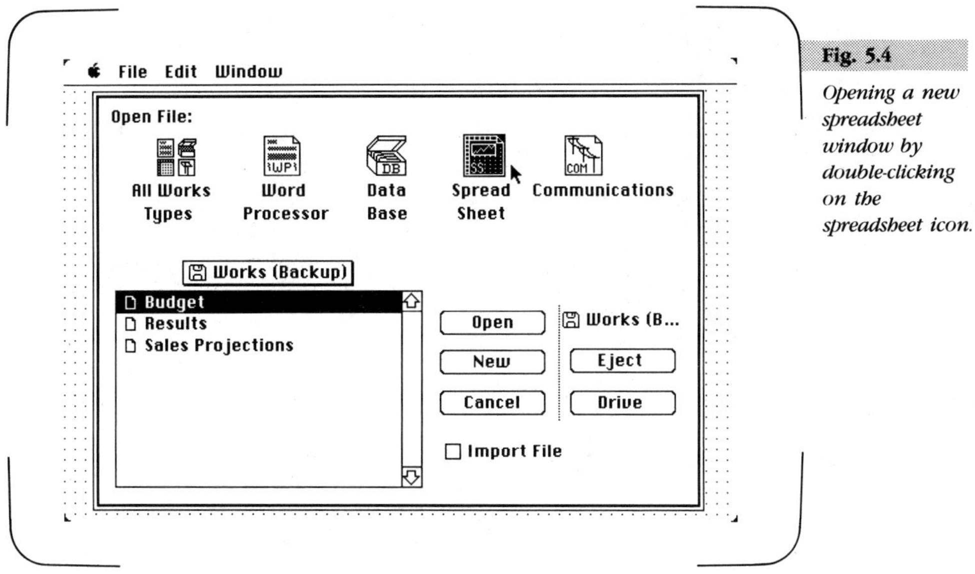

Fig. 5.4

Opening a new spreadsheet window by double-clicking on the spreadsheet icon.

Making Simple Cell Entries

One obvious way to enter items into cells is to do the following:

1. Make a cell active by pointing to it and clicking.
2. Enter the label, value, or equation.
3. Click the enter box next to the entry bar (or press **return**).
4. Point and click again to make a new cell active.
5. Repeat the process until you're finished.

If you've entered something in cell A1, pressing the *return* key instead of clicking on the enter box automatically makes cell A2 the next active cell. This feature is one of many shortcuts built into the Works spreadsheet. If you click on the enter box next to the entry bar or if you press the *enter* key on the keyboard, A1 is still the active cell. Terminating an entry with the *return* key always makes the cell immediately below active. You'll learn more about similar shortcuts in the section "Shortcuts for Creating Spreadsheets."

Selecting and Deselecting Single Cells and Ranges

As already mentioned, a simple click is all that's necessary to select single cells. This process also activates the selected cell. Works also lets you select ranges in rows, columns, or blocks (see fig. 5.5). The ranges are highlighted so that they're easy to see. To select any block of cells, you drag. You can select a block of rows and columns by dragging diagonally.

Fig. 5.5

Selected ranges of rows, columns, or areas.

	A	B	C	D	E
1					
2		Q1 Actual	Q2 Actual	Q3 Plan	Q4 Plan
3	SALES				
4	WEST	$123,568	$107,232	$140,000	$140,000
5	CENTRAL	$113,454	$110,785	$140,000	$140,000
6	EAST	$98,876	$101,867	$140,000	$140,000

	A	B	C	D	E
1					
2		Q1 Actual	Q2 Actual	Q3 Plan	Q4 Plan
3	SALES				
4	WEST	$123,568	$107,232	$140,000	$140,000
5	CENTRAL	$113,454	$110,785	$140,000	$140,000
6	EAST	$98,876	$101,867	$140,000	$140,000

	A	B	C	D	E
1					
2		Q1 Actual	Q2 Actual	Q3 Plan	Q4 Plan
3	SALES				
4	WEST	$123,568	$107,232	$140,000	$140,000
5	CENTRAL	$113,454	$110,785	$140,000	$140,000
6	EAST	$98,876	$101,867	$140,000	$140,000

By clicking on a column heading or a row number, you select the entire corresponding row or column. The first cell in the selected row or column becomes the active cell.

You select a range by clicking on the first cell in a range and *shift*-clicking on the last cell. This method works equally well for rows, columns, or blocks. To select a rectangle, click in one corner and *shift*-click diagonally across from it. The clicked (as opposed to the *shift*-clicked) cell always becomes the active cell.

The Select menu offers a Select All Cells option, which highlights everything from the first to the last cell you have used for your spreadsheet. For instance, if you have something in A1 and something in A13, but cells A2 through A12 are empty, the entire range A1 through A13 is selected. This choice also activates the first cell in your spreadsheet.

To deselect a range, you click anywhere on a spreadsheet. In the process, you also activate the cell in which you click. The spreadsheet screen also has a deselect box, located above row 1 and to the left of column A (see fig. 5.6). Clicking this box deselects the entire spreadsheet without activating any cells.

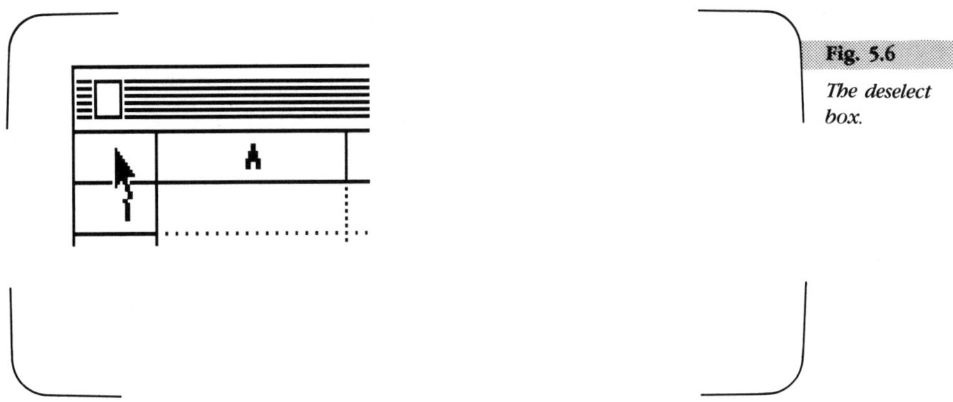

Fig. 5.6

The deselect box.

Changing Column Widths

Works sets all columns on a new spreadsheet at 12 characters wide. You may want to make a column wider than 12 columns so that it can accept long labels or big numbers. Or you may want to reduce the size of columns that will contain short entries. Narrow columns enable you to fit more columns on your screen and paper.

Works has two ways to change the width of a column. One way is to point to the top part of the line separating two columns. The pointer then changes to a thick bar with two arrows (see fig. 5.7). Drag the column to the desired width, and watch the width change as you drag.

The Format menu offers another way to change column widths (see fig. 5.8). Make any cell in the column the active cell, and choose Column Width from the Format menu. Works displays a dialog box. Enter the desired number of characters for the column width; then either click OK or press the *return* key (see fig. 5.9). Columns can be from 1 to 40 characters wide.

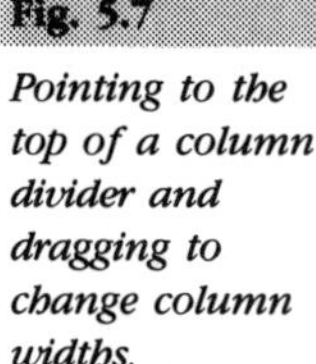

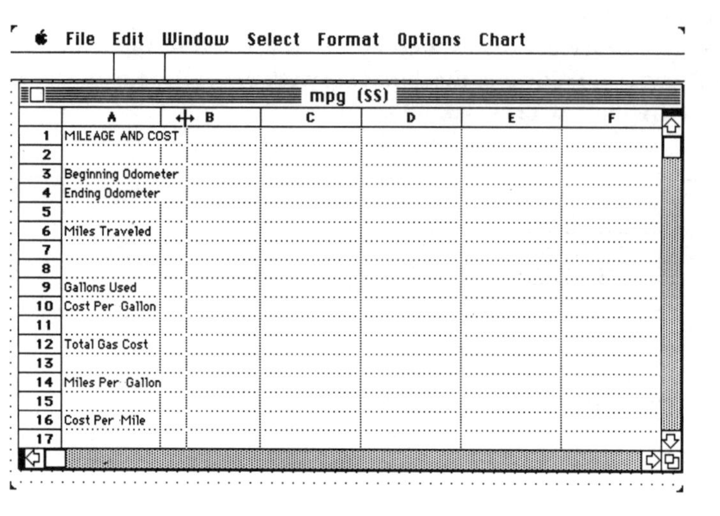

Fig. 5.7

Pointing to the top of a column divider and dragging to change column widths.

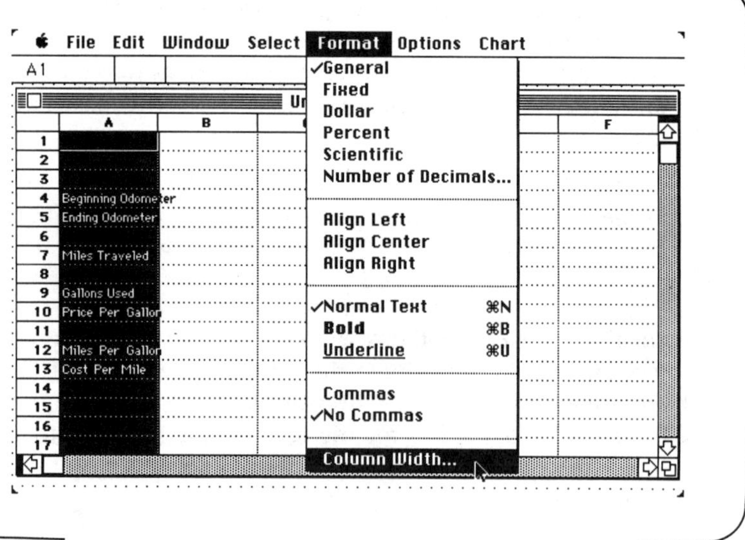

Fig. 5.8

Choosing Column Width on the Format menu.

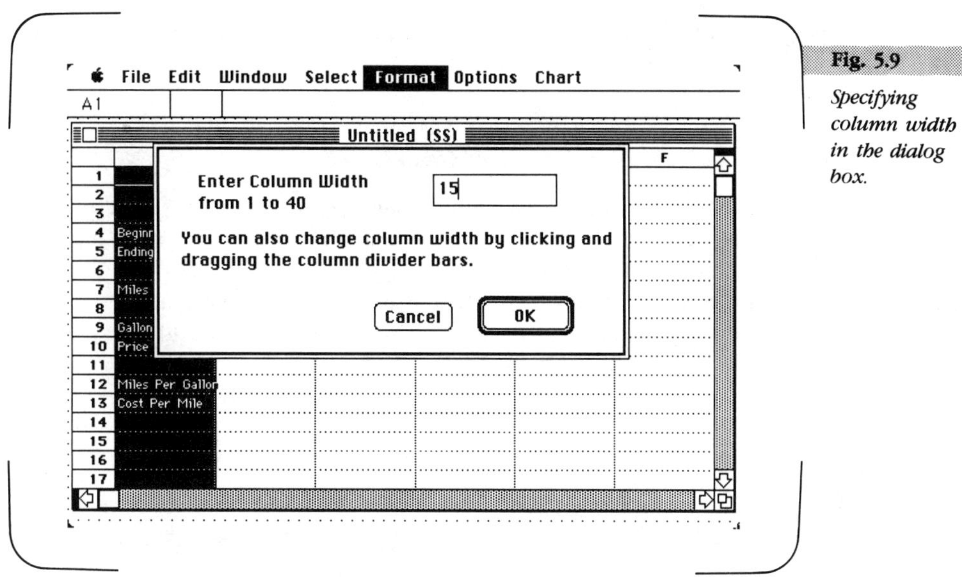

Fig. 5.9

Specifying column width in the dialog box.

You can change the widths of all columns at once. Here's how:

1. Select any row or the whole spreadsheet.
2. Choose the Column Width option on the Format menu.
3. When Works asks you for a width, enter a new width.
4. Click OK or press **return**. Works then adjusts all columns to the new width.

Entering Numbers (Values)

You use virtually the same techniques to enter numbers (values) as you do to enter labels. You can use the number keys along the top row of the keyboard, or if your keyboard has a ten-key pad, you can use it. When entering numbers with decimal points, you can use either the period key or the decimal point key on the ten-key pad.

You can enter numbers by making a cell active and typing an entry. What you type appears in the entry bar. Clicking the enter box and pressing the *return* key are two ways to finish, or terminate, entering a number.

NOTE: Precede negative numbers with a minus sign. Don't enter dollar signs, parentheses, or commas. Farther into this chapter, you learn how to display and print these embellishments. Don't enter spaces, letters, or any punctuation other than decimal points (periods); otherwise, Works may mistake your value for a label.

Creating Simple Equations

Equations always begin with an equal sign (=). For example, the equation in B6 in figure 5.10, =B4–B3 (shown in the entry bar), subtracts the beginning from the ending odometer readings. The result of the calculation appears in B6. Any change in the odometer readings causes Works to recalculate automatically the miles traveled and every other equation in the spreadsheet.

Fig. 5.10

Equation in cell B6 subtracts the beginning from the ending odometer readings. Equation appears in entry bar, result in B6.

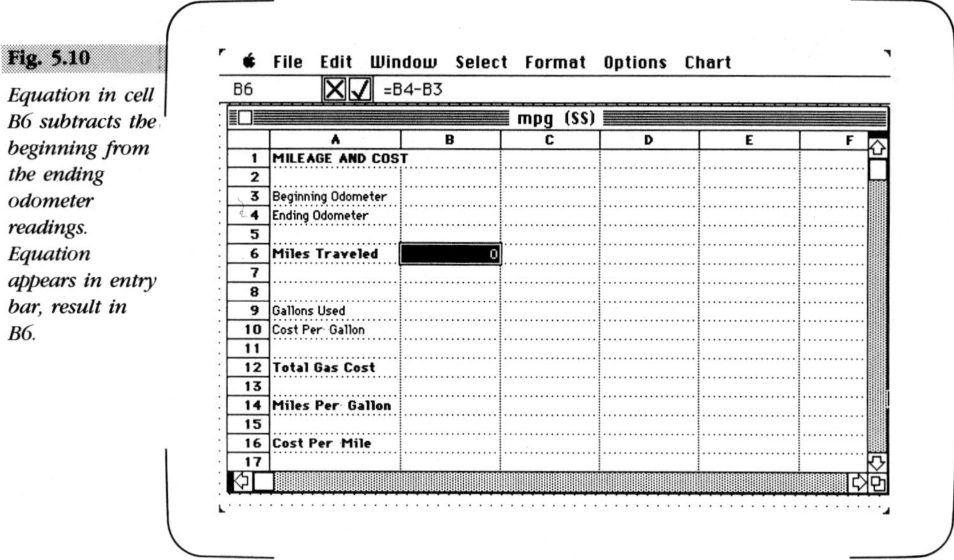

The procedure for creating an equation is the following:

1. Activate the cell location of the answer (B6 in fig. 5.10).
2. Type the equation (=B4–B3, in this example).
3. Either press **return** or click on the enter box.

Formula Error Messages

Works can spot some but not all your equation errors. (No spreadsheet package can detect all equation errors, so be certain to check your work carefully.) When Works does find an error, the system warns you either by displaying a message in the offending and affected cells or by displaying a dialog box (see fig. 5.11). In the example, the equation includes a nonexistent cell location (BO). Works has placed the cursor at the location of the suspected error and offers the user an opportunity to edit that equation. After correcting an error, you click OK to return to the spreadsheet. If you click Treat As Text, Works converts the entire equation into text and inserts leading quotation marks.

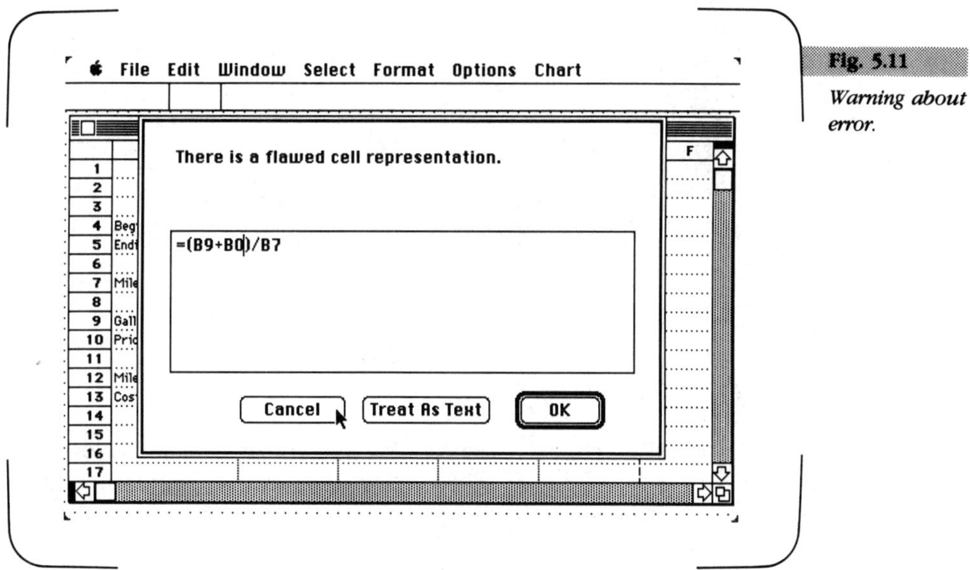

Fig. 5.11
Warning about error.

The Show Formulas Option

Another way to spot equation errors is to use the Show Formulas command on the Options menu (see fig. 5.12). This option displays all the formulas in the cells so that you can inspect your work visually. You also can print the spreadsheet with the formulas showing. To cancel this option, choose Show Values from the same menu.

Saving Spreadsheets

To save a spreadsheet, you use the techniques you learned in Chapter 2. Choose Save As on the File menu, and name the spreadsheet the first time you save it. Then get into the habit of using the *command*-S shortcut about every 15 minutes, or whenever you're interrupted.

Fig. 5.12

The Show Formulas option and its results.

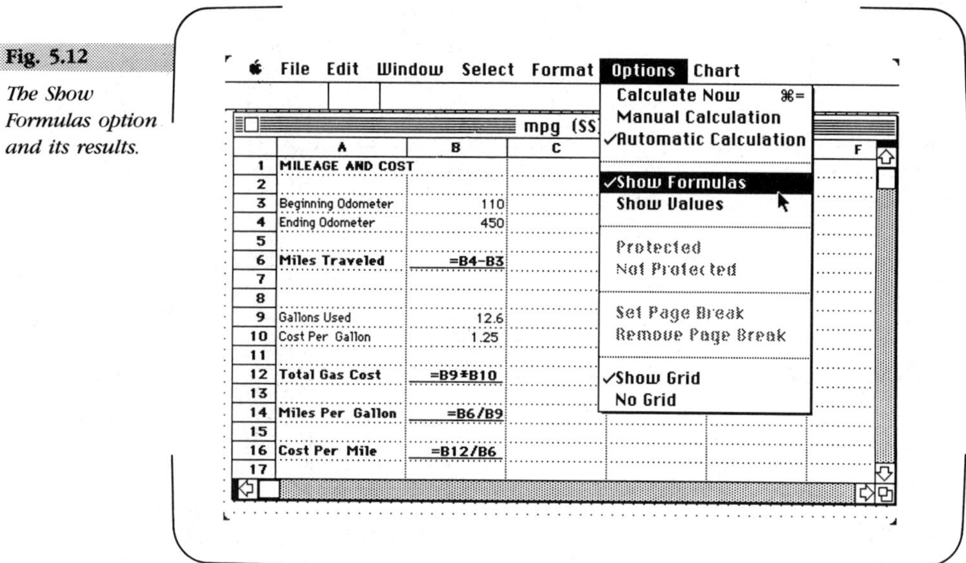

Testing Spreadsheets

I can't say it often enough: It's very easy to make spreadsheet errors that can go undetected for years. These errors can cost companies thousands or even millions of dollars. Spreadsheet errors have even caused bankruptcies.

Before using even the simplest spreadsheet for real work, be sure to examine and test the spreadsheet. Get into the habit of running examples through both your new spreadsheet and a calculator. Test under enough different conditions to check each spreadsheet operation. People have lost their jobs—and lawsuits—because they've failed to test spreadsheets. Don't join their ranks.

Spreadsheet Printing Techniques

To print spreadsheets, you use the same techniques you used to print word-processing documents. Either select Print from the File menu or use the *command*-P shortcut.

When printing spreadsheets, you have the same control over Page Setup options that you have with Works' word-processing window. You can request page numbers, headers, footers, special paper sizes, and more.

Spreadsheet Page Setup Tips

The spreadsheet Page Setup dialog box has a few more choices than the one you see in a word-processing window (see fig. 5.13). However, the familiar paper-size, margin, header, footer, and orientation features are particularly helpful when you are printing spreadsheets.

The appearance of your Page Setup dialog box may differ from the figure. The LaserWriter dialog box does not contain a custom paper-size choice, for example. The word AppleTalk doesn't appear in the upper left corner of the ImageWriter dialog box if the printer is not connected to AppleTalk. As new printers are introduced, you can expect to see still more choices and changes in the appearance of these dialog boxes.

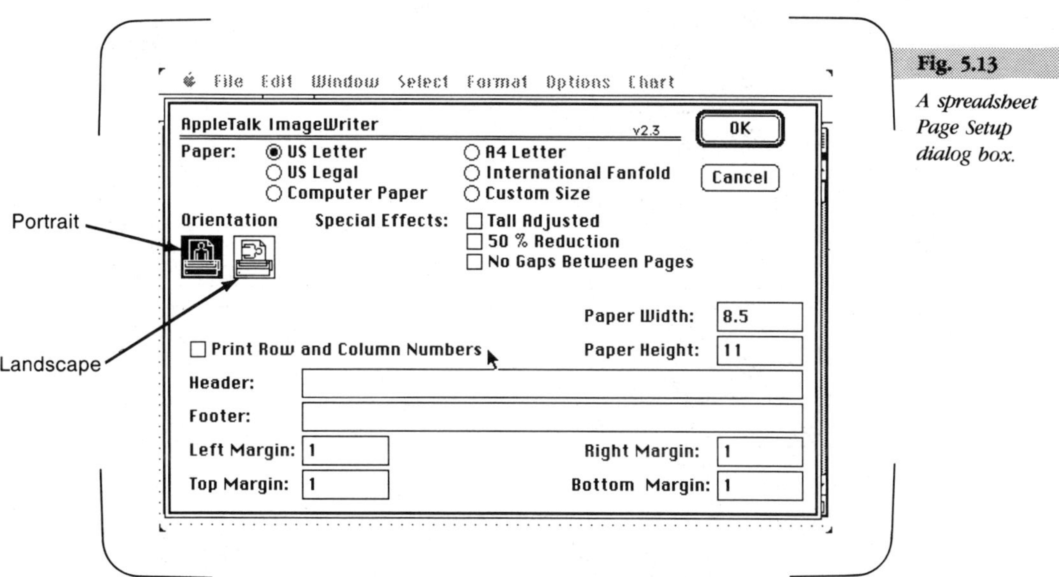

Fig. 5.13
A spreadsheet Page Setup dialog box.

Orientation and Reduction

The default Orientation choice—Portrait—in the Page Setup dialog box is great for printing long spreadsheets (see fig. 5.14). This orientation causes Works to print rows across the short edge of your paper. Use this choice if you have many rows and only a few columns. Clicking on the Landscape icon causes Works to print rows along the long edge of the paper. This orientation is helpful for wide spreadsheets. The choices are named after the way most people hold a camera to take pictures of people and to take pictures of landscapes.

Fig. 5.14

Spreadsheet printed in Portrait and Landscape orientations.

	A	B	C	D	E	F
1	MILEAGE AND COST					
2						
3	Beginning Odometer	110				
4	Ending Odometer	325				
5	**Miles Traveled**	215				
6						
7	Gallons Used	12.6				
8	Cost Per Gallon	$1.25				
9						
10	**Total Gas Cost**	$15.75				
11						
12	**Miles Per Gallon**	17.06				
13						
14	**Cost Per Mile**	$0.073				
15						
16						
17						

	A	B	C	D	E	F	G
1	MILEAGE AND COST						
2							
3	Beginning Odometer	110					
4	Ending Odometer	325					
5							
6	**Miles Traveled**	215					
7							
8							
9	Gallons Used	12.6					
10	Cost Per Gallon	$1.25					
11							
12	**Total Gas Cost**	$15.75					
13							
14	**Miles Per Gallon**	17.06					
15							
16	**Cost Per Mile**	$0.073					

You'll also find yourself frequently using the 50% Reduction box on your ImageWriter dialog box or the Reduce or Enlarge box on your LaserWriter dialog box. As you'd expect, checking the 50% Reduction box on an ImageWriter dialog box prints everything half the normal size. Thus, you can fit twice as much on each sheet of paper. The Reduce or Enlarge box on the LaserWriter dialog box lets you specify the percentage of reduction or enlargement. The 100% setting prints things normally and is the default; 50, 40, 32, or any other whole number less than 100 makes things smaller. Entering numbers larger than 100 causes the printer to use bigger type. Fewer cells fit on a sheet of paper.

Row Numbers and Column Letters

You can print spreadsheets with or without column letters and row numbers. Usually, these identifiers aren't printed, but sometimes they're handy to have when you are testing a new spreadsheet or discussing a spreadsheet over the phone (see fig. 5.15). To print row and column identifiers, you click the Print Row and Column Numbers box in the Page Setup dialog box.

	A	B	C
1	Real Estate Sales Year to Date		
2			
3		Sales	3% Commission
4	Bill	$11,147,844	$334,435.32
5	Mary	$15,587,882	$467,636.46
6	Phil	$8,878,557	$266,356.71
7	George	$447,877	$13,436.31
8	Larry	$17,877,893	$536,336.79
9			
10	Totals	$53,940,053	$1,618,201.59

Fig. 5.15

Spreadsheet with printed row numbers and column letters.

Grids

Usually, Works displays and prints the square boxes that surround each cell. You can turn off the grids by choosing No Grid on the Options menu. This option affects the entire spreadsheet.

You can also turn off the grid but still print the row numbers and column letters. You use No Grid option with the Print Row and Column Numbers choice in the dialog box. When you do this, Works encloses the spreadsheet in a box, as illustrated in figure 5.16.

Page Breaks

Works shows you how much of the spreadsheet will fit on a printed sheet, based on your Page Setup choices. Heavier dashed lines appear on the screen, indicating spreadsheet page breaks and the positions of edges of printed pages. These lines change as you change Page Setup options.

Fig. 5.16

Suppressing the grid, but printing the row numbers and column letters.

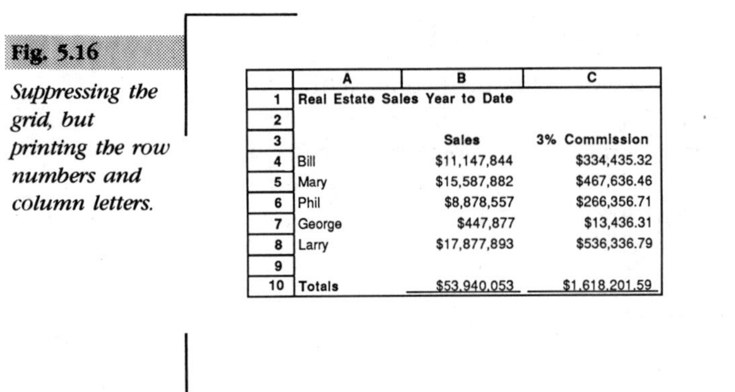

	A	B	C
1	Real Estate Sales Year to Date		
2			
3		Sales	3% Commission
4	Bill	$11,147,844	$334,435.32
5	Mary	$15,587,882	$467,636.46
6	Phil	$8,878,557	$266,356.71
7	George	$447,877	$13,436.31
8	Larry	$17,877,893	$536,336.79
9			
10	Totals	$53,940,053	$1,618,201.59

If a spreadsheet is too wide or too long to fit on one printed sheet, Works prints the spreadsheet on multiple pages. For example, in figure 5.17, Works will print a new page starting at row 15. After that side of the spreadsheet is printed, Works will print the next page starting at column G. At least four sheets of paper are required to print this spreadsheet.

Fig. 5.17

Darker dashed lines showing where printer page breaks will appear.

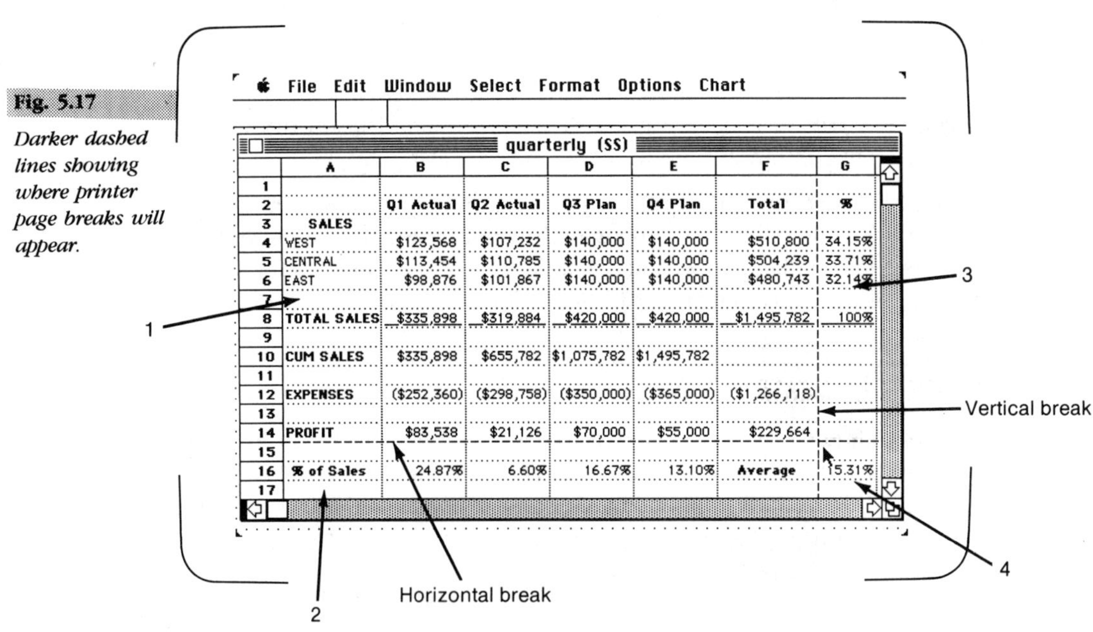

	A	B	C	D	E	F	G
1							
2		Q1 Actual	Q2 Actual	Q3 Plan	Q4 Plan	Total	%
3	SALES						
4	WEST	$123,568	$107,232	$140,000	$140,000	$510,800	34.15%
5	CENTRAL	$113,454	$110,785	$140,000	$140,000	$504,239	33.71%
6	EAST	$98,876	$101,867	$140,000	$140,000	$480,743	32.14%
7							
8	TOTAL SALES	$335,898	$319,884	$420,000	$420,000	$1,495,782	100%
9							
10	CUM SALES	$335,898	$655,782	$1,075,782	$1,495,782		
11							
12	EXPENSES	($252,360)	($298,758)	($350,000)	($365,000)	($1,266,118)	
13							
14	PROFIT	$83,538	$21,126	$70,000	$55,000	$229,664	
15							
16	% of Sales	24.87%	6.60%	16.67%	13.10%	Average	15.31%
17							

Setting Your Own Page Breaks

You can force Works to insert page breaks just about wherever you want them. You can't, however, choose page breaks that won't fit on the paper size you've selected during the Page Setup process. To insert a page break,

1. Select the cell you want to be the upper left corner of the new page.
2. Choose Set Page Break on the Options menu. Works then displays the new vertical and horizontal breaks and repaginates the rest of the spreadsheet.
3. Review the new breaks and revise them if you like. When printing, Works uses the new breaks.

In figure 5.18, for example, a break is set between columns C and D. Works prints columns A through C on one page; the cells to the left, on another page or pages.

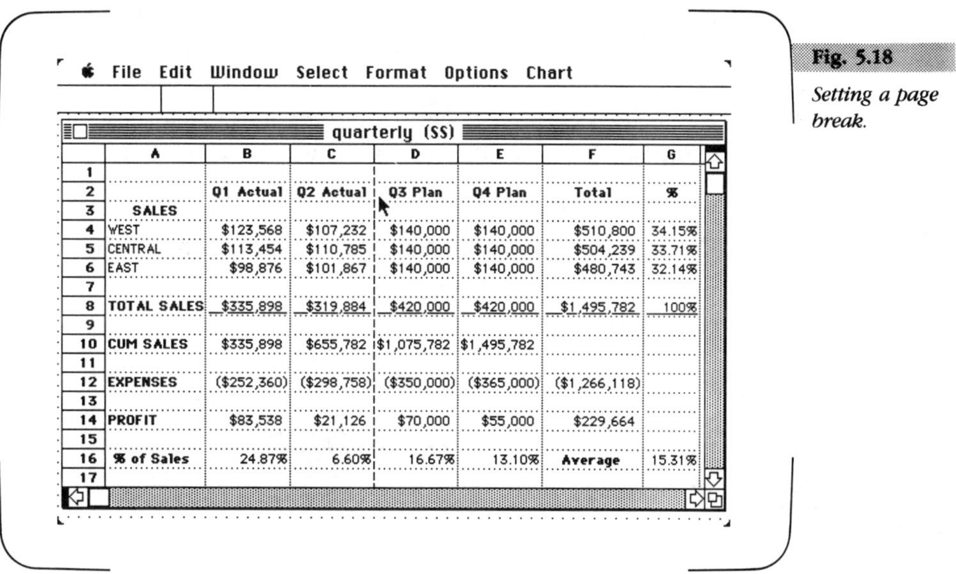

	A	B	C	D	E	F	G
1							
2		Q1 Actual	Q2 Actual	Q3 Plan	Q4 Plan	Total	%
3	SALES						
4	WEST	$123,568	$107,232	$140,000	$140,000	$510,800	34.15%
5	CENTRAL	$113,454	$110,785	$140,000	$140,000	$504,239	33.71%
6	EAST	$98,876	$101,867	$140,000	$140,000	$480,743	32.14%
7							
8	TOTAL SALES	$335,898	$319,884	$420,000	$420,000	$1,495,782	100%
9							
10	CUM SALES	$335,898	$655,782	$1,075,782	$1,495,782		
11							
12	EXPENSES	($252,360)	($298,758)	($350,000)	($365,000)	($1,266,118)	
13							
14	PROFIT	$83,538	$21,126	$70,000	$55,000	$229,664	
15							
16	% of Sales	24.87%	6.60%	16.67%	13.10%	Average	15.31%
17							

Fig. 5.18

Setting a page break.

Removing Vertical and Horizontal Page Breaks

At times, you may want to remove a page break you have previously inserted. At other times, you may decide to move a page break in order to create a more balanced page or to divide the printed spreadsheet more effectively. With Works, this procedure is easy. Following are the steps for removing vertical page breaks:

1. Select a cell immediately to the right of the page break.
2. Choose Remove Page Break on the Options menu. Works then repaginates for you.
3. Check the new page breaks.

To remove horizontal page breaks, you

1. Select a cell immediately below the page break.
2. Choose Remove Page Break from the Options menu. Works then repaginates for you.
3. Check the new page breaks.

You can remove vertical *and* horizontal page breaks at the same time. The trick is to combine the horizontal and vertical removal techniques. You choose a cell that is immediately below the horizontal break and just to the right of the vertical break. Highlight this cell; then use the Remove Page Break choice from the Options menu. In figure 5.19, for example, highlighting F15 causes Works to remove two page breaks. The steps are as follows:

1. Locate the cell immediately below the horizontal break and immediately to the right of the vertical break.
2. Click on this cell.
3. Choose Remove Page Break from the Options menu. Works then repaginates for you.
4. Check the results.

Selective Printing of Ranges and Windows

Usually, Works prints an entire spreadsheet. You can, however, print parts of a large spreadsheet by selecting them before executing the print request. Figure 5.20 shows an example of a specific area selected. Only that area is printed, as is shown in figure 5.21.

Using the Print Window option on the File menu, you can print only the part of the spreadsheet that is displayed (see fig. 5.22). The row letters and column numbers are always printed, but the entry bar, scroll

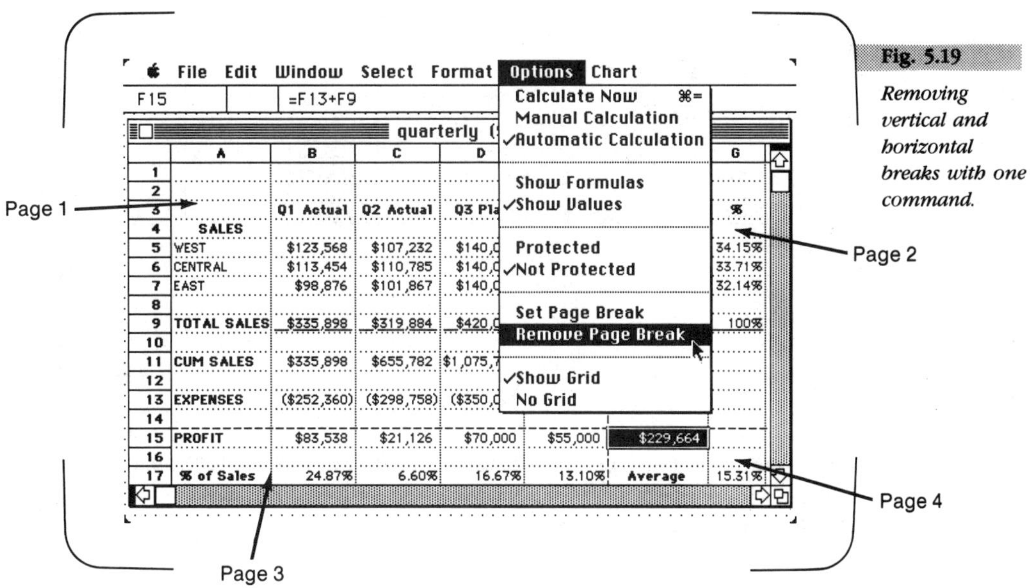

Fig. 5.19 *Removing vertical and horizontal breaks with one command.*

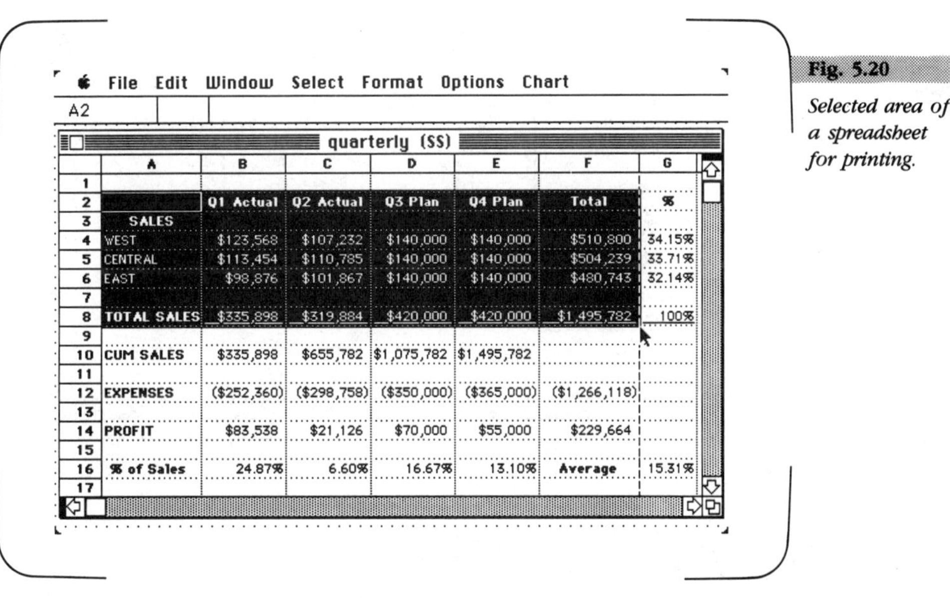

Fig. 5.20 *Selected area of a spreadsheet for printing.*

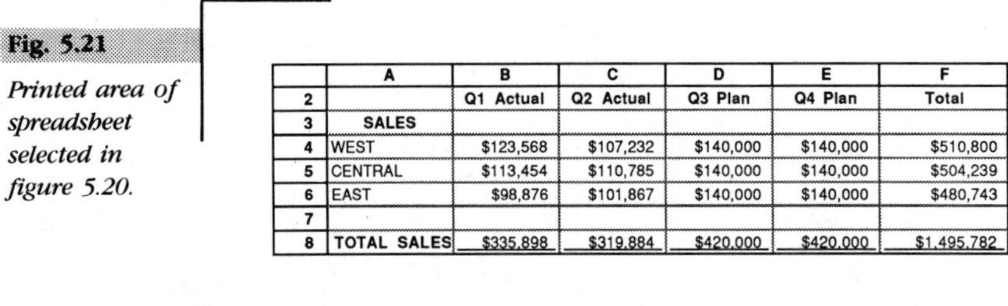

	A	B	C	D	E	F
2		Q1 Actual	Q2 Actual	Q3 Plan	Q4 Plan	Total
3	SALES					
4	WEST	$123,568	$107,232	$140,000	$140,000	$510,800
5	CENTRAL	$113,454	$110,785	$140,000	$140,000	$504,239
6	EAST	$98,876	$101,867	$140,000	$140,000	$480,743
7						
8	TOTAL SALES	$335,898	$319,884	$420,000	$420,000	$1,495,782

Fig. 5.21

Printed area of spreadsheet selected in figure 5.20.

bars, menu, and so on, are not printed. If the spreadsheet shares the screen with something else (a word-processing document, for example), Works prints only the spreadsheet window.

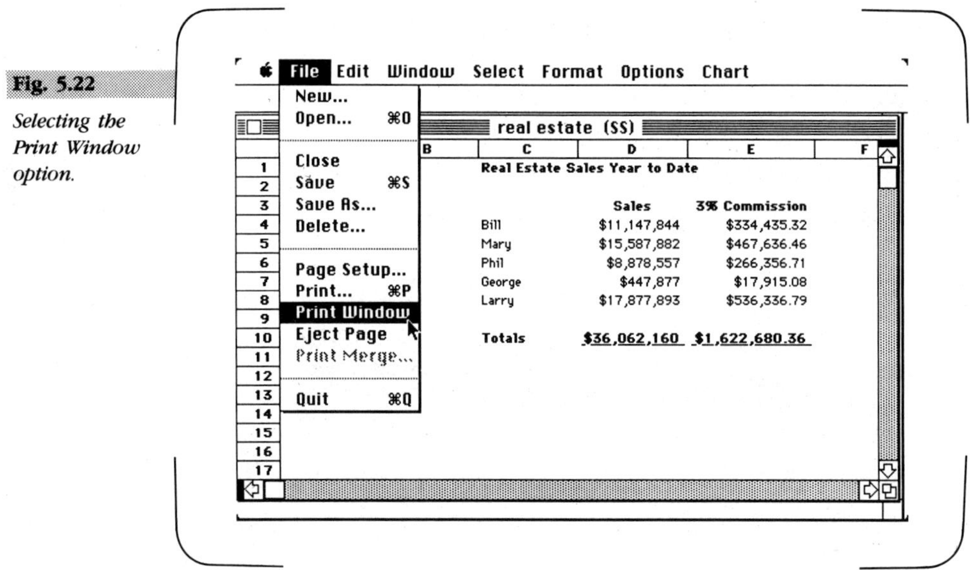

Fig. 5.22

Selecting the Print Window option.

The Format Menu

As you've learned, you can vary the appearance of Works spreadsheets to meet your needs. Changing the width of column A in the mileage spreadsheet is an example. Other ways of making changes also are available. For example, you can control the precision and appearance of the display of numbers and the alignment of numbers within cells. You also can print in boldface type and with or without the grid.

To reformat cells in your spreadsheet, select them and then pull down the Format menu (see fig. 5.23). All the options on the menu are applicable to numbers; but text entries can be affected only by the alignment choices and the Normal Text, Bold, and Underline options.

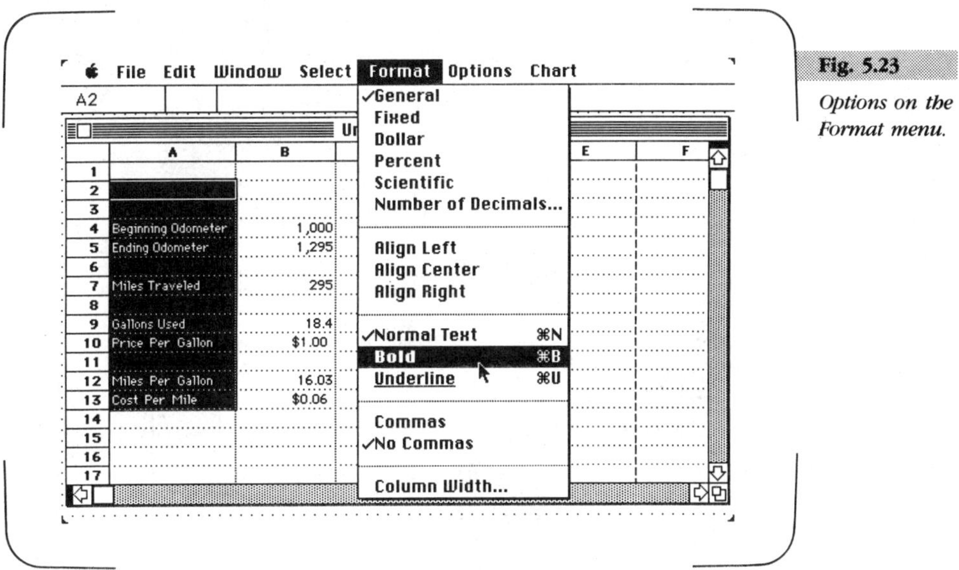

Fig. 5.23

Options on the Format menu.

Controlling Precision, Number of Decimals, and Dollar Signs

Within the spreadsheet, you want numbers calculated precisely. In the displayed or printed spreadsheet, however, numbers shown with 8, 10, or 12 decimal places are difficult to read and remember. You may need a display of 10 decimal places in some instances; but more often than not, you will prefer seeing only 2 or 3 numbers to the left of the decimal point. In the same way, although dollar signs are not at all necessary in calculations, having dollar signs in total lines makes your displayed or printed spreadsheet more attractive and clearer. Through the Format menu, Works provides many ways for you to control the appearance of your spreadsheet.

General is the normal, or default, format for numbers. When you choose the General format, Works displays numbers to the greatest precision possible in a given cell. This precision varies with the cell's width, of course. The wider the cell, the greater the precision of the display. Leading zeros are not displayed; for example, 0.05 is displayed as .05. You can't specify the number of decimal places displayed when you choose the General format.

Notice the Miles per Gallon and Cost per Mile answers in figure 5.24. Works displays the decimal parts of the numbers to 9 and 10 places, respectively. That's too much precision for many applications, so Works offers fixed formats as well.

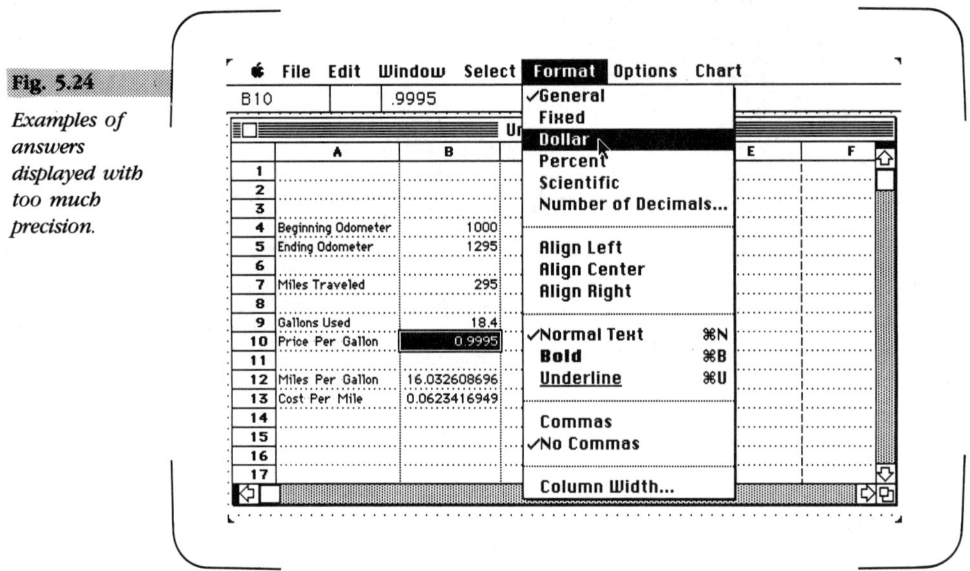

Fig. 5.24 *Examples of answers displayed with too much precision.*

Selecting the Fixed format or Dollar format option (rather than General) enables you to define the number of places displayed to the right of the decimal point. The default is two decimal places.

You can change the number of decimal places, using the dialog box that appears when you choose Number of Decimals on the Format menu (see fig. 5.25). Works permits a maximum of 15 places to the right of the decimal point.

The Scientific option is used to display very small and very large numbers. Each scientific notation number has three parts:

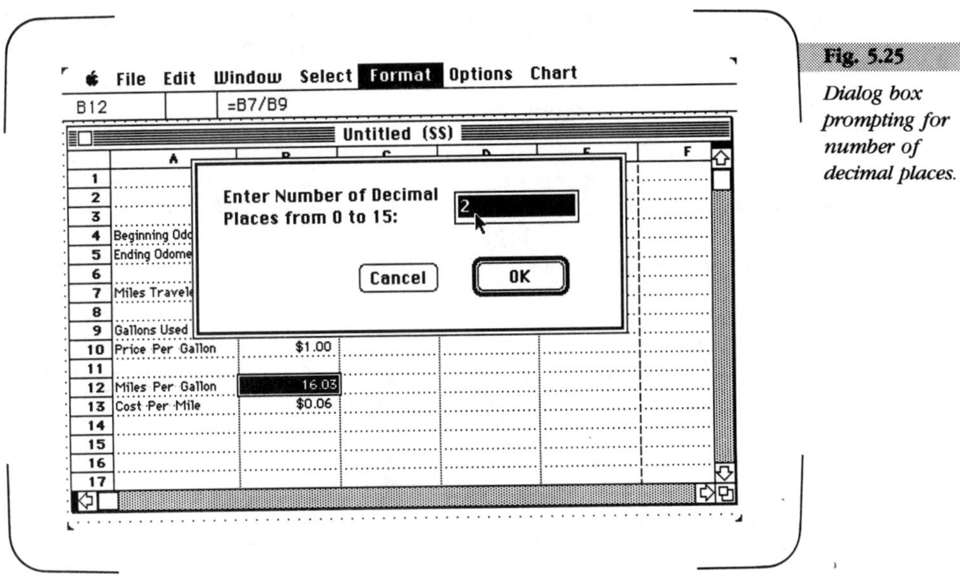

Fig. 5.25

Dialog box prompting for number of decimal places.

- A decimal number in the form *n.nn*, called the mantissa
- The exponentiation letter (*E* or *e*)
- The exponent itself, separated from the *E* by a plus sign

Here are some examples of numbers and how Works displays them in scientific notation:

1,000,000	becomes	1.00E+06
150,000	becomes	1.50E+05
255,000,000	becomes	2.55E+08
−478,555	becomes	−4.79E+05

In the first example, 1.00 is the mantissa, E is the exponentiation letter, and 06 is the exponent.

If you choose Dollar on the Format Menu, the selected cells will contain dollar signs and default to two decimal places unless you tell Works otherwise.

When displayed and printed, the contents of dollar-formatted cells appear to be rounded. This arrangement doesn't affect the actual values, which you can see by activating the cell and viewing the contents in the entry bar. How Works rounds numbers depends on the number of decimal places you specify. For example, 9.505 appears as $10 if you choose no decimal places; $9.51, if you choose two places; and $9.505, if you specify three places.

NOTE: When setting up column widths, be sure to take into account the space occupied by dollar signs, decimal points, and decimal places. Negative numbers displayed and printed in the Dollar format appear in parentheses; make room for these, too.

Controlling Percentages, Commas, Alignment, and Typeface

When you select the Percent formatting option, Works displays numbers as percentages. That is to say, the system multiplies numbers by 100. For example, 0.03 appears as 3.00%; 1.0, as 100.00%. The number remains unmodified in the entry bar.

Works uses two decimal places as the default, but you can change this. And Works rounds percentages in the same way it rounds dollars for display and printing purposes: according to the number of decimal places specified. In figure 5.26, column A shows four numbers in the General format, and column B shows the same entries in the Percent format. Equation answers can be automatically formatted like this, too.

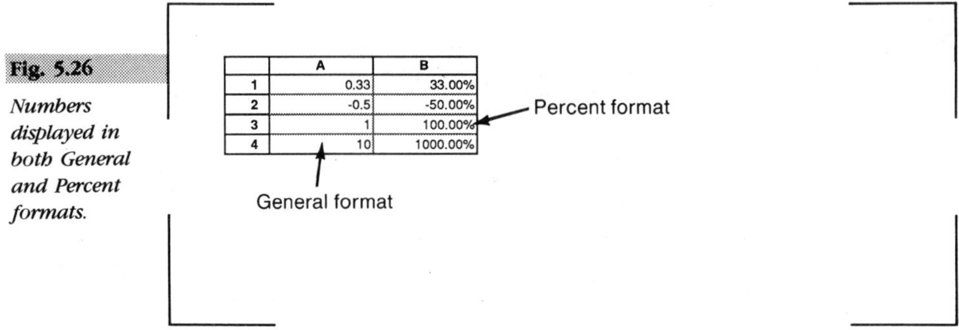

	A	B
1	0.33	33.00%
2	-0.5	-50.00%
3	1	100.00%
4	10	1000.00%

Fig. 5.26
Numbers displayed in both General and Percent formats.

To specify numbers with or without commas, you select one choice or the other on the Format menu. Remember to allow room for commas when you set up column widths.

On the Format menu, the three choices Align Left, Align Center, and Align Right tell Works where to place numbers and labels in the cells. Align Left is the default format for labels. That is, the first character of a label usually is placed at the left edge of the cell. Works usually right-aligns numbers. You can center numbers or text if you want (see fig. 5.27).

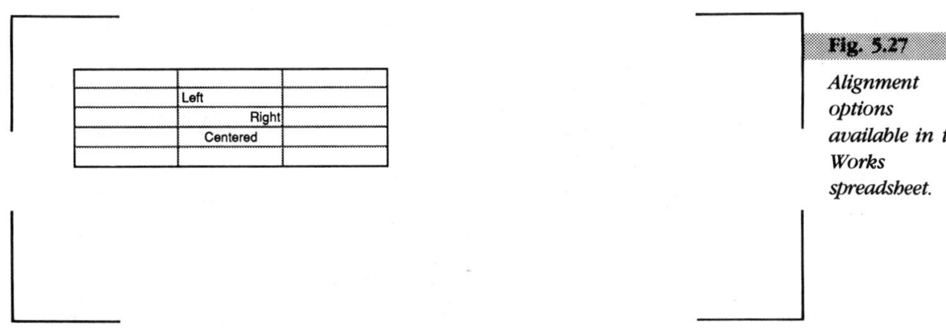

Fig. 5.27
Alignment options available in the Works spreadsheet.

You can enhance labels and numbers by selecting them, then choosing the Bold or Underline option on the Format menu. To turn off these options, you specify Normal Text. When entering and editing, you can use three *command*-[letter] shortcuts. They are the same as those used in word processing:

command-B	Bold
command-U	Underline
command-N	Normal Text (turns off Bold and Underline)

Ranges

Frequently, you may want to affect a collection of rows or columns or a block. For example, you may want to make all the labels in a column boldface or have all the number formats in an area of the spreadsheet contain dollar signs, commas, and two decimal places.

Speeding Formatting by Selecting Ranges

By altering large sections of a spreadsheet at once, you can save yourself a great deal of work. For example, you can tell Works that you want boldfaced, centered column headings along a whole row, as shown in figure 5.28.

The procedure is the following:

1. Select a row by clicking on the row number.
2. Press **command-B** (for bold).
3. With the row still highlighted, pull down the Options menu.
4. Choose Align Center.

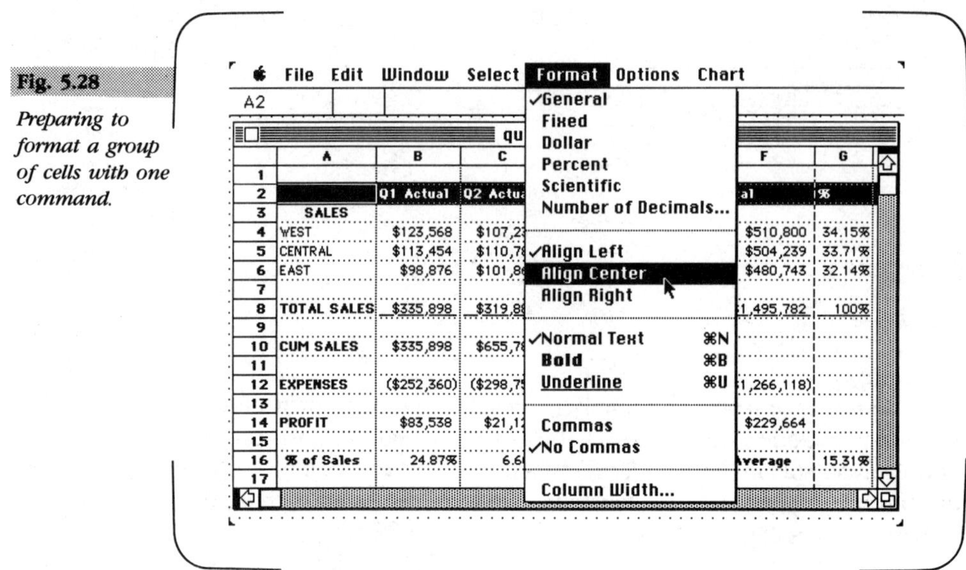

Fig. 5.28

Preparing to format a group of cells with one command.

5. If you haven't already done so, enter the column headings (use the *tab* key to move horizontally across the selected row).

Steps 1 through 4 can be performed either before or after the headings are entered. The column labels will be boldfaced and centered within their respective columns.

Formatting Ranges of Numbers

Using similar techniques, you can format large areas of cells that will contain numbers in your spreadsheet:

1. Using the *shift*-click technique, select the area that needs formatting.

2. Pull down the Format menu, and change the format of the entire range.

3. Enter some numbers and inspect the results.

NOTE: Although cells appear empty, they may contain formatting information. To confirm this possibility, check the cell by activating it and pulling down the Format menu. The options in effect have check marks beside them. In figure 5.29, for example, cell A2 looks empty but contains Dollar, Bold, Underline, and Commas format options.

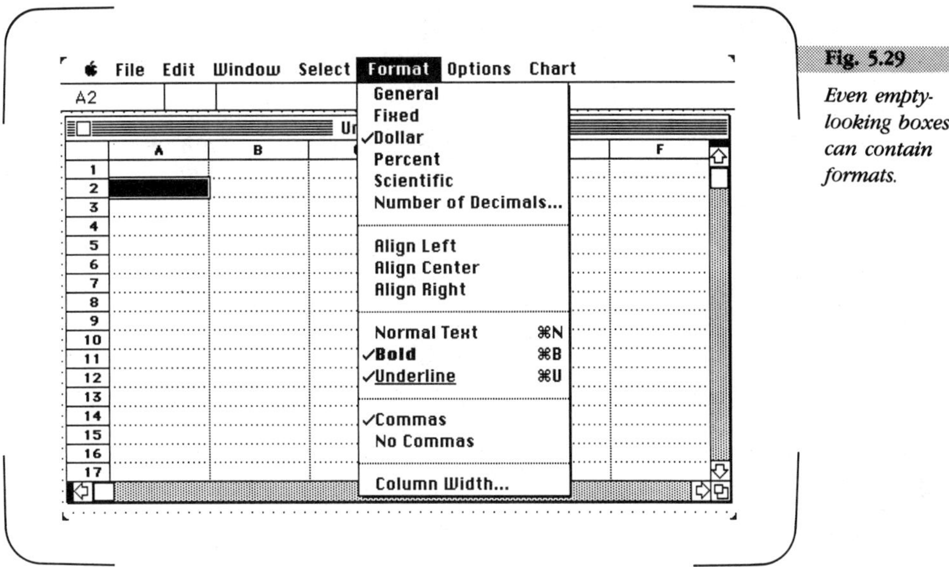

Fig. 5.29

Even empty-looking boxes can contain formats.

Cell Protection

As you've already seen, spreadsheets are easy to alter. This facility is both a blessing and a curse. A moment of carelessness can damage or delete a vital equation. You can make the mistake yourself, or someone else using your spreadsheet can do the damage. Unless you catch and undo the mistake immediately, you lose the equation forever. The spreadsheet will never give the right answers again unless the problem is spotted and the equation is rewritten.

Fortunately, Works offers a protection feature. You can specify cells that can never be changed without your authorization. Protection "locks" the specified cells. You can protect all the cells in your spreadsheet or just some of them. Protection is easy. Here's a suggested way to do it:

1. Enter and format your labels.
2. Enter and test your equations; format these cells as needed.
3. Select a range to be protected (usually, only labels and equations).
4. Choose Protected on the Options menu.
5. Continue selecting ranges and choosing the Protected option until you've protected all important areas.
6. Don't forget to save the protected spreadsheet.

NOTE: Usually, you won't want to protect areas of the spreadsheet that will contain values unless you don't want anyone to change the values accidentally.

If you try to modify a protected cell, Works displays a warning in a dialog box (see fig. 5.30). You must acknowledge the warning before Works lets you continue.

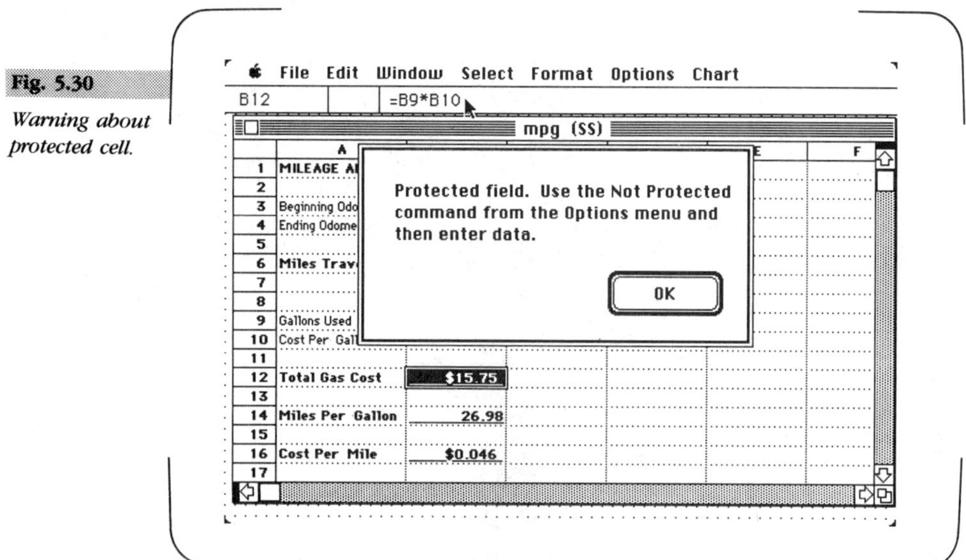

Fig. 5.30

Warning about protected cell.

To modify that cell, you must unprotect it. To unprotect cells or ranges of cells, you select them and then choose Not Protected on the Options menu. You turn off protection everywhere by choosing Select All Cells from the Select menu and then specifying Not Protected on the Options menu.

When designing the spreadsheet, you can protect things as you go rather than wait until you finish, but you need to unprotect areas that need changing. Most people find it easier to wait until a spreadsheet is completed and tested before protecting it.

Shortcuts for Creating Spreadsheets

Works offers a number of powerful shortcuts for creating spreadsheets. These shortcuts are summarized in the following sections.

Quick Ways To Enter and Activate

As you've learned already, you don't have to click the enter box after each entry. You don't even need to click a new cell after each entry. Press the *tab* key to terminate your entry and make the cell to the right of the one you just completed the new active cell. You can accomplish the same task by pressing the right-arrow key on your keyboard.

Pressing the *return* key terminates an entry and activates the cell immediately below. Pressing the *enter* key terminates without changing the active cell. Pressing *shift-tab* activates the cell to the left of your preceding entry; pressing *shift-return* activates the cell above the preceding entry. Those of you with arrow keys will find that they do what you expect. If you select a portion of a spreadsheet (cells B4 through E6 in fig. 5.31, for instance), the tabbing and entry techniques described here keep your cursor within the selected area. Tabbing after entering E4 moves the cursor tabs. Table 5.1 provides a summary of the quick ways to make entries and change active cells.

Table 5.1
Quick Ways To Make Entries and Change Active Cells

Action or Key	*Result*
Click enter box	Terminates entry, same cell remains active
enter	Terminates entry; same cell remains active
tab	Terminates entry, moves to right
shift-tab	Terminates entry, moves to left
return	Terminates entry, moves down
shift-return	Terminates entry, moves up
right arrow	Terminates entry, moves to right
left arrow	Terminates entry, moves to left
up arrow	Terminates entry, moves up
down arrow	Terminates entry, moves down

Equation-Building Shortcuts

Much of the time you spend building a spreadsheet consists of creating equations. One way to build an equation containing cell references is to type the locations (A1, B2, C3). A quicker way is to point and click. Another shortcut is to copy equations, and a third way involves using cell references.

Clicking To Build Equations

You can click to build equations. For example, in figure 5.31, one way to enter into cell B8 an equation that adds the contents of B4, B5, and B6 is to type the entire equation (=B4+B5+B6) on the keyboard. But Works offers a shortcut. Simply by clicking on a cell, you include its location in the equation under development. Works "watches" where you click and adds those cell references to your equation in the entry bar. Here are the steps:

1. Select the cell where you want the equation to appear (B8, in this example).
2. Enter an equal sign (=) to start the equation.
3. Click on the first cell (B6) to be included; Works then outlines that cell.
4. Click on the next cell and the next (B5, then B4), until you're done. Each cell is outlined when you click on it.
5. Click on the enter box or otherwise terminate the entry. The results then appear in the cell (B8) containing the equation.

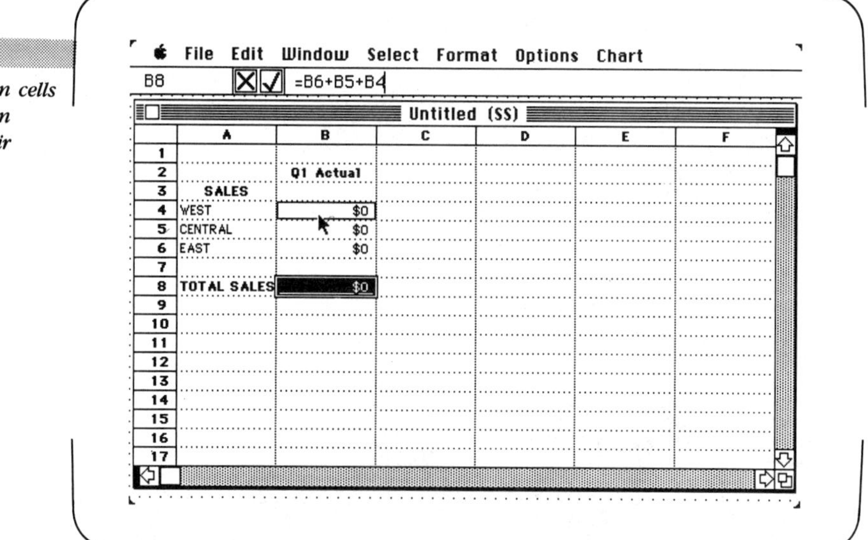

Fig. 5.31

Clicking on cells rather than typing their locations.

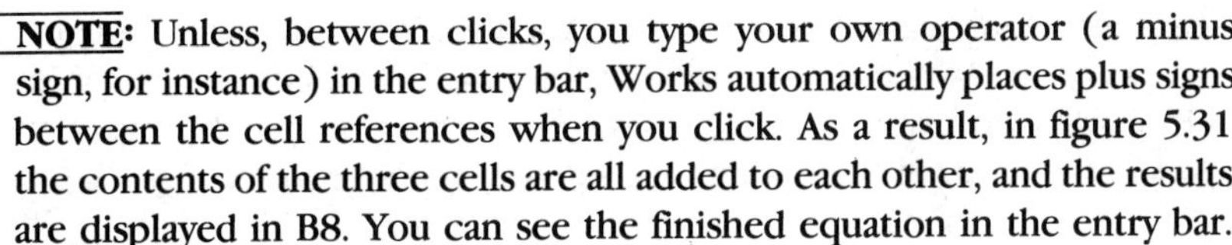

NOTE: Unless, between clicks, you type your own operator (a minus sign, for instance) in the entry bar, Works automatically places plus signs between the cell references when you click. As a result, in figure 5.31 the contents of the three cells are all added to each other, and the results are displayed in B8. You can see the finished equation in the entry bar.

You can instruct Works to subtract the numbers from each other instead, by entering minus signs between the clicks. You can enter asterisks to make Works multiply the numbers.

Copying Equations

In figure 5.32, the equations for adding the sales in each quarter are similar. The only things that change are the locations of the equations and the references to the cells containing values to be added. For example, the Total Sales equation in C8 is C6+C5+C4; the equation in cell D8 is D6+D5+D4; and so on. Rather than retyping similar equations over and over again, you can copy equations and adapt them to different situations. You use the Copy and Paste features that you're familiar with, but a new "wrinkle" is described in the following sections.

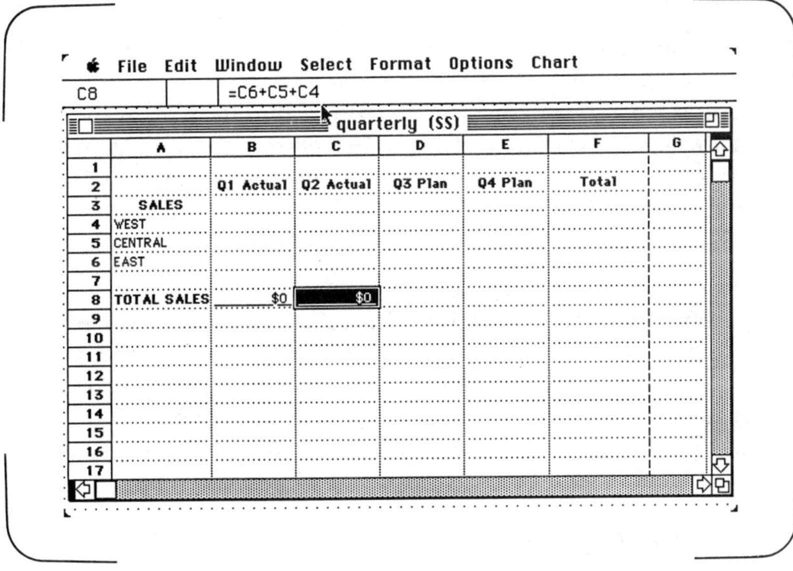

Fig. 5.32 *Preparing to use a special form of copying to speed spreadsheet construction.*

Using Cell-Referencing Shortcuts

The new "wrinkle" is relative addressing. In this process, Works modifies equations when it copies them so that the new equations work properly in their new locations. Because Works changes the letters and numbers in the new equation cell in relation to the location of the original equation, the process is called ***relative addressing***. The following examples help clarify this concept, which new spreadsheet users may find confusing. Stick with it. This is a powerful and important tool.

Relative Cell References

When you copy and paste spreadsheet equations, Works makes assumptions about the relative positions of the cell that you copy from and the cell you copy to. Therefore, if you copy the equation from B8 and paste it in C8, all the cell references in C8's equation contain Cs rather than Bs.

Perform the following steps to copy an equation.

1. Select a cell containing an equation (like B8 in fig. 5.32).
2. Copy by pressing **command-C** or choosing Copy on the Edit menu.
3. Select the destination cell (C8).
4. Paste by using **command-V** or choosing Paste on the Edit menu.

Relative referencing works vertically as well as horizontally. You can create an equation in cell F4 that totals the western region's quarterly sales figures (=E4+D4+C4+B4) and then copy the equation for the other regions. Works automatically changes the cell references to include appropriate row numbers. Thus, the central region's equation is (=E5+D5+C5+B5). The east's cells automatically contain 6s rather than 4s or 5s.

Moreover, relative addresses can be combinations of "over and down." For example, take the cumulative sales equations required for row 10 in figure 5.33. The equation for C10 is =B10+C8; the similar equation in D10 is =C10+D8; in cell E10, the equation is =D10+E8; and so on. Works automatically tries to create copies that relate correctly to their origins. Obviously, you need to check to see whether Works has done what you require.

Absolute Cell References

Automatic relative addressing is a handy and powerful feature. Sometimes, however, you want to overrule Works' automatic provision of relative addresses when copying. You can take control by forcing absolute cell addresses.

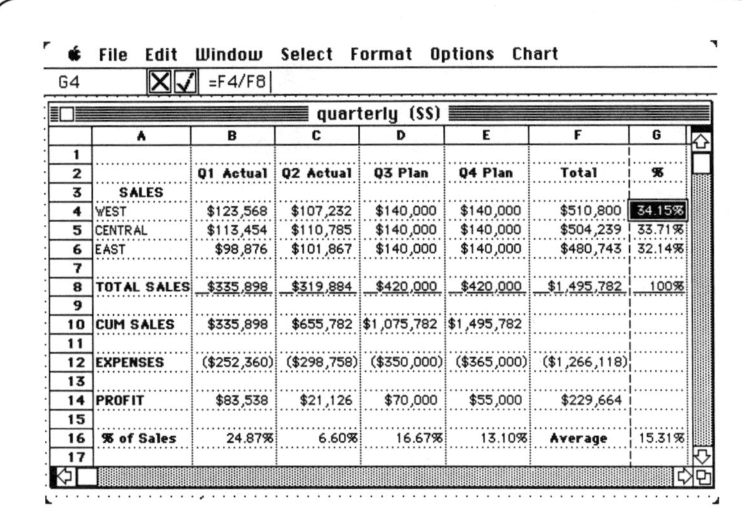

	A	B	C	D	E	F	G
1							
2		Q1 Actual	Q2 Actual	Q3 Plan	Q4 Plan	Total	%
3	SALES						
4	WEST	$123,568	$107,232	$140,000	$140,000	$510,800	34.15%
5	CENTRAL	$113,454	$110,785	$140,000	$140,000	$504,239	33.71%
6	EAST	$98,876	$101,867	$140,000	$140,000	$480,743	32.14%
7							
8	TOTAL SALES	$335,898	$319,884	$420,000	$420,000	$1,495,782	100%
9							
10	CUM SALES	$335,898	$655,782	$1,075,782	$1,495,782		
11							
12	EXPENSES	($252,360)	($298,758)	($350,000)	($365,000)	($1,266,118)	
13							
14	PROFIT	$83,538	$21,126	$70,000	$55,000	$229,664	
15							
16	% of Sales	24.87%	6.60%	16.67%	13.10%	Average	15.31%
17							

Fig. 5.33

Building fairly complex equations by making copies of equations that contain either relative or absolute addresses.

For example, in figure 5.33, to show the percentage of total sales contributed by each region, you need to divide each region's sales (cells F4, F5, and F6) by the total sales in cell F8.

Assume that you set the format of cell G4 to display percentages so that Works takes care of moving the decimal place and displaying the percent sign for you. Then, the equation to find the percentage of total sales contributed by the western region is located in cell G4 and written =F4/F8 (see the entry bar in fig. 5.33).

If you copy this perfectly good equation from G4 and paste it into G5 and G6, however, the two new equations won't work properly. Instead of using the contents of F8 (Total Sales) for the percentage calculation, the central region's equation in G5 uses the contents of F9. Works, unless told to do otherwise, replaces the Total Sales address (F8) with a location relative to F8, based on the new equation's relative position to G4 after pasting.

Similarly, if you simply paste another copy of the equation from G4 into G6, that new equation uses the contents of F10 rather than F8. The resulting division by zero creates error messages in cells G5 and G6. Some errors are more subtle. The problem is that you may still get answers; they just won't be right.

In this example, you want all three regional percentage calculations to use the contents of F8 in calculations, regardless of the equation's relative position. You can accomplish this task by an absolute cell reference.

Preceding row numbers and column letters with dollar signs tells Works that you want to address things absolutely. Therefore, to force Works always to use F8 (Total Sales) in all three regional calculations, you make the original equation in G4 =F4/$F$8.

When you copy and paste this equation, Works still changes the F4 reference to F5 or F6, but does not change $F$8—ever. You can change absolute references to relative and back by using the entry bar. You may want to experiment with your spreadsheet. When you finish, be certain that the percentage equations use absolute references for the divisor.

You can create absolute references by typing the dollar signs in cell references, or you can use the following shortcut:

1. Activate the cell containing the reference.
2. Select the reference you want to make absolute.
3. Either press **command-A** or choose Absolute Cell Ref on the Edit menu.

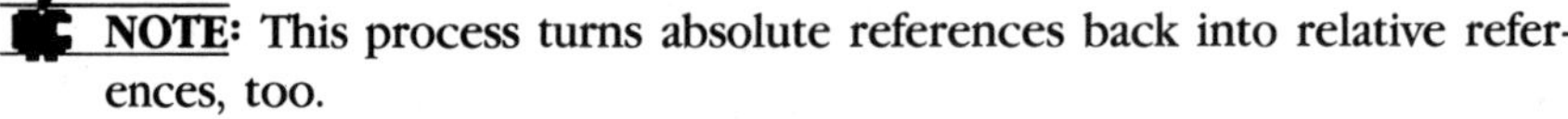

NOTE: This process turns absolute references back into relative references, too.

Mixed Absolute and Relative References

You can mix absolute and relative references. For example, any of the following cell addresses is valid, but the references all do different things:

$A$1
$A1
A$1

In the first case, A1 is always the cell used. In the second reference, new equations refer to different row numbers but always refer to cells in column A. The third example, A$1, creates copies of equations that always refer to cells in row 1, but the column changes.

Don't feel bad if this information doesn't sink in right away. Just remember always to test new spreadsheets carefully, and be certain to examine equations that you've created by using the Copy and Paste features. The best way to learn this material is to see what Works does to your equations when it assigns relative locations during pasting. You also need to pay attention to references when using the Fill Right and Fill Down features (described in the following section).

Copying by Filling Cells

A faster way to copy and paste, this shortcut uses the Fill commands to duplicate the contents of single cells or entire rows or columns. Here are the general procedures:

1. Select the cells, rows, or columns to be copied.
2. Select the cells, rows, or columns to receive the copies.
3. Either choose Fill Right or Fill Down on the Edit menu, or press **command-R** or **command-D**, respectively.
4. Works copies the contents of the active cells to the selected cells.
5. Equations (if copied) get proper relative and absolute references.

NOTE: You can fill with labels, equations, values, formats, and other elements you want to duplicate. The examples that follow show equations, but other cell types can be filled just as easily.

Using Fill Right

Obviously, a command this powerful has much for you to know about, so start with a simple example. Look at figure 5.34. Suppose that you want to create the Total Sales equation in D9 and copy it into cells E9 through G9. Using the Fill Right feature, you can accomplish this task quickly:

1. Activate the first cell (D9) and enter the equation **=D7+D6+D5**
2. Select the equation and cells that will receive copies (D9 through G9).
3. Press **command-R** to fill to the right (or choose Fill Right on the Edit menu). Works then copies properly addressed equations.

In figure 5.35, examine cells D8 through F8. Notice how Works copied the equation into cells to the right of the active cell and automatically assigned relative cell addresses. If a source equation contains absolute references, Works also honors them.

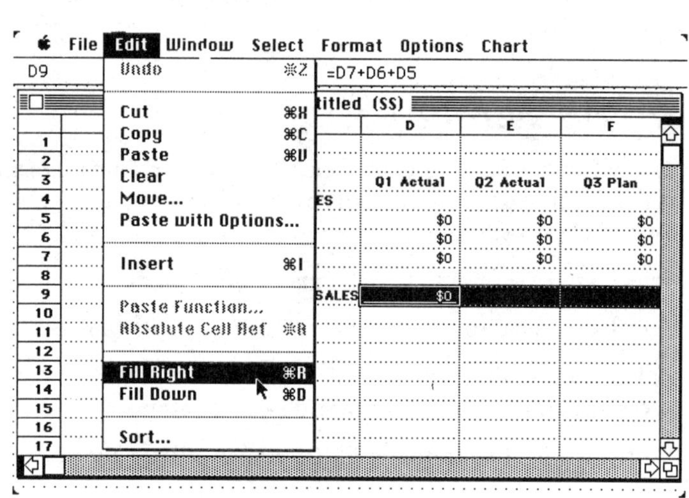

Fig. 5.34

Using Fill Right to copy the contents of the active cell to selected cells to the right.

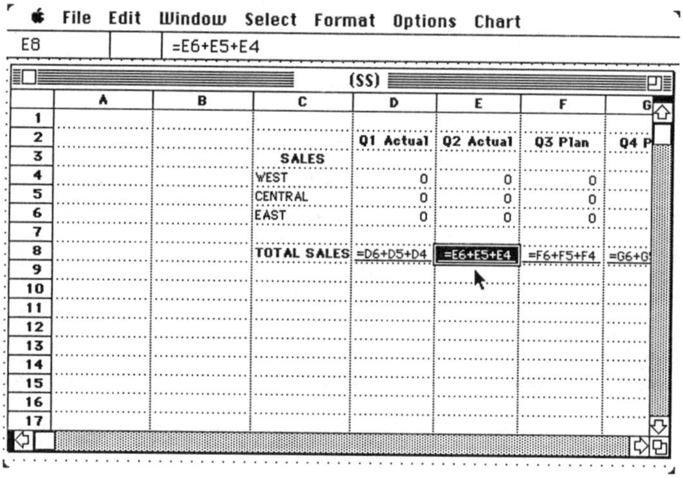

Fig. 5.35

When you use the Fill Right feature, relative and absolute references work as you expect.

Using Fill Down

The Fill Down feature works the same way as Fill Right, with one difference: Works copies the contents of the active cell down instead of to the right. Figure 5.36 provides an example; in this case, Works is copying the value $1,000 from E5 to E6 and E7.

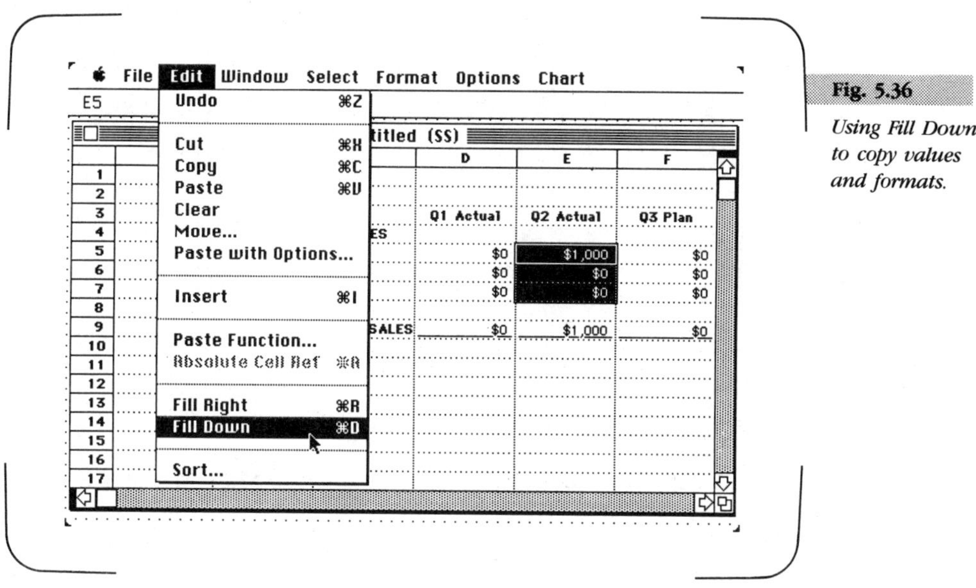

Fig. 5.36

Using Fill Down to copy values and formats.

Here's how to use Fill Down:

1. Activate the source cell (E5 in fig. 5.36).
2. Highlight cells to receive copies (E6 and E7).
3. Use either Fill Down on the Edit menu or the **command-D** shortcut.
4. Selected cells (E6 and E7) contain copies of the value from the active cell (E5).
5. If equations are copied, references are altered appropriately.

Works then recalculates the spreadsheet, displaying the results of the Fill Down activity (see fig. 5.37).

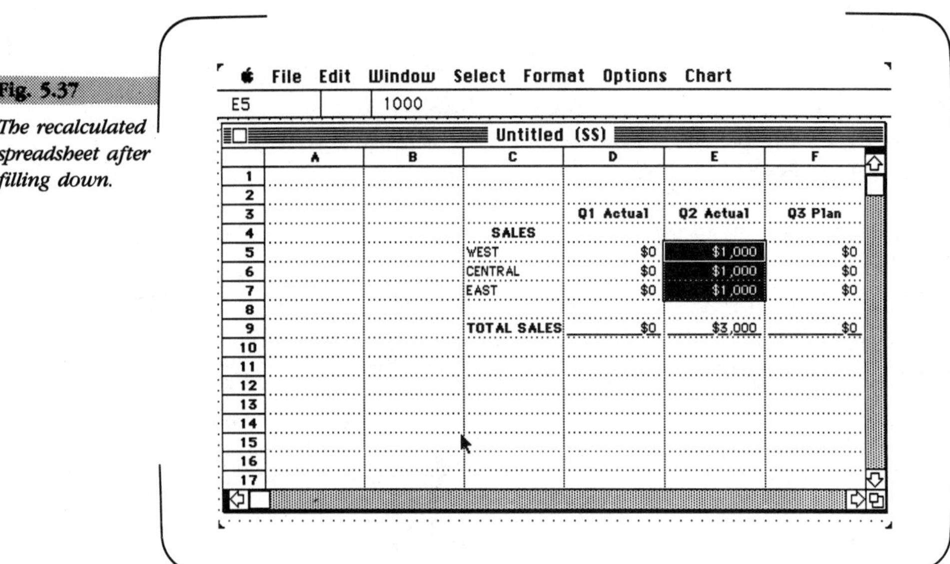

Fig. 5.37

The recalculated spreadsheet after filling down.

Copying Multiple Cells with Fill

You can copy selected portions of columns or rows by using the Fill features. For example, suppose that you want to copy the $1,000 value from cell D5 to the entire selected area (see fig. 5.38). You can do a two-step fill:

1. Select the cell to be copied (D5).
2. Drag to select the destination (D5 through G7).
3. Fill down first (press **command-D** or use the Fill Down Edit menu option).
4. Fill right (press **command-R** or use the Fill Right Edit menu choice).

In this example, Works first fills column D with the value from D5. Then, the program fills columns E through G with copies of the values in column D. Figure 5.38 shows the filled spreadsheet. You can do the same thing by selecting rows and the Fill Down feature instead.

Taking Care When Filling

You need to think ahead when defining ranges used with the Fill features; otherwise, you may unintentionally alter cells. For example, if you use

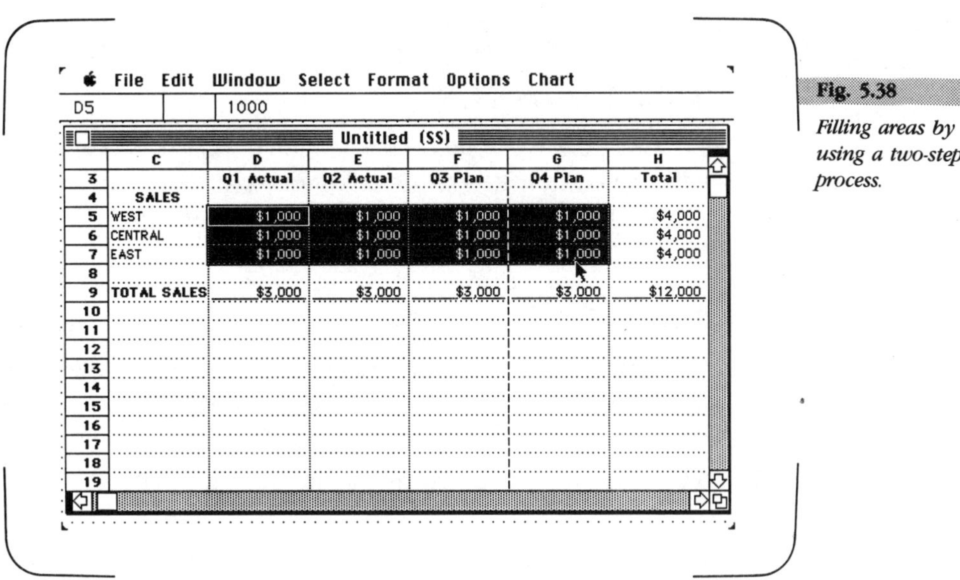

Fig. 5.38

Filling areas by using a two-step process.

Fill Right with cells selected as in figure 5.39, Works replaces the equations in column H with values and so destroys the equations.

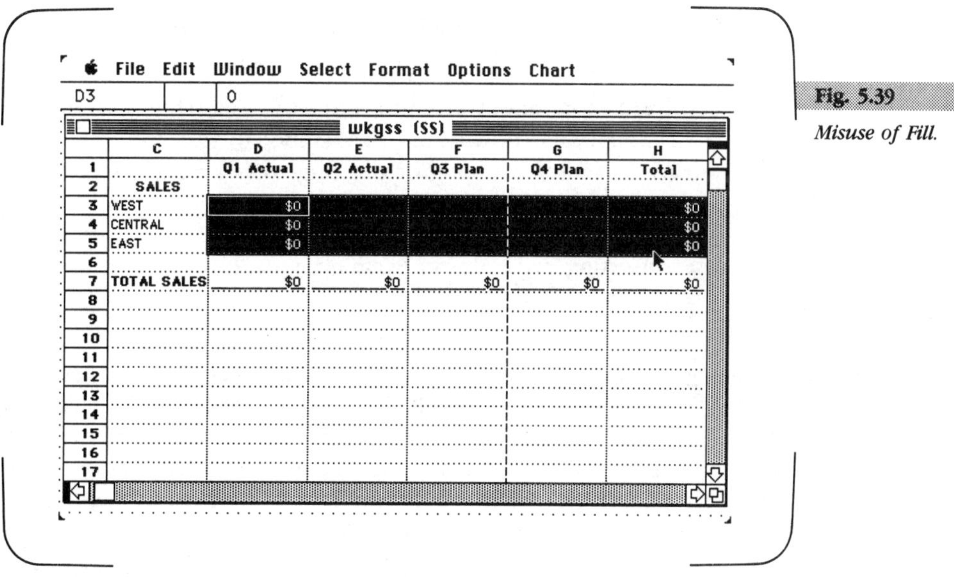

Fig. 5.39

Misuse of Fill.

Inserting and Deleting Rows and Columns

Most good spreadsheets evolve over time. You'll want to add an extra row—a new region, for instance—or a column containing subtotals. Fortunately, Works makes it easy to insert new columns or rows. The program even helps with cell referencing.

Inserting Rows

Suppose, for example, that you need to add a fourth region, New England to the spreadsheet. You'll need to add a row after WEST (row 5). Works does most of the hard stuff, but you must be alert. Here are the steps:

1. Select the row immediately below the desired insertion (row 6).
2. Either press **command-I** or choose Insert from the Edit menu.
3. A blank row 6 appears between row 5 and the old row 6. Works pushes lines down and renumbers them; old 6 becomes 7, and so on (see fig. 5.40).
4. You can repeat the process to insert multiple rows.
5. Works automatically modifies parts of your old equations, but you may need to change other parts manually.

   You learn more about this subject in the following section and in Chapter 6. For now, simply remember to test the spreadsheet after inserting or deleting rows or columns.
6. The new cells may need formatting and/or filling.
7. After inserting cells, always examine equations and test the spreadsheet.

WARNING: Many equations won't automatically include values entered in new lines; other equations will. For example, when you add a new region between CENTRAL and WEST in figure 5.40, Works doesn't automatically include the new row's values in equations. The old Total Sales equations is modified to take into account the movement of row 6 down to row 7, but the new row (row 6) isn't included.

Thus, before insertion, the totals equation (at B9) is =B7+B6+B5. After insertion, the Total Sales equation is in cell B10 and reads =B8+B7+B5. Notice that B6 isn't included in the equation without your help. Later

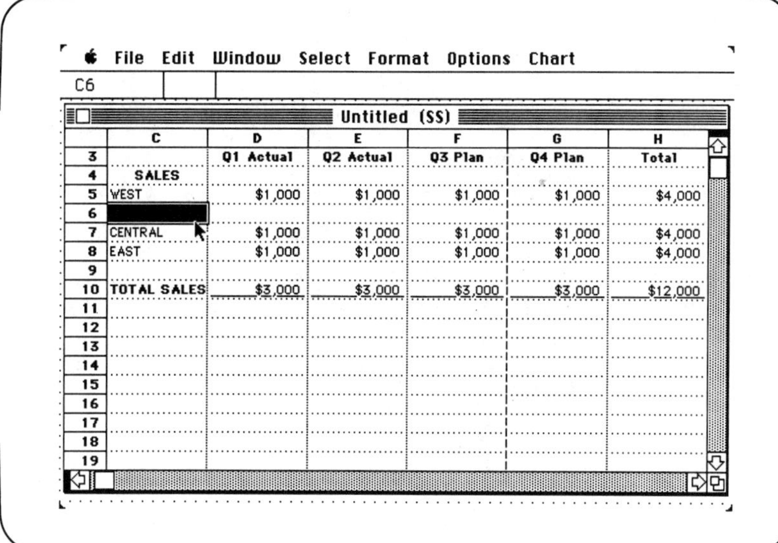

Fig. 5.40
Inserting a blank row to make room for new information.

you'll learn about Works functions (SUM and SSUM) that minimize problems like these, but even these functions don't eliminate the requirement to test carefully after insertions.

Inserting Columns

Column insertion works much like row insertion. Suppose that you want to insert a new column after column C (see fig. 5.41). Here are the steps you follow:

1. Select the column immediately to the right of where you want to insert a column.
2. Either press **command-I** or choose Insert on the Edit menu. A new blank column appears. Columns to the right of the new one are pushed right.
3. Repeat the process to insert multiple columns.
4. Works automatically modifies portions of your old equations, such as relettering columns and many cell references, but you may need to make modifications to some equations.
5. The new cells may need formatting and/or filling.
6. Examine equations and test the spreadsheet after inserting columns.

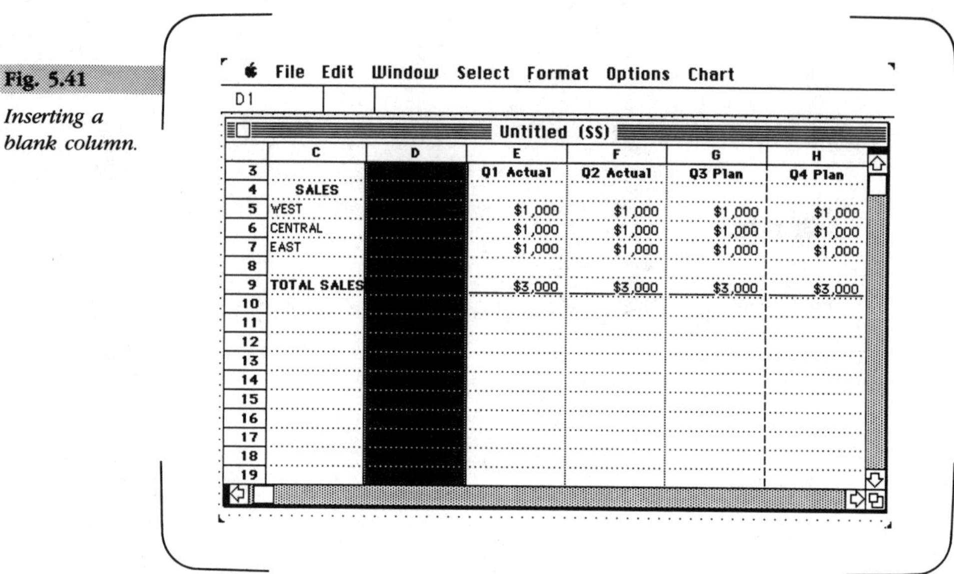

Fig. 5.41

Inserting a blank column.

WARNING: Many equations won't automatically include values entered in new columns; other equations will. You need to test carefully. For more information, see the warning in the "Inserting Rows" section.

Deleting Rows or Columns

Deleting is as simple as selecting the undesired row or column and using Works' Cut feature. You can select multiple rows or columns at once. Use the Edit menu choice or the **command-X** shortcut. Here's how:

1. Select a row or column (click on the row number or column letter).
2. Either press **command-X** or use the Cut option on the Edit menu. The selected row or column disappears, and Works renumbers the affected rows, columns, and references.
3. Examine and test your spreadsheet to ensure proper operation.

Remember that the cut column or row replaces the contents of your Clipboard. You can undo cuts if you spot your error in time.

NOTE: If you remove cells needed for equations, your spreadsheet won't work properly. Usually, but not always, Works warns you by presenting a dialog box or by displaying N/A or *Error* in the affected cells.

Moving Cells

You can quickly move a cell or group of cells within a spreadsheet by using the Move command. Sometimes you'll want to move cells to a space that is already empty. At other times, you'll need to make room first by inserting blank rows or columns. (To learn how to move cells from one spreadsheet to another, see the discussion of the Paste with Options command.)

Here are the steps to move cells within a spreadsheet:

1. If necessary, use the insertion features to prepare a place big enough to accept the cells to be moved.
2. Select the range of cells to be moved.
3. Choose Move on the Edit menu (see fig. 5.42). Works then displays a dialog box.
4. Enter the reference of the upper left cell of the new position (see fig. 5.43).

Works does most of the renumbering and referencing for you when you use the Move command, but you should still check your work.

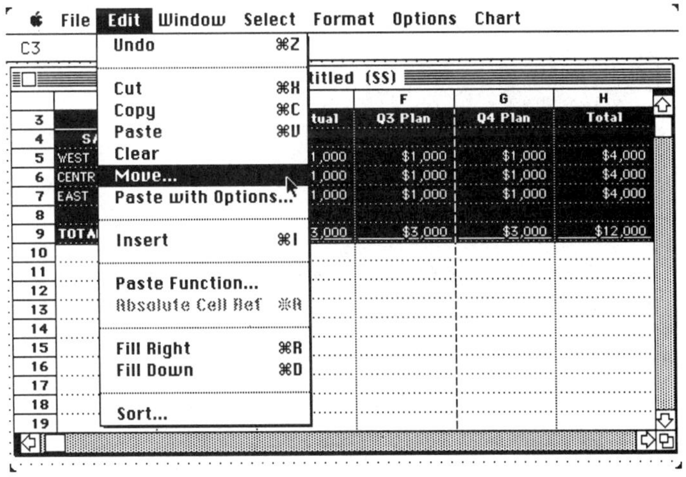

Fig. 5.42

Moving cells.

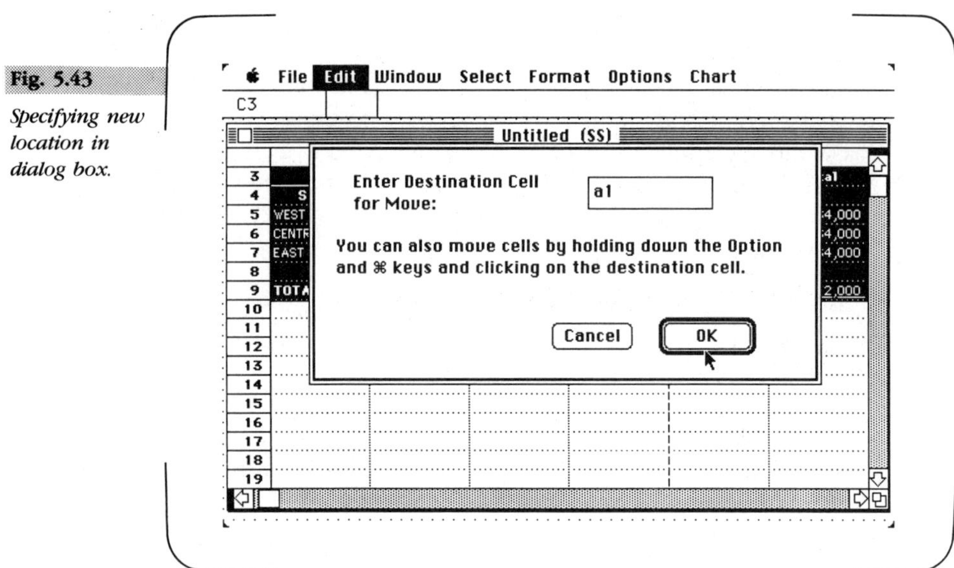

Fig. 5.43

Specifying new location in dialog box.

NOTE: When you move a range of cells to a new location, the moved cells replace whatever was there before. Sometimes this replacement is desirable; at other times, it is not. Look before you move. Be sure that the destination area is big enough to accept the cells you're moving. Works warns you if you're about to replace values, labels, or equations (see fig. 5.44).

Moving Cells—A Shortcut

Once you understand how the Move feature behaves, you don't have to go to the Edit menu to use Move. Instead, use the following procedure:

1. Select what you want to move.
2. Hold down the **option** and **command** keys and click on the destination.

Don't try this shortcut from the Move dialog box. The steps don't work if a dialog box is on the screen.

Using the Paste with Options Feature

The Paste with Options feature lets you indicate whether you want to move only values from a cell or both the values and their equations. With the Transpose option, you can paste rows into columns or vice

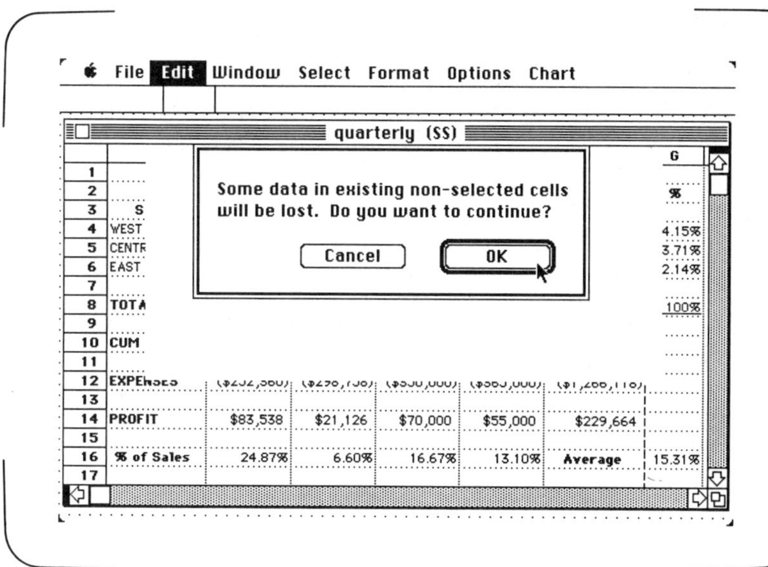

Fig. 5.44

Warning that you're about to replace values, labels, or equations.

versa. This capability is useful for some graphing functions, as you'll see in Chapter 7.

The Paste with Options choice is on the Edit menu (see fig. 5.45). You can use Paste with Options to paste items within a spreadsheet or to paste items from one spreadsheet to another. If you paste values and formulas (equations), Works adjusts cell references when it pastes.

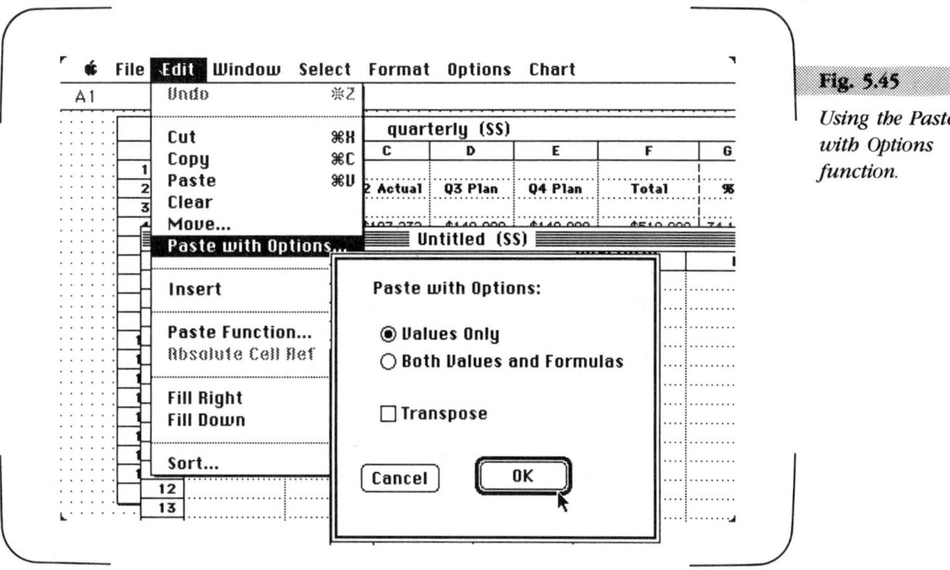

Fig. 5.45

Using the Paste with Options function.

Moving Cells to Another Spreadsheet

You use the Clipboard or Scrapbook to move cells from one spreadsheet to another. You can't use the Move feature; instead, you must cut or copy, open the other window, and then paste. Follow these steps for using the Clipboard to move cells:

1. Select the range to be copied.
2. Copy or cut the cell contents to the Clipboard.
3. Open the second spreadsheet, or make it the active one.
4. Prepare room for pasting, if necessary.
5. Choose the Paste with Options feature. Works then tries to renumber and correctly reference pasted cells.
6. Examine and test the pasted cells.

You can use the Scrapbook to store frequently used ranges of cells. Use the Paste with Options command to bring these ranges in from the Scrapbook.

Sorting

You can quickly rearrange the rows (but not the columns) on your spreadsheet by sorting them. Works Version 1.0, however, contains a bug that makes certain sorts risky. Moreover, sorting selected portions of any spreadsheet can create problems if you aren't careful, regardless of what software you use.

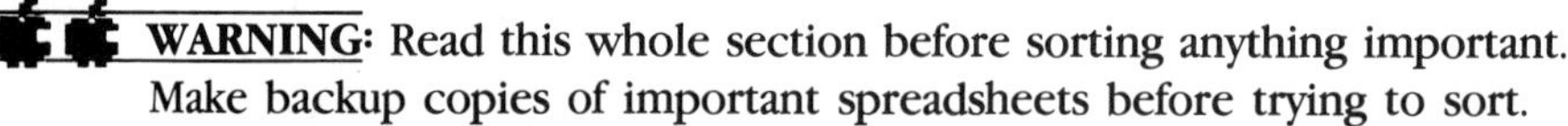

WARNING: Read this whole section before sorting anything important. Make backup copies of important spreadsheets before trying to sort.

You can sort rows in either ascending or descending order. In ascending order, Works arranges the values from small to large. The program places the most negative numbers at the top of the spreadsheet. The negative numbers are followed by zero and then positive numbers starting with 1, for example, −7, −5, −1, 0, 1, 8. Labels appear in A–to–Z order. Blanks always end up on the bottom. Descending order is the opposite of ascending. See "Sort Order" at the end of this chapter for other details.

For an example of sorting, suppose that you want regions to be ordered based on their annual sales contribution. Works can do that for you. Here's how:

1. Select the cells to be sorted (A4 through E6, in the example) and choose Sort from the Edit menu (see fig. 5.46). Do *not* select the Total column (F) if you are using Version 1.0.
2. Works displays a Sort dialog box (see fig. 5.47).
3. Decide which column will be used as the basis of the sort (F). This column is called a *sort key*.
4. Click on Ascending or Descending.
5. Click the OK button or press **return** to sort.
6. Check the results before doing anything else; undo, if necessary.

Multilevel Sorts

You can perform multilevel sorts by choosing more than one key in the Sort dialog box. For instance, in a more complex spreadsheet, you can sort branch offices within regions, people within departments, and so forth.

Works remembers previous sorts, so sorting more than three levels "deep" is possible. For example, you can perform a three-level sort, then another sort again on the sorted spreadsheet. Look at the example in

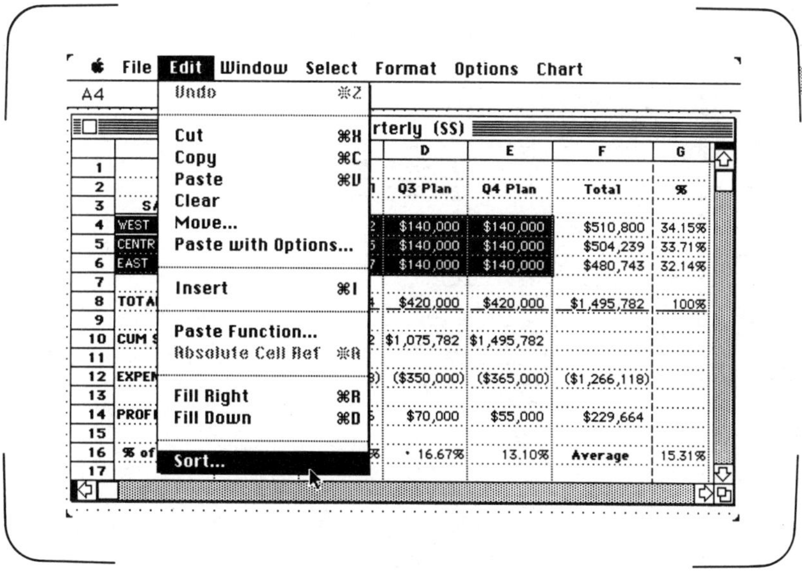

Fig. 5.46

Selecting the Sort option.

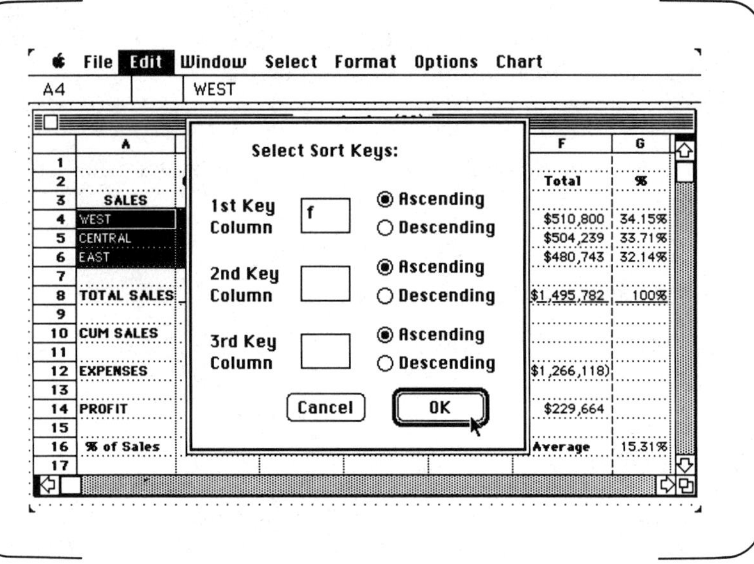

Fig. 5.47

Sorting regional offices in ascending order, based on their total sales.

figure 5.48. You can sort all three columns: first by region, then state, and then by city name. You enter A as the first key column, C as the second, and B as the third sort column (see fig. 5.49). The result of the sort is shown in figure 5.50.

Fig. 5.48

Spreadsheet entries before sorting.

	A	B	C
1	Region	City	State
2	WEST	Los Angeles	CA
3	EAST	Buffalo	NY
4	CENTRAL	Chicago	IL
5	EAST	New York	NY
6	CENTRAL	Indianapolis	IN
7	EAST	Boston	MA
8	CENTRAL	St Louis	MO
9	CENTRAL	Detroit	MI
10	WEST	Oakland	CA
11	EAST	Cambridge	MA
12	EAST	Albany	NY
13	WEST	San Diego	CA
14	CENTRAL	Peoria	IL
15	WEST	San Francisco	CA
16	WEST	Seattle	WA
17			

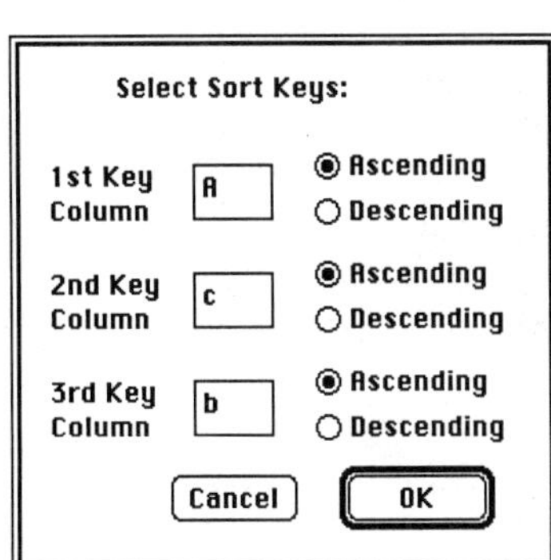

Fig. 5.49

Setting up a three-level sort.

	A	B	C
1	Region	City	State
2	CENTRAL	Chicago	IL
3	CENTRAL	Peoria	IL
4	CENTRAL	Indianapolis	IN
5	CENTRAL	Detroit	MI
6	CENTRAL	St Louis	MO
7	EAST	Boston	MA
8	EAST	Cambridge	MA
9	EAST	Albany	NY
10	EAST	Buffalo	NY
11	EAST	New York	NY
12	WEST	Los Angeles	CA
13	WEST	Oakland	CA
14	WEST	San Diego	CA
15	WEST	San Francisco	CA
16	WEST	Seattle	WA
17			

Fig. 5.50

Result of a multilevel sort by region, state, and city.

Cautions about Sorting

When selecting the cells to be sorted, you can easily select too many or too few cells. Both errors can create havoc. For example, if you don't include cells A4, A5, and A6 when sorting the spreadsheet in figure 5.51, Works rearranges the sales numbers, but the region names stay in their old locations. Therefore, all the numbers are improperly labeled. This problem occurs in most spreadsheet software and is not unique to Works.

Fig. 5.51

Choose all necessary cells when sorting.

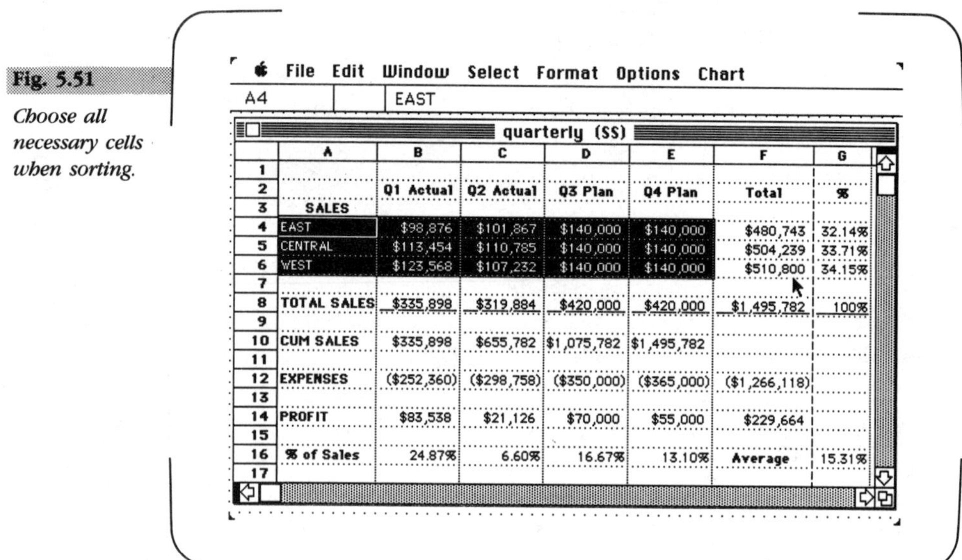

	A	B	C	D	E	F	G
1							
2		Q1 Actual	Q2 Actual	Q3 Plan	Q4 Plan	Total	%
3	SALES						
4	EAST	$98,876	$101,867	$140,000	$140,000	$480,743	32.14%
5	CENTRAL	$113,454	$110,785	$140,000	$140,000	$504,239	33.71%
6	WEST	$123,568	$107,232	$140,000	$140,000	$510,800	34.15%
7							
8	TOTAL SALES	$335,898	$319,884	$420,000	$420,000	$1,495,782	100%
9							
10	CUM SALES	$335,898	$655,782	$1,075,782	$1,495,782		
11							
12	EXPENSES	($252,360)	($298,758)	($350,000)	($365,000)	($1,266,118)	
13							
14	PROFIT	$83,538	$21,126	$70,000	$55,000	$229,664	
15							
16	% of Sales	24.87%	6.60%	16.67%	13.10%	Average	15.31%
17							

But you should consider something else. Until Microsoft gets the bugs out of the Works sort routine, you shouldn't try to sort cells containing equations or cell references. Frequently but not always, Works reassigns cell references improperly when cells are moved using the Sort feature.

In figures 5.52 and 5.53, for example, notice what happens to the cell references in column F. After sorting occurs, the references point to incorrect cells and provide inaccurate totals. Before the sort, cell F4 contains an equation that adds the contents of cells B4 through E4. Cells F5 and F6 contain similar equations (see fig. 5.52). After the sort, cell F4 contains the sum of cells B6 through E6 (see fig. 5.53). The spreadsheet is adding numbers from the wrong rows. The equation in F6 is also incorrect.

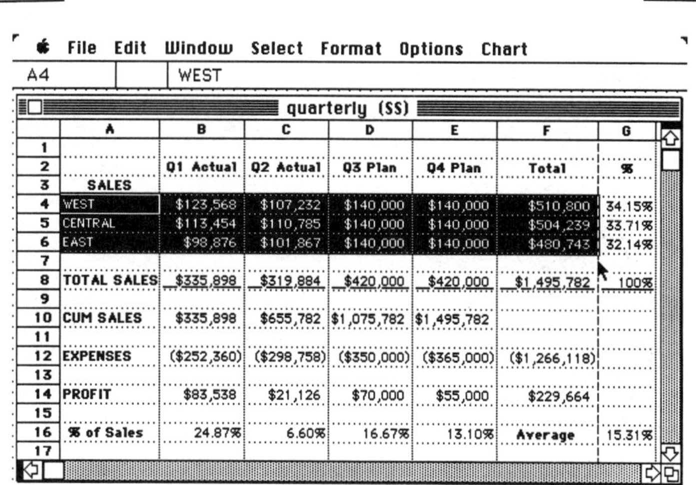

File Edit Window Select Format Options Chart

A4 WEST

quarterly (SS)

	A	B	C	D	E	F	G
1							
2		Q1 Actual	Q2 Actual	Q3 Plan	Q4 Plan	Total	%
3	SALES						
4	WEST	$123,568	$107,232	$140,000	$140,000	$510,800	34.15%
5	CENTRAL	$113,454	$110,785	$140,000	$140,000	$504,239	33.71%
6	EAST	$98,876	$101,867	$140,000	$140,000	$480,743	32.14%
7							
8	TOTAL SALES	$335,898	$319,884	$420,000	$420,000	$1,495,782	100%
9							
10	CUM SALES	$335,898	$655,782	$1,075,782	$1,495,782		
11							
12	EXPENSES	($252,360)	($298,758)	($350,000)	($365,000)	($1,266,118)	
13							
14	PROFIT	$83,538	$21,126	$70,000	$55,000	$229,664	
15							
16	% of Sales	24.87%	6.60%	16.67%	13.10%	Average	15.31%
17							

Fig. 5.52

Spreadsheet before sorting values and equations with Version 1.0.

File Edit Window Select Format Options Chart

quarterly (SS)

	A	B	C	D	E	F	G
1							
2		Q1 Actual	Q2 Actual	Q3 Plan	Q4 Plan	Total	%
3	SALES						
4	WEST	123,568	107232	140000	140000	=Sum(B4:E4)	=F4/F
5	CENTRAL	113454	110785	140000	140000	=Sum(B5:E5)	=F5/F
6	EAST	98876	101867	140000	140000	=Sum(B6:E6)	=F6/F
7							
8	TOTAL SALES	=B6+B5+B4	=C6+C5+C4	=D6+D5+D4	=E6+E5+E4	=F6+F5+F4	=Sum(G3
9							
10	CUM SALES	=B8	=C8+B10	=D8+C10	=E8+D10		
11							
12	EXPENSES	-252360	-298758	-350000	-365000	=Sum(E12:B12)	
13							
14	PROFIT	=B12+B8	=C12+C8	=D12+D8	=E12+E8	=F12+F8	
15							
16	% of Sales	=B14/B8	=C14/C8	=D14/D8	=E14/E8	Average	=Averag
17							

Because of this problem, you should not include any column containing relative references when you are selecting the range to be sorted. In certain cases, Works improperly changes some or all of the cell references in the equations after the sort. Microsoft knows about this "disfunction," and the company is working on the necessary corrections.

Fig. 5.53

Spreadsheet damaged after sorting.

File Edit Window Select Format Options Chart

A4 | EAST

quarterly (SS)

	A	B	C	D	E	F	G
1							
2		Q1 Actual	Q2 Actual	Q3 Plan	Q4 Plan	Total	%
3	SALES						
4	EAST	$98,876	$101,867	$140,000	$140,000	$510,800	34.15%
5	CENTRAL	$113,454	$110,785	$140,000	$140,000	$504,239	33.71%
6	WEST	$123,568	$107,232	$140,000	$140,000	$480,743	32.14%
7							
8	TOTAL SALES	$335,898	$319,884	$420,000	$420,000	$1,495,782	100%
9							
10	CUM SALES	$335,898	$655,782	$1,075,782	$1,495,782		
11							
12	EXPENSES	($252,360)	($298,758)	($350,000)	($365,000)	($1,266,118)	
13							
14	PROFIT	$83,538	$21,126	$70,000	$55,000	$229,664	
15							
16	% of Sales	24.87%	6.60%	16.67%	13.10%	Average	15.31%
17							

File Edit Window Select Format Options Chart

A4 | EAST

quarterly (SS)

	A	B	C	D	E	F	G
1							
2		Q1 Actual	Q2 Actual	Q3 Plan	Q4 Plan	Total	%
3	SALES						
4	EAST	98876	101867	140000	140000	=Sum(B6:E6)	=F4/F
5	CENTRAL	113454	110785	140000	140000	=Sum(B5:E5)	=F5/F
6	WEST	123,568	107232	140000	140000	=Sum(B4:E4)	=F6/F
7							
8	TOTAL SALES	=B6+B5+B4	=C6+C5+C4	=D6+D5+D4	=E6+E5+E4	=F6+F5+F4	=Sum(G3
9							
10	CUM SALES	=B8	=C8+B10	=D8+C10	=E8+D10		
11							
12	EXPENSES	-252360	-298758	-350000	-365000	=Sum(E12:B12)	
13							
14	PROFIT	=B12+B8	=C12+C8	=D12+D8	=E12+E8	=F12+F8	
15							
16	% of Sales	=B14/B8	=C14/C8	=D14/D8	=E14/E8	Average	=Averag
17							

Sort Order

If the key column contains elements besides numbers, Works performs ascending sorts in the following order:

error values
numbers
spaces
text (including numbers typed as text)
blanks

Figure 5.54 shows a random collection of cell entries in column A. Column B shows how they appear after being sorted in ascending order; column C shows the same values sorted in descending order. Notice that the blank always ends up on the bottom. Notice also what happens when a number is the first character in a label. Works ignores capitalization when text is sorted.

BEFORE SORT	AFTER ASCENDING SORT	AFTER DESCENDING SORT
9	-1.26E+11	9
	-1	6
a label	0	0.5
A LABEL	0.5	0
-1	6	-1
0	9	-1.26E+11
1 NUMBER IN A LABEL	1 NUMBER IN A LABEL	b
0.5	a label	B
-1.26E+11	A LABEL	a label
6	b	A LABEL
b	B	1 NUMBER IN A LABEL
B		

Fig. 5.54

Results of ascending and descending sorts.

Moving around the Spreadsheet

Frequently, spreadsheets are larger than the screen. To move around a spreadsheet, you can use scroll bars. They appear on spreadsheet windows just like on other Works windows.

You also can tell Works that you want "to go to" a specific cell, to the last cell in a worksheet, or to the active cell.

The Go To Cell Option

In spreadsheets that greatly exceed the size of your screen, scrolling from place to place can be cumbersome and time-consuming. The Go To Cell option speeds navigation (see fig. 5.55). If you choose Go To Cell on the Select menu or use the *command*-G key sequence, Works displays a dialog box (see fig. 5.56).

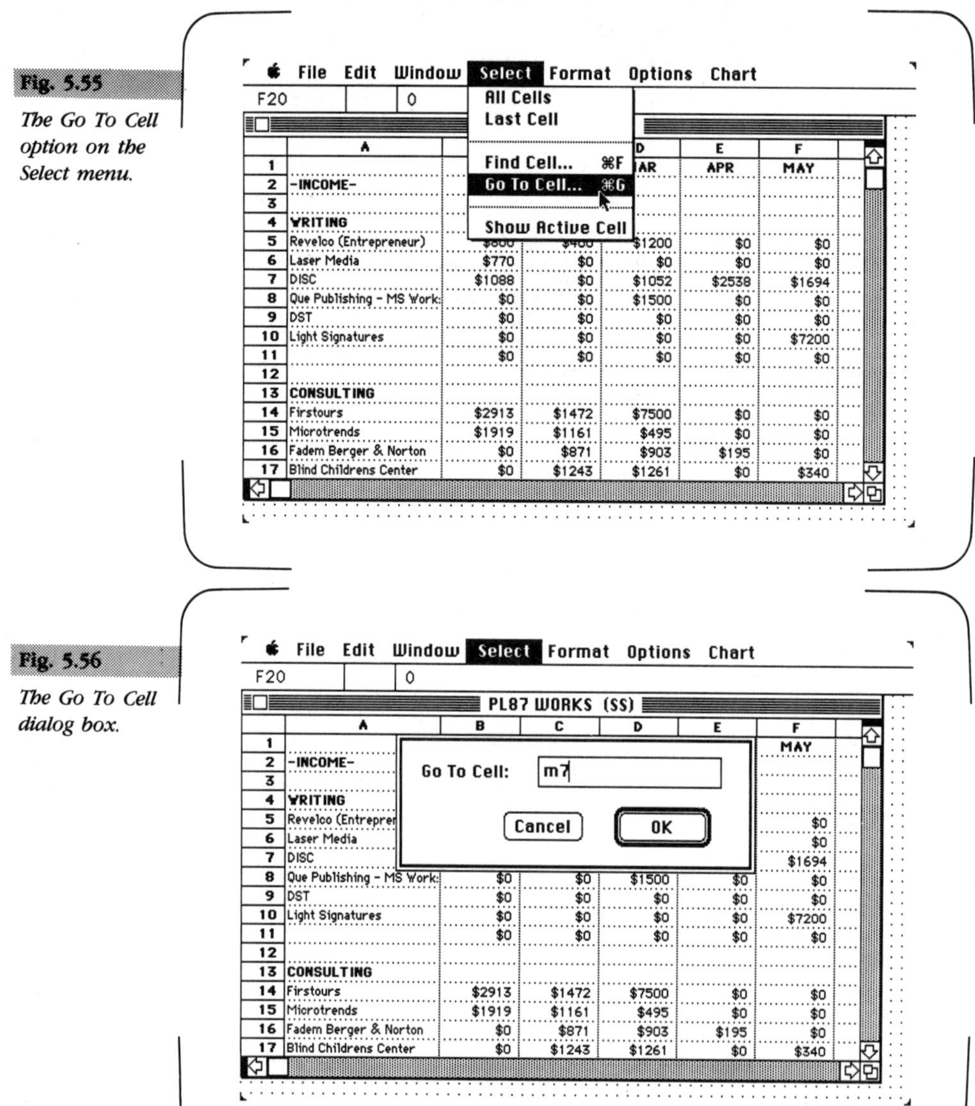

Fig. 5.55

The Go To Cell option on the Select menu.

Fig. 5.56

The Go To Cell dialog box.

Enter a cell number or the contents of a cell that you want to find. For example, you can enter A5, "Total", or an equation. You also can enter the answers displayed in equation cells. When you click the OK button or press the *return* key, Works quickly scrolls you to the area containing the cell you've specified. The specific steps follow:

1. Either press **command-G** or choose Go To Cell from the Select menu. The dialog box then appears.
2. Enter a cell address (such as Total, Error, or M7).
3. Either press **return** or click the OK button. The cell and its neighbors come into view.
4. Click the Find Next button or press **return** to see whether there are other occurrences.

Because the Go To Cell feature does not activate the cell or include the cell's location in any equation you're building, this feature is ideal for "looking around" while you're writing new equations.

The Find Cell Option

The Find Cell feature acts like the Go To Cell feature, except that Find Cell activates the requested cell in addition to scrolling the display. Because Find Cell activates the cell, the cell's contents appear in the entry bar, ready for editing or other use.

1. Either press **command-F** or choose Find Cell on the Select menu. The dialog box then appears (see fig. 5.57).
2. Enter a request (A1, profit, =A1+B1, and so forth).
3. Either press **return** or click on the Find Next button. The first matching cell and its neighbors appear.
4. The first matching cell becomes the active cell.

Tips for Using Go To Cell and Find Cell

In cases of multiple occurrences of the item you request (a repeated label or value, for instance), Works takes you to the occurrence closest to the upper left corner of the spreadsheet (A1). Repeat your request to find the next occurrence. Use **command-F** to speed the process.

Works ignores dollar signs and commas when searching spreadsheets, so you can type them or not. If a cell is formatted using the Percent option, however, you need to type the percent sign when searching.

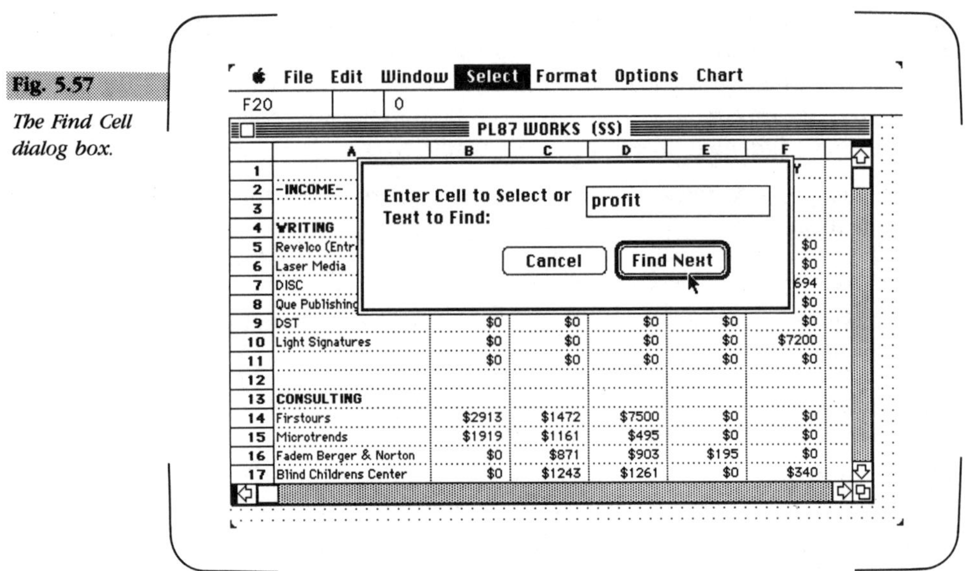

Fig. 5.57

The Find Cell dialog box.

The Show Active Cell and Find Last Cell Options

The Show Active Cell option brings the active cell into view when it has scrolled off the screen. This feature is at the bottom of the Select menu.

The Select menu also contains an option called Find Last Cell. It takes you to the last cell on a spreadsheet that contains a value, a label, or an equation. Works activates that cell when you get there.

NOTE: Sometimes, apparently blank cells contain spaces. This is why a cell that appears to be unused is considered by Works to be the last cell.

Using Multiple Window Panes

When dealing with large spreadsheets, you'll find yourself scrolling back and forth frequently. For example, you'll change an income estimate and then scroll down several pages to see the impact on profitability. Or you'll change a January number and scroll to the right to inspect the change on the year's total. All this scrolling can be time-consuming and annoying. Works offers a "window pane" feature that lets you look at up to four different parts of a spreadsheet at once, even if they're widely separated.

In figure 5.58, four panes are visible in the spreadsheet window. Each pane has its own scroll bars and boxes, and each pane can be scrolled independently of the others.

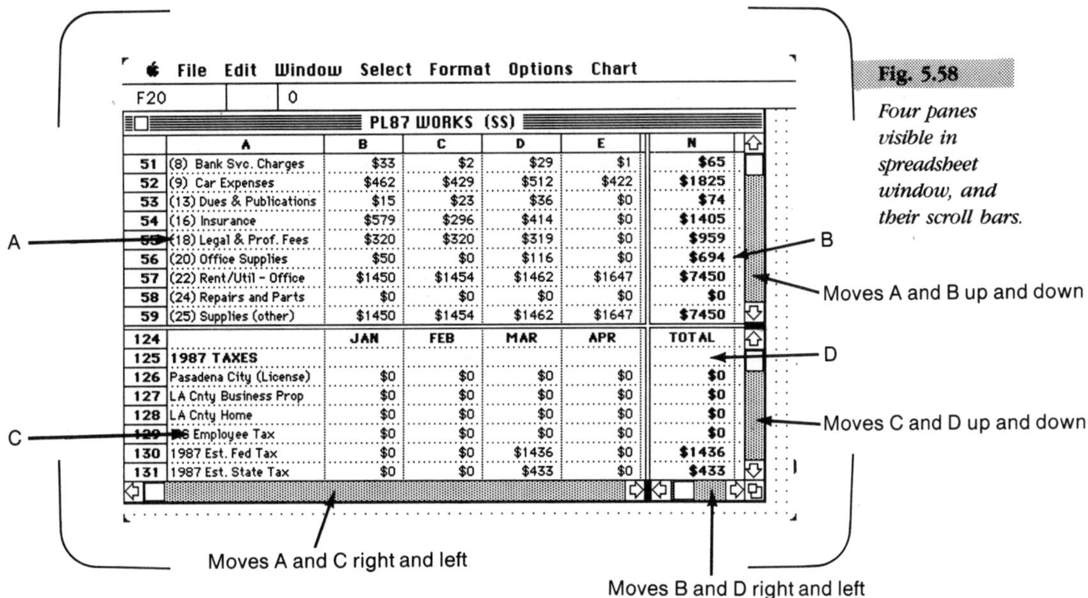

Fig. 5.58

Four panes visible in spreadsheet window, and their scroll bars.

To create a pane, you do the following:

1. Point to the black space next to the left or top scroll boxes. The pointer then changes to a two-headed arrow.
2. Drag the black space until the window pane bar appears. Keep dragging the window pane bar to its desired position.
3. Scroll the contents of the various panes as needed.

To reposition or eliminate a pane, you point to the black area between the scroll arrows and then move the pane off-screen.

Spreadsheet Design Considerations

After you've created a few simple spreadsheets, you'll be tempted to tackle a big one or two. Before you do, give some thought to the design of the spreadsheet. You may even want to sketch your design first; this process can save you a great deal of editing and testing time later. The following sections provide tips for designing spreadsheets.

Circular References

One common mistake is to include in an answer cells that are affected by the answer, causing the answer to change. In these cases, the answer is always changing and never right; these are called *circular references.*

Consider figure 5.59, for example. This simple spreadsheet computes the effect of commissions on profitability. The sales people's commissions, however, are based on profit. Because commissions are a form of expense, they affect profit, which affects commissions, and so on. Cells B16 and B14 constitute a circular reference.

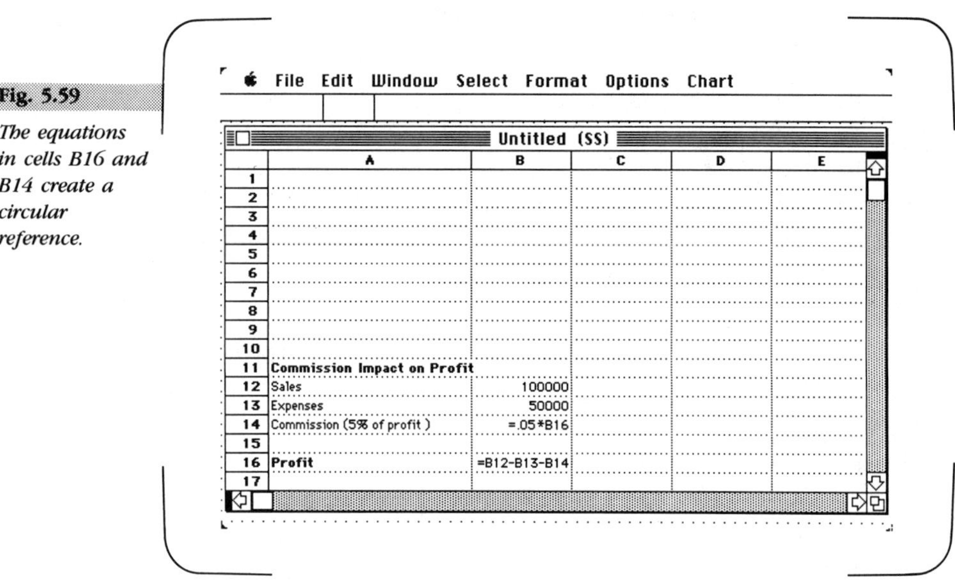

Fig. 5.59

The equations in cells B16 and B14 create a circular reference.

Works usually warns you when it spots circular references (see fig. 5.60). After you acknowledge the warning, Works tries to perform the computation anyway.

Sometimes you can eliminate circular references by rearranging the locations of items on your spreadsheet. In other cases, such as in this example, a policy change or interim step may be required. For instance, you can base commissions on precommission profits.

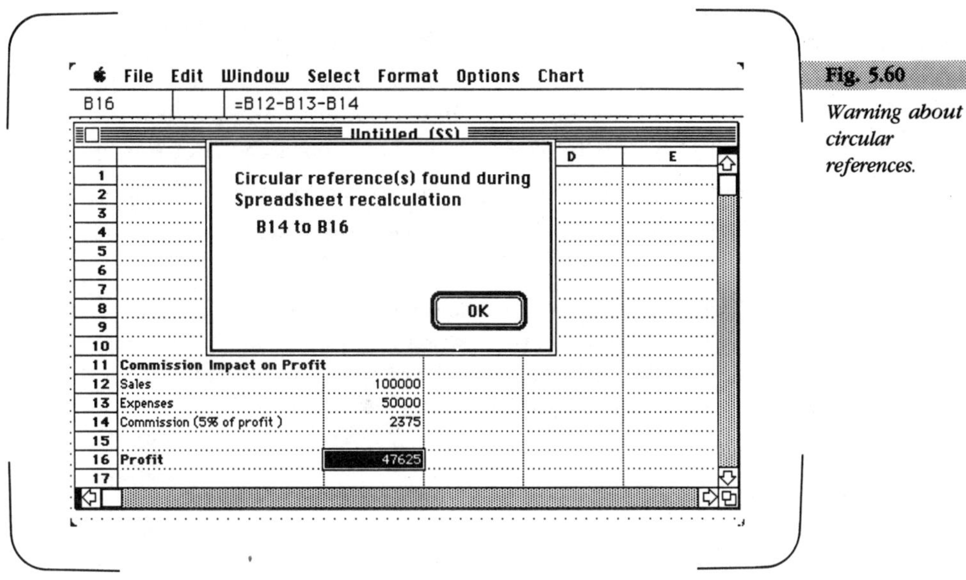

Fig. 5.60 *Warning about circular references.*

Order of Computations

If your spreadsheet equations contain multiple operators, Works performs the requested operations in the following order:

^	Exponentiation
–	Negation
* and /	Multiplication and division
+ and –	Addition and subtraction
= < <= > >= <>	Comparisons

Keep this order in mind when you are writing equations for your spreadsheet calculations.

Automatic and Manual Recalculation and the Calculate Now Option

Usually, each time you enter a new value into a spreadsheet—or change an old value—Works recomputes everything, a process called *automatic recalculation.* Works starts a new spreadsheet in automatic recalculation mode. In large spreadsheets, recalculation takes enough time that you may need to wait a few seconds between entries.

By selecting the Manual Recalculation option, you can avoid this delay, but you must remember to ask Works to recalculate after you finish making changes. The Manual Recalculation option is available on the Options menu. Simply pull it down and click on Manual Recalculation. Thereafter, you will need to remember to tell Works to recalculate.

WARNING: If you choose the Manual Recalculation option, you're responsible for remembering to recalculate after changing values on the spreadsheet. If you forget, your answers may be wrong.

The Calculate Now function causes Works to recalculate the spreadsheet any time you evoke it. You can either choose the Calculate Now command from the Options menu or use the shortcut: Hold down the *command* key and press the equal key (=).

Conclusion

This chapter has covered the basic concepts of spreadsheet creation. You know how to create, make entries in, edit, and print your spreadsheet. As you use your spreadsheets, you will be able to take advantage of the shortcuts that have been explained. The following chapter describes the spreadsheet functions, which can simplify spreadsheet designs and increase their power. Then, in Chapter 7, you learn how to use your spreadsheet to create different kinds of graphs.

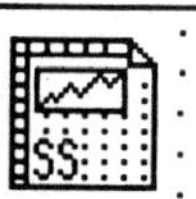

Quick Start: Creating a Spreadsheet

This Quick Start introduces you to the fundamental spreadsheet operations: creating a spreadsheet window, entering items in spreadsheet cells, editing entries, and formatting and printing the spreadsheet. In addition, you learn several shortcuts that eliminate typing.

Opening a Spreadsheet Window

The quickest way to begin a new spreadsheet project is to double-click on the spreadsheet icon in the Works Open File dialog box. Another way to begin is to select Open from the pull-down File menu. Whichever method you choose, you see a spreadsheet screen with the title Untitled and the letters *(SS)*, for spreadsheet.

A spreadsheet can contain four types of data: labels, numbers, equations, and operators. *Labels* are text entries used to describe or explain things in the spreadsheet. *Values* are the numbers used in spreadsheet calculations. *Equations*, or formulas, tell Works what to do with the values you've entered. *Operators* are used in equations to indicate the relationships between values.

The following sections introduce you to the steps involved in entering numbers, labels, and equations into the spreadsheet.

Entering Labels

If an entry contains letters—or if it differs from the conventional format for numbers—Works regards the entry as a label. (An exception is the letter *e* within a number, which is used in scientific notation.) To be treated as a label, a number must be preceded by a double quotation mark (").

To practice entering labels in the Works spreadsheet, open a spreadsheet window as described previously, and then perform the following steps.

1. Activate cell A3 by pointing and clicking.
2. Press **Caps Lock** and enter the label **SALES**.
3. Press **return**. Notice that cell A4 becomes active. (You could press *enter*, but if you press *return* you avoid having to point and click to make A4 active.)

4. Enter **WEST** in cell A4, and press **return.**
5. Enter **CENTRAL** in cell A5, and press **return.**
6. Enter **EAST** in cell A6, and press **return.**
7. Activate cell A8, enter **TOTAL SALES**, and press **return.**

When you are finished, your spreadsheet should look like figure 5.61.

Fig. 5.61

Cells with labels.

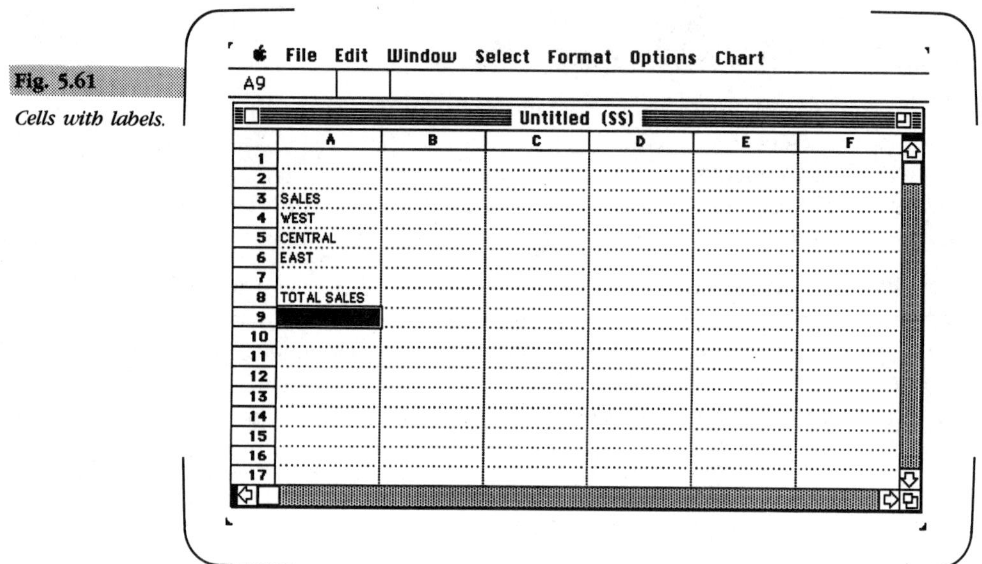

For additional practice, enter the labels *Q1 Actual*, *Q2 Actual*, *Q3 Plan*, *Q4 Plan* and *Total* in cells B2 through F4, respectively. Use the *tab* key instead of *return* to move from column to column (see fig. 5.62).

Entering Numbers

Numeric entries can contain the digits 0 through 9, the minus sign (–), and the decimal point (.). Your entries must be in appropriate form to be interpreted as numbers, however: the entry *12.34.56* is interpreted as a number, as is *–12.34.56.*

Other characters (with the exception of all letters but *e*) can be entered, but Works either ignores them or performs appropriate conversions. Dollar signs and commas are ignored, for instance, and entries followed by the percent sign (%) are converted to decimals.

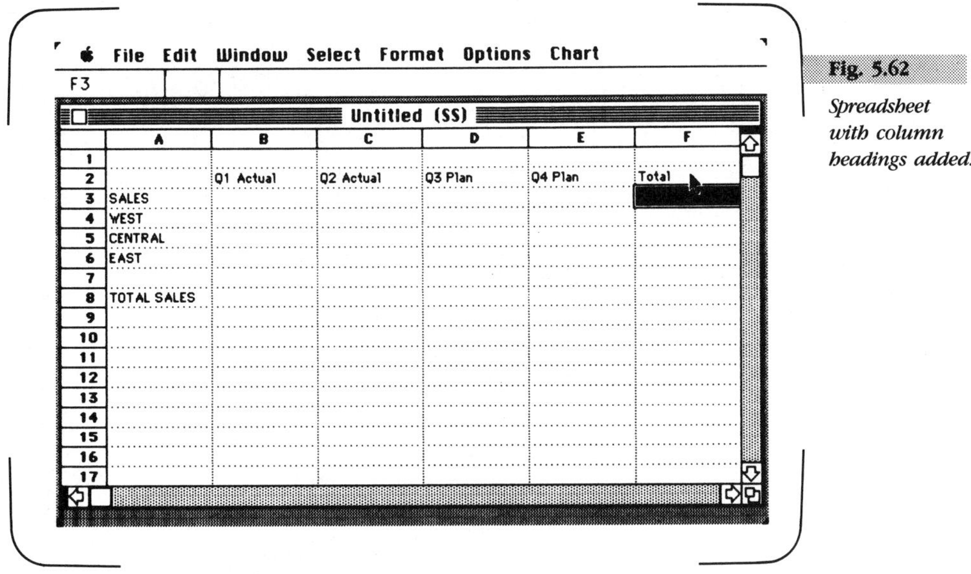

Fig. 5.62 *Spreadsheet with column headings added.*

To practice entering numbers in your spreadsheet, work through these steps:

1. Point and click on cell B4.
2. Enter **123568** and press **return**. The number appears in cell B4, and B5 is activated.
3. Repeat steps 1 and 2 for cells B5 and B6, entering the values **113454** and **98876**, respectively.

The result should look like figure 5.63.

To work through the examples given in later Quick Start sections, you'll need to enter more numbers in the spreadsheet. Perform these steps to enter those numbers and to learn an easy way of making entries into a range of cells:

1. Point to cell C4.
2. Press the mouse button and hold it down as you drag the mouse pointer to cell E6.
3. Release the mouse button. Notice that the entire range from C4 to E6 is black, and C4 has a white border (see fig. 5.64).

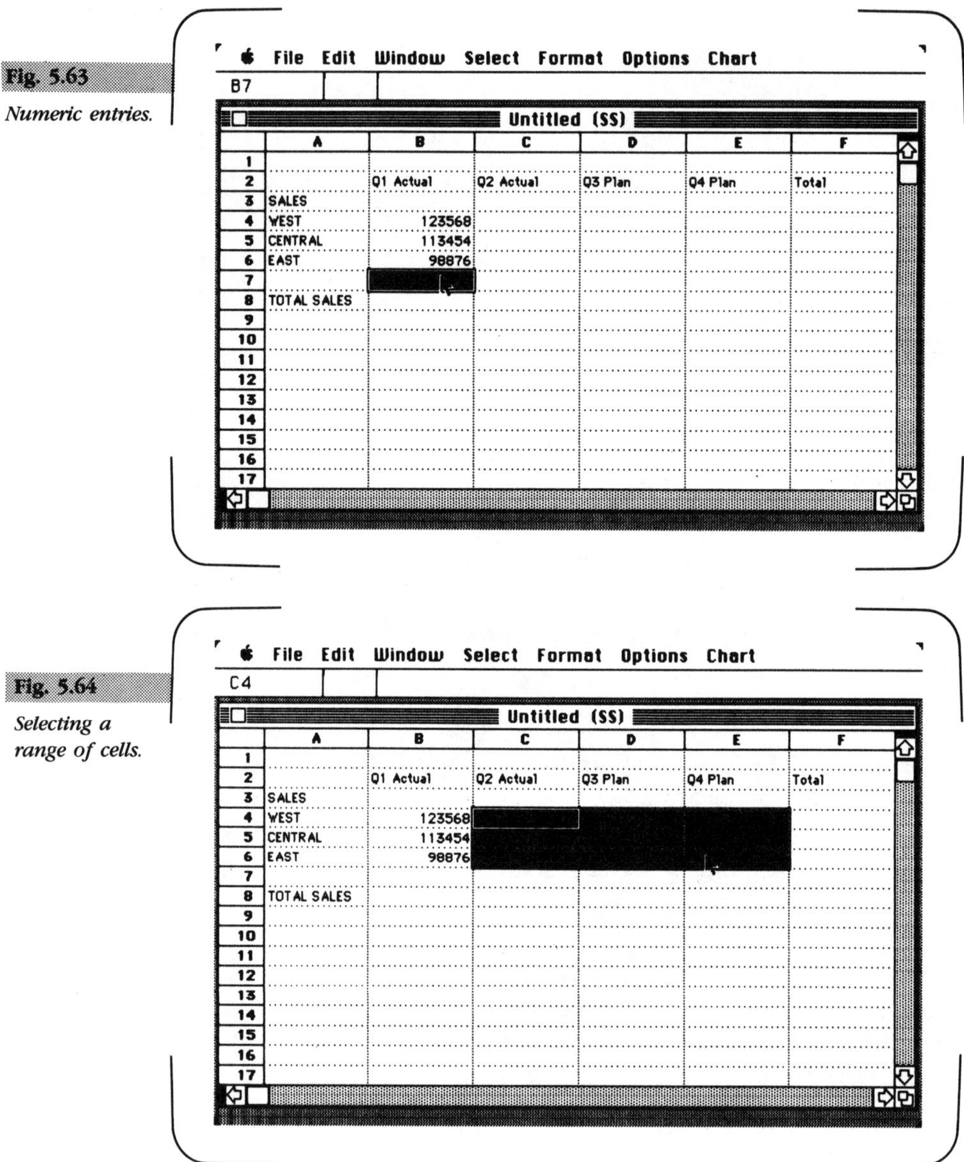

Fig. 5.63

Numeric entries.

Fig. 5.64

Selecting a range of cells.

4. Enter **107232**, **110785**, and **101867** in cells C4, C5, and C6, respectively; press **return** after each entry.

5. Notice that cell D4 now is active. (When a range is selected, pressing return at the bottom of a selected column causes the

cell at the top of the next column of the range to become active.)

6. Enter the other numbers shown in figure 5.65.

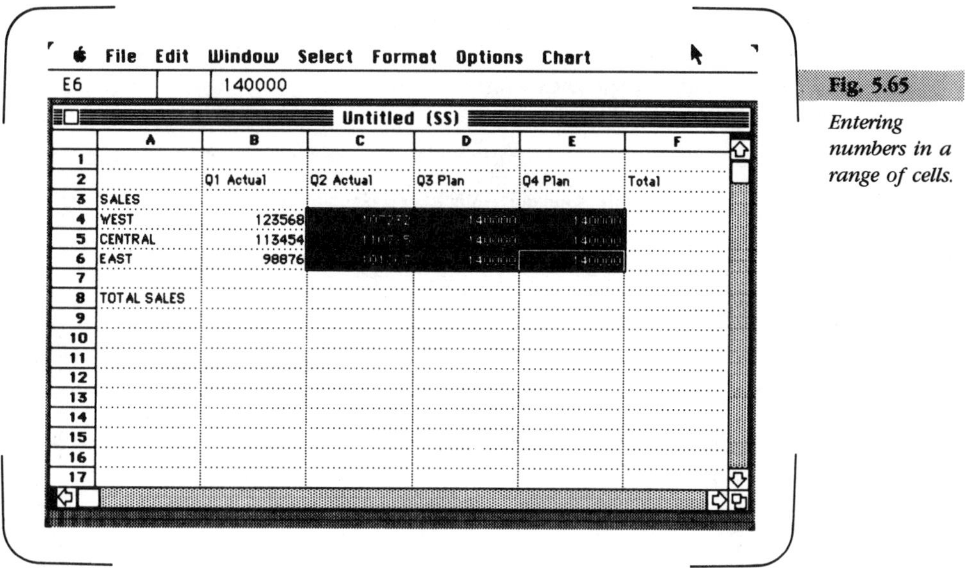

Fig. 5.65 *Entering numbers in a range of cells.*

Entering Equations

Equations are the workhorses of electronic spreadsheets. Without the capability for performing calculations automatically, spreadsheets would be little more than expensive alternatives to the traditional columnar pad.

Works spreadsheet equations always begin with the equal sign (=). For example, the equation in cell B8 contains the formula =B6+B5+B4. As soon as you have entered an equation, the result appears in the cell containing the equation; if you change a value in any cell to which the equation refers, the result changes automatically.

To practice entering a simple equation, activate cell B8 and enter **=B6+B5+B4**. Notice that the total appears as soon as you press *return* or *enter* or click the enter box. If you like, you can change one of the values in B4, B5, or B6 and watch the change in cell B8.

Entering cell references by hand is tedious. Works, however, provides an easier way: instead of entering the address of a cell, you can just point to the cell. For practice in doing so, follow these steps:

1. Activate cell C8.
2. Type an equal sign (=).
3. Point to cell C6 and click; notice that C6 is enclosed in a solid line and that the cell address appears in the entry box.
4. Point to cell C5 and click. Notice that now C5 is enclosed in a solid line, and that Works has automatically provided a plus sign, as shown in figure 5.66.

Fig. 5.66

Using the mouse to enter a cell reference.

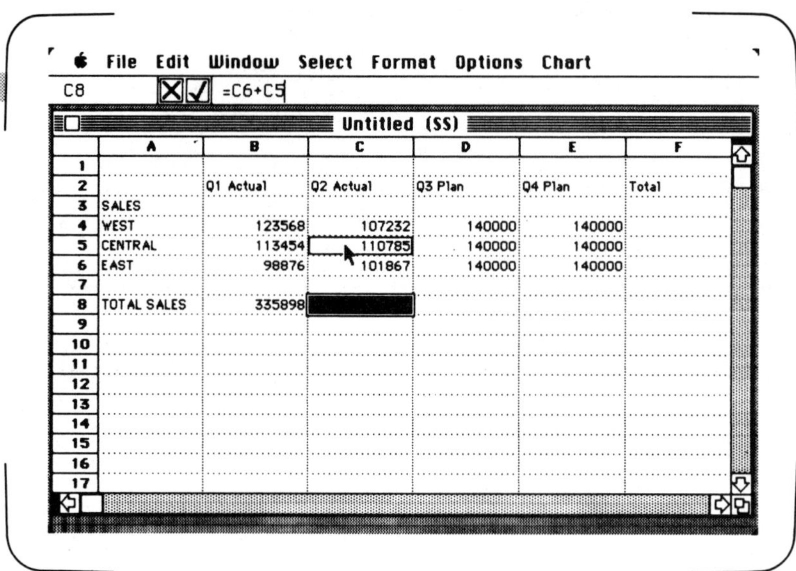

5 Point to cell C4 and click.
6. Click on the enter box, or press **return** or **enter**.

When you are finished, the total of the values in C4 through C6 should appear in cell C8. Repeat this procedure for columns D and E.

For further practice, create formulas for regional subtotals in cells F4, F5, and F6. Each of those cells should show the total for columns B, C, D, and E in the respective row. Cell F6, for example, sums the values in B6, C6, D6, and E6. Enter the equations in cells F4 and F5. Then, create an equation in cell F8 to add the regional totals that are in F4, F5, and F6. The final result should look like figure 5.67.

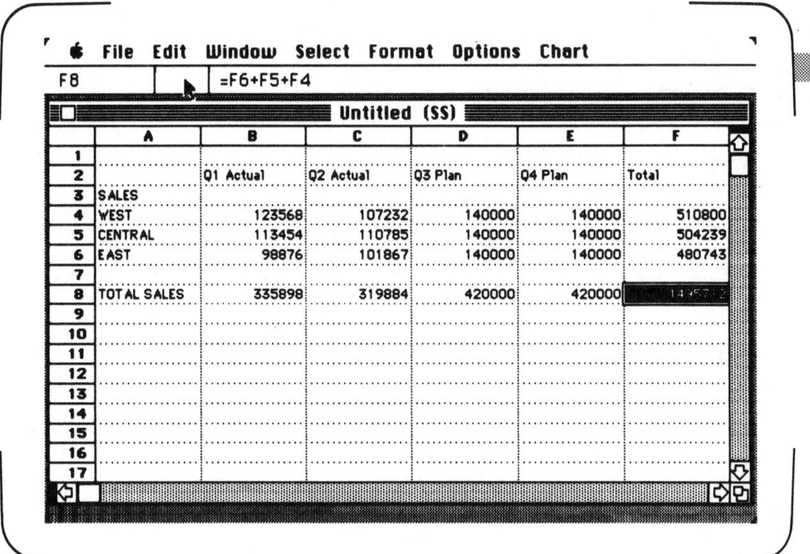

Fig. 5.67

Adding regional subtotals and a grand total to the worksheet.

Formatting the Spreadsheet

This section shows you how to change the appearance of your spreadsheet with boldface, underlining, and other embellishments. You can change single cells; entire rows, columns, or spreadsheets; or selected ranges of cells. The process is always the same. Try a few examples.

1. Click on the A label in your spreadsheet to highlight the entire column A.
2. Pull down the Format menu and choose Bold.
3. Click on the row number 2 to highlight all of row 2.
4. Choose the Align Center and Bold options from the Format menu.
5. Select the cell range B4 through F8.
6. Select the Dollar option from the Format menu.
7. With the same range selected, choose Commas from the Format menu. Notice what happens to cell F8 (see fig. 5.68). The number is too big to fit with dollar signs, commas, decimal points, and cents. You can make the column wider or—better yet—eliminate the cents.

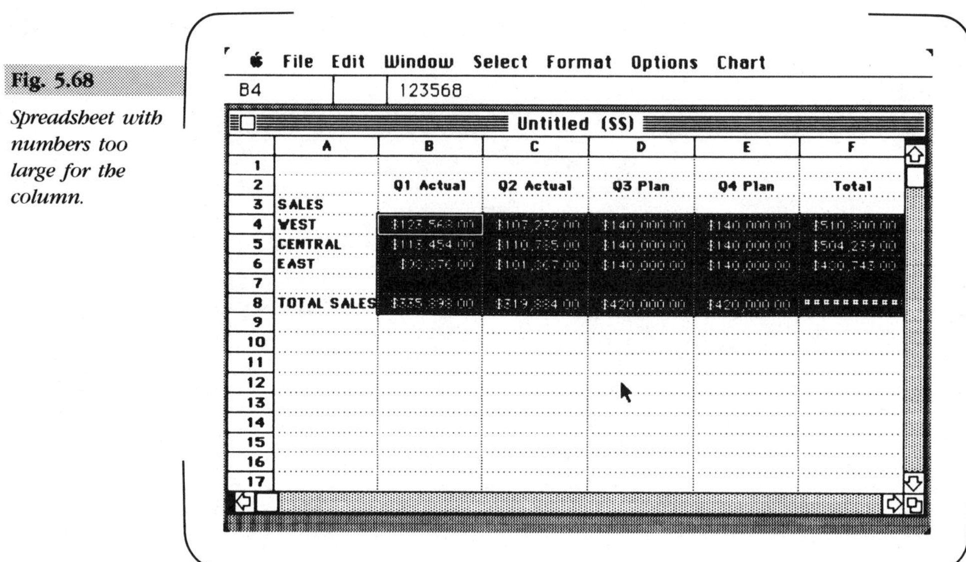

Fig. 5.68

Spreadsheet with numbers too large for the column.

8. With B4 through F8 still selected, choose Number of Decimals from the Format menu. In the dialog box, specify 0 as the number of decimal places. Now the numbers fit.

9. Click the deselect box (above the row 1 marker and to the left of the column A label). Inspect your work. It should look like figure 5.69.

10. Experiment with the choices on the Options menu, such as Show Grid/No Grid, Show Formulas, Show Values. Make your spreadsheet look like figure 5.69 before you save it, however.

Printing the Spreadsheet

You've entered all your sales data and the equations used to provide totals. Now you are ready to prepare a quick printout of the spreadsheet so that you can check your work:

1. Select Print from the File menu. You are offered the opportunity to select the print quality, page range, and other options (depending on your printer). For this Quick Start lesson, just use the defaults.

2. Click OK in the Print dialog box (see fig. 5.70). (Your Print dialog box may look different from the one shown in the figure.)

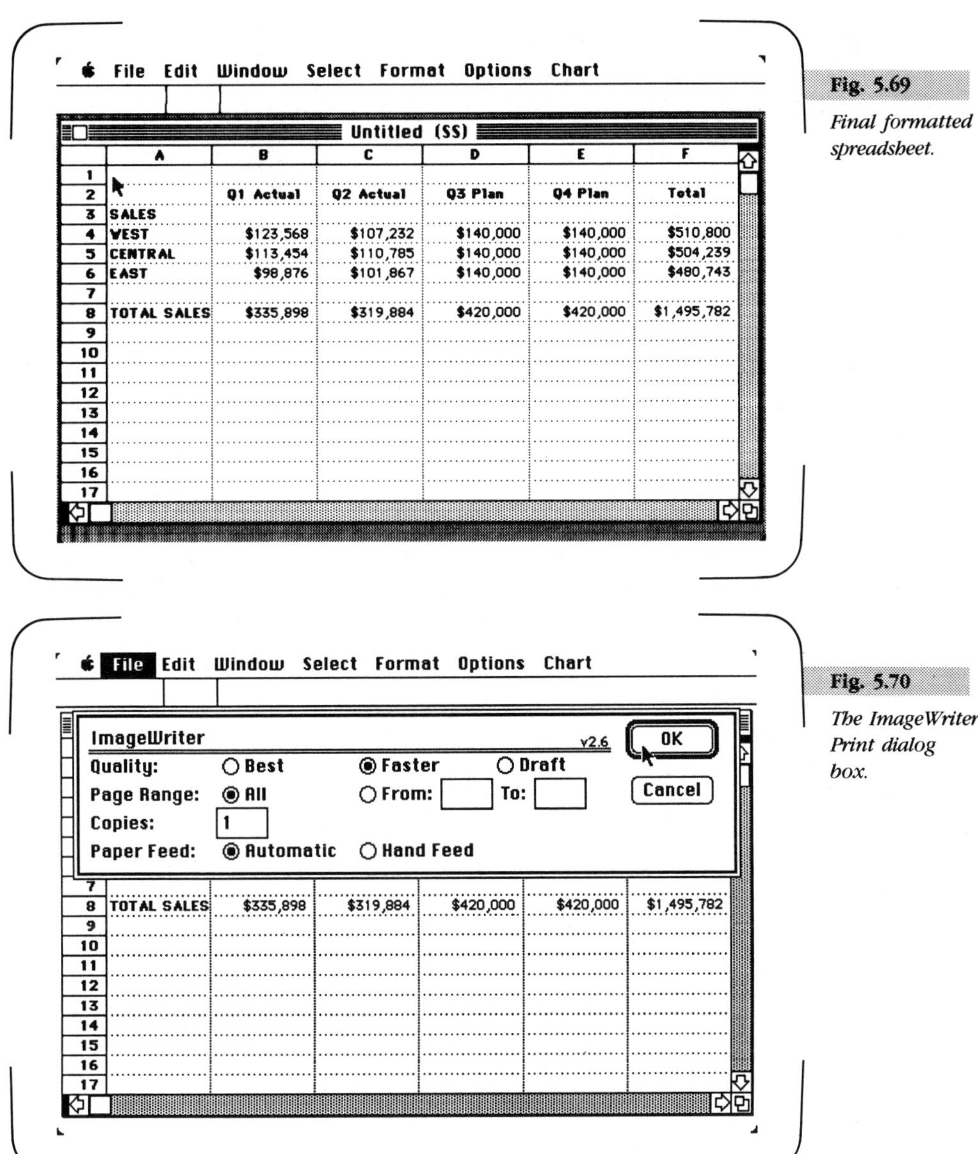

	A	B	C	D	E	F
1						
2		Q1 Actual	Q2 Actual	Q3 Plan	Q4 Plan	Total
3	SALES					
4	WEST	$123,568	$107,232	$140,000	$140,000	$510,800
5	CENTRAL	$113,454	$110,785	$140,000	$140,000	$504,239
6	EAST	$98,876	$101,867	$140,000	$140,000	$480,743
7						
8	TOTAL SALES	$335,898	$319,884	$420,000	$420,000	$1,495,782
9						
10						
11						
12						
13						
14						
15						
16						
17						

Fig. 5.69 *Final formatted spreadsheet.*

Fig. 5.70 *The ImageWriter Print dialog box.*

With Works, you don't need to specify how much of the spreadsheet is to be printed unless you want to print only a portion of it. The program is "smart" enough to print only the active part of the spreadsheet. The resulting printout is shown in figure 5.71.

Fig. 5.71

Printout of the spreadsheet.

	Q1 Actual	Q2 Actual	Q3 Plan	Q4 Plan	Total
SALES					
WEST	$123,568	$107,232	$140,000	$140,000	$510,800
CENTRAL	$113,454	$110,785	$140,000	$140,000	$504,239
EAST	$98,876	$101,867	$140,000	$140,000	$480,743
TOTAL SALES	$335,898	$319,884	$420,000	$420,000	$1,495,782

Saving Your Work

The easiest way to save your new spreadsheet is to press **command-S**. The first time you save a spreadsheet, a dialog box appears, and you are prompted to enter a name for the spreadsheet, as shown in figure 5.72. Name this spreadsheet Quarterly. Get into the habit of saving regularly as you work, particularly when you are interrupted.

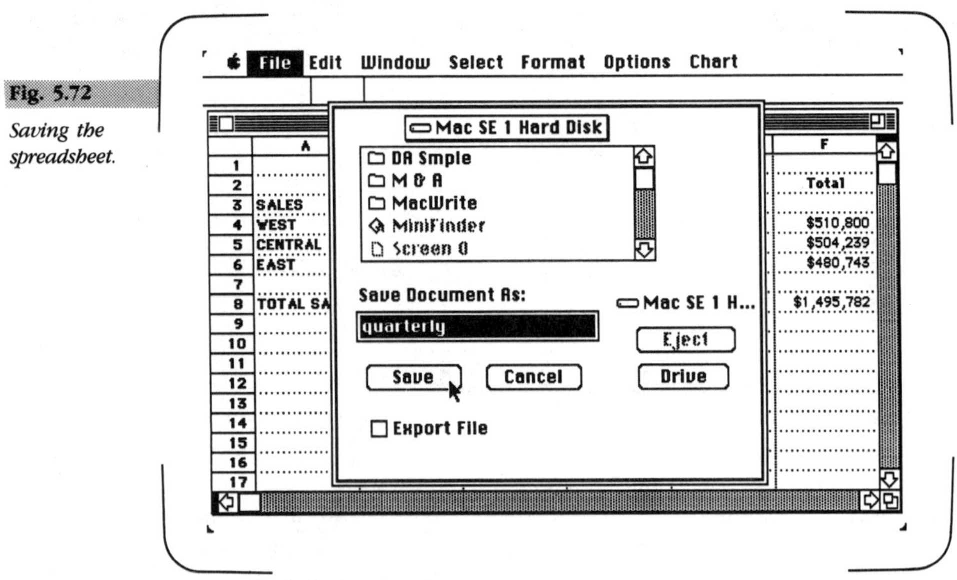

Fig. 5.72

Saving the spreadsheet.

Editing the Spreadsheet

Editing spreadsheet entries is simple. This section shows you how to edit the spreadsheet by changing individual entries, moving and copying cells and ranges of cells, and inserting rows and columns.

The spreadsheet you have just created will be used again in later Quick Starts. Before you begin working on editing techniques, you need to create a new copy of the spreadsheet with a different name.

Follow these steps to create a new copy of the spreadsheet with a different name:

1. Select Save As from the File menu. A dialog box appears, and you are prompted to enter a name for the spreadsheet.

2. Enter a new name for the spreadsheet. For this exercise, call the new version Quarterly 2.

3. Press **return** or **enter**, or click the Save button in the dialog box.

When the dialog box disappears, notice that the name in the spreadsheet window changes to the new name you have entered. Because the spreadsheet has already been saved under another name, the version saved earlier remains intact and unaltered. Any changes you make from this point on do not affect the previous version.

Changing Cell Entries

For practice in fundamental editing techniques, follow these steps; they show you how to change one of the numbers you have entered. The techniques for editing labels and equations are the same.

1. Point and click on cell B4. Notice that the contents of the cell appear in the entry bar.

2. Position the pointer between the 1 and the 2 in *123568*; then click the mouse button. Notice that the pointer becomes an I-beam when it is within the entry bar; after you click, a vertical bar appears between the *1* and the *2*.

3. Press the **backspace** key once to delete the *1*.

4. Press **2** to insert that number in the place formerly occupied by the *1*.

5. Press **enter** or **return**, or click the enter box. Notice that the total in cell B8 changes, reflecting the change you have made.

Erasing Cells

Imagine that your planned sales figures for Quarter 4 have been increased to $150,000, so you need to revise the spreadsheet. Works provides several ways to make these changes. Follow these steps to make the necessary changes.

1. Select the range E4 through F6.
2. Select Cut (or Clear) from the Edit menu, or press **command-X** to cut. (Works has no shortcut for the Clear command.

Copying Cells

Now you're ready to enter the new sales figures, and you'd like to avoid repetitive typing. Follow these steps to take advantage of Works' copy command.

1. Select cell E4.
2. Enter **150000** and press **enter** or **return**, or click the enter box. The best action is to click the enter box or press the **enter** key: the following step requires that E4 be selected, and pressing **return** causes E5 to become the selected cell.
3. With E4 still selected, select Copy from the Edit menu or press **command-C**.
4. Make E5 active, and select Paste from the Edit menu or press **command-V**. The entry *150000* appears in E5.
5. Repeat step 4 for cell E6.

Equations can be copied, as well. For additional practice, copy the equation in F4 to F5 and F6. The final edited spreadsheet looks like figure 5.73.

If you select any of the copied equation cells, you'll notice something that may surprise you if you have done little work with spreadsheets before: the cell references have been adjusted automatically. For example, the equation in C8 refers to cells C6 through C4; the copy in D8 refers to D6 through D4. For further information on this convenient feature of the Works spreadsheet, see the section "Cell-Referencing Shortcuts."

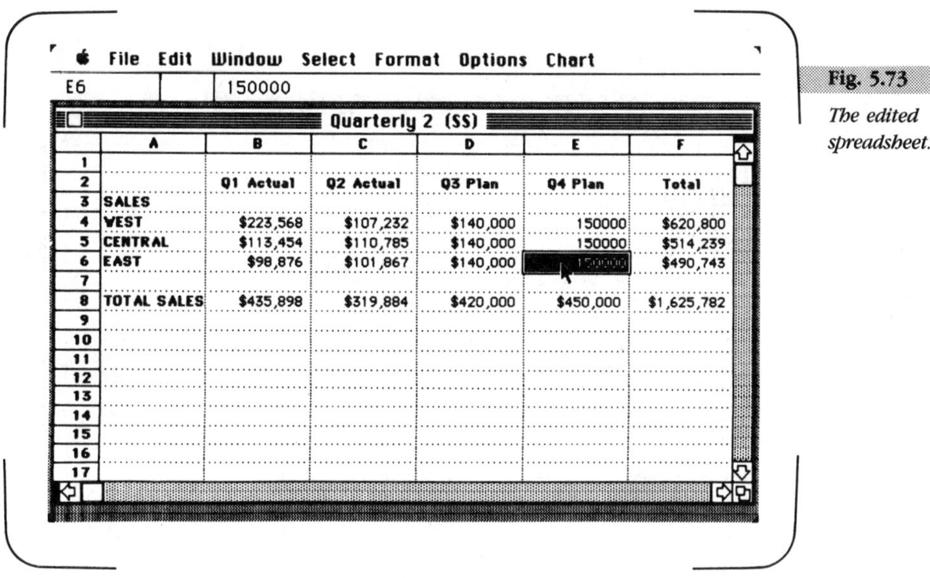

	A	B	C	D	E	F
1						
2		Q1 Actual	Q2 Actual	Q3 Plan	Q4 Plan	Total
3	SALES					
4	WEST	$223,568	$107,232	$140,000	150000	$620,800
5	CENTRAL	$113,454	$110,785	$140,000	150000	$514,239
6	EAST	$98,876	$101,867	$140,000	150000	$490,743
7						
8	TOTAL SALES	$435,898	$319,884	$420,000	$450,000	$1,625,782
9						
10						
11						
12						
13						
14						
15						
16						
17						

Fig. 5.73

The edited spreadsheet.

Moving Cells

Assume that you want to move the totals (row 8) so that they're directly below the figures. Moving cells is just as easy as copying them, as you'll learn from these simple steps:

1. Select the range A8 to F8.
2. Choose Move from the Edit menu.
3. In the Move dialog box, enter the Destination Cell for the Move. The destination cell is the upper left cell of the range to which you want to move the selected cells—in this example, cell A7.

Notice, again, that cell references have been adjusted (see fig. 5.74).

Inserting Rows and Columns

Sometimes inserting a row or column is simpler than moving parts of the spreadsheet around. To practice inserting a row, you can insert a row above row 7 in the spreadsheet shown in figure 5.74. The insertion will restore the spreadsheet to its previous condition, as shown in figure 5.73. To insert a row or column, follow these steps:

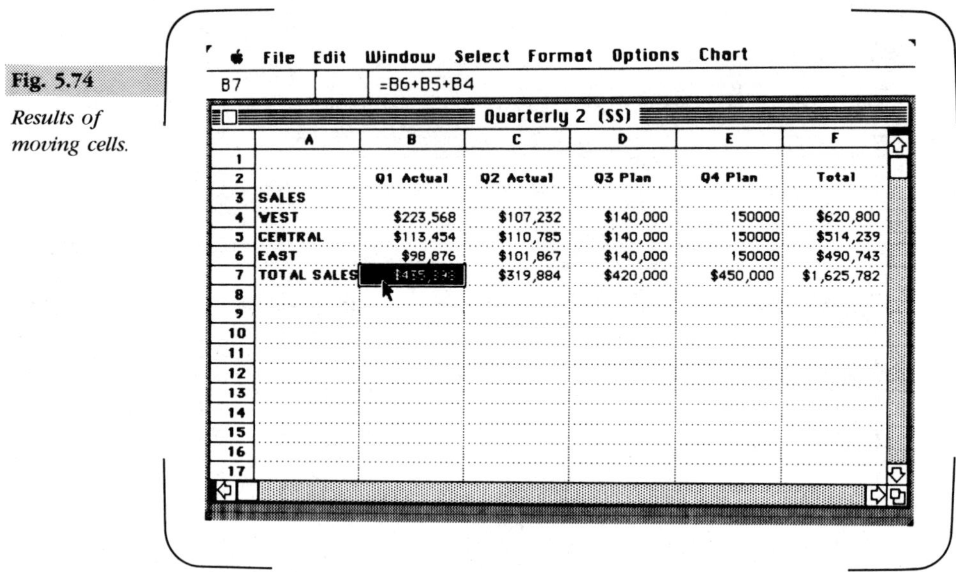

	A	B	C	D	E	F
1						
2		Q1 Actual	Q2 Actual	Q3 Plan	Q4 Plan	Total
3	SALES					
4	WEST	$223,568	$107,232	$140,000	150000	$620,800
5	CENTRAL	$113,454	$110,785	$140,000	150000	$514,239
6	EAST	$98,876	$101,867	$140,000	150000	$490,743
7	TOTAL SALES	$435,898	$319,884	$420,000	$450,000	$1,625,782
8						
9						
10						
11						
12						
13						
14						
15						
16						
17						

Fig. 5.74

Results of moving cells.

1. Select row 7 by clicking on the row label (the number to the left of the row).
2. Choose Insert from the Edit menu, or press **command-I**.

A new row is inserted above the selected row.

The steps for inserting a column are the same, with one exception: before selecting Insert or pressing *command*-I, you click on a column label (the letter above a column). A new column is inserted to the left of the selected column.

When you add a row or column within a range that's referenced by an equation, the cell references are adjusted but are not augmented to accommodate the new row or column. If you add a new row above row 5, for example, the equation in B8 reads =B7+B6+B4. The former references to B5 and B6 are adjusted because the values previously in B5 and B6 are now in B6 and B7. But the equation is not adjusted to include references to values in the new row. Be careful. Always test your spreadsheets after moving parts of them.

If you want more practice, you can save this altered spreadsheet under a name different from Quarterly 2. Otherwise, you may simply abandon this version.

Closing Your Spreadsheet Window

Closing the spreadsheet window is simple: just click on the small box at the upper left corner of the spreadsheet window or choose Close from the File menu. If you have changed the spreadsheet since the last time you saved it, a dialog box appears; and you are asked whether you want to save the changes. Click the Yes button to save changes, the No button to abandon your changes, or the Cancel button to return to the spreadsheet without closing it. After closing the window, you are returned to the Open File screen.

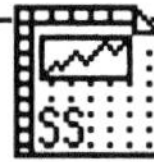

6

Spreadsheet Functions

This chapter looks at a few of the more popular Works spreadsheet functions. Works provides more than 50 functions, which simplify and speed the development of spreadsheets. You can think of functions as built-in equations. All you need to do is provide the variables, and the functions produce the answers. For instance, the Sqrt function finds the square root of a value, and the Sum function adds a specific range of cells. You can, of course, write your own equations in Works, but the built-in functions save you the time and trouble. Works also has functions that help with financial modeling. Still others perform trigonometric and statistical computations. You can use functions by themselves or include them in complex formulas.

After reading about these functions, you probably will want to explore others to use in your specific applications. Following the explanation of functions is a list of all Works functions, classified by subject (mathematical, financial, and so on). And following this list are detailed descriptions of the functions themselves.

As you read about the functions, you may want to try using some of them. Open a new spreadsheet if you like.

Specifics about Functions

Before you can use functions effectively, you need to know a few terms and concepts. You need to learn about the parts of a function and the different ways you can provide input to be used by functions. The following text also discusses the way to enter a function, the types of functions built into Works, and the options and commands you can use with functions.

The Parts and Construction of Functions

Functions usually consist of at least two parts: the function name and an argument or arguments. Arguments are enclosed in parentheses; multiple arguments are separated by commas. A few functions, like ERROR( ), do not use arguments.

Function Arguments

Arguments are the information you provide a function for its calculation. For example, if you use the Sqrt function to find the square root of 9, *9* is the argument; if you want to find the square root of the contents of cell B2, the argument is B2. As mentioned, you enclose arguments in parentheses. Figure 6.1 shows how these two examples look in a spreadsheet.

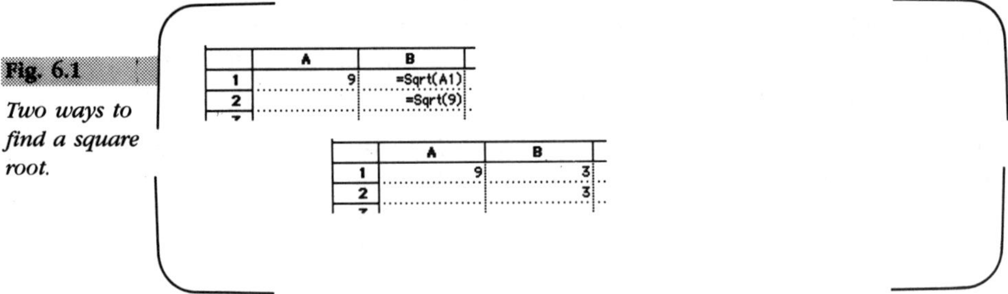

Fig. 6.1

Two ways to find a square root.

As you can see, arguments can be either values or references to cells or ranges containing values. Works displays, or *returns*, the results of its computation in the cell containing the function.

Function Syntax

When you use functions, you must follow rules. Certain things must occur in a certain order; this order is called the *syntax* of a function. It's a little like grammar.

Some general syntax rules apply to all functions; in addition, each function has its own specific syntax. Following are some general syntax rules:

- Precede a function with an equal sign if the function starts a cell entry.
- Works ignores upper- and lowercase.

- Spell functions correctly.
- Don't use spaces between function names and parentheses.
- Provide all required arguments.
- Separate multiple arguments with commas.
- Functions consider cells containing text to be blank.

If Works "suspects" that you've done something wrong, it warns you by displaying a dialog box that shows the entry and warns that it is incorrect. For example, some format choices are applicable to numbers only, and other choices are for text only. In figure 6.2, Works expected a cell address, like A1, or a number, like 12.5. A label was entered by mistake.

Don't, however, expect Works to find all your mistakes; test your work.

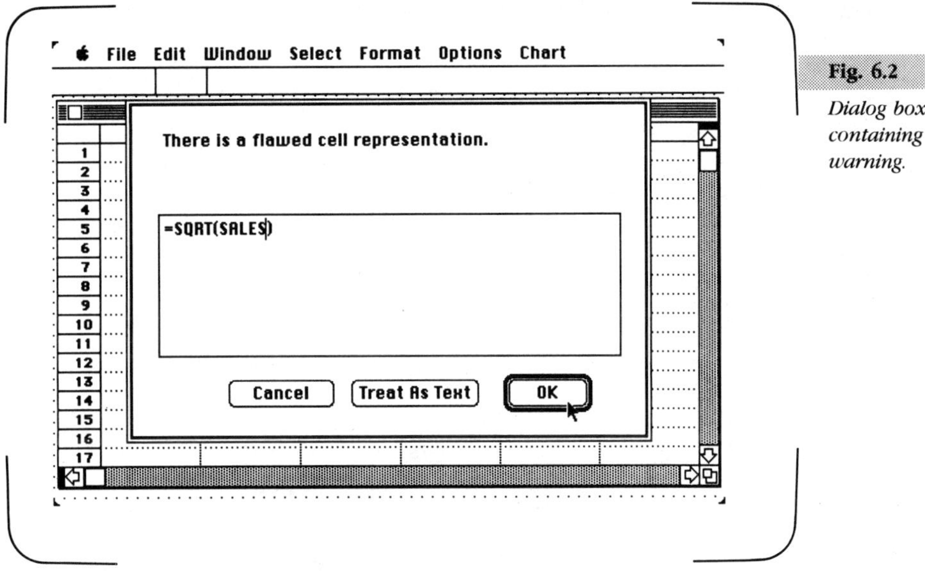

Fig. 6.2
Dialog box containing warning.

The Paste Function Option

Remembering the exact spelling of all 54 functions is hard, and making typos is easy. Therefore, Works provides a Paste Function option on the Edit menu so that you can paste the function and parentheses without having to type the function name. The Paste Function displays a dialog box containing the names of all Works functions (see fig. 6.3). You choose the one you want, and Works pastes a copy for you. Then, you enter the arguements within the parentheses.

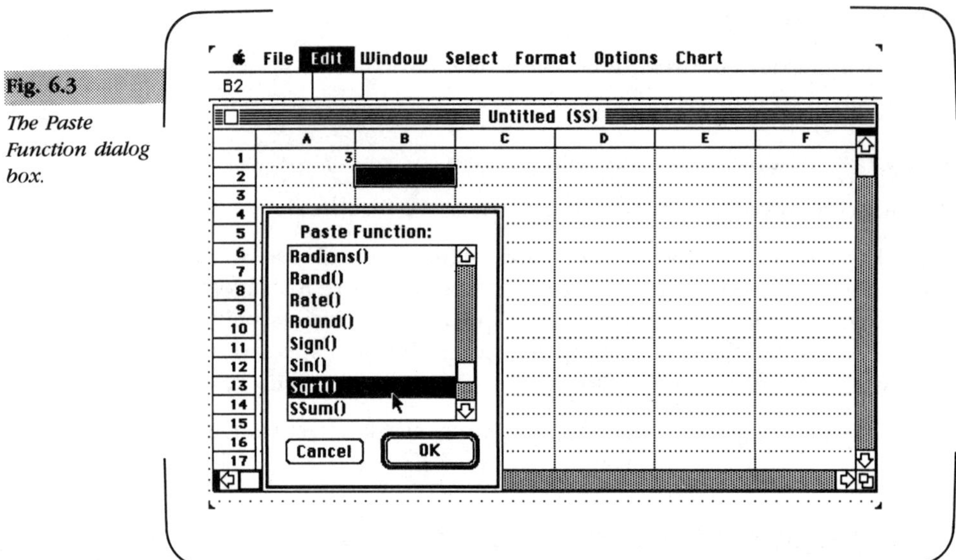

Fig. 6.3

The Paste Function dialog box.

Using the Paste Function option is a shorthand method of placing functions in the entry bar. Here's what you do:

1. Select (make active) the cell in which you want the function to reside.
2. Choose Paste Function on the Edit menu.
3. Use the scroll bars, if necessary, to find the function you want.
4. Either double-click on the function's name or click the OK button. The function then appears in the spreadsheet edit bar.
5. Add the necessary arguments and continue.

Ranges in Function Arguments

Many functions, such as Sum, use ranges of values for computations. For example, you can use Sum to develop the quarterly subtotals and totals in the sample spreadsheet in Chapter 5. Figure 6.4 shows Sum functions in row 8 and column F.

You enclose function ranges and other arguments in parentheses. To enter ranges, you either type them or use the pointing, clicking, and dragging techniques you've already learned.

	A	B	C	D	E	F
2		Q1 Actual	Q2 Actual	Q3 Plan	Q4 Plan	Total
3	SALES					
4	WEST	123,568	107232	140000	140000	=Sum(B4:E4)
5	CENTRAL	113454	110785	140000	140000	=Sum(B5:E5)
6	EAST	98876	101867	140000	140000	=Sum(B6:E6)
7						
8	TOTAL SALES	=Sum(B4:B6)	=Sum(C4:C6)	=Sum(D4:D6)	=Sum(E4:E6)	=Sum(F4:F6)

Fig. 6.4

Sum functions in row 8 and column F

Function ranges can define blocks, parts or all of a row or column, or even noncontiguous cells. You can reference multiple ranges for one function. Here are some examples of ranges used with the Sum function:

=Sum(B4:E4)	References cells in a row
=Sum(A1:Z1)	References cells in a column
=Sum(B4:E6)	References a block of cells
=Sum(A1,B2,C3)	References noncontiguous cells separated by commas
=Sum (B4:E4,G4,A6:E6)	References two ranges and a specific cell

As you can see, you use a colon (:) to separate a range's starting and ending locations, and you use commas to separate cell addresses or ranges.

Logical Functions

Unlike most functions, which return a variety of answers based on given arguments, logical functions return only one of two answers—usually 0 or 1—after performing their operations or inspecting the contents of a cell. For example, in figure 6.5, the If function places either a 1 or a 0 in cell B3, depending on whether specified conditions are met. In this case, the contents of cell B1 must be greater than 5 in order to meet the conditions indicated.

The If function located in B3 is displayed in the entry bar. The first part of the argument (B1) is what the function is to test. Because a cell location has been used, the If function tests any number placed in B1. The "greater than 5" (>5) tells Works to test the value in B1 to see whether it is a number larger than 5. Works is told to return a 1 if cell

B1 is greater than 5 and a 0 if B1 is less than or equal to 5. Replacing the 0 in this example with a 9 would cause Works to return a 9 when B1 is 5 or less.

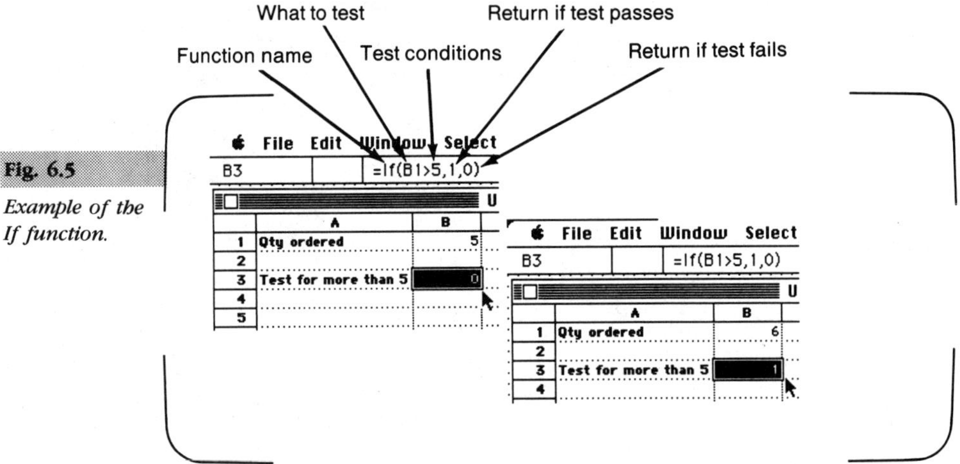

Fig. 6.5

Example of the If function.

Lookup Functions

With Works, you can create lookup tables and have Works enter data into cells from the tables, based on specific conditions. Lookup tables are cell ranges containing reference data that Works uses for computations. In figure 6.6, for example, the range B1 through G2 is a lookup table. The Lookup function in cell B5 checks the quantity-ordered cell, B4. The prices and quantities are listed in the lookup table, and the prices vary according to quantity ordered. In this example, the Lookup function places the appropriate price in cell B5, based on the quantity ordered. Several other Works functions use this lookup approach.

Categories of Functions

This section consists of tables that list Works' spreadsheet functions by category: special-purpose, mathematical, trigonometric, logical, and financial. Use the tables to find functions you want; then read more about the functions in the alphabetical function section that follows this one.

Table 6.1 describes Works' special-purpose functions.

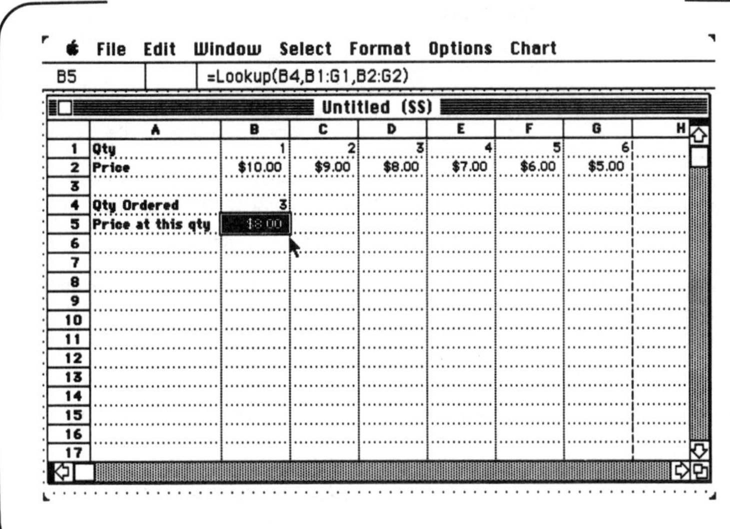

Fig. 6.6

Example of the Lookup function.

Table 6.1
Special-Purpose Functions

Function Name	*Action*
Error( )	Returns value *Error*
HLookup(lookup-number, compare-range,index-number)	Selects value in table, according to *lookup-number*
Index(range,row,column)	Selects reference in *range*, according to Index value's *row* and *column*
Lookup(lookup-number, compare-range,result-range)	Selects value in table, according to *lookup-number*
Match(lookup-number, compare-range, type)	Selects number of value according to *lookup-number*
NA( )	Returns value N/A
Type(value)	Returns type of *value*
VLookup(lookup-number, compare-number,index-number)	Selects value in table, according to *lookup-number*

Table 6.2 describes mathematical functions.

Table 6.2
Mathematical Functions

Function Name	*Action*
Abs(number)	Returns absolute value of *number*
Exp(number)	Raises *e* to power of *number*
Int(number)	Returns integer part of *number*
Ln(number)	Returns logarithm, base *e*, of *number*
Log10(number)	Returns logarithm, base 10, of *number*
Mod(number,divisor-number)	Returns remainder of *number* divided by *divisor-number*
Pi( )	Returns value of pi
Rand( )	Returns random number between 0 and 1
Round(number,number-of-digits)	Rounds *number* to *number-of-digits*
Sign(number)	Returns sign of *number*
Sqrt(number)	Returns square root of *number*

Table 6.3 gives descriptions of statistical functions.

Table 6.3
Statistical Functions

Function Name	*Action*
Average(values-1,values-2,...)	Returns average of values in *values*
Count(values-1,values-2,...)	Returns count of values in *values*
Max(values-1,values-2,...)	Returns maximum value in *values*
Min(values-1,values-2,...)	Returns minimum value in *values*
SSum(values-1,values-2,...)	Returns sum of *values* displayed
StDev(values-1,values-2,...)	Returns standard deviation of *values*
Sum(values-1,values-2,...)	Returns sum of *values*
Var(values-1,values-2,...)	Returns variance of *values*

Table 6.4 lists Works' trigonometric functions.

Table 6.4
Trigonometric Functions

Function Name	*Action*
ACos(number)	Returns arccosine of *number*
ASin(number)	Returns arcsine of *number*
ATan(number)	Returns arctangent of *number*
ATan2(x-number,y-number)	Returns arctangent of point (*x-number,y-number*)
Cos(number)	Returns cosine of *number*
Degrees(number)	Converts *number* from radians to degrees
Radians(number)	Converts *number* from degrees to radians
Sin(number)	Returns sine of *number*
Tan(number)	Returns tangent of *number*

Table 6.5 contains descriptions of logical functions.

Table 6.5
Logical Functions

Function Name	*Action*
And(values-1,values-2,...)	Returns 1 (True) if all *values* are not zero (True); otherwise, returns 0 (False)
Choose(index,number-1,number-2,...)	Uses *index* to select value from *numbers*
False( )	Returns value 0 (False)
If(number,number-if-true, number-if-false)	Returns *number-if-true* if number is not zero (True); returns *number-if-false* if number is 0 (False)
IsBlank(values-1,values-2,...)	Returns 1 (True) if all *values* are blank or text; otherwise, returns 0 (False)
IsError(value)	Returns 1 (True) if *value* is any error value
IsNA(value)	Returns 1 (True) if *value* is error value N/A
Not(number)	Returns 1 (True) if *number* is 0; returns 0 (FALSE) if *number* is not zero (True)
Or(values-1,values-2,...)	Returns 1 (True) if any logical value in *values* arguments is not zero (True); otherwise, returns 0 (False)
True( )	Returns value 1 (True)

Table 6.6 lists the names and uses of Works' financial functions.

Table 6.6
Financial Functions

Function Name	*Action*
FV(rate,nper,pmt,pv,type)	Computes future value of investment
IRR(range,guess)	Calculates internal rate of return of *range*
MIRR(range,safe,risk)	Returns modified internal rate of return of *range*
NPer(rate,pmt,pv,fv,type)	Computes number of payments of investment
NPV(rate,values-1,values-2,...)	Determines net present value of *values*
Pmt(rate,nper,pv,fv,type)	Calculates periodic payment of investment
PV(rate,nper,pmt,fv,type)	Computes present value of investment
Rate(nper,pmt,pv,fv,type,guess)	Determines rate returned on investment

Descriptions of Functions

The rest of this chapter provides explanations and examples of Works functions, which are discussed in alphabetical order.

Abs(number)

With Abs you can enter or reference a number and find its absolute value, which is the "distance" (positive or negative) between *number* and 0. For example, =Abs(−4) produces a result of 4. This function is useful if you want to find the difference between two numbers without first knowing which is larger. For example, =Abs(10−12) and =Abs(12−10) both return the answer 2. One use of this function is to change negative financial-function results to positive numbers for later use.

ACos(number)

ACos is one of Works' trigonometry functions. The arccosine is sometimes know as the "inverse cosine." Works' ACos function yields the radian measure of the angle whose cosine is presented as the argument. For example, the cosine of 0.785 radians (45 degrees) is 0.707; hence, ACos(0.707) returns the value 0.785. Because the interval for the cosine is from −1 to 1, the argument of the ACos function is restricted to that interval.

And(values-1,values-2,...)

The And function analyzes all the *values* in arguments you reference. If all the values are True (not 0), the And function returns a 1 (True). If any argument is False (0), And returns a 0 (False). For example, cell A2 in figure 6.7 contains an And function that checks the range B1 through E1. Notice how the results change (in A2) when even one of the cells in the tested range changes (C1). The function ignores cells containing text and blank cells.

Fig. 6.7

Using the And function.

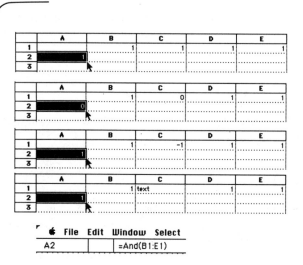

	A	B	C	D	E
1		1	1	1	1
2	1				
3					

	A	B	C	D	E
1		1	0	1	1
2	0				
3					

	A	B	C	D	E
1		1	-1	1	1
2	1				
3					

	A	B	C	D	E
1		1	text	1	1
2	1				
3					

File Edit Window Select

A2 =And(B1:E1)

ASin(number)

The ASin function returns the radian measure of a sine. For example, the sine of 1.570 ($\pi/2$ radians, or 90 degrees) is 1; the function ASin(1) returns the value 1.570.

ATan(number)

The ATan function returns the measure of the angle whose tangent is supplied as an argument. The tangent of 0.785 ($\pi/4$, or 45 degrees) is 1; the equation =ATan(1) returns the value 0.785.

ATan2(x-number,y-number)

The ATan2 function returns the radian measure of the angle defined by x-number and y-number; those numbers represent coordinates in two dimensions. For instance, the point (3,4) lies on the terminal side of an angle whose measure is 0.927 radians, or 53.13 degrees. The equation =ATan2(3,4) consequently returns the value 0.926.

Average(values-1,values-2,...)

The Average function finds the average of all numbers listed in the function's argument, as illustrated in figure 6.8. If the range(s) contain text or blanks, the function ignores them.

The function and its results reside in cell B12; the function is displayed in the entry bar. The argument (B4:B8) tells Works to find the average of the sales figures found in cells B4, B5, B6, B7, and B8. The argument could contain numbers rather than cell references. For instance, =Average(10,20,30) produces the answer 20.

Choose(index,number-1,number-2,...)

The Choose function returns a number based on the *index* argument. The *index*, the first part of the argument, tells Works where to look in the rest of the arguments to find the result. For example, the following function yields 30:

=Choose(3,10,20,30,40)

In this example, Works uses the third entry (30) because the *index* is 3.

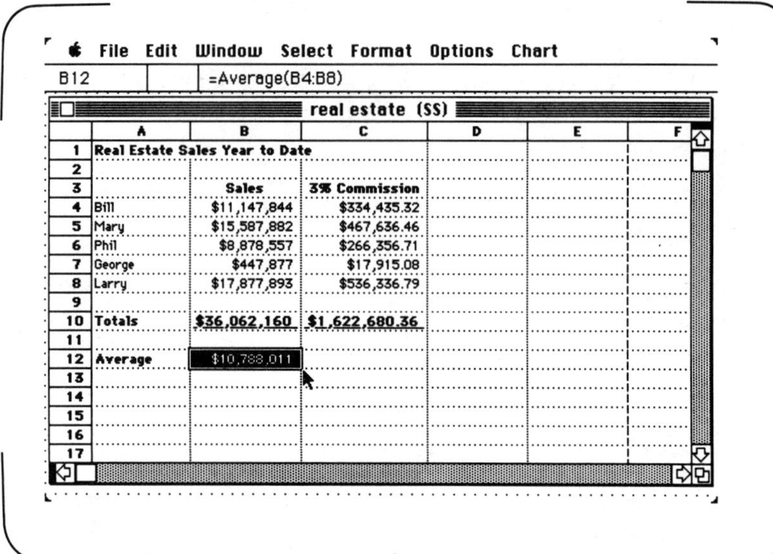

	A	B	C	D	E	F
1	Real Estate Sales Year to Date					
2						
3		Sales	3% Commission			
4	Bill	$11,147,844	$334,435.32			
5	Mary	$15,587,882	$467,636.46			
6	Phil	$8,878,557	$266,356.71			
7	George	$447,877	$17,915.08			
8	Larry	$17,877,893	$536,336.79			
9						
10	Totals	$36,062,160	$1,622,680.36			
11						
12	Average	$10,788,011				
13						
14						
15						
16						
17						

Fig. 6.8

Using the Average function to compute averages for a specified range.

Remember that you can substitute cell locations for numbers, so you could use the contents of a cell as the *index* or for any of the numbers in the argument. Here's an example:

=Choose(A1,10,30,A5)

In this case, Works inspects the content of cell A1 to determine which of the following arguments to use. If an index value is less than 1 or exceeds the number of available numbers in an argument, Choose returns *Error*.

Cos(number)

The Cos function returns the cosine of an angle measured in radians. If you remember your trigonometry, you know that the cosine of an angle is the ratio between the x-coordinate of a point on the angle's terminal side and the length of a line from the origin to the point. Radian measure assumes that the length of the radial line is 1. Consequently, the cosine of a 90-degree angle is 1. Ninety degrees is equal to 1.570 (or $\pi/2$) radians, so the equation =Cos(1.570) returns the value 0.

Count(values-1,values-2,...)

Count counts the numbers in your argument. You can use numbers or references, but you can't count cells containing text or blanks.

The range can be a column, a row, or any group of cells. For instance, in figure 6.9, the Count function counts the range of values in cells F91 through F102 and displays the count in B106. You could just as easily count B91 through F103, although you'd get a different answer. Because Works ignores text and blanks when counting, however, you can't specify A91 through A102, all of which contain text. The results would be *Error*.

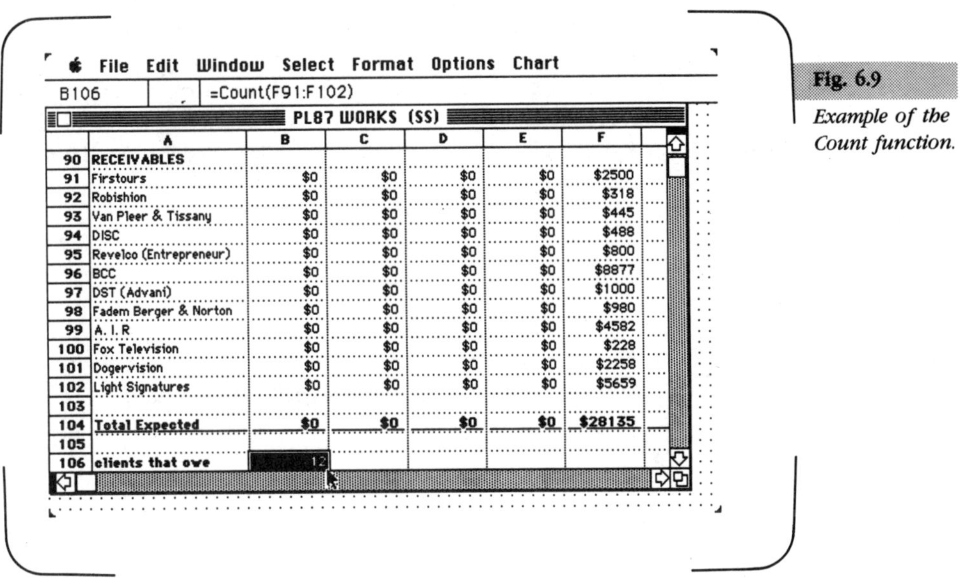

	A	B	C	D	E	F
90	RECEIVABLES					
91	Firstours	$0	$0	$0	$0	$2500
92	Robishion	$0	$0	$0	$0	$318
93	Van Pleer & Tissany	$0	$0	$0	$0	$445
94	DISC	$0	$0	$0	$0	$488
95	Reveloo (Entrepreneur)	$0	$0	$0	$0	$800
96	BCC	$0	$0	$0	$0	$8877
97	DST (Advani)	$0	$0	$0	$0	$1000
98	Fadem Berger & Norton	$0	$0	$0	$0	$980
99	A. I. R	$0	$0	$0	$0	$4582
100	Fox Television	$0	$0	$0	$0	$228
101	Dogervision	$0	$0	$0	$0	$2258
102	Light Signatures	$0	$0	$0	$0	$5659
103						
104	Total Expected	$0	$0	$0	$0	$28135
105						
106	clients that owe	12				

Fig. 6.9 *Example of the Count function.*

Degrees(number)

With the Degrees function, you can convert radians into degrees. A full circle contains 360 degrees, or 2π radians. The equation used to convert radian measure to degree measure is

Degrees = Radians * $180/\pi$

Figure 6.10 shows an example. The answer is slightly less than 180 because of the precision limitations in your Macintosh and Works.

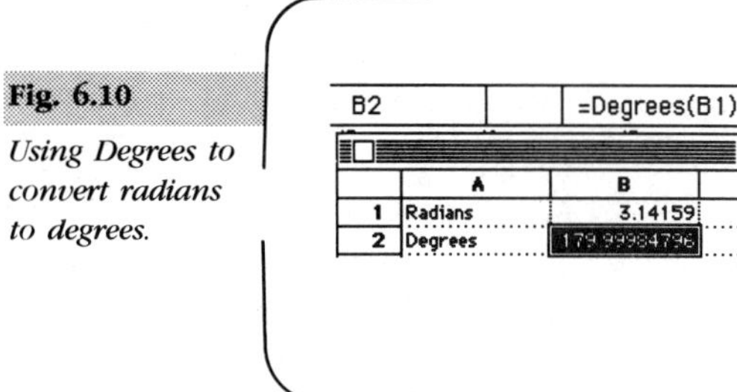

Fig. 6.10
Using Degrees to convert radians to degrees.

Error( )

The Error function, which has no arguments, enables you to force an error in your spreadsheet while you are testing it. Then, you can see which other cells in your spreadsheet are affected by an error at the chosen point. For instance, if you place an error in cell B1 of figure 6.10, `*Error*` is displayed in B2, indicating that an error in B1 affects the results in B2.

Exp(number)

The Exp function returns the result of raising the natural number e(2.7182818) to the power of the function's argument. This function therefore is the inverse of the natural logarithm function, Ln. For example, the equation =Ln(10) returns 2.303, and the equation =Exp(2.303) returns 10.

False( )

The False function takes no arguments, but the parentheses are required. False is primarily a testing tool that forces False in a cell where you want the false value. This function is useful when you are testing spreadsheets that use logical functions because you can force the logical situation you want [see also True( )].

FV(rate,nper,pmt,pv,type)

The financial function FV, or future value, usually determines the amount that an investment will be worth after a given time. FV can use other

Works financial functions in the process. Here's what FV's arguments mean:

- *rate:* the annual interest rate in percentage points (for example, 8 percent)
- *nper:* periods, or length of time in years
- *pmt:* payments, or annual dollar amount (a negative number)
- *pv:* present value, or optional dollar amount (a negative number)
- *type* (optional): either 0 for payments made at the end of each period or 1 for payments made at the beginning

Some arguments can be other Works financial functions. If you don't enter optional parameters, Works substitutes zeros. Payments and present values are negative numbers because Works treats payments as such. Future value is positive because it's money you will receive rather than give.

For example, suppose that you have $20,000 in an account earning 6.5 percent annual interest, and you plan to add an additional $250.00 at the beginning of each each month ($3,000 per year) over a 20-year period. To find out how much you'll have in 20 years, you use

=FV(6.5%,20,–3000,–20000,0)

The answer is $186,948.83—not a bad 20 years' work. You can compute a 1-point increase in interest rate by changing one parameter, *rate.* At 7.5 percent, the yield jumps to $214,871.07. In the argument, Works percentages are entered as shown or as 0.065 with no percentage sign.

HLookup(lookup-number, compare-range,index-number)

The HLookup function examines the first row in a range you define (the *compare-range*). Once HLookup finds the largest value that is less than or equal to the *lookup-number* in a column, the function moves up or down the column the number of rows called for in the *index-number.*

For example, in figure 6.11, the equation in cell A9 uses the block of cells A1 through D6. Each cell in row 1 is tested against the *lookup-number* (2,000). When the function finds the column containing 2,000 (column C), Works goes down the column the number of rows specified in the *index-number* portion of the argument (4). The value in cell B4 appears in the cell containing the HLookup equation (A9). Remember that you can substitute cell addresses for the *lookup-number* or *index-number* in your arguments.

NOTE: Values in the *compare-range* must be in ascending order.

File Edit Window Select Format Options Chart

A9 =HLookup(2000,A1:D6,4)

Hlookup (SS)

	A	B	C	D	E	F
1	1000	2000	3000	4000		
2	$20.00	$70.00	$120.00	$170.00		
3	$30.00	$80.00	$130.00	$180.00		
4	$40.00	$90.00	$140.00	$190.00		
5	$50.00	$100.00	$150.00	$200.00		
6	$60.00	$110.00	$160.00	$210.00		
7						
8						
9	90					
10						
11						
12						
13						
14						
15						
16						
17						

Fig. 6.11
Using the HLookup function.

If(number,number-if-true, number-if-false)

With the If function, you can replace the contents of a cell based on the results of tests. For example, you can specify two different values for a cell based on the results of a test. In figure 6.12, If puts the number 10 in cell B1 if A1 is less than 1, or If puts 20 in cell B1 if A1 is 1 or more.

You can have Works use the If function to perform calculations based on test results. The equation in figure 6.13 tests to see whether the beginning odometer reading in a mileage spreadsheet is smaller than the ending reading. If the beginning reading is smaller, then Works subtracts the two numbers, and the miles traveled appear in cell B5. Otherwise, Works is asked to divide by zero, which causes `*Error*` to appear in B5 and affected cells (see fig. 6.14). You can accomplish the same

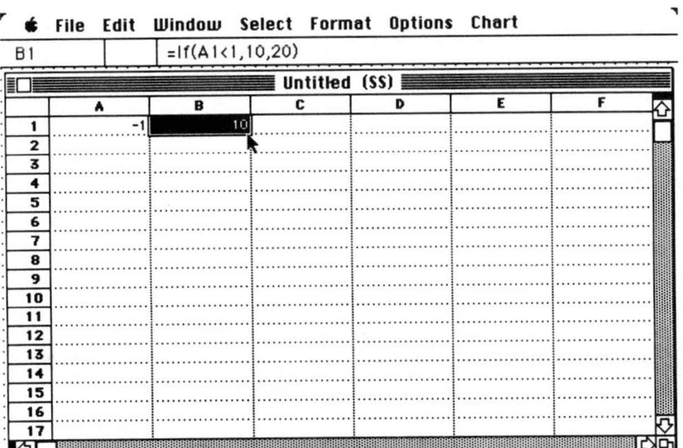

Fig. 6.12

Using If to replace a cell's contents based on test results.

thing in other ways, for example, =If(B4<B3,1/0,B4-B3). As another alternative, instead of dividing by zero you can use the Error function:

=If(B4<B3, Error( ),B4-B3)

or

=IF(B3>B$,Error( ),B4-B3)

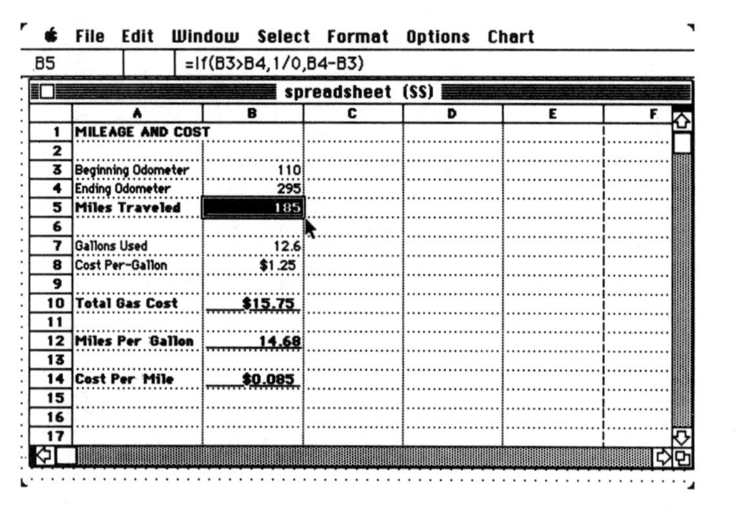

Fig. 6.13

Using the If function to perform calculations based on test results.

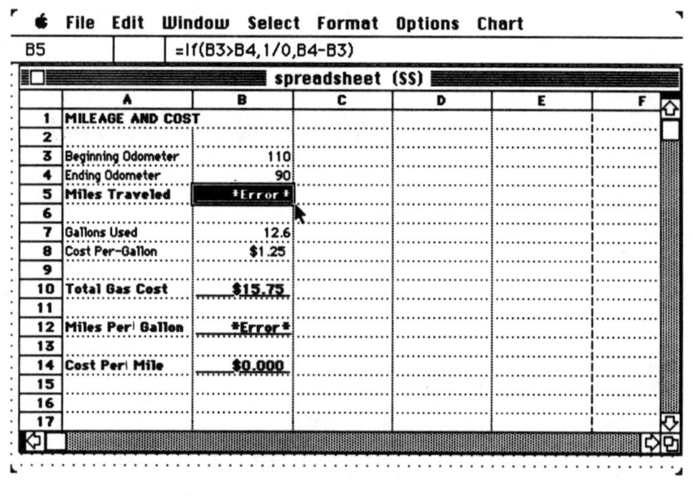

Fig. 6.14

Causing Works to display `*Error*` *if an error condition exists.*

Index(range,row,column)

Index returns the value contained in a specific cell or range of cells. The first part of the argument is the *range*. Regardless of where the range is in the spreadsheet, Works counts down and then across the specified number of cells, starting in the upper right corner of the specified range.

Indexing can be based on computations or other cell contents or can be specific numbers, as is the case in figure 6.15. Here, Works begins at cell B1 and counts down three rows and over two columns to locate the contents of cell C3. This value is displayed in cell A1.

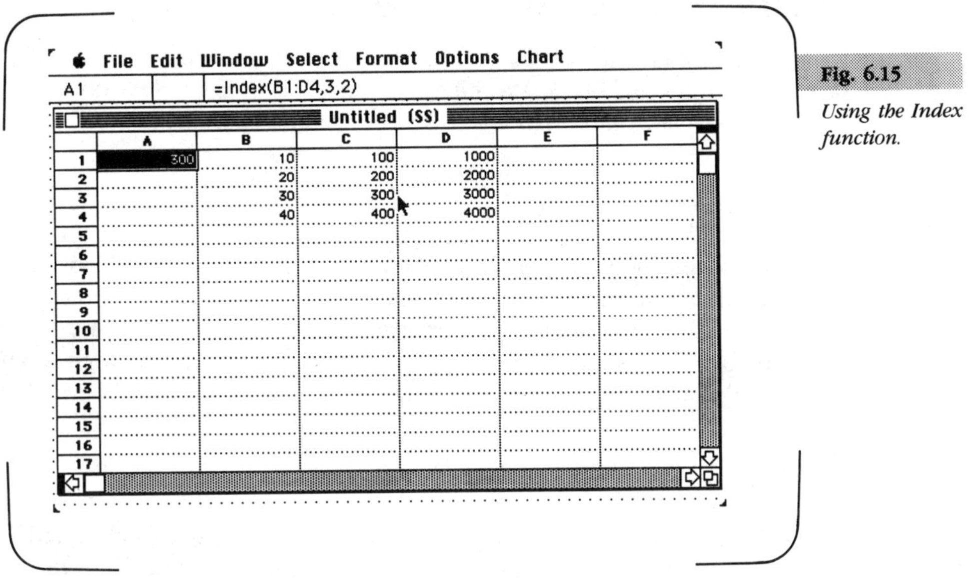

Fig. 6.15 *Using the Index function.*

Int(number)

The Int function rounds numbers down. For example, Int(3.4) rounds down to 3, but a negative number such as -3.4 rounds to -4.

NOTE: Other spreadsheets truncate numbers (cut off numbers to the right of the decimal point) with their Int functions. Works rounds. This difference is definitely worth noting if you are used to spreadsheets like 1-2-3.

IRR(range,guess)

IRR takes a series of cash flows (the *range*) and makes 20 attempts at computing the internal rate of return (the interest rate that gives the range a zero net present value). This procedure is called the *iterative technique* because the function makes 20 attempts (iterations) before giving up.

You specify the starting range for the iterations by entering a *guess*; try 0 or 1 to start. If IRR fails after 20 tries, the message `*Error*` appears. The function ignores blanks and labels.

IsBlank(values-1,values-2,...)

IsBlank tests cells or ranges of cells to see whether they're blank. If all tested cells are blank, the function returns a 0; if any cell contains a number, IsBlank returns a 1. IsBlank treats text as blanks.

IsError(range)

IsError returns a value of 1 if a cell or any cell in a range of cells contains an `*Error*` warning. If IsError finds no warning, the function returns a 0. You can use this function to prevent `*Error*` messages from appearing on your worksheets, although this practice is generally not recommended because it masks spreadsheet problems.

IsNA(range)

IsNA returns a value of 1 if a cell or any cell in a range of cells contains an N/A warning. If IsNA finds no N/A warnings, the function returns a 0. You can use this function to prevent N/A from appearing on your spreadsheets. Again, this practice is not recommended because it masks problems.

Ln(number)

This function returns the natural logarithm—that is, the logarithm to base e (2.7182818)—of the number provided as the function argument. The logarithm is the power to which the base is raised to yield the number; for example, $e^2 = 7.389056$, so the natural logarithm of 7.389 is 2. Similarly, the Works equation =Ln(7.389056) returns the result approximately equal to 2.

Log10(number)

Log10 yields the base 10 logarithm of a positive number. This function is the inverse of base 10 exponentiation. For example, the equation to find the log of 10 is =Log10(10), and the result is 1. As always, you can substitute a cell reference for the number.

Lookup(lookup-number, compare-range,result-range)

The Lookup function examines a range you define (the *compare-range*) and returns the largest value that is less than or equal to the *lookup-number*. Lookup puts the results in *result-range*. See figure 6.6 for an example of the Lookup function.

NOTE: Values in the *compare-range* must be in ascending order. Both *result-range* and *compare-range* must be the same length.

Match(lookup-number,compare-range,type)

The Match function compares the *lookup-number* with the numbers in the *compare-range* and returns a number indicating the position in the *compare-range* where the match was found.

The numbers in the *compare-range* are scanned from left to right and from top to bottom. If the *compare-range* is A1:B2, for example, the cells are scanned in this order: A1, A2, B1, B2. A match is found only when a number in the *compare-range* matches the *lookup-number* in accordance with the *type* of match specified in the third argument of the function. If match *type* is 1, the match is the largest number in the *compare-range* that is less than or equal to the *lookup-number*. If the match *type* argument is 0, the number in the *compare-range* must be equal to the *lookup-number*; if no number in the range matches the *lookup-number*, the function returns an error message. If the match *type* argument is -1, the match is the smallest number in the *compare-range* that is greater than or equal to the *lookup-number*.

NOTE: The order of the *compare-range* values is important when match *types* 1 and -1 are used. For match *type* 1, the values must be in ascending order. For match *type* -1, the values must be in descending order.

One possible use of the Match function is shown in figure 6.16. This spreadsheet classifies clients according to the number of orders they have placed in the past year. Those who've placed the fewest orders are assigned customer status 1; those who've placed the most orders are assigned status 5. The matching is done by an equation in colum C. The equation in C2, for instance, is

=Match(B2,$A$12:$A$16,1)

Notice that the specified match type is 1, which specifies that the matching number be the largest value in the *compare-range* that is less than or equal to the *lookup-number*. The number meeting that specification in the *compare-range* (A12:A16) is 0. Because 0 is the first number in the range, the equation returns the value 1.

This function is especially useful with other table-oriented functions, such as HLookup, VLookup, Index, and Lookup. The advantage to Match is that it always returns an integer value, which can be used as an argument for one of the other functions. You might use the status number generated in the preceding example to index into a table of values so that your spreadsheet can automaticlly determine discounts, set the frequency of sales calls, or provide other handy information.

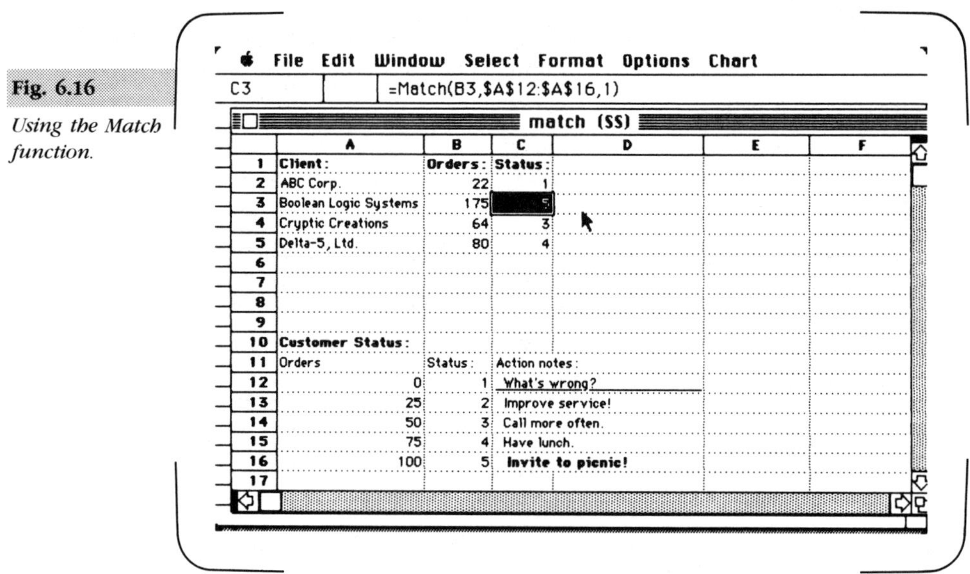

	A	B	C	D	E	F
1	Client:	Orders:	Status:			
2	ABC Corp.	22	1			
3	Boolean Logic Systems	175	5			
4	Cryptic Creations	64	3			
5	Delta-5, Ltd.	80	4			
6						
7						
8						
9						
10	Customer Status:					
11	Orders	Status:	Action notes:			
12	0	1	What's wrong?			
13	25	2	Improve service!			
14	50	3	Call more often.			
15	75	4	Have lunch.			
16	100	5	Invite to picnic!			
17						

Fig. 6.16

Using the Match function.

Max(values-1,values-2,...)

Max yields the highest number in the range specified in the argument. You can use values, cell locations, or ranges as arguments. The function ignores text and blanks.

Figure 6.17 shows an example of the Max function. Here, Works searched the range F4:F6 and displayed in cell F10 (the location of the Max function) the highest value found.

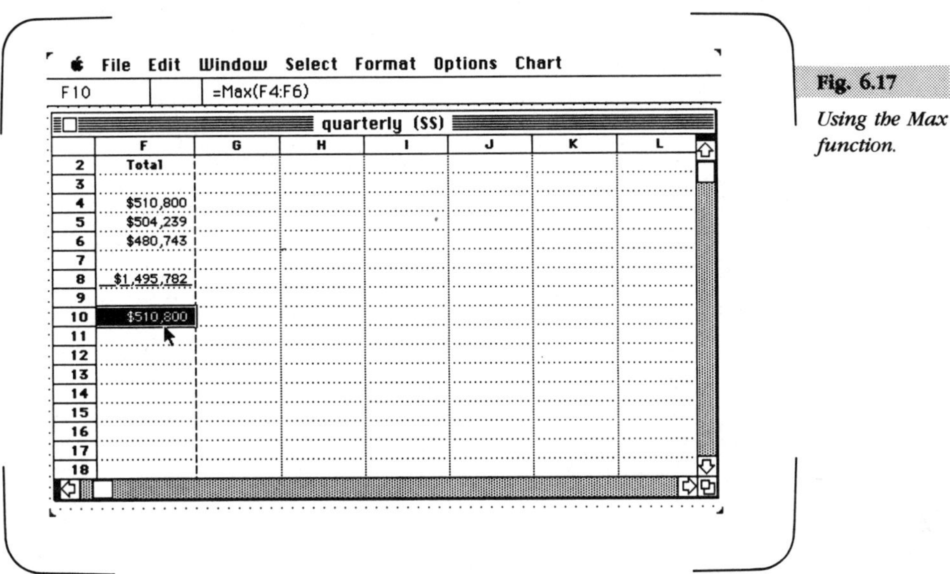

Fig. 6.17

Using the Max function.

Min(values-1,values-2,...)

Min is identical to the Max function, except that Min yields the lowest number in the range specified in the argument. Arguments can contain values, cell locations, or ranges. Mix ignores text and blanks.

MIRR(range,safe,risk)

MIRR computes modified internal rates of return, taking into consideration the *safe* and *risk* arguments. *Safe* is the rate returned by an investment that will finance negative cash flows. *Risk* is the return from reinvestment rate of positive cash flow. For instance, suppose that you have these cash flows in cells A1 through A5:

A1	-50000
A2	20000
A3	-3000
A4	30000
A5	5000

Suppose also that you borrow money at 18 percent to finance the negative cash flows while reinvesting the positive cash flows at 19 percent. The modified internal rate of return would be 9.29 percent. The equation is =MIRR(A1:A5,18%,19%).

Mod(number,divisor-number)

The Mod function returns the remainder after division. For example, 5 divided by 3 leaves a remainder of 2, so the equation =Mod(5,3) returns the value 2. Similarly, =Mod(–5,–3) returns the value –2.

All is well as long as the dividend and the divisor have the same sign: the result is positive for a positive dividend and divisor, and negative for negative numbers. But erroneous results occur when the dividend and divisor have different signs. Notice, for example, in figure 6.18, that the equation =Mod(5,–3), in cell C4, returns –1, and that =Mod(–9,4), in cell C5, returns 3.

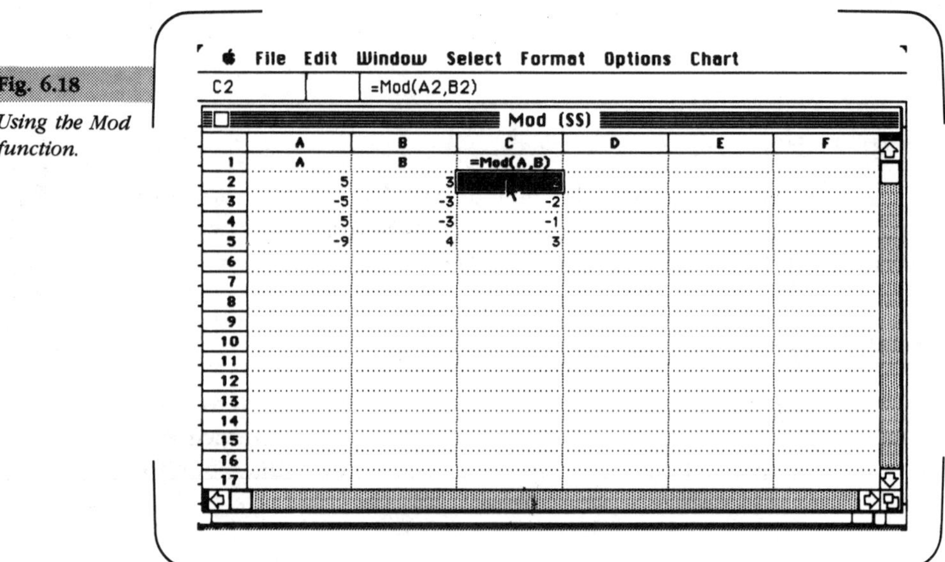

Fig. 6.18

Using the Mod function.

Apparently, this unusual behavior results from a bug in the Works. If you experiment with the Mod function, you'll find that it returns the difference between the divisor and the expected answer. For instance, the answer you'd expect from =Mod(5,–3) is either 2 or –2. (Opinion differs on whether the result of modulus division of mixed numbers should reflect the sign of the dividend or of the divisor.) But =Mod(5,–3) returns –1, which is equal to the difference between the divisor, –3, and the expected result, –2. Similar results obtain with the equation =Mod(–9,4), which returns 3 rather than the expected result, 1. And 1 is, of course, the difference between 4 and 3. Be careful in using this function!

NA( )

The NA function takes no arguments, but the parentheses are required. NA is primarily a testing tool that forces N/A in a cell where you want the N/A value.

Not(argument)

Not returns a 0 (false) if the result of the *argument* is false, that is, a value other than 0. Arguments can be values, equations, or cell locations.

Here are two examples of this function:

=Not(1+2=4) yields a 1.

=Not(1+2=3) yields a 0.

NPer(rate,pmt,pv,fv,type)

NPer computes the number of periods of an investment involving constant cash flows. For instance, you can use NPer to determine how long you need to pay off a loan at a particular monthly payment level.

NPer uses the following arguments:

- *rate:* the interest rate in percentage points (for example, 1 percent)
- *pmt:* payments
- *pv:* present value
- *fv* (optional): future value

- *type* (optional): either 0 for payments made at the end of each period or 1 for payments made at the beginning

Look at how NPer is used. Suppose that you want to find out how long you need to pay back an $18,000 car loan at 12 percent, by making $400 monthly payments at the beginning of each month. You use

=NPer(1%,-400,18000,0,1)

The answer is 59.271277992 months. (You could have substituted 0.01 for 1% in the equation; Works accepts both forms.)

This simple example uses a monthly interest rate of 1 percent because the payment periods are months. Payments are always negative numbers. Optional arguments such as *fv* and *type* default to 0 if you don't specify them.

NPV(rate,values-1,values-2,...)

The NPV function computes the net present value of future cash flows, given a constant rate of interest (*rate*). Cash flows occur at the beginning of constant intervals. Values can be numbers, equations, or cell or range references. NPV ignores text and blanks if they occur in the ranges you specify.

Or(values-1,values-2,...)

The Or function returns either a 1 (True) if any value in the argument is true or a False (0) if all arguments are false. Arguments can be values, equations, or cell references.

Here are two examples of Or:

=Or(1+2=4,1+2=3) yields a 1.

=Or(1+2=4, 1+2=5) yields a 0.

Pi( )

Pi inserts an approximation of the mathematical constant that is its namesake: 3.15159. No arguments are required, but the parentheses are.

Pmt(rate,nper,pv,fv,type)

Pmt yields an investment's periodic payment, assuming constant cash flows. In other words, if you know the amount, interest rate, and duration of a loan, you can use this function to determine the amount of your regular payments. The arguments include

- *rate:* interest rate per period
- *nper:* net present value
- *pv:* present value
- *fv* (optional): future value
- *type* (optional): either 1 for payments at beginning of period or 2 for payments at end of period

Here's an example. Suppose that you want to buy a house and require a $300,000 loan for 30 years. The going rate for fixed mortgages is 10 percent, and you plan to make payments at the first of each month. To calculate your approximate monthly payments, you use the following function:

```
Pmt(10.0%/12,360,300000,0,1)
```

You also can enter 0.10/12 rather than 10.0%/12.

The answer is $2,610.96 per month. The annual interest rate (10 percent) is divided by 12 months to get the appropriate interest rate for the rest of the assumptions. Notice the use of an equation (10%/12) in the function.

PV(rate,nper,pmt,fv,type)

One of Works' financial functions, PV, or present value, can be used by itself or with the other financial functions. PV's elements are

- *rate:* interest rate per period
- *nper:* net present value
- *pmt:* payment (a negative number)
- *fv* (optional): future value
- *type* (optional): either 0 for payments at beginning of period or 1 for payments at end of period

Imagine that you have $1,200 dollars a month to spend on house payments. With PV, you can calculate how much you can afford to borrow, given current interest rates and the length of the mortgage. Assume that the rate is 10 percent, the mortgage is for 30 years, and you'll make payments at the beginning of each month. You use

=PV(10%/12,30*12,–1200,0,1)

According to this function, you can afford a house that costs roughly $137,880. But if interest rates go back to 18 percent, you'd better find a house with an $80,818 mortgage.

Notice the use of two equations in the example; they save you some manual calculations. The first equation (10%/12) makes the interest rate compatible with the periods (months). The second equation (30*12) computes the number of months in 30 years (360). Works substitutes 0s if you omit the optional arguments *type* and *fv*.

Radians(number)

With Radians, you can convert degrees to radians. You can use values, equations, or cell references as arguments.

Rand( )

Each time Works recalculates the spreadsheet, the Rand function generates a new positive random number between 0 and 0.999. No arguments are accepted, but the parentheses are required. To see Rand( ) at work, enter =Rand( ) in a cell; then hold the *command* key and repeatedly press the equal key (=), causing Works to recalculate the spreadsheet. Each recalculation yields a new random number in the cell containing the Rand( ) function.

Rate(nper,pmt,pv,fv,type,guess)

Another financial function, Rate determines the probable rate of growth for an investment, given the initial value of the investment and its probable value at the end of a known time period. This function's arguments are

- *nper:* period
- *pmt:* payment (an optional negative number)

- *pv:* present value
- *fv* (optional): future value
- *type* (optional): either 0 for payments at beginning of period or 1 for payments at end of period
- *guess:* a starting point for solving the equation

Suppose that you purchase a 1964 Mustang convertible for $8,000 and plan to keep it for 10 years, at which point you think it will be worth $13,000. You can estimate the percentage yield of this investment by using

=Rate(10,0,–8000,13000,0,.1)

The investment yields 4.97 percent, ignoring any expenses, such as storage costs or insurance and maintenance if you drive the car. If you have extra predictable expenses—for example, $400 per year for storage—you enter that amount as a payment (*pmt*):

=Rate(10,–400,–8000,13000,0,.1)

The results look even worse: Your yield is less than 1 percent.

NOTE: Works substitutes 0s if you leave out the optional arguments *type* and *fv*. If your *guess* (starting point) is too high or low, Works gives up trying to find an answer after 20 iterations. Choose another *guess*, and have Works try again.

Round(number,number-of-digits)

The Round function yields numbers rounded to the precision specified by the *number-of-digits* in the argument. If you specify 0 digits, Works rounds to the nearest integer. Thus, the expression =Round(1.23456,3) produces the answer 1.235. Remember that you can use cell locations in place of numbers, so =Round(A1,3) is also acceptable.

Sign(number)

The Sign function tests for positive or negative numbers. Again, you can substitute cell references or equations for numbers in the argument. Here's what happens:

- Positive numbers produce a 1.
- Negative numbers produce a -1.

- Zeros produce 0.

Note the following examples:

=Sign(10) yields 1.

=Sign(-3) yields -1.

=Sign(0) yields 0.

=Sign(3-3) yields 0.

=Sign(3+1) yields 1.

Sin(number)

Sin calculates a number's sine when the number is an angle in radians.

Sqrt(number)

Sqrt yields the square root of positive numbers. If you use negative numbers, `*Error*` warnings appear.

SSum(values-1,values-2,...)

You have control over the precision with which numbers are both displayed and printed, but usually numbers are computed in the General (unrounded) format. Therefore, sometimes the numbers on the screen (or printout) may not match the numbers entered. This problem is particularly troublesome when you have formatted cells for dollars or percentages.

For example, in figure 6.19, cells B2 through C3 all contain 0.333, and cells B4 and C5 contain 0.334. Cell B5 contains the equation =Sum(B4:B2). Cell C5, however, uses the SSum function: =SSum(C4:C2). If the cells are displayed in the General format, both columns add up to 1, just as they would on most pocket calculators. But if all 6 cells are formatted for dollars and cents with two decimal places, things get sticky (see fig. 6.20). Because B5 contains the regular Sum function, it doesn't produce the results you'd get if you added the displayed numbers with your calculator. Instead, the answer in B5 is provided based on the actual cell contents of B4 through B2. Remember that in both figures 6.19 and 6.20, cells B4 and C4 contain 0.334. In figure 6.20, the cells display 0.33 because of rounding done by the dollar formatting option. Even when numbers are rounded for display, computation takes place using the unrounded cell values.

Cell C5 contains the SSum function, which makes the results consistent with the precision used to display and print the other cells. That is, the SSum function ensures that if you add a column of numbers from the screen (or printout) with your calculator, the calculator and screen agree. Which column in figure 6.20 contains the correct total? The answer is a matter of personal preference or company policy.

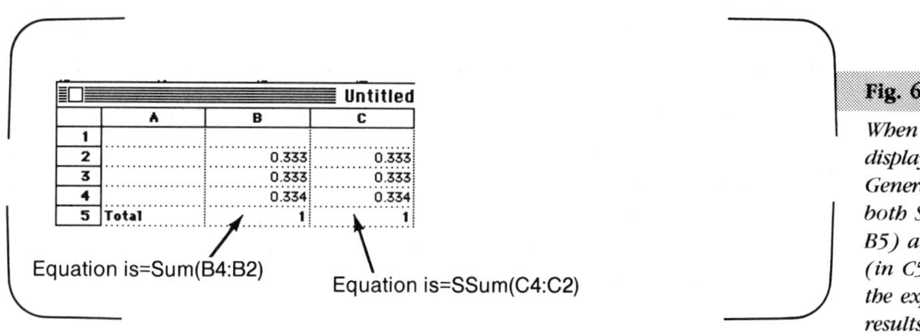

Fig. 6.19

When cells are displayed in the General format, both Sum (in B5) and SSum (in C5) produce the expected results.

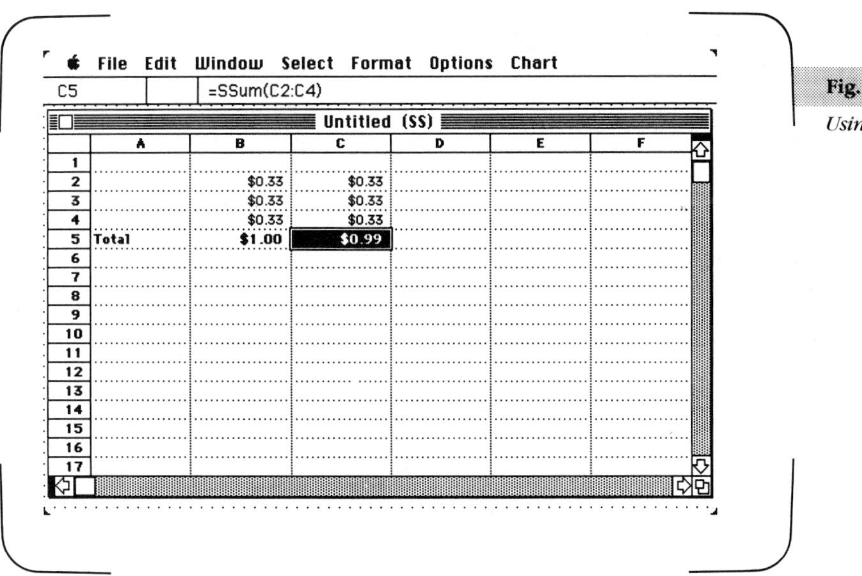

Fig. 6.20

Using SSum.

StDev(values-1,values-2,...)

Given numbers, equations, or appropriate cell references, StDev yields simple standard deviations. The function ignores text and blanks.

Sum(values-1,values-2,...)

Sum adds the numbers found in the specified range. You can use values, cell references, or ranges.

NOTE: Be careful when inserting rows and columns in areas of a spreadsheet containing Sum or SSum functions (see fig. 6.21). In this example, the NORTHEAST region has been inserted as row 7, but the Sum function does not include row 7 in its computations. As you can see in the entry bar, the Sum function looks only at rows B4 through B6. Also note the problem in the percentage column, G. You may need to redefine the Sum range because rows aren't automatically included in the Sum totals.

Fig. 6.21

Inserting rows at the top or bottom of columns containing Sum or SSum functions.

File Edit Window Select Format Options Chart

B8 =Sum(B4:B6)

quarterly (SS)

	A	B	C	D	E	F	G
1							
2		Q1 Actual	Q2 Actual	Q3 Plan	Q4 Plan	Total	%
3	SALES						
4	WEST	$123,568	$107,232	$140,000	$140,000	$510,800	34.15%
5	CENTRAL	$113,454	$110,785	$140,000	$140,000	$504,239	33.71%
6	EAST	$98,876	$101,867	$140,000	$140,000	$480,743	32.14%
7	NORTH EAST	$120,000	$78,955	$48,878	$44,774	$292,607	19.56%
8	TOTAL SALES	$335,898	$319,884	$420,000	$420,000	$1,495,782	100%
9							
10	CUM SALES	$335,898	$655,782	$1,075,782	$1,495,782		
11							
12	EXPENSES	($252,360)	($298,758)	($350,000)	($365,000)	($1,266,118)	
13							
14	PROFIT	$83,538	$21,126	$70,000	$55,000	$229,664	
15							
16	% of Sales	24.87%	6.60%	16.67%	13.10%	Average	15.31%
17							

Tan(number)

The Tan function returns the tangent of the angle (expressed in radian measure) supplied as an argument to the function. Remember that the tangent is the ratio of the x-coordinate to the y-coordinate on a unit circle. The x-coordinate is 0 for the angles $\pi/2$, $3 * \pi/2$, $5 * \pi/2$, and so on (equivalent to 90 degrees, 270 degrees, 450 degrees, respectively). Consequently, the Tan function returns an error message for those values because division by 0 is not defined.

True( )

The True function takes no arguments, but the parentheses are required. This function is primarily a testing tool for equations containing logical functions. True( ) forces True in a cell where you want the True value. You then can see the effect of True entries on other areas of the spreadsheet.

Type(value)

The Type function checks a cell and returns a number based on the type of cell entry the function finds. This function displays a 1 if the cell contains a number, a 2 if the cell contains text or is blank, a 16 if the cell contains `*Error*`, an 8 if the cell contains N/A. Formulas and cell references are treated as numbers.

In figure 6.22, for example, column C shows the results returned when the Type function encounters the cell contents shown in column B.

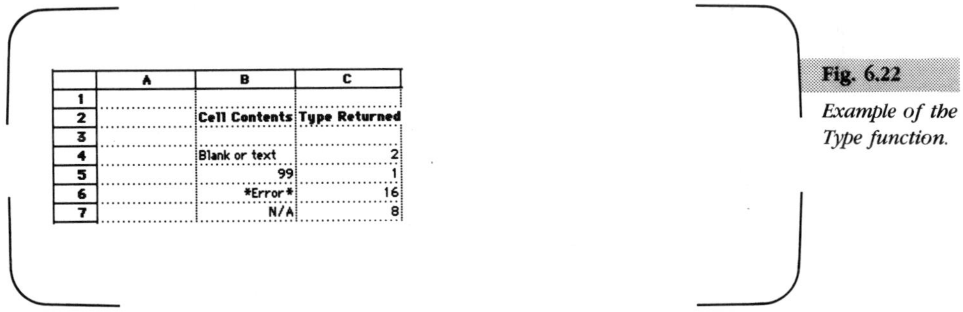

	A	B	C
1			
2		Cell Contents	Type Returned
3			
4		Blank or text	2
5		99	1
6		*Error*	16
7		N/A	8

Fig. 6.22

Example of the Type function.

Var(values-1,values-2,...)

Var returns the variance of numbers in a range. Adding the population average as the last argument yields the population variance. In figure 6.23, A6 illustrates a typical use of the Var function. Cell B6 shows the Var and Average functions used together to get a true population variance by including an average of the entire population. Cells containing text or blanks are ignored.

Fig. 6.23

Using the Var and Average functions.

	A	B	C	D
1	12	12		
2	5	5		
3	18	18		
4	20	20		
5	2	2		
6	61.8	49.44		
7				
8				
9				
10				
11				
12				
13				
14				
15				
16				
17				

	A	B	C	D
1	12	12		
2	5	5		
3	18	18		
4	20	20		
5	2	2		
6	=Var(A1:A5)	=Var(B1:B5,Average(B1:B5))		
7				
8				
9				
10				
11				
12				
13				
14				
15				
16				
17				

VLookup(lookup-number, compare-range,index-number)

The VLookup function examines the first column in a range you define (the *compare-range*). Once VLookup finds the largest value in a row that is less than or equal to the *lookup-number*, the function returns the value in the row that is *index-number* of columns to the right or left of the leftmost column in *compare-range*.

In figure 6.24, Works went down to row 4 (because of the *lookup-number*, 4). At row 4, the VLookup moved right to the third column because of the *index-number* of 3 supplied in the entry bar. The range used was A1 to D6. Remember that the *lookup-number* and *index-number* can be cell references or equations instead.

NOTE: Values in the *compare-range* must be in ascending order.

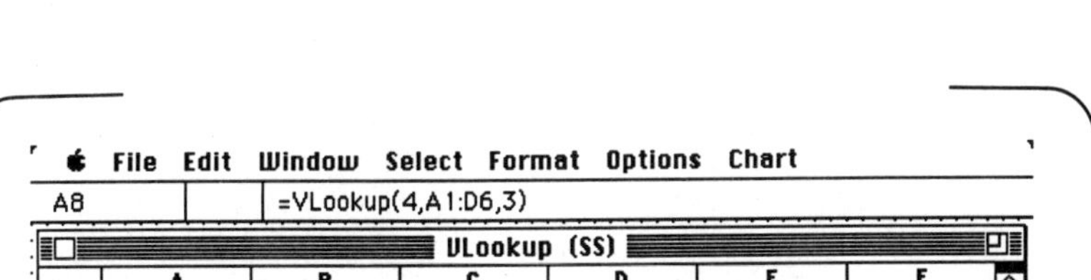

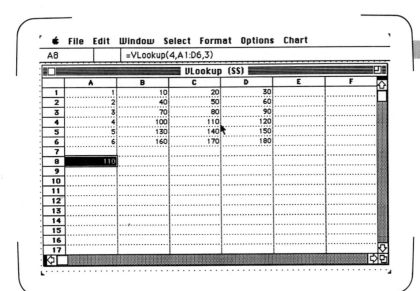

Fig. 6.24

Using the VLookup function.

7

Graphs

Spreadsheets are valuable sources of data about your business. You probably use them many times a day. Sometimes, however, you need a way to compare statistics visually—a way to view information without having to think about what those figures represent. You need a graphic representation of the data in your spreadsheet.

Works enables you to create four types of series graphs—line, bar, stacked bar, and combination—and pie graphs (see figs. 7.1, 7.2, 7.3, and 7.4). All these graphs can be developed from your spreadsheets.

This chapter contains instructions for creating series and pie graphs from the data in your spreadsheets. You find out how to define a graph and how to specify data. You learn about the options for graphs, such as horizontal and vertical titles and grids. The discussions also tell you how to plot and print your graphs; how to save graph definitions with your spreadsheets; and how to duplicate, modify, and erase graph definitions. You also learn about ways of finding errors in your graphs. Finally, a Quick Start is included so that you can have practical experience working with graphs.

Is It a Chart or a Graph or a Plot?

One person's chart is another's graph, or so it seems. In the authors' guidelines provided by the publishers of this book, authors are encouraged to use the term *graph*, rather than *chart*, because charts are lists of things, like best-selling records, whereas graphs are—you know—pictures.

Microsoft and many other producers in the computer industry, however, have taken to calling graphs charts—not only in manuals but on screens

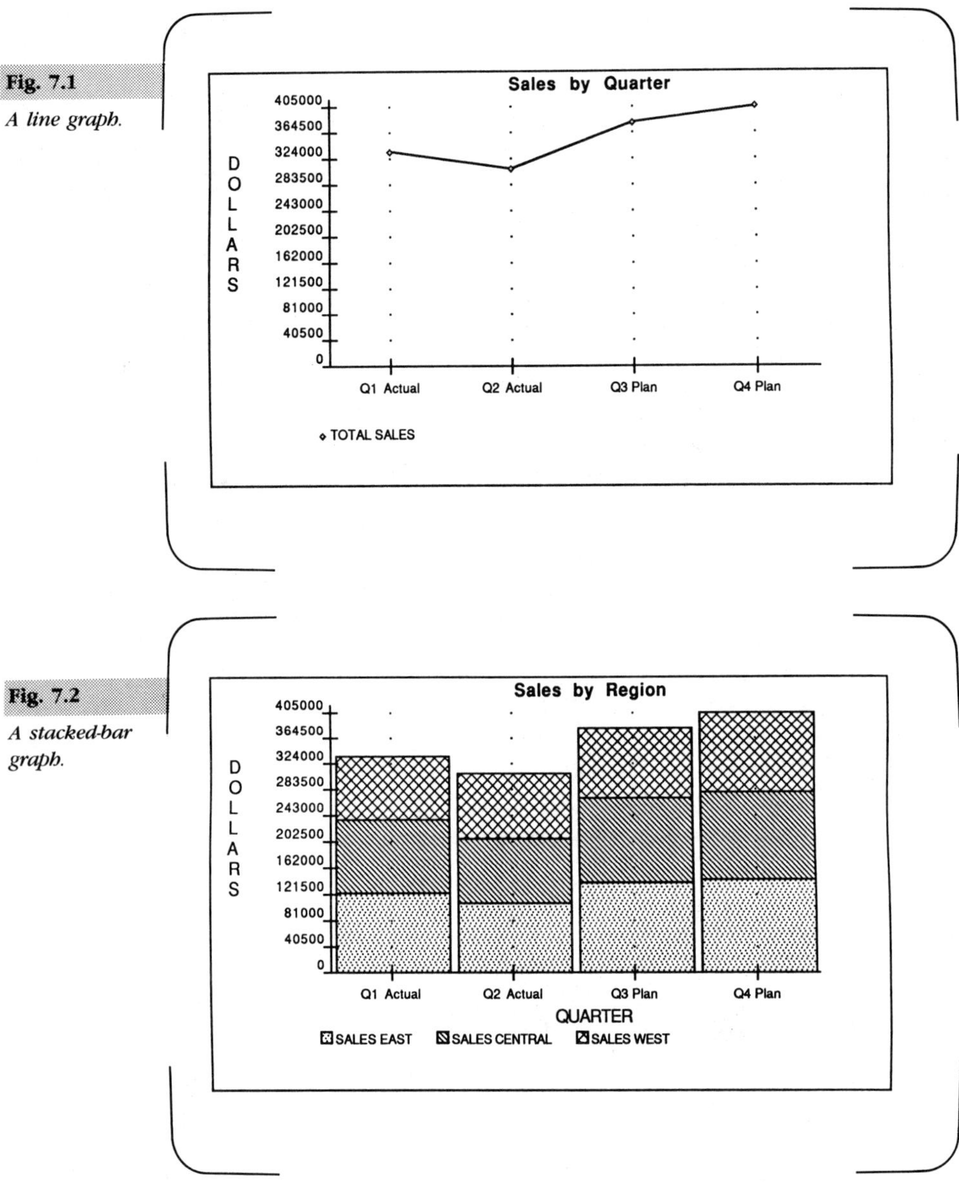

Fig. 7.1

A line graph.

Fig. 7.2

A stacked-bar graph.

as well. For example, the Works menu for creating graphs is called the Chart menu, and the dialog boxes refer regularly to charts. Sometimes Microsoft also calls charts (I mean graphs) *plots*. Rather than add to the confusion, this book uses the term *graph* except in commands and names of screens and dialog boxes.

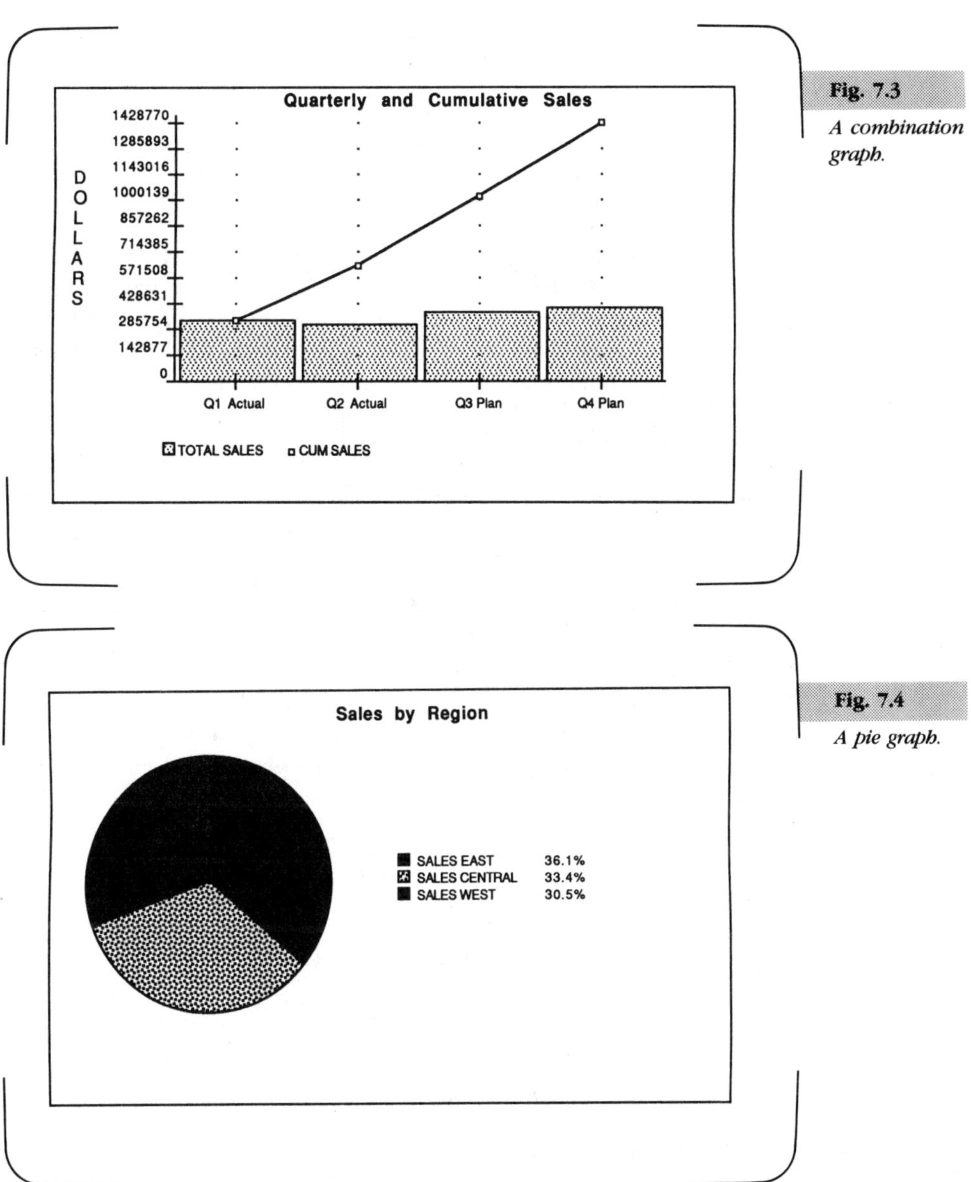

Fig. 7.3
A combination graph.

Fig. 7.4
A pie graph.

Learning Basic Graphing Concepts

To generate Works graphs, you use data from your spreadsheets. You start by creating graph definitions, which tell Works the data to use from your spreadsheet and the location of that data. When defining a graph, you also can specify optional graph titles, scale titles, and the scale itself. You can make other style decisions as well.

Once you have created a graph definition, Works saves it automatically, so you don't need to reenter it. You can save up to eight different definitions per spreadsheet, so you can have as many as eight different graphs for one spreadsheet.

Works automatically assigns sequentially numbered definition names. Using a separate command (which is described in a following section), you can change these sequential definition names to make them more meaningful. Moreover, you easily can delete unwanted definitions to make room for new ones.

You can display graphs—a capability that Microsoft calls *plotting*. You also can print graphs by using the Print Window command on the File menu. And you can include graphs in other documents (as pictures) by using the Mac's familiar cut-and-paste techniques.

Creating Series Graphs

With Works, you can create several different types of graphs. You can create series graphs, which display progressive relationships among data—changes in income over time, for example. Series graphs are divided into line graphs, bar graphs, stacked-bar graphs, and combinations. You also can create pie graphs, which are used to show the relationships between the parts and the whole.

Works' graphing feature is quite flexible. You can do most of the steps in any order:

1. Open a spreadsheet (always the first step).
2. Choose New Series Chart on the Chart menu.
3. Select the desired type of series chart (line, bar, and so on).
4. Define the range(s) to be plotted.
5. Enter titles (optional).
6. Change scale type (optional).
7. Define minimum and maximum scales (optional).
8. Make style decisions—grid, no grid, and so on (optional).
9. Plot the graph (on-screen).
10. Print the graph.

To illustrate this procedure, the Quarterly spreadsheet developed in Chapter 5 is used. With that spreadsheet window open, you choose New Series Chart from the spreadsheet Chart menu (see fig. 7.5). The chart definition dialog box then appears, as shown in figure 7.6. Notice that Works has assigned a name to this new definition. The program abbreviates the spreadsheet name and adds *Chart* and a sequential number from 1 to 8.

Moving around the Chart Definition Dialog Box

To move around the chart definition dialog box, you click the screen buttons and navigate among the entry boxes by using the *tab* key. When text entries are required, you use the word-processing techniques you've already learned (see Chapters 2 through 4). Works saves your definitions and plots your graphs when you press the *return* key.

NOTE: Some options in the dialog box are applicable only to selected graph types or are for use with other option choices. If a choice is dimmed, it is unavailable.

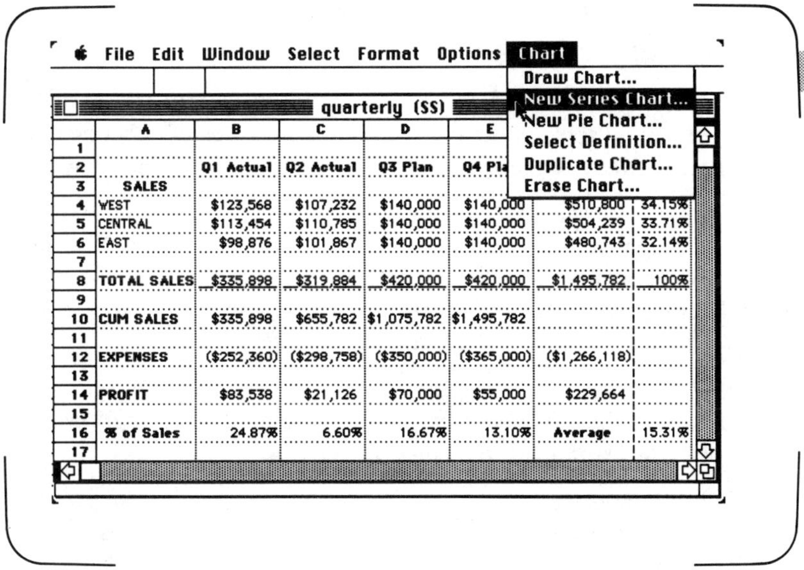

Fig. 7.5

Quarterly spreadsheet window opened and New Series Chart option selected.

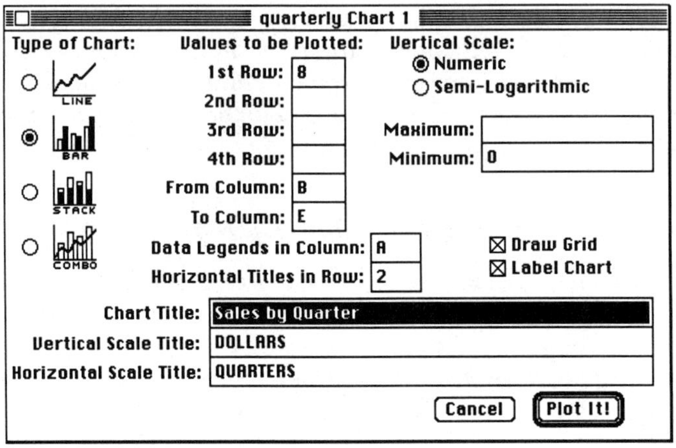

Fig. 7.6

The chart definition dialog box.

Specifying the Graph Type and Defining the Values To Be Graphed

To specify the type of series graph you want to create, click on the button next to the appropriate illustration. You can select only one type of graph at a time. The example in figure 7.6 shows the bar graph selected.

In a series graph, you can plot from one to four rows of data. You also can control the number of columns plotted. To define these ranges, enter spreadsheet location references in the Values to be Plotted boxes. Works even proposes some row and column choices for you.

In figure 7.6, the definition specifies that Works should graph sales dollars by quarter. The 1st Row box contains the number 8, the location of the total sales data from the spreadsheet (fig. 7.5).

You can tell Works that you want to plot the sales data from all four quarters. Enter **B** (the column of the first quarter's sales figures) in the From Column box and **E** (the column of the last quarter) in the To Column box.

Entering Horizontal Titles

Just as you label columns on a spreadsheet, in a series graph, you can label horizontal points (like the quarters in the example). Works uses spreadsheet column labels for this purpose. If you don't have appropriate labels and you want to plot horizontal row titles, you need to add the labels to your spreadsheet first. The labels should be short and descriptive.

Row 2 in figure 7.5 already contains the horizontal labels. To tell Works to use them, you enter the number **2** in the Horizontal Titles in Row box. Works centers the labels when it plots the graph.

Adding Horizontal and Vertical Scale Titles

In addition to labeling horizontal points, you may want to add a title that describes the purpose or title of the horizontal scale. On a 12-month graph, the title might be *Months*. In the quarterly sales example, the word *QUARTERS* or *1987* is appropriate. Horizontal scale titles are optional, so you don't have to enter anything; but if you do, Works centers the scale title.

When vertical scale titles are appropriate, you can add them too. In the example, *DOLLARS* as the vertical scale title makes the graph easier to understand. You type the entry in the Vertical Scale Title box and tab or click to move on to another option.

Using the Draw Grid and Label Chart Options

With the Draw Grid option in the dialog box, you can place horizontal and vertical reference points on your graph in order to improve readability. Click to turn the option on or off. The default is on (indicated by an x in the box).

If you don't want Works to display any labels, you can use the Label Chart option to turn off labels. For example, you may want to cut and paste the graph to another application, such as MacPaint, and add labels later. Click the Label Chart box to toggle labeling on and off. The default is on.

Plotting Your Graph

After you finish your definition, click the Plot It! button to see the results. You can accomplish the same result by pressing the *return* key. Figure 7.7 shows the sample graph displayed. It shows the dollar volume of sales in two quarters (Q1 and Q2) and the planned sales for the third and fourth quarters. You use the size box in the lower right corner of the window to make the graph smaller, as explained in the following section. As with all Works windows, you click in the close box at the top left of the screen to close the window.

Fig. 7.7

The displayed graph.

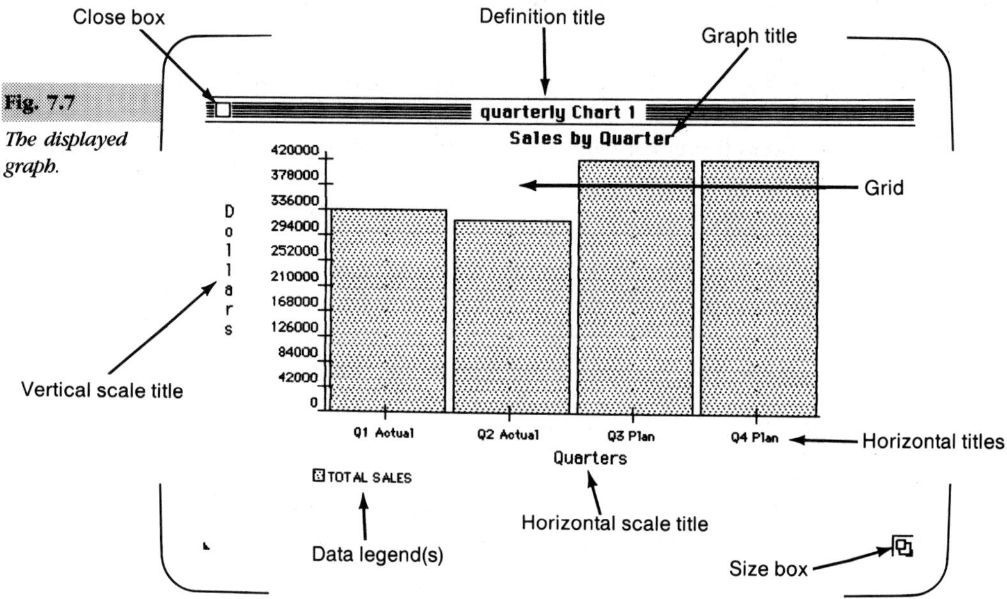

NOTE: Works assigns sequentially numbered definition names, so the names for various definitions on a spreadsheet all look alike. Before you choose Plot It!, you should get in the habit of noting the number that Works assigns at the end of your definition name. Then, later, you can find the definition you want without having to view all definitions.

Printing Your Graph

The process of printing graphs differs slightly from most other Works printing procedures. With the graph on the screen, you choose Print Window from the File menu. Because Print Window does not display a dialog box, you can't make any page setup decisions when printing graph windows. The graph does, however, reflect elements such as window size, grid options, and other characteristics seen on-screen. For example, to print a small copy of a graph, you simply drag the graph window to a smaller size.

Moving, Resizing, and Closing Graph Windows

You can move and resize graph windows just as you do other types of windows. You drag windows by their title bars. Choose the appropriate window size from the Window menu, or drag the window to its new size by using the size box in the lower right corner. If you are using a big screen, you may accidentally make a graph so big that it won't fit on the printed page. Works truncates your graph without warning.

You can copy or cut Works graphs to the Clipboard or Scrapbook. Once there, they can be pasted into word-processing documents or used with applications such as MacPaint. See Chapter 1 or consult your Macintosh manual for specific instructions for using the cut, copy, paste, and related features.

To return to your spreadsheet from the graph window, click the close box in the upper left corner of the graph window. Works then saves the existing definition.

Viewing a Graph and Spreadsheet Together

You can see the effect of spreadsheet changes on your graph almost immediately if you display both the spreadsheet and graph windows simultaneously (see fig. 7.8). Here's what you do:

1. Display your graph.
2. Choose Small Window on the Window menu.
3. Using the size box, drag the graph to an even smaller size if you like.
4. Activate the spreadsheet and make that window smaller if you like.
5. Rearrange the windows to your liking.
6. Change spreadsheet data and watch the graph results.

Figure 7.8 shows two views of a spreadsheet and graph on the same screen. Note the differences between the top and bottom views. In the bottom view, figures in column E (Q4) have been changed, producing corresponding differences in the line on the graph.

Fig. 7.8

Viewing changes in your graph as you alter spreadsheet contents.

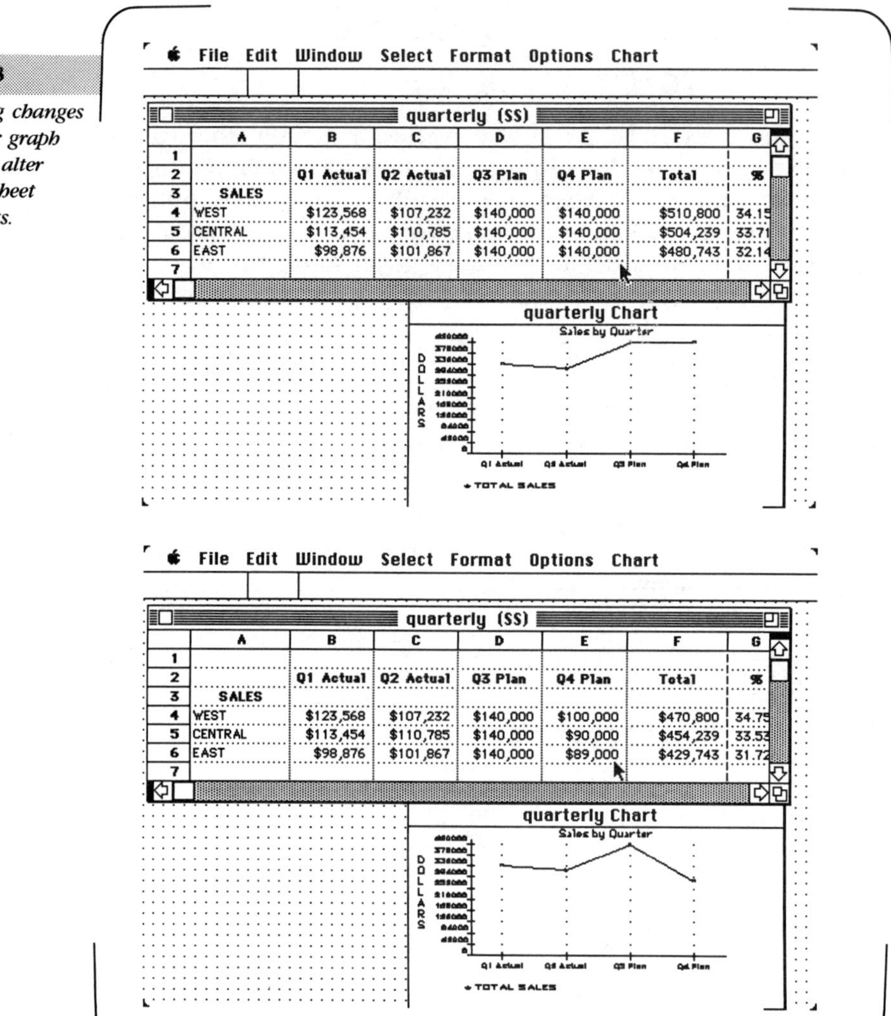

Modifying a Graph Definition

After viewing a graph, you may want to change the design. Works saves new definitions automatically, so you have only to request the right definition and then modify it. The procedure is the following:

1. Choose Select Definition on the Chart menu (see fig. 7.9).
2. Double-click on the definition of your choice.

3. Make your changes.
4. Replot the graph (Works saves your changes).

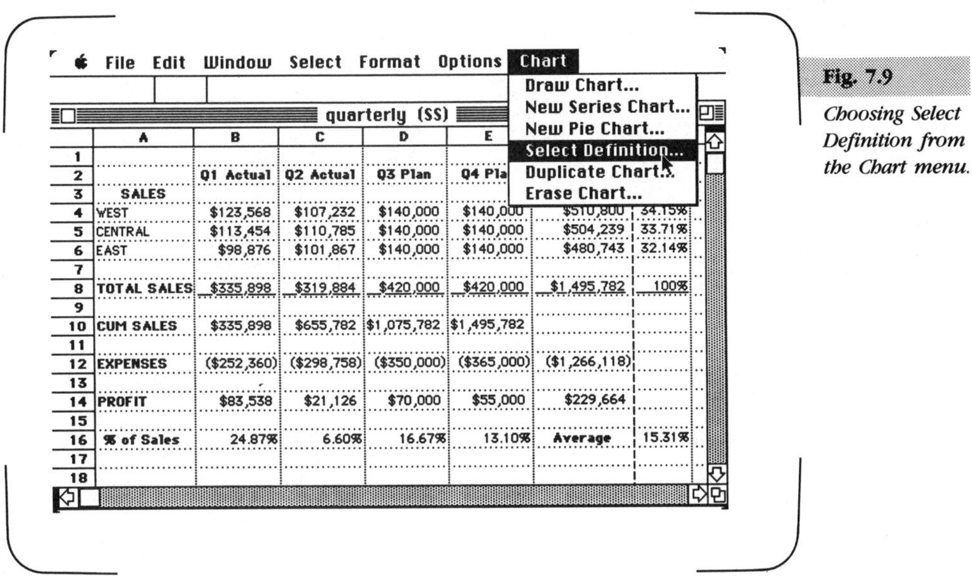

Fig. 7.9
Choosing Select Definition from the Chart menu.

For example, in figures 7.10, 7.11, and 7.12, changing one definition option turned a line graph into a bar graph. Figure 7.10 shows the original line graph. To display the chart definition dialog box, you choose Select Definition from the Chart menu. Then choose BAR as the chart type (see fig. 7.11). You click Plot It! to see the new bar graph (see fig. 7.12).

Here's a shortcut for modifying graph definitions. When a graph is on the screen, you can get to the graph's definition quickly by double-clicking anywhere on the graph. This procedure is a quick way to test new graph design options because you can see the results before making permanent choices.

Saving Graph Definitions without Plotting

If you click on the graph definition's close box, Works saves your definition and returns you to the spreadsheet. No plot appears.

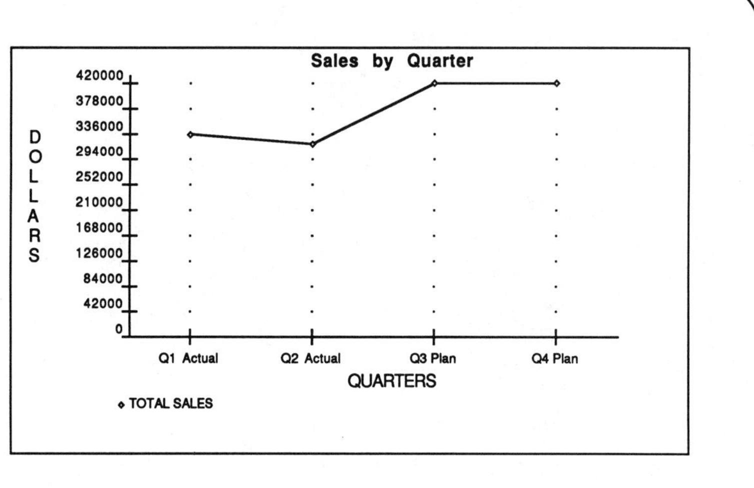

Fig. 7.10

The original line graph.

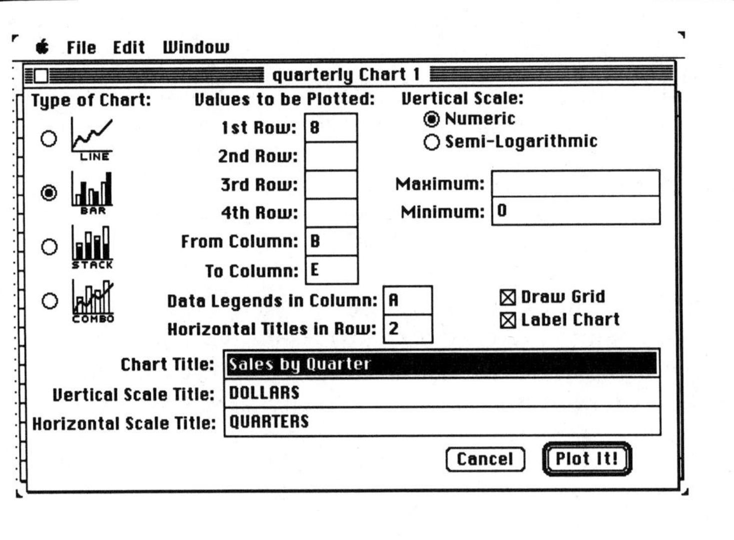

Fig. 7.11

Choosing BAR in the chart definition dialog box.

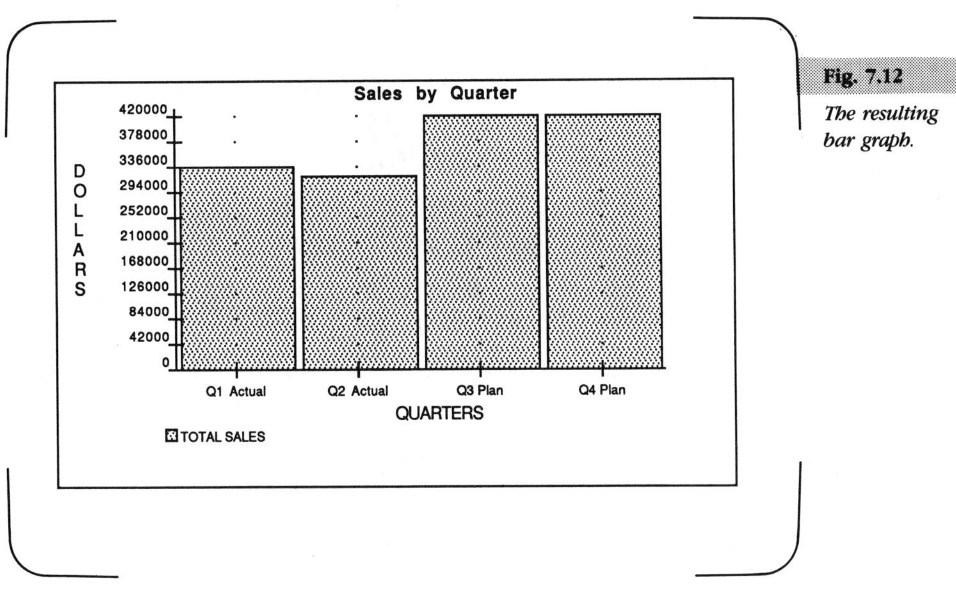

Fig. 7.12

The resulting bar graph.

Using Existing Graph Definitions

If you have defined more than one graph for the current spreadsheet, Works displays the definition names when you choose the Select Definition option on the Chart menu. Works displays a list of your chart definitions (see fig. 7.13).

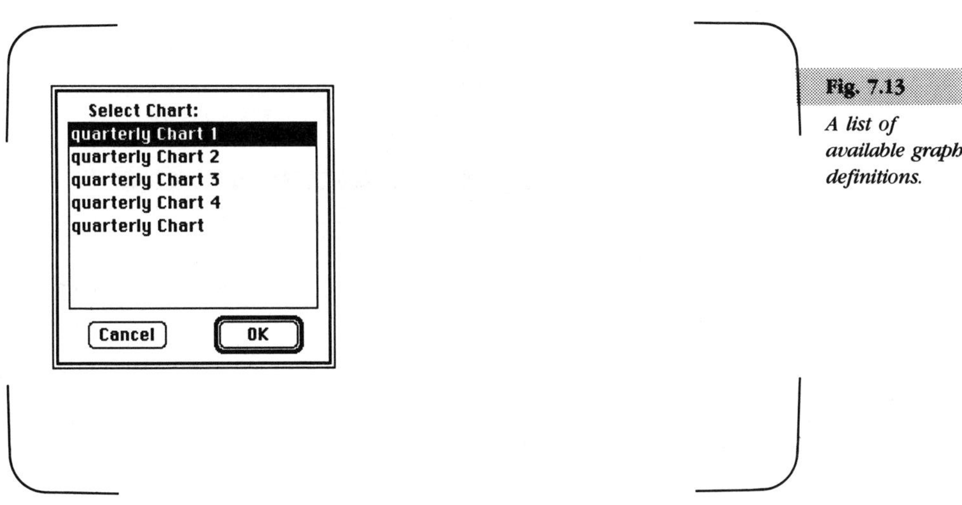

Fig. 7.13

A list of available graph definitions.

Double-click on the desired title to display the definition. You then can either modify the definition or click Plot It! to see the results. Pressing the *return* key is another way to execute the Plot It! command.

Renaming Graph Definitions

To avoid confusion, you may want to assign more meaningful names to your favorite graph definitions. Here's how:

1. Display the chart definition dialog box by choosing Select Definition or clicking on the graph window.
2. Pull down the Edit menu and select Change Chart Name (see fig. 7.14).
3. Type a new name in the Enter Chart Name box (see fig. 7.15).
4. Either press **return** or click Plot It!

NOTE: The Change Chart Name choice is available only when you have an active chart definition dialog box on your screen.

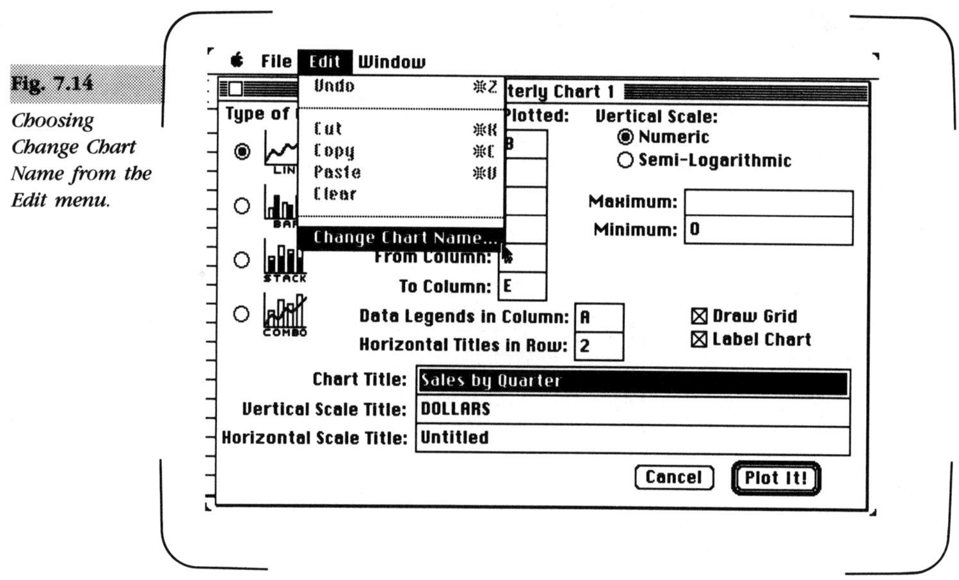

Fig. 7.14

Choosing Change Chart Name from the Edit menu.

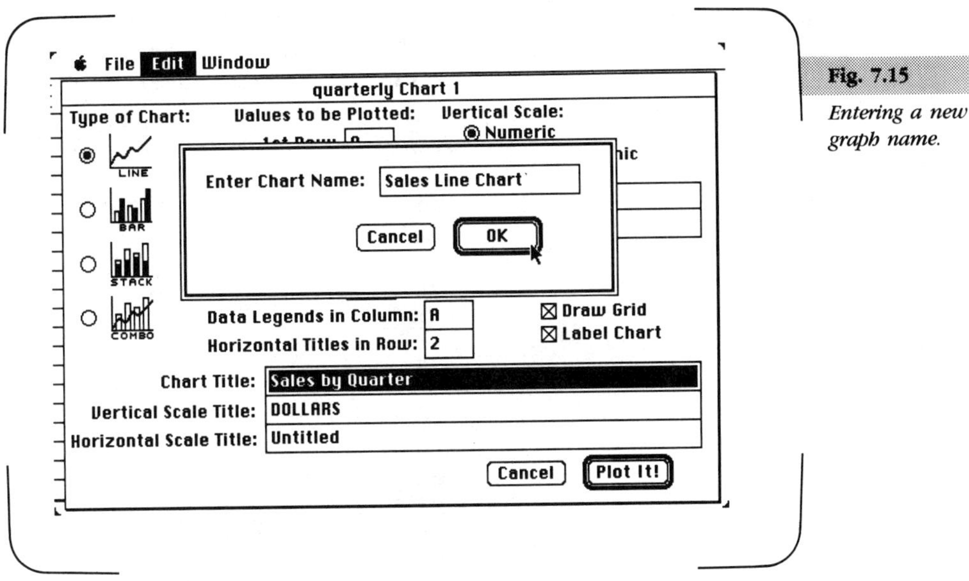

Fig. 7.15

Entering a new graph name.

Using Numeric Vertical Scales

Usually, Works automatically scales graphs for you, taking into consideration the graph's smallest and largest numbers. When necessary, Works creates scales that include negative numbers and automatically uses scientific notation.

The default vertical scale is ten units per increment—what Microsoft calls *numeric vertical scaling*. You may want to experiment with different sales values on your spreadsheet and watch Works adjust the graph's scale for you.

To determine the top of the scale, Works uses the largest number in the graph. Works then divides that number by ten to create the increments. Therefore, every time you change the largest number in your graph, the scale is likely to change. If this arrangement bothers you, you can define the upper and lower vertical scales.

The chart definition dialog box lets you specify the maximum and minimum numbers that appear on your vertical scale. Setting your own scale overrides Works' automatic scaling feature and sometimes improves the graph's appearance, unless your scales are too small to contain the data. For example, if you make the maximum scale 10,000 and try to plot a value of 15,000, Works overrides your maximum scale. In such a case, Works scales automatically (without warning you).

Sometimes, when displaying a range of numbers that contain very big and very small numbers, you may find a semilogarithmic scale useful. Choose the Semi-Logarithmic option in the chart definition dialog box. Semilogarithmic scales are not uniform throughout (see fig. 7.16). They are used to display very large and very small numbers on the same plot.

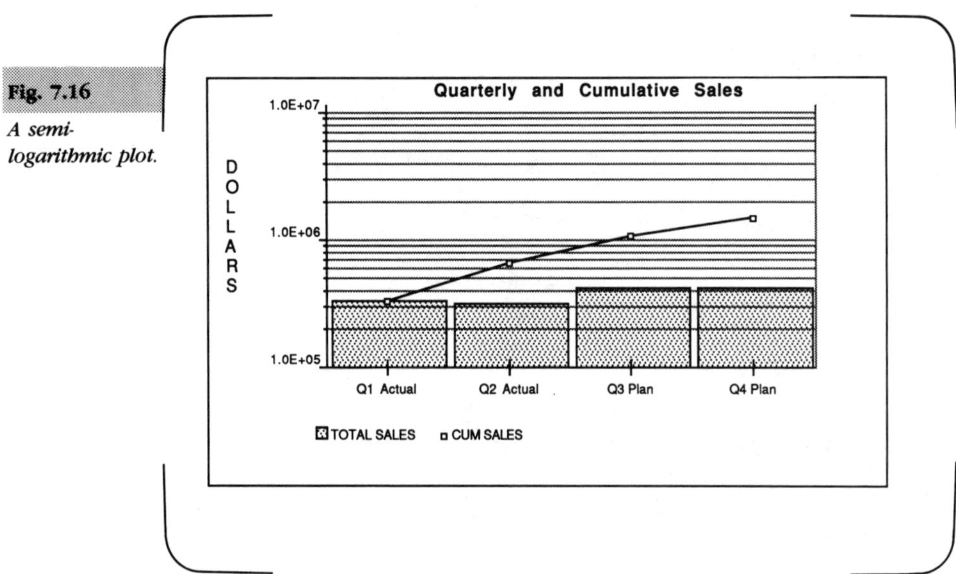

Fig. 7.16
A semi-logarithmic plot.

NOTE: This option distorts the relative appearance of small and large numbers but allows you to see both types on the same graph. All the data must be greater than zero. You can't scale stacked-bar graphs by using the semilogarithmic scale.

Creating More Series Graph Types

Besides simple line and bar graphs, Works easily produces other types of series graphs. You can create a graph consisting of several lines, a graph that combines lines and bars, and even a stacked-bar graph. With this variety, you can pick the style that presents your data most clearly and effectively.

Multiline Graphs

You can plot more than one range on a single graph. For example, suppose that you want to plot cumulative sales in addition to the quarterly sales figures. By defining row 10 from the Quarterly spreadsheet as the 2nd Row on the line chart definition, you add the cumulative sales line (see figs. 7.17 and 7.18).

Works rescales graphs, if necessary, to accommodate the highest value in a multiline plot.

Combination Line and Bar Graphs

You can combine line and bar graphs easily. Works plots the first row as a bar graph and the second as a line graph, as shown in figures 7.19 and 7.20. The COMBO chart type is selected to plot the material in the quarterly spreadsheet (see fig. 7.19). The TOTAL SALES row of the spreadsheet (8B through 8E) is plotted as a bar graph. Row 10 (CUM SALES) becomes a line graph. Notice the locations of the graph titles entered in the dialog box.

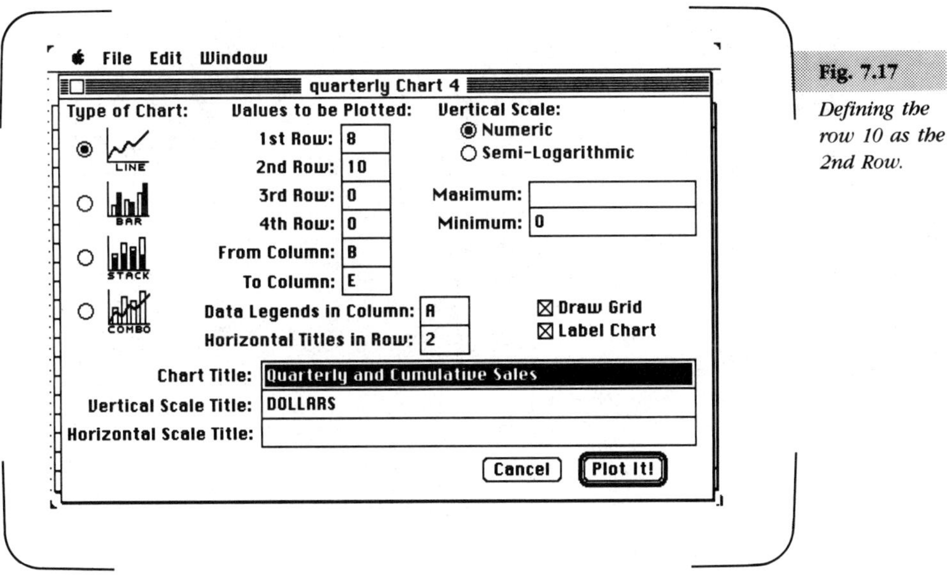

Fig. 7.17

Defining the row 10 as the 2nd Row.

Fig. 7.18

A multiline graph resulting from the definition in figure 7.17.

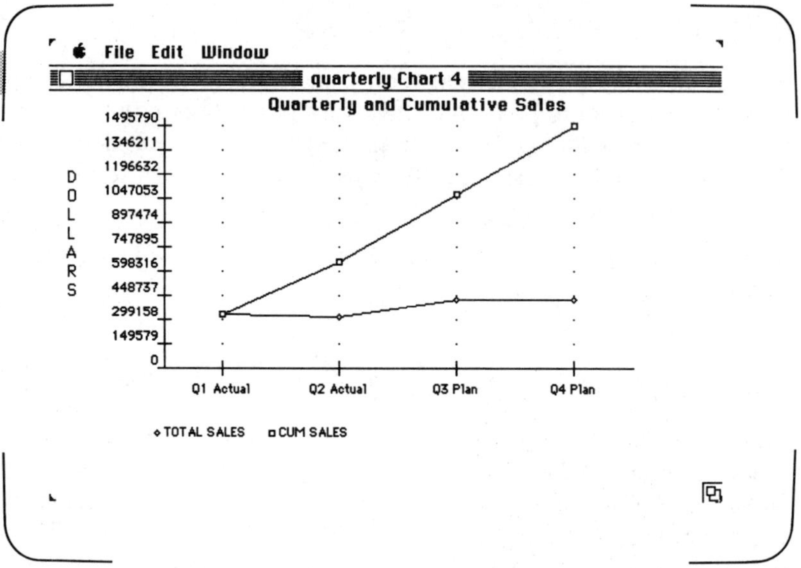

File Edit Window

quarterly Chart 4

Quarterly and Cumulative Sales

DOLLARS

1495790
1346211
1196632
1047053
897474
747895
598316
448737
299158
149579
0

Q1 Actual Q2 Actual Q3 Plan Q4 Plan

◇TOTAL SALES □CUM SALES

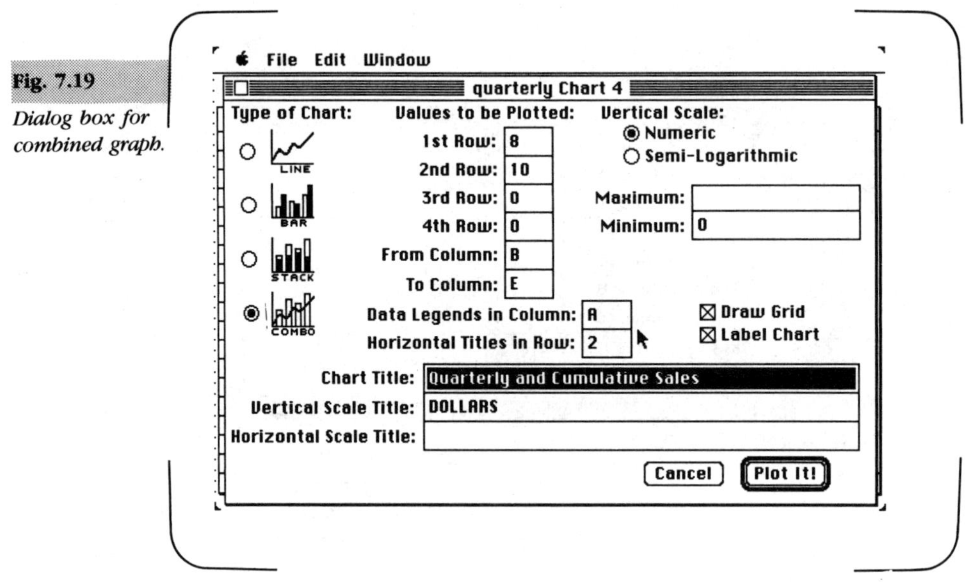

Fig. 7.19

Dialog box for combined graph.

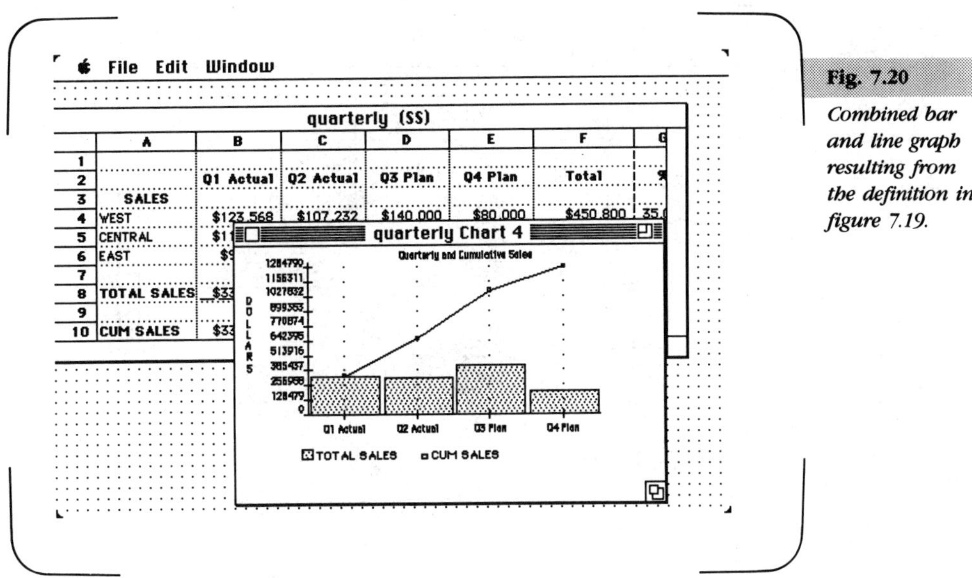

Fig. 7.20

Combined bar and line graph resulting from the definition in figure 7.19.

Stacked-Bar Graphs

Stacked-bar graphs show the portions that make up the whole of a bar. For example, figure 7.21 shows the definition for a graph illustrating the quarterly contribution made by each region and the quarterly totals; figure 7.22 shows the resulting graph.

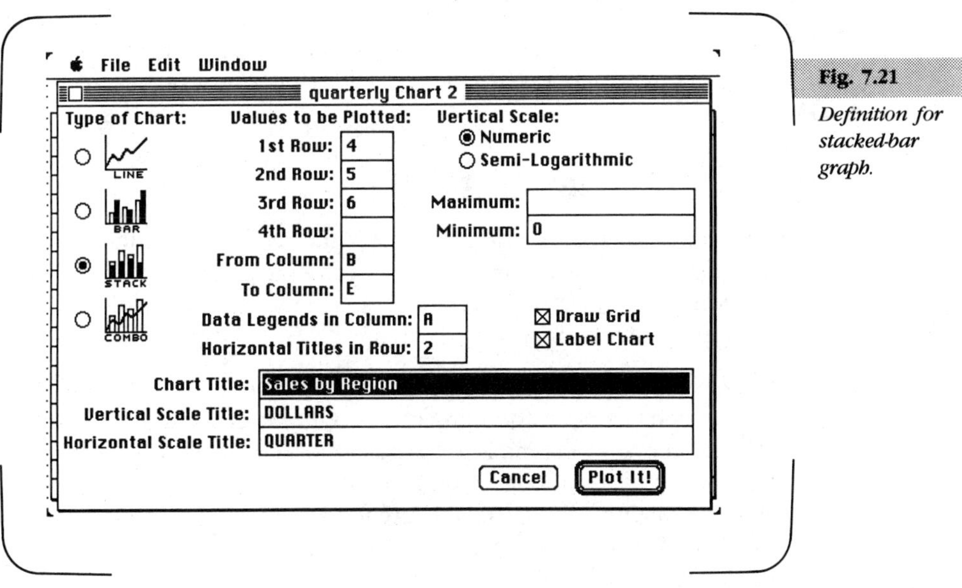

Fig. 7.21

Definition for stacked-bar graph.

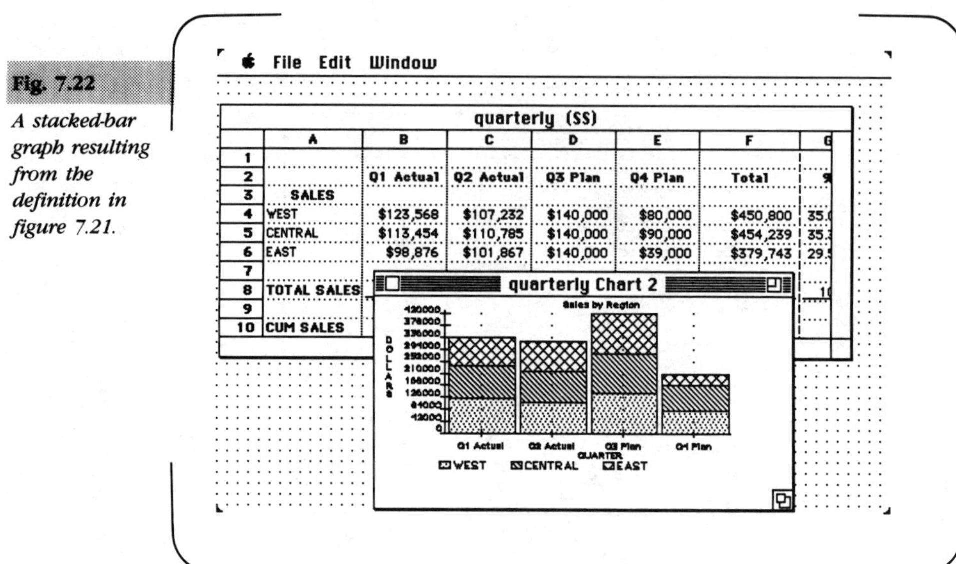

Fig. 7.22

A stacked-bar graph resulting from the definition in figure 7.21.

In this graph, each region's sales figures are graphed separately, and the combined regional figures are stacked for each quarter. This stacking is accomplished by making spreadsheet row 4 (WEST) the first row to be plotted. It becomes the bottom segment of each bar. Row 5 on the spreadsheet (CENTRAL) is next in the stack, and the EAST (row 6) is on top. If the spreadsheet had included a fourth region, its row number could have been entered in the 4th Row dialog box.

You can plot up to four portions (segments) per bar this way. Simply enter the row number that corresponds to each portion.

Creating Pie Graphs

Works pie graphs represent percentages and are plotted from columns, rather than rows. For example, you can use a pie graph to compare sales by region in the Quarterly spreadsheet example, as shown in figure 7.24. The graph's definition appears in figure 7.23.

You can have Works compute percentages for you if the cells you want to graph don't contain the percentages. Or you can tell Works to use cells that contain percentages. Because Works rounds to one decimal place when plotting, the spreadsheet percentage and the plot percentage may differ slightly. Notice the difference in percentages shown in the spreadsheet column G (fig. 7.25) and those shown in the graph (fig. 7.24).

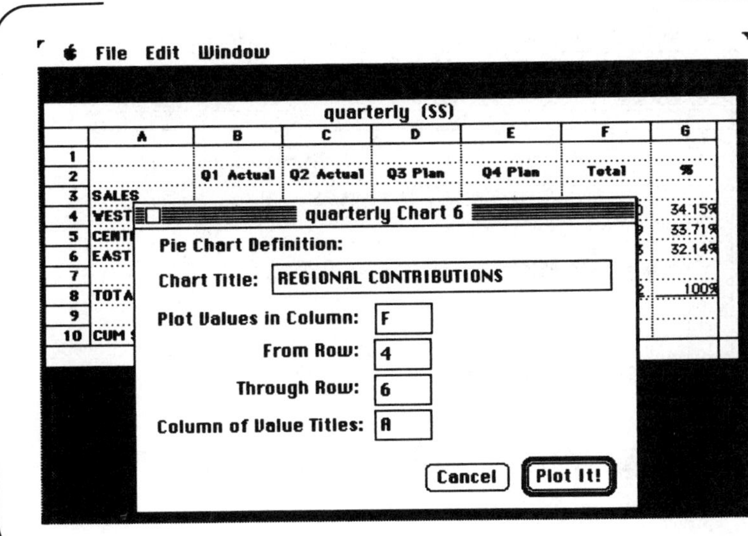

Fig. 7.23

Definition for pie graph.

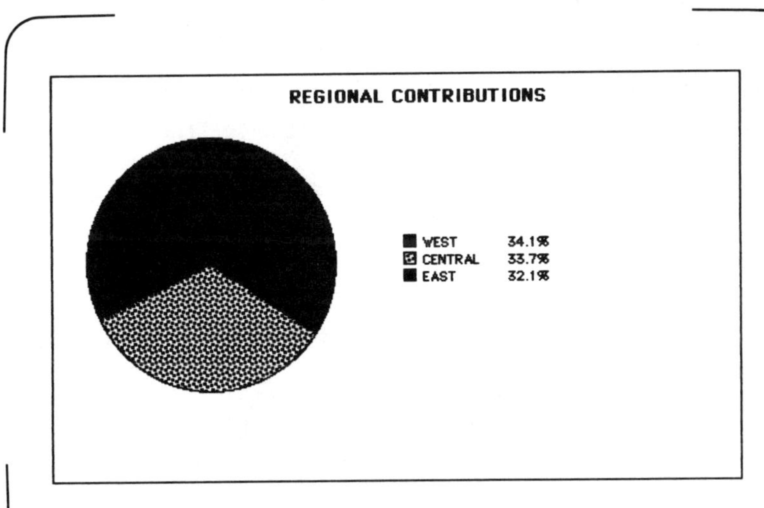

Fig. 7.24

A pie graph resulting from the definition in figure 7.23.

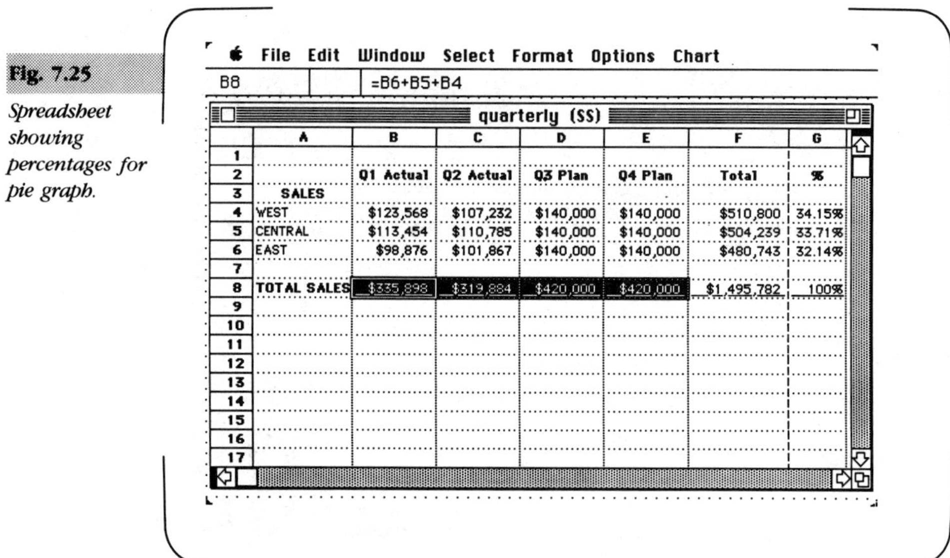

	A	B	C	D	E	F	G
1							
2		Q1 Actual	Q2 Actual	Q3 Plan	Q4 Plan	Total	%
3	SALES						
4	WEST	$123,568	$107,232	$140,000	$140,000	$510,800	34.15%
5	CENTRAL	$113,454	$110,785	$140,000	$140,000	$504,239	33.71%
6	EAST	$98,876	$101,867	$140,000	$140,000	$480,743	32.14%
7							
8	TOTAL SALES	$335,898	$319,884	$420,000	$420,000	$1,495,782	100%
9							
10							
11							
12							
13							
14							
15							
16							
17							

Fig. 7.25

Spreadsheet showing percentages for pie graph.

You do not define pie graphs from the chart definition dialog box. You choose New Pie Chart from the Chart menu. Works then displays the Pie Chart Definition dialog box. The specific steps are as follows:

1. Open the spreadsheet containing the column to be graphed.
2. Choose New Pie Chart from the Chart menu. The Pie Chart Definition dialog box appears (fig. 7.23).
3. Enter the title in the Chart Title box.
4. Enter the letter of the column to be graphed in the Plot Values in Column box.
5. Enter the first and last rows to be plotted in the From Row and Through Row boxes.
6. In the Column of Value Titles box, enter the letter of the spreadsheet column containing the slice labels to be used in the graph.
7. Click Plot It! or press **return**.

Resize the graph if you wish and try some "what if" figures.

The Transpose Option

As just stated, pie graphs require data in columns, not rows. Suppose that you want to create a pie graph that shows the total year's sales broken into quarters—one slice per quarter.

The Quarterly spreadsheet has quarterly subtotals, but they're in row 8, not in a column. (The same is true for the titles you need for the pie graph. They're in row 2.) You can find some empty room on the spreadsheet and retype the numbers and labels by hand, or you can use the Transpose feature.

Transpose, a special cut-and-paste technique on the spreadsheet's Edit menu, is pretty well hidden. You find Transpose by first copying something to the Clipboard and then choosing Paste with Options from the Edit Menu. That choice reveals a dialog box containing the Transpose choice.

Again, look at figure 7.25. Suppose that you want to transpose the sales numbers in cells B8 through E8. You want to copy these values into cells A10 through A13 (all in the same column) so that you can use the values for a pie graph. Perform the following steps to transpose the numbers:

1. Decide where you want to put the copied data. Make room, if necessary, in cells A10 through A13.
2. Select the cells to copy (B8 through E8).
3. Copy the cells to the Clipboard (press **command-C**).
4. Activate (click on) the cell to receive the first number (A10). *Don't forget this essential step!*
5. Choose Paste with Options from the Edit menu (see fig. 7.26).
6. When the Paste with Options dialog box appears, choose Transpose by clicking to place an *x* in the box (see fig. 7.27). Click OK or press **return**.
7. The numbers are pasted automatically; a copy of B8 appears in A10, C8 in A11, and so on.
8. Repeat these steps to transpose the labels. The results look like figure 7.28.

9. Define or redefine the pie graph so that it uses the columnar data and labels you've just created (see fig. 7.29).

10. Click Plot It!

The resulting pie graph is shown in figure 7.30.

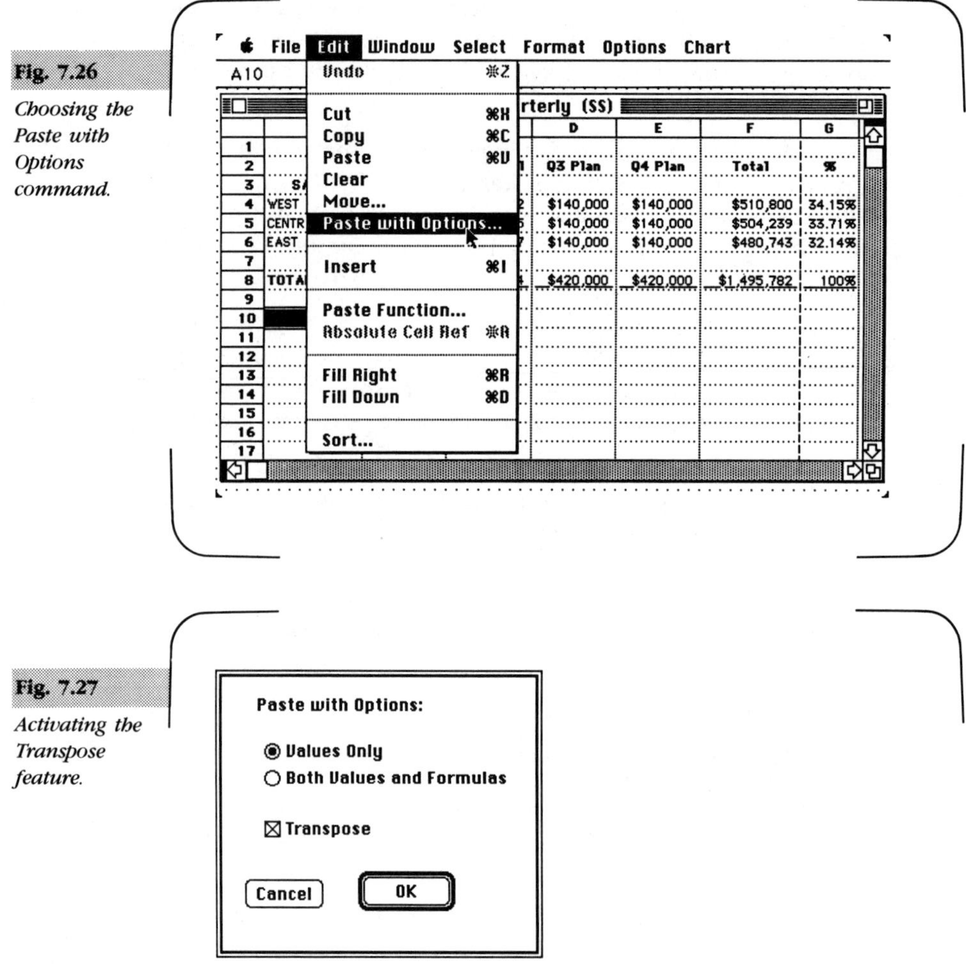

Fig. 7.26

Choosing the Paste with Options command.

Fig. 7.27

Activating the Transpose feature.

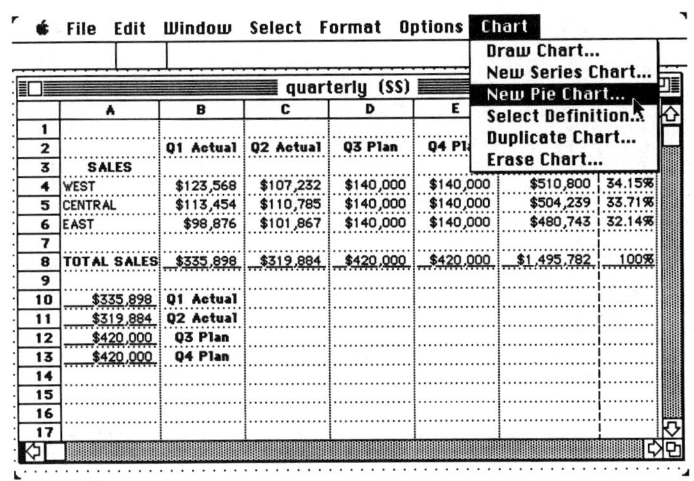

	A	B	C	D	E		
1							
2		Q1 Actual	Q2 Actual	Q3 Plan	Q4 Pl		
3	SALES						
4	WEST	$123,568	$107,232	$140,000	$140,000	$510,800	34.15%
5	CENTRAL	$113,454	$110,785	$140,000	$140,000	$504,239	33.71%
6	EAST	$98,876	$101,867	$140,000	$140,000	$480,743	32.14%
7							
8	TOTAL SALES	$335,898	$319,884	$420,000	$420,000	$1,495,782	100%
9							
10	$335,898	Q1 Actual					
11	$319,884	Q2 Actual					
12	$420,000	Q3 Plan					
13	$420,000	Q4 Plan					
14							
15							
16							
17							

Fig. 7.28

The spreadsheet after transposing rows to columns.

quarterly Chart

Pie Chart Definition:

Chart Title: Quarterly Sales

Plot Values in Column: a

From Row: 10

Through Row: 13

Column of Value Titles: b

Cancel | Plot It!

Fig. 7.29

Pie Chart Definition dialog box.

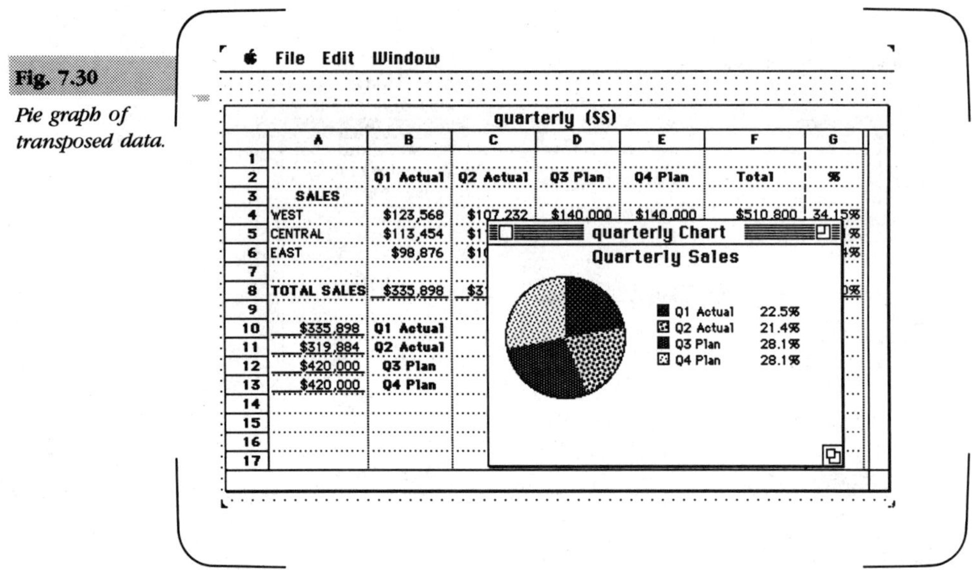

Fig. 7.30

Pie graph of transposed data.

The Problem with Transpose

The Transpose option has one major drawback. If you change the sales data in your spreadsheet after transposing, the transposed numbers *will not* reflect your changes. Neither will the graph because it's based on the unchanging cells. For this reason, I recommend a different approach to setting up pie graphs like this. Forget transposing.

Just as before, set aside an out-of-the way section of the spreadsheet for the columnar data you want plotted. For this discussion, assume that area is the same one used for the transpose trick: cells A10 through A13.

Here's where things get different. Place the simple equation =B8 in cell A10, =C8 in A11, and so on (see fig. 7.31). These simple equations make cell A10 equal to cell B8, A10 equal to C8, and so on, whatever their contents. When cell B8 changes, so does A10.

Now, when a subtotal on row 8 changes, the subtotals in column A (cells A10 through A13) change too. So does your graph.

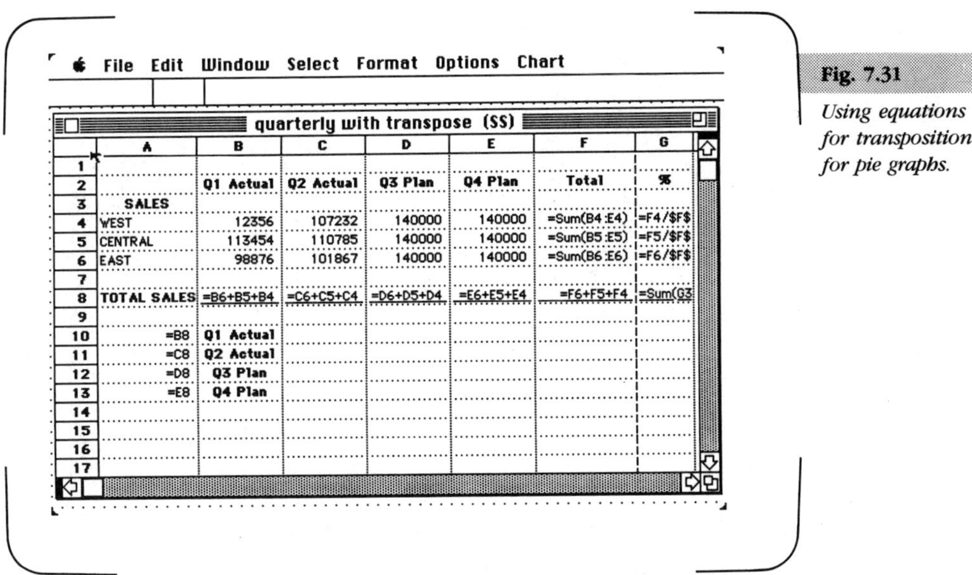

	A	B	C	D	E	F	G
1							
2		Q1 Actual	Q2 Actual	Q3 Plan	Q4 Plan	Total	%
3	SALES						
4	WEST	12356	107232	140000	140000	=Sum(B4:E4)	=F4/F
5	CENTRAL	113454	110785	140000	140000	=Sum(B5:E5)	=F5/F
6	EAST	98876	101867	140000	140000	=Sum(B6:E6)	=F6/F
7							
8	TOTAL SALES	=B6+B5+B4	=C6+C5+C4	=D6+D5+D4	=E6+E5+E4	=F6+F5+F4	=Sum(G3
9							
10	=B8	Q1 Actual					
11	=C8	Q2 Actual					
12	=D8	Q3 Plan					
13	=E8	Q4 Plan					
14							
15							
16							
17							

Fig. 7.31
Using equations for transposition for pie graphs.

Duplicating and Erasing Graph Definitions

To save time when creating similar but not identical graphs, you can duplicate a graph definition and modify it. Here's how:

1. Choose Duplicate Chart from the Chart menu (see fig. 7.32).
2. Select the definition you want to duplicate. Click only once on the graph name (see fig. 7.33).
3. Either click OK or press the **return** key.
4. Works assigns a sequential graph name.
5. Make the changes you want in the chart definitions dialog box.
6. Plot, save, or cancel as usual.

NOTE: Works can store only eight definitions per spreadsheet. If the Duplicate Chart option is dimmed, you must erase unneeded definitions before copying.

Because you can have no more than eight graph definitions for each spreadsheet, you will eventually want to erase unwanted definitions. The steps are

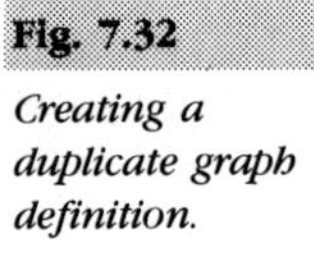

Fig. 7.32

Creating a duplicate graph definition.

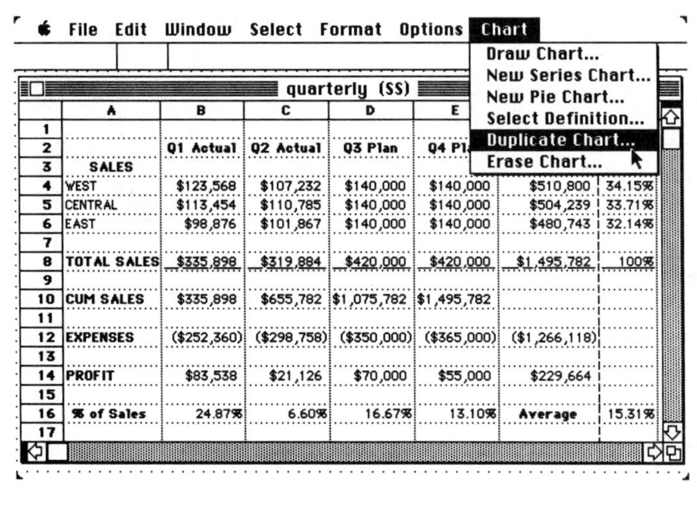

Fig. 7.33

Selecting a definition to be modified.

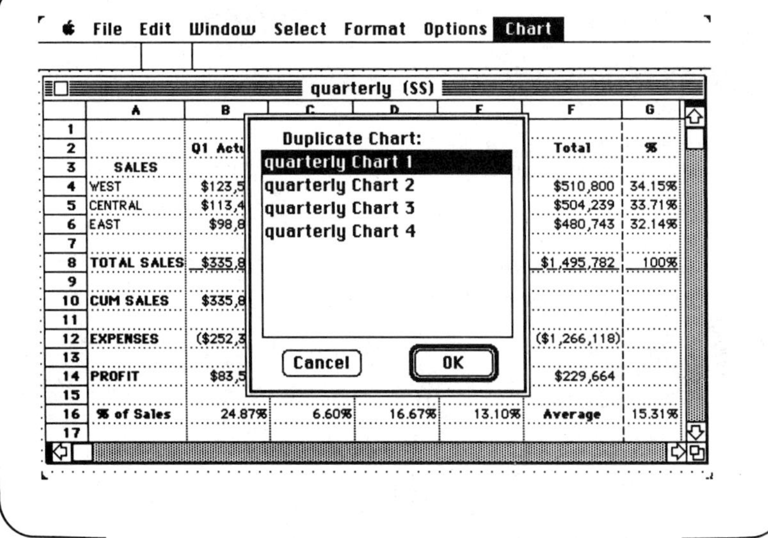

1. Choose Erase Chart from the Chart menu (see fig. 7.34).
2. Double-click on the unwanted graph, or click on a title to select it and then click the OK button (see fig. 7.35).
3. Either click OK or press the **return** key.

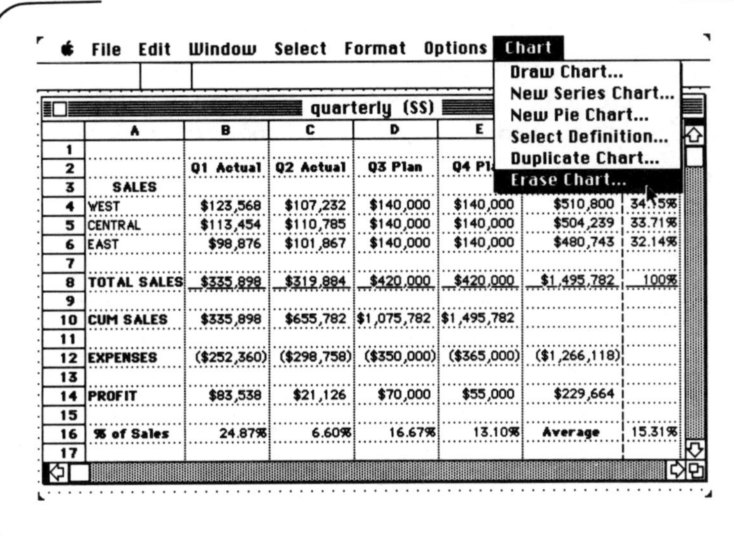

Fig. 7.34

Choosing Erase Chart from the Chart menu.

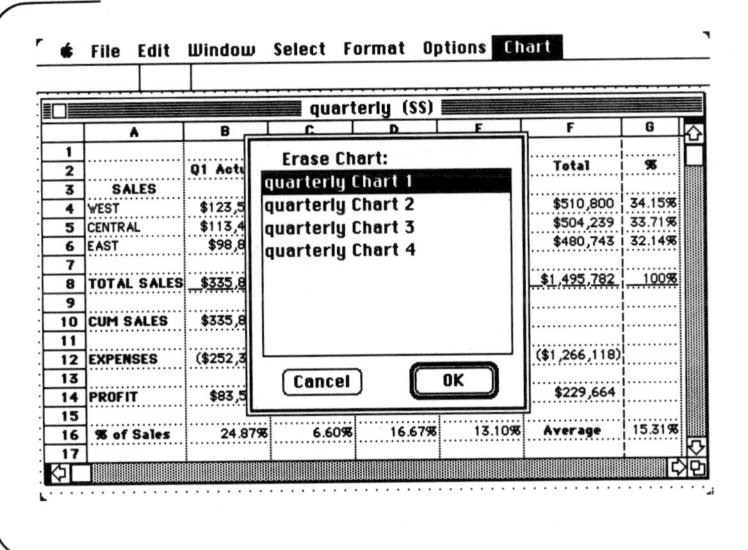

Fig. 7.35

Choosing a graph definition to be erased.

The graph-definition file is erased from your disk, and you can create a new graph definition for that spreadsheet.

CAUTION: Double-clicking is an Erase shortcut. When selecting, be careful that you don't double-click accidentally. If you do erase the wrong definition this way, you can't use the Undo feature (*command*-Z).

Finding Errors in Graphs

Works warns you about most graphing errors. For example, Works displays the warning in figure 7.36 because a pie graph was defined with too many pie slices. Before continuing, you must acknowledge these warnings.

Fig. 7.36

Warning about graphing error.

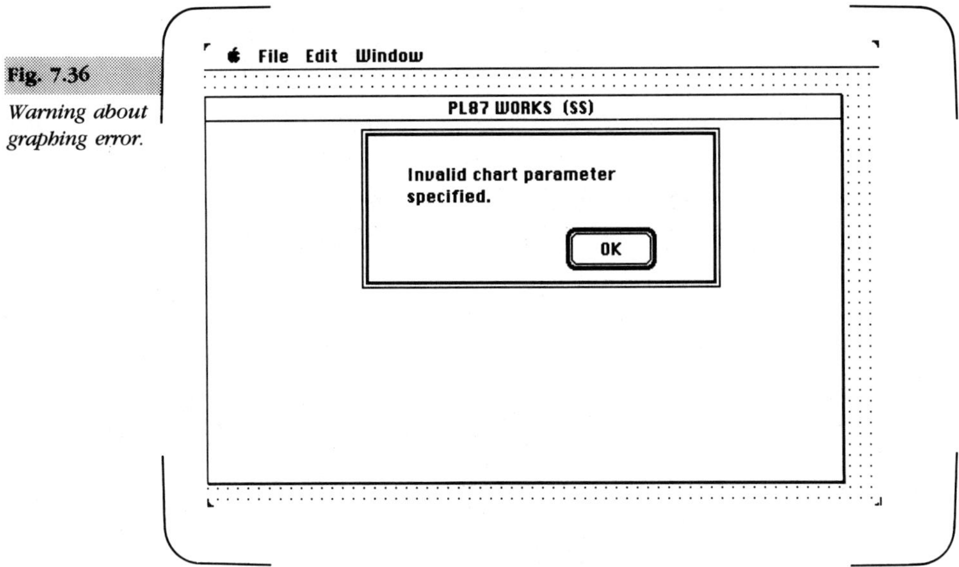

As you become more familiar with the Works graphing features, you will find more and more ways to use these effective, easily produced graphs.

Quick Start: Graphs from Your Spreadsheet

This Quick Start uses the Quarterly spreadsheet that you created in Chapter 5. Because Works graphs always require a spreadsheet as their starting point, you need to use the Quarterly spreadsheet or to create another spreadsheet like Quarterly.

In this Quick Start you learn how to create a simple bar graph based on the Quarterly spreadsheet. You specify the graph titles, definitions, and labels through the chart definition dialog box. Then, you change your graph: you change the name, size, and position of the graph and change the graph type to a line graph. Finally, you create a pie graph from the same spreadsheet.

Your First Series (Bar) Graph

If you don't have the Quarterly spreadsheet on your screen now, open the spreadsheet. Choose the Quarterly spreadsheet from the Open dialog box by double-clicking on the Quarterly file name or by clicking once on Quarterly and then choosing Open from the File menu. Quarterly should look like figure 7.37. Don't worry if you've entered different dollar values, however.

CAUTION: Don't ever press *enter* or *return* until you have made all the necessary changes to the chart definition dialog box. Pressing *enter* or *return* causes Works to plot the graph based on the information at hand, even if the information is wrong or incomplete. Plotting the wrong information produces a graph with erroneous results that can confuse you. If you do press *enter* or *return* or click the Plot It! button by mistake, simply double-click anywhere on the resulting graph to return to the dialog box.

1. With the Quarterly spreadsheet on your desktop, choose New Series Chart from the Chart menu (see fig. 7.38). A chart definition dialog box appears, listing the Works graph options and default settings (see fig. 7.39).

You create your graph titles and definitions in this dialog box (see fig. 7.39). After you work through the rest of the steps, your chart definition dialog box should look like the one shown in figure 7.40.

2. With the chart definition dialog box on your screen, click the BAR button under Type of Chart.

Fig. 7.37

The Quarterly spreadsheet.

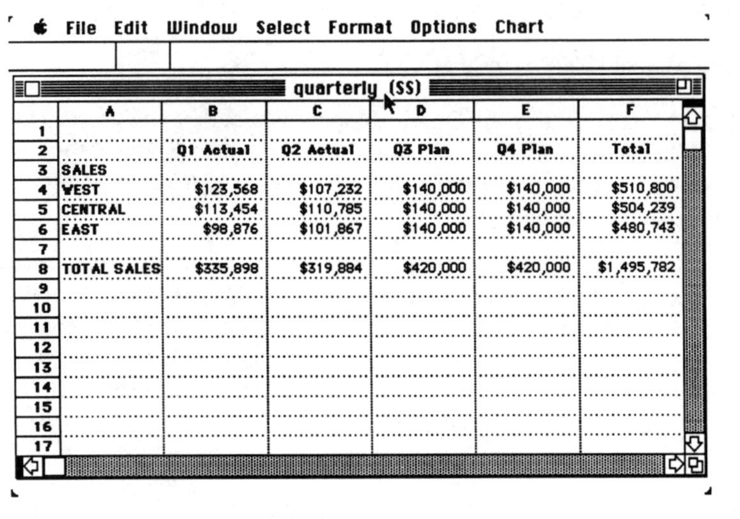

	A	B	C	D	E	F
1						
2		Q1 Actual	Q2 Actual	Q3 Plan	Q4 Plan	Total
3	SALES					
4	WEST	$123,568	$107,232	$140,000	$140,000	$510,800
5	CENTRAL	$113,454	$110,785	$140,000	$140,000	$504,239
6	EAST	$98,876	$101,867	$140,000	$140,000	$480,743
7						
8	TOTAL SALES	$335,898	$319,884	$420,000	$420,000	$1,495,782
9						
10						
11						
12						
13						
14						
15						
16						
17						

Fig. 7.38

Choosing the New Series Chart command.

	A	B	C	D		
1						
2		Q1 Actual	Q2 Actual	Q3 Plan		
3	SALES					
4	WEST	$123,568	$107,232	$140,000	$140,000	$510,800
5	CENTRAL	$113,454	$110,785	$140,000	$140,000	$504,239
6	EAST	$98,876	$101,867	$140,000	$140,000	$480,743
7						
8	TOTAL SALES	$335,898	$319,884	$420,000	$420,000	$1,495,782
9						
10						
11						
12						
13						
14						
15						
16						
17						

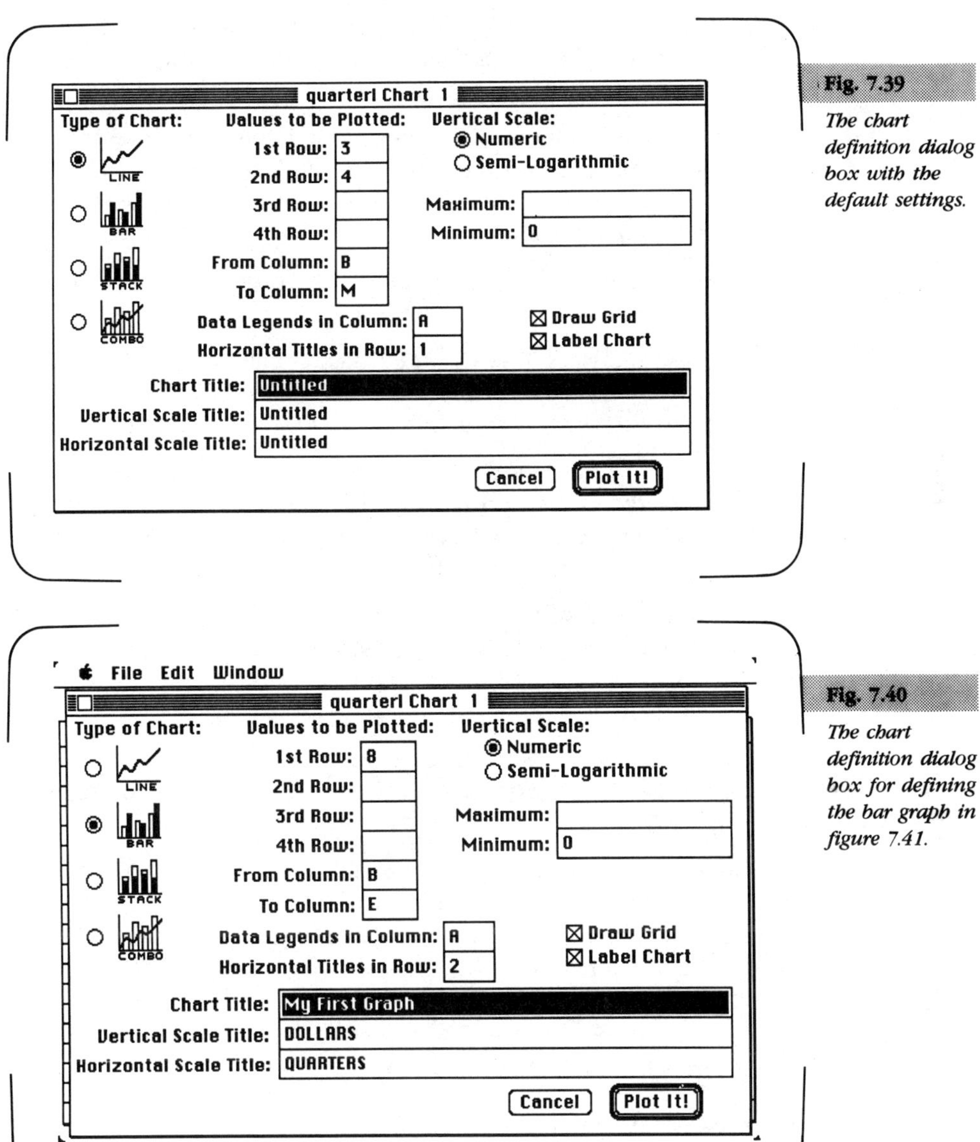

Fig. 7.39

The chart definition dialog box with the default settings.

Fig. 7.40

The chart definition dialog box for defining the bar graph in figure 7.41.

3. Double-click in the 1st Row box. You are going to change the suggested row that Works offers. Enter the number **8** (don't press *enter* or *return*). The *8* corresponds to the TOTAL SALES row on your Quarterly spreadsheet.

4. Double-click on the 2nd Row box containing the number 4. Press **backspace** to eliminate row 4, because you are plotting data from only one spreadsheet row.
5. If the From Column box contains the letter *B*, leave it as is. If not, double-click on the From Column box and type the letter **B**. Do not press *enter* or *return*. If you do, double-click on the resulting incomplete graph to return to the dialog box.
6. Double-click on the To Column letter, probably M, and change it to **E**.
7. To use the label TOTAL SALES from column A of your Quarterly spreadsheet as the data legend, double-click on the box to the right of Data Legends in Column. Type the letter **A** in the box.
8. To use the labels in row 2 of your spreadsheet (Q1 Actual, Q2 Actual, and so on) as labels for the four bars you are about to view, enter **2** in the box next to Horizontal Titles in Row.
9. If you can stand the suspense, double-click on the title boxes and enter **My First Graph** in the Chart Title box, **Dollars** in the Vertical Scale Title box, and **Quarters** in the Horizontal Scale Title box.
10. Now, if you haven't peeked already, click on the Plot It! button, or simply press **return**. Voila! Does the bar graph look like figure 7.41?

The appearance of your bar graph should be similar to the graph in figure 7.41, although the size of the bars can vary if your sales data is different. If the appearance is not similar, compare your chart definition dialog box to figure 7.40, make any necessary changes, and replot the graph.

Changing the Graph Size and Position

With the bar graph on the screen, point to the size box in the lower right corner of the window. With the mouse button held down, drag up and to the left, making the plot smaller. You soon see the spreadsheet underneath. For now, make your plot about the size shown in figure 7.42.

You can make the plot even smaller and move it around. You also can change spreadsheet numbers and watch the graph change.

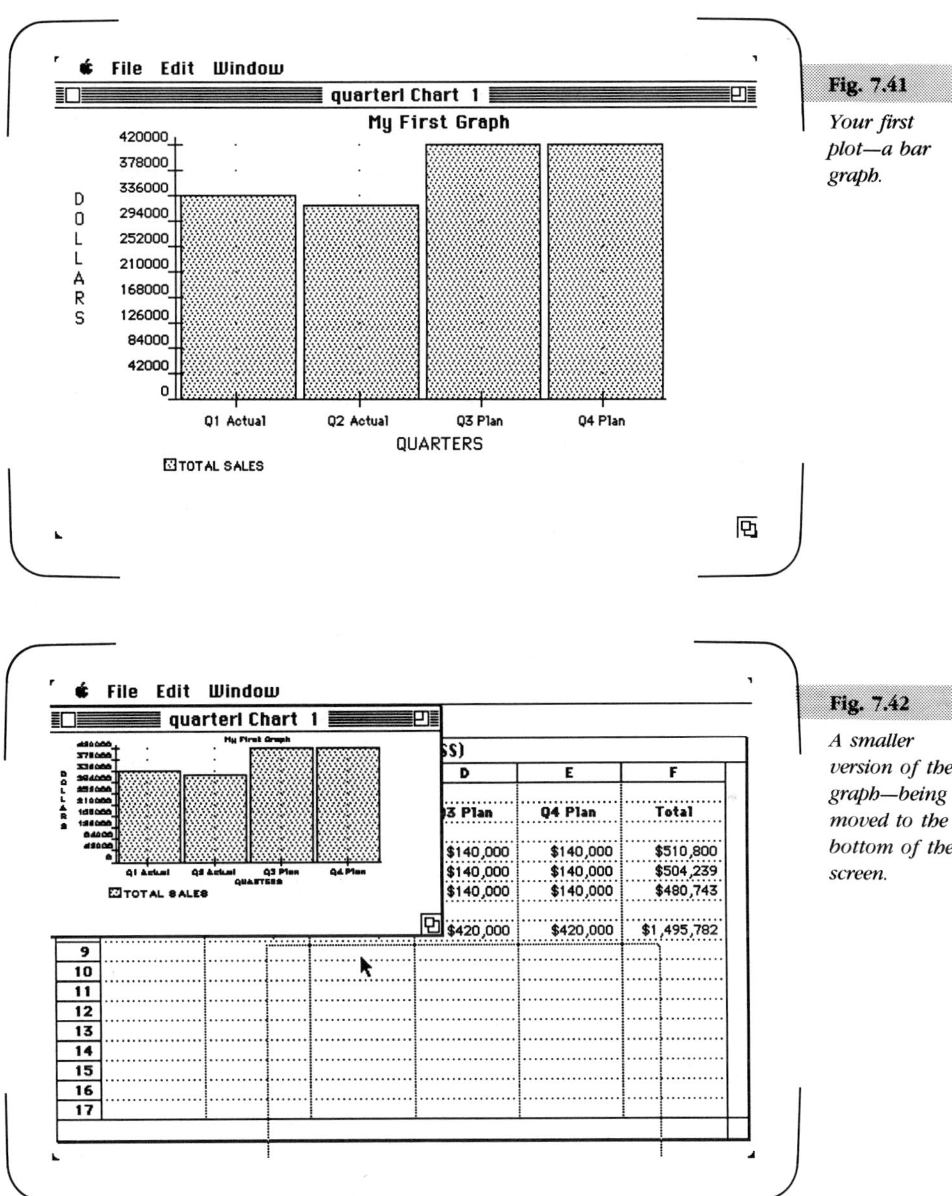

Fig. 7.41

Your first plot—a bar graph.

Fig. 7.42

A smaller version of the graph—being moved to the bottom of the screen.

Try a few changes on your graph.

1. Point to the title bar at the top of the graph and hold down the mouse button.

2. Drag down on the outline of the graph so that the spreadsheet numbers and the bulk of the graph are both visible. When you release the mouse button, the graph moves to the position of the outline.

3. Make the spreadsheet window shorter so that you can see both the spreadsheet and the plot. While holding down the mouse button, drag up from the bottom of the spreadsheet. Your screen now looks like figure 7.43.

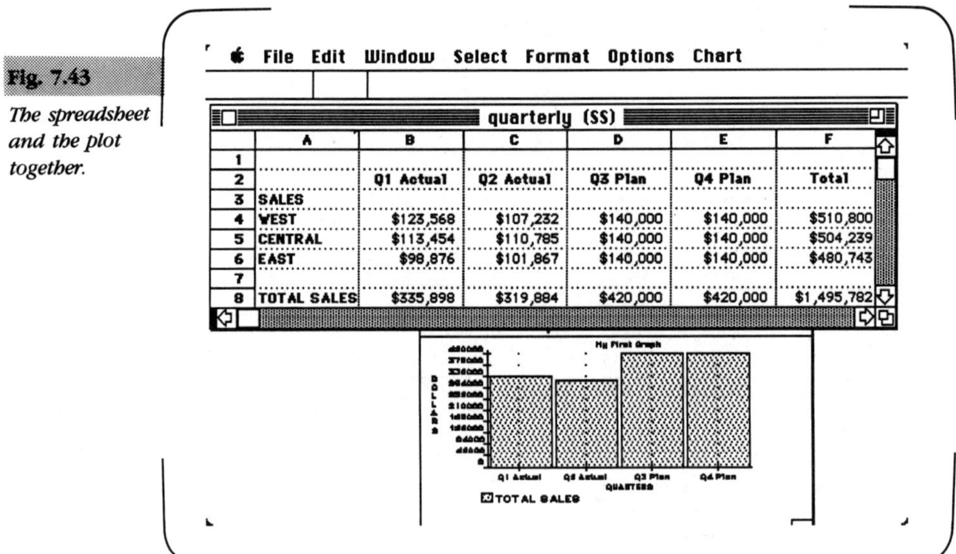

	A	B	C	D	E	F
1						
2		Q1 Actual	Q2 Actual	Q3 Plan	Q4 Plan	Total
3	SALES					
4	WEST	$123,568	$107,232	$140,000	$140,000	$510,800
5	CENTRAL	$113,454	$110,785	$140,000	$140,000	$504,239
6	EAST	$98,876	$101,867	$140,000	$140,000	$480,743
7						
8	TOTAL SALES	$335,898	$319,884	$420,000	$420,000	$1,495,782

Fig. 7.43

The spreadsheet and the plot together.

Clicking on a spreadsheet cell, like B4, makes the spreadsheet the active window, but you can still see the graph. While you make changes in the sales numbers contained in the cells, you see the results of the changes on the graph at the same time. Make some big changes in the numbers in the cells so that the changes are easy to see on the graph (see fig. 7.44).

Changing Chart Type

You can change the bar graph to a line graph with only a few clicks.

1. Double-click anywhere on the graph to return to the chart definition dialog box.

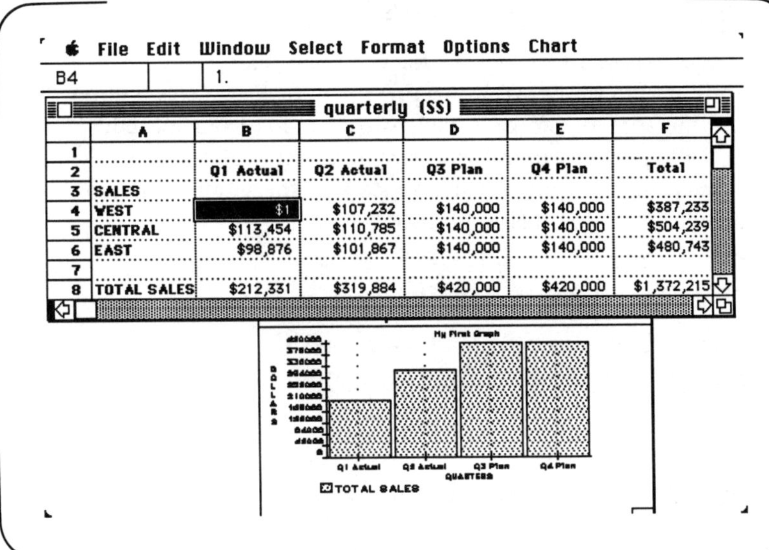

	A	B	C	D	E	F
1						
2		Q1 Actual	Q2 Actual	Q3 Plan	Q4 Plan	Total
3	SALES					
4	WEST	$1	$107,232	$140,000	$140,000	$387,233
5	CENTRAL	$113,454	$110,785	$140,000	$140,000	$504,239
6	EAST	$98,876	$101,867	$140,000	$140,000	$480,743
7						
8	TOTAL SALES	$212,331	$319,884	$420,000	$420,000	$1,372,215

Fig. 7.44

A change in the spreadsheet is seen immediately on the graph.

2. Click the LINE button.
3. Press **return** or click Plot It!.
4. The bar graph becomes a line graph like figure 7.45.

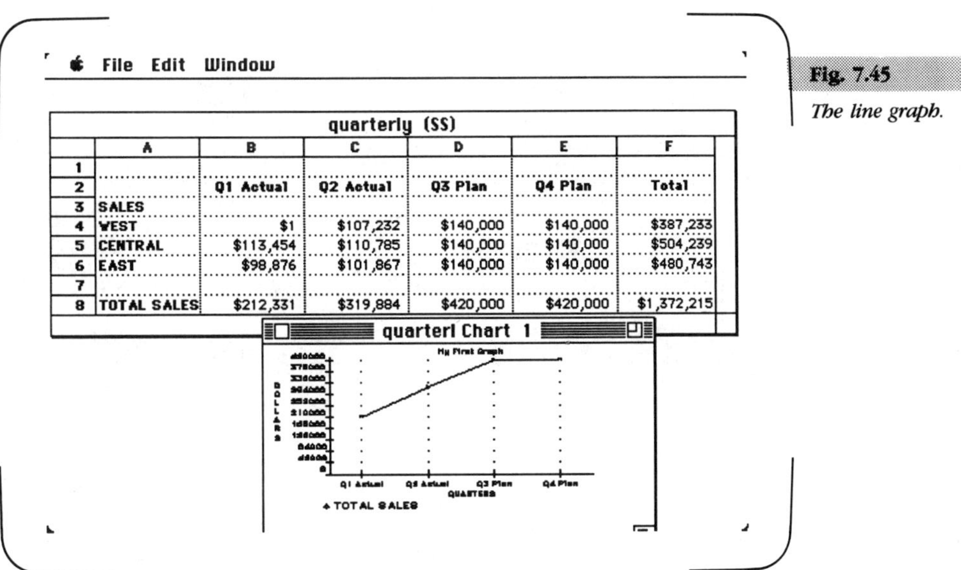

	A	B	C	D	E	F
1						
2		Q1 Actual	Q2 Actual	Q3 Plan	Q4 Plan	Total
3	SALES					
4	WEST	$1	$107,232	$140,000	$140,000	$387,233
5	CENTRAL	$113,454	$110,785	$140,000	$140,000	$504,239
6	EAST	$98,876	$101,867	$140,000	$140,000	$480,743
7						
8	TOTAL SALES	$212,331	$319,884	$420,000	$420,000	$1,372,215

Fig. 7.45

The line graph.

Changing the Graph Name

The name that Works proposes for your first masterpiece is neither inspiring nor descriptive. Take control! With the chart definition dialog box on the screen, choose Change Chart Name from the Edit Menu. A dialog box appears. Enter a title that suits you. Click OK or simply tap the **return** key. The new name appears in the graph's title bar and in the Select Definition dialog box.

Saving Your New Graph

Works saves graph definitions with the spreadsheet. Be sure to save your spreadsheet before quitting if you want to maintain new graph definitions.

A First Pie Graph

Pie graphs have fewer options than series graphs. Experiment by creating a pie graph of the regional totals in column F of the Quarterly spreadsheet. The pie graph has three slices, one slice for each region on the spreadsheet.

1. From the Quarterly spreadsheet, choose New Pie Chart from the Chart menu (see fig. 7.46). A Pie Chart Definition dialog box appears (see fig. 7.47)

File Edit Window Select Format Options Chart

Draw Chart...
New Series Chart...
New Pie Chart...
Select Definition...
Duplicate Chart...
Erase Chart...

B4 110110

quarterly (SS)

	A	B	C	D		
1						
2		Q1 Actual	Q2 Actual	Q3 Plan		
3	SALES					
4	WEST	$110,110	$107,232	$140,000	$140,000	$497,342
5	CENTRAL	$113,454	$110,785	$140,000	$140,000	$504,239
6	EAST	$98,876	$101,867	$140,000	$140,000	$480,743
7						
8	TOTAL SALES	$322,440	$319,884	$420,000	$420,000	$1,482,324

Fig. 7.46

Choosing the New Pie Chart from the Chart menu.

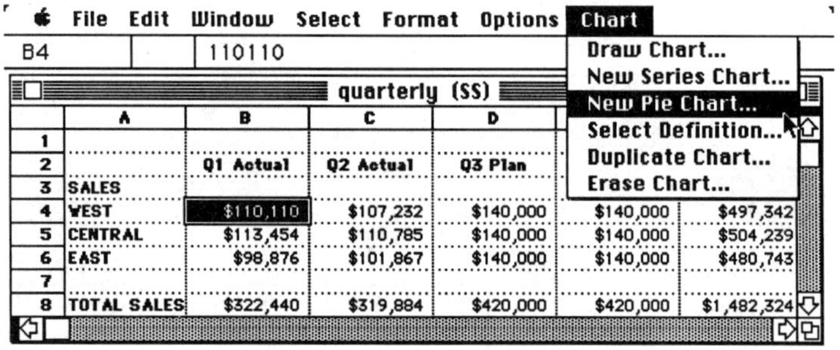

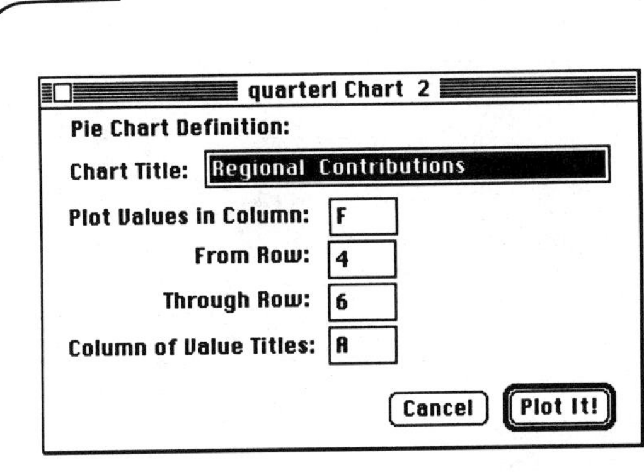

Fig. 7.47

The Pie Chart Definition dialog box.

2. Double-click on the Chart Title box and enter a descriptive title, **Regional Contributions**. This title will be displayed and printed on your graph.

CAUTION: Do not press *enter* or *return* until you have made all your entries in the dialog box. If you do press *enter* or *return* by mistake, double-click on the resulting graph to return to the dialog box.

3. The regional totals are in column F. Double-click on the Plot Values in Column box and enter the letter **F**, upper- or lowercase letter.

4. The regional totals you want to use in your pie graph are located on lines 4, 5, and 6 of the spreadsheet. Double-click on the From Row box and type **4**; then double-click on the Through Row box and type **6**. You have just told Works to make three pie slices, one for each region.

5. Label the pie slices with the region names that Works suggests in column A of your spreadsheet. Double-click on the Column of Value Titles box and type the letter **A**, if it is not already in the box.

6. Either press **return**, press **enter**, or click Plot It! The result should look like figure 7.48.

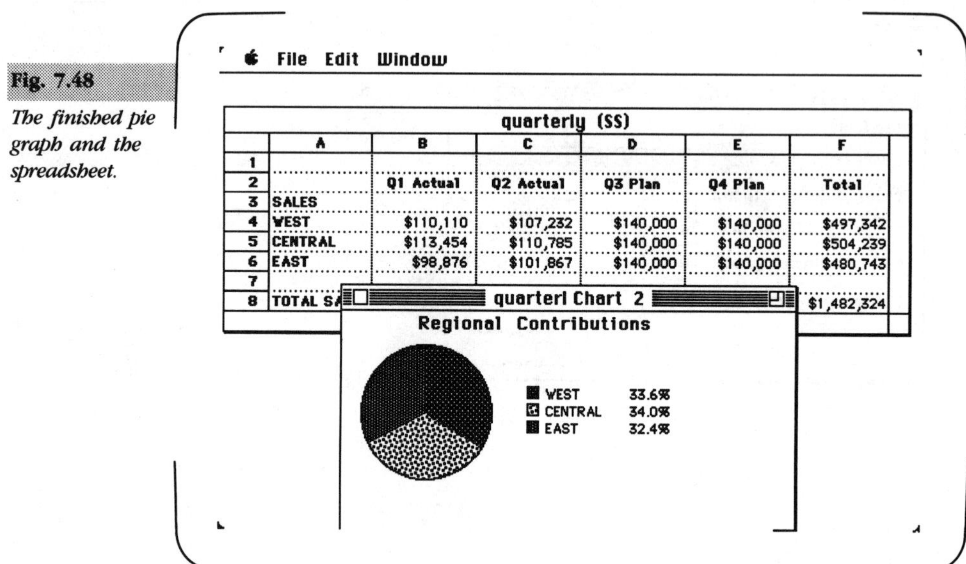

Fig. 7.48

The finished pie graph and the spreadsheet.

If you have a problem with your pie graph, return to the dialog box by double-clicking anywhere on the graph. Entering the wrong row or column number is easy to do. If your data is different from the data on the sample Quarterly spreadsheet, the size of your slices can vary. Alter the pie graph slices by changing the numbers and letters in the boxes on the dialog box screen. Then rename the graph definition and save your spreadsheet before quitting.

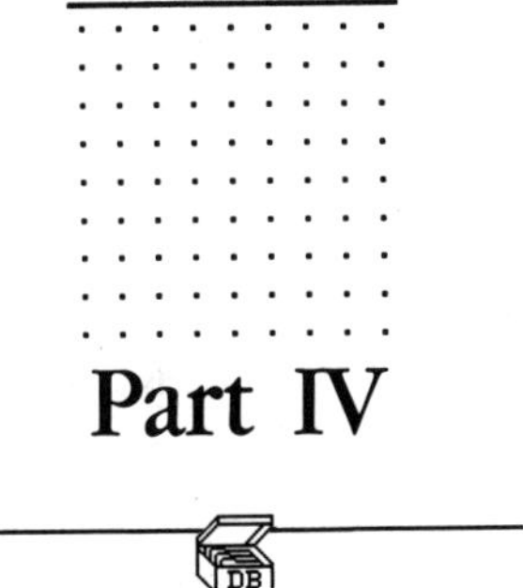

Part IV

DATABASES

8

Databases

With Works, you can organize information in much the same way that you would set up card files. These organized collections of information are called *databases*, and they are stored on computer disks rather than on paper. You can set up as many different databases as you like, each with a different file name.

Why use Works instead of a paper card file? Because with Works you can locate and rearrange your information quickly. And, as you know, data that is computerized is easy to edit. Moreover, you can produce lists and reports from your databases and merge your database information with word-processing documents to create personalized form letters, mailing labels, preprinted forms, and more.

This chapter first presents basic database terminology and explains the special database features of Works. Then, you learn how to design, create, and edit databases. Next, you are given ways to use your database—to move through the records, to select specified records, and to create on-screen reports. (Chapter 9 focuses on printing information from your database.) Finally, this chapter explains how to change the design of a database and gives shortcuts and tips for working with databases.

Understanding Database Terms and Features

The following sections define terms that will help you understand this chapter and the next. You learn the definitions of records, forms, fields, and report definitions. You also are introduced to Works' basic database features: sorting, searching, and matching capabilities and the list and form windows.

Records, Forms, Fields, and Reports

As mentioned, a database is any organized collection of records. To use an analogy, a card file filled with cards containing people's names and addresses is an example of a database. The individual cards are the *records*. Figure 8.1 shows an example of records in a database.

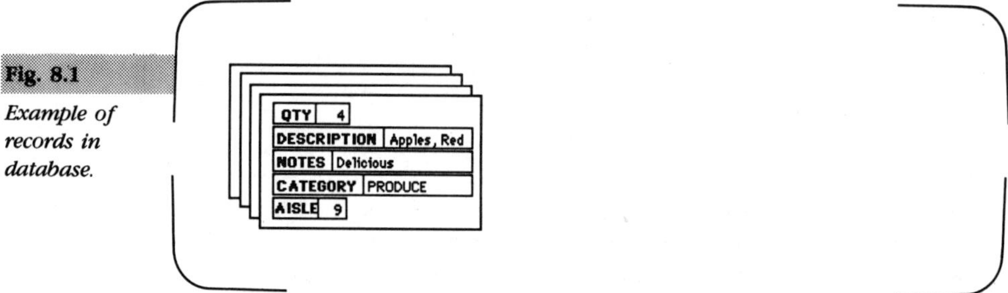

Fig. 8.1 *Example of records in database.*

To help you enter and edit records, Works displays *forms* that may remind you of printed paper forms. You fill in the blanks on the forms while entering or editing information in your database.

Records consist of *fields*, which are like the blanks on printed paper forms. Most records contain more than one field. For example, figure 8.2 shows a membership record in a Chamber of Commerce database. This record contains 12 fields.

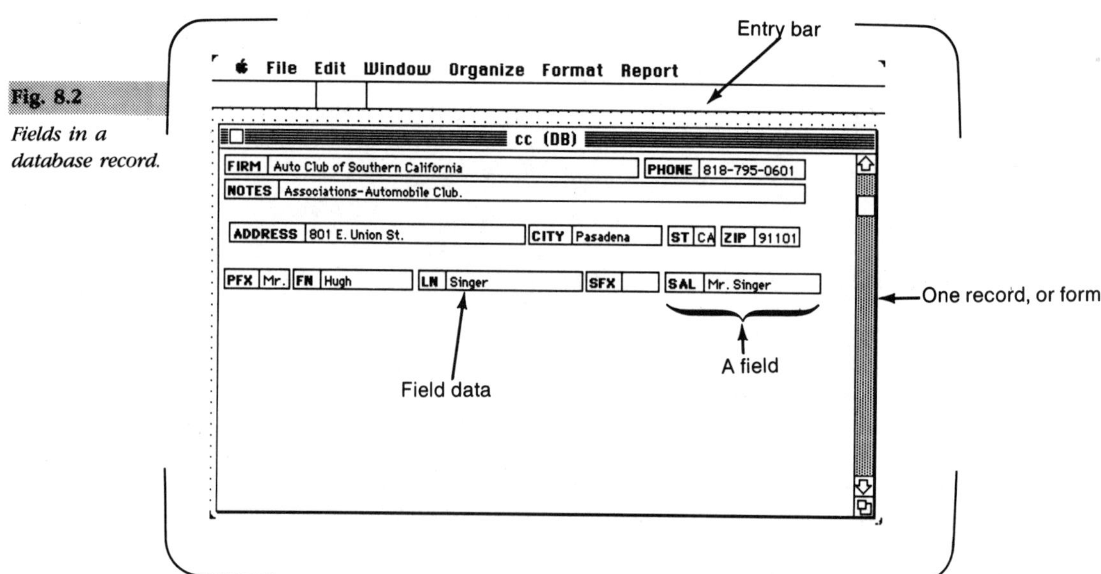

Fig. 8.2 *Fields in a database record.*

When you design a new database, you create the fields and therefore the form used to organize your data. You can change the size of fields, move them around, and change their appearance. Even after you finish designing a form, you can rearrange it and add or delete fields.

When you need paper copies of information from a Works database, you print *reports*, which are printed documents. You create *report definitions* to specify totals, subtotals, headers, footers, and other features for the printed report. These topics are covered in Chapter 9.

Sorting, Searching, and Matching Capabilities

Unless you tell Works to do otherwise, it stores your records in the order in which you enter them. You can, however, easily rearrange the records. In database terms, reorganizing is called *sorting*. With Works' sorting features, reorganization is so simple that you'll probably find yourself doing it frequently. For example, you can rearrange the list of names of Chamber of Commerce members in figure 8.3 alphabetically by last name of the individual instead of by firm as it is now.

FIRM	PHONE	FN	LN	PFX	S
Auto Club of Southern California	818-795-0601	Hugh	Singer	Mr.	
Automated Systems Program	818-355-4013	Carrie	Joseph	Ms.	
Avera B Lewis Jr.	213-792-5224	B. Lewis	Avera	Mr.	J
Avery International	818-304-2000	Diane	Dixon	Ms.	
Avis Rent A Car	818-449-6122	Rick	Simonson	Mr.	
Avon Products, Inc.	818-578-8000	William	Roy	Mr.	
B & J Janitorial Service	(?)794-0746	Norman	Taylor	Mr.	
B W & C Investments, The dba The Bral	213-624-1001	Tony	Canzoneri	Mr.	
B.C.D. Software Services	818-796-1764	Chris	Leu	Mr.	
Babaeian Transportation Co. Inc.	818-956-2227	Masood	Babaeian	Mr.	
Badger-Carmichael	818-793-7910	Gary	Badger	Mr.	
Bahama Bowling Lanes	818-351-8858	Billy	Meyers	Mr.	
Bailey, Soleno & Associates	818-304-0555	Lucinda	Bailey	Ms.	
Bank of America	818-578-5091	Jim Fang	Ding	Mr.	
Bank of America	818-578-5163	Alan	Hancock	Mr.	
Barker Brothers	818-796-0133	Don	Glasgow	Mr.	
Barnes, Edwin A (Ned)	818-799-6201	Ron	Barnes	Mr.	

Fig. 8.3

List of names of Chamber of Commerce members.

After entering records into your database, you can use Works' *search* features to find specific items of interest. You do not need to scroll through your entire database to find one specific record. If you want to find items that occur in multiple records, you can use Works' *matching* feature to locate all records that meet your search criteria.

The Show List Feature

For many applications, you'll find yourself using the list window more often than the form window. To display the list window, you use the Show List option on the Format menu (see fig. 8.4).

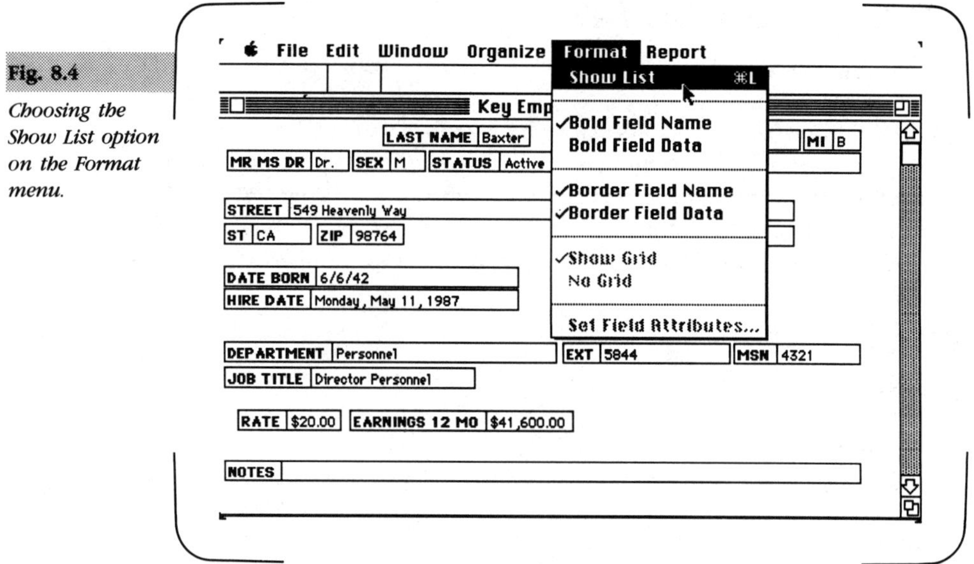

Fig. 8.4

Choosing the Show List option on the Format menu.

Show List may be Works' most powerful and useful database option. In fact, Show List may be the wrong name. Not only can you use Show List to display multiple records, as shown in figure 8.5, but you also can use Show List to rearrange records and to copy parts of one record to another, with your records displayed in list format. Show List frequently speeds the entry and editing of records as well. Manage List might be a better name for the Show List feature.

In the list window, records become rows, fields become columns, and field names become column headings. If a record is too long to fit on the screen, you can use the horizontal scroll bar to view the record's

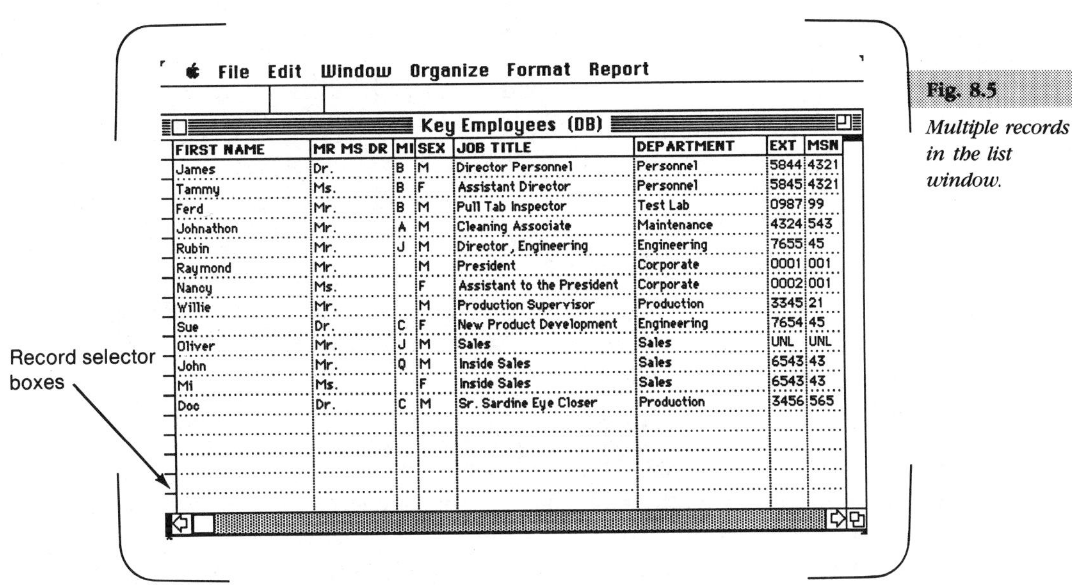

FIRST NAME	MR MS DR	MI	SEX	JOB TITLE	DEPARTMENT	EXT	MSN
James	Dr.	B	M	Director Personnel	Personnel	5844	4321
Tammy	Ms.	B	F	Assistant Director	Personnel	5845	4321
Ferd	Mr.	B	M	Pull Tab Inspector	Test Lab	0987	99
Johnathon	Mr.	A	M	Cleaning Associate	Maintenance	4324	543
Rubin	Mr.	J	M	Director, Engineering	Engineering	7655	45
Raymond	Mr.		M	President	Corporate	0001	001
Nancy	Ms.		F	Assistant to the President	Corporate	0002	001
Willie	Mr.		M	Production Supervisor	Production	3345	21
Sue	Dr.	C	F	New Product Development	Engineering	7654	45
Oliver	Mr.	J	M	Sales	Sales	UNL	UNL
John	Mr.	Q	M	Inside Sales	Sales	6543	43
Mi	Ms.		F	Inside Sales	Sales	6543	43
Doc	Dr.	C	M	Sr. Sardine Eye Closer	Production	3456	565

Fig. 8.5
Multiple records in the list window.

entire contents. If all your records won't fit on the screen at once, use the vertical scroll bar to display the records that don't fit. Clicking Show Form on the Format menu returns Works to the form window.

Works provides two shortcut methods of switching between the list and form windows. You can press *command*-L (for list) to toggle between the two views, or you can double-click. To move from the form to the list window, you double-click on any white section of a form that isn't part of a field or field name. To move from the list to the form window, you double-click on any record selector box to the left of a record (or blank), as shown in figure 8.5.

If you double-click on a field, Works gives you the opportunity to change field names or attributes. Click the Cancel button if you activate this feature accidentally.

Designing a Database

Whole books have been written about the art of designing databases. Fortunately, Works enables you to change designs if they need improvement, so your initial attempt doesn't have to be perfect. The process of developing those first few databases is always a learning experience. Creating a database involves the following basic steps:

1. Think about the organization of your new database.

2. Open a new database window.
3. Enter and name fields to create the rough form.
4. Alter field sizes as necessary.
5. Rearrange field locations (optional).
6. Enter your records.
7. Name and save the database.

These steps are explained in more detail in the rest of this chapter. During the process of designing and creating a database, you should keep in mind the following basic principles.

Keep your database simple.

Designing a fancy database is easier than maintaining one. Updating complex databases can take hours or even days, and large databases take up memory and disk space, too. You should avoid the temptation to collect trivia; otherwise, you may run out of room for new records because you're tracking too much unneeded information.

Consider your future requirements.

If you plan to create a mailing list and search or sort it by ZIP code, you probably need a separate field for the ZIP code. Many people don't create enough separate fields in their first database design. Instead, they create a single field for city, state, and ZIP code. When this approach is used, the database can be sorted by the city name only.

If you plan to create personalized form letters, you probably need a salutation field in addition to the usual first and last name fields. For example, you address a letter to a judge *The Honorable Judge Smith*, but you probably want the salutation of the letter to read *Dear Judge Smith*. If the judge were a close friend, however, you might want the salutation to read *Dear Mary* instead.

If you plan to sort the list by people's last names, you either have to have a last name field in your database or always enter names with the last name first in a single name field.

Establish standards.

Computers take things more literally than humans do. You may treat *Washington D.C.*, *The District of Columbia*, *our nation's capital*, and even *DC* as the same place, but Works won't. So write down the rules you plan to use and make them available to anyone who enters and edits records.

Test your database by using a representative data sampling.

You can add fields later, but before entering much data, you should think things through and try out the database. Otherwise, later, you'll need to update hundreds or even thousands of records manually. Be certain to test your database with enough data to catch potential problems. If you need an additional field for some unanticipated reason, you're better off making that discovery when you have only a few records in the database.

Defining a New Database

Enough theory. Let's get started. To learn the basics of database creation, you can look at a database that you can use at home: a grocery database containing the names of frequently purchased items and their aisle locations. You can use the finished database to prepare convenient shopping lists.

The *quickest* way to open a new database window is by double-clicking on the Data Base icon on the Works Greeting screen, as illustrated in figure 8.6. (You also can click once to highlight the Data Base icon and then click the Open button.)

Fig. 8.6

Opening a new database window by double-clicking on the Data Base icon.

Works opens an untitled database window and displays a Field Name dialog box in which you must type the first field name. Works "suggests" using the name *Untitled1* (see fig. 8.7). You can use that name or type a new one of your own.

To add the field to the file, you either click the Add Field button or press the *return* or *enter* key. You can rename the field before clicking the Add Field button, or you can place all untitled fields on the screen and name them later.

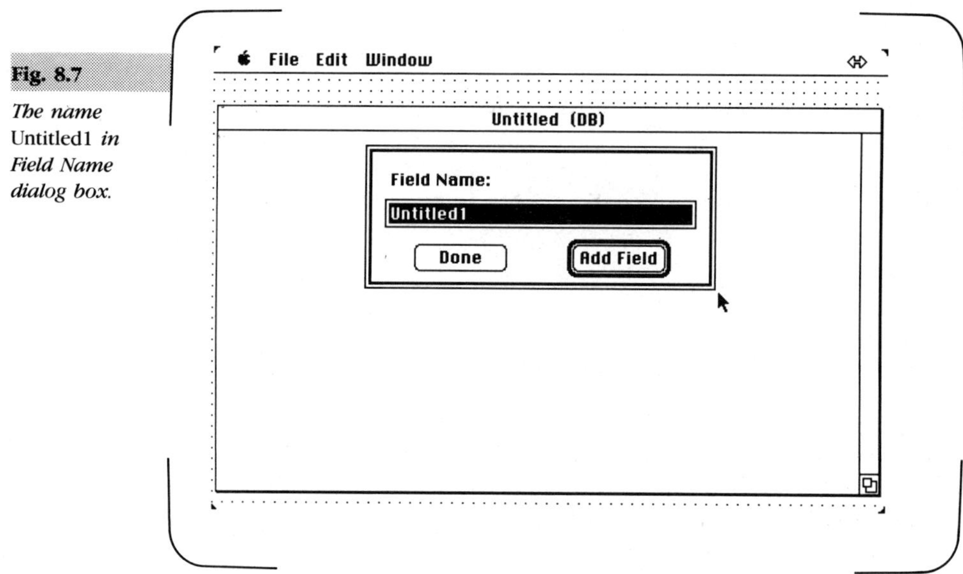

Fig. 8.7

The name Untitled1 *in Field Name dialog box.*

Whenever you click the Add Field button or press the *return* or *enter* key, Works adds the new field to the screen and displays another Field Name dialog box (see fig. 8.8). Works keeps adding new fields until you click the Done button (see fig. 8.9).

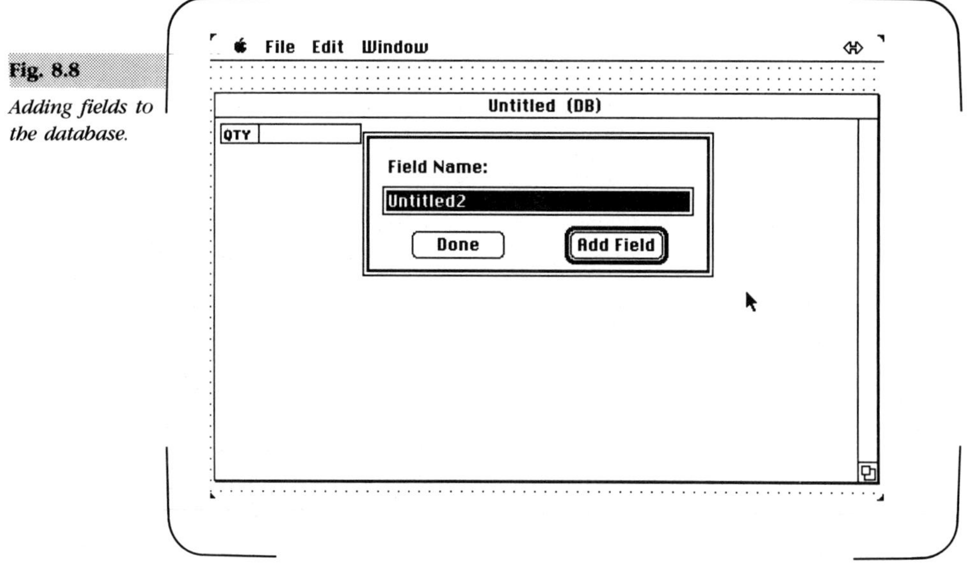

Fig. 8.8

Adding fields to the database.

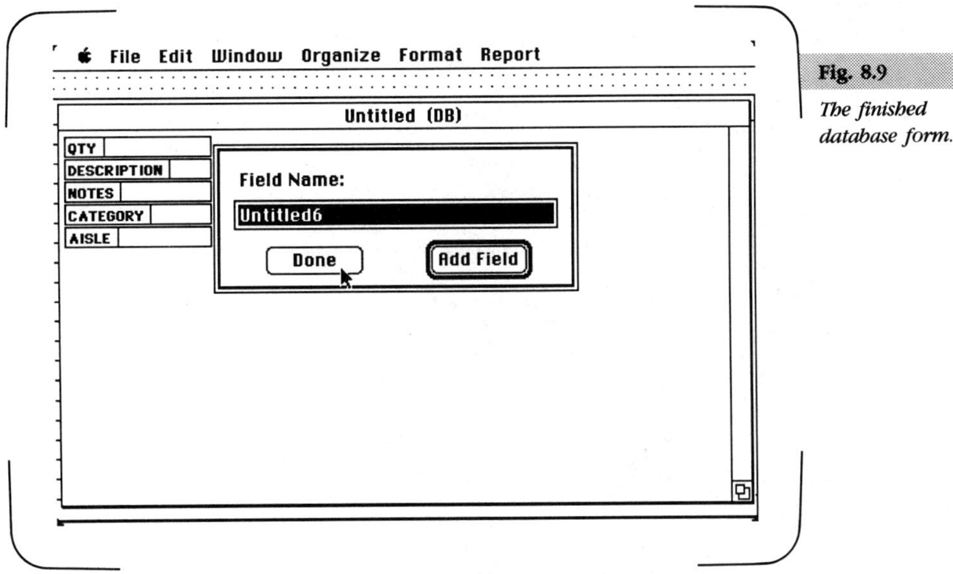

Fig. 8.9

The finished database form.

Naming Fields

Try to use short but descriptive field names. They can be up to 64 characters long, but a name that long would be difficult to remember and cumbersome to work with. A name that is too short, N, for example, is meaningless to anyone else—and even to the creator of the name after some time has passed. Note the names in the sample database: QTY, DESCRIPTION, and CATEGORY are easy to understand and to enter.

Field names must start with a letter, not a number or a space. Most punctuation marks—hyphens, parentheses, and periods—are not permitted. You can, however, use colons and dollar signs. If you enter an illegal character, Works warns you, as shown in figure 8.10. Then, you can click the OK button and enter an acceptable field name.

Moving Fields on a Form

While you are designing your form or after you have used it for a while, you may want to change the location of a field. Appearance may be an issue. Convenience when moving from entry to entry may be another consideration. Or you may need to move the labels around to make room for bigger fields.

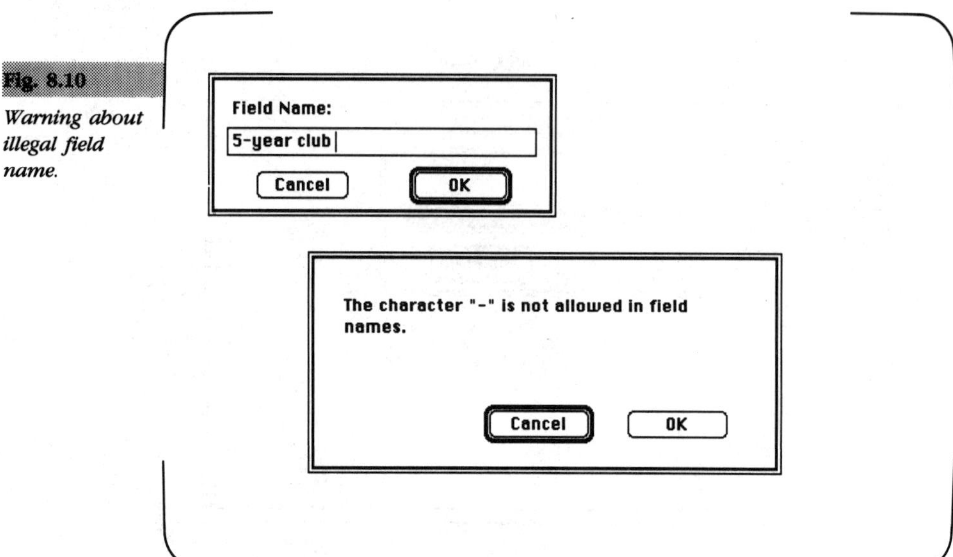

Fig. 8.10

Warning about illegal field name.

In Works, moving fields is easy. To move a field on a form, you do the following:

1. Point to the field name. The cursor becomes a hand, as illustrated in figure 8.11.
2. Press the mouse button and drag the field where you want it (see fig. 8.12). A box outlined in dashes appears to show you where the field will be placed.
3. Release the mouse button to move the field to the place indicated by the box outlined in dashes.

NOTE: Don't overlap fields; if you do, Works displays a warning message.

You can drag a field so far that part of it runs off the left or right edge of the screen, which is okay for temporary "parking" while designing a form.

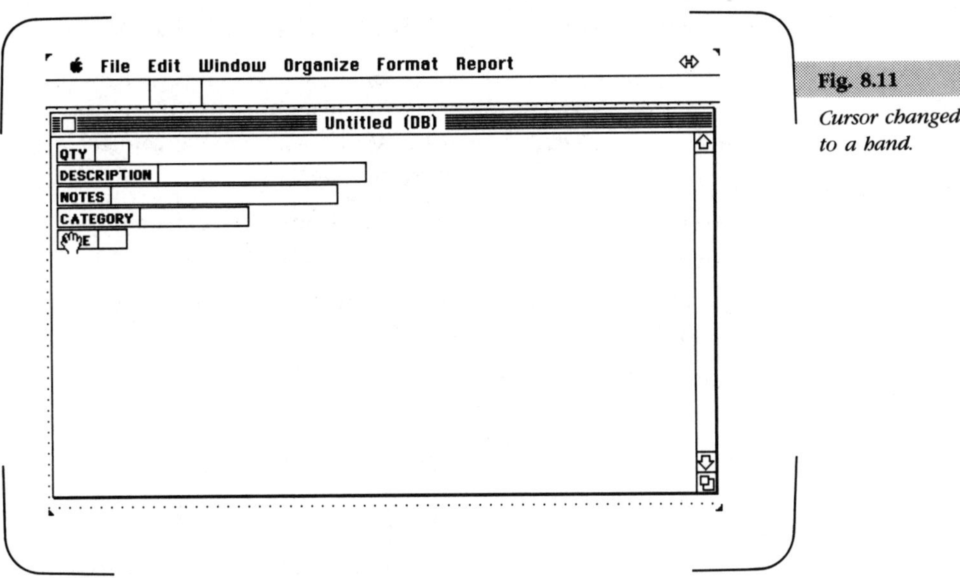

Fig. 8.11

Cursor changed to a hand.

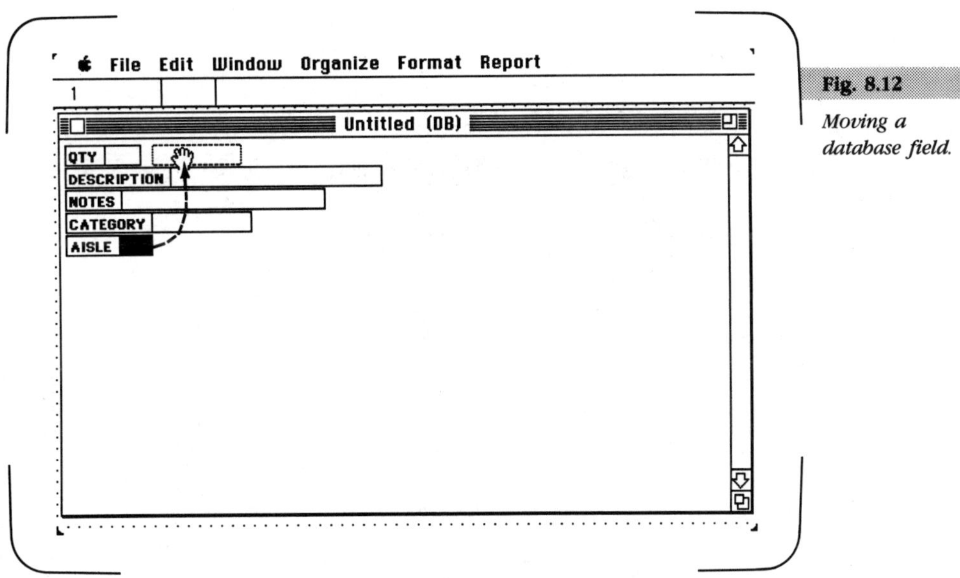

Fig. 8.12

Moving a database field.

Changing the Size and Style of Fields

The white part of the field box is where you enter your database information. Whenever you like, you can make this white area larger or smaller than the sizes assigned by Works when you create the fields. Adjusting a field's size is simple. Here's what you do:

1. Point to the right edge of the field box. The cursor then becomes a double-headed arrow, as shown in figure 8.13.
2. Hold down the mouse button and drag the box to the size you want, as illustrated in figure 8.14.
3. Release the mouse button.

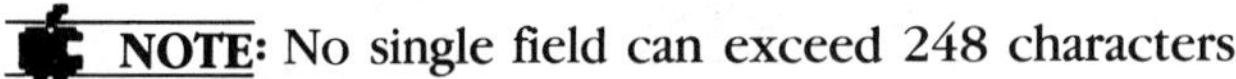

NOTE: No single field can exceed 248 characters.

You can change the size of a field any time, even after you've entered data. When you change size, you don't affect the field's content. For example, if you make a field shorter than its content, the content remains unchanged; you just can't see everything. To reveal the entire entry, make the box bigger again.

Fig. 8.13

Cursor changed to a double-headed arrow.

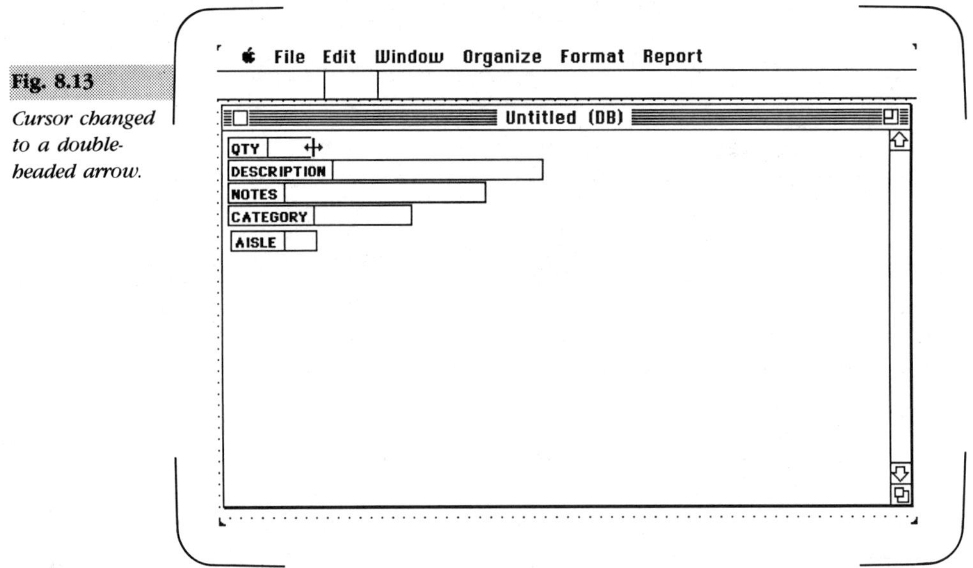

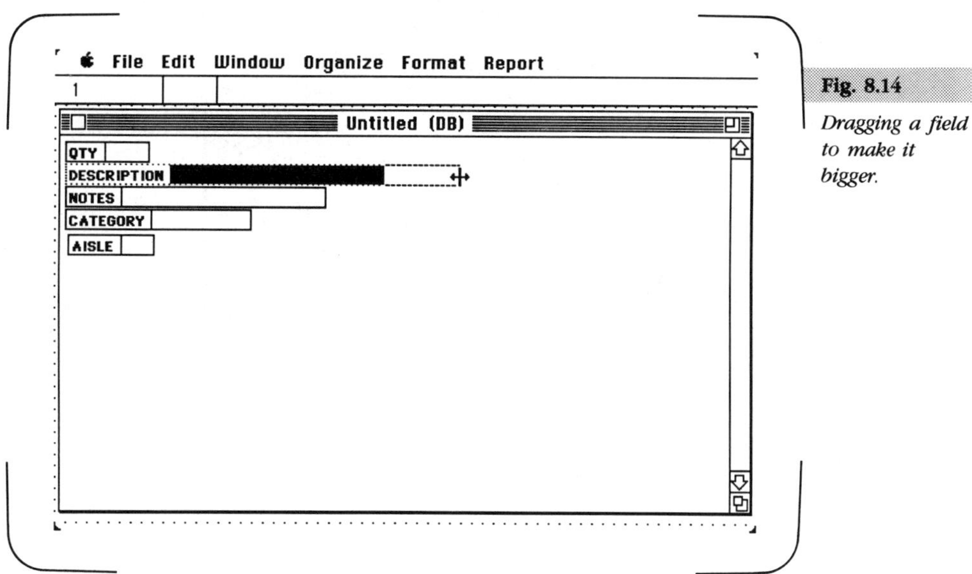

Fig. 8.14

Dragging a field to make it bigger.

NOTE: If you change the size of a field box in one record, you change that field box in the rest of the records in the database.

You can alter the appearance of a form by selecting from a variety of formats on the Format menu (see fig. 8.15). For example, you can bold-face field names or keep them as is, and you have the same control over the data you enter. You can box the border and data. The format defaults are

Boldface field names
Normal data
Boxed field names
Boxed data

Experiment if you like. When options are active, check marks appear to their left. Figures 8.16, 8.17, and 8.18 illustrate how the options on the Format menu affect the appearance of a form. In figure 8.16, the Border Field Data and Bold Field Name options have been chosen. You can see that the field names have no borders but are in boldface and the field data entries are enclosed in boxes. In figure 8.17 only Bold Field Name has been checked. No borders appear on-screen, and the field names appear in boldface. Finally, in figure 8.18 both field names and field data entries are bordered and in boldface. The Format menu affords you considerable variety for displaying your forms in clear and effective ways.

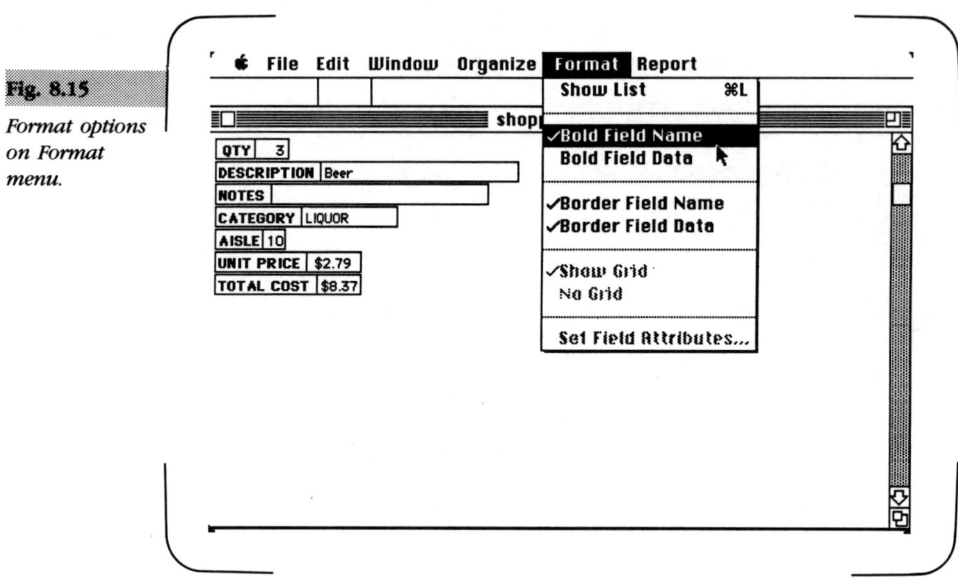

Fig. 8.15

Format options on Format menu.

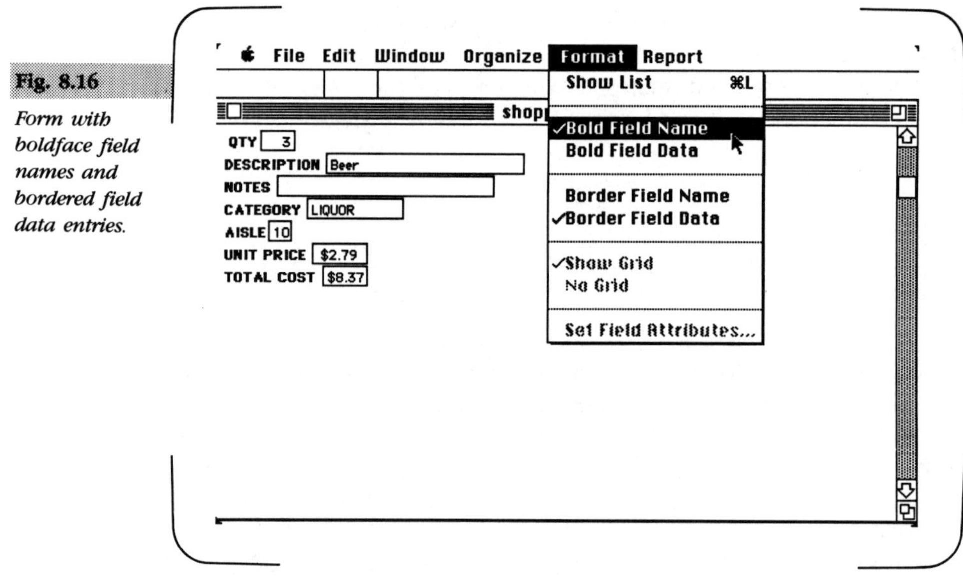

Fig. 8.16

Form with boldface field names and bordered field data entries.

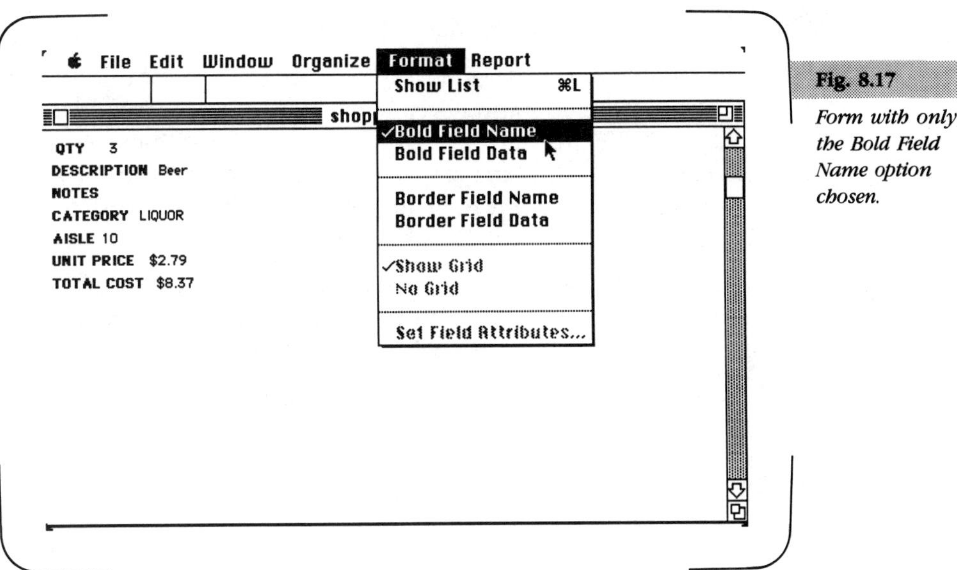

Fig. 8.17

Form with only the Bold Field Name option chosen.

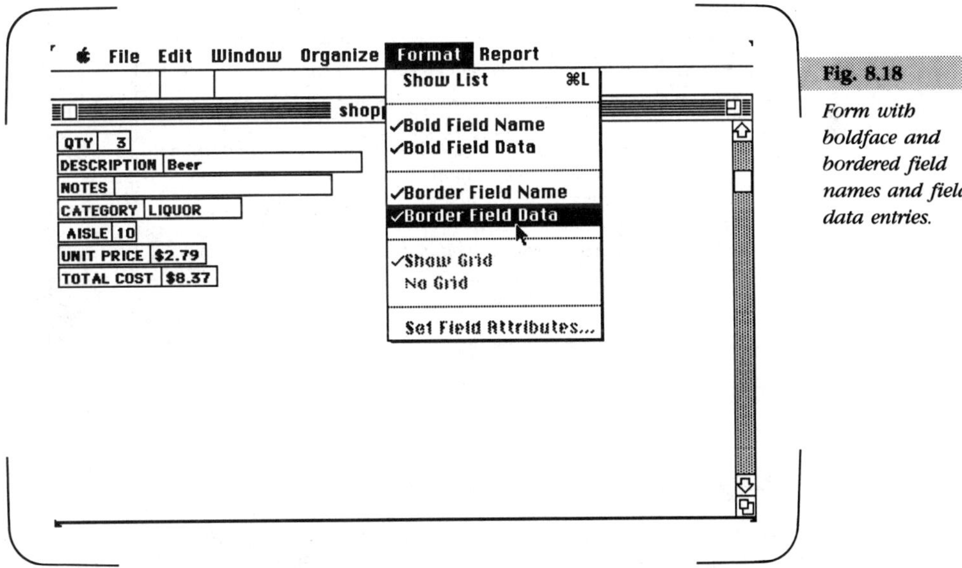

Fig. 8.18

Form with boldface and bordered field names and field data entries.

Specifying Field Attributes

Just as the spreadsheet portion of Works lets you specify cell formats, the database gives you control over field formats. The controls are called *field attributes* in the database. By specifying field attributes, you tell Works two things: what kind of information will be stored in a field and how you want the contents to be displayed. Each field can have its own attributes.

To change field attributes, you select the appropriate field and then choose Set Field Attributes on the Format menu. Or you can use this shortcut: Double-click on the right half of any field.

Works then displays the Set Field Attributes dialog box for the selected field (see fig. 8.19). The choices you make here affect the way Works both displays and treats field entries. This dialog box is crowded, so we'll take its contents a little at a time.

Fig. 8.19

Set Field Attributes dialog box.

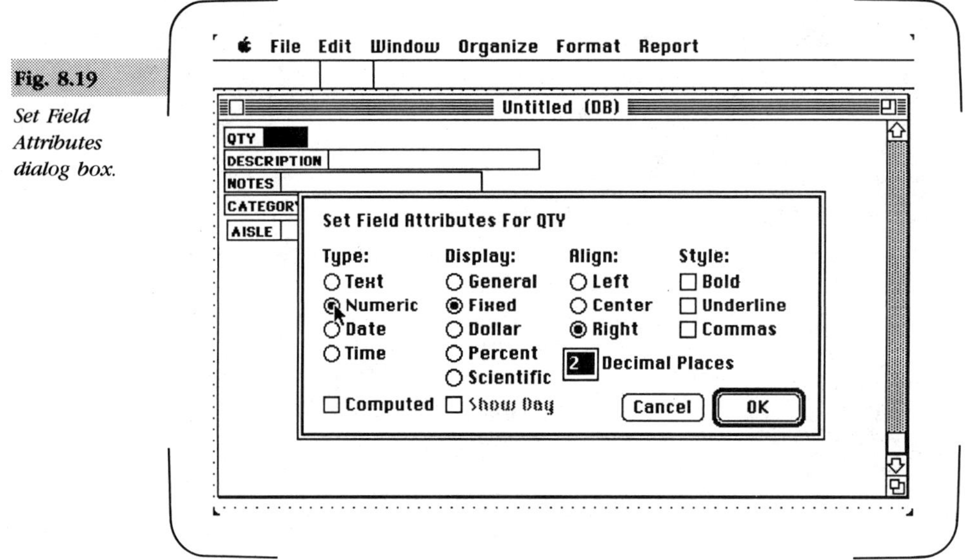

Making Field Attribute Choices

To make field attribute choices, you click the appropriate buttons in the Set Field Attributes dialog box. Dimmed choices are not available for the selected field type; for example, you can't select the Commas option for text fields.

Specifying Field Type and Display

The first choice you make in the Set Field Attributes dialog box should be the Type: Text, Numeric, Date, or Time. As already noted, this choice determines what other options are available. For example, numeric field types can be displayed in several different formats, chosen under Display.

Text Format

Many entries you make in a database are simple text, such as names, addresses, and notes. Therefore, Works "assumes" that all fields contain text unless you tell the program otherwise.

It is sometimes better to let Works "believe" that a column contains text even if the fields always contain numbers, such as a ZIP code or telephone number. This reason is explained in the following section and in the discussion on searches. For now, you need remember only that you can type anything you want in a text field and the text will be displayed as entered. Unless you make a different alignment choice, Works displays text fields left-aligned.

Numeric Format

The Numeric option tells Works that you intend always to enter numbers—and only numbers—in the selected field. If you choose the Numeric attribute, Works challenges any nonnumeric entries, as illustrated in figure 8.20.

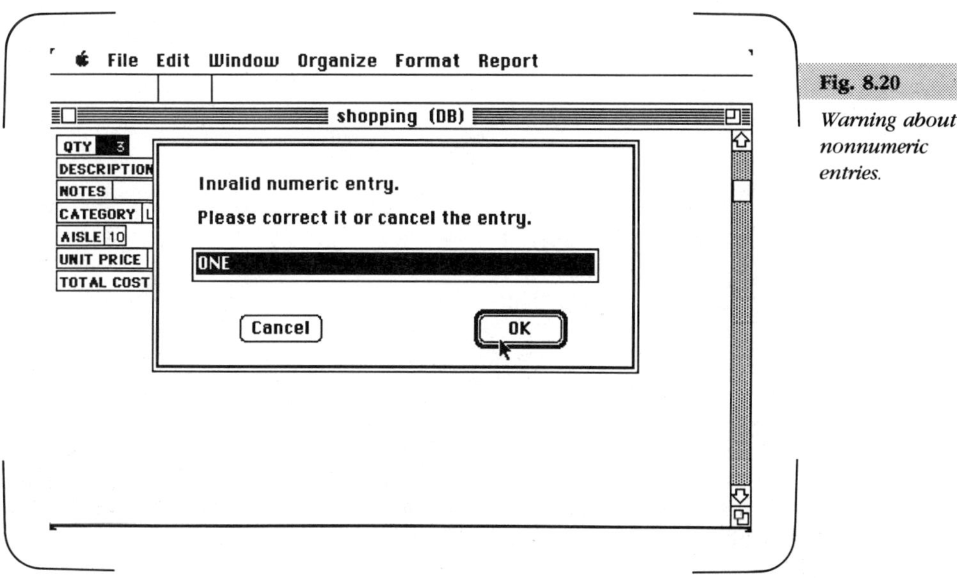

Fig. 8.20

Warning about nonnumeric entries.

When you define a field as numeric, you have a choice of display formats as well. Spreadsheet users will find them familiar:

- General (the default)
- Fixed
- Dollar
- Percent
- Scientific
- Commas

With Fixed format, you can specify the number of decimal places displayed. The Dollar format displays numbers with a dollar sign and two decimal places ($5.00). Refer to Chapter 5 for a full discussion of these formats.

NOTE: Works drops leading zeros when you enter them in numeric fields. For example, Works stores and displays the numeric version of a ZIP code 01234 as 1234. Besides upsetting the post office, this arrangement produces incorrect results if you sort by ZIP code. If you define telephone number fields as numeric, Works won't like dashes or parentheses either. Define your telephone numbers as text, not numbers, if you want telephone numbers to look like (818)555-1212 or 818/555-1212, or even 818-555-1212.

Date Format

If you tell Works that a field will contain dates, you can enter them in a variety of formats. All the following entries are permissible:

11-7-47
11-07-47
11/7/47
11.7.47
Nov 7, 1947
November 7, 1947
Friday, November 7, 1947

For storage purposes, Works converts these entries to their shortest form: 11-7-47.

Works offers a number of options for displaying as well as entering dates. These options appear under the Display heading in the Field Attributes dialog box when you select the Date type. For example, you can enter a date in any of the preceding formats and have Works display it in any of the formats shown in figure 8.21. Notice the way the date appears in the entry bar. That single entry can be displayed in five different formats, as shown here.

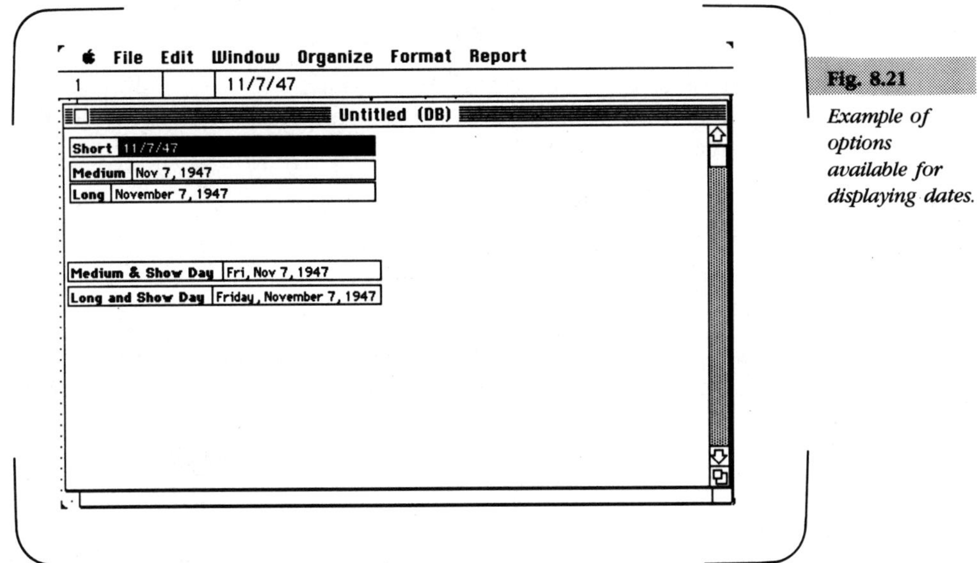

Fig. 8.21

Example of options available for displaying dates.

NOTE: Works Versions 1.0 and 1.1 don't support European date formats or date math.

Time Format

If you tell Works that a field will contain time, you can enter hours and minutes in a variety of formats, including both 12- and 24-hour formats. Works deals with only hours and minutes, not seconds, and assumes AM unless you enter PM or the 24-hour equivalent of a time. Table 8.1 shows some examples.

Table 8.1
Examples of Time Formats

What you enter	*What Works displays*
9:10	9:10 AM
9:10 PM	9:10 PM
22:10	9:10 PM
9:1	9:01 AM

NOTE: You must leave a space between the numbers and AM or PM when you make entries. You can shorten AM to A or PM to P if you like; Works adds the M for you.

Specifying Field Style and Alignment

You can boldface and underline data in fields, and you can display numbers either with or without commas. You also can define the number of decimal places in numbers.

The alignment of cell contents can be

Left-aligned (the default for text, dates, and times)
Right-aligned (the default for numbers)
Centered

These alignments are the same as the alignment choices for the Works spreadsheet (see Chapter 5 for more information).

Using Computed Fields

You can have Works compute data for a field, based on the contents of other fields in a record. In this respect, the Works database is like the Works spreadsheet. For example, if your form contains an hourly rate field, you can have Works use the arguments you provide and compute annual earnings and place the results in a computed field.

The edit bar in figure 8.22 contains a typical equation. Works calculates the annual salary by multiplying the contents of the RATE field times the number of hours in a week (40) and then the number of weeks in a year (52).

You can create computed fields by using the spreadsheet operators and some of the spreadsheet functions discussed in Chapters 5 and 6. Here are the general steps:

1. Create the field or fields that will hold the values.

2. Define a separate computed field. Use the Set Field Attributes dialog box in the same way as explained in the preceding sections, but check the computed choice in the dialog box (see fig. 8.19).

3. When you click OK, the Set Field Attributes dialog box disappears, and an equal sign appears in the entry bar. Supply the equation for the field.

4. Data in the value field(s) creates results in the equation field.

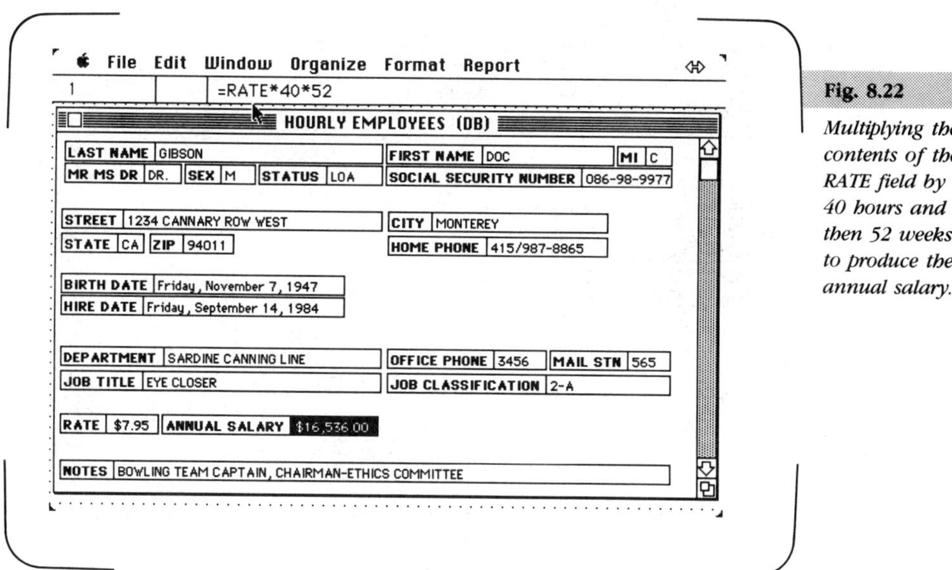

Fig. 8.22

Multiplying the contents of the RATE field by 40 hours and then 52 weeks to produce the annual salary.

A Sample Computed Field

Computed database fields always start with an equal sign and contain at least one field name, sometimes many. In addition, one or more operators are required. Spreadsheet functions are optional.

Look at an example: the grocery database in figure 8.23. Suppose that you want to add a computed TOTAL COST field, which computes the cost of purchasing the number of items specified in the QTY field. The figure shows a computed field that multiplies the quantity purchased times the unit price to provide the total cost. The equation is displayed in the edit bar.

You build equations in much the same way you create spreadsheet equations. Begin with an equal sign, and click on field names to include them. (You can type field names, but this process is slower and error prone.) Use functions if they help. Formulas can contain up to 238 characters.

Figures 8.24 and 8.25 illustrate some of the steps involved in adding a computed field:

1. Create a new field (TOTAL COST in the example).
2. Define the field as Numeric, using the Set Field Attributes dialog box (see fig. 8.24).

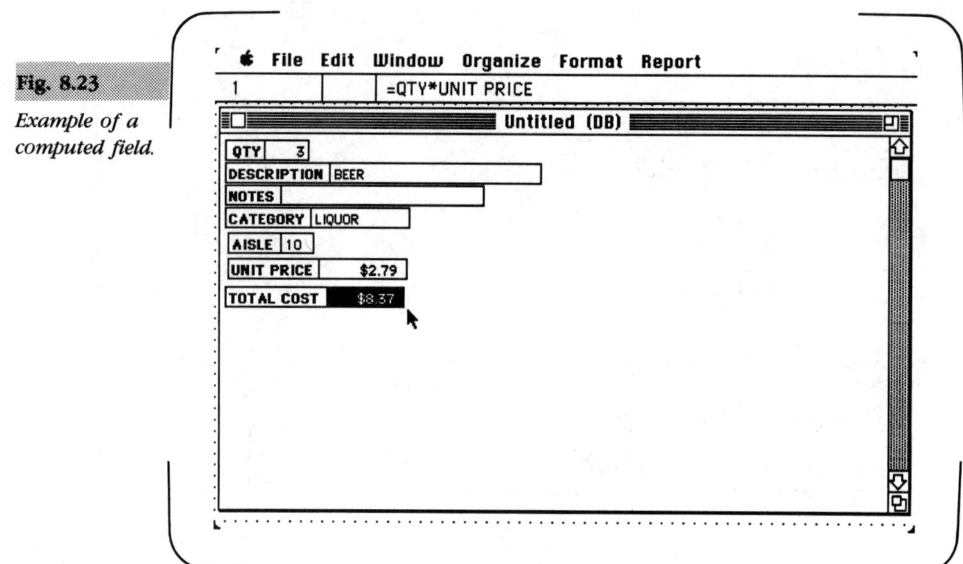

Fig. 8.23

Example of a computed field.

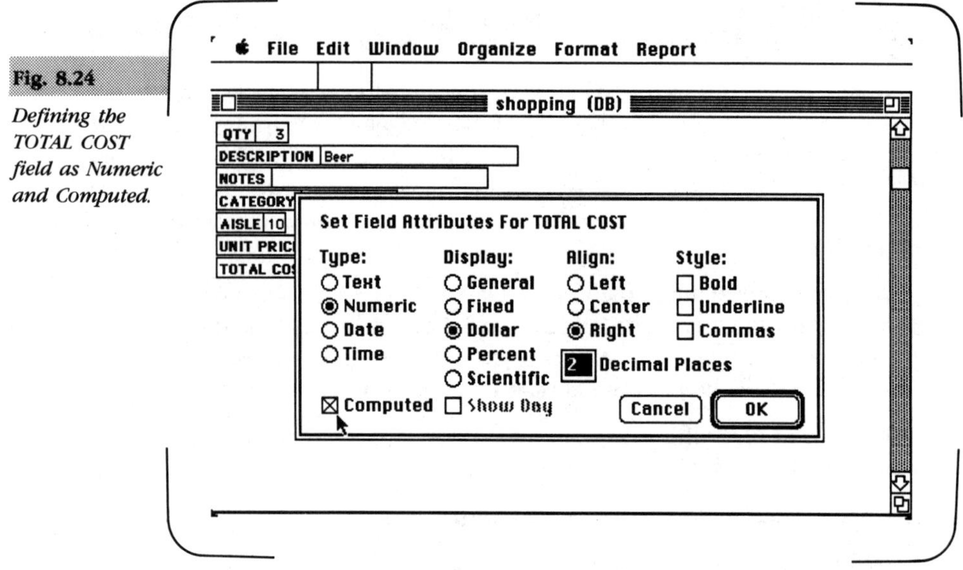

Fig. 8.24

Defining the TOTAL COST field as Numeric and Computed.

3. Further define the field as a computed field (check the dialog box).
4. Format the field if you like (dollars and two decimal places, for instance).
5. Either click OK or press the **return** key. An equal sign appears in the entry bar.
6. Click on the value field (QTY, in the example).
7. Enter the rest of the equation and field names (as needed).
8. Enter data in the necessary field (UNIT PRICE, in the example).
9. Watch the contents of the computed field (TOTAL COST) change (see fig. 8.25).

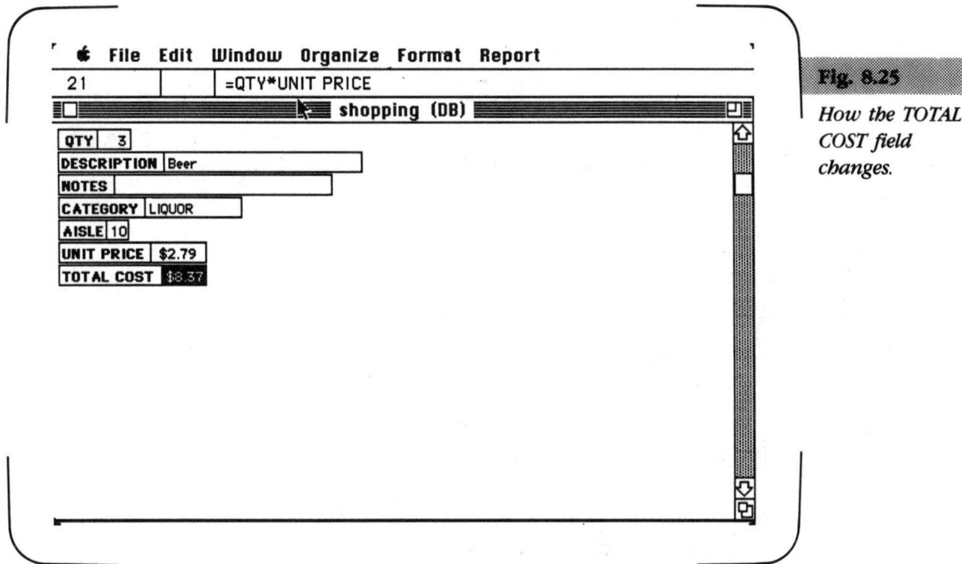

Fig. 8.25
How the TOTAL COST field changes.

Arithmetic Operators in Computed Fields

Arithmetic operators tell Works what you want done with values. Works supports the following operators in database computed fields:

+	Addition
-	Subtraction
*	Multiplication

/ Division
^ Exponentiation (raises to a power)
- Negation (changes a positive number to a negative number)

See Chapters 5 and 6 for more information about the arithmetic operators.

Functions Supported in Computed Fields

Spreadsheet functions that do not require ranges of values can be used in database computed fields. For definitions of these functions, see Chapter 6. Functions supported by the database are listed in table 8.2.

Table 8.2
Works Database Functions

Special-Purpose

Error( )
Returns the value *Error*
NA( )
Returns the value N/A
Type(value)
Type of value

Mathematical

Abs(number)
Absolute value of number
Exp(number)
e to the power number
Int(number)
Integer part of number
Ln(number)
Logarithm, base e, of number
Log10(number)
Logarithm, base 10, of number
Mod(number,divisor-number)
Remainder of number divided by divisor-number
Pi( )
value of pi
Rand( )
Random number between 0 and 1

Table 8.2—*continued*

Round(number,number-of-digits)
    Number rounded to number-of-digits
Sign(number)
    Sign of number
Sqrt(number)
    Square root of number

Statistical

None are offered because they all require ranges that aren't supported in databases.

Trigonometric

ACos(number)
    Arccosine of number
ASin(number)
    Arcsine of number
ATan(number)
    Arctangent of number
ATan2(x-number,y-number)
    Arctangent of point (x-number,y-number)
Cos(number)
    Cosine of number
Degrees(number)
    Converts number from radians to degrees
Radians(number)
    Converts number from degrees to radians
Sin(number)
    Sine of number
Tan(number)
    Tangent of number

Logical

And(values-1,values-2, . . .)
    1 (TRUE) if all values are non-zero (TRUE); otherwise 0 (FALSE)
False( )
    Returns the value 0 (FALSE)
If(number,number-if-true,number-if-false)
    Number-if-true if number is non-zero (TRUE);
    Number-if-false if number is 0 (FALSE)

Continued on next page

Table 8.2—*continued*

IsBlank(values-1,values-2, . . .)
  1 (TRUE) if all values are blank or text; otherwise 0 (FALSE)
IsError(value)
  1 (TRUE) if value is any error value
IsNA(value)
  1 (TRUE) if value is the error value N/A
Not(number)
  1 (TRUE) if number is 0
  0 (FALSE) if number is non-zero (TRUE)
Or(values-1,values-2, . . .)
  1 (TRUE) if any logical value in values is non-zero (TRUE); otherwise, 0 (FALSE)
True( )
  Returns the value 1 (TRUE)

Financial

FV(rate,nper,pmt,pv,type)
  Future value of investment
NPer(rate,pmt,pv,fv,type)
  Number of payments of investment
NPV(rate,values-1,values-2, . . .)
  Net present value of values
Pmt(rate,nper,pv,fv,type)
  Periodic payment of investment
PV(rate,nper,pmt,fv,type)
  Present value of investment
Rate(nper,pmt,pv,fv,type,guess)
  Rate returned on investment

Entering, Saving, and Editing Data

After defining a new database, you can enter data in the first record, using the empty form that is already on the screen. You also can enter data in the list window. Either way, you enter data one field at a time; use the typing techniques you've already learned. When you finish entering data, you need to save it in a disk file—something that Works reminds you to do. You can enter more records or change (edit) existing information later. In the editing process, you use the word-processing techniques you've already learned.

The Data Entry Process

When you begin to enter data, Works displays an entry bar that contains an enter box and a cancel box, just like the spreadsheet entry bar (see fig. 8.26). The key you press to terminate an entry affects what happens after you make the entry (see "Shortcuts for Entering Data, Date, and Time").

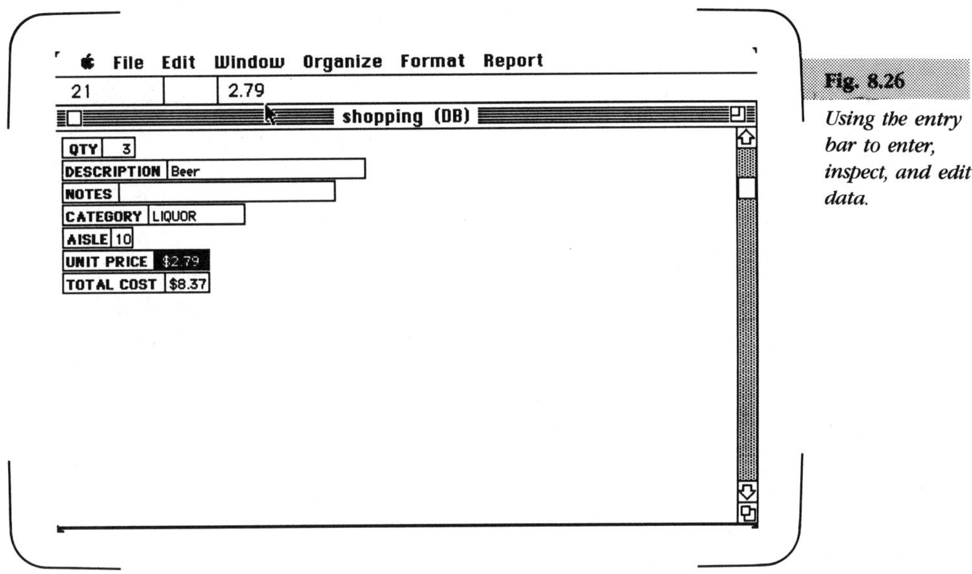

Fig. 8.26

Using the entry bar to enter, inspect, and edit data.

Following are the basic steps for entering data into fields:

1. Select the record in which you want to make the entry.
2. Select the field in which you want to make an entry.
3. Start typing.
4. Your entry appears in the entry bar at the top of the screen. You both enter and edit text and numbers in this entry bar.
5. When you have finished entering and editing the entry, you terminate the entry by clicking the enter box or pressing **return**, **tab**, and so on.

   Works then checks the entry to ensure proper type (date, number, and so forth) and uses the new data to update your record (in memory only; the disk copy of your database has not been changed).

6. Select another field in either the current record or a new record, and make another entry.
7. Continue the process until you have finished all entries.
8. To update the disk copy of your database, you must use one of the save commands, as described in the next section.

Saving Database Entries

You can ask Works to save your changes whenever you like. Get into the habit of saving your work every 15 minutes or so (and whenever you're interrupted). Use the techniques you've already learned: Choose the Save option on the File menu, or hold down the *command* key and press S (for save).

When you make changes in a database (such as adding entries or editing records), Works doesn't automatically save those changes to disk. They exist in memory only. When you try to close a database window, Works asks you whether you want to save the changes you've made.

If you click the Yes button or press the *return* key, Works saves the changes, thus updating the disk copy of your database.

If you answer No, or if you leave Works without saving because of a hardware, software, or power problem, Works doesn't save your changes.

Editing Procedures for Records

You can edit any field in any record either while you are first entering the record or later. Here's how:

1. Select the appropriate record if it's not already on the screen (see "Moving from Form to Form").
2. Click on the field you want to edit. The entry then appears in the entry bar.
3. Use the standard selecting, deleting, and inserting techniques to change the entry in the entry bar.
4. Click the enter box or press the **return** key.
5. To update the disk copy of your database, use the save features.

Shortcuts for Entering Data, Date, and Time

As you've learned already, you don't have to click the enter box after each entry. You can press the *enter* key to terminate an entry without changing the active field. You can then click the next field of your choice, but you don't even need do that. Pressing the *tab* key terminates your entry and activates the next field in the record.

To activate the preceding field on a form, you press *shift-tab*. Use the *return* key to terminate an entry and make the same field in the next record active. With *shift-return*, you activate the same field in the preceding record.

Those of you with cursor-arrow keys will find that they do what you expect. The arrow keys provide handy shortcuts. Table 8.3 lists the methods you can use to enter items and change active fields.

Table 8.3
Methods of Entering Items and Changing Active Fields

Do this	*To do this*
Click enter box	Terminate entry, same field remains active
Press *enter*	Terminate entry, same field remains active
Press *tab*	Terminate entry and move to next field
Press *shift-tab*	Terminate entry and move to preceding field
Press *return*	Terminate entry and move to next record
Press *shift-return*	Terminate entry and move to preceding record
Press right-arrow key	Terminate entry and move right
Press left-arrow key	Terminate entry and move left
Press up-arrow key	Terminate entry and move up
Press down-arrow key	Terminate entry and move down

If your system clock is set correctly, you can enter the current date by holding down the *command* key and pressing D.

Here's a shortcut for entering the current time (again, your system clock must be set properly): Select the appropriate field, and then hold down the *command* key and press T.

Using the Database

After your database is entered and edited to your satisfaction, you are ready to start using it. Here you discover the beauty of a computerized database. You can scroll through the entire database easily and quickly. You can move directly to specific entries to check facts or figures. With the searching and matching capabilities, you can create special reports or pull out certain records for comparisons or demonstrations. The possibilities are numerous. After you have mastered the techniques of using the Works database, you will continue to think of more ways to use it.

Moving from Form to Form

You can move from form to form by using the scroll bar at the right edge of the database window. To move back one record, click on the scroll bar's up arrow; to move forward one record, click on the down arrow. You can also click on the shaded scroll area, which takes you forward or backward one record (form) at a time.

If you're browsing through information in an existing database, you can scroll through the records to find the one you want. Or you can scroll to the end of the database, where Works displays an empty form.

Sorting Your Data

With the Works sort features, you can rearrange the contents of your database at any time. You can sort in either the form or the list window, but the results of sort requests are easier to see in the list window.

You sort (reorganize) according to the contents of a single field in the database. For example, you can sort addresses by city, state, or ZIP code. You can organize your grocery list according to product, aisle, or price. As you work with the sort feature, you will find more ways to use it.

The sorting procedure is simple, as are all of Works' features. You select the field you want to use for sorting by clicking on the field name. Then, you pull down the Organize menu and specify the Sort option. In the example in figure 8.27, the database is to be sorted by category.

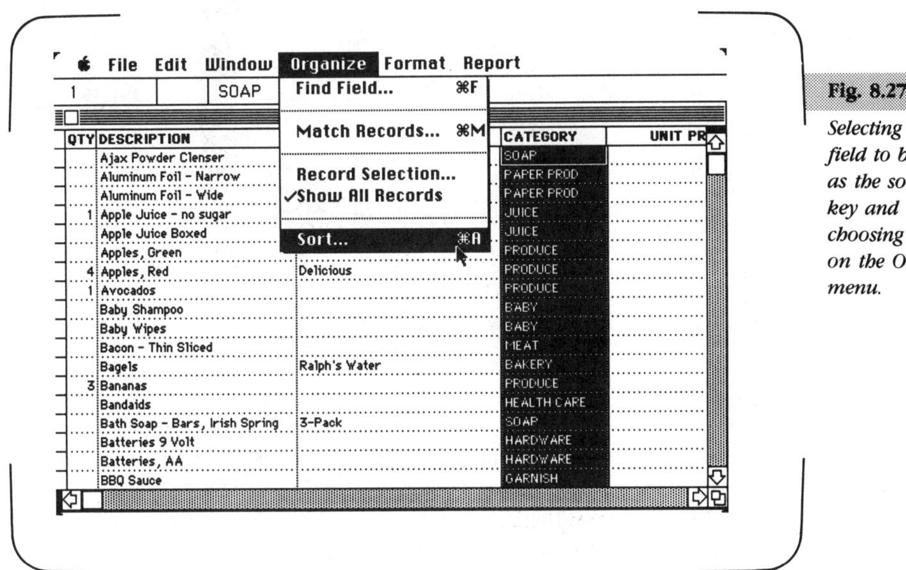

Fig. 8.27

Selecting the field to be used as the sorting key and then choosing Sort on the Organize menu.

The Sort dialog box appears, as shown in figure 8.28. In this box, you define the method of sorting you want to use.

As you can see, you can sort alphabetically, numerically, or chronologically, depending on the type of the field you've chosen. And you can arrange records in ascending or descending order. The Sort dialog box highlights the available choices. For example, if the field is text, the options From A to Z and From Z to A are highlighted. In figure 8.28, you can sort alphabetically on the field CATEGORY. Click on the option you want, and watch Works rearrange things for you.

If you sort using a field that contains numbers but is defined as a text field, the results may surprise you. When a field is defined as text, Works treats the digits as characters, and the first digit is the first character in the alphanumeric sort. Therefore, the first character is the most important sorting criteria and one (1) precedes two (2)—always. For instance, in an ascending text sort, 10,200 appears before 20 because Works ignores the numeric value of the two entries and arranges them according to rules about sorting text. Notice how the result of a sort

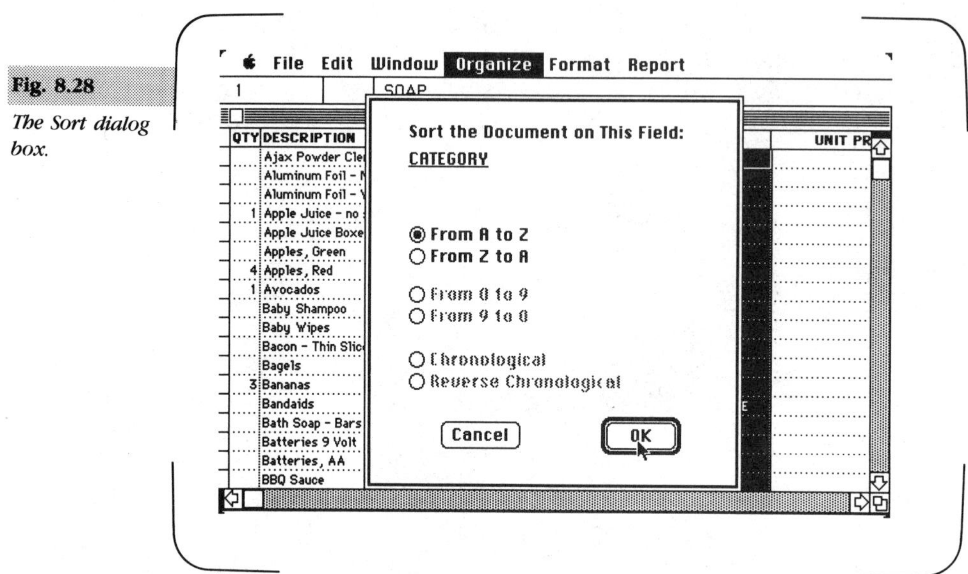

Fig. 8.28

The Sort dialog box.

on the MSN field changes in figures 8.29 and 8.30 when the field is defined first as text and then as numeric. When the field is defined as text, 1 always comes before 2 and so on, regardless of the size of the number (fig. 8.29). When the field is defined as numeric, the numbers are sorted into correct numerical order (fig. 8.30)

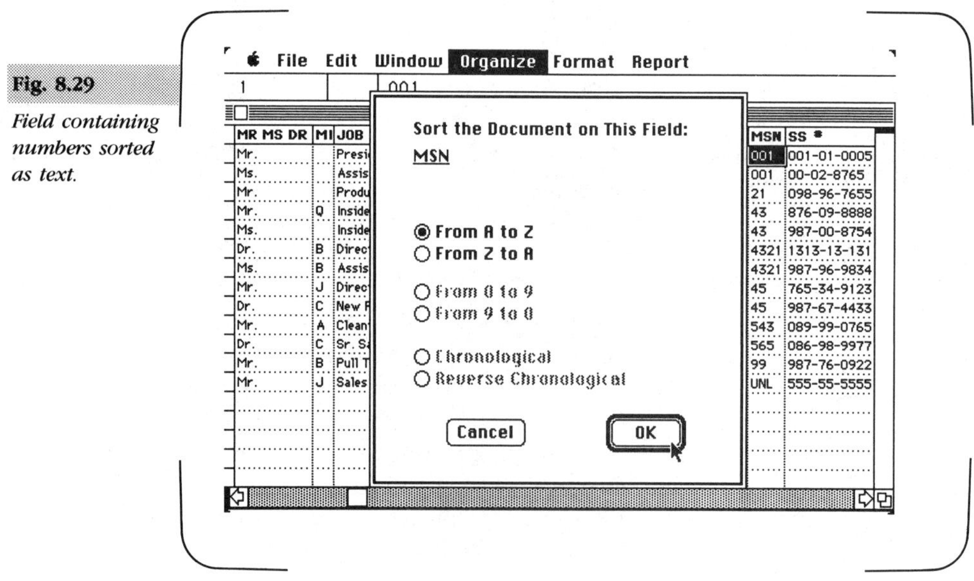

Fig. 8.29

Field containing numbers sorted as text.

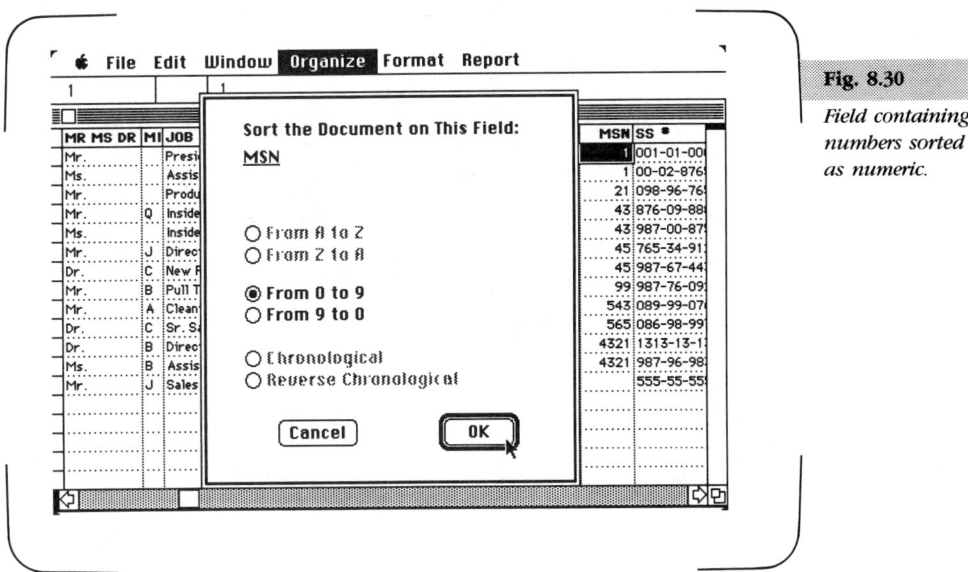

Fig. 8.30
Field containing numbers sorted as numeric.

If you make the wrong sort request, you usually can use Undo to put your database in the order it was in before the sort. You must, however, use Undo immediately. Sorts take place only in memory, so the disk copy of your database stays in the old order until you update the database by using the Save command.

Searching the Database

With the Find Field command on the Organize menu, you can have Works find a specific record. To find groups of records, you use the Match Records command, also on the Organize menu. Both options have command shortcuts: *command*-F and *command*-M, respectively.

Using the Find Field Command

With Find Field, you can search for specific single occurrences of information. When you select this option, Works presents a dialog box and prompts you to enter what you want to find. This entry can be either text or numbers. For example, in figure 8.31, Works is told to find the word *chip* in any text field in the database.

Usually, Works checks all fields. You can, however, ask Works to check only fields that are defined as text fields (the default). Or you can expand

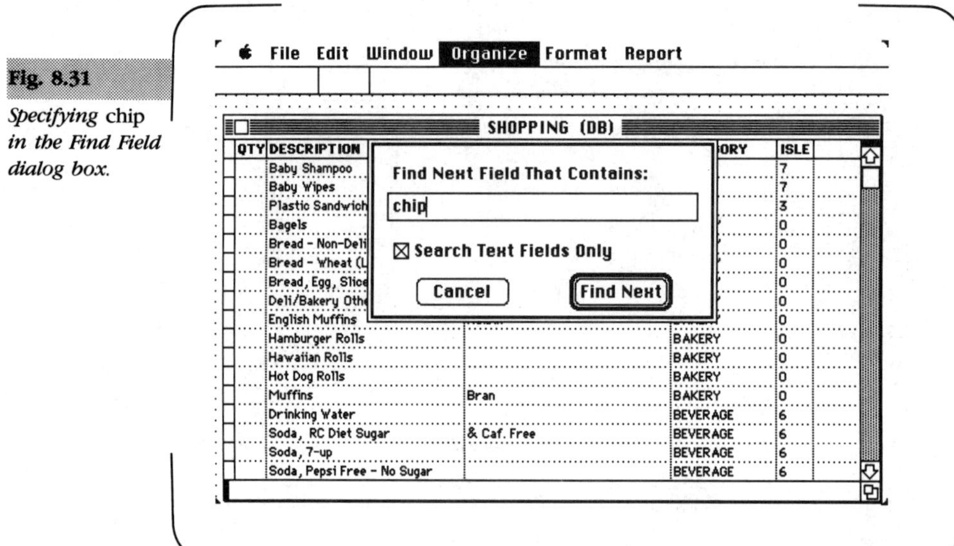

Fig. 8.31

Specifying chip *in the Find Field dialog box.*

the search to include numeric and date fields. To expand the search, click to remove the *X* from the Search Text Fields Only box.

When you click the Find Next button or press the *return* key to begin the search, Works finds and highlights the first occurrence of the item specified, as shown in figure 8.32.

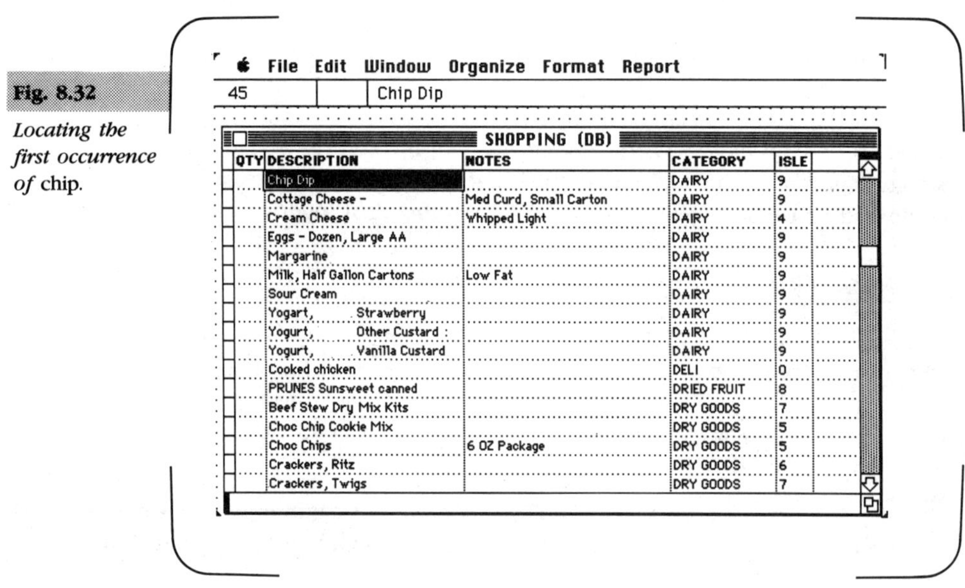

Fig. 8.32

Locating the first occurrence of chip.

To search for another occurrence of the same word, select the Find Field option again. Works displays your previous search request, which you can use again to look for additional occurrences. Either press *return* or click Find Next to search again or modify your request. To speed things up, get in the habit of using the *command*-F shortcut. Works tells you when it finds the last occurrence of the word specified. Click OK to make this dialog box disappear.

Using the Match Records Command

When you specify the Match Records option, Works displays all the records that meet your search criteria. Although this command works in the form window, Match Records is most useful in the list window. After you choose Match Records on the Organize menu, Works displays a dialog box that looks like the Find Field dialog box. To enter the search criteria, you use the same techniques as for Find Field. For example, in figure 8.33, Works is told to match only records containing the word *PARK*.

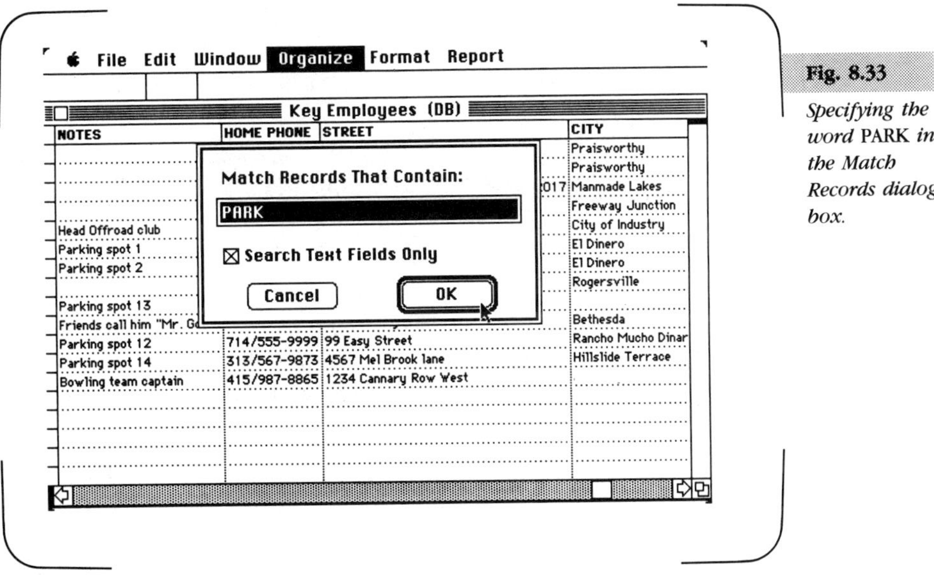

Fig. 8.33

Specifying the word PARK *in the Match Records dialog box.*

To find the word(s) you're searching for, Works looks either in every text field or everywhere in the database. For example, Works finds employees with the last name of *Park* or the first name of *Parker*. If someone in your database lives on Park Lane, Works finds that occurrence of the word, too. And if the NOTES field contains *Parking spot*, that also qualifies. You tell Works to search the entire database by clicking to remove the check mark in the Search Text Fields Only box, as you do in the Find Field dialog box.

When you use the Match Records feature, Works displays a collection (or subset) consisting of the records that meet your search criteria (see fig. 8.34, which shows records containing the word *park*). You can scroll through the list in either the form or list window; you can print the window; and you can cut or clear the entries.

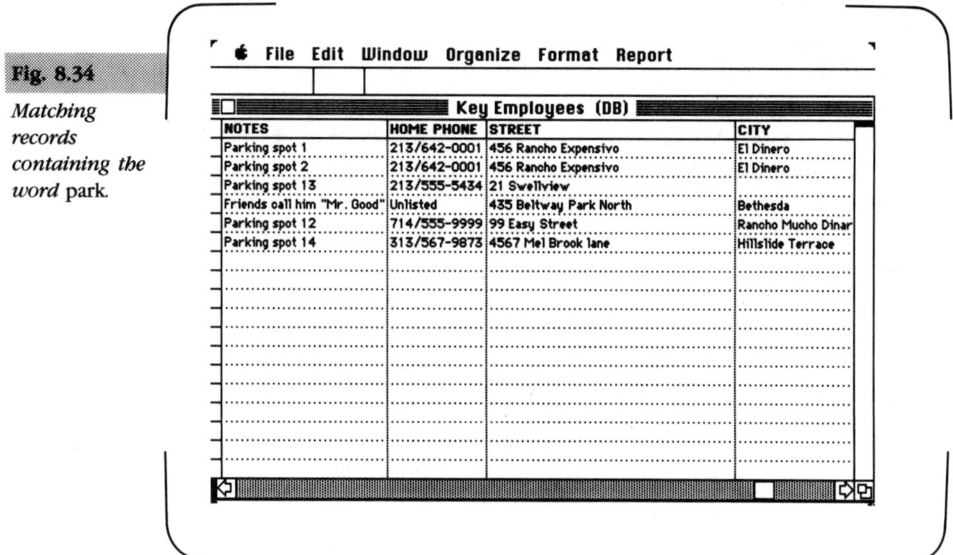

NOTES	HOME PHONE	STREET	CITY
Parking spot 1	213/642-0001	456 Rancho Expensivo	El Dinero
Parking spot 2	213/642-0001	456 Rancho Expensivo	El Dinero
Parking spot 13	213/555-5434	21 Swellview	
Friends call him "Mr. Good"	Unlisted	435 Beltway Park North	Bethesda
Parking spot 12	714/555-9999	99 Easy Street	Rancho Mucho Dinar
Parking spot 14	313/567-9873	4567 Mel Brook lane	Hillside Terrace

Fig. 8.34

Matching records containing the word park.

To remove the check mark from the option and return to the full database, click the Match Records option on the Organize menu a second time. You also can use the *command*-M shortcut to return to the full database.

Using Special Search Tips and Techniques

Works search features have certain characteristics you need to understand. Otherwise, you may not be able to find entries that you know are in your database. This section covers some of those important characteristics.

Special characters, accent marks, and spaces are important in searches. For example, if you search for *La Canada*, Works won't find *La Cañada*.

If you put a space in front of a search request, Works finds only the occurrences preceded by at least one space. For example, if you search for " wood", Works doesn't find *dogwood* but does find *woodwork*. Spaces at the end of search requests are important, too. If you request "clean ", Works won't find records containing *cleaning*, and so on.

In figure 8.35, Works is told to find all occurrences of "chip dip ". But, as shown in figure 8.36, Works doesn't find *Chip Dip*, even though it's in plain sight. A space is included in the search request, and, in this case, no space follows *Dip*.

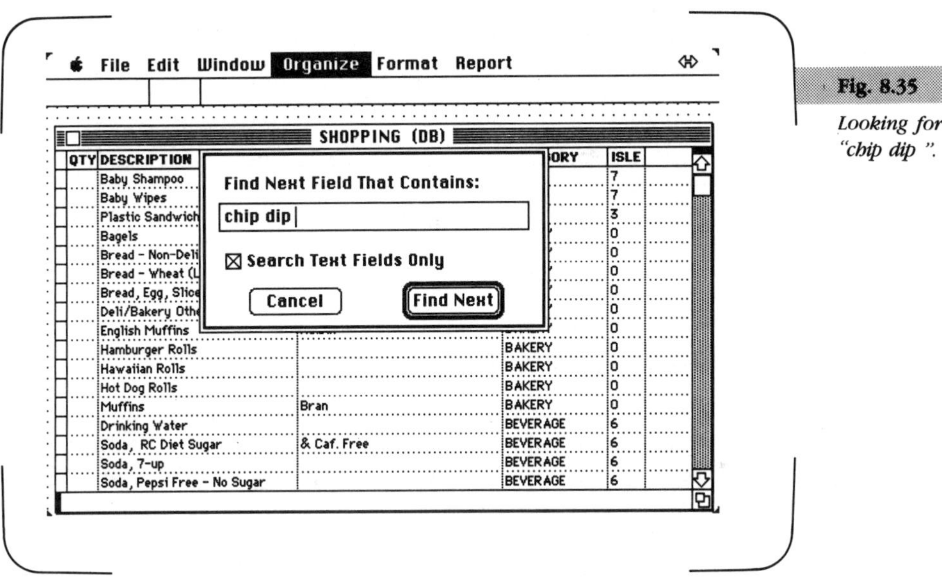

Fig. 8.35
Looking for "chip dip ".

As you have probably noticed, Works doesn't distinguish between uppercase and lowercase letters when you use the Find Field and Match Records commands. For example, as far as Works is concerned, the words *Parks, parks, PARKS,* and *pArks* all match.

Works Versions 1.0 and 1.1 treat searching for dates and times a little differently than you might expect. These versions won't even look at date or time fields unless you remove the Search Text Fields Only restriction. When these versions do look at date and time fields, however, the program searches these fields as if they were text. That is to say, if a date field is displayed in the long form, you need to search for the date in the long form. For example, if you search for 4-19-82, Works won't find Monday, April 19, 1982.

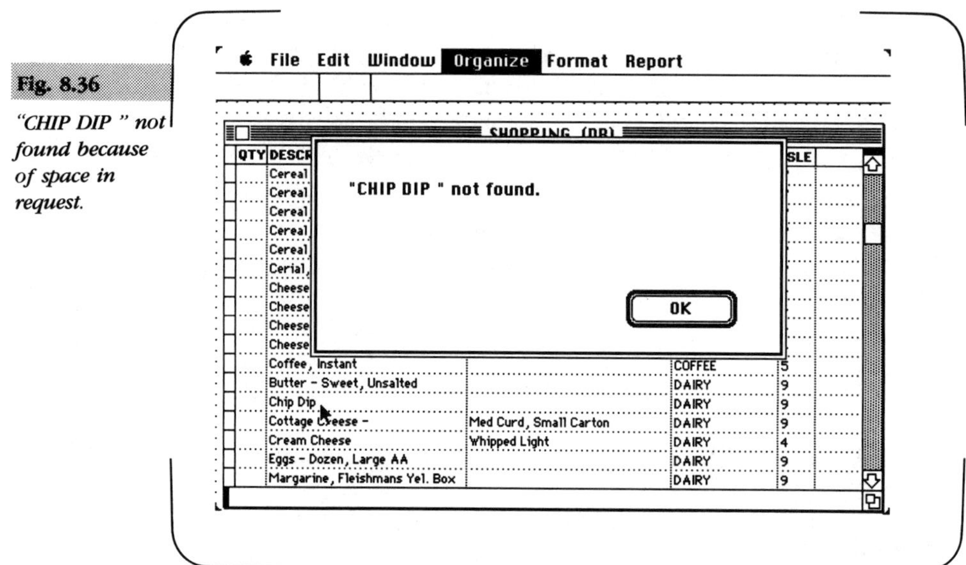

Fig. 8.36

"CHIP DIP " not found because of space in request.

Understanding Selection Rules

When your database grows, looking for all the records containing *park* or everybody in *Marketing* may not be easy or practical. You may need to find more specific groups, such as *everybody in Marketing or Sales who earns more than $20,000.00 but less than $50,000.00 and is female*. Works enables you to set up *selection rules*, also called *comparison phrases*, to help with this kind of searching.

Selection rules are also an important part of report designing, so you need to understand how they work. Don't be put off by their seeming complexity. All you need to do is tell Works three things:

1. Which field(s) should be searched
2. What the rules are (comparison phrases)
3. What to look for (comparison information)

Choosing Selection Rules

You use selection rules all the time in conversation—for example, "Who earns more than I do?" and "Does he live on the same street as you do?"

Works answers questions just like these. In Works, you must use specific phrases that the program can interpret. Works has 14 comparison phrases:

equals
is greater than
is greater than or equal to
is less than
is less than or equal to
is not equal to
is blank
is not blank
contains
begins with
ends with
does not contain
does not begin with
does not end with

By combining these phrases with field names from your database and your specific requirements, you can make almost limitless comparisons and selections.

You complete the phrases by indicating which field(s) to search and by entering your own comparison criteria. For instance, if your database has a SALARY field, you can use a complete selection rule like this:

SALARY is greater than or equal to 20000

To minimize needless typing, Works provides a dialog box containing a list of the field names in the currently active database and a second window containing up to 14 comparison phrases (see fig. 8.37). You scroll through these windows and select the items you need to construct your selection rules. The dialog box also contains a place for you to enter your comparison information.

At the bottom of the dialog box are buttons for implementing the rules once you've created them. After you've created and installed the rule, you can use it to select only records that meet the rule's selection criteria.

NOTE: Some types of fields can't be compared by all 14 phrases, so only applicable comparisons (based on the type of field you've selected) are shown in the phrase window. For example, if you select a date field, Works won't display *contains, begins with, ends with,* and other text-related comparison phrases.

Suppose that you want to find the names of all employees in a database who were hired before a specific date. The selections shown in figure 8.37 accomplish that task for you. When the Select button is clicked, the new rule will be installed.

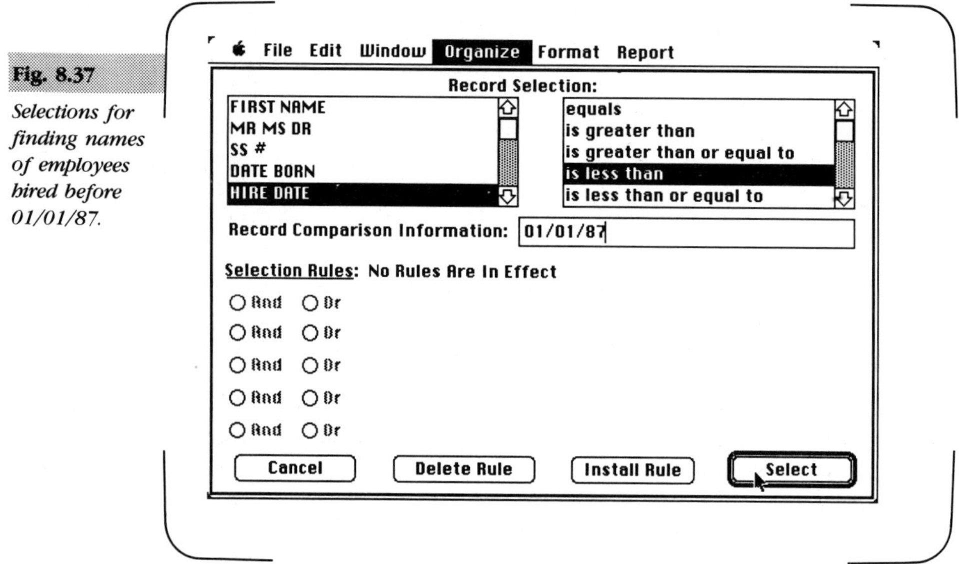

Fig. 8.37

Selections for finding names of employees hired before 01/01/87.

Here are the steps you follow for this example:

1. Choose Record Selection from the Organize menu.
2. Click to select the HIRE DATE field name (scroll, if necessary).
3. Select the *is less than* phrase by clicking (scroll, if necessary).
4. Enter the "before" date; use any Works date format (see the "Date Format" section).
5. Click on the Install Rule button. The rule you've written appears next to the Selection Rules box.
6. Either press the **return** key or click the Select button to see the results.

If all goes well, Works displays only records containing hire dates that fall before the comparison date you entered (see fig. 8.38). You can scroll to see the column containing employee names.

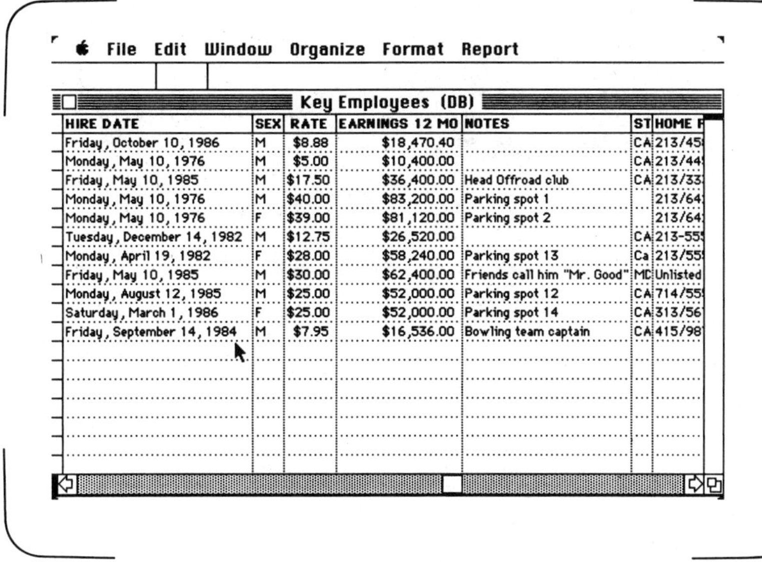

HIRE DATE	SEX	RATE	EARNINGS 12 MO	NOTES	ST	HOME F
Friday, October 10, 1986	M	$8.88	$18,470.40		CA	213/45
Monday, May 10, 1976	M	$5.00	$10,400.00		CA	213/44
Friday, May 10, 1985	M	$17.50	$36,400.00	Head Offroad club	CA	213/33
Monday, May 10, 1976	M	$40.00	$83,200.00	Parking spot 1		213/64
Monday, May 10, 1976	F	$39.00	$81,120.00	Parking spot 2		213/64
Tuesday, December 14, 1982	M	$12.75	$26,520.00		CA	213-55
Monday, April 19, 1982	F	$28.00	$58,240.00	Parking spot 13	Ca	213/55
Friday, May 10, 1985	M	$30.00	$62,400.00	Friends call him "Mr. Good"	MD	Unlisted
Monday, August 12, 1985	M	$25.00	$52,000.00	Parking spot 12	CA	714/55
Saturday, March 1, 1986	F	$25.00	$52,000.00	Parking spot 14	CA	313/56
Friday, September 14, 1984	M	$7.95	$16,536.00	Bowling team captain	CA	415/98

Fig. 8.38

The results of the selection rules for finding names of employees hired before 01/01/87.

If Works can't find any records, the program tells you so. Works also tells you whether you made an error when constructing your rule. Common errors include forgetting to enter comparison phrases and trying to enter text when comparing numeric fields. When these situations arise, correct your entry and try again.

Specifying Multiple Selection Rules

You can limit choices further by specifying up to six restrictions. For instance, you can select records for employees hired before January 1, 1987, earning more than $10.00 per hour, and working in California (see fig. 8.39). Figure 8.40 shows the records Works displays for these selection rules. You can enter multiple rules when you first start the selection process, or you can add to the selection rules after you've tried a selection or two. Works remembers the last rules you used and lets you add to them.

Understanding the And/Or Selection Rules

And and *or*: We use these two words in conversation all the time. "I'll take a pound of clams and a pound of the fresh trout." "How many Beatles albums do I have that are on either compact disks or cassette tapes?" "I want something that's both hot and spicy."

With Works, you can make selection requests like these, too. You've seen how And works by itself in figure 8.39. In that example, And re-

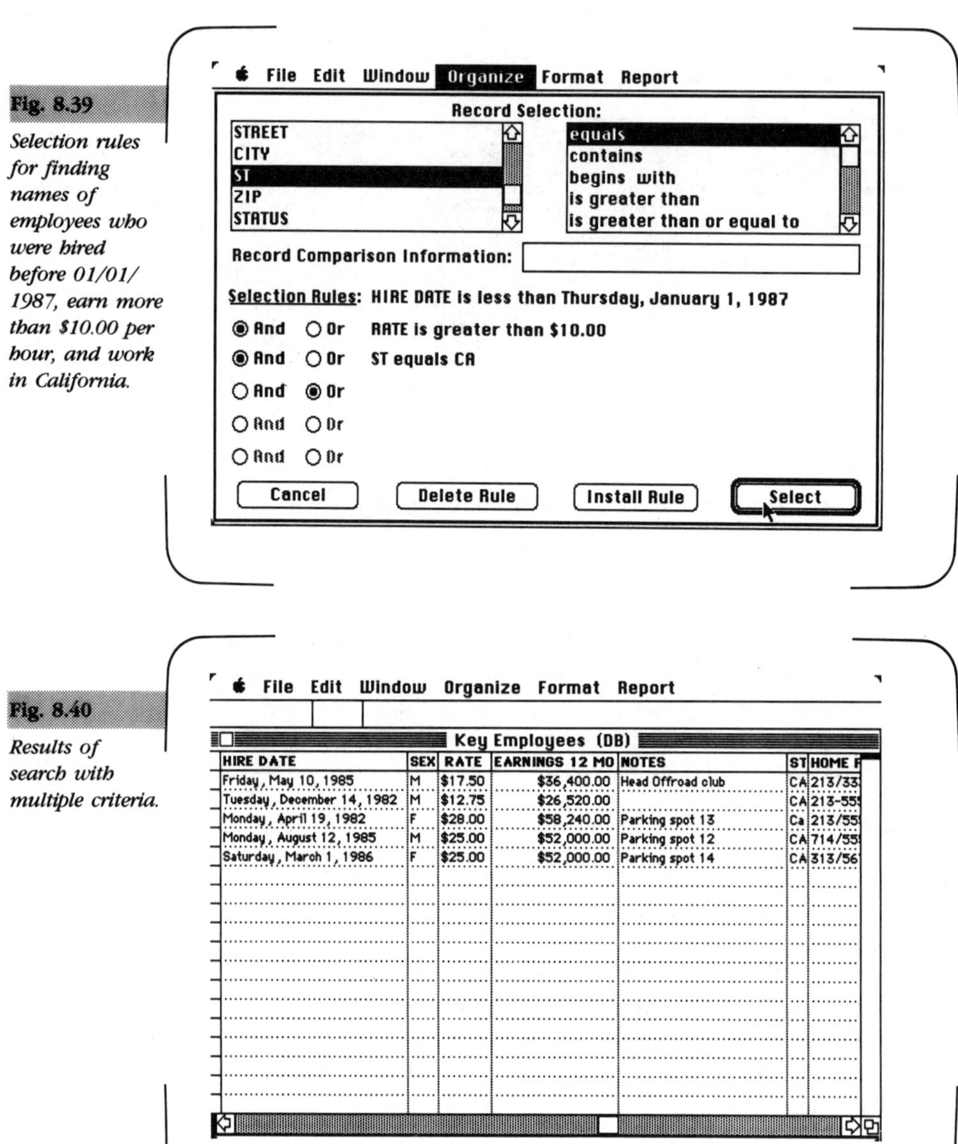

HIRE DATE	SEX	RATE	EARNINGS 12 MO	NOTES	ST	HOME
Friday, May 10, 1985	M	$17.50	$36,400.00	Head Offroad club	CA	213/33
Tuesday, December 14, 1982	M	$12.75	$26,520.00		CA	213-55
Monday, April 19, 1982	F	$28.00	$58,240.00	Parking spot 13	Ca	213/55
Monday, August 12, 1985	M	$25.00	$52,000.00	Parking spot 12	CA	714/55
Saturday, March 1, 1986	F	$25.00	$52,000.00	Parking spot 14	CA	313/56

Fig. 8.39 *Selection rules for finding names of employees who were hired before 01/01/1987, earn more than $10.00 per hour, and work in California.*

Fig. 8.40 *Results of search with multiple criteria.*

stricts the display to only records that meet all three conditions: employees hired before 01/01/87 And earning more than $10.00 per hour And working in California.

You can also use And to refine the selection further, by using multiple And selection criteria like this:

And RATE is greater than $10.00
And RATE is less than $40.00

And what about the Or feature? By adding Or selection criteria, you can widen your search to include other possibilities. For example, by adding "Or HIRE DATE less than 01/01/70" to the selection rules in figure 8.39, you can have Works find the names of employees hired before that date, regardless of their sex or location.

Practice will help you perfect these selection skills. The key point to remember is that And restricts, while Or expands the number of records that will be selected.

Deleting a Selection Rule

To delete the last selection rule you entered, you click the Delete Rule button. You can't move back through your list of selection rules. If you're unhappy with an earlier selection rule, you'll probably have to erase some good ones to reach it.

Saving Copies of Selected Data

Usually, during the selection process, Works simply displays the results. You can, however, save a copy of the records you've selected, using a different file name. This arrangement gives you, for example, a "California" version of your personnel database or a "Marketing Department" personnel database. You even can alter the design of the smaller (or subset) database. Here's what you do:

1. Save any changes you've recently made (maybe even back up the database).
2. Select the desired records by using the steps outlined in the preceding sections.
3. Make any modifications to the new subset (delete fields and so forth).
4. Use the Save As (not the Save) command.

If you select data and use the Save command or *command*-S shortcut rather than Save As, you may permanently damage the disk copy of your large database. You will, in effect, replace the big database with the new smaller subset. If you do make this blunder, rest assured that the big database is still in memory and can be saved under its old file name. But you need to catch your mistake soon after you've made it; Undo won't help here.

You need to keep another point in mind. If you copy records from one database into a new database, you have to keep both the original and new databases up-to-date thereafter. For example, suppose that you have both a national personnel database and a California database containing the names of the same employees. When someone moves, you must record that employee's change of address in both databases. Don't make extra work for yourself without a good reason.

Changing Database Design

Once you've defined a database—or even after you've used it for a while—you may want to make design changes. Works is extremely flexible this way. You can add or delete fields, change field attributes, move things around, insert records, and more.

WARNING: Before modifying a database, make a backup copy, particularly if you've invested a great deal of time and effort in the original design or have spent hours editing data. Then, if things go badly, you won't have to redesign the database or re-enter hours' worth of work to get back to where you started.

Changing Field Names and Attributes

You can change the name of a field whenever you like. Here's what you do:

1. Double-click on the field name. A dialog box then appears.
2. Make the change.
3. Either click the OK button or press **return**.

You also can change a field's attributes whenever you like, regardless of whether Works is in the form or the list window. The procedure is the following:

1. Double-click on the field name. Works then displays a dialog box.
2. Make the change.
3. Click the OK button or press **return**.

CAUTION: Feel free to change choices like bold, text alignment, and commas. If the database contains important records, however, be careful about changing the field type (see the following section).

Changing Field Types—Risky Business

You can change field type (one of the attributes) *after* entering data into your database, but doing so *before* is preferable. Otherwise, you run the risk of losing all or some of your entries in the changed field. This loss might occur for a variety of reasons. For example, if you change a text field to a date field, you eliminate any entries that don't conform to Works' date formats.

If you must change the definition of a field that contains data, keep in mind the following guidelines:

- Save a copy (backup) of your database first.
- You can always change time, date, or number fields to text. If you try other conversions, you'll probably lose data; in such cases, Works warns you about the problem, as shown in figure 8.41.
- You can recover data by using the Undo command if you use it immediately.

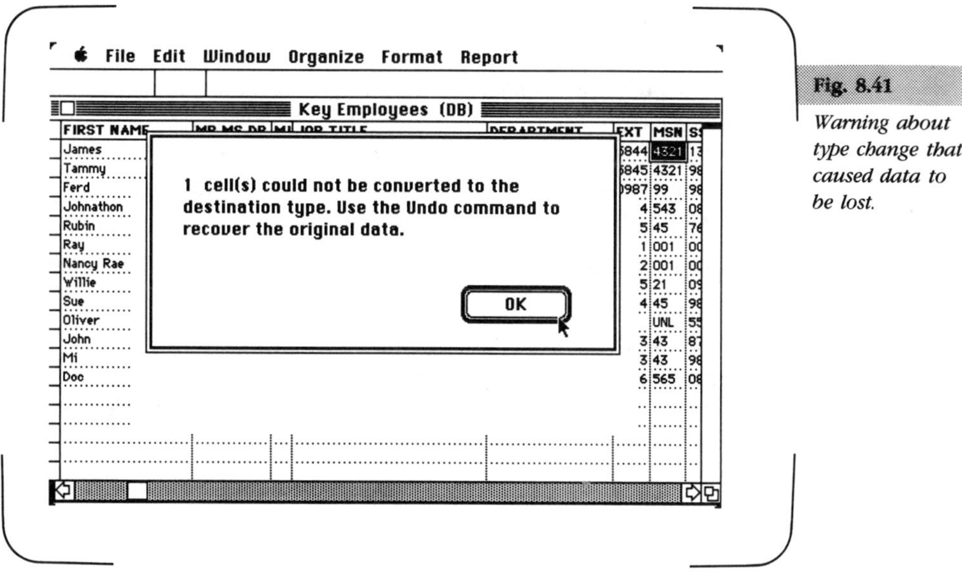

Fig. 8.41

Warning about type change that caused data to be lost.

Adding Fields

You can add a field any time, using a variety of methods. Works can be in either the form or list window.

One way to add a field in the form window is to choose Add New Field from the Edit menu. You name the field and change its size and location the same way you change fields when you are creating your database. If you're adding a field in the form window, Works determines the field's initial location for you. In either case, you can move the field to wherever you want.

Here's a shortcut for adding fields in the form window. It seems like magic, but it works. Point to the position where you want the upper left corner of the field to appear, and then drag a brand-new field box to its desired length. The box will appear the moment you start dragging. Besides saving you a trip to the Edit menu, this technique puts the field right where you want it. The method is worth learning; try using it on any open database form window.

In the list window, Works adds the field at the end of the record. The field is the rightmost entry on your screen. To move the field to the desired position, point to the field name and drag the field to its new location.

Deleting Fields

You can delete entire fields (and their contents) at any time by choosing the Delete Field option on the Edit menu. (Works can be in either the form or list window.) Works then removes the field and its contents from every record in your database. Before deleting fields, you should back up your database.

To restore data that has been deleted with this option, you must use Undo.

Don't confuse the Delete Field option with cutting and pasting or back-spacing to delete data in a specific field. Unless you use the Undo option immediately after deleting a field, the deletion is irreversible. Deleted fields do not go to the Clipboard.

Deleting Records

The best way to delete an entire record is to select it in the list window. Here's what you do:

1. Click on the box to the left of the record you want to delete; Works then highlights that record.

2. Cut by using either the **command-X** shortcut or the Cut option on the Edit menu. If you make a mistake, use Undo on the same menu.

NOTE: To delete multiple, adjacent records, drag rather than simply clicking as described in step 1. Works then highlights the records starting where you begin to drag and ending where you release the mouse button. Cut, as described in step 2. Works then removes all the highlighted records. (They'll be on the Clipboard but no longer in the database.)

Shortcuts and Tips for Using Databases

As you know, Works is easy to use. The Works database is simple and straightforward in its operation. You can, however, save time by learning some shortcuts and special tips. With the information in this section, you can increase both your speed and your efficiency in working with your database.

Selecting and Deselecting Records in a List

Figure 8.42 shows small boxes to the left of each record. These are called record selector boxes. By clicking on one of them, you select the entire record. You'll see why this procedure is handy.

The box to the left of the field names is called the deselect box. You click it to deselect whatever you've selected—an entire record, multiple records, or a single field. This box is similar to its namesake in a spreadsheet window.

Inserting Records in a List

You can always add records at the end of a database and have Works sort them into place. But you also can add new records precisely where you want them without sorting. Just as you can insert rows in a spreadsheet, you can insert records in a list. Here's what you do:

1. Select the record below where you want the insert to appear, as shown in figure 8.43.

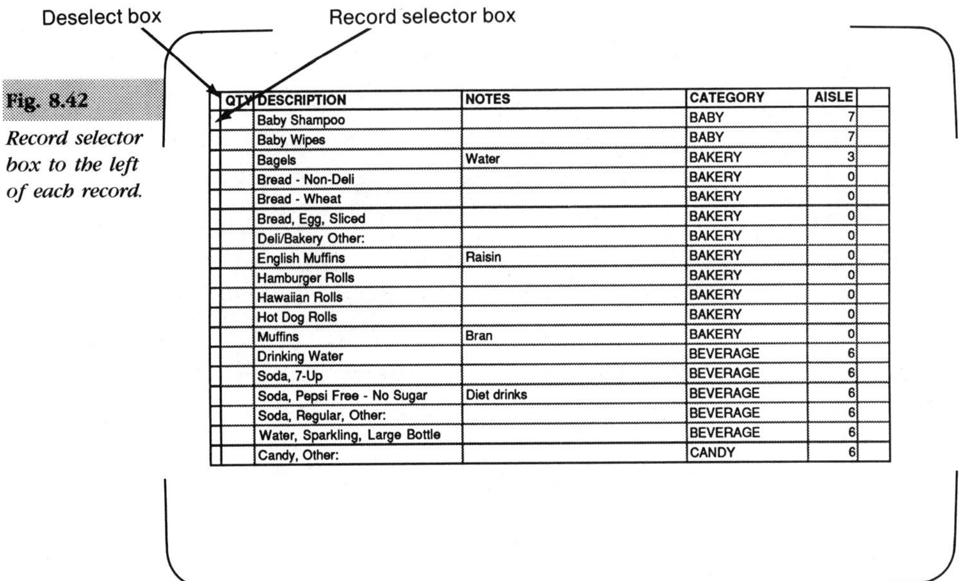

QTY	DESCRIPTION	NOTES	CATEGORY	AISLE
	Baby Shampoo		BABY	7
	Baby Wipes		BABY	7
	Bagels	Water	BAKERY	3
	Bread - Non-Deli		BAKERY	0
	Bread - Wheat		BAKERY	0
	Bread, Egg, Sliced		BAKERY	0
	Deli/Bakery Other:		BAKERY	0
	English Muffins	Raisin	BAKERY	0
	Hamburger Rolls		BAKERY	0
	Hawaiian Rolls		BAKERY	0
	Hot Dog Rolls		BAKERY	0
	Muffins	Bran	BAKERY	0
	Drinking Water		BEVERAGE	6
	Soda, 7-Up		BEVERAGE	6
	Soda, Pepsi Free - No Sugar	Diet drinks	BEVERAGE	6
	Soda, Regular, Other:		BEVERAGE	6
	Water, Sparkling, Large Bottle		BEVERAGE	6
	Candy, Other:		CANDY	6

Fig. 8.42

Record selector box to the left of each record.

2. Either choose Insert Record from the Edit menu (see fig. 8.43) or press **command-I**. A blank record then appears, as illustrated in figure 8.44.

3. Enter the data (use the cut-and-paste feature if it will speed things up).

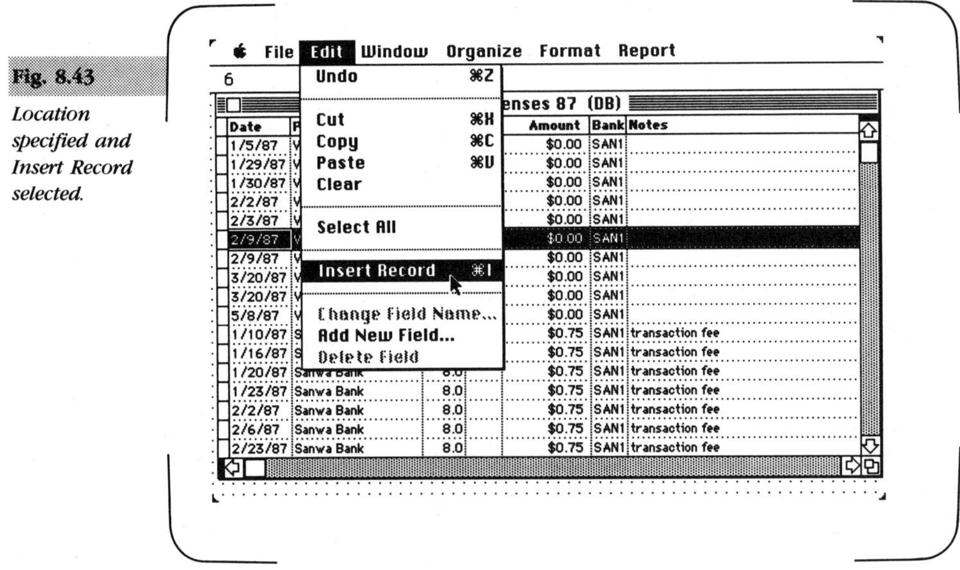

Fig. 8.43

Location specified and Insert Record selected.

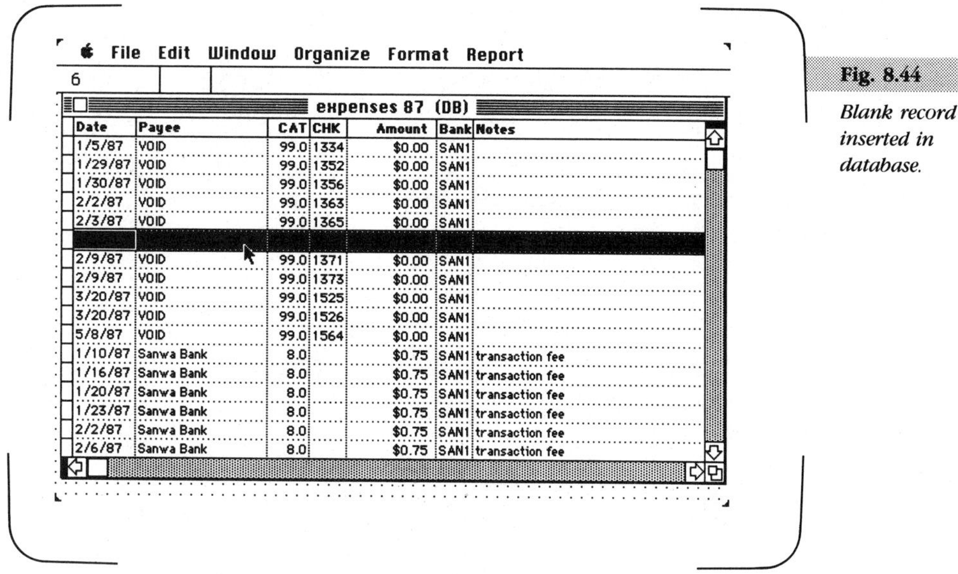

Date	Payee	CAT	CHK	Amount	Bank	Notes
1/5/87	VOID	99.0	1334	$0.00	SAN1	
1/29/87	VOID	99.0	1352	$0.00	SAN1	
1/30/87	VOID	99.0	1356	$0.00	SAN1	
2/2/87	VOID	99.0	1363	$0.00	SAN1	
2/3/87	VOID	99.0	1365	$0.00	SAN1	
2/9/87	VOID	99.0	1371	$0.00	SAN1	
2/9/87	VOID	99.0	1373	$0.00	SAN1	
3/20/87	VOID	99.0	1525	$0.00	SAN1	
3/20/87	VOID	99.0	1526	$0.00	SAN1	
5/8/87	VOID	99.0	1564	$0.00	SAN1	
1/10/87	Sanwa Bank	8.0		$0.75	SAN1	transaction fee
1/16/87	Sanwa Bank	8.0		$0.75	SAN1	transaction fee
1/20/87	Sanwa Bank	8.0		$0.75	SAN1	transaction fee
1/23/87	Sanwa Bank	8.0		$0.75	SAN1	transaction fee
2/2/87	Sanwa Bank	8.0		$0.75	SAN1	transaction fee
2/6/87	Sanwa Bank	8.0		$0.75	SAN1	transaction fee

Fig. 8.44

Blank record inserted in database.

Changing Field Lengths in a List

You can make a field in a list wider or narrower by dragging the line separating the fields. This process resembles that used to resize spreadsheet columns. You do this:

1. Point to the right edge of the field name box. The pointer becomes a double-headed arrow.
2. Drag the field to the desired size.

Moving Fields in a List

You can rearrange the order in which fields appear in list windows—a process similar to that used to move columns in a spreadsheet. This rearranging does not affect the location of fields when in the form window. Here's what you do:

1. Point to the name of the field you want to move. The pointer then becomes a hand.
2. Drag the field to its new position. Fields to its right are pushed right to accommodate the moved field.

Dividing a List Window into Panes

With Works displaying the list window, you can create a split screen similar to a split spreadsheet window (see fig. 8.45). You can create horizontal, vertical, and combined window panes. These arrangements make it easy to view different parts of long records without rearranging field order. To control the panes, you pull split bars, which are small black rectangles at the upper right and lower left corners of the database windows.

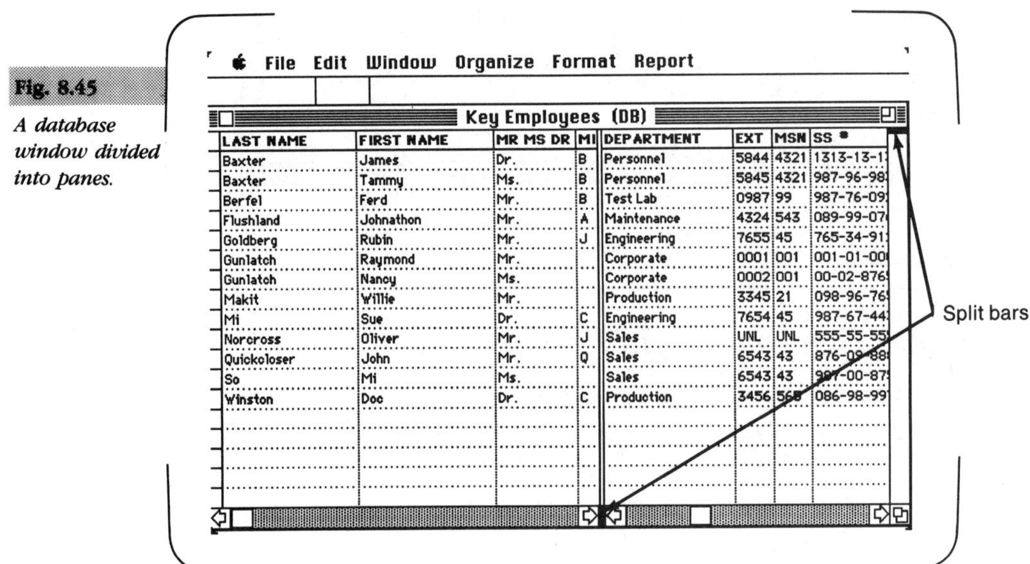

LAST NAME	FIRST NAME	MR MS DR	MI	DEPARTMENT	EXT	MSN	SS #
Baxter	James	Dr.	B	Personnel	5844	4321	1313-13-1
Baxter	Tammy	Ms.	B	Personnel	5845	4321	987-96-98
Berfel	Ferd	Mr.	B	Test Lab	0987	99	987-76-09
Flushland	Johnathon	Mr.	A	Maintenance	4324	543	089-99-07
Goldberg	Rubin	Mr.	J	Engineering	7655	45	765-34-91
Gunlatch	Raymond	Mr.		Corporate	0001	001	001-01-00
Gunlatch	Nancy	Ms.		Corporate	0002	001	00-02-876
Makit	Willie	Mr.		Production	3345	21	098-96-76
Mi	Sue	Dr.	C	Engineering	7654	45	987-67-44
Norcross	Oliver	Mr.	J	Sales	UNL	UNL	555-55-55
Quickcloser	John	Mr.	Q	Sales	6543	43	876-0[illegible]-88
So	Mi	Ms.		Sales	6543	43	9[illegible]7-00-87
Winston	Doc	Dr.	C	Production	3456	56[illegible]	086-98-99

Fig. 8.45

A database window divided into panes.

To divide a list window into panes, you do the following:

1. Point at a split bar. The pointer then becomes a two-way arrow.
2. Drag the split bar to create the desired pane.
3. Repeat the process on the other axis, if you want.

Controlling the List Grid

The Show Grid/No Grid option on the Format menu does what you'd expect. Figure 8.46 shows how the screen looks when the No Grid option is specified.

QTY	DESCRIPTION	NOTES	CATEGORY	AISLE
1	Baby Shampoo		BABY	7
	Baby Wipes		BABY	7
	Bagels	Water	BAKERY	3
	Bread - Non-Deli		BAKERY	0
	Bread - Wheat		BAKERY	0
	Bread, Egg, Sliced		BAKERY	0
	Deli/Bakery Other:		BAKERY	0
1	English Muffins	Raisin	BAKERY	0
	Hamburger Rolls		BAKERY	0
	Hawaiian Rolls		BAKERY	0
	Hot Dog Rolls		BAKERY	0
	Muffins	Bran	BAKERY	0
1	Drinking Water		BEVERAGE	6
	Soda, 7-Up		BEVERAGE	6
	Soda, Pepsi Free - No Sugar	Diet drinks	BEVERAGE	6
	Soda, Regular, Other:		BEVERAGE	6
	Water, Sparkling, Large Bottle		BEVERAGE	6
	Candy, Other:		CANDY	6

Fig. 8.46

Grid turned off in the list window.

Cutting and Copying Information

You can highlight database information and copy or cut it to the Clipboard and Scrapbook. This procedure works for single words, entire field contents, complete records, or even an entire database. Remember that if you cut (rather than copy), you delete information from the database. (See Chapter 2 for more information about cutting, copying, and pasting.)

Duplicating Fields from Previous Entries

When entering data into a database, press *command-*" (quotation mark) to reproduce the entry from the same field in the preceding record. This procedure helps eliminate repetitive typing.

Conclusion

In this chapter, you have learned how to design, create, and use a Works database. As noted, Works displays these databases only. You need to learn new techniques in order to print your database on paper. Those procedures are explained in Chapter 9.

Quick Start: Creating a Database

This Quick Start helps you to set up fields with understandable field names, to vary the length of fields, and to make data entries and corrections. You create and experiment with a simple database that collects the names, positions, departments, phone numbers, and salaries of fictitious employees. You also save your work so that it can be used with the Report Quick Start in Chapter 9 and in Chapter 11.

Opening a New Database Window

The quickest way to open a new database is to double-click on the Data Base icon in the Open File dialog box. The window opens with a Field Name dialog box containing the name Untitled. To label the fields, you simply type the appropriate name in the Untitled box.

Naming the Fields

When the first Field Name dialog box appears, type **LAST NAME**; then press **return**. If you prefer, use the Caps Lock key to enter the field names in all capitals.

Works prompts you for additional fields and gives you the opportunity to name them as you go. Enter and name the seven fields shown the example in figure 8.47. Then click Done.

Changing Field Sizes

To make each field box larger or smaller, point to the right edge of the field box. Then drag the box to its new size while holding down the mouse button. Use figure 8.48 as a guide for the length of your boxes.

Setting Field Attributes

Most of your fields contain simple text, but the ANNUAL SALARY field holds dollar amounts. Works displays the amounts with dollar signs, cents (two decimal places), and even commas, if you so specify. Works also challenges unlikely entries. For example, Works challenges any text in the ANNUAL SALARY field, knowing that the salary field contains only dollar amounts.

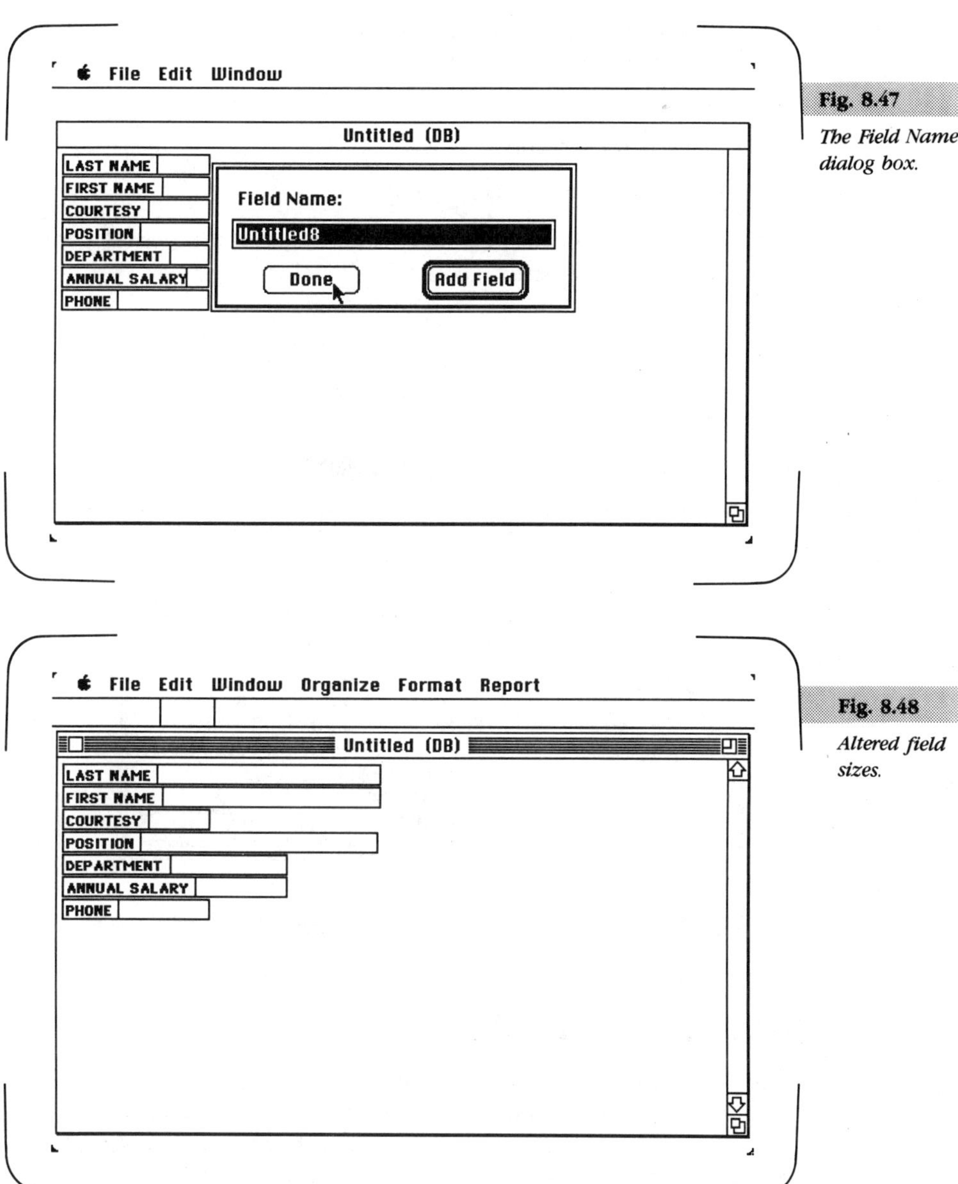

Fig. 8.47

The Field Name dialog box.

Fig. 8.48

Altered field sizes.

To set the field attributes for the ANNUAL SALARY field, double-click on the empty field box to the right of the ANNUAL SALARY field label box. Do not click on the field label box itself. When the Set Field Attributes for ANNUAL SALARY dialog box appears, do the following steps (see fig. 8.49):

1. Click Numeric under Type.
2. Click Dollar under Display.
3. Leave the *2* in the Decimal Places box and the default choice for right alignment.
4. Click Commas under Style.
5. Click OK or press **return**.

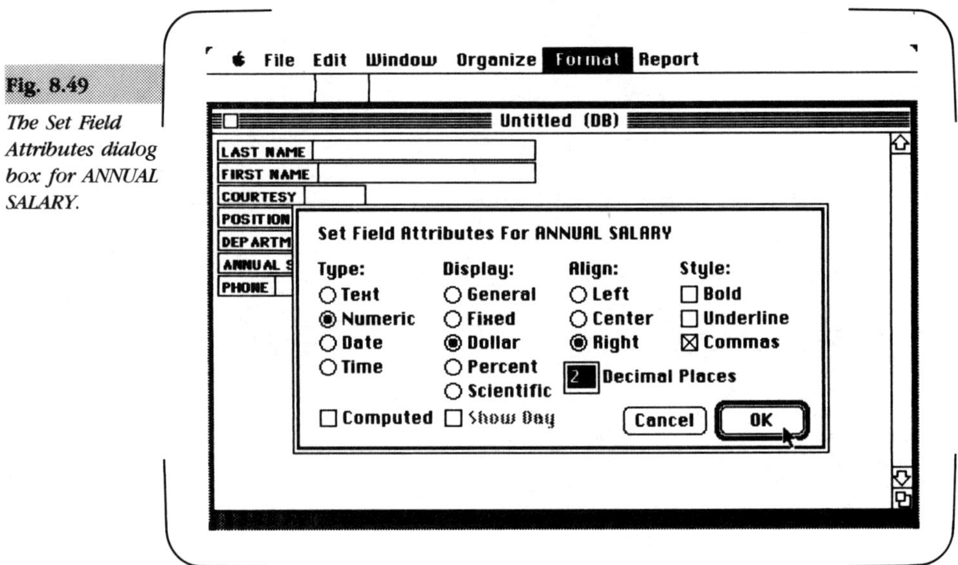

Fig. 8.49

The Set Field Attributes dialog box for ANNUAL SALARY.

Changing Field Names

The function of the COURTESY field on your database is to provide such courtesy titles as Mr and Ms to the names on your list, but the field name is not clear. To change the field name, double-click on COURTESY. A dialog box appears, asking for your changes. Simply start typing to replace the previous name, or point with the mouse and insert or delete as described in the word processing chapter.

The easiest way to change the field name is to type over the old name. Replace COURTESY with MR OR MS. Do not use periods or other punctuation marks because Works doesn't allow most punctuation or special characters in field names. Your screen now should look like figure 8.50.

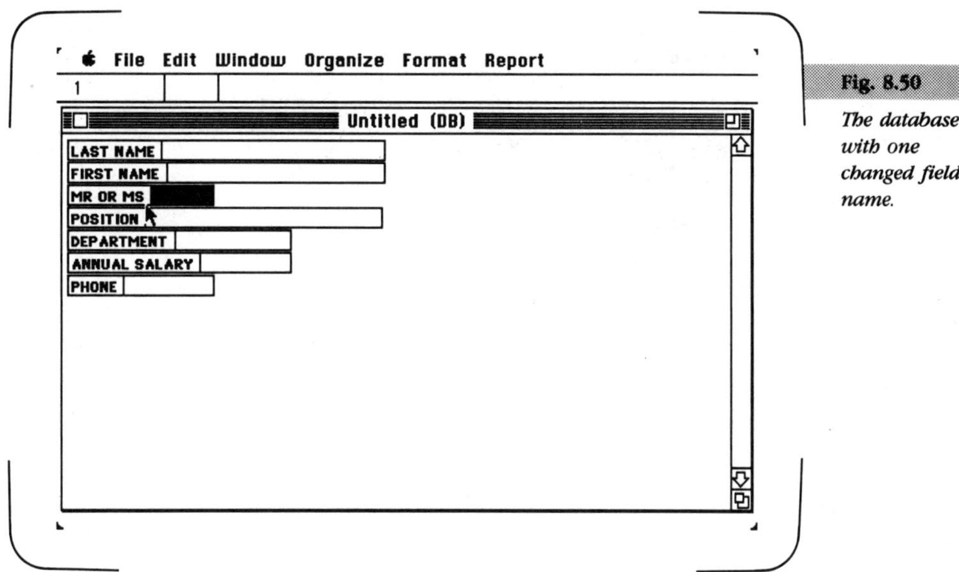

Fig. 8.50

The database with one changed field name.

Because the field name ANNUAL SALARY is long, use the *backspace* key to delete the word *ANNUAL* from the field name.

Entering Sample Data

Try entering your own records. Make up names as you go along, or use names of people you know.

Start by clicking on the empty field box to the right of the LAST NAME field label. The highlighted box turns black. Type a last name; press **return**. The First Name box is now highlighted. Continue to enter information and to press **return** until you reach the last box (see fig. 8.51). After you type the information in the last box, check the database file for typographical errors before you press **return**. If you spot an error, backspace or select the text to be corrected and make the corrections.

After you make the last entry in the PHONE box and check for errors, press **return**. A blank database form appears. Now, you can invent the specifics for another new employee. Have fun by creating five or six new records. Be sure to put some of the employees in different departments.

Fig. 8.51

A sample employee database file

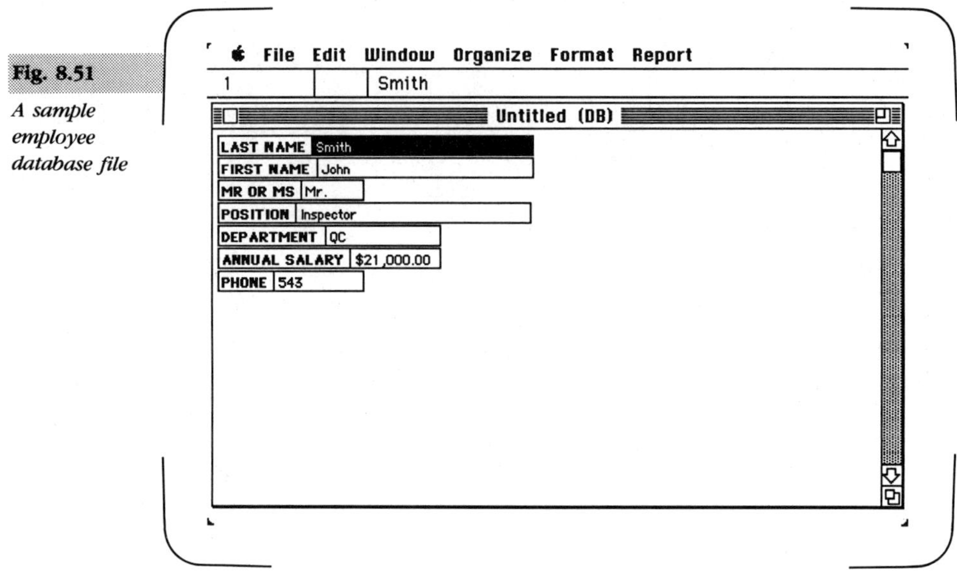

Displaying Records in the List Window

To switch from the form view to the list view, click anywhere on the blank portion of your screen, or use the Show List option in the Format menu. The employee information you have entered into your database files should look like figure 8.52.

Moving Fields in List Windows

To view the remaining fields, you need to scroll the screen. Drag the right arrow on the horizontal scroll bar at the bottom of the screen until the PHONE field comes into view. Move the field from its current location to a new location by following the steps listed below:

1. Point to the PHONE field name with the mouse pointer. The pointer becomes a hand.

2. Press the mouse button and drag the field to the left until the PHONE field is just to the right of the MR OR MS field. The window scrolls as necessary to bring MR OR MS into view.

3. Release the mouse button. The PHONE field is now in its new location. Your screen should look something like figure 8.53, except for the width of your fields and the presence of SALARY on the screen.

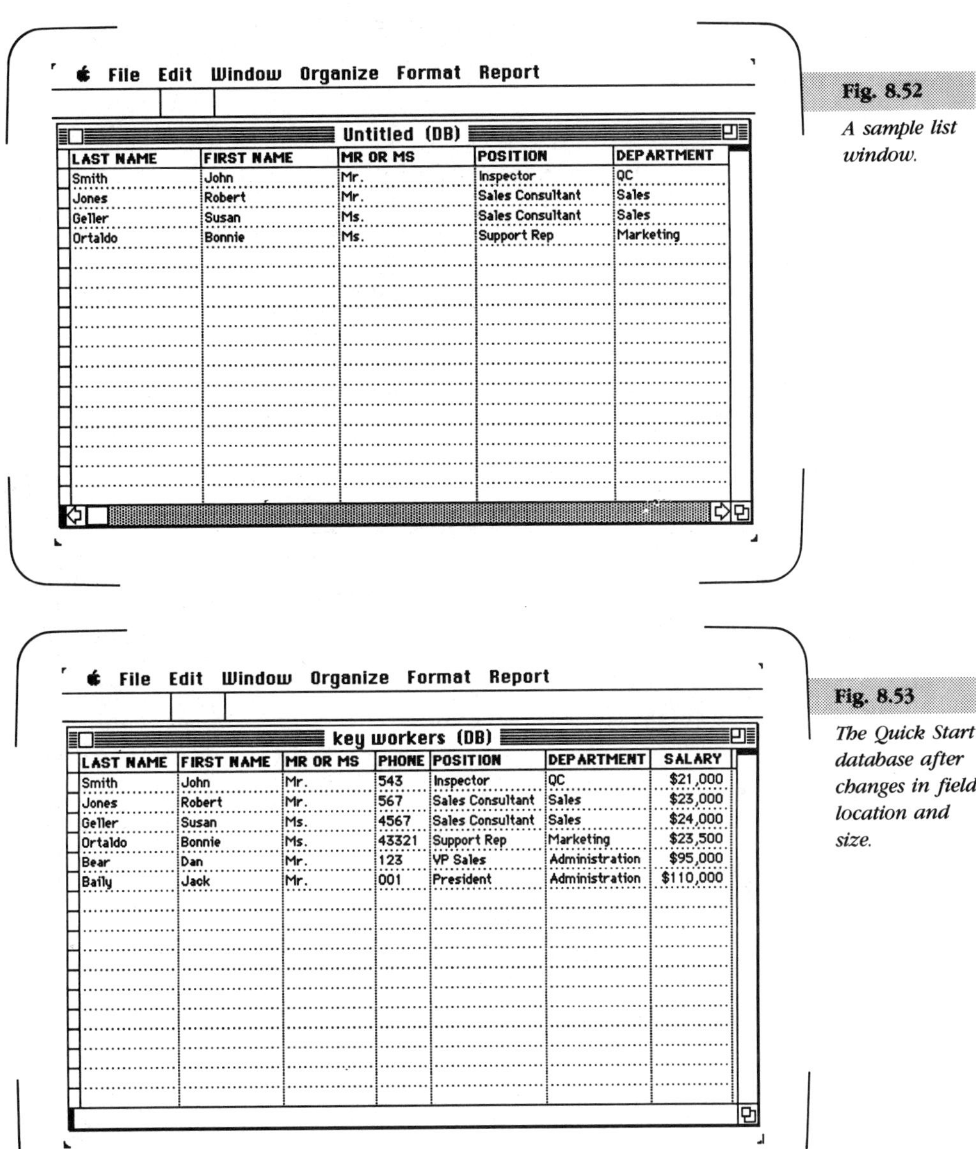

LAST NAME	FIRST NAME	MR OR MS	POSITION	DEPARTMENT
Smith	John	Mr.	Inspector	QC
Jones	Robert	Mr.	Sales Consultant	Sales
Geller	Susan	Ms.	Sales Consultant	Sales
Ortaldo	Bonnie	Ms.	Support Rep	Marketing

Fig. 8.52

A sample list window.

LAST NAME	FIRST NAME	MR OR MS	PHONE	POSITION	DEPARTMENT	SALARY
Smith	John	Mr.	543	Inspector	QC	$21,000
Jones	Robert	Mr.	567	Sales Consultant	Sales	$23,000
Geller	Susan	Ms.	4567	Sales Consultant	Sales	$24,000
Ortaldo	Bonnie	Ms.	43321	Support Rep	Marketing	$23,500
Bear	Dan	Mr.	123	VP Sales	Administration	$95,000
Baily	Jack	Mr.	001	President	Administration	$110,000

Fig. 8.53

The Quick Start database after changes in field location and size.

Changing Field Sizes for Lists

Many of the fields are bigger than necessary in the example. You can drag fields to smaller sizes by pointing the mouse at the vertical lines that separate field names in the list window. When the cursor turns into a two-headed arrow, press the mouse button and drag the field to its desired size. Practice adjusting field widths by making your screen look like figure 8.53.

Performing a Simple Sort

While you are still in the list window, practice sorting the sample records. You can see the results quickly.

1. Click the LAST NAME field title to highlight the records in that field.
2. From the Organize menu, choose Sort; a dialog box appears (see fig. 8.54).

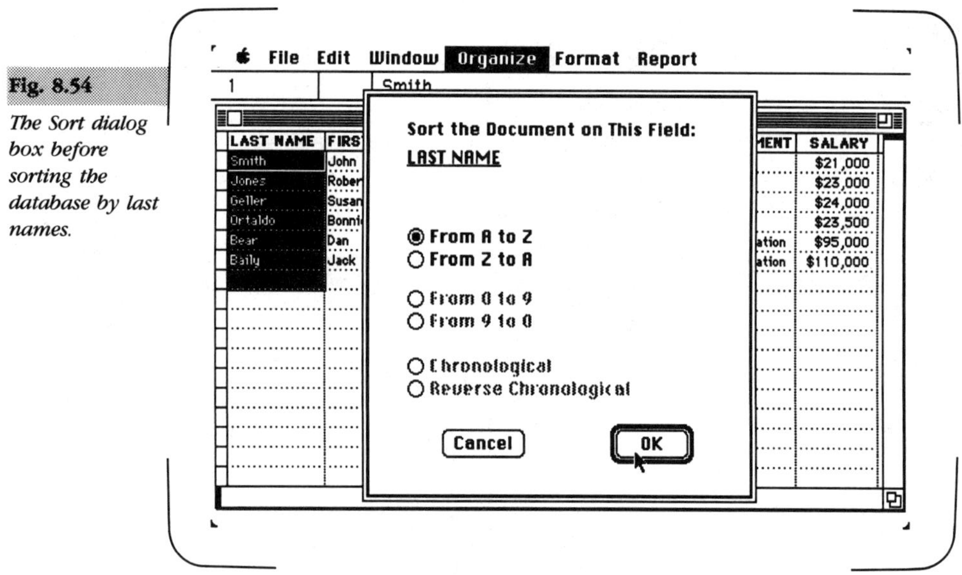

Fig. 8.54

The Sort dialog box before sorting the database by last names.

3. Choose the desired Sort order by clicking From A to Z if that option is not chosen already.
4. Click OK or press **return**. While viewing the results, experiment with sorts on other fields.

Saving the Quick Start Database

You want to use your database for the Quick Start report exercise in Chapter 9 and for the integration exercises in Chapter 11. To save your database, use the Save As command from the File menu. When prompted for a name, use QUICK DATABASE. Click the close box or choose Quit from the File menu if it's time for a break.

9

Database Reports

If you want paper copies of your Works database information to mark up, pass around, or examine, you must print that information. The printing process involves sorting the database and creating report definitions, page setups, and so forth. In Works, you can choose from two printing procedures. You use the Print Window command if you need to print only a few items that fit on a screen. If, on the other hand, you need to print longer reports, you use the report-generation feature, which provides subtotals, totals, and labeling options. In this chapter, you learn how to print both windows and longer reports.

Defining and Printing Short Reports

With the Print Window command, you can quickly produce short reports (which fit in one or two screens). This procedure is the same one you learned in the word-processing section of this book (see Chapter 2).

Here's how the procedure works:

1. You place the database in the desired order (sort the database). You can use the selection features to create a subset, if you like.

2. Scroll so that the appropriate data appears in the database window.

3. Choose Print Window from the File menu, as shown in figure 9.1.

To "kick" the page out of the printer, you use the Eject Page option on the File menu.

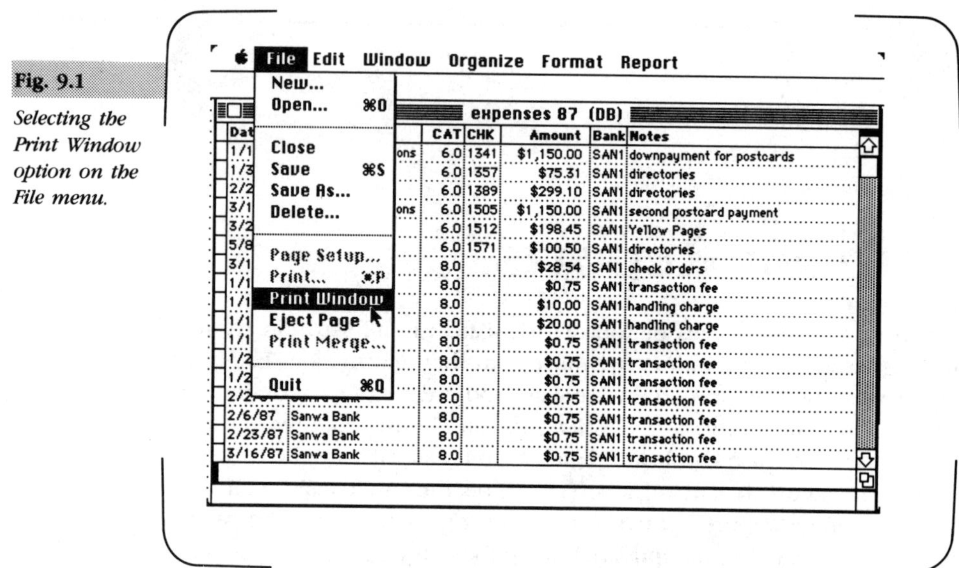

Fig. 9.1

Selecting the Print Window option on the File menu.

When you use Print Window, you can't specify page setup information. Nor can you title reports or total or subtotal data. The Print Window command prints the data exactly as it appears on your screen.

Defining and Printing Long Reports

Versions 1.0 and 1.1 of Works offer a useful database-reporting feature. Although the capabilities have some limitations compared to dedicated database programs, you can print lists of items from your database and compute subtotals and totals on numeric fields. You can print all fields or only specific ones, in any order you choose. And you can define paper sizes and add page numbers, headers, footers, and so on, by using Works' page setup features.

To restrict the records to be included in your reports, use the record-selection procedures described in Chapter 8. If you don't use these procedures, your report(s) will contain all the records in your database. Figure 9.2 shows the record-selection procedures used to produce the report in figure 9.3. The selection rule "CAT equals 9.0" results in a printed report of only the records in category 9.0.

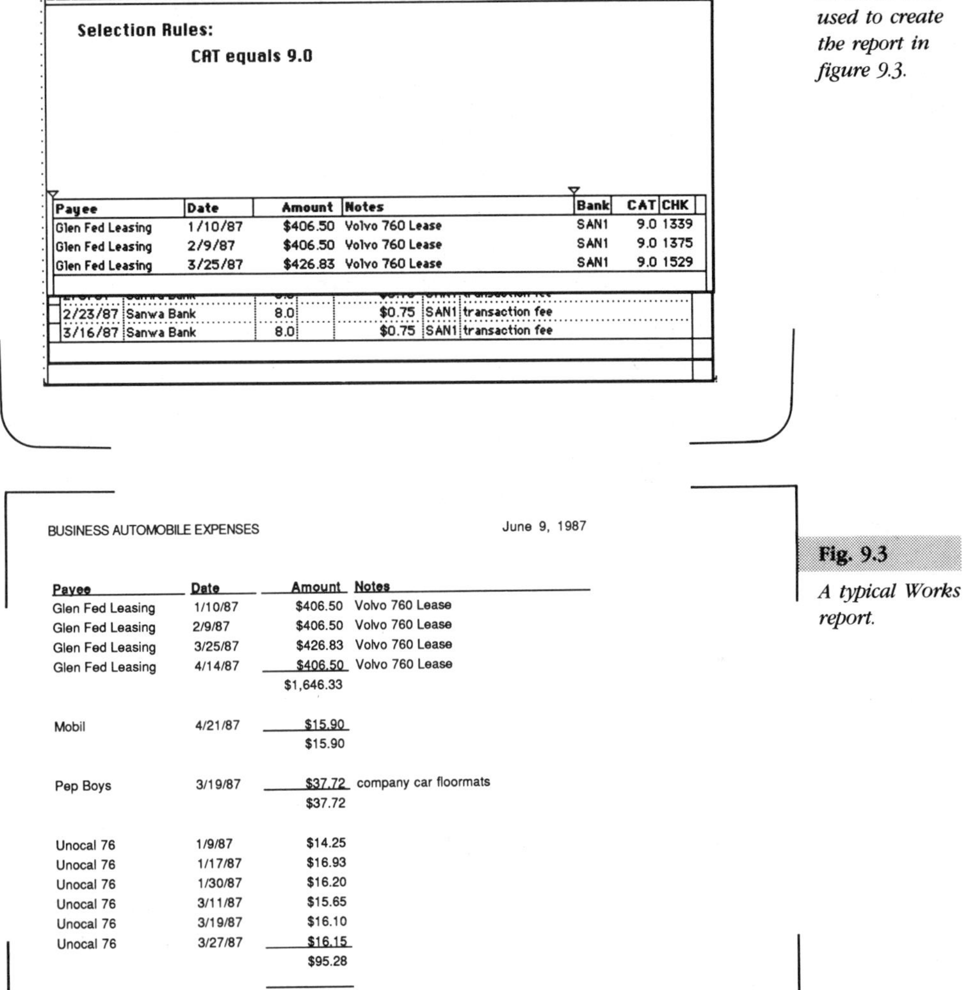

Fig. 9.2

Selection rules used to create the report in figure 9.3.

BUSINESS AUTOMOBILE EXPENSES June 9, 1987

Payee	Date	Amount	Notes
Glen Fed Leasing	1/10/87	$406.50	Volvo 760 Lease
Glen Fed Leasing	2/9/87	$406.50	Volvo 760 Lease
Glen Fed Leasing	3/25/87	$426.83	Volvo 760 Lease
Glen Fed Leasing	4/14/87	$406.50	Volvo 760 Lease
		$1,646.33	
Mobil	4/21/87	$15.90	
		$15.90	
Pep Boys	3/19/87	$37.72	company car floormats
		$37.72	
Unocal 76	1/9/87	$14.25	
Unocal 76	1/17/87	$16.93	
Unocal 76	1/30/87	$16.20	
Unocal 76	3/11/87	$15.65	
Unocal 76	3/19/87	$16.10	
Unocal 76	3/27/87	$16.15	
		$95.28	
		$1,795.23	

Page 1

Fig. 9.3

A typical Works report.

To set up reports, you create *report definitions*, in which you designate the fields to include in a report and specify where the fields will appear. You also have some control over when new pages begin. For example, when printing a list of expenses, you can have Works start a new page for each expense type (account number).

You can store up to eight report definitions in each database file. This arrangement enables you to choose and then view or print a variety of reports quickly. Figure 9.4, for example, shows a selection list of four report definition titles.

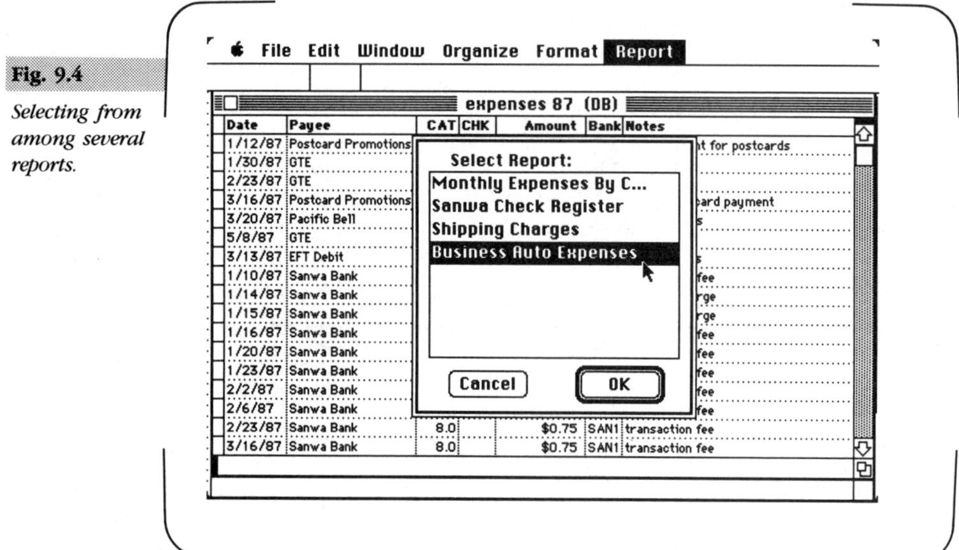

Fig. 9.4

Selecting from among several reports.

NOTE: Report definitions don't alter the contents or arrangement of your database. If you want records to appear in a particular order in your reports—for example, employees' last names according to state—you must rearrange your database before you print the report.

Creating a New Report

The process of creating a new report involves careful preparation. You need to determine the organization of your report and specify to Works the page setup information and printing details. The steps are as follows:

1. Open the appropriate database window.
2. Rearrange the records in your database if necessary (sort it).
3. Choose New Report from the Report menu.
4. Specify page setup information (paper size, margins, headers, and so on).
5. Create or modify record-selection criteria (if any).

6. Arrange the fields in the order they will be printed.
7. Alter field sizes if necessary.
8. Specify subtotals, page breaks, grid or no grid, and so forth.
9. Rename the report definition if you want.
10. Preview report totals and subtotals on-screen if you want.
11. Print the report.

You need to look at some of these steps in more detail. This information is given in the following paragraphs.

Sorting before Reporting

Works' report features do not sort your database for you. If you want items to appear in a particular order, you must sort the database before you run a report. This process is particularly important if you want your report to contain subtotals or page breaks.

Using the Report Window

When you choose the New Report option on the Report menu, as shown in figure 9.5, a report window appears (see fig. 9.6). Works assigns your report definition a sequential name containing the database name and a number. You can change the report definition title at any time. An additional menu item, TotalsPage, appears in the menu bar.

If you have already defined any selection rules for the database, they appear in the top of the window. You can keep them, eliminate them, or change them.

When you open a report window, the first three records in your database, along with their field names, appear in the order in which they will be printed. The report window is slightly smaller than the database window, so you may see part of your entire database at the bottom of the screen (see fig. 9.6).

Defining the Page Setup

You can simplify the report-definition process by setting paper sizes, margins, reduction ratios, and page orientation before you display the report window. Use the Page Setup command from the File menu. If you have done this, Works shows you (on-screen) how much of your proposed report will fit on a printed page.

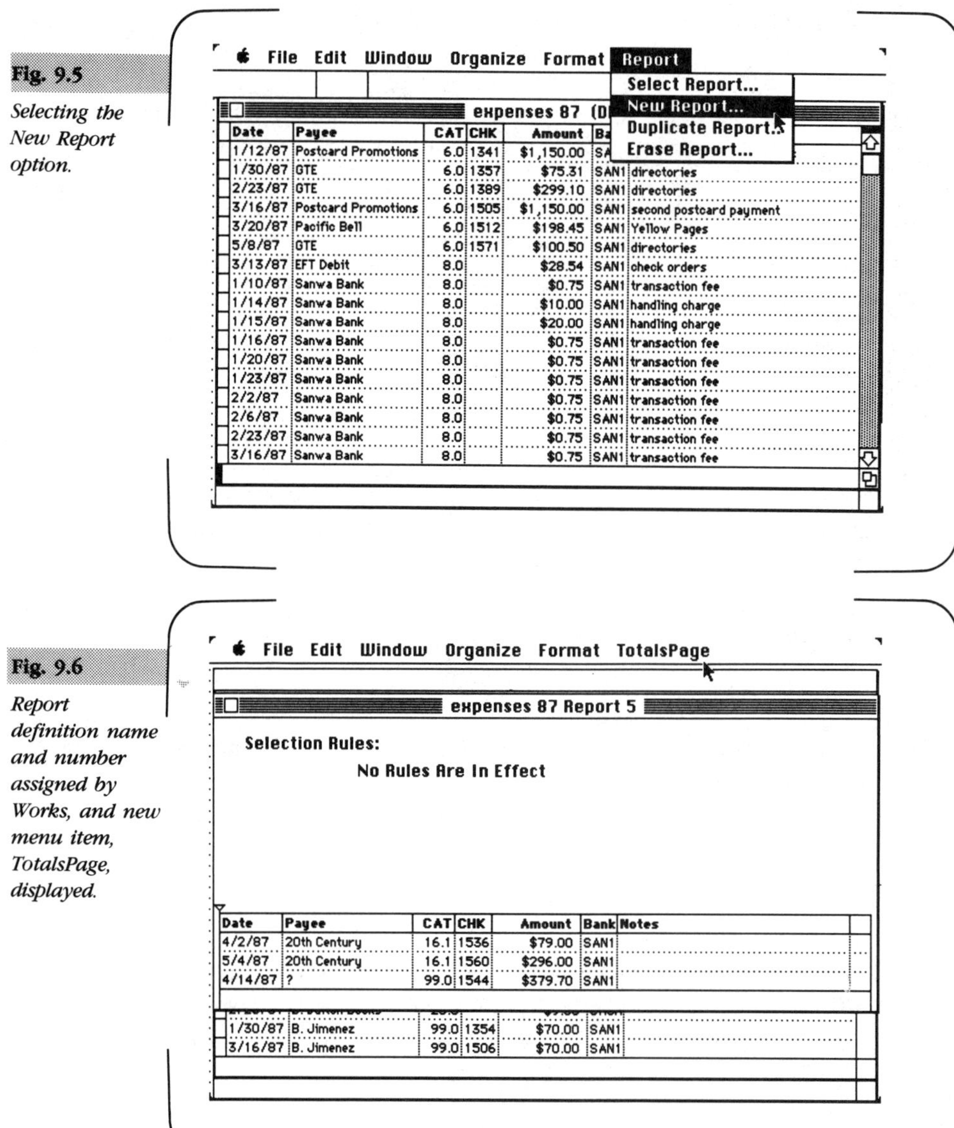

Fig. 9.5

Selecting the New Report option.

Fig. 9.6

Report definition name and number assigned by Works, and new menu item, TotalsPage, displayed.

You alter the page setup options, shown in figure 9.7, by using the techniques you learned in the word-processing chapters. As you've done before, choose Page Setup from the File menu. Here are some tips to keep in mind:

- Use the header feature to create printed report titles.

- Use reduction and landscape orientation for wide reports.
- Use enlargement for reports with only a few short fields.
- You can't control fonts (except to reduce or enlarge everywhere).

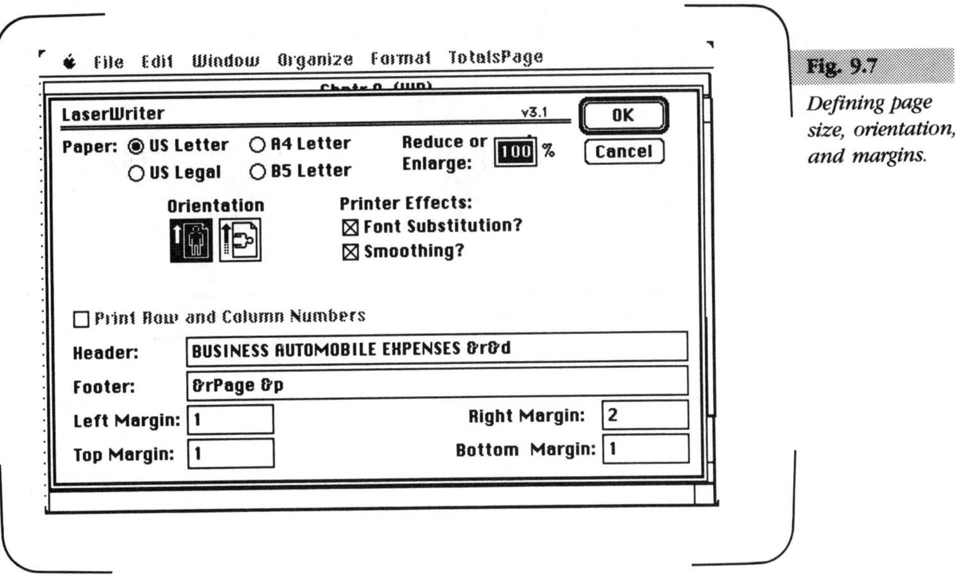

Fig. 9.7
Defining page size, orientation, and margins.

Specifying Report Selection Criteria

To restrict the number of records you want in your report, use the database record-selection techniques you learned in Chapter 8. Choose Record Selection from the Organize menu. You can create and store one set of selection criteria for each report definition.

For example, in figure 9.8, the selection rules tell Works to select only shipping-expense records. The category (account number) is 31.1 and the amount is greater than 0. The report in figure 9.9 is the result.

Arranging Fields

Unless you specify differently, Works automatically prints the first few (the leftmost) fields in your database. You use the edge markers to tell Works exactly which fields to print. Look at the area above the field names in figure 9.10. You see two downward-pointing triangles. These triangles are the left and right edge markers, which define the printing area.

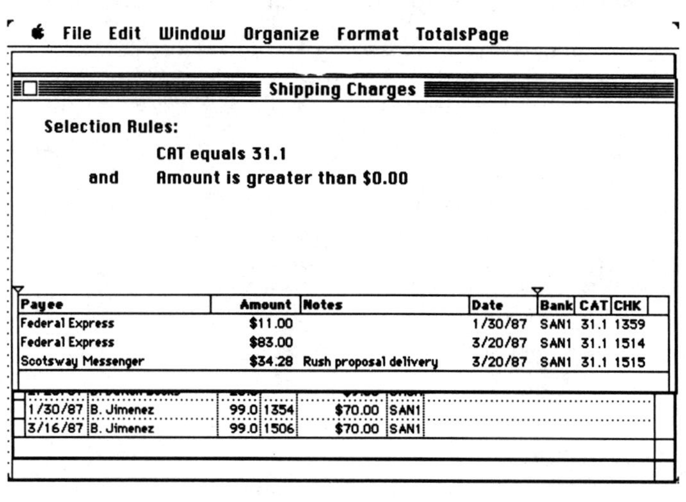

Fig. 9.8

Selection rules for shipping-expense report.

Fig. 9.9

Shipping expense report.

SHIPPING CHARGES BY CARRIER June 9, 1987

Payee	Amount	Notes	Date
Federal Express	$11.00		1/30/87
Federal Express	$83.00		3/20/87
	$94.00		
Scotsway Messenger	$34.28	Rush proposal delivery	3/20/87
	$34.28		
UPS	$5.73		1/7/87
UPS	$87.27		1/19/87
UPS	$2.01		1/22/87
UPS	$23.25		2/23/87
UPS	$64.43		3/3/87
UPS	$22.70		4/14/87
UPS	$11.09		4/20/87
	$216.48		
	$344.76		

Page 1

Payee	Date	Amount	Notes	Bank	CAT	CHK
Postcard Promotions	1/12/87	$1,150.00	downpayment for postcards	SAN1	6.0	1341
GTE	1/30/87	$75.31	directories	SAN1	6.0	1357
GTE	2/23/87	$299.10	directories	SAN1	6.0	1389

2/23/87	Sanwa Bank	8.0	$0.75	SAN1	transaction fee
3/16/87	Sanwa Bank	8.0	$0.75	SAN1	transaction fee

Fig. 9.10

The two triangles that define the part of the database which will be printed.

Using the page setup information you've provided, Works moves the markers to indicate which fields it will or won't print. You could say that Works uses the markers to expand or contract the available printing area.

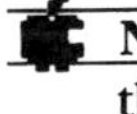

NOTE: If you've chosen landscape orientation or specified reduction in the Page Setup window, the right marker may not be visible. You can find it by scrolling to the right with the horizontal scroll bar.

Works prints any field that is completely to the *left* of the right-edge marker, but Works doesn't print fields that are completely or partially to the *right* of the right-edge marker. If the marker falls anywhere in the middle of a field, the program won't print that field. For example, in figure 9.11, Works will print the Payee, Amount, Notes, and Date fields, but not Bank and the other fields to the right of the right-edge marker.

Frequently, after an initial inspection of the screen, you may decide that you want to print fields falling outside the defined printing area. Sometimes, you may not want to print items that are in the printing area. To accomplish these changes, you can use several techniques:

- Change the size of the printing area by changing the page setup specifications.

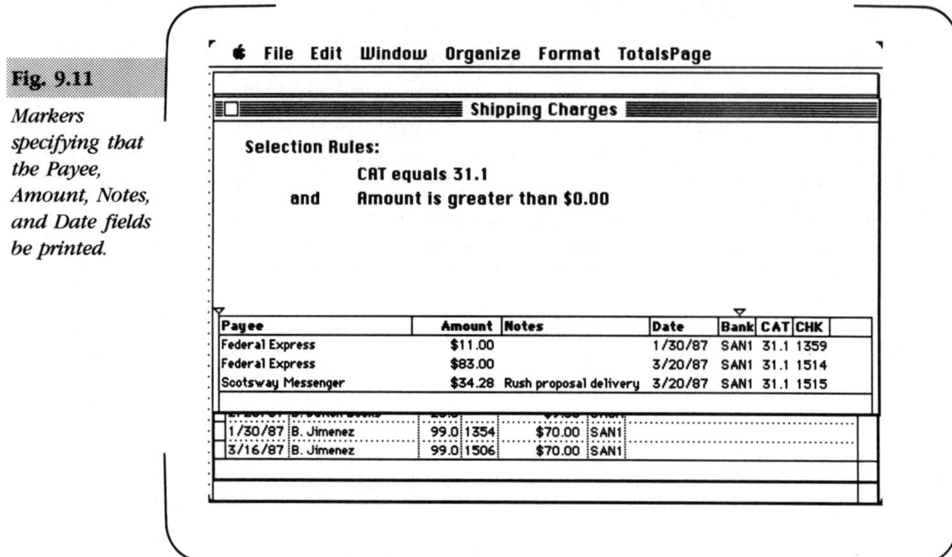

Fig. 9.11

Markers specifying that the Payee, Amount, Notes, and Date fields be printed.

- Drag fields into and out of the printing area.
- Adjust the size of the fields to make them fit.

Moving Fields

You can move fields by dragging them. As you know, when you point to a field title, the pointer becomes a hand. Use the pointer to drag fields into or out of the printing area. You also can use this method to rearrange the order of fields within the printing area.

NOTE: When you drag a new field into the printing area, you may push other fields to the right and out of the printing area. By dragging a field out of the area, you create space that will be automatically filled by other fields.

When you move fields in the report window, you don't rearrange them in your database. Each report definition can have its own arrangement.

Changing Field Size

You already know how to change the size of a field: You point to the right edge of a field title, and when the pointer changes to a two-headed arrow, you drag the field to its new size and release the mouse button.

When you change a field's size in a report window, you change the field size only for the report definition. The change does not affect the actual database or other report definitions. This technique is a handy way to "push" an unwanted field far enough to the right that Works doesn't print it.

You can squeeze in additional fields by reducing field sizes, thereby fitting more fields in the printing area. When you do so, however, you may truncate some of your records and obscure part of the field's title. By changing a field's size, you also change the length of the line that underscores the column heading.

Figure 9.12 shows an example. Here, the report in figure 9.9 has been modified. Notice that the Payee column has been shortened and the Date column has been moved to the beginning of the row (see "Moving Fields"). Fields have been added—Bank, CAT, and CHK—and reduction and orientation in the Page Setup dialog box have been changed. A header was also entered in the Page Setup dialog box, containing the report title (SHIPPING CHARGES BY CARRIER) and the &R&D shorthand for printing today's date, right-justified. A footer was used to print the page number preceded by the word page. Because it was right-justified, the footer entry was &RPage&P. For additional information on page setup techniques, see the word-processing chapter.

SHIPPING CHARGES BY CARRIER June 9, 1987

Date	Payee	Amount	Notes	Bank	CAT	CHK
1/30/87	Federal Express	$11.00		SAN1	31.1	1359
3/20/87	Federal Express	$83.00		SAN1	31.1	1514
		$94.00				
3/20/87	Scotsway Messenger	$34.28	Rush proposal delivery	SAN1	31.1	1515
		$34.28				
1/7/87	UPS	$5.73		SAN1	31.1	1336
1/19/87	UPS	$87.27		SAN1	31.1	1346
1/22/87	UPS	$2.01		SAN1	31.1	1347
2/23/87	UPS	$23.25		SAN1	31.1	1390
3/3/87	UPS	$64.43		SAN1	31.1	1396
4/14/87	UPS	$22.70		SAN1	31.1	1546
4/20/87	UPS	$11.09		SAN1	31.1	1548
		$216.48				
		$344.76				

Page 1

Fig. 9.12

Rearranged shipping-expense report.

Renaming Fields

In Works Versions 1.0 and 1.1, database field names are used as the column headings for reports. Unfortunately, you can't rename field titles in the report window, so if you need different titles, you must change them in the database itself. This change affects the database and all other reports as well.

Computing Totals and Subtotals

Works computes totals from your numeric fields. Under certain conditions, you also can create subtotals. To define totals and subtotals, you use the TotalsPage menu, which you access through the report window. A check mark preceding an option indicates that that feature has been selected for the highlighted column.

Computing totals is simple. You can do so for any numeric field. Here's how:

1. Select the numeric field that you want totaled (click on the field).
2. Choose Sum This Field on the TotalsPage menu. Works then prints a total for the field.

In figure 9.13, for example, the Amount field is selected, and the check mark by the Sum This Field option indicates that Works will total the Amount field when printing it.

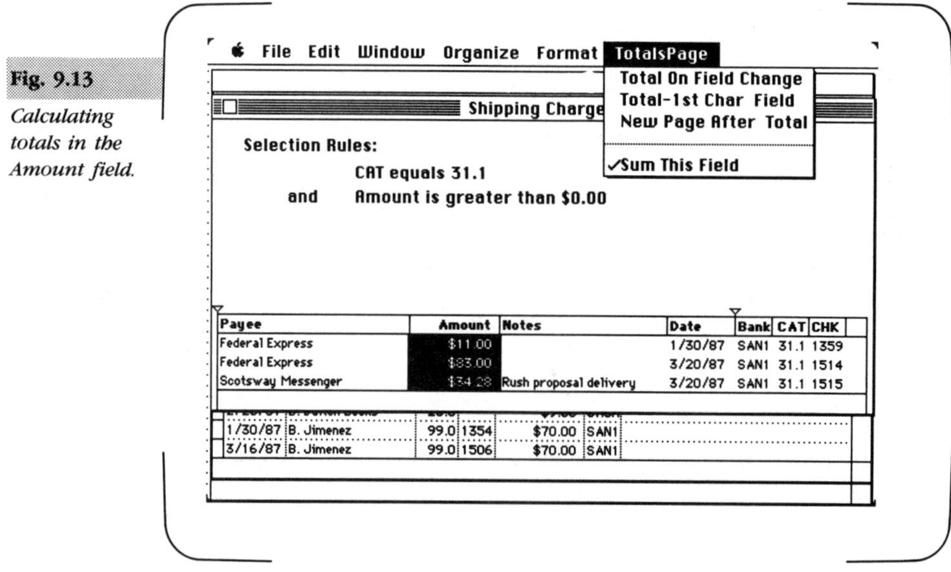

Fig. 9.13
Calculating totals in the Amount field.

Frequently, you'll also want to create subtotals in reports (for example, expense category subtotals). You can use two options on the TotalsPage menu for this purpose:

Total On Field Change
Total-1st Char Field

NOTE: When you use either of these features, Works expects you to sort your database into a useful order before running the report. Works report definitions don't sort for you.

In figure 9.14, Works computes a subtotal whenever the name of the Payee changes in this alphanumeric field. One or more numeric fields may be called out by using the Sum This Field choice, as well.

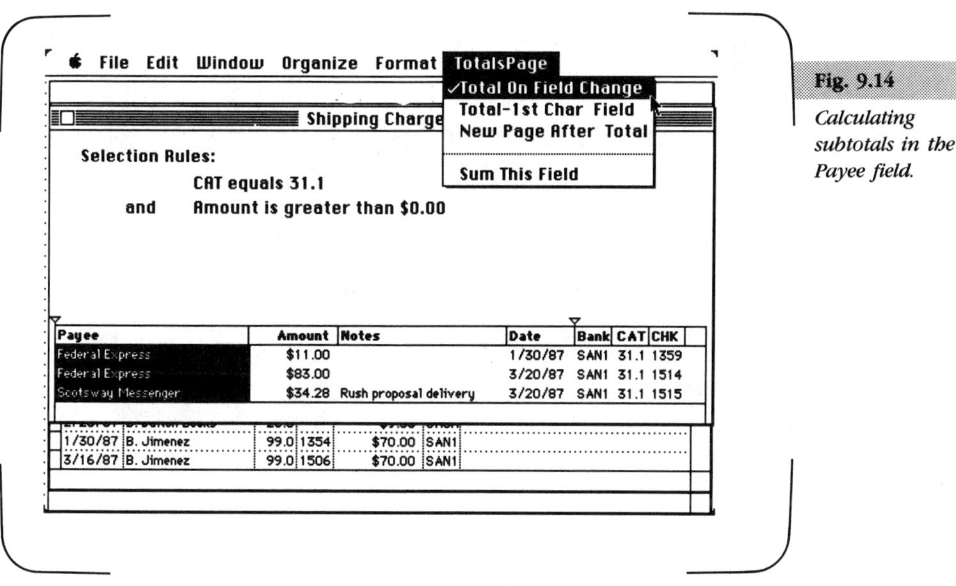

Fig. 9.14 *Calculating subtotals in the Payee field.*

When you use Total On Field Change, Works computes a new subtotal whenever the content of a field changes in any way. For instance, if you use *both* the options specified in figures 9.13 and 9.14 (Sum This Field and Total On Field Change), Works calculates subtotals in the Amount field each time the name of a payee in the Payee field changes.

Using the Totals On Field Change Feature

Suppose that you want a report to list the names of key employees by department and to subtotal their earnings by department. Figure 9.15

shows the appropriate TotalsPage menu selections—Totals On Field Change and Sum This Field. Figure 9.16 shows the final report. Notice the added totals lines.

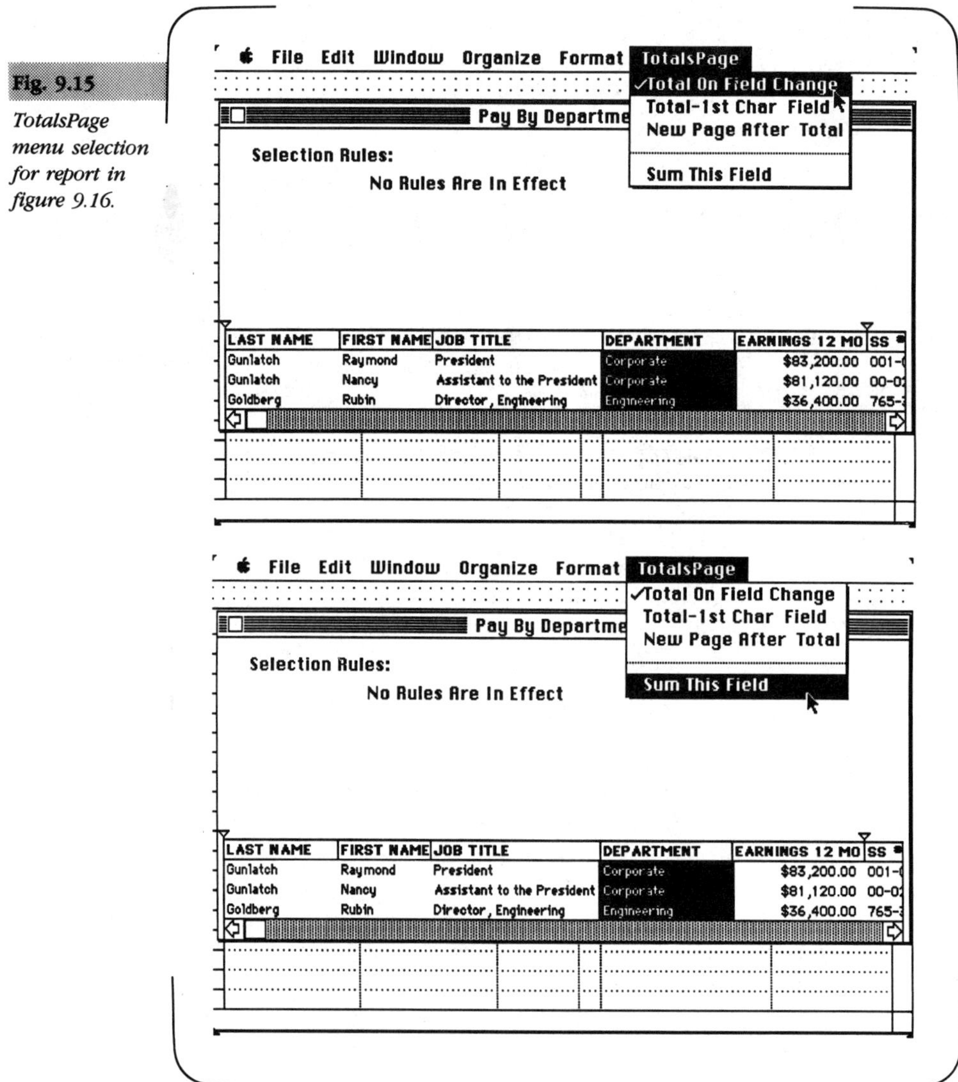

Fig. 9.15 *TotalsPage menu selection for report in figure 9.16.*

KEY EMPLOYEE PAY BY DEPARTMENT August 26, 1987

LAST NAME	FIRST NAME	JOB TITLE	DEPARTMENT	EARNINGS 12 MO
Gunlatch	Raymond	President	Corporate	$83,200.00
Gunlatch	Nancy	Assistant to the President	Corporate	$81,120.00
				$164,320.00
Goldberg	Rubin	Director, Engineering	Engineering	$36,400.00
Mi	Sue	New Product Development	Engineering	$58,240.00
				$94,640.00
Flushland	Johnathon	Cleaning Associate	Maintenance	$10,400.00
				$10,400.00
Baxter	James	Director Personnel	Personnel	$41,600.00
Baxter	Tammy	Assistant Director	Personnel	$37,440.00
				$79,040.00
Makit	Willie	Production Supervisor	Production	$26,520.00
Winston	Doc	Sr. Sardine Eye Closer	Production	$16,536.00
				$43,056.00
Norcross	Oliver	Sales	Sales	$62,400.00
Quickcloser	John	Inside Sales	Sales	$52,000.00
So	Mi	Inside Sales	Sales	$52,000.00
				$166,400.00
Berfel	Ferd	Pull Tab Inspector	Test Lab	$18,470.40
				$18,470.40
				$576,326.40

Page 1

Fig. 9.16

Report listing names of key employees by department, with subtotals of their earnings by department.

If you plan to use a field for subtotals, you should be consistent when making entries in your records. For example, if you enter *Sales* as the department name for some employees and *Sales Dept.* for others, you'll get two subtotals instead of the single total you want.

Figure 9.17 illustrates a subtotal problem caused by data entry inconsistency. In this case, a space appears before the *S* in *Sales* for employee Quickcloser's department field. Because any difference in a field can cause a new subtotal, you should avoid abbreviations, indiscriminate punctuation and spaces, and other discrepancies.

Using the Total-1st Char Field Feature

When you use Total-1st Char Field, Works creates a new subtotal whenever the first character in a record differs from the one preceding it. Sometimes the first character in an entry tells you something about the group to which the item belongs. For instance, first numbers in ZIP codes specify National Postal Areas. Some inventory managers use part-numbering schemes that have significant first numbers, too. If you deal with numbers like these and need to compute subtotals by groups based

Fig. 9.17

Subtotal problem caused by inconsistency in data entry.

KEY EMPLOYEE PAY BY DEPARTMENT — August 27, 1987

LAST NAME	FIRST NAME	JOB TITLE	DEPARTMENT	EARNINGS 12 M
Baxter	James	Director Personnel	Personnel	$41,600.00
Baxter	Tammy	Assistant Director	Personnel	$37,440.00
				$79,040.00
Berfel	Ferd	Pull Tab Inspector	Test Lab	$18,470.40
				$18,470.40
Flushland	Johnathon	Cleaning Associate	Maintenance	$10,400.00
				$10,400.00
Goldberg	Rubin	Director, Engineering	Engineering	$36,400.00
				$36,400.00
Gunlatch	Raymond	President	Corporate	$83,200.00
Gunlatch	Nancy	Assistant to the President	Corporate	$81,120.00
				$164,320.00
Makit	Willie	Production Supervisor	Production	$26,520.00
				$26,520.00
Mi	Sue.	New Product Development	Engineering	$58,240.00
				$58,240.00
Norcross	Oliver	Sales	Sales	$62,400.00
				$62,400.00
Quickcloser	John	Inside Sales	Sales	$52,000.00
				$52,000.00
So	Mi	Inside Sales	Sales	$52,000.00
				$52,000.00
Winston	Doc	Sr. Sardine Eye Closer	Production	$16,536.00
				$16,536.00
				$576,326.40

Unwanted breaks

Space before "S"

Page 1

only on the first character in a field, use Total-1st Char Field instead of Total On Field Change. Total-1st Char Field subtotals when—and only when—the first character in a field changes.

NOTE: This feature is not particularly handy. Even Microsoft admits that Total-1st Char Field has limited appeal. At first glance, you'd think that the feature would calculate subtotals by month in date fields; but it can't. If you use Total-1st Char Field on a field containing the dates 10/01/86, 11/15/86, 12/25/86, and 1/01/87, they all appear in the same group.

Starting a New Page after a Subtotal

Sometimes you may want Works to begin a new page after each subtotal. For example, you may want each region or expense category to appear on a separate page. To accomplish this division, you use the New Page After Total option on the TotalsPage menu. You use New Page After Total with either Total On Field Change or Total-1st Char Field.

You select New Page After Total immediately after you define a field to be subtotaled and while the field is highlighted. Here's what you do:

1. Click on the field you want to subtotal.
2. Choose either Total On Field Change or Total-1st Char Field.
3. With the field still selected, choose New Page After Total.
4. Complete the report definition and print the report.

Turning the Grid On or Off

When defining reports, you can use the Show Grid or No Grid option on the Format menu. You may want to turn off the grid before printing reports.

Printing

After you create a report definition, you print the report by using the Print option on the File menu. The report definition must be on the screen when you request printing.

Previewing and Copying Subtotals and Totals

Unfortunately, when using Works, you can't preview entire database reports on your screen. You must print the reports, a process that can be time-consuming. You can, however, preview subtotals and totals by using the Copy Totals feature. Sometimes this preview gives you an idea of how well you have defined the report before printing.

The Copy Totals command, which is on the Edit menu, copies to the Clipboard totals and subtotals you've defined by using the Total On Field Change, Total-1st Char Field, and Sum This Field options. You can use Copy Totals any time after you've defined at least one total or subtotal. You then can view the information or copy it into a different Works window.

To view the Clipboard's contents, select Show Clipboard on the Window menu. Then use the zoom box or the Clipboard's scroll bars (if necessary) to see the entire Clipboard contents. You can use Works' Print Window option to produce hard copy if you like.

Figure 9.18 shows the Copy Totals command. The DEPARTMENT field has been selected. In figure 9.19, notice that the first record from each category (each department, in the example) has been copied to the Clipboard. The summed field (EARNINGS 12 MO), however, contains the total for the category rather than the field value for the record displayed.

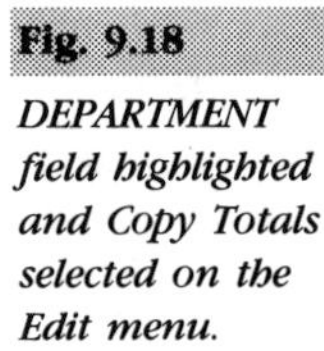

Fig. 9.18

DEPARTMENT field highlighted and Copy Totals selected on the Edit menu.

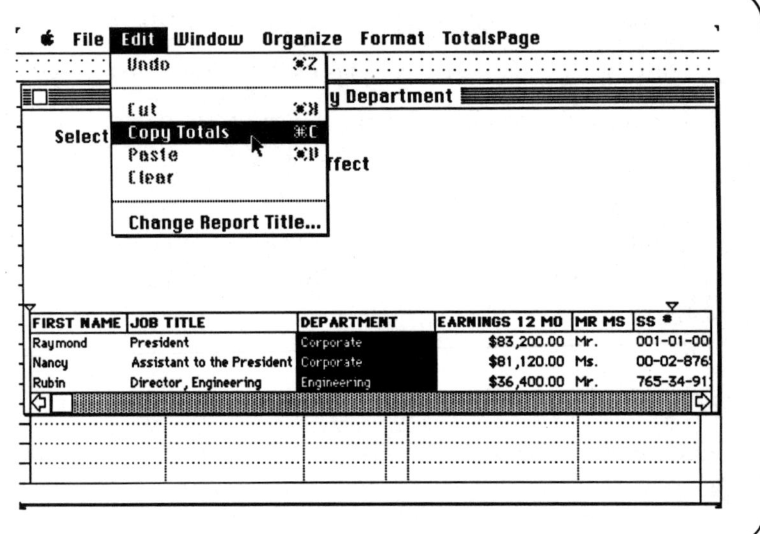

Fig. 9.19

Information copied to Clipboard.

Clipboard (DB)

LAST NAME	FIRST NAME	JOB TITLE	DEPARTMENT	EARNINGS 12 M
Baxter	James	Director Personnel	Personnel	$79,040.00
Berfel	Ferd	Pull Tab Inspector	Test Lab	$18,470.40
Flushland	Johnathon	Cleaning Associate	Maintenance	$10,400.00
Goldberg	Rubin	Director, Engineering	Engineering	$36,400.00
Gunlatch	Raymond	President	Corporate	$164,320.00
Makit	Willie	Production Supervisor	Production	$26,520.00
Mi	Sue	New Product Development	Engineering	$58,240.00
Norcross	Oliver	Sales	Sales	$62,400.00
Quickcloser	John	Inside Sales	Sales	$52,000.00
So	Mi	Inside Sales	Sales	$52,000.00
Winston	Doc	Sr. Sardine Eye Closer	Production	$16,536.00
				$576,326.40

The steps involved in this process are straightforward:

1. Create a report definition containing at least one subtotal field.
2. With the report window active, either choose Copy Totals from the Edit menu or press **command-C**.
3. Paste the resulting subtotals that can be found on the Clipboard.

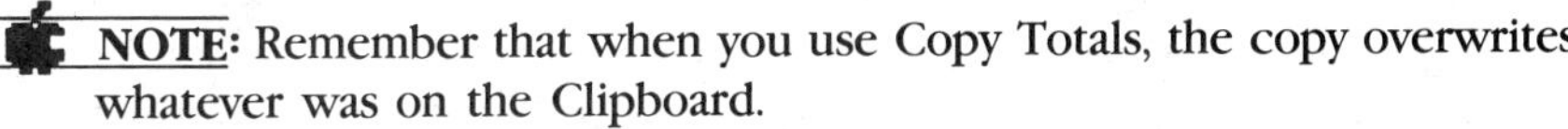

NOTE: Remember that when you use Copy Totals, the copy overwrites whatever was on the Clipboard.

Once you've used the Copy Totals command to place totals and subtotals on the Clipboard, you can transfer (paste) them to word-processing windows, a spreadsheet, and so on. Grids aren't copied even if they're displayed. Copy Totals does copy field names (column titles) to the Clipboard—and to subsequent windows. In other words, the field names are *always* copied to the Clipboard.

Choosing Existing Report Definitions

As mentioned, Works stores up to eight report definitions. To choose a report, you use Works' Select Report feature:

1. Choose Select Report on the Report menu. Works then displays the list of available report definitions.
2. Specify a report by double-clicking on its name (or highlighting it and clicking OK).
3. Redefine and/or run the report. (You may want to rename the report with a more descriptive name than the one given by Works so that you can identify the report quickly.)

Changing, Duplicating, and Erasing Report Definitions

Another advantage of Works is the ease with which you can change, duplicate, or erase report definitions. As you work with database reports, you will find more and more uses for the capabilities of changing and duplicating these definitions.

Modifying stored report definitions is easy. You start by using Works' Select Report feature:

1. Choose Select Report from the Report menu. The list of available report definitions appears.

2. Select the report you want by double-clicking on its name (or highlighting it and clicking OK).
3. Redefine the report (page setup, field locations, totals, and so on).
4. Run the report.

When you're creating similar reports, you can save time by copying an existing report definition, then modifying it. For instance, in figure 9.20, you can choose the report definition, "Hired Before 1986." Then, by changing the comparison date, you can find the names of employees hired before a different cut-off point.

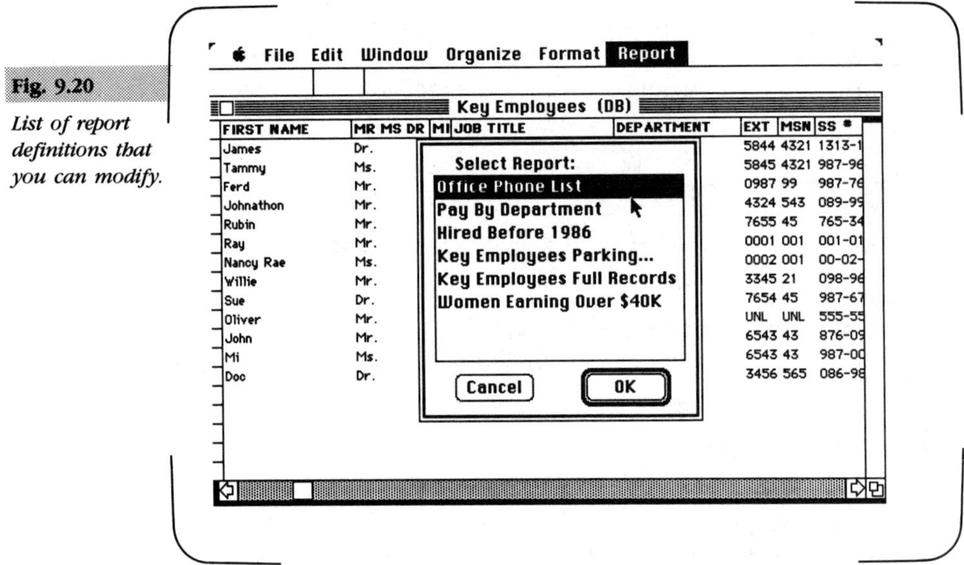

Fig. 9.20

List of report definitions that you can modify.

To duplicate reports, you use Works' Duplicate Report feature. Here's what you do:

1. Choose Duplicate Report from the Report menu. Works then displays the list of available report definitions.
2. Double-click (or highlight and click OK) to select a report name. Works then displays a copy of the report definition (sequentially numbered).
3. Redefine the report as needed (page setup, field locations, totals, and so on).

4. Change the report name if you want.
5. Run the report.

Erasing Reports

To eliminate unwanted reports, you use the Erase Report option on the Report menu. Here's how this feature works:

1. Choose Erase Report from the Report menu. The screen then displays the list of available report definitions.
2. Select the unwanted report by double-clicking on its name (or highlighting it and clicking OK). Works then eliminates the report.

CAUTION: You can't use Undo to recover erased report definitions, so, when erasing them, select with care.

The Quick Start, which follows, gives you instructions for quickly printing a report from the database you created in the preceding Quick Start.

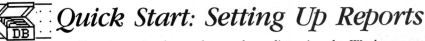

Quick Start: Setting Up Reports

To print a simple employee phone list using the Works report features, use the Quick Database that you began in Chapter 8. Start by opening Works and the Quick Database. If Works is running, choose the database from the Works Open File dialog box. To launch Works if Works isn't running, click on the icon for the database itself. Clicking the database icon both invokes Works and opens the database.

Preparing Data for Reporting

Use the Show List command to display your records in the list window. If you have not already sorted, sort the records alphabetically by last name by using the Sort option from the Organize menu. (See the Quick Start in Chapter 8 for instructions.)

If necessary, move and resize your fields until they look like figure 9.21 (again see the Quick Start in Chapter 8). Then choose New Report from the Report Menu.

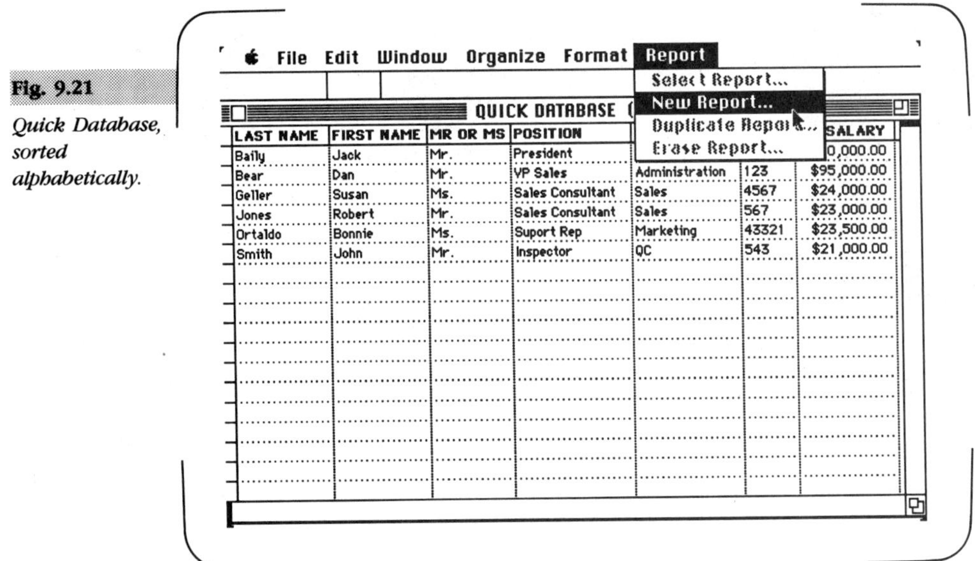

Fig. 9.21

Quick Database, sorted alphabetically.

Determining the Fields To Print

The Report window displays a part of your database. Triangular markers above the database indicate the left and right report margins. Sometimes, however, no marker appears at the right edge of the screen. If no marker appears near the right edge, every field will be printed on the report. If a marker does appear on the screen, only the fields completely to the left of the marker will be printed on the report. If you have a visible marker on the screen, the marker is probably pointing somewhere in the SALARY field.

To create a phone list, you don't want to include salaries. Adjust your fields so that last names, first names, titles, positions, departments, and phone extensions are completely to the left of the right marker. If you don't have a right marker on your screen, salaries will be printed on the report unless you force a marker.

Your goal is to position the triangular marker to the right of the PHONE field, anywhere inside the SALARY field (see fig. 9.22). The easiest way to force the marker onto the screen is to increase the size of the left margin, thereby reducing the available printing space on the page.

To increase the size of the left margin, choose Page Setup from the File menu (see fig. 9.22). Click in the box next to Left Margin setting, and enter the number **1.5** in the white area. Do not press *enter* or *return* yet.

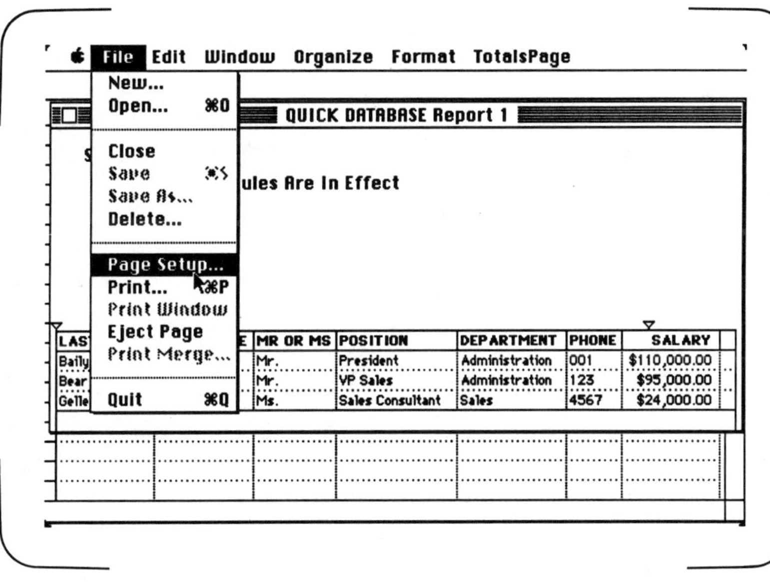

Fig. 9.22

Preparing the database for printing a phone list.

Adding a Report Title

While the Page Setup dialog box is still on your screen, you can add a header, a footer, and other embellishments to your report; formatting commands, preceded by the ampersand, can be used to control text alignment. In the header line in figure 9.23, for example, the formatting command &c causes the text *PHONE LIST – CONFIDENTIAL* to be centered on the page. The command &r specifies that text following the command is to be aligned with the right margin, and the command &d specifies what that text is to be: the date. More information on these formatting commands is given in the section "Headers and Footers" in Chapter 4.

Fig. 9.23

Page Setup dialog box for the report.

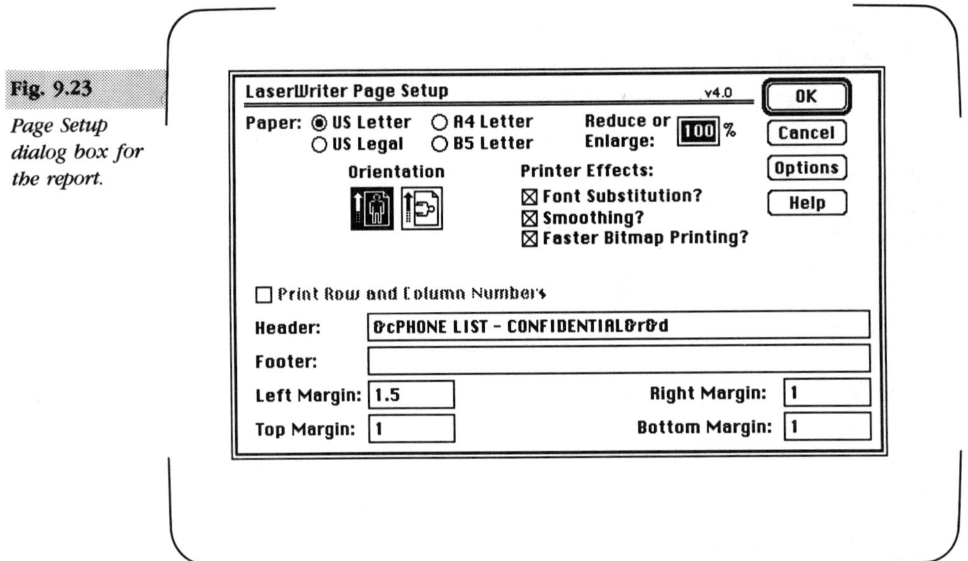

Printing the Report

Now that you have defined the report, choose Print from the File menu, or use the *command*-P shortcut. Your report should look like figure 9.24. Experiment with various options like Show Grid, No Grid, field widths, page setups, and so forth.

PHONE LIST - CONFIDENTIAL September 2, 1987

LAST NAME	FIRST NAME	MR OR MS	POSITION	DEPARTMENT	PHONE
Baily	Jack	Mr.	President	Administration	001
Bear	Dan	Mr.	VP Sales	Administration	123
Geller	Susan	Ms.	Sales Consultant	Sales	4567
Jones	Robert	Mr.	Sales Consultant	Sales	567
Ortaldo	Bonnie	Ms.	Suport Rep	Marketing	43321
Smith	John	Mr.	Inspector	QC	543

Fig. 9.24

The sample phone list report.

Saving Report Definitions

When you finish experimenting, save your database changes. You can press *command*-S, select Save from the File menu, or click the Yes button in the dialog box that appears when you close a window in which you have made changes. Remember, you need to save report definitions with the database. When you add or change a report definition, resave the database!

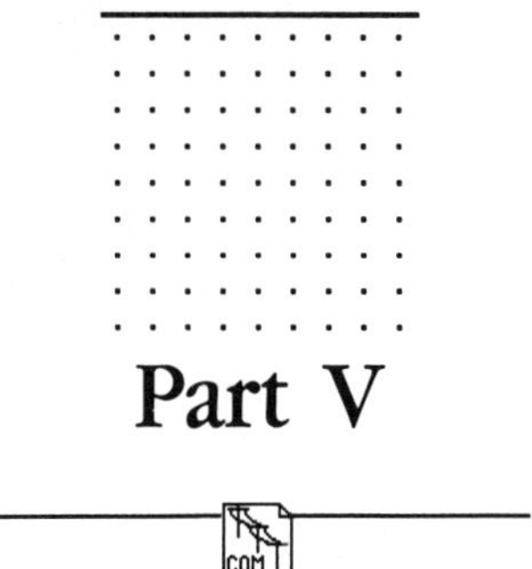

Part V

COMMUNICATIONS

10

Communications

With a modem, you can use your Mac to exchange information over regular telephone lines with other modem-equipped computers anywhere (see fig. 10.1). Works' communications feature helps make this process possible. This capacity also can turn your Mac into a "terminal" that can be connected, via telephone, to large time-sharing computers such as those run by CompuServe, The Source, and hundreds of other information vendors. You can access smaller low-cost or free services called bulletin board services or BBSs. (Appendix B provides information, including telephone numbers, about information vendors as well as bulletin boards throughout the United States.)

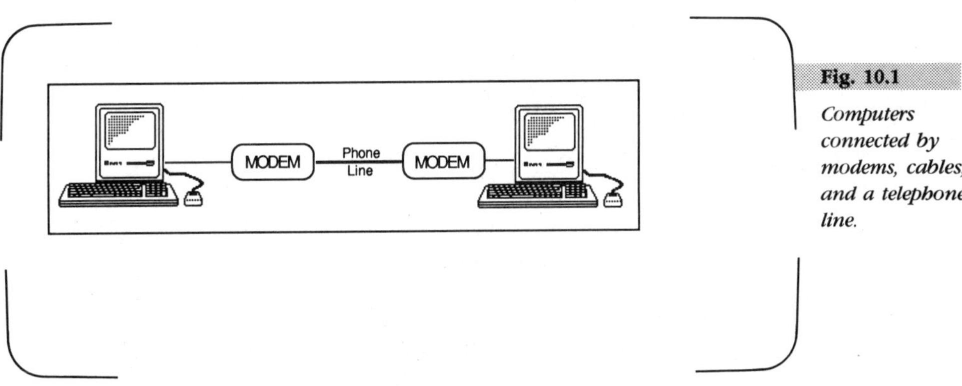

Fig. 10.1

Computers connected by modems, cables, and a telephone line.

Works also communicates directly with other personal computers; you send and receive information from either your keyboard or your disk drive. Works can exchange data this way even while you're busy doing other things—such as working on a spreadsheet or word-processing document—a process called *background communications.*

Works' communications feature supports a wide variety of *protocols,* or communications methods, which make your Mac compatible with many different types of computers. These protocols enable you to collect and convert selected information from non-Macintosh computers such as IBM PCs. Chapter 11 offers more insight into this capability.

Businesses use these procedures to exchange spreadsheets, databases, and interoffice memos with far-flung offices. Hobbiests exchange programs, graphics, and ideas the same way. In this chapter, you learn about the terms and processes involved in these types of data sharing.

Communications Terms

Works' communications feature can be explained in everyday English, but unfortunately a technically correct description requires the use of some "computerese." You'll be bombarded by these technical terms when you visit computer stores or try to connect your computer to other computers, but the terms soon will become part of your vocabulary (and then you won't need to walk away from cocktail party conversations when the talk turns technical). The important terms that you learn about in this chapter include the following:

Modems

Auto-dialing
Auto-answering
Touch-Tone
Pulse dialing
Call waiting
Direct connection
Acoustic coupling
Smart modem
Dumb

Communications Settings

Type (terminal emulation)
Auto-wrap
NewLine
Baud rate (or bits per second, or BPS)
Data size
Stop bits
Parity
Handshake
Line delay
Character delay
Echo On/Off (full- and half-duplex)

Protocols

MacBinary
Xmodem
Asynchronous (Stop/start or Xon/Xoff)

These terms may seem a little overwhelming, but hang in there. They'll be introduced a few at a time. As you'll see, the important thing to know is that you must set up your computer and modem to be compatible with the system on the other end of the telephone line.

Modems

For practically all communications applications, you need a modem to connect your Macintosh to a regular telephone line. Any computers with which you exchange data must be similarly equipped.

Modems convert the computer signals coming out of the back of your Macintosh into tones that can be carried over regular telephone lines. This process is called *modulation*. Modems also convert the tones that arrive over telephone lines back into computer signals through a process called *demodulation*. The term *modem* is a contraction of *mo*dulation and *dem*odulation.

A number of vendors, including Apple, Hayes, Prometheus, and U.S. Robotics, offer Macintosh-compatible modems. They range in price from less than $100.00 to more than $500.00. Features that affect the price include brand name, information-exchange speed, and the number of automated features provided.

Direct-Connect Modems and Acoustic Couplers

A *direct-connect modem* plugs into a modular phone jack and sends signals from the computer directly into the phone line. An *acoustically coupled modem*, on the other hand, requires that you place the phone handset into the modem's rubber cups in order to exchange data. Acoustic couplers are less reliable and offer fewer features than today's more popular direct-connect modems. And acoustic couplers don't fully use the Works communications features.

Smart Modems

You can use Works with "dumb" acoustically coupled modems, but most users opt for today's more full-featured "smart" direct-connect modems. *Smart modems* contain their own microprocessors and help with the communications process. For instance, these modems can dial the outgoing computer phone calls for you and automatically answer incoming computer calls.

Works can simplify things for you by taking advantage of the smart modem's automatic features. Works knows how to carry on "conversations" with the modem itself. That is, Works tells the modem what to do and then waits for its response. Works also keeps you informed of what's going on. For instance, Works might have the following "dialog" with your modem. (I've taken some artistic license here.)

Works	*Modem*
Hey, modem, are you ready?	Yep.
Let's use Touch-Tone and the highest speed.	Fine.
Ron wants you to dial 555-2345.	Sure. I'm dialing. It's ringing.
	A computer answered.
Swell. I'll tell Ron.	
(Ron and Works exchange information with the remote computer.)	
(After they're done . . .)	
Hey, modem, you listening to me?	Yep.
Hang up, he's done.	OK. The phone line's free.
I'll tell Ron.	

For Works to control and monitor the modem this way, Works must "speak" the modem's control language. Some industry standards have developed for controlling smart modems. The most popular among microcomputer users is the Hayes AT standard, which Works supports. Using this standard, the preceding exchange between Works and the smart modem might look something like the following. (Again, I've taken some artistic license.)

Works	*Modem*
ATB1	OK
ATDT5552345	OK
	DIALING
	RINGING
	CARRIER DETECT
(Data is exchanged.)	OK
+++	
ATHO	OK

When you use Works, command exchanges like this appear on your screen from time to time. Fortunately, you won't need to learn how to understand them or even how to issue such commands directly to your smart modem. Works takes care of those tasks for you. You control Works by using simple menus and screen buttons as usual.

The Right Modem Purchase

To take full advantage of Works' communications features (in the United States and Canada), your modem should have at least the following features:

- "Intelligence" based on the Hayes AT standard—that is, a Hayes-compatible smart modem. (See "Smart Modems.")
- The capability to answer the telephone line automatically
- Compatibility with Bell 212A (1200 BPS asynchronous), a common standard used by most microcomputer users and time-sharing vendors, such as CompuServe
- A cable compatible with your Macintosh model
- Direct connection to telephone lines (through a modular telephone jack)

Works supports additional modem features, including faster speeds and advanced security systems. A knowledgeable dealer can help you pick the right modem for your application. Users outside of the United States and Canada probably will want appropriate non-Bell compatibility (in addition to or instead of Bell 212A).

Communications Documents

A Works communications document consists of a collection of stored settings, a list of phone numbers, and a place to view information as it is exchanged. You can save multiple communications documents on disk, but you can have only one communications document open at once. You select and open a communications document as you do other Works documents, by using the Open File dialog box, shown in figure 10.2.

Fig. 10.2

Opening a communications document, using the Open File dialog box.

Open File:

All Works Types | Word Processor | Data Base | Spread Sheet | Communications

WORKS 1.0

Beta Works
M&A
NCM
test

Open | New | Cancel

HARD DISK

Eject | Drive

Import File

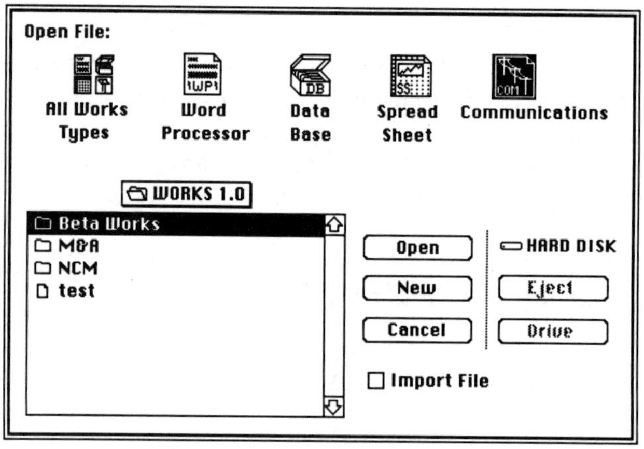

NOTE: You can have a communications document on your desk with other types of documents, such as spreadsheets and databases or word-processing projects. While using a communications document, you can create and exchange other types of Works documents (see fig. 10.3).

The Communications Settings Dialog Box

Perhaps the biggest stumbling block to successful communications is the wide variety of communications settings available. In addition to setting modems to send and receive information at the same speed, you must make other decisions. You make most of them in the Works Communications Settings dialog box. Figures 10.4. and 10.5, respectively, show the dialog boxes for Works Version 1.0 and 1.1.

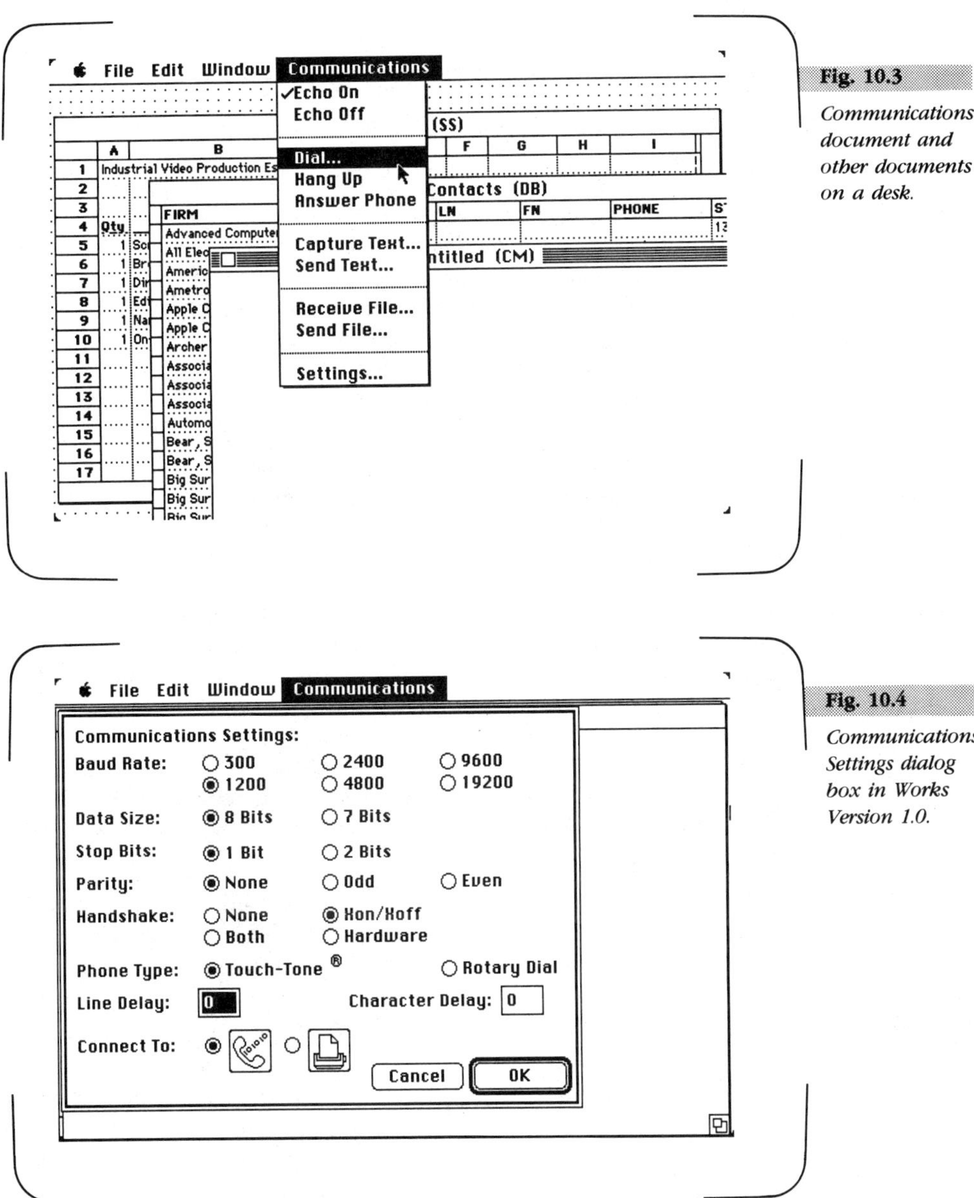

Fig. 10.3 *Communications document and other documents on a desk.*

Fig. 10.4 *Communications Settings dialog box in Works Version 1.0.*

When you open a new communications window, Works asks you to click buttons and otherwise fill in the Communications Settings dialog box. You can change these settings any time by choosing the Settings option on the Communications menu.

Fig. 10.5

Communications Settings dialog box in Works Version 1.1.

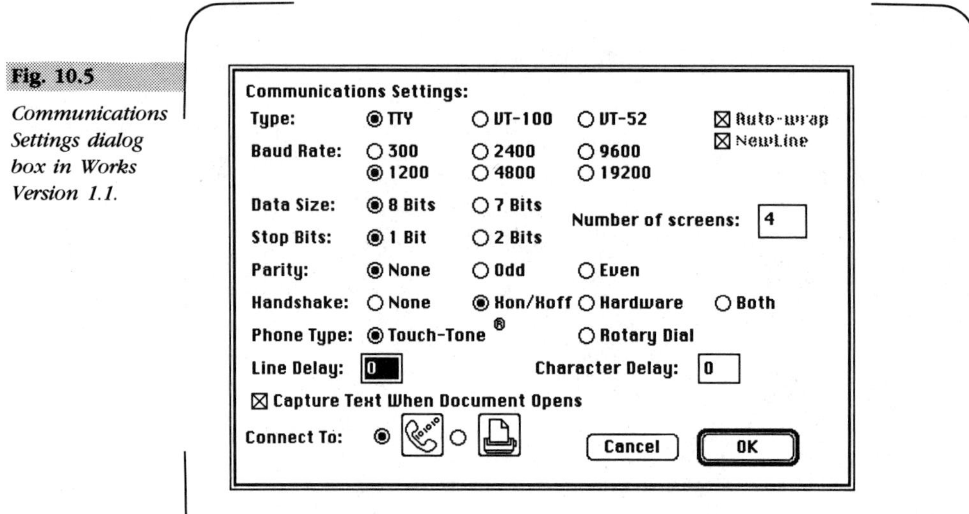

Which options should you select? Your choices depend on the computer at the other end. Before using the communications features, you should understand the choices available and gather some information about the computers you intend to call.

Works 1.1 offers settings options not found in the Version 1.0 Communications Settings dialog box. This discussion starts by reviewing the settings available in both Works 1.0 and 1.1; then the text discusses the options available only in Version 1.1.

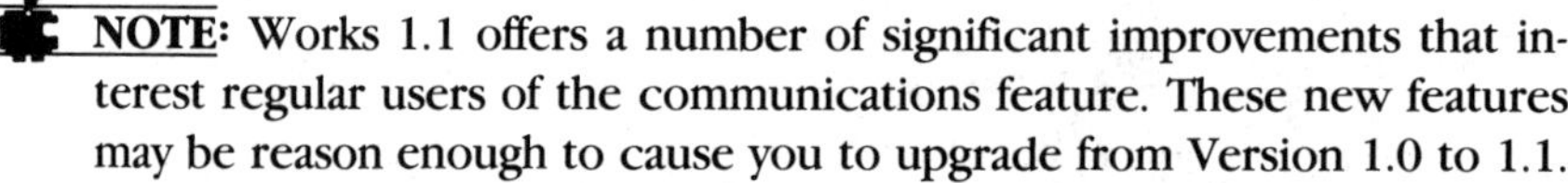

NOTE: Works 1.1 offers a number of significant improvements that interest regular users of the communications feature. These new features may be reason enough to cause you to upgrade from Version 1.0 to 1.1.

Baud Rate

All versions of the Works communications feature offer a choice of baud rate. *Baud* is an antiquated term used to refer to the speed of information transmission. A more accurate term is *bits per second*, abbreviated BPS. Nonetheless, people have the habit of referring to modems as being 300 baud, 1200 baud, 2400 baud, and so forth. These rates are commonly used modem communications speeds. For now, all you need to know is that baud (or BPS) refers to the approximate speed at which information travels between the two computers. The higher the baud rate, the faster the information travels.

Modems on both ends of an exchange must be set for the same speed. Not all modems operate at all speeds. Generally (but not always), faster modems cost more than slower ones. Many modems offer a variety of speeds to ensure compatibility with the largest possible number of other systems. Sometimes people with fast modems purposely slow them to improve the reliability of data transmission over noisy telephone lines. Find out which baud rates are supported by the modem connected to the computer you intend to call. Then tell Works.

NOTE: The highest baud rates offered by Works (9600 and 19200) aren't normally used with modems. These baud rates can be useful when two computers are directly connected to each other through a cable. This procedure is sometimes used for data conversion tasks. See Chapter 11 for more information.

Just because two modems are set at the same speed doesn't mean that they're automatically compatible. Other operating characteristics usually need to be matched. Works is set to start with the most commonly used settings, but you may have to change one or more of them from time to time. Read on.

Data Size

As you may know, computers represent letters and numbers internally, using combinations of 0s and 1s, which are also called *bits*. Over the years, several data-representation standards have developed. Some systems use eight bits to represent each character; other systems use only seven bits.

When computers exchange information, they need to use the same number of bits to represent characters at both ends. If you use the wrong Data Size option, data may be "scrambled," as shown in figure 10.6.

Stop Bits

Another variable is the number of bits used to separate characters when they're exchanged; these extra 0s and 1s are called *stop bits*. Works offers a choice of one or two stop bits. You should, when possible, match the number of stop bits used by the other system.

Parity

Many communications devices use a simple kind of error detection called *parity checking*. As with the distinction between baud rate and BPS, you

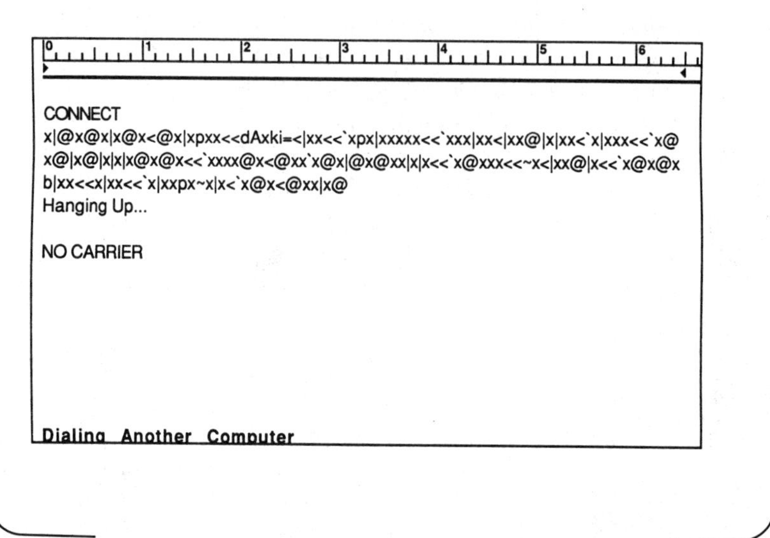

Fig. 10.6

Scrambled data resulting from incompatible settings.

need not be too concerned with these technicalities; parity checking, briefly, is a method of adding extra bits to each transmitted character so that the number of 1s is either even or odd. All you really need to know is that your computer and the remote computer should both use the same parity setting. Works offers three choices:

- None
- Odd
- Even

You and the other computer user should agree on a parity-checking technique (odd or even). Or you both can choose to exchange data without parity checking by clicking the None button in your Communications Settings dialog boxes.

Handshake

When data is "flying" back and forth at high speeds, both Works itself and the hardware (your Mac and modem) may need to pause from time to time to catch up. Therefore, you need to be able to tell the sending computer to stop sending momentarily while your system "catches its breath." And you must notify the sender when your system is ready to begin receiving again. The methods used to accomplish this starting and stopping are numerous—and beyond the scope of this book—but you should know that the process is called ***handshaking***.

Requests to stop and start data transmission can come from the Works software itself, your Macintosh, or both. Works usually uses a simple handshaking technique called Xon/Xoff, or *asynchronous* handshaking. In unusual circumstances, you may need to use hardware handshaking in addition to or in place of the Xon/Xoff approach. Even more rarely, technical people may want to defeat handshaking altogether. Works provides all these options.

The default, and most frequently used, technique is Xon/Xoff. To select a different scheme, click on the button next to the option you want. Remember that both your modem and the other system must support the choice you make.

Phone Type

Most telephone lines today can support Touch-Tone dialing, the fastest, most efficient way for your smart modem to dial. If your phone line doesn't work with Touch-Tone, select Rotary Dial (sometimes called pulse dial) in the Communications Settings dialog box by clicking the appropriate button.

If, using the Touch-Tone method, you hear your modem trying to dial but you can't reach the designated computer, try Rotary Dial. If that procedure doesn't work, contact the phone company, a knowledgeable colleague, or your dealer for help.

Line and Character Delays

Some computers and software packages can't receive data as quickly as Works can send the data. Moreover, they may not be able to handshake (see "Handshake"). In these cases, you may find that the receiving software misses characters or even entire lines that you send.

You may be able to correct the problem by having Works pause briefly after each line or character sent. To produce pauses between lines or characters, you change the 0s in the Line Delay and Character Delay boxes to small numbers. Then observe the results. Obviously, these pauses slow the whole communications process, so no delay is the best—and the default—choice.

Connect To

You can connect your modem to either of two connectors on the back of your Mac. Usually, you connect the modem to the connector labeled with the telephone handset icon; and Works "assumes" that you have done so. If you must connect the modem to the printer jack instead, tell Works by clicking the button to the left of the printer icon in the Communications Settings dialog box.

Additional Settings for Version 1.1

Works 1.1 offers additional features that require more settings choices. These features are described in the following sections.

Terminal Type

Works 1.0 emulates, or mimics, only one terminal type and behaves like a simple "teletype" terminal. This capability makes Works 1.0 compatible with most of today's popular systems, such as CompuServe, The Source, and so on.

Works 1.1, on the other hand, emulates three popular terminal types, so it is compatible with many other computers that expect to be connected to a specific type of terminal. The three terminal types emulated are

- TTY (also called teletype, or dumb, terminals)
- VT-100 (similar to the Digital Equipment terminal of the same number)
- VT-52 (similar to the Digital Equipment terminal of the same number)

In Works 1.1, the default terminal type is TTY. To change terminal types, you click on the button next to the desired alternative. The other terminal types offer a few additional features not found in TTY mode.

Auto-Wrap

In VT-100 or VT-52 mode, Version 1.1 provides an Auto-wrap feature. (Version 1.0 does not provide this feature.) Auto-wrap "compensates" for long lines of text by automatically reformatting them on the screen, much the same way that the Works word-processing feature automatically wraps text when you type it. Text is then easier to read, and words aren't broken up arbitrarily, as is the case when the feature isn't used.

You select or disable Auto-wrap by clicking that button in the Communications Settings dialog box. This option usually is enabled, as indicated by an X in the box.

Notice that if you select the TTY terminal type, the Auto-wrap option appears dimmed in the Communications Settings dialog box. In TTY mode, Auto-wrap is not available.

NewLine

Version 1.1 offers a NewLine option, which isn't available in Version 1.0. The following background information makes this valuable feature easier to understand.

Many telecommunications systems differentiate between a carriage-return character and a line-feed character. Usually, when a carriage-return character is received, the cursor on the receiving computer's screen moves back to the leftmost position on the current line. A separate line-feed character must be sent to move the cursor down one line to a "clean" part of the screen. Therefore, if you are receiving information from a system that sends only carriage returns (as opposed to carriage returns plus line feeds), new lines of text overwrite preceding lines on your screen.

This arrangement isn't a problem if you don't need to read the text and are simply saving it to disk for later use. But if you want to read the text as it comes in, you want Works to display each new line below the one preceding it.

The NewLine option in VT-100 or VT-52 mode of Version 1.1 enables you to accomplish this task if the sending computer cannot. When you invoke this feature (an X appears in the box), Works executes a "carriage return plus line feed" whenever the program receives a carriage return. That is, Works moves the cursor down one line each time the system receives a carriage-return character.

To disable the NewLine option, you click its box.

If you select TTY as the terminal type, the NewLine option appears dimmed in the Communications Settings dialog box. This feature is not available for the TTY terminal type.

Number of Screens

Some more background is necessary before a discussion of the Number of screens option in Version 1.1. Version 1.0 does not offer a scrolling feature; so as Works receives text, the system displays the text and then pushes it up toward the top of the screen into "alphabet heaven." Once text disappears from the screen in Version 1.0, that text is gone forever. If you don't read quickly or if you want to review something, you need to have the sending computer resend the material (unless you've also saved it to a disk file, in which case you can review the text with Works' word-processing feature).

Obviously, being able to look back is nice. With Works 1.1, you can review up to 100 previous screens, and you can specify how far back you want to look. Here's how.

Set the Number of screens option in the Version 1.1 Communications Settings dialog box to a number greater than zero. Works then sends the latest text that has scrolled off the screen to temporary storage in memory rather than sending the text directly to "alphabet heaven."

When Works has received more than a screen of text, familiar-looking scroll bars appear in the communications window. You can look at old text by—you guessed it—using the scroll bars. For example, in figure 10.7 the name of the restaurant has been pushed off the screen. In figure 10.8, the text has been scrolled so that the name of the restaurant is seen.

To scroll up or down, you click on the arrows. You can scroll up to review things while new information is still coming in; Works keeps things in order for you. To move in page-sized increments, click on the scroll bar itself. When you finish looking around, you return to the "bottom" of the window to pick up the communications dialog where you left off.

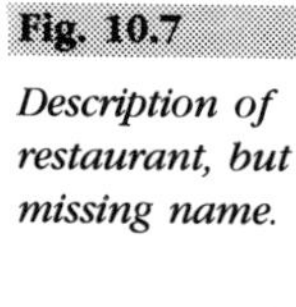

Fig. 10.7

Description of restaurant, but missing name.

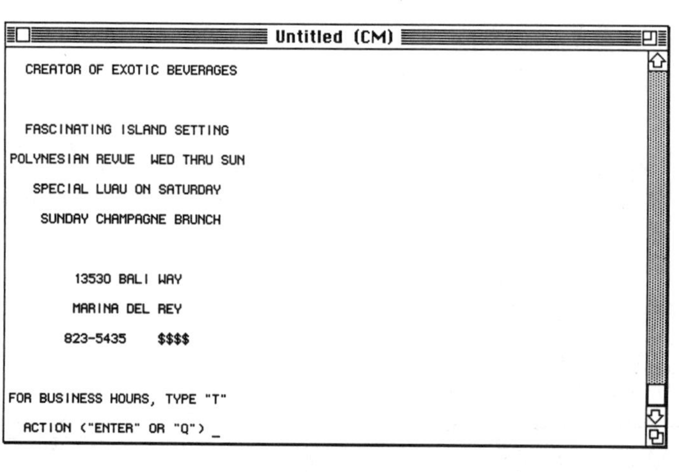

Untitled (CM)
CREATOR OF EXOTIC BEVERAGES
FASCINATING ISLAND SETTING
POLYNESIAN REVUE WED THRU SUN
SPECIAL LUAU ON SATURDAY
SUNDAY CHAMPAGNE BRUNCH
13530 BALI WAY
MARINA DEL REY
823-5435 $$$$
FOR BUSINESS HOURS, TYPE "T"
ACTION ("ENTER" OR "Q") _

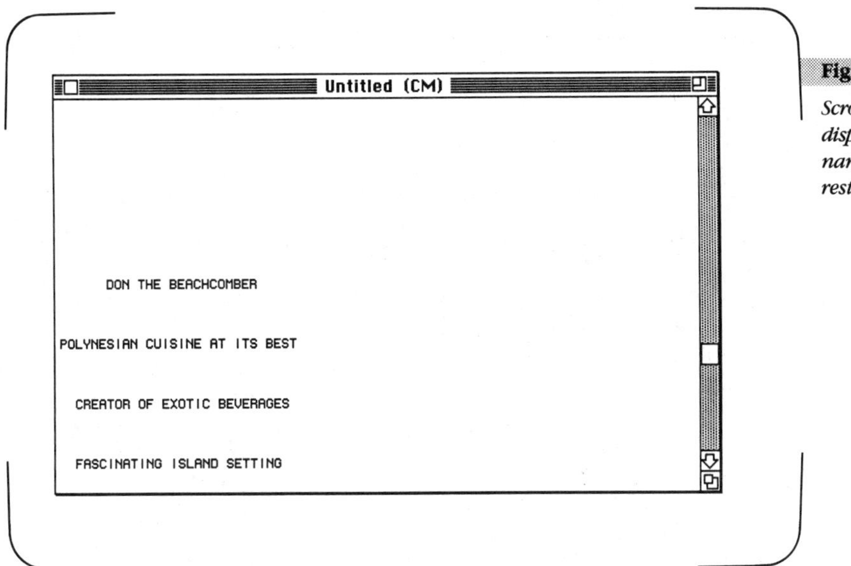

Fig. 10.8

Scrolling back displays the name of the restaurant.

Obviously, the scrolling feature is useful. But why does Works give you a choice of number of screens? The answer is this: To conserve memory. This technique is particularly useful if you have a 512K Macintosh or if you keep many open documents on your desktop simultaneously.

Remember that in Works you can have many projects going on at once. Works stores everything that you've placed on your desktop—spreadsheets, word-processing documents, and so on—in memory (RAM). Sometimes not enough RAM is available for you to have many documents open and still be able to scroll through 100 screens of old communications text. You can, however, specify how much of your computer's memory should be reserved for temporary storage of old text. The more old screens you want to review, the less room you have for other active projects, such as spreadsheets and word-processing documents.

The default setting is four screens, which should be plenty for most casual data-communications sessions. (Remember that you can always save entire sessions to disk for later review as word-processing documents; see "Receiving and Storing Simple Text.") To define the number of screens you want to be able to review, tab to or click on the Number of screens box and enter a number from 0 to 100.

If not enough memory is available in your computer to save the requested number of screens, Works warns you, as illustrated in figure 10.9. The system then saves as many screens as possible. You can sometimes free up additional memory for screen scrolling by closing unneeded documents.

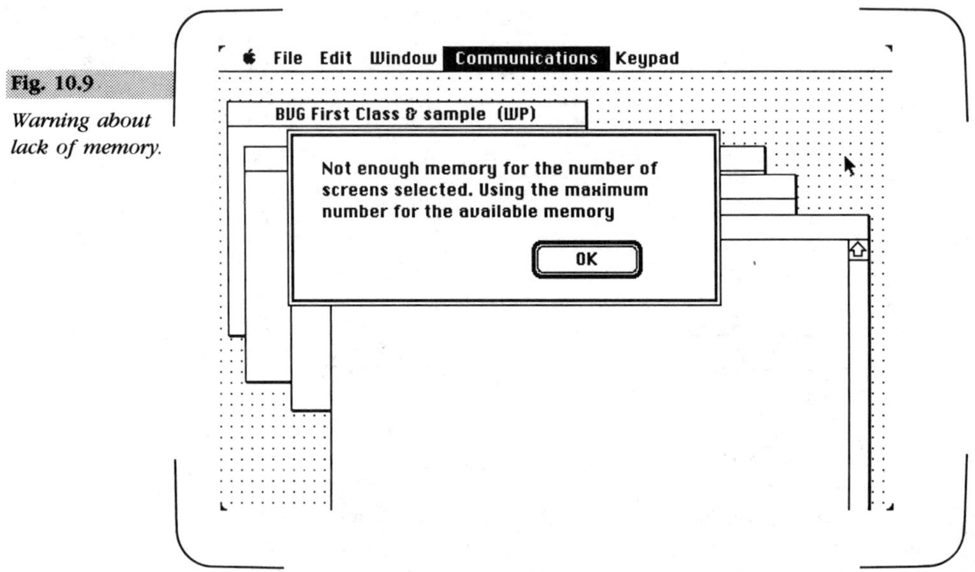

Fig. 10.9

Warning about lack of memory.

Any text that you can see by scrolling you can select, copy, cut, paste, and so on, by using the familiar Macintosh techniques. Because you can have other documents open, you can use the Clipboard to pass text from the communications window to other documents, such as word-processing or spreadsheet projects.

Changing and Saving Settings

After making changes in the Communications Settings dialog box, you must decide whether, and where, to save the new settings. This decision is covered in more detail in the "Communications Tips and Techniques" section of this chapter.

If you want to save the settings as part of the current communications document, you save the document as you would any other. Press *command*-S or choose the Save option on the File menu.

To create a new communications document containing the modified settings, you use Save As on the File menu. Works then preserves the old settings under the old document name and creates a new communications document with the new name you choose. The new document becomes the active one.

If you need to change communications settings in an active communications document, select Settings on the Communications menu. Make any desired changes, and test the results. Remember that you'll need to save the communications document if you want the changes to be permanent.

Echo On and Echo Off

Not all settings are in the Communications Settings dialog box. Two settings worth remembering are Echo On and Echo Off, which are on the Communications menu (see again fig. 10.3). Works sets this option to the most popular choice, but sometimes you'll want to change this setting. Take a moment now to tuck the following concept away in the back of your mind.

When you're communicating with another computer and you press a key on your keyboard, you usually want your screen to display what you've typed. In communications mode, characters appear on your screen in two ways. Either your Mac displays the characters directly, as occurs when you perform word-processing or other tasks; or the screen displays copies, or *echoes*, of what you've typed. These echoes have been sent back to you over the telephone line by the other computer, a procedure that is usually called either *echoing* or *full-duplex operation.*

Many computers can echo what you've sent. By looking at these echoes, you can be more confident that what you are sending is being received correctly at the other end.

Both computers need to be in agreement about echoing. To make them agree, you use the Echo On and Echo Off options on the Communications menu. Clicking one option overrides the other. Use Echo On, the default, if the computer at the other end will send the characters to your screen. Choose Echo Off only if the other computer can't or won't echo.

The most common echo problem occurs when both computers update your screen. This problem happens when you have selected Echo Off and the other computer echoes anyway. "YYoouurr ssccrreeeenn wwiillll ccoonnttaaiinn ddoouubbllee cchhaarraacctteerrss lliikkee tthheessee." To remedy this problem, pull down the Communications menu and select Echo On. Things will look normal thereafter.

A more bizarre problem occurs when the other computer should be echoing and doesn't. You type on your keyboard, and the other computer gets what it needs, but your screen doesn't show anything you've typed. The screen does, however, display the other computer's responses to your typing. To remedy this problem, select Echo Off. Some software makers refer to the equivalent of the Works Echo On feature as full duplex and to Echo Off as half duplex.

NOTE: Some modems have switches and software commands that can cause additional echoing. If you're seeing three of every character, consult your modem manual, dealer, mentor, or eye doctor.

The Telephone List

Works enables you to enter and save the telephone numbers of up to eight computers that you call frequently. You enter these numbers in a phone list, which is stored as part of a communications document. You can type descriptive names next to each telephone number. Figure 10.10 shows an example of such a list.

Fig. 10.10

A typical telephone list.

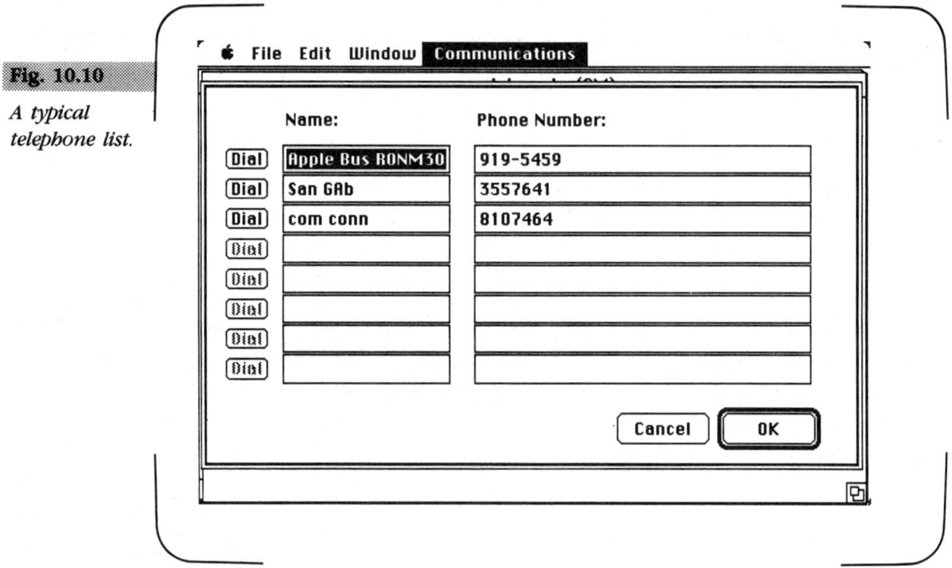

To access the phone list, you chose Dial on the Communications menu. You can use the list as a reference for manually dialed calls. If you have a compatible smart modem, Works automatically instructs the modem to dial the number, which you choose by clicking the Dial button next to the number.

Entering New Auto-Dial Phone Numbers

Before you can use your modem's automatic dialing feature, you need to enter at least one telephone number in a communications document phone list. And you should know certain things about automatically dialed phone numbers. For example, Works and most smart modems ignore parentheses, slashes, spaces, and dashes. Therefore, all the following entry styles are usually allowed:

1 800 555 1212
1-800-555-1212
1(800)555-1212
1-800/555-1212
18005551212

Don't type letters instead of numbers—for example, 1-800-CAR-CARE—in the telephone number box. You won't reach the desired party, and you may confuse your modem.

NOTE: Works accepts up to 50 characters per phone number. This number is plenty, even for complex international numbers with accounting-access codes.

To move from entry box to entry box in the phone list, you click or use the *tab* key. Enter, edit, and delete phone numbers or names as you do any other Macintosh entry.

CAUTION: Works saves changes in your phone list to disk only when you save an edited communications document. You don't save your changes by clicking OK; Works accepts them only until you close the communications window. If you've made important changes to your telephone list, be sure to press Y (for yes) in response to the Save changes? prompt when you close the communications window.

Pausing While Dialing

The auto-dial feature dials more quickly than you could possibly dial with your own finger. For example, a modem using this feature can dial an entire 11-digit long-distance number in about 1 second. This feature is great if your system is connected directly to an outside line (like the ones at your home), but what if you're calling from an office phone that requires that you dial 9 (or some other access number) and then pause for connection to an outside line?

Works and your smart modem offer a simple and moderately effective solution to this problem: the pause feature. By using one or more commas in a telephone number, you cause Works and the modem to pause in the dialing sequence. For example, if you type **9,1 800 555 1212**, the modem dials 9 and then pauses briefly before dialing the rest of the telephone number.

To extend the length of the pause, use more commas. The exact length of the pause achieved by placing a comma in a phone number is determined by your modem. Usually, a comma produces a two-second pause. For example, if you type **9,,1-800-5551212**, the system dials 9, waits about 4 seconds for an outside line, and then dials the telephone number. This "art" is an inexact one, and you need to experiment with the number of commas required to produce a delay that works reliably.

You can use commas and extra numbers at the ends of telephone numbers, too. This capability is helpful if your phone service requires accounting codes for long-distance calls.

Auto-Dialing from the Phone List

Once you've specified or confirmed the communications settings and entered at least one phone number in your phone list, you're ready to dial another computer. With your modem turned on, select Dial on the Communications menu. Then click the Dial button next to the desired number.

Works sends setup and dialing instructions to the modem and then clears the window so that you can watch the progress. If your modem has a built-in speaker and it's turned on, you can hear the call's progress as well. When the screen displays the word *CONNECT* (or your modem's message for connection), you're ready to exchange information.

Here are the steps involved in this process:

1. Choose Dial from the Communications menu.
2. The phone list appears.
3. Click the Dial button to the left of the number you want to dial.
4. Works and your smart modem dial for you and then let you communicate.

Dialing with Non-Hayes-Compatible Smart Modems

Some smart modems have command languages that differ from the Hayes AT standard. By reading the modem manual, you can find out what commands to send to instruct the modem to do things Works can't do. (For example, you may need to send the DIAL command rather than Hayes' ATD command.) You can send commands to any smart modem from your keyboard. An explanation follows.

When Works opens a communications window, the system immediately connects your keyboard with the modem. Therefore, you should be able to type modem commands from the keyboard and have the modem execute them. Refer to your modem manual to learn more about entering commands.

Dialing Manually

If you don't have an auto-dial modem, you must dial phone numbers on a regular telephone and then "trick" Works. First, to get a Dial button to light, you place a comma in one of the phone number fields. Before you click the Dial button, use the dial on your phone to dial the number. Then, click the Dial button to get the modem and Works working together. If you're using an acoustic coupler, place the phone handset in the coupler cups. If you're using a direct-connect manual modem, hang up the phone.

Here's a list of the steps you perform:

1. Place a comma in a phone number entry box on the telephone list.
2. Use your telephone to dial the desired number.
3. Click the Dial button next to the comma.
4. Listen for a ring followed by a high-pitched tone.
5. Either place the handset in the cups (if you're using an acoustic coupler), or hang up the telephone (if you're using a manual direct-connect modem).
6. Communicate.

What To Do When a Computer Answers

If you're using a direct-connect modem that has a speaker, you know when another computer answers. You hear a high-pitched, continuous tone or whistling on the line; this tone is called the *carrier*.

Shortly, you'll hear a second, different tone in addition to the first one. Your modem and the other are trying to agree on a communications speed. If all goes well, the speaker soon mutes, and you see CONNECT and perhaps other things on your screen. What happens after that depends on what type of computer you've dialed and what you want to accomplish.

If you've dialed another Macintosh that is also using the Works communications feature and if you both have selected compatible settings and echo techniques, you can start typing. Everything you type appears on the other Mac user's screen, and vice versa.

Many non-Works communications packages operate the same way. For example, figure 10.11 shows a typical exchange between Works and Hayes Smartcom II® software running on an IBM computer. This exchange could just as easily have taken place between two Macs or a Mac and an Apple II. (Notice that boldfaced, underscored, and otherwise special characters are received as plain text.)

Fig. 10.11

A typical exchange between IBM and Macintosh computers.

```
Setting modem to answer calls...
ATS0=1

OK

RING

CONNECT

Hi Ron! I am typing this from the keyboard of my IBM PC. How does the
connection look at your end?

Hi! 'Looks great. Go ahead and send the text file.

This is a sample of a file sent from an IBM PC
to the Works Communications option over phone lines.
Notice that all text refinements have been lost:

Bold, Italic, Underscore, Superscript, Subscript

Got it. Thanks & bye!
Hanging Up...

NO CARRIER
```

If your system is connected to a different service, such as Telenet®, CompuServe, or a local bulletin board, instead of to another personal computer, you must follow the appropriate procedures to identify yourself to the other system. Usually, these procedures, collectively called *logging on*, include typing an account number, password, and, possibly, some other information. Consult the manuals for the services you intend to use or get help from their customer service people.

Figure 10.12 illustrates a short session between a Macintosh Works user and the U.S. Department of Commerce's Economic Bulletin Board.

I dialed the number, and the Economic BBS answered as shown in the first few lines of the figure.

```
OK

Dialing...

CONNECT
WELCOME TO ECONOMIC BBS

      THE U.S. DEPARTMENT OF COMMERCE'S ECONOMIC BULLETIN BOARD

This bulletin board service provides current economic news and information
produced by the Department of Commerce and other Federal government agencies.

FULL ACCESS TO THIS SERVICE IS LIMITED TO PAID SUBSCRIBERS WHO HAVE A VALID
ACCOUNT NUMBER, BUT "GUEST" USERS MAY VIEW BULLETINS AND DOWNLOAD TWO FILES
THAT DESCRIBE THE EBB AND HOW TO REGISTER FOR THE SERVICE.

IF YOU ARE A GUEST USER, we suggest you download: 1) FILES - a description
of all files available on the system, and  2) REG-FORM - a registration form
that you can complete and mail.

If you have trouble using this service, please call (202) 377-1986 for
assistance.


What is your FIRST Name? RRoonn
What is your LAST Name? Mansfield
RON MANSFIELD
Is your name correct ([Y],N)? y
What is your ACCOUNT # (GUEST if none)? guest
guest, right (Y=[ENTER],N)? yep
Checking Users...
What is your CITY and STATE? Los Angeles, CA

                              WELCOME

                                 TO

      THE U.S. DEPARTMENT OF COMMERCE'S ECONOMIC BULLETIN BOARD

If you are new to using computer bulletin boards, the EBB provides you with
three types of services, reading bulletins, downloading files, and sending
messages to us or receiving messages from us.  Functions available on other
computer bulletin board services such as uploading files or sending messages to other
users are not available on this service.

Press [ENTER] to continue? (Return)

BULLETINS will provide you with general economic news, a calendar of release
dates for upcoming economic news, contacts in economic statistical agencies,
and instructions on how to use the bulletin board. (etc.)
                             THANK YOU FOR USING
                          THE ECONOMIC BULLETIN BOARD

RON MANSFIELD from LOS ANGELES, CA
<C>hange name/address, <D>isconnect, <R>egister? d
b'\=E dm2a(#
NO CARRIER
```

Fig. 10.12

Communications with the U.S. Government's ECO BBS on-line.

The BBS requested identification from me. If I had been a registered user, an account number would have been required and possibly a password as well. Because I'm just a visitor on this friendlier-than-usual system, my name was enough.

Notice that I had to change the Echo On/Off setting on the Communications menu to eliminate the double characters that appeared when the other computer "echoed back" what I typed. Both the government computer and my Mac were putting characters on the screen.

The service then explained its features. The explanation would fill more than one screen on most computers, so the BBS paused to let the user read the first screen. (Not all services have this capability.) At times like this, Works 1.1's scrolling feature comes in handy. If I had been using either VT-100 or VT-52 mode in Works 1.1, I could have scrolled back to reread previous information. When I was ready to continue, I pressed the *return* (*enter*) key to see the next screen.

The BBS then gave me the chance to register as a regular user. I declined, and the BBS hung up (disconnected itself from the telephone line). The garbage that followed (`b'\=E` and so on at the bottom of the figure) appeared because the BBS hung up. When my smart modem detected the government computer's disconnection, my modem displayed `NO CARRIER` and also hung up.

Hanging Up

As demonstrated in the sample BBS session, most smart modems hang up automatically if the connection to the other computer is broken. If, however, you reach a wrong number, make a bad connection, hear a busy signal, or finish exchanging data, *you* must hang up. Two methods are available: Either choose Hang Up on the Communications menu or press *command*-= (equal sign). Works then tells your smart modem to disconnect. You'll see `Hanging Up, +++`, and probably something like `NO CARRIER` (as shown in fig. 10.12). Closing the communications window also causes your modem to hang up.

A problem on the phone line can cause one or both systems to hang up without asking you first.

To hang up a dumb modem, use the Hang Up option on the Communications menu. If you're using an acoustic coupler, hang up the telephone.

Transmission of Data

Now that you have learned the necessary communications terms and the settings you need, you are ready to transmit data. You can send messages just by typing. You also can send and receive files—both simple and complex.

Sending Text from Your Keyboard

The process of sending text from a computer keyboard is perhaps the easiest of all data exchanges. Once your system is connected to a compatible computer, you simply type as usual; and what you type appears almost simultaneously on both your computer screen and that of the other machine. Likewise, anything typed at the other end appears on your screen. Figure 10.13 illustrates this process.

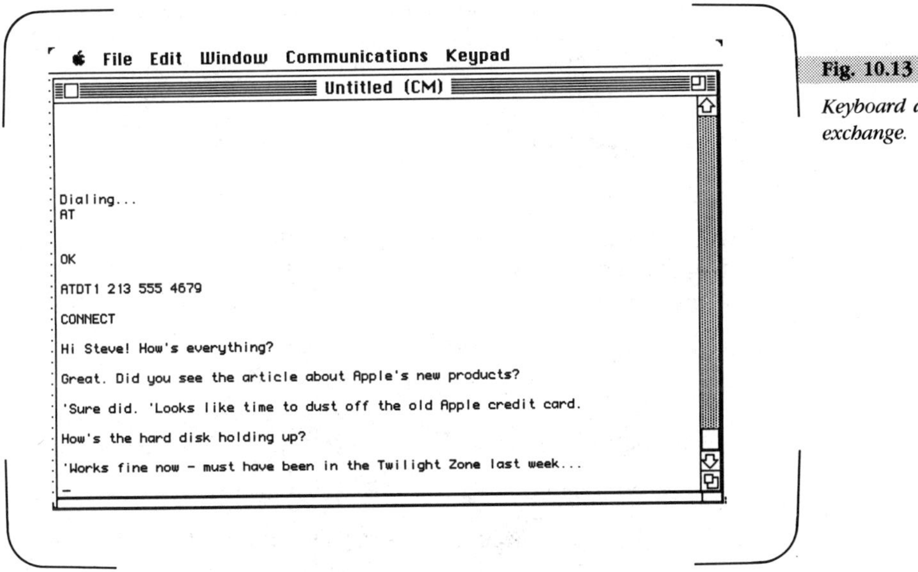

Fig. 10.13

Keyboard data exchange.

Obviously, you'll want to take turns typing, much the way polite people take turns talking. If you both type at once, your screens probably will be illegible.

Why type to each other when you can talk over the same telephone line instead? One reason is to let someone know that you're ready to send or receive a file. Typing back and forth this way is easier than picking up the telephone and talking—something that may be impossible if the computers are already connected over your only telephone line.

Typing is also a great communications tool for the deaf. Works 1.0 and all three emulation modes (Type options) of Works 1.0 should be compatible with most TTY terminals for the deaf. You may want to start with the 300-baud setting when testing compatibility.

Many bulletin boards and computer services such as CompuServe and The Source have "round tables" where multiple users log on simultaneously and take turns discussing topics of common interest through their keyboards. These people think typing is more fun than talking.

Here are the steps involved in exchanging keyboard data:

1. Open a communications document and dial the other computer. Log on, if necessary.
2. When the computers are connected, take turns typing and reading.
3. Hang up by choosing the Hang Up option on the Communications menu or by pressing **command**-=.
4. Close the communications window.

Sending Simple Text Files

Before making the telephone connection, you can prepare plain text to be sent. You type the text in a word-processing window, save the text to disk, and choose the Send Text option on the Communications menu. Works then displays the Send Text dialog box, as shown in figure 10.14.

Here's a step-by-step description of what you do:

1. Create a word-processing file.
2. Save the file on a disk.
3. Open communications and connect with the other computer.
4. With the text disk in a drive, select Send Text.
5. Select the file to send and click OK or double-click.
6. Watch the text transfer.
7. Continue with other communications or hang up.

NOTE: Pictures and text attributes can't be sent with this technique. Some receiving systems ignore or are confused by special Macintosh characters and accent marks. Text is sent without line feeds, which can cause the receiving computer to display lines one on top of the other.

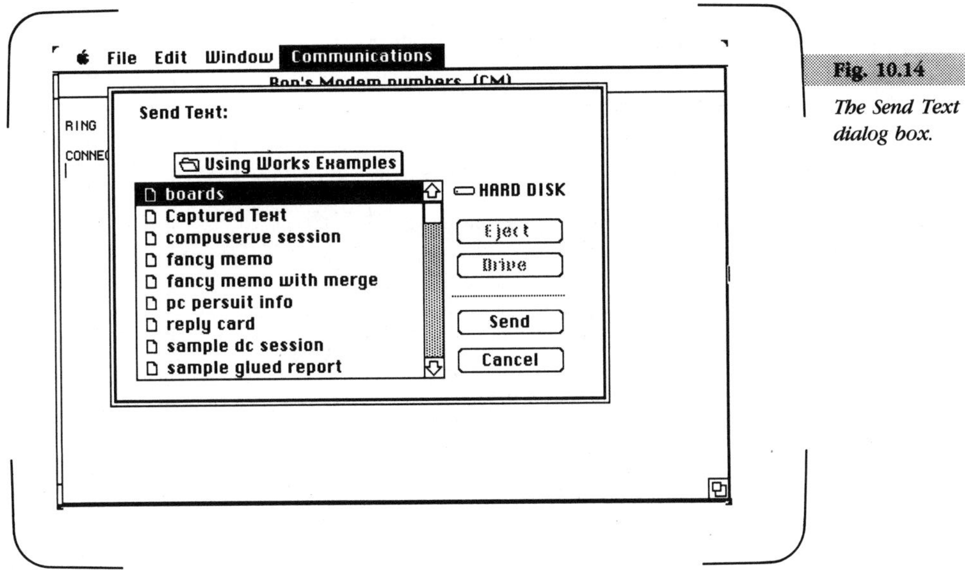

Fig. 10.14

The Send Text dialog box.

If the recipient saves the text to disk and looks at the text with a word-processing package, everything should be all right.

Sending Complex Files

When sending files that contain more complicated text, you'll probably want to use the Send File option rather than the Send Text feature. Send File enables you to send programs, complete word-processing documents (including text attributes, pictures, margins, and so on), databases, spreadsheets—virtually anything that you can save on a Macintosh disk. Figure 10.15 shows the Send File dialog box.

To take advantage of this capability, the communications software on both ends must be compatible. Moreover, the receiving computer must be compatible with the files that you send if they're to be useful at that end. For example, sending a Works spreadsheet file to someone who doesn't own a compatible spreadsheet program does little good.

Xmodem Protocols

These complex exchanges use one of three Xmodem protocols. A *protocol* is a set of data-exchange procedures and rules that two computers use together. They usually do this exchange without your intervention,

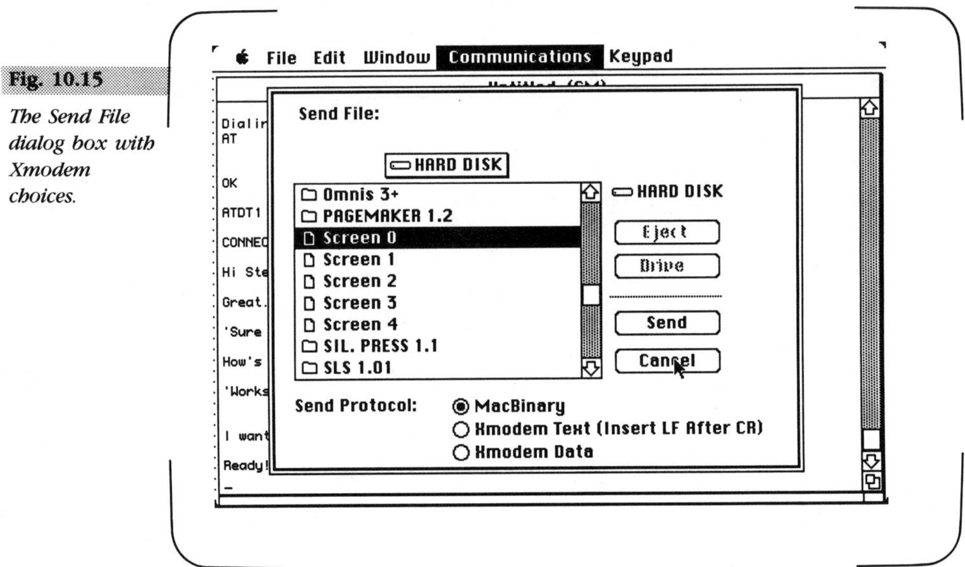

Fig. 10.15

The Send File dialog box with Xmodem choices.

once you get things rolling. Xmodem protocols were designed to facilitate relatively fast and error-free exchanges of complex files containing pictures, control codes, text, and just about anything else found on a disk. The original Xmodem protocol has a number of variations, and Works supports three of them:

MacBinary
Xmodem Text (Insert LF After CR)
Xmodem Data

You make your choice in the Send File and Receive File dialog boxes, which you access through the Communications menu. Both computers should be using the same protocol.

You can't hurt anything if you try to send or receive data with the wrong protocol. Works informs you of problems as it attempts to perform the exchange you've requested.

MacBinary

The MacBinary protocol is an Xmodem protocol used by Macintosh computers and others that support MacBinary. This protocol is also the one that Works automatically uses to exchange Works files of any kind. In figure 10.16, Works is trying to transmit a file named Screen 4, using the MacBinary protocol. Works has checked the size of the disk file and specifies that the file will be sent in 52 chunks, or *blocks*.

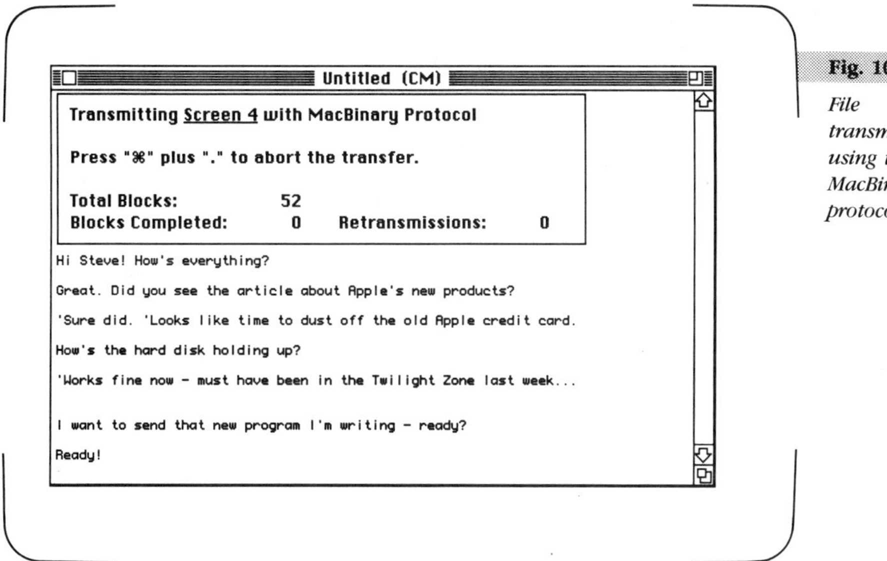

Fig. 10.16 *File transmission using the MacBinary protocol.*

Works tells you how many blocks have been sent successfully, (none, in this example) and how many times blocks need to be sent again because of transmission errors. If Works keeps trying to send and resend most blocks, you may have a bad telephone connection or incompatible communications software.

To abort an Xmodem file transfer, press **command-.** (period).

Xmodem Text and Xmodem Data

Use the Xmodem Text protocol at both ends if you're going to exchange text with a non-Macintosh system. Don't try to exchange formats, pictures, and so on.

Try using the Xmodem Data protocol if your Mac is connected to non-Macintosh systems sending programs and other files that contain more than just simple text.

Procedure for Sending Complex Files

As you have seen, sending complex files involves more steps and decisions than sending simple text files. Here's a more detailed explanation of what the procedure involves:

1. Locate the files you plan to send.

2. Save the files on a disk.

3. Open a communications window, and connect with the other computer.
4. With the disk in a drive, select Send File.
5. Pick the correct protocol.
6. Specify the file to send and click Send or double-click.
7. Watch the screen as the transfer progresses.
8. Continue with other communications, or hang up.

Receiving and Storing Simple Text

You can easily capture incoming text to disk, using the Capture Text dialog box shown in figure 10.17.

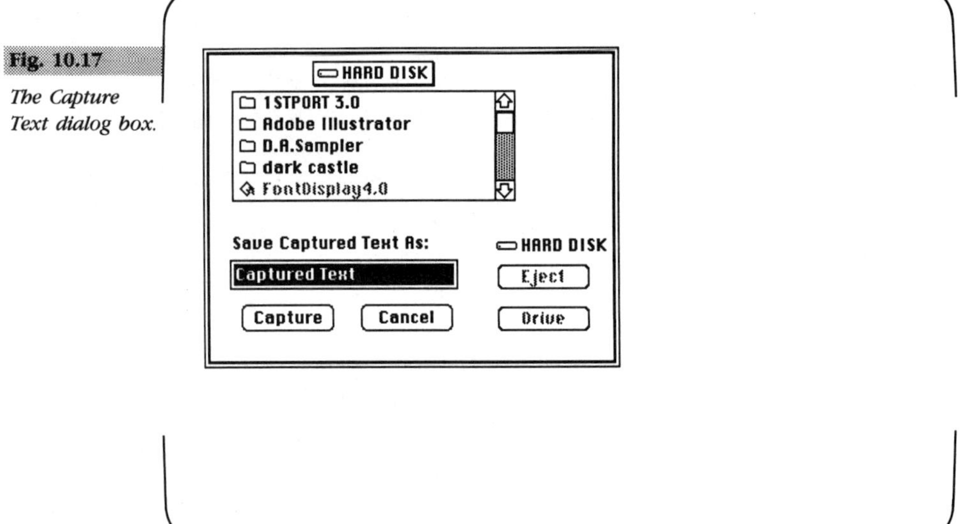

Fig. 10.17

The Capture Text dialog box.

1. Choose the Capture Text option on the Communications menu.
2. Works uses Captured Text as the default file name for storage. Change this name to something meaningful if you want.
3. Click Capture or double-click the file name.
4. Choose End Capture Text when you're finished.

Receiving and Storing Complex Files

After the connection has been established and the sender is prepared to transmit files, select Receive File on the Communications menu. Works then proposes a file name, which you can change. Choose the appropriate protocol. The protocols, explained in the instructions for sending complex files, must be the same for both computers. Click the Receive button. Works and the other system take it from there, informing you of progress and problems.

Printing Incoming Information

Use the Print Window option on the File menu to print the contents of the communications window. You can print only one screenful of word-processing communications information.

If, for any reason, you think that you may need to print more than a screenful of incoming information, use the Save Text feature at the beginning of your session. Then open the resulting text file with the Works word processor to print what was sent and received. If you don't remember to use Save Text and are using Works 1.1, you may be able to copy and paste text from the temporary memory where text is saved for scrolling. This approach, however, is limited and cumbersome compared to the Save Text feature.

Using the Keypad Menu

The Keypad menu is used to send VT-100 and VT-52 special function key codes. To send a code, pull down the menu and point to the number or code you wish to send (see fig. 10.18). It will be highlighted. Releasing the mouse button sends the code.

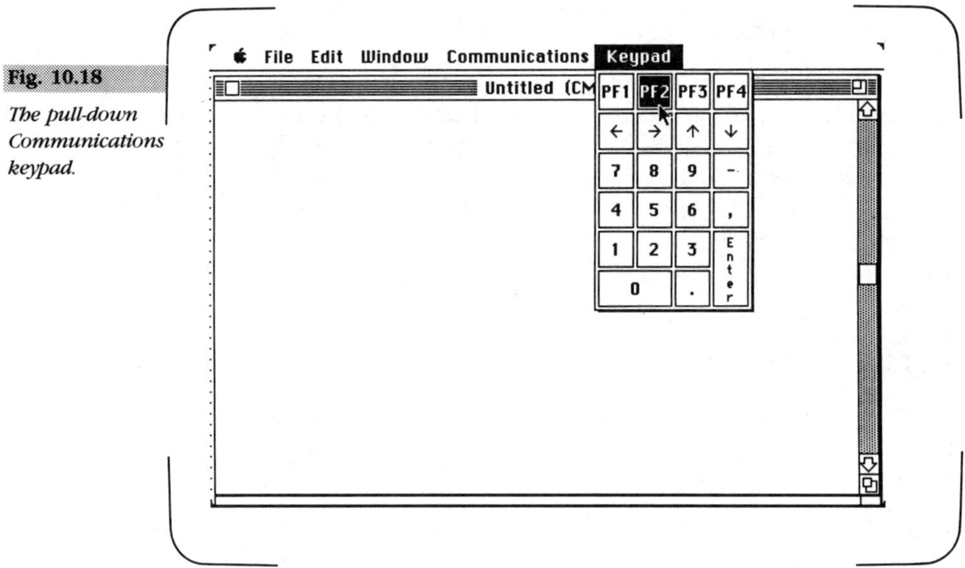

Fig. 10.18

The pull-down Communications keypad.

Using Control Codes and Special Function Keys

Just as you use special key combinations and function keys on your Macintosh for word processing and other tasks, computer-terminal users do equivalent things with their keyboards. For example, the operator of a teletype can ring the bell on another teletype by pressing *control*-G—a keystroke sequence sometimes called the ASCII BEL function.

Many other control codes and special function keys are used on terminals such as the VT-100 and VT-52 (see table 10.1). The control codes and special function keys that you may be asked to send include BEL (rings the bell or beeps the beeper), Backspace (BS), TAB, Form Feed (FF), any of the device control codes (DC1-DC4), Escape (ESC), and BREAK. Table 10.2 lists the popular control codes and special function keys, and also shows how to send the codes from Works (when doing so is possible).

NOTE: With the exception of sending the ampersand, you don't need to press the *shift* key when sending control codes. Lowercase letters work just fine.

Table 10.1
VT-100 And VT-52 Functions And Keys

Key or Function	*How To Use from Works*
132-column mode	Not currently available
Smooth scrolling	Not currently available
Split screen	Not currently available
Double-high characters	Not currently available
Double-wide characters	Not currently available
PF1	Click on PF1 on Keypad menu
PF2	Click on PF2 on Keypad menu
PF3	Click on PF3 on Keypad menu
PF4	Click on PF4 on Keypad menu
PRINT ENTER	Click on ENTER on Keypad menu
Up arrow	Click on [↑] on Keypad menu
Down arrow	Click on [↓] on Keypad menu
Right arrow	Click on [→] on Keypad menu
Left arrow	Click on [←] on Keypad menu
Switch Key	Not currently available

Table 10.2
ASCII Control Codes

ASCII	*Mnemonic*	*Hex*	*Value*	*How To Send From Works*
NUL	@	00		Hold down *option* or *control* and press @.
SOH	A	01		Hold down *option* or *control* and press a.
STX	B	02		Hold down *option* or *control* and press b.
ETX	C	03		Hold down *option* or *control* and press c.
EOT	D	04		Hold down *option* or *control* and press d.
ENQ	E	05		Hold down *option* or *control* and press e.
ACK	F	06		Hold down *option* or *control* and press f.
BEL	G	07		Hold down *option* or *control* and press g.

Continued on next page.

Table 10.2—*continued*

ASCII	*Mnemonic*	*Hex*	*Value*	*How To Send From Works*
BS	H	08		Hold down *option* or *control* and press h.
TAB	I	09		Hold down *option* or *control* and press i.
LF	J	0A		Hold down *option* or *control* and press j.
VT	K	0B		Hold down *option* or *control* and press k.
FF	L	0C		Hold down *option* or *control* and press l.
CR	M	0D		Hold down *option* or *control* and press m.
SO	N	0E		Hold down *option* or *control* and press n.
SI	O	0F		Hold down *option* or *control* and press o.
DEL	P	10		Hold down *option* or *control* and press p.
DC1 (Xon)	Q	11		Hold down *option* or *control* and press q.
DC2	R	12		Hold down *option* or *control* and press r.
DC3 (Xoff)	S	13		Hold down *option* or *control* and press s.
DC4	T	14		Hold down *option* or *control* and press t.
NAK	U	15		Hold down *option* or *control* and press u.
SYN	V	16		Hold down *option* or *control* and press v.
ETB	W	17		Hold down *option* or *control* and press w.
CAN	X	18		Hold down *option* or *control* and press x.
EM	Y	19		Hold down *option* or *control* and press y.
SUB	Z	1A		Hold down *option* or *control* and press z.

Table 10.2—*continued*

ASCII	*Mnemonic*	*Hex*	*Value*	*How To Send From Works*
ESC	[	1B		Hold down *option* or *control* and press [.
FS		1C		
GS		1D		
BREAK	3			Hold down *option* or *control* and press 3.

NOTE: Older Macintoshes don't have control keys. Use the option key instead.

Let Works Answer the Phone

If your direct-connect modem has a Hayes-compatible auto-answer feature and you enable it, Works and your hardware can answer incoming calls made by other computers. If the other caller has Works or compatible software, the caller can send files to your Macintosh disks or *download* files from your disks to his or her system.

This process can take place while you use Works for something else (word processing, for instance) or even when you're away from your computer. Some users use this capability to take advantage of low late-night and early-morning long-distance telephone rates.

Procedure for Automatic Answering

To have Works answer the phone automatically, do the following:

1. Turn on the modem.
2. Open a communications document.
3. Choose Answer Phone from the Communications menu.
4. Watch Works set up your modem for auto-answer.
5. Do other Works projects if you want, but don't close the communications window or quit Works.

As long as you leave the communications window open and the Answer Phone option checked on the Communications menu, Works and your modem answer the telephone and try to establish communications with the caller. They accomplish this task by sending a high-pitched carrier tone, which other modems recognize and respond to.

If you plan to use the auto-answer feature regularly, you need a separate telephone line for this purpose because you don't want your computer to answer calls from humans—unless they're bill collectors or oil lease sales people.

Disabling Auto Answer

To disable auto-answer mode, remove the check mark from the Answer Phone option in the Communications menu by clicking on that option. Closing the communications window also disables auto-answer mode, but, to be sure, you can make the choice yourself before closing the window.

Turning off the modem usually disables the feature as well. And so does quitting Works. To be safe, issue the disable command yourself anyway by removing the check mark from the communications menu.

Security Considerations

Auto-answer is a powerful and desirable feature but presents some obvious security risks. Works offers no password protection, so unauthorized computerists could obtain copies of your important files. Intentional damage, although unlikely, is possible. For obvious reasons, destructive techniques are not described here, but some security precautions are outlined.

The modem itself is your first line of defense. Get in the habit of turning off the modem when you're not using it. If you never intend to use the modem's auto-answer feature, disable it. Read the modem manual. Some manufacturers provide a DIP switch that disables answer mode. Other makers (such as Apple) disable auto-answer through software commands you can send through Works. In fact, Works does this disabling for you.

Communications Tips and Techniques

This section contains tips and techniques for less common situations. Perhaps you have the problem of call waiting on your phone, or you are using an extension phone. You also learn what happens when you try to use your modem on a phone connected to a central telephone system. Finally, you learn how to simplify and speed complicated log-on procedures.

The Case for Multiple Communications Documents

You should remember that if you store multiple computer telephone numbers in a document's phone list, a single set of settings applies to all numbers. Some computers require different settings than other computers do, so you may need to create multiple communications documents even if you regularly call fewer than eight different computers. Then, you can save the telephone numbers of computers with similar settings in files containing the appropriate settings. For example, you might create a file for 300-baud computers and another for 1200-baud numbers. Simply use the Save As choice from the File menu. Use meaningful file names like "1200BPS ECHO" or "300BPS VT100 4screens".

Call Waiting

If your phone line has a call-waiting feature that beeps when someone is trying to reach you while you're using the phone, problems will arise when you're communicating. This problem is a general one and not specific to Works.

When using a modem, you need to disable the call-waiting feature temporarily, or get a separate phone line without the call-waiting feature, or put up with the aggravation of having call waiting garble your transmissions. In severe cases call waiting can cause computers to abort communications with each other.

Ask your telephone company how you can disable call waiting temporarily by yourself. In many areas, you can accomplish this task by dialing *70 (asterisk, seven, zero) on Touch-Tone phones. You can add this string to the telephone numbers in the Works telephone list. You may need to add a comma or two to pause.

If you have a pulse-dialing (rotary-dial) line, try dialing 1170 (one, one, seven, zero) to defeat call waiting temporarily. When disabling call waiting, don't hang up after entering the disable instructions. Wait until you hear the disable confirmation tone; then dial the computer number immediately.

For instance, if you have Touch-Tone service, the number in your phone list might be

*70,,555 1212

Rotary-dial customers might use the following numbers instead:

1170,,555 1212

You may need to vary the number of commas, and therefore the length of the pause, to give your phone company's equipment enough time to disable call waiting and send the confirmation tone. Experiment, young pioneers, experiment.

When you (or your modem) finish communicating and hang up, the call-waiting feature probably will be reenabled automatically, so you'll have to disable call waiting every time you use the modem. The easy way to do this is to add the disable command to each phone number in your phone lists.

Here's a list of the steps you need to perform:

1. Dial either *70 (Touch-Tone) or 1170 (rotary).
2. Listen for the confirmation tone.
3. Without hanging up, dial the other computer.
4. Repeat the preceding steps for each new call.

Other Telephone Extensions

When you're using your modem and someone picks up an extension phone, information exchange may be garbled or aborted. If asking people to keep their hands off the telephones doesn't help, get a separate modem line or check with a phone store for devices that lock out other extensions when you're using your modem.

Multiline Installations

Most direct-connect modems require a single-line modular telephone jack, which most telephone companies call an RJ-11. If you have a two-line phone (an RJ-14) or a multiline business phone, you probably will need an adapter. Check with Radio Shack or a local telephone store for these items.

PBX Considerations

If you have an electronic or other central phone system in your office, you may want to get a separate outside line for the modem. If you can't, you may need a special adapter for your modem. Your office phone jack may not be an RJ-11, even if it looks like the one you have at home. Contact the makers or sellers of your telephone equipment for details. Your life will be much simpler if you don't run your modem through the office telephone-switching equipment.

Some PBX systems are pretty "impatient": They expect you to begin dialing promptly after getting an outside line. Certain combinations of modem types or commas in your phone list don't work well with some PBX systems. For example, a smart modem (or comma-laden phone number) that takes a long time to start dialing after requesting an outside line may find that the PBX "got bored" and took back the line for use by someone else.

If you suspect that this problem is happening, try removing unnecessary commas in phone lists. Or try having the phone repair person extend the amount of time that the PBX waits for you to start dialing. Most PBX systems can be modified this way, but you may need to persist to get someone to make the necessary changes. A better approach is to avoid the PBX altogether and get an outside line hooked directly to your modem.

Automated Log-on Procedures

Logging on to CompuServe and other services can be fairly time-consuming. You need to remember codes and passwords and account numbers. Some communications programs remember all these procedures for you; you simply replay "scripts" that perform the log-on for you. Works, however, does not offer this feature. Therefore, if you plan to use Works for fancy log-ons, consider purchasing Tempo™ or another macro product.

The Most Common Communications Problems

Thousands of things can go wrong with a data communications setup, but millions of successful data calls are made each day. Once you get the hang of it, data communications are easy. A few problems, however, seem to crop up regularly, particularly for first-time users. Those problems are outlined in the following sections, along with some suggested solutions.

Modem Won't Respond

If your modem won't respond, check to see that the modem is on and plugged into a working outlet. Also make sure that the cable connecting the modem to the computer is secure at both ends. And be certain that Works knows which Macintosh connector you're using for the modem (see the Communications Settings dialog box), as shown in figure 10.19.

Fig. 10.19

Be sure to connect the modem properly.

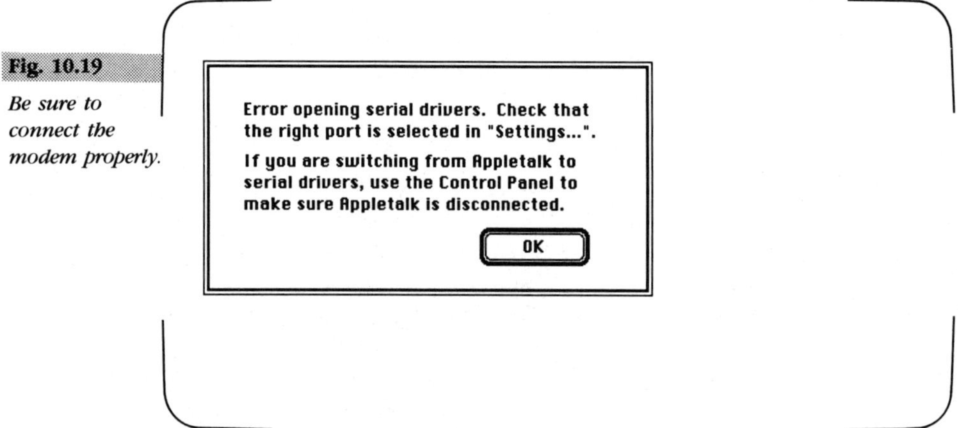

Error opening serial drivers. Check that the right port is selected in "Settings...".
If you are switching from Appletalk to serial drivers, use the Control Panel to make sure Appletalk is disconnected.
OK

Turn off the modem, wait a second, and turn the modem back on again. This sequence of steps is a necessity with smart modems when they get "confused."

If you've never used the modem with your computer before, be sure that the modem is truly Hayes-compatible. Suspect the cable. Get dealer help.

No Dial Tone

Check both ends of the phone cable running between the wall and modem. If your modem has two jacks, make sure that you've used the right jack on the back of your modem. Also be sure that someone else isn't using the line and has placed a caller on hold.

Check the wall jack (and any phone-line extension cord you're using) with a regular telephone. If you've never used the modem with this particular jack, suspect the jack. Check your modem manual. Most modems need RJ-11, single-line, modular phone jacks. If you have a multiline jack, you may need an inexpensive adapter. Many electronic business phone systems use jacks that look like RJ-11 modular jacks but aren't electrically compatible.

The Other Computer Won't Answer

If the other computer won't answer, double-check the telephone list. You may have made a typo.

If a typo is not the problem, call a human who knows the other computer's status. That computer may be down for service. Some services have restricted operating hours as well. Moreover, telephone numbers are sometimes changed for security or technical reasons.

Privately owned BBS systems disappear frequently. Operators lose interest, their equipment breaks, they move away to college—you name it. Ask around at users' meetings and on other bulletin boards.

Screen Contents Garbled or Computers Disconnect

For computers to be able to communicate, they both must have compatible settings (communications parameters). If the computers disconnect, try talking to a human at the other end. Match baud rates, type of parity checking, data length (that is, word length), and so on. Write down the settings or create a separate communications document for later use.

Expect minor compatibility problems when exchanging text with dissimilar computers, particularly if your text or the other person's contains foreign characters, accent marks, and so on. So-called standards aren't.

If text transmissions appear fine for a while and then start to look garbled or if the computers hang up for no apparent reason, suspect the telephone connection. This problem is a big one in rural areas—and during electrical storms.

Try redialing or waiting for a while. If people in your building pick up extension telephones on the same line as your modem, text will be scrambled.

Can't Log On

If the telephone rings and a computer answers but won't let you log on, check the following.

Have you entered your name and password properly? Some systems are case-sensitive. That is, they may require passwords in all uppercase or all lowercase letters.

Sometimes the log-on process requires communication through a money-saving "front end" computer service such as Telenet. The front-end computer (for example, Telenet) may be working, but the second computer, which you really want to use (CompuServe, for instance), may be down for service. Sometimes the important computer is available, but the front-end computer can't reach the other computer because of problems at the front-end. Try a different front-end (for example, Tymnet®), dial the important computer directly, or call back later.

Xmodem File Transfers Won't Work

Not all Xmodem protocols are compatible. This lack is the "standards" problem again. Try different Xmodem combinations on both ends. Your best bet is to communicate from Works to Works using MacBinary when possible.

Works Won't Auto-Answer When Telephone Rings

If Works won't auto-answer when the telephone rings, check whether the modem is connected to the line that's ringing. Some modems have switches and software commands that disable the auto-answer feature. Check your modem manual. Bad cables may make the modem "think" your Macintosh isn't ready to take calls. See your dealer. The modem may be set to answer after a number of rings rather than on the first ring. Have callers let the phone ring longer, or read the modem manual and set the modem to answer sooner.

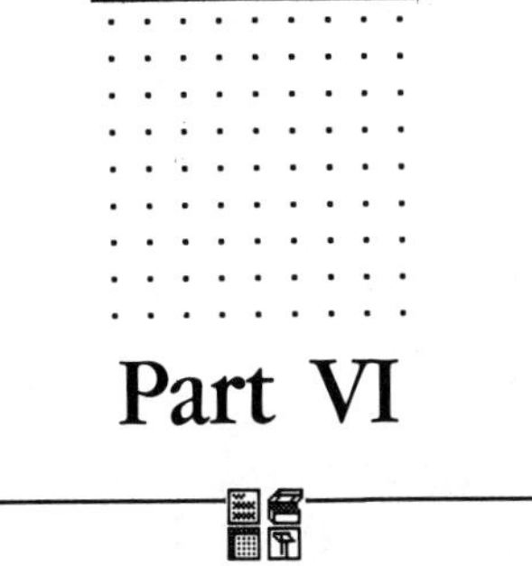

Part VI

INTEGRATING APPLICATIONS

11

Tying It All Together

Now that you know how to create spreadsheets, graphs, word-processing documents, databases, and communication documents, you are ready to learn how to use the different capabilities together. The process is sometimes referred to as *integration* or *information sharing*.

Works offers two ways to share information between windows. For most people, the simplest method to understand is copying, which is done with the help of the Clipboard and, possibly, the Scrapbook. If you've done any of the Quick Starts in this book, you've probably already used the Clipboard. You can use the copying techniques with word-processing documents, spreadsheets, and databases. Merging, the second method, is used to combine information from databases with a word-processing document.

In this chapter, you add to your understanding of the use of the Clipboard, Scrapbook, and other information-sharing tools. You also see how to use Works to merge database and word-processing documents.

If you've been creating the Quick Start examples, you can use them as you read this chapter. Get the Quick Start Simple memo, Quick Database, and Quarterly spreadsheet out on your desktop (see fig. 11.1). You simply start Works and use the Open command three times, selecting a different file each time. If you prefer to use your own spreadsheet, word-processing, and database files, load them instead and experiment as you read along. To confirm that you have the three documents available, use the Window menu; it should show all three file names at the bottom of the menu (see fig. 11.2).

Copying

Works was designed so that you can pass information easily from one window to another through the Clipboard. The windows can be of the same type (say, two word-processing windows) or different. For example, you can create a spreadsheet and then include the results in a

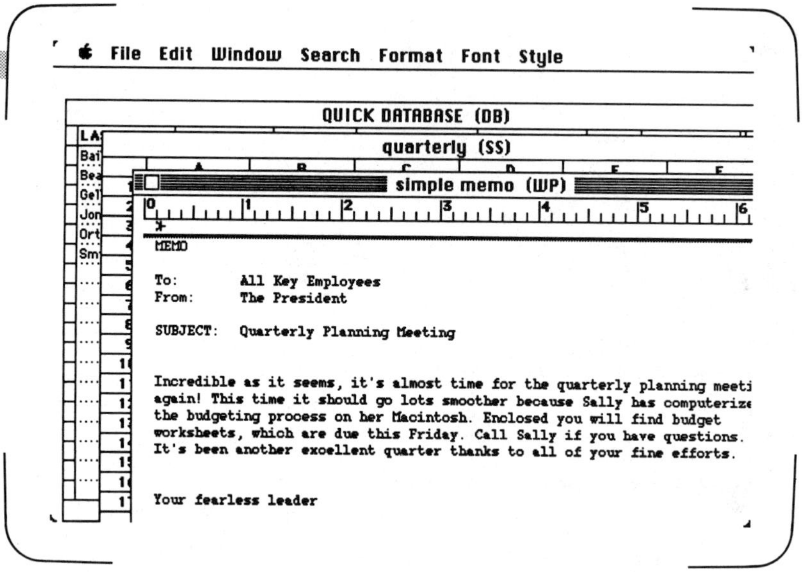

Fig. 11.1

A spreadsheet, database, and word-processing document opened on the desktop.

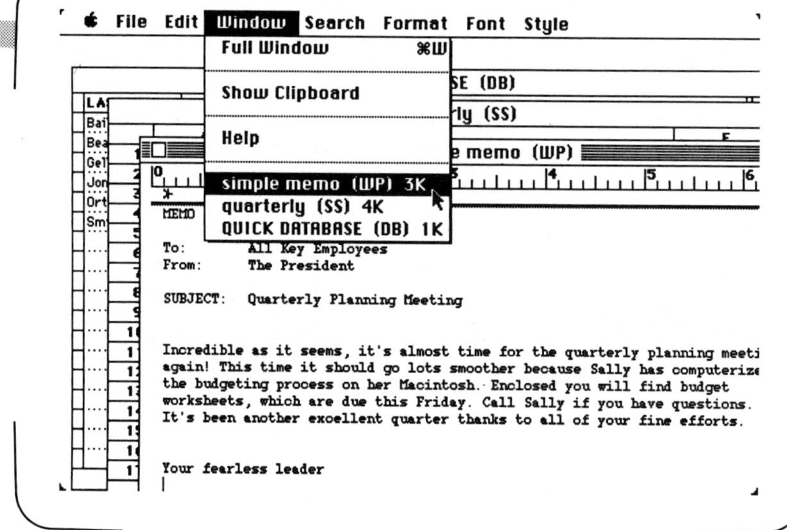
File Edit Window Search Format Font Style
Full Window ⌘W
Show Clipboard
Help
simple memo (WP) 3K
quarterly (SS) 4K
QUICK DATABASE (DB) 1K
MEMO
To: All Key Employees
From: The President
SUBJECT: Quarterly Planning Meeting
Incredible as it seems, it's almost time for the quarterly planning meeti
again! This time it should go lots smoother because Sally has computerize
the budgeting process on her Macintosh. Enclosed you will find budget
worksheets, which are due this Friday. Call Sally if you have questions.
It's been another excellent quarter thanks to all of your fine efforts.
Your fearless leader

Fig. 11.2

The Window menu showing three open documents.

report you've written in a word-processing window. And with a few more keystrokes, you can add a graph to the report. Items from your database can be copied into a spreadsheet, and vice versa.

The main thing to remember about this type of copying is that both documents must be on your desktop. You should also remember that when you use the Clipboard to move or copy information from one window to another, you lose the Clipboard's previous contents. During copying, the amount of available memory also can be a consideration.

Copying Capabilities and Limitations

You can copy or move most of your creations from one Works window to another. Table 11.1 lists the types of moves you can accomplish.

Table 11.1
Types of Moves Available in Works

From	*To*	*Notes*
Spreadsheet	Word processing	Answers only, not equations
Spreadsheet	Database	Converts rows to records
Spreadsheet	Spreadsheet	Converts cell references
Word processing	Spreadsheet	
Word processing	Database	
Word processing	Word processing	
Database	Spreadsheet	Copies records to rows
Database	Word processing	
Database	Database	
Report	Word processing	Totals and subtotals only

Some types of transfers you can't do directly through Works. Most notably, you can't copy entire database reports to word-processing windows. You can paste database report totals and subtotals to the Clipboard, but you can't paste complete reports without using special utilities from other vendors or the public domain (for example, Image Saver, which is described in Chapter 12).

When you copy a spreadsheet to a word-processing window, the equations stay behind. Database and spreadsheet windows have limited font choices, so information from word-processing documents destined for databases or spreadsheets automatically conforms to its new environment. When database and spreadsheet information is pasted to a word-processing document, the information arrives in its original font, size, and style. You can change these elements in the word-processing document. Works databases and spreadsheets can't handle pictures, so they are left behind when you copy from a word-processing window to a spreadsheet or database.

Works accomplishes most data exchanges by making copies of information in your computer's RAM, or random-access memory. Suppose, for example, that you copy the entire contents of a big database into a spreadsheet. After the copying takes place, three copies of the data are in memory: the database itself, the Clipboard copy of the data, and the spreadsheet copy of the data. Other information Works needs also is stored in RAM.

Sometimes your computer won't have enough memory for Works to accomplish the desired task. For instance, if you had a database that contained more than 1,100 records, like the Chamber of Commerce example in Chapter 9, you might have trouble copying the entire database to a spreadsheet, even with a Macintosh Plus containing a million bytes of RAM. When you have this problem, Works displays a warning so that you can cancel the move (see fig. 11.3).

Fig. 11.3

Warning about lack of memory.

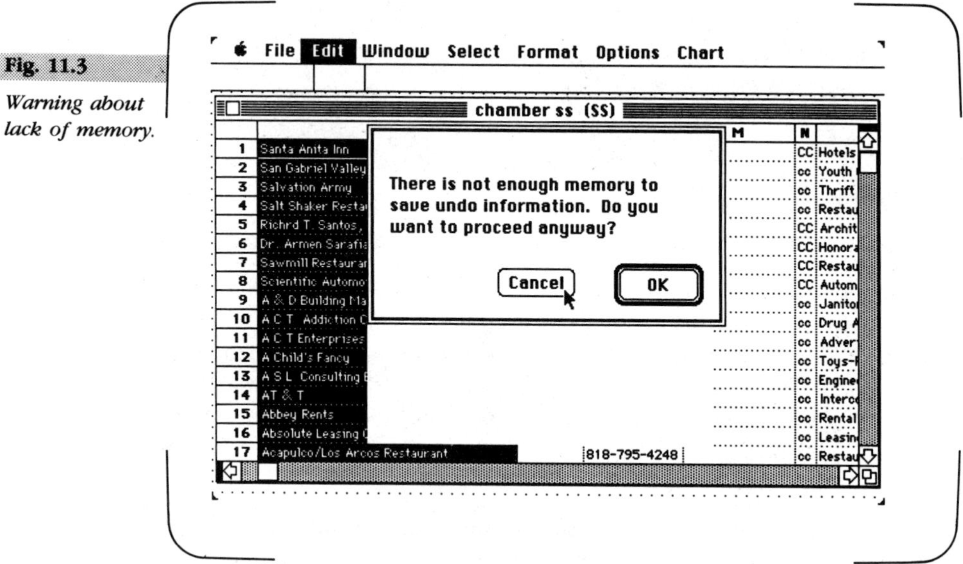

Frequently (but not always), you can avoid this problem by copying small sections of data and repeating the process until you're done. At other times, you will have to break up your database, spreadsheet, or word-processing document into smaller pieces. Another strategy is to copy only what you need—no unnecessary fields, columns, and so on.

Copying from Spreadsheets to Word-Processing Windows

Let's try some integration. How often have you wished that you could include the results of a complex spreadsheet computation in a report or memo, without having to retype hundreds of numbers and proofread the typing job? With Works, you easily copy spreadsheet answers from a spreadsheet window to a word-processing window. Not surprisingly, this method of moving information is one of the most popular.

Although Works moves the spreadsheet answers to a word-processing window, you can't have Works recalculate anything in the word-processing window. All the calculations must take place in the spreadsheet window before you move the answers to the word-processing window. If you want to make spreadsheet changes and have Works recompute them for you after you paste the results into a word-processing window, you must make those changes in the spreadsheet window and repeat the moving process.

Here's what you do to move finished spreadsheet answers to a word-processing window:

1. Open the word-processing document and make it active either by choosing it from the window menu or by "rotating" through the three documents by using the **command-,** shortcut.
2. Point to the insertion point (where you'll put the spreadsheet results). Click once. For this example, click after the end of the paragraph and before "Your fearless leader."
3. Activate the spreadsheet (create or alter it if necessary).
4. Select the spreadsheet cells you want to copy (highlight them). In this example, highlight cells A2 through F8.
5. Copy the spreadsheet cells to the Clipboard (press **command-C**).
6. Switch to the word-processing window (press **command-,** once or twice, as needed).
7. Paste the Clipboard contents (press **command-V**).
8. Reformat the word-processing document (adjust margins, change fonts, and so on), if needed.

Figure 11.4 shows the results of the preceding steps. Notice that Works repaged automatically. The program pushed "Your fearless leader" down to make room for the spreadsheet information. Works even set custom tabs for the spreadsheet. (To confirm this fact, click anywhere on the spreadsheet information in the word-processing window and look at the tab indicators.) Boldface spreadsheet characters are still boldface after pasting. The font used in the spreadsheet also is the same after pasting.

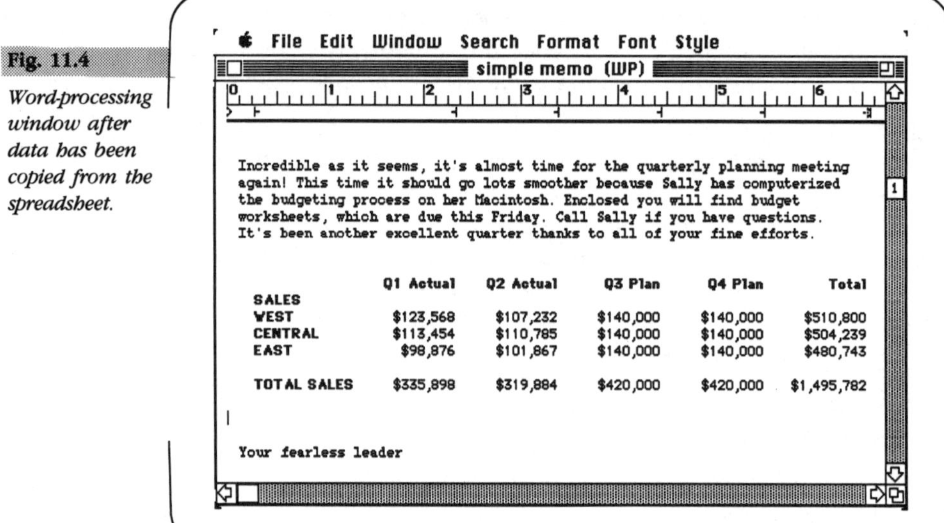
File Edit Window Search Format Font Style
simple memo (WP)
Incredible as it seems, it's almost time for the quarterly planning meeting again! This time it should go lots smoother because Sally has computerized the budgeting process on her Macintosh. Enclosed you will find budget worksheets, which are due this Friday. Call Sally if you have questions. It's been another excellent quarter thanks to all of your fine efforts.
Q1 Actual Q2 Actual Q3 Plan Q4 Plan Total
SALES
WEST $123,568 $107,232 $140,000 $140,000 $510,800
CENTRAL $113,454 $110,785 $140,000 $140,000 $504,239
EAST $98,876 $101,867 $140,000 $140,000 $480,743
TOTAL SALES $335,898 $319,884 $420,000 $420,000 $1,495,782
Your fearless leader

Fig. 11.4

Word-processing window after data has been copied from the spreadsheet.

NOTE: You can open a spreadsheet window first and then a word-processing window, rather than following the order outlined in this example. The order doesn't matter.

Once pasted into a word-processing document, all the columns in a spreadsheet are separated automatically by tabs. Rows are separated by Return characters. To make room for large spreadsheets, you may need to modify the word-processing document's format (page setup, tab locations, and so on); you can make the changes after pasting.

Usually, spreadsheet contents arrive in the word-processing window in the Geneva 9 font. After the contents have been moved, you can change the font and size. Grids aren't pasted even if they're shown in the spreadsheet window.

Copying Graphs to Word-Processing Windows

Copying graphs to word-processing windows is another popular use of Works' integration capabilities. Graphs are attractive, show concepts quickly, and make good use of the Mac's graphics powers. Once you've perfected a graph, you can copy it to a word-processing window and then resize and position the graph as desired. Works treats the graph like a picture. You also can overlay additional text on a graph after it's pasted, but you can't edit words that were created by the charting function itself.

Here are the steps you follow:

1. Activate the word-processing document.
2. Point to the insertion point (where you want to put the graph—just below the spreadsheet insertion, if you are using the Quick Start files). Make room for the graph by pressing **return** as many times as necessary.
3. Activate the spreadsheet.
4. Display the appropriate graph (see fig. 11.5). You may want to use the size box to make the graph smaller.

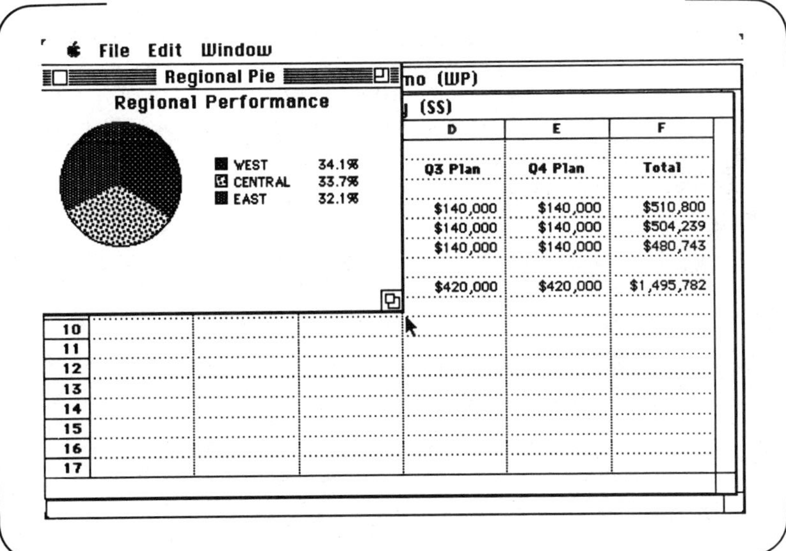

Fig. 11.5

A graph to be inserted into a word-processing document.

5. Copy the graph to the Clipboard (use **command-C** or the Copy command on the Edit menu).

6. Switch to the word-processing window (use **command-,** or the Window menu).

7. Paste the Clipboard contents (use **command-V** or the Edit menu).

8. Move and resize the graph as required.

You can paste series graphs with or without grids and labels. You make this choice in the chart definition dialog box. To label graphs, you can use the word-processing feature.

Notice that when you pasted your graph, Works did not repage the text. The graph could have covered "Your fearless leader" because text can be "covered" by pictures. Move the graph and then make room for "Your fearless leader" again by adding carriage returns. Experiment with the graph. Practice selecting it (press **command-A**), moving it (drag when the pointer is a hand), and resizing it (drag the lower right corner). Finally, use the Draw feature to draw a rectangle around the graph and add lines for a shadow effect. When you are done, your screen will look something like figure 11.6.

Copying from One Word-Processing Window to Another

Sometimes you may want to combine parts of two or more word-processing documents. Because you can store text on disk, you no longer need to retype paragraphs or pages in order to use them in different documents. Copying items from one word-processing document to another is easy. Here's what you do:

1. Place both documents (source and destination) on the desktop.

2. Activate to the destination document (use the Window menu).

3. Point to the location in the destination document where you want the copied information.

4. Switch to the source document (use **command-,** or the Window menu).

5. Highlight the source item(s) you want to copy.

MEMO

Fig. 11.6

A printed memo using data from a spreadsheet and a graph.

To: All Key Employees
From: The President

SUBJECT: Quarterly Planning Meeting

Incredible as it seems, it's almost time for the quarterly planning meeting again! This time it should go lots smoother because Sally has computerized the budgeting process on her Macintosh. Enclosed you will find budget worksheets, which are due this Friday. Call Sally if you have questions. It's been another excellent quarter thanks to all of your fine efforts.

	Q1 Actual	Q2 Actual	Q3 Plan	Q4 Plan	Total
SALES					
WEST	$123,568	$107,232	$140,000	$140,000	$510,800
CENTRAL	$113,454	$110,785	$140,000	$140,000	$504,239
EAST	$98,876	$101,867	$140,000	$140,000	$480,743
TOTAL SALES	$335,898	$319,884	$420,000	$420,000	$1,495,782

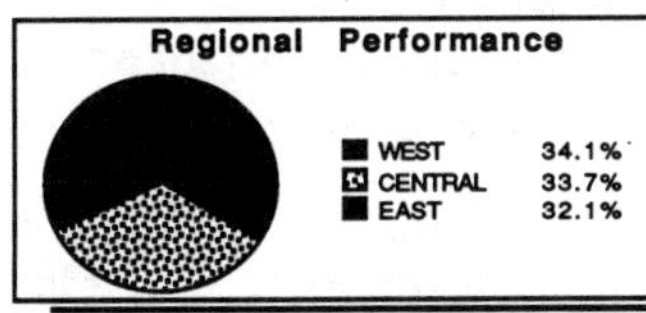

Your fearless leader

-CONFIDENTIAL-

6. Copy the source items to the Clipboard (use **command-C** or the Edit menu).
7. Switch to the destination document (use **command-,** or the Window menu).
8. Paste at the appropriate spot (use **command-V** or the Edit menu).

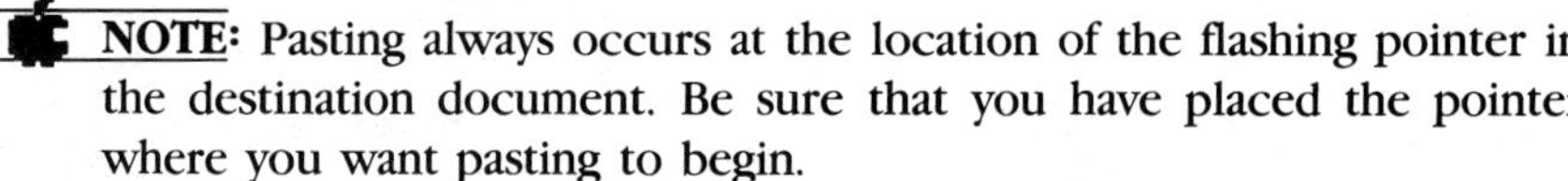

NOTE: Pasting always occurs at the location of the flashing pointer in the destination document. Be sure that you have placed the pointer where you want pasting to begin.

Works copies and pastes attributes, such as size and style of type, from the source document to the destination document. Paragraph-formatting information (tabs, temporary margins, line spacing, and so on) also is copied from the source document to the destination, thereby retaining the style of the text. Remember that this type of moving uses the Clipboard, so its prior contents are replaced. You can use Cut instead of Copy if you want to remove the items from the source document.

Copying from Spreadsheet to Spreadsheet

Copying items from one spreadsheet window to another is easy, but one important warning is in order: Because you can copy equations and other cell references to any location in a destination spreadsheet, Works tries to take care of any necessary cell reference changes. This feature usually works properly, but you may inadvertently create situations that Works can't handle. Therefore, you need to examine and test the destination spreadsheet carefully after any copying.

Suppose, for example, that you want to combine mileage information from two spreadsheets (Truck 1 and Truck 2) into the Truck 1 spreadsheet. Following are the steps involved in copying from one spreadsheet to another:

1. Place both spreadsheets (source [Truck 2] and destination [Truck 1]) on the desktop (see fig. 11.7).
2. Switch to the source spreadsheet (use **command-,** or the Window menu).
3. Highlight the source cells to be copied (column B of the Truck 2 spreadsheet).
4. Copy them to the Clipboard (use **command-C** or the Edit menu).
5. Switch to the destination spreadsheet (Truck 1) by using the Window menu, and use the zoom box to make the Truck 1 window full size.
6. In the destination spreadsheet (Truck 1), point to the upper left cell of the area to receive the information—column C (see fig. 11.8).

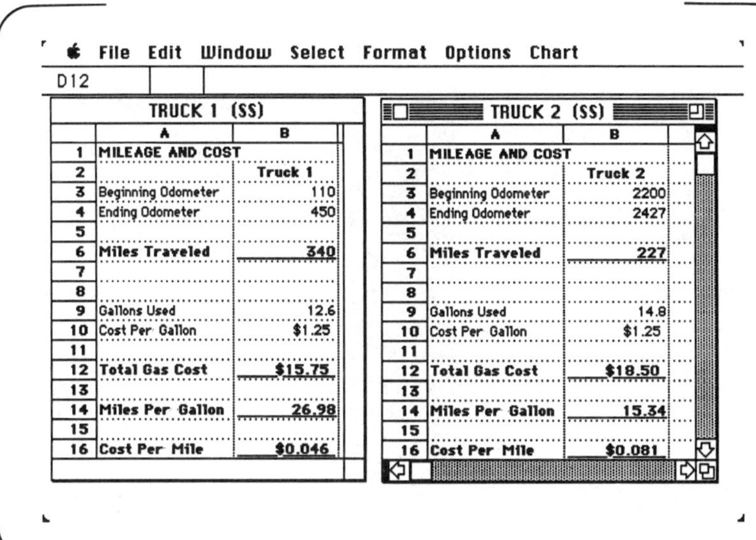

File Edit Window Select Format Options Chart

D12

TRUCK 1 (SS)

	A	B
1	MILEAGE AND COST	
2		Truck 1
3	Beginning Odometer	110
4	Ending Odometer	450
5		
6	Miles Traveled	340
7		
8		
9	Gallons Used	12.6
10	Cost Per Gallon	$1.25
11		
12	Total Gas Cost	$15.75
13		
14	Miles Per Gallon	26.98
15		
16	Cost Per Mile	$0.046

TRUCK 2 (SS)

	A	B
1	MILEAGE AND COST	
2		Truck 2
3	Beginning Odometer	2200
4	Ending Odometer	2427
5		
6	Miles Traveled	227
7		
8		
9	Gallons Used	14.8
10	Cost Per Gallon	$1.25
11		
12	Total Gas Cost	$18.50
13		
14	Miles Per Gallon	15.34
15		
16	Cost Per Mile	$0.081

Fig. 11.7

Preparing to copy from one spreadsheet to another.

File Edit Window Select Format Options Chart

TRUCK 1 (SS)

	A	B	C	D	E	F
1	MILEAGE AND COST					
2		Truck 1				
3	Beginning Odometer	110				
4	Ending Odometer	450				
5						
6	Miles Traveled	340				
7						
8						
9	Gallons Used	12.6				
10	Cost Per Gallon	$1.25				
11						
12	Total Gas Cost	$15.75				
13						
14	Miles Per Gallon	26.98				
15						
16	Cost Per Mile	$0.046				
17						
18						

Fig. 11.8

Selecting the column to receive the information.

7. Paste at the appropriate spot (use **command-V** or the Edit menu). Figure 11.9 shows the spreadsheet just after this step.

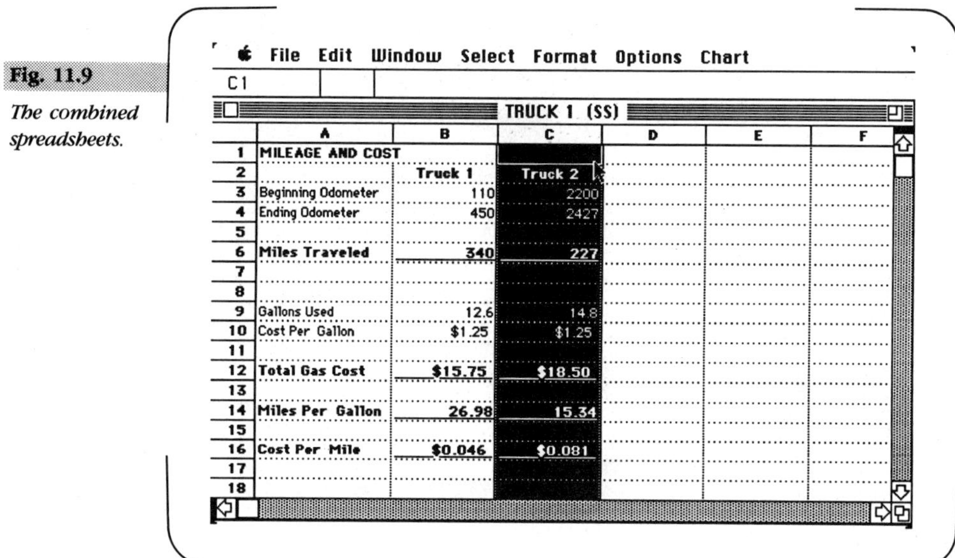

	A	B	C	D	E	F
1	MILEAGE AND COST					
2		Truck 1	Truck 2			
3	Beginning Odometer	110	2200			
4	Ending Odometer	450	2427			
5						
6	Miles Traveled	340	227			
7						
8						
9	Gallons Used	12.6	14.8			
10	Cost Per Gallon	$1.25	$1.25			
11						
12	Total Gas Cost	$15.75	$18.50			
13						
14	Miles Per Gallon	26.98	15.34			
15						
16	Cost Per Mile	$0.046	$0.081			
17						
18						

Fig. 11.9

The combined spreadsheets.

8. Examine and test the destination spreadsheet carefully.

Obviously, this procedure can be repeated for other spreadsheets.

NOTE: Remember that the Clipboard is used for this type of move, so the Clipboard's prior contents are replaced. If you want to remove the items from the source spreadsheet, you can use Cut instead of Copy.

When pasting between spreadsheets, Works copies formulas, values, and attributes (boldface, underscore, commas, dollar signs, and so forth). Because Works automatically modifies copied formulas containing cell references, the formulas usually work in their new (destination) environment.

CAUTION: You must be certain that you "take with you" everything copied cell references need to use in their new "home." For example, if a formula in the source spreadsheet references a value in cell F8, you probably need either to take the data to the new spreadsheet from F8 in the source file or have data in the right place in the destination spreadsheet. In figure 11.10, the percentage calculations need the Total Sales cell, which the program expects to find in cell F8, but that cell was not copied and pasted. (Notice the absolute address $F$8 in the equation, which is visible in the edit bar.) Usually, but not always, Works warns you about such situations. Here, error messages are placed in affected cells.

File Edit Window Select Format Options Chart

G6 =F6/$F$8

Untitled (SS)

	B	C	D	E	F	G
1						
2	Q1 Actual	Q2 Actual	Q3 Plan	Q4 Plan	Total	%
3						
4	$123,568	$107,232	$140,000	$140,000	$510,800	*Error*
5	$113,454	$110,785	$140,000	$140,000	$504,239	*Error*
6	$98,876	$101,867	$140,000	$140,000	$480,743	*Error*
7						
8						
9						
10						
11						
12						
13						
14						
15						
16						
17						

Fig. 11.10

Error messages in cells after pasting equations that expect data in cell F8 (see edit bar).

You also must be certain that you don't accidentally take along from the source spreadsheet cells that reference or replace inappropriate cell locations on the destination spreadsheet. This warning is particularly important if the destination spreadsheet already contains information of any kind.

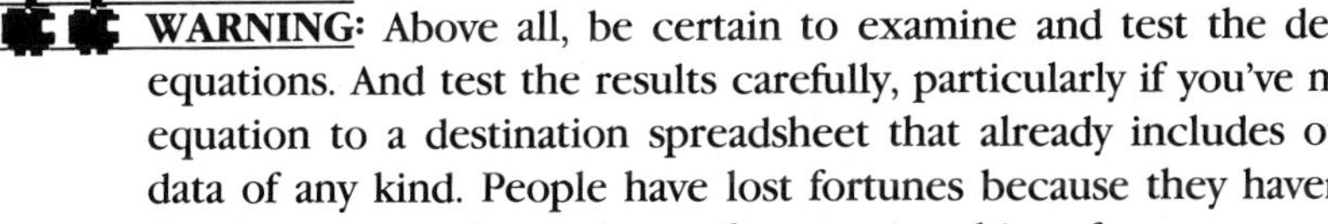

WARNING: Above all, be certain to examine and test the destination equations. And test the results carefully, particularly if you've moved an equation to a destination spreadsheet that already includes other cell data of any kind. People have lost fortunes because they haven't taken the time to examine and test after copying things from one spreadsheet to another.

Copying from Spreadsheets to Databases

Suppose that you've created a spreadsheet containing details of your expenses and want to convert it to an expense database. With Works, you can convert spreadsheet rows into database records. The cells in a row become fields in a record, as shown in figure 11.11. Note that row 12 in the spreadsheet has become the first displayed record in the database. You can move spreadsheet data to a new database or into an existing database.

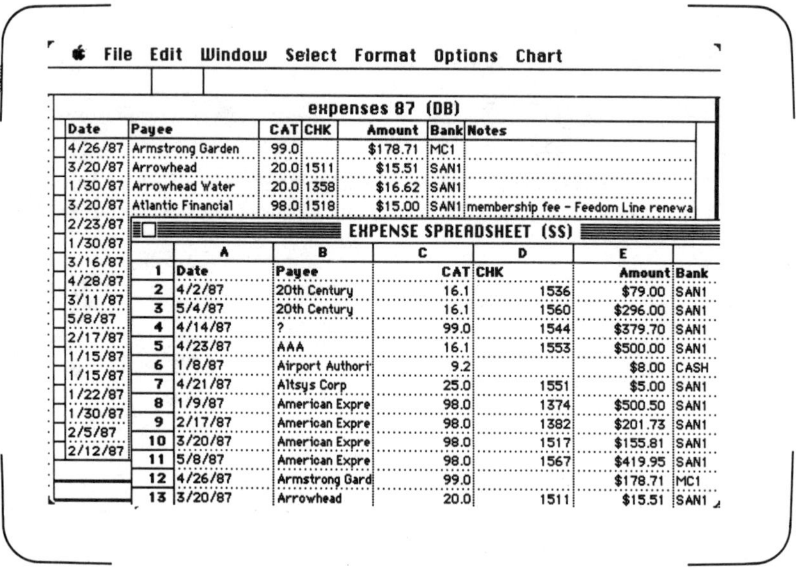

Fig. 11.11

Items moved from a spreadsheet to a database (rows become records).

File Edit Window Select Format Options Chart

expenses 87 (DB)

Date	Payee	CAT	CHK	Amount	Bank	Notes
4/26/87	Armstrong Garden	99.0		$178.71	MC1	
3/20/87	Arrowhead	20.0	1511	$15.51	SAN1	
1/30/87	Arrowhead Water	20.0	1358	$16.62	SAN1	
3/20/87	Atlantic Financial	98.0	1518	$15.00	SAN1	membership fee - Feedom Line renewa
2/23/87						
1/30/87						
3/16/87						
4/28/87						
3/11/87						
5/8/87						
2/17/87						
1/15/87						
1/15/87						
1/22/87						
1/30/87						
2/5/87						
2/12/87						

EXPENSE SPREADSHEET (SS)

	A	B	C	D	E	
1	Date	Payee	CAT	CHK	Amount	Bank
2	4/2/87	20th Century	16.1	1536	$79.00	SAN1
3	5/4/87	20th Century	16.1	1560	$296.00	SAN1
4	4/14/87	?	99.0	1544	$379.70	SAN1
5	4/23/87	AAA	16.1	1553	$500.00	SAN1
6	1/8/87	Airport Authori	9.2		$8.00	CASH
7	4/21/87	Altsys Corp	25.0	1551	$5.00	SAN1
8	1/9/87	American Expre	98.0	1374	$500.50	SAN1
9	2/17/87	American Expre	98.0	1382	$201.73	SAN1
10	3/20/87	American Expre	98.0	1517	$155.81	SAN1
11	5/8/87	American Expre	98.0	1567	$419.95	SAN1
12	4/26/87	Armstrong Gard	99.0		$178.71	MC1
13	3/20/87	Arrowhead	20.0	1511	$15.51	SAN1

Here are the steps you follow to copy from a spreadsheet to a database:

1. Open or create the database in the list window.
2. Be sure that the database contains enough fields to receive the spreadsheet rows.
3. Choose the database location in which you want to paste the first record.
4. Open the spreadsheet.
5. Highlight the cells you want to copy.
6. Copy spreadsheet cells to the Clipboard (press **command-C**).
7. Switch to the database window (press **command-,**).
8. Point to the upper left destination cell.
9. Paste the cells into the database (press **command-V**).
10. Modify database field sizes, names, and so on, if necessary.

NOTE: If you're moving spreadsheet contents into an existing database, be certain that the order of the database fields matches that of the spreadsheet rows. Otherwise, Works may paste dates from the spreadsheet into fields meant for names in the database, and so on.

When pasting to a database that already contains records, you must take care to avoid overwriting good records in the receiving database. Be sure to put the database pointer on the last (the empty) record, unless you want to overwrite existing records. The easiest way to see where the data will be pasted is to place the database window in the list window and select the upper left corner where you want pasting to begin. If the location you choose will cause existing data to be overwritten, Works warns you.

Remember that when you transfer spreadsheet information to databases, Works moves the answers, not the equations or functions. Moreover, numbers, dollar signs, commas, and decimal points all become text. The best way to transfer numbers is to convert them to Standard format in the spreadsheet before copying and pasting. After pasting the numbers into the database, redefine them as numbers and then add other desired attributes (dollar signs, commas, and so forth).

Copying from Word-Processing Windows to Spreadsheets

Sometimes a document that starts out as a memo ends up as a spreadsheet. Suppose that you've started a new real estate sales department. After writing a memo about the first month's sales, you decide to track monthly sales in a spreadsheet. Figure 11.12 shows how you copy tabular typed material into a spreadsheet. Notice that the typed numbers have dollar signs and commas, which Works strips away when pasting from the Clipboard to the spreadsheet. You can use the spreadsheet's formatting options to get back the dollar signs and commas. Numbers that are separated by tabs become separate cells in a row. Return characters (forced line endings) in word-processing documents are interpreted by Works' spreadsheet feature as row endings.

Pasting columns of numbers from a word-processing window to a spreadsheet window is easy, as the following steps demonstrate.

1. Open or create a new spreadsheet.
2. Open (or type) the word-processing document containing the tabular material.
3. Highlight the cells you want to copy.
4. Copy the word-processing data to the Clipboard (press **command-C**).

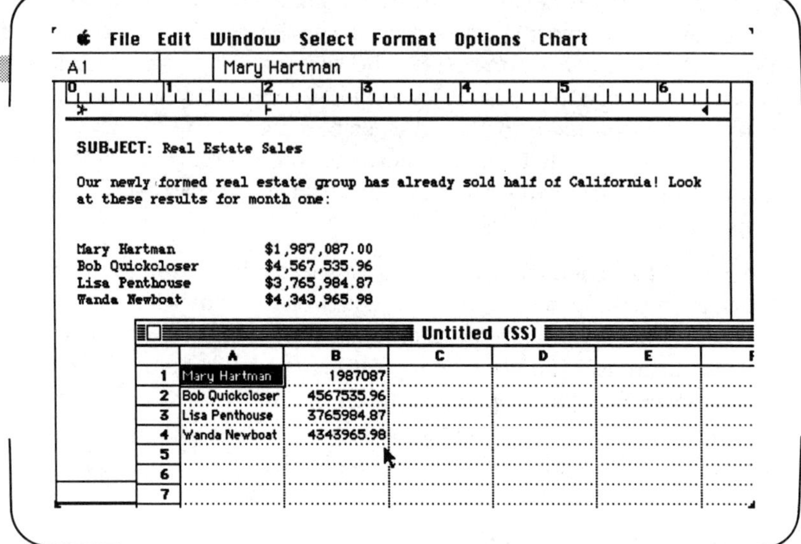

Fig. 11.12

Copying tabular text to a spreadsheet to eliminate retyping.

5. Switch to the spreadsheet window (press **command-,**).
6. Point to the upper left destination cell (A1 in the example).
7. Paste the cells to the spreadsheet (press **command-V**).
8. Modify the spreadsheet column sizes and add headings, equations, and so forth.

NOTE: If you're moving word-processing contents into an existing spreadsheet, be sure that the order of the word-processing items matches that of the spreadsheet rows. Otherwise, dates from the document may be pasted into fields meant for names in the spreadsheet, and so forth.

When you are pasting to a spreadsheet that already contains cell data, be careful not to overwrite good cells in the receiving spreadsheet. Place the spreadsheet pointer in the upper left cell to receive information. If the cell location you choose will cause data to be overwritten, Works warns you.

Word-processing fonts and type of all sizes are converted to Geneva 9 when pasted to the spreadsheet.

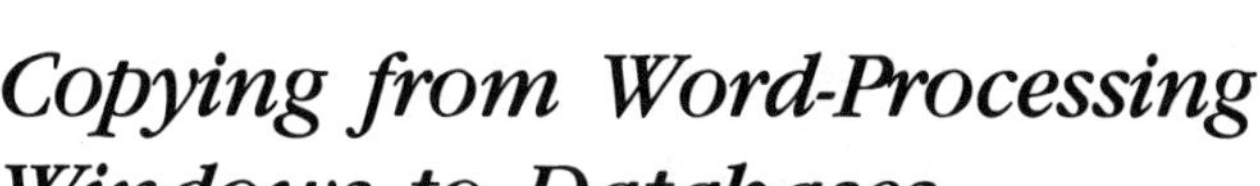

Copying from Word-Processing Windows to Databases

Suppose that you have created the slightly more formal version of the real estate sales memo shown in figure 11.13. You've decided to set up a Works database to track monthly sales by employee. You will have one record for each employee each month.

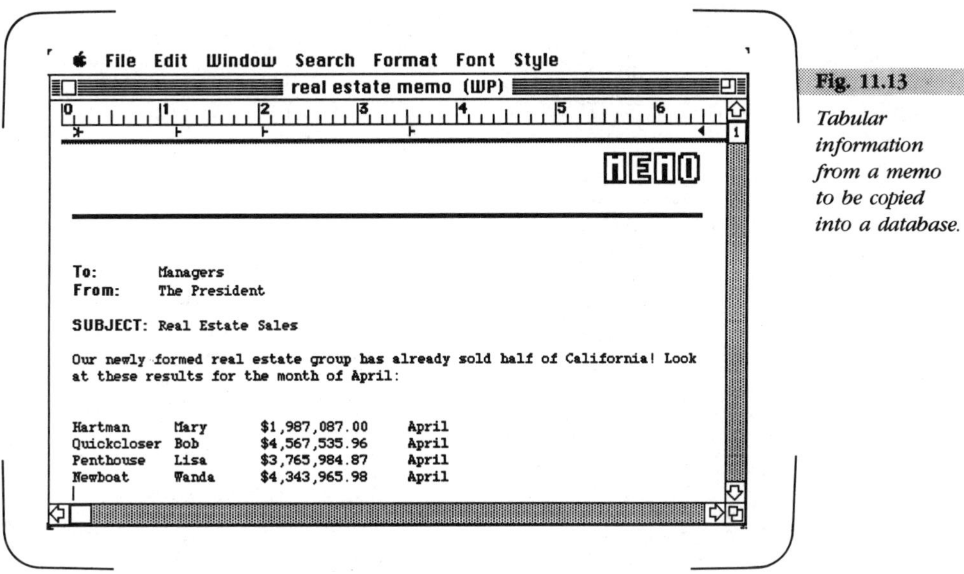

Fig. 11.13

Tabular information from a memo to be copied into a database.

Copying from a word-processing document to a database is similar to copying from a word-processing window to a spreadsheet. Items that are separated by tabs become separate fields in a record. Return characters (forced line endings) in word-processing documents are interpreted by Works' spreadsheet feature as record endings. To see what's happening, place the receiving database in the list window. Here's what you do:

1. Open or create a database.
2. Open (or type) the word-processing document containing tabular information to be transferred.
3. Highlight the word-processing items you want to copy.
4. Copy the word-processing data to the Clipboard (press **command-C**).

5. Switch to the database window (press **command-,**).
6. Point to the upper left destination field.
7. Paste the cells into the database by pressing **command-V** (see fig. 11.14).
8. Modify database field sizes, field types, and so on.

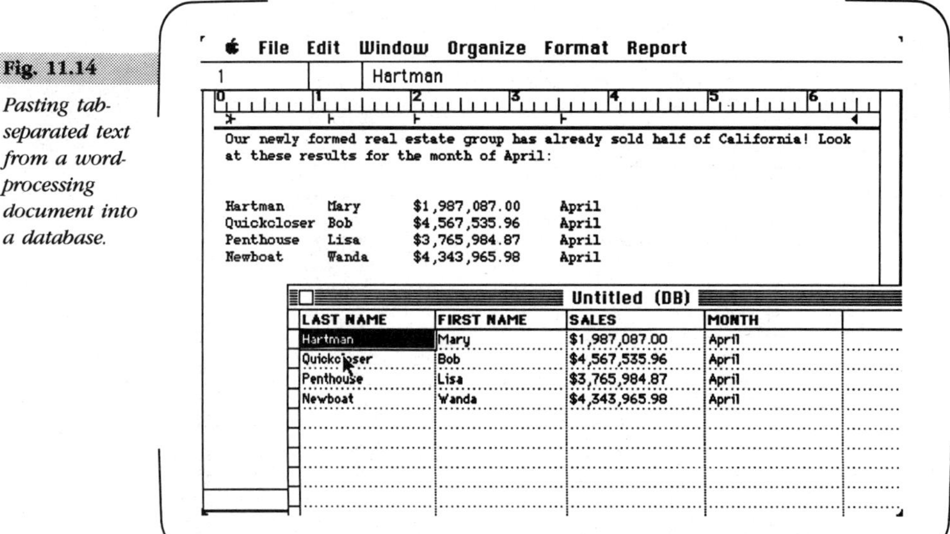

Fig. 11.14

Pasting tab-separated text from a word-processing document into a database.

NOTE: If you're moving word-processing contents into an existing database, be certain that the order of the word-processing items matches that of the database fields. Otherwise, Works may paste dates from the word-processing document into fields meant for names in the database, and so on. If you match field attributes in the database (Date or Numeric format, for instance), Works treats the data properly. Otherwise, everything is imported as text.

When pasting to a database that already contains records, take care to avoid overwriting good records in the receiving database. Be sure to place the database pointer on the last (the empty) record unless you want to overwrite existing records. The easiest way to see where the data will be pasted is to put the database window in list view and select the upper left corner where you want pasting to begin. If the chosen location will cause existing data to be overwritten, Works warns you.

IMPORTANT: Unless you set up the database field attributes otherwise, Works transfers numbers as text. Therefore, you should paste numbers from the word processor without commas, dollar signs, parentheses, and so forth. After pasting the numbers into the database, you can define fields as numeric and choose appropriate attributes. You also can define database fields properly before pasting. In the example the SALES field attributes match the style of the numbers in the memo (see fig. 11.15).

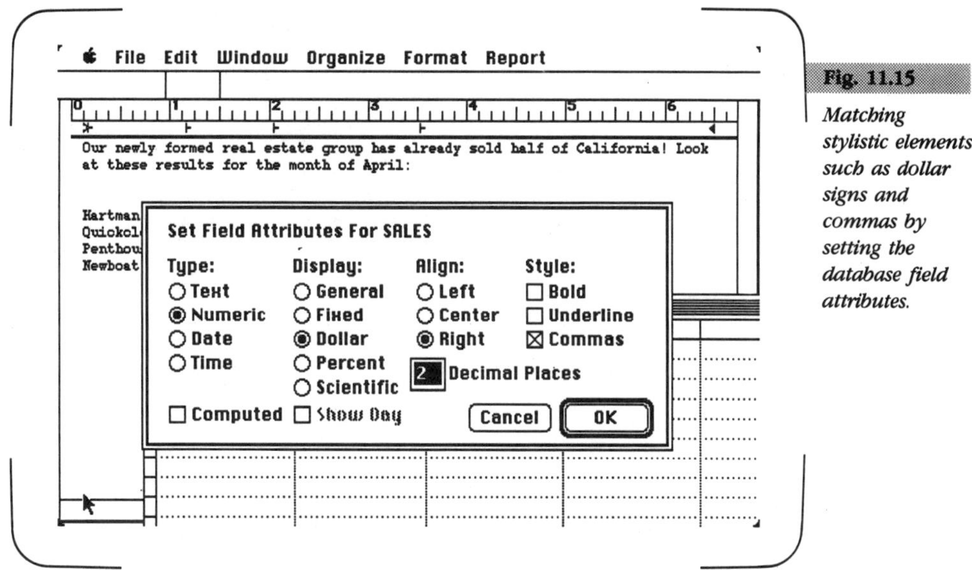

Fig. 11.15
Matching stylistic elements such as dollar signs and commas by setting the database field attributes.

Copying from Databases to Spreadsheets

Remember the Quick Database containing the names and salaries of employees? Assume that you want to convert that database into a spreadsheet so that you can make a graph. Works helps you convert database records into spreadsheet rows. Fields in database list rows become rows in a spreadsheet. You can move database data to a new spreadsheet or into an existing spreadsheet (see fig. 11.16).

Here are the general steps:

1. Open or create a spreadsheet.
2. Click to specify the location in the spreadsheet where you want Works to paste the first record. Usually, this location is the first empty cell in a row.

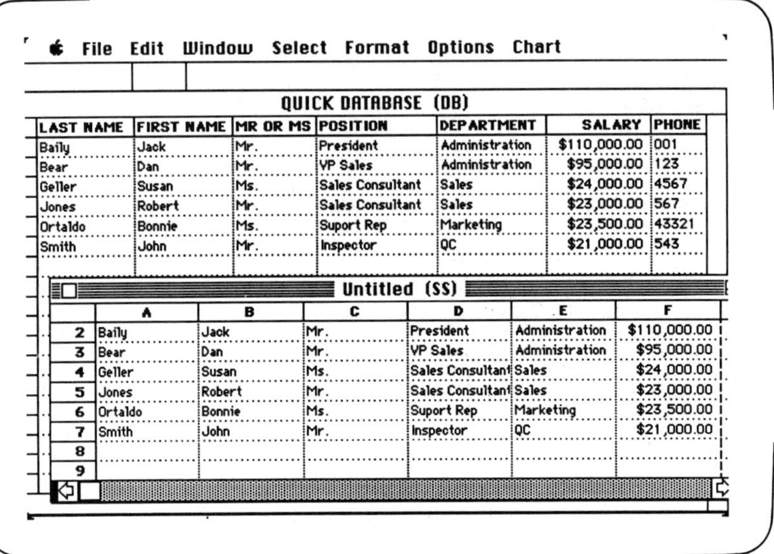

Fig. 11.16

Records copied from a database to rows in a spreadsheet.

3. Open the database (which probably is in list view).
4. Highlight the fields to be copied.
5. Copy fields to the Clipboard (press **command-C**).
6. Switch to the spreadsheet window (press **command-,**).
7. Point to the upper left destination cell.
8. Paste the fields into the spreadsheet (press **command-V**).
9. Modify spreadsheet column sizes and so on.
10. Add equations, graph definitions, and so forth.

NOTE: If you're moving database contents into an existing spreadsheet, be sure that the order of the database fields matches that of the spreadsheet rows. Otherwise, dates from the database may be pasted into cells meant for names in the spreadsheet, and so on.

NOTE: Works spreadsheets recognize numbers from Works databases. Most attributes are transferred as well. If dollars appear in the database, they'll also show up in the spreadsheet after transferring occurs.

When pasting to a spreadsheet that already contains cell data, be careful not to overwrite good cells in the receiving spreadsheet. Put the spread-

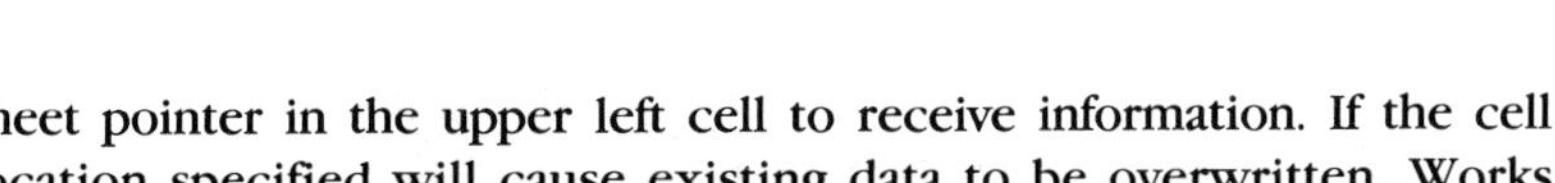

sheet pointer in the upper left cell to receive information. If the cell location specified will cause existing data to be overwritten, Works warns you.

Copying from Database to Database

If you need to copy the contents of selected database records to a new database, you can use the record-selection and Save As techniques described in Chapter 8. Using these procedures is the best way to create a similar database because Works copies field names, attributes, and other important elements. In effect you make an exact copy of the source database, but probably with fewer records if you've used record selection.

If you need to copy records from one existing database to another existing but differently structured database, a few more steps are required. Suppose, for example, that you are using the Quick Database, and you want to copy parts of those records into a new database containing only names, home addresses, and home phones. You don't want people to have access to the salary information in the Quick Database.

You need to organize the source and destination databases so that the field orders are compatible with each other. You don't need the same number of fields, and they don't need the same field names. At a minimum, however, the necessary fields in the destination database must be in the correct order, in anticipation of the transfer. Obviously, the destination database can have additional fields for data not in the source database. Moreover, you don't have to copy all fields from the source database. If you plan to try this procedure, set up a new database like figure 11.17. Call the new database Employee Home Info or something similar.

Here's what you do:

1. Open the source and destination databases in the list window (in the example, Quick Database and Employee Home Info database, respectively).

2. Arrange the source fields and destination fields to coincide with each other (see fig. 11.17). Field names need not match, but their order must be the same.

3. Activate the source database.

4. Highlight the source items you want Works to copy (in the example, LAST NAME, FIRST NAME, and MR OR MS).

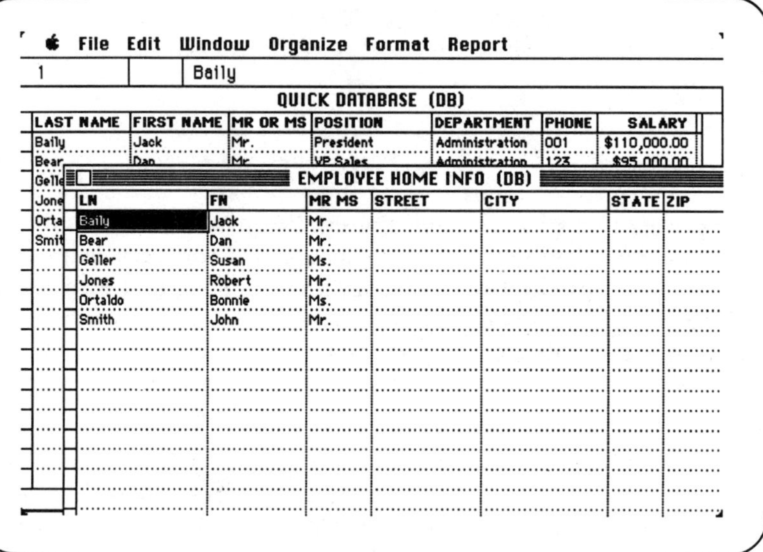

Fig. 11.17

Selected items from the Quick Database copied to the Employee Home Info database.

5. Copy the source items to the Clipboard (press **command-C**).
6. Switch to the destination database window (press **command-,**).
7. Point to the upper left destination field.
8. Paste the items to the destination database (press **command-V**).
9. Modify database field sizes, names, and so on, if necessary.
10. Add the missing employee information (home addresses and phones).

NOTE: When pasting to a database that already contains records, you must take care not to overwrite good records in the destination database. Be certain to position the database pointer on the last (the empty) record, unless you want to overwrite existing records. If the location specified will cause Works to overwrite existing data, the program warns you.

Copying from Databases to Word-Processing Windows

At times, you may need information from your database to use in a report or a letter. In particular, you may need statistical information to support points or explain decisions. Instead of having to type all the data in your word processor, you can copy material from a database to a word-processing window. For instance, suppose that you want to paste last names, first names, positions, and salaries from the Quick Database into a memo (see fig. 11.18.)

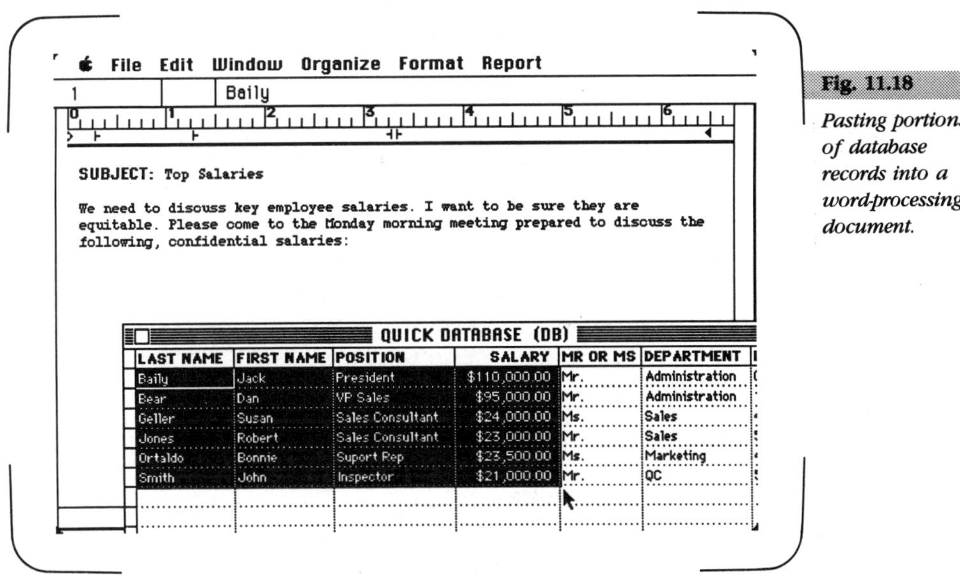

Fig. 11.18

Pasting portions of database records into a word-processing document.

Here are the general steps involved in moving database items to a word-processing window:

1. Open the word-processing document.
2. Point to the insertion point (where you'll put database results).
3. Open the database (create or alter it, if necessary).
4. Use the Show List option.
5. Rearrange the list, if necessary, as in figure 11.18.
6. Select the database items to be copied (highlight them).
7. Copy the database items to the Clipboard (press **command-C**).

8. Switch to the word-processing window (press **command-,**).
9. Paste the Clipboard contents (press **command-V**).
10. Reformat the word-processing document, if necessary.

NOTE: When pasted this way, fields in the database are separated by tabs, which appear automatically in the word-processing document. Records are separated by Return characters. You may need to modify the word-processing document's page setup, (margins, reduction, and so forth) to make room for large records; you can do so after pasting.

Database contents usually arrive in the word-processing window in the Geneva 9 font. Once the contents have been moved, you can change the font. Grids aren't pasted even if they're shown in the database window.

Copying Database Report Totals to Word-Processing Windows

If you've read Chapter 9, you probably already know how to move database report totals and subtotals to the Clipboard. Once there, they can be moved to any word-processing document available on your desktop. Following is a review of the information about copying totals and subtotals.

The Copy Totals command, which is on the Edit menu, copies totals and subtotals you've defined by using the Total On Field Change, Total-1st Character, and Sum This Field options. You can use Copy Totals any time after you've defined at least one total or subtotal. When you invoke this command, Works puts copies of the totals and subtotals on the Clipboard. You then can view the Clipboard's contents or copy the information into a different Works window.

Look at figure 11.19, which shows a report from the Quick Database. The data has been sorted by department. The report definition instructed Works to total on field changes (in the DEPARTMENT field) and to sum on the SALARY field.

The Copy Totals option from the Edit menu was used to create the Clipboard contents shown in figure 11.20. Remember that the first record from each category (each department, in the example) is copied to the Clipboard but that the summed field contains the total for the category rather than the field value for the record displayed.

LAST NAME	FIRST NAME	POSITION	MR OR MS	DEPARTMENT	SALARY
Baily	Jack	President	Mr.	Administration	$110,000.00
Bear	Dan	VP Sales	Mr.	Administration	$95,000.00
					$205,000.00
Ortaldo	Bonnie	Suport Rep	Ms.	Marketing	$23,500.00
					$23,500.00
Smith	John	Inspector	Mr.	QC	$21,000.00
					$21,000.00
Geller	Susan	Sales Consultant	Ms.	Sales	$24,000.00
Jones	Robert	Sales Consultant	Mr.	Sales	$23,000.00
					$47,000.00
					$296,500.00

Fig. 11.19

Database report with totals ready to be copied.

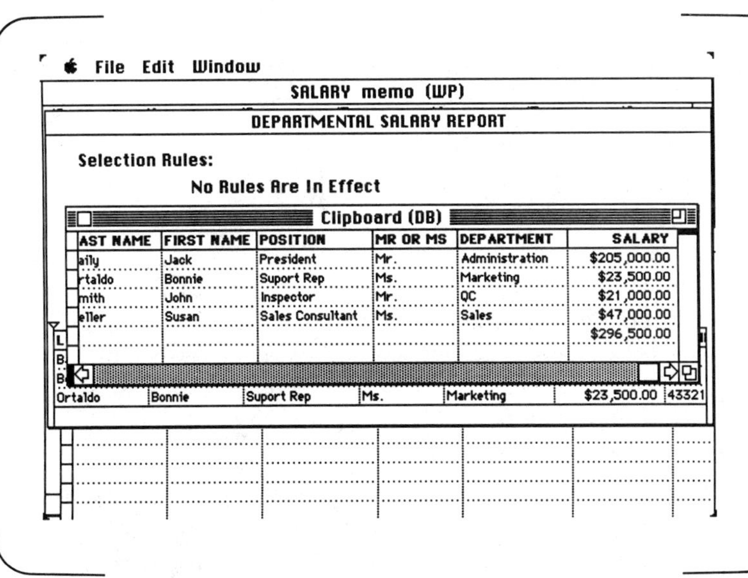

Fig. 11.20

The Clipboard after the Copy Totals option is used.

After the salary totals have been copied to the Clipboard, they can be pasted to a word-processing document (see fig. 11.21). Word-processing techniques can be used to deleted unwanted text after pasting.

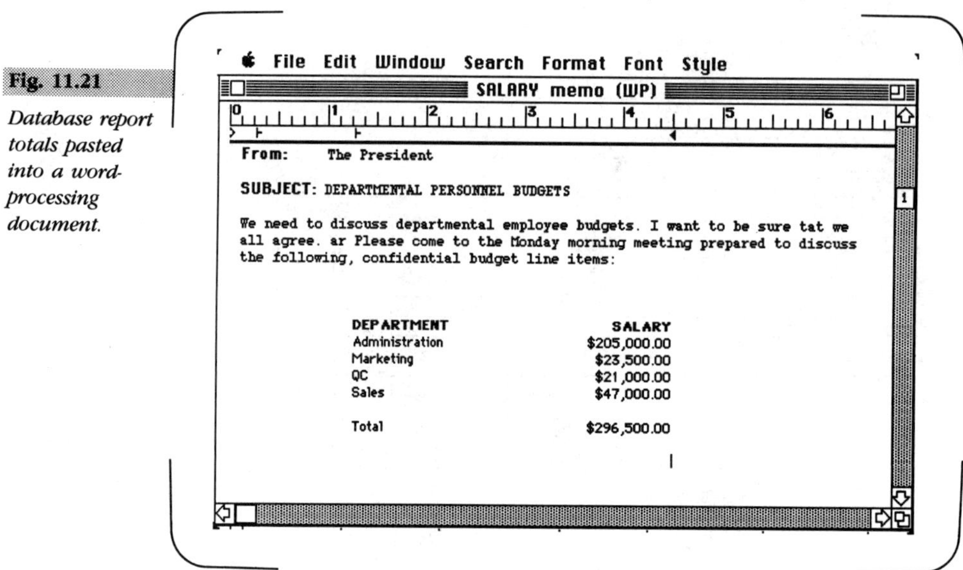

Fig. 11.21

Database report totals pasted into a word-processing document.

Even if you have turned off the report's grid option, Works displays the Clipboard copies of your totals with a grid. If you transfer the contents of the Clipboard to another window (spreadsheet, word-processing, and so on), the grid isn't transferred.

Merging

The Merge option has many uses. For example, you can use a Works database to create a mailing list and send out personalized mailings. Works enables you to merge names, addresses, and other items from your databases with word-processing documents to create personalized form letters, to fill in forms automatically, and so forth. During this process, you don't use the Clipboard.

Figure 11.22, for example, shows mailing labels that were created with a LaserWriter and Works' Merge feature. If you plan to print labels on an ImageWriter, see "Printing Small Labels with an ImageWriter" at the end of this chapter.

Creating and Printing Merge Documents

A merge document looks like a normal word-processing document except that the merge document contains *placeholders* where you would

Abbey Rents
Mr. Steve Brown
1901 E. Colorado Blvd.
Pasadena CA 91107

First Class Mail

A S L Consulting Engineers
Mr. William D. Lewis
3280 E. Foothill Blvd., #160
Pasadena CA 91107

First Class Mail

A Child's Fancy
Ms. Merle Einstein
20 E. Colorado Blvd.
Pasadena CA 91105

First Class Mail

A & D Building Maintenance Co.
Mr. Andre Chambers
2120 E. Foothill Blvd. #1
Pasadena CA 91107

First Class Mail

Fig. 11.22
Mailing labels created with a LaserWriter and Works' Merge feature.

otherwise type information such as names, addresses, and so on. These placeholders tell Works to get specific information from one of your databases when printing. When you print a merge document, Works fills in the blanks, using information from the records in your database.

Each placeholder contains the name of the database and the database field name containing the desired information. The two items are separated by a colon (see fig. 11.23). Theoretically, a merge document can pull information from more than one database, but this procedure is tricky and seldom done.

Assume that you want to use the Simple memo and the Quick Database to print personalized memos. Here are the steps involved in creating merge documents containing placeholders:

1. Place the database on the desktop (open the Quick Database).
2. Open the word-processing document (the Simple memo).
3. Type, edit, and proof the word-processing text that will always be printed—the body of the memo (delete "All Key Employees" and add "Dear:").
4. Point to the position in the word-processing document where you want to add a placeholder (between "Dear" and the colon).

Fig. 11.23

Placeholders showing the name of the database and the fields to be used.

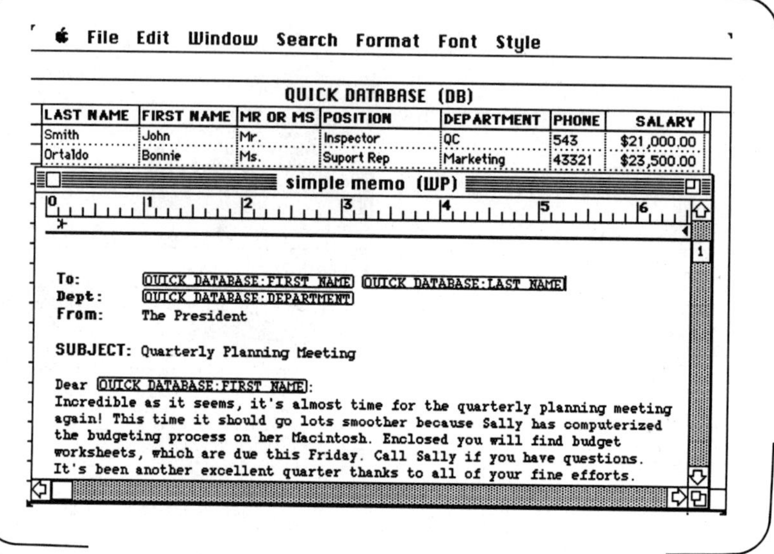
File Edit Window Search Format Font Style
QUICK DATABASE (DB)
LAST NAME FIRST NAME MR OR MS POSITION DEPARTMENT PHONE SALARY
Smith John Mr. Inspector QC 543 $21,000.00
Ortaldo Bonnie Ms. Suport Rep Marketing 43321 $23,500.00
simple memo (WP)
To: QUICK DATABASE:FIRST NAME QUICK DATABASE:LAST NAME
Dept: QUICK DATABASE:DEPARTMENT
From: The President
SUBJECT: Quarterly Planning Meeting
Dear QUICK DATABASE:FIRST NAME:
Incredible as it seems, it's almost time for the quarterly planning meeting
again! This time it should go lots smoother because Sally has computerized
the budgeting process on her Macintosh. Enclosed you will find budget
worksheets, which are due this Friday. Call Sally if you have questions.
It's been another excellent quarter thanks to all of your fine efforts.

5. Choose Prepare to Merge from the Edit menu (see fig. 11.24). You'll see a list of available databases and fields like that shown in figure 11.25.

Fig. 11.24

Choosing Prepare to Merge from the Edit menu.

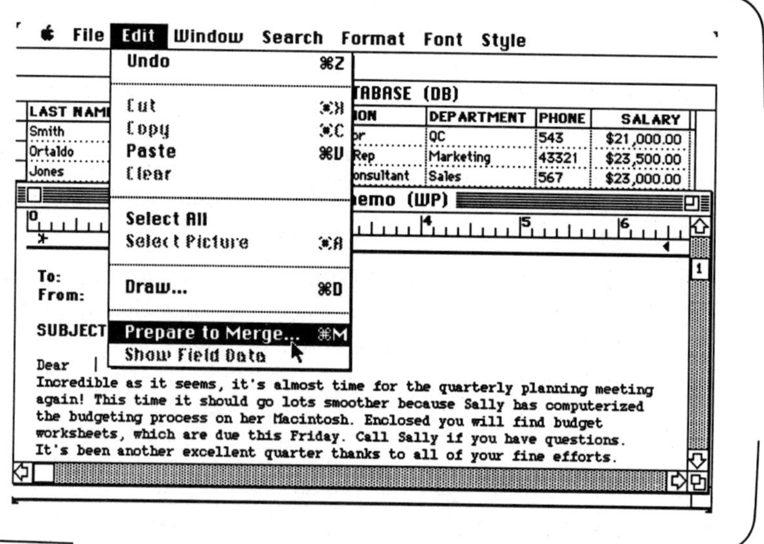
File Edit Window Search Format Font Style
Undo ⌘Z
Cut ⌘X
Copy ⌘C
Paste ⌘V
Clear
Select All
Select Picture ⌘A
Draw... ⌘D
Prepare to Merge... ⌘M
Show Field Data
LAST NAME
Smith
Ortaldo
Jones
DEPARTMENT PHONE SALARY
QC 543 $21,000.00
Marketing 43321 $23,500.00
Sales 567 $23,000.00
To:
From:
SUBJECT
Dear
Incredible as it seems, it's almost time for the quarterly planning meeting
again! This time it should go lots smoother because Sally has computerized
the budgeting process on her Macintosh. Enclosed you will find budget
worksheets, which are due this Friday. Call Sally if you have questions.
It's been another excellent quarter thanks to all of your fine efforts.

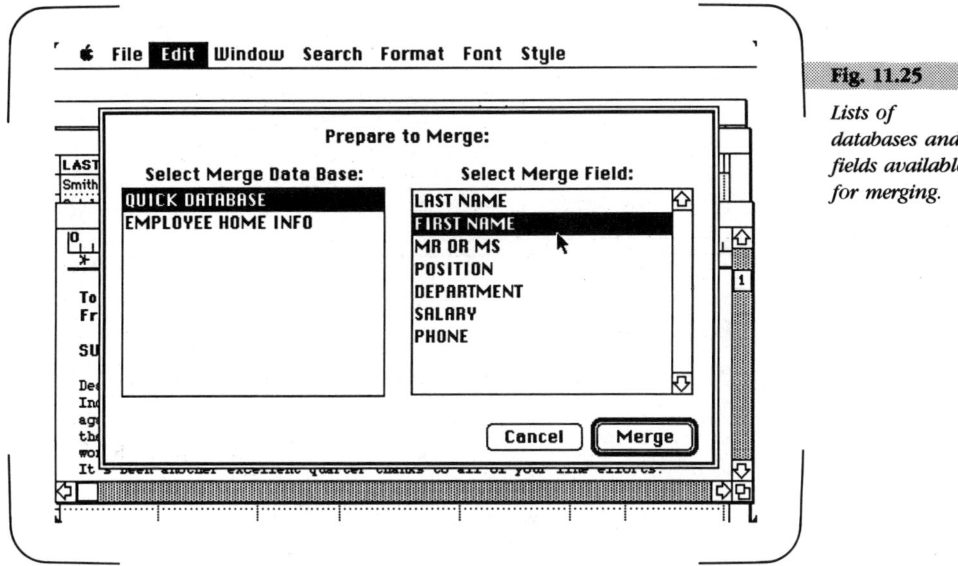

Fig. 11.25
Lists of databases and fields available for merging.

6. Select the database you want (Quick Database).
7. Choose the appropriate field (click OK or double-click). Works then puts the placeholder containing the name of the database and field into your document at the location specified.
8. Insert necessary spaces, commas, and so forth. For example, put a space between the first-name and last-name placeholders after "To:" in the memo.
9. Repeat the process until you've installed all the placeholders you need. Your practice memo should look like figure 11.23.
10. Preview your work by choosing Show Field Data from the Edit menu (see fig. 11.26).

After viewing the data, you can redisplay the placeholders by picking the Show Field Names option, which replaces the Show Field Data option on the Edit menu. The screen again looks like figure 11.23.

After you've set up a merge document, you're almost ready to print. First, you must be certain that your database is in the order you want (sort it) and that you have selected only the records you want to print. If you don't restrict the records, Works prints them all. (See the section in Chapter 8 on record-selection features.)

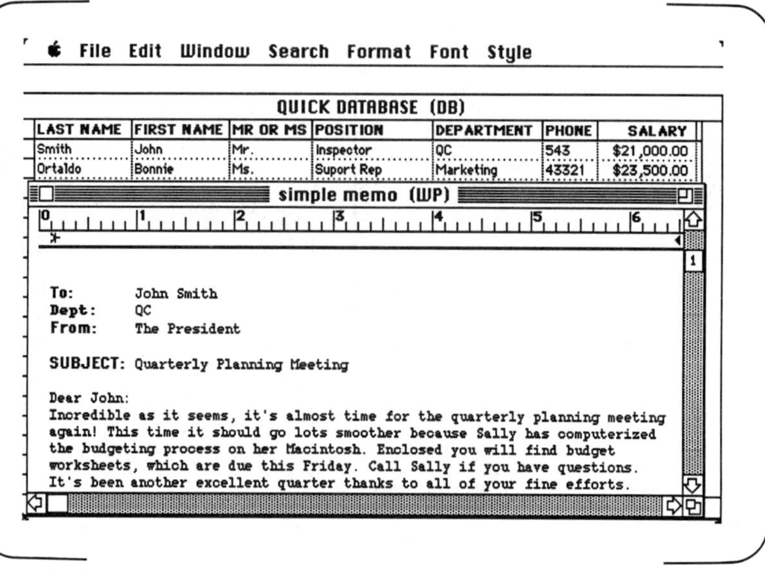
File Edit Window Search Format Font Style
QUICK DATABASE (DB)
LAST NAME FIRST NAME MR OR MS POSITION DEPARTMENT PHONE SALARY
Smith John Mr. Inspector QC 543 $21,000.00
Ortaldo Bonnie Ms. Suport Rep Marketing 43321 $23,500.00
simple memo (WP)
To: John Smith
Dept: QC
From: The President
SUBJECT: Quarterly Planning Meeting
Dear John:
Incredible as it seems, it's almost time for the quarterly planning meeting
again! This time it should go lots smoother because Sally has computerized
the budgeting process on her Macintosh. Enclosed you will find budget
worksheets, which are due this Friday. Call Sally if you have questions.
It's been another excellent quarter thanks to all of your fine efforts.

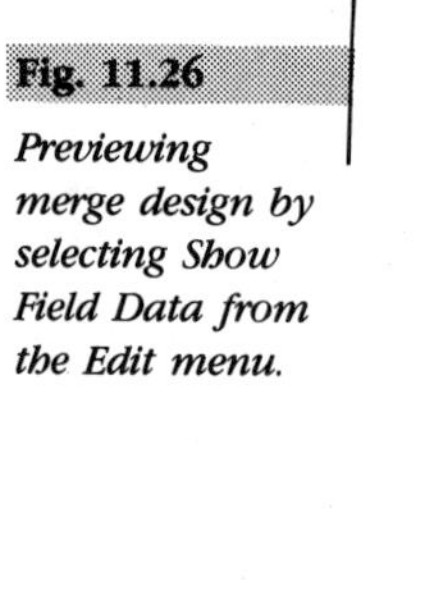

Fig. 11.26

Previewing merge design by selecting Show Field Data from the Edit menu.

When the selected records are in order, choose Print Merge from the Edit menu. You can use the *command-*. [period] feature to abort printing.

Using Word-Processing Attributes in Merge Documents

You can print the information from your database in merge documents, using any available word-processing font attribute, size, and so on. Simply select the placeholder and change its type as you would any word-processing text (see fig. 11.27). In this example, text was centered and printed in a variety of type sizes and in boldface and italics. The Draw feature and clip art from the Scrapbook also were used.

Dealing with Placeholder Wrap

Sometimes, placeholders wrap down to the next line because they're too long to fit on one line due to the word-processing margin and page-size definitions. This wrap does not mean that the database information wraps automatically when printed. For example, figure 11.28 shows a placeholder that has wrapped because of long database names and a small document size. Regardless of this arrangement, the document was

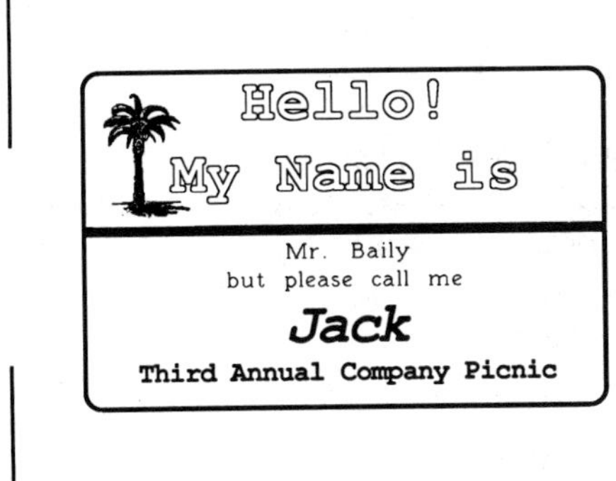

Fig. 11.27

Most word-processing attributes, including typestyles, formatting, and so on, are supported by the Merge function.

used to print the badge in figure 11.27. You can preview merge printing on the screen to see how the finished document will look. You use the Show Field Data option on the Edit menu. Choosing Show Field Names, which replaces Show Field Data, returns you to the preceding view.

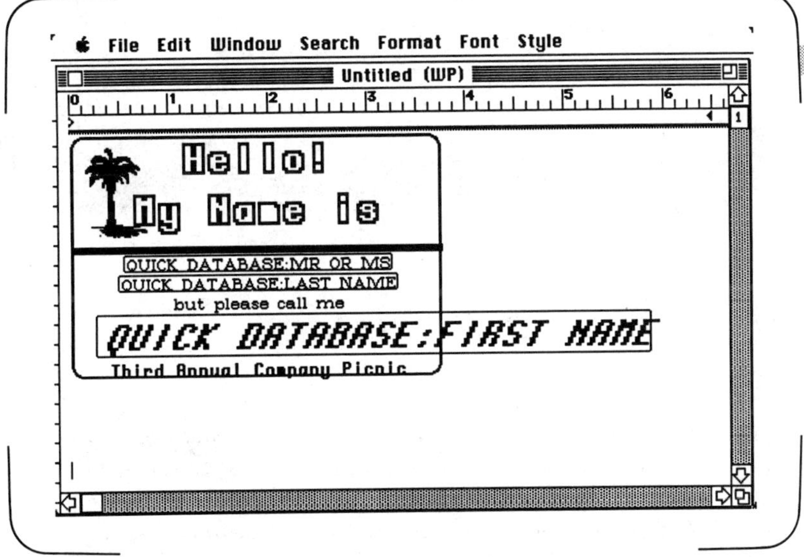

Fig. 11.28

Narrow document margins and long placeholder names, which cause placeholder wrap.

HINT: If you know that you'll be using a database for merging, give the database and fields short names, and the placeholders will be shorter. If you decide to rename a database, remember to edit the placeholders; the database file names must agree.

Changing Database and Field Names: Cautions

Don't change database or database field names that are referenced in placeholders. If you do, you will have to update the merge documents manually to reflect the changes; otherwise, Works displays error messages like those shown in figure 11.29. In this case, the database called Key Employees is not open on the desktop.

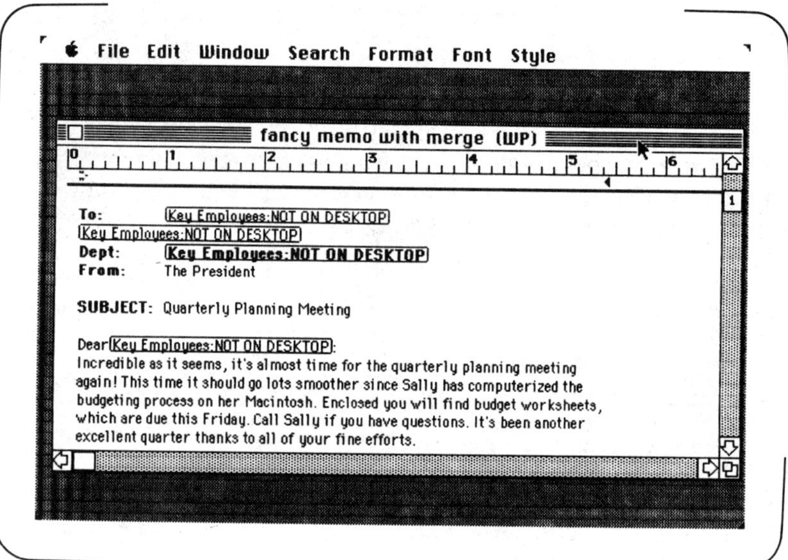

File Edit Window Search Format Font Style
fancy memo with merge (WP)
To: Key Employees:NOT ON DESKTOP
Key Employees:NOT ON DESKTOP
Dept: Key Employees:NOT ON DESKTOP
From: The President
SUBJECT: Quarterly Planning Meeting
Dear Key Employees:NOT ON DESKTOP:
Incredible as it seems, it's almost time for the quarterly planning meeting again! This time it should go lots smoother since Sally has computerized the budgeting process on her Macintosh. Enclosed you will find budget worksheets, which are due this Friday. Call Sally if you have questions. It's been another excellent quarter thanks to all of your fine efforts.

Fig. 11.29

Error messages that appear if you forget to open your database.

Merge Document Formatting Considerations

Works wraps merged data to make it fit, and it usually looks just fine. In extreme cases, however, a large insertion could turn a one-page document into a multipage document. When designing the fixed text, which is repeated in every merge document, be certain to allow enough white space so that all the merge data will fit where you want it.

Do you plan to use merge documents to fill out printed forms with six-lines-per-inch spacing and boxes in fixed locations? Then, pick a font that is not proportionally spaced and has typewriter line spacing—for example, Courier.

Adding and Deleting Placeholders

You can add or delete placeholders at any time by using the inserting, cutting, and backspacing techniques you've already learned. Remember, however, that if you plan to add placeholders, the database must be on your desktop.

Printing Small Labels with an ImageWriter

Microsoft does not recommend printing small (one-inch) labels on the ImageWriter with Works Versions 1.0. Due to incompatibilities in the printer and software, labels will jam frequently, which may cause printer damage. Larger labels usually work.

Works Version 1.1 offers an improved method of label printing for small labels. With this version, you should be able to print even one-inch labels. Sometimes, you may notice a brief delay while Works 1.1 calculates necessary parameters for label printing. If you print more than 128 labels, you will see a blank label (#129) and additional blanks after every 128 labels. Once label printing starts, Works 1.1 is faster than Version 1.0. Version 1.1 uses disk space for label printing, so you may see an alert when you are printing labels on a system not equipped with a hard disk. Remove from the disk unnecessary files, like the Works Help file, and try again.

Personalized Form Filling

With Works' drawing features, you can create forms, labels, continuous envelopes, name tags, and so on. Figure 11.30 shows an example of the merge document that created the forms shown in figure 11.31. You use the database to produce a worksheet for each employee in the database.

Fig. 11.30

Merge document for creating personalized forms.

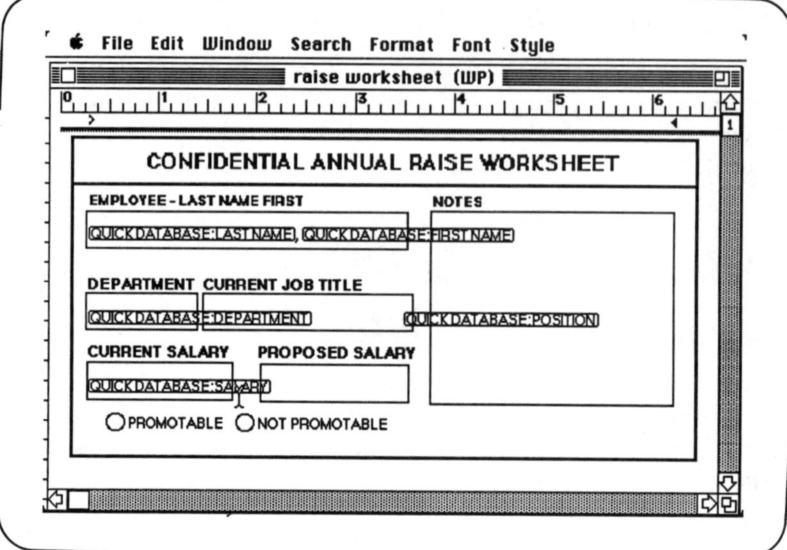

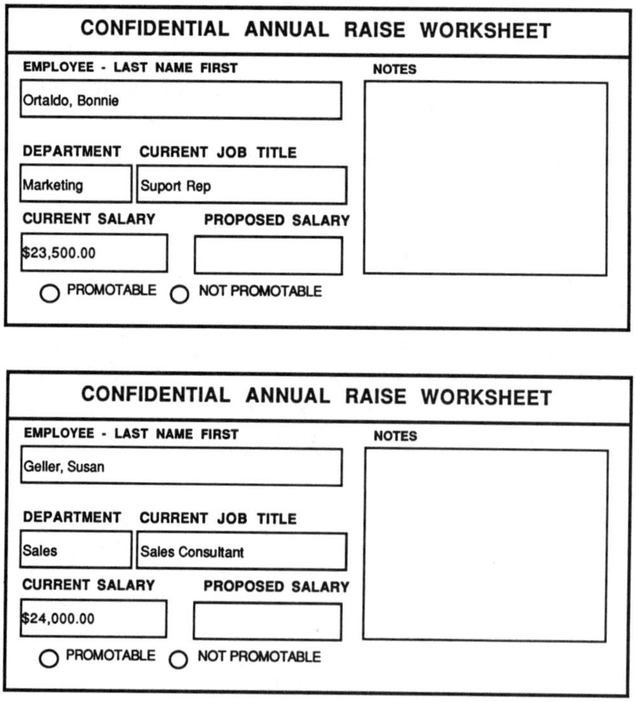

Fig. 11.31

Examples of personalized forms.

CONFIDENTIAL ANNUAL RAISE WORKSHEET

EMPLOYEE - LAST NAME FIRST

Ortaldo, Bonnie

NOTES

DEPARTMENT Marketing

CURRENT JOB TITLE Suport Rep

CURRENT SALARY $23,500.00

PROPOSED SALARY

○ PROMOTABLE ○ NOT PROMOTABLE

CONFIDENTIAL ANNUAL RAISE WORKSHEET

EMPLOYEE - LAST NAME FIRST

Geller, Susan

NOTES

DEPARTMENT Sales

CURRENT JOB TITLE Sales Consultant

CURRENT SALARY $24,000.00

PROPOSED SALARY

○ PROMOTABLE ○ NOT PROMOTABLE

12

Using Works with Other Products

As powerful as Microsoft Works and your Macintosh are, you may want to augment them sometimes with other software and special-purpose hardware. Works has been designed to work with a variety of other programs, and a number of vendors have designed their programs with Works in mind. Because Works has become a best-seller, this trend will continue.

This chapter explores products that can be used with Works. Most of them you can find at your local Apple dealer. If you need help obtaining them, refer to Appendix A for a list of the manufacturers' addresses and telephone numbers.

Graphics

You probably purchased your Macintosh partly because of its graphics power. Works was designed to be compatible with many of today's popular graphics products: MacPaint, MacDraw, SuperPaint, ThunderScan®, MacVision, and others. You can capture most Macintosh screens as "paint files" and include them in Works word-processing documents. Put simply, if you can get a MacPaint-compatible image to your Clipboard or Scrapbook, Works can integrate that image into your word-processing document. Once a picture has been pasted into a Works word-processing document, the picture can be moved and resized.

Paint Programs

Any paint program that can create MacPaint-style (picture, or PICT) files can generate pictures for Works word-processing documents. Figure 12.1 shows two examples of these pictures, which are referred to sometimes as *bit images*, *bit-mapped images*, or *bit-mapped graphics*. Table

12.1 lists a few of the many programs that can create these pictures. You can even paste and display color pictures using your Mac II.

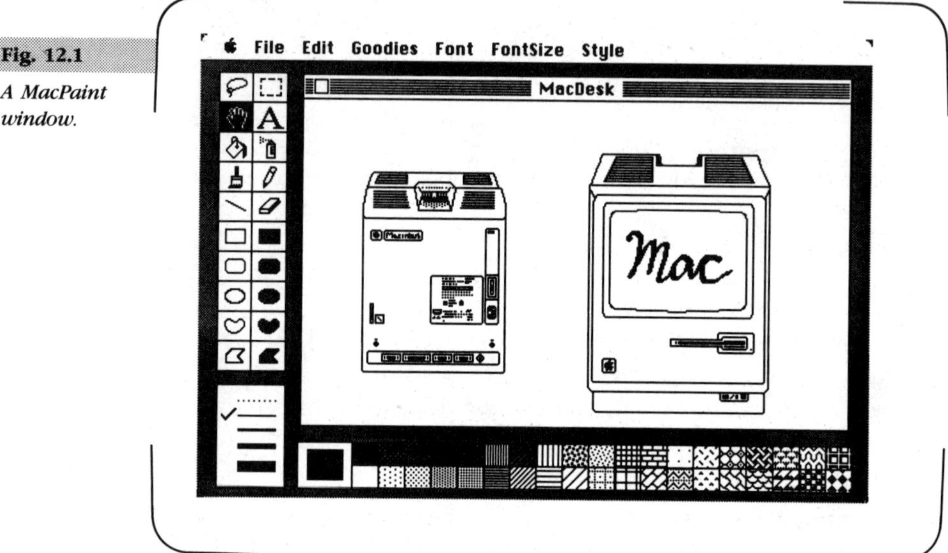

Fig. 12.1

A MacPaint window.

Table 12.1
Paint Programs

Product	*Notes*	*Sold by*
MacPaint		Apple, Inc.
MacDraw		Apple Inc.
SuperPaint		Silicon Beach Software, Inc.
FullPaint™		B. Knick Drafting
MacPerspective		3-D drafting ADAPSO
Easy 3D	3-D drafting	Enabling Technologies
Mac3D®	3-D drafting	Challenger Software
Housebuilder™		Alternative Enterprises

To create many of the illustrations in this book, both MacPaint and SuperPaint were used. MacPaint is small enough to be used with Works and the Switcher program (described elsewhere in this chapter). A powerful trilogy, Works, MacPaint, and Switcher (or Apple's new MultiFinder) enable you to create pictures and drop them quickly into a Works word-processing document without constantly loading and then leaving Works and MacPaint.

Clip Art

If you're not feeling artistic—or if you're in a hurry—you can purchase other people's art work and include it in your Works word-processing documents. A number of companies offer Macintosh *clip art*, and thousands of free or low-cost drawings are available in the public domain through clubs and shareware publishers.

Many of these collections of drawings are cartoonlike; others are quite realistic, as you can see in figure 12.2. Drawings of people, places, maps, flags—you name it—are available.

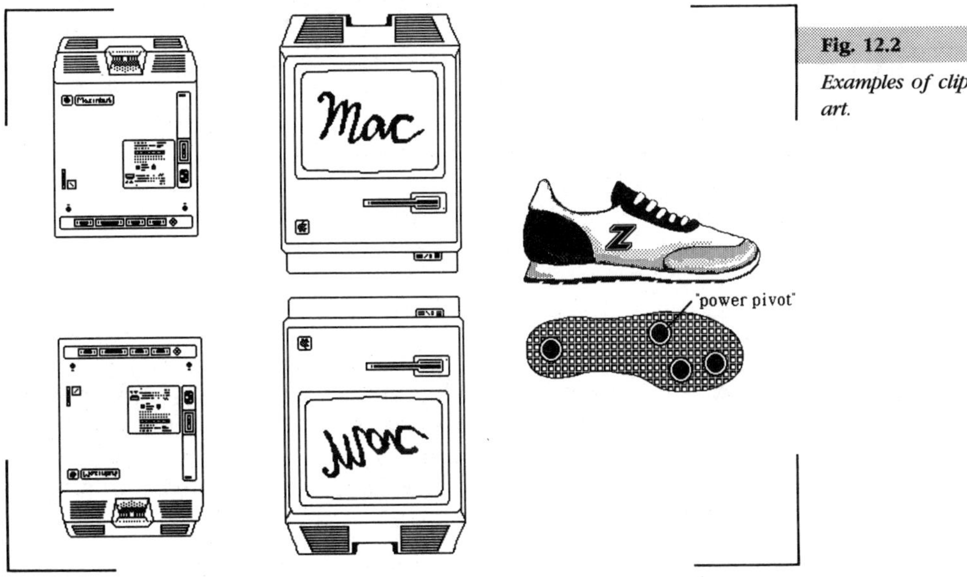

Fig. 12.2
Examples of clip art.

You can assemble and modify most drawings by using the paint tools described in this chapter. After the drawings are in MacPaint-compatible format, Works can use them.

The low-cost and free clip art collections are suitable for school publications, newsletters, bulletin board announcements, and so forth. The more expensive professional-quality collections of art work are used by graphic artists to design ads, company logos, forms, and so on. Table 12.2 lists a few of the many sources of clip art. Appendix A contains the addresses and telephone numbers of the manufacturers; call or write them for current catalogs and pricing information.

Table 12.2
Clip Art Sources

Product	*Notes*	*Sold by*
Art ala Mac™	Some used in this book	Springboard Software, Inc.
ClickArt®	Some used in this book	T/Maker Graphics
Byte Series	Collection of drawings	A. A. H. Computer Graphics
Various	Some used in this book	Educomp (shareware)
Mac-Art Library	Collections	CompuCraft
Various	Collections	ImageWorld
Graphic Accents™	Collections	Kensington Graphics
McPic!™	Collections	Magnum Software
MacAtlas™	Map Collections	MicroMaps
Mac Art Dpt.	Collections	Simon and Schuster
Various	Collections	Spinnaker Software
Various	Collections	Sunshine

Screen Dumps

Have you ever wondered how writers create the sample screens used in operators' manuals and books like this one? A feature called the *screen dump* is the answer. The Macintosh offers a built-in screen dump capability, which creates a paint file that can be modified with programs like MacPaint or used as is by Works.

To create screen dumps, you hold down three keys simultaneously: *shift*, *command*, and 3. Works then creates a paint file that is an exact rendering of what's on the screen at the time you press the keys. Works automatically assigns each file one of ten names in the format *Screen n*, where *n* is a number from 0 to 9. When you've saved ten screens this way, you must rename them, move them to another disk, or trash them before you can create more. If you have a Macintosh II with a color monitor, you may need to switch to the two-color characteristic setting on your Control Panel in order to do screen dumps.

Camera

Application programs sometimes prevent you from doing screen dumps with *shift-command-*3. For example, you can't use this keystroke sequence to create a screen dump of the Works Greeting Screen. Macintosh Plus and SE users can't generate screen dumps with the mouse button held down; therefore, capturing screens displaying menus, for example, is impossible.

Several companies offer desk accessories that get around these problems. Perhaps the best known of these products is Camera, an accessory available from many public domain catalogs and many of the utility collections sold by dealers.

Camera enables you to take screen snapshots after a time delay you set. This arrangement gives you time to invoke Camera, set up the screen that you want to capture, and even pull down and hold menus in place (see fig. 12.3). Macintosh Plus and SE users can then capture screens with the mouse button down. Camera was used for all the figures in this book that have menus pulled down. The program also gives you the option of hiding the pointer.

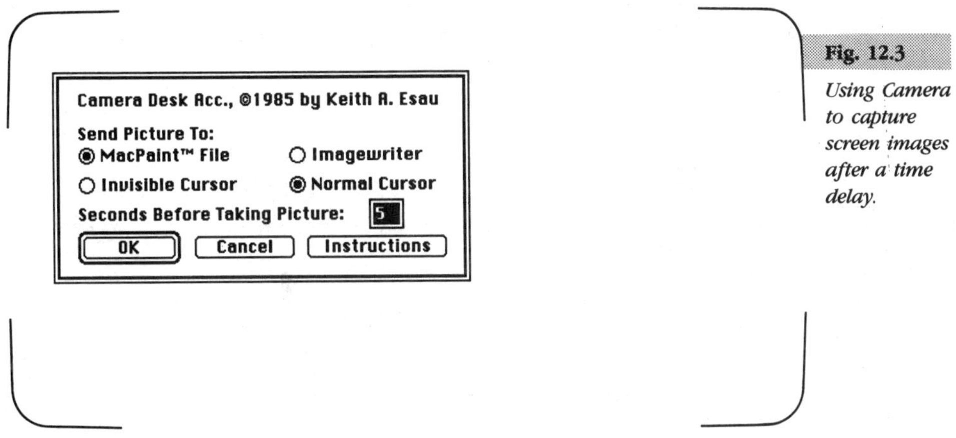

Fig. 12.3

Using Camera to capture screen images after a time delay.

GLUE and SuperGlue

The package called GLUE™ and its recent replacement SuperGlue™ contains two programs. One, ImageSaver, redirects any output that would go to your printer to a disk file instead. This redirected printer output is always stored as a series of QuickDraw commands, regardless of whether you've sent text, pictures, or both to the disk. You can use ImageSaver to capture items that otherwise are unavailable to the Works word-processing feature—for example, complete database reports.

When you install GLUE or SuperGlue, an additional option is added to your Chooser (see fig. 12.4). The icon looks like a 35mm camera.

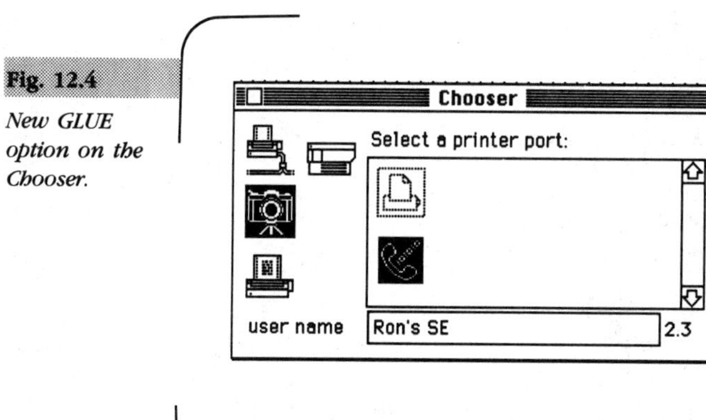

Fig. 12.4

New GLUE option on the Chooser.

When you click on the ImageSaver icon in the Chooser dialog box (see figure 12.5), anything that usually is printed is converted into a file and stored to disk instead. You provide the name under which GLUE saves the file, as shown in figure 12.6.

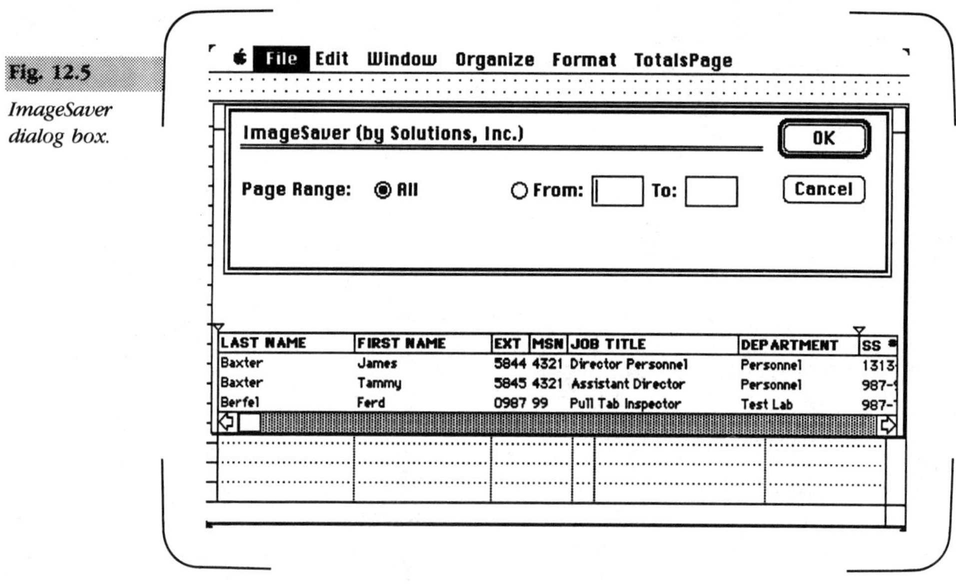

Fig. 12.5

ImageSaver dialog box.

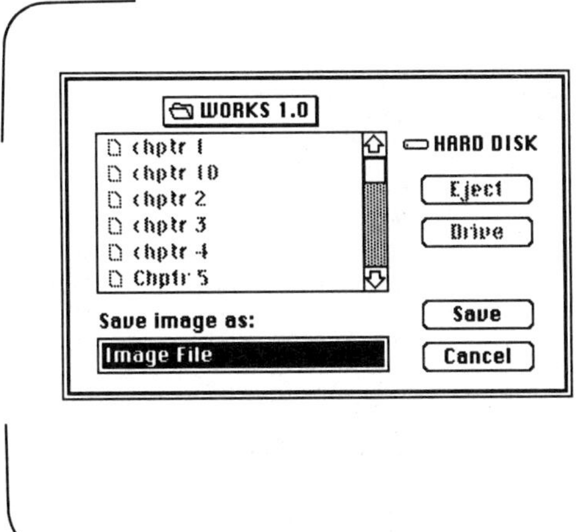

Fig. 12.6

Specifying the name under which GLUE saves the picture image (of a database report, in this case).

After you save the image you created with GLUE, you can view and modify the image by using the second program in the GLUE package, Viewer. It enables you to see the contents of the ImageSaver files you've created. You can also print the files or convert them to MacPaint files.

Using GLUE with Works offers at least three important advantages. First, you can capture images larger than the screen even if your paint program (MacPaint, for example) won't let you copy them directly to the Clipboard. Second, if you have a program that doesn't generate bit-mapped graphics and you want to include its output in a Works word-processing document, GLUE helps you accomplish this task. The third and most interesting use of GLUE involves Works' Report feature and word-processing windows.

With Works Versions 1.0 and 1.1, you can't copy database reports directly to a word-processing window. If you use GLUE to send a report to a bit-mapped file, however, you can import the report into a Works word-processing window as a picture. You can resize the report, draw lines, and so on. But remember that the report is a picture, so you can't use Works to edit the text in the report.

In figure 12.7, for instance, a Works report has been pasted into a Works word-processing document, where Works' Draw feature was used to add a box around part of the report. Then the Line Draw feature was used to add "drop shadow" lines at the bottom and to the right of the box.

Fig. 12.7

A report pasted as a picture into a word-processing window and enhanced with Works' drawing features.

CONFIDENTIAL KEY EMPLOYEE PHONE LIST August 27, 1987

LAST NAME	FIRST NAME	EXT	MSN	JOB TITLE	DEPARTMENT
Baxter	James	5844	4321	Director Personnel	Personnel
Baxter	Tammy	5845	4321	Assistant Director	Personnel
Berfel	Ferd	0987	99	Pull Tab Inspector	Test Lab
Flushland	Johnathon	4324	543	Cleaning Associate	Maintenance
Goldberg	Rubin	7655	45	Director, Engineering	Engineering
Gunlatch	Raymond	0001	001	President	Corporate
Gunlatch	Nancy	0002	001	Assistant to the President	Corporate
Makit	Willie	3345	21	Production Supervisor	Production
Mi	Sue	7654	45	New Product Development	Engineering
Norcross	Oliver	UNL	UNL	Sales	Sales
Quickcloser	John	6543	43	Inside Sales	Sales
So	Mi	6543	43	Inside Sales	Sales
Winston	Doc	3456	565	Sr. Sardine Eye Closer	Production

SuperGlue offers a text-extraction mode that lets you capture reports as text (ASCII) and then paste the text into word-processing windows for normal editing. A complete description of the GLUE and SuperGlue programs is beyond the scope of this book. The following procedure, however, can get you started using GLUE (once you've purchased, installed, and read about it):

1. Prepare a report for printing, but don't print it.
2. Select the GLUE option (camera-shaped icon) on the Chooser.
3. Print the desired report, using either the Print command on the File menu or the **command-P** shortcut. (ImageSaver sends the report to a file, not to your printer.)
4. Give the file a meaningful name (GLUE prompts you for it).
5. Quit Works (or use the Switcher or MultiFinder).
6. Open the picture (report), using GLUE's Viewer.
7. Copy the report from the disk to the Clipboard or Scrapbook.
8. Open Works and the appropriate word-processing document.
9. Paste the report (picture) into the word-processing document.
10. Resize, move, and draw as desired.
11. Reset the Chooser to a printer.

You can use GLUE for many different kinds of projects. With its added convenience and speed, you can produce attractive and professional-looking reports and brochures. If you don't already own GLUE, purchase the newer, more powerful SuperGlue instead.

Graphics Scanners

Several hardware manufacturers have created devices called *graphics scanners*. These devices scan art work to create bit images your Macintosh can store and manipulate. Once these images are in MacPaint-compatible format, Works can modify them with paint programs or use them in word-processing documents. Table 12.3 lists a few of the better known scanners.

Table 12.3
Scanners

Product	*Notes*	*Sold by*
ThunderScan®	Uses your ImageWriter	Thunderware®, Inc.
MacVision	Video capture	Koala
Turboscan		DEST
Abaton Scan 300		Abaton Technology Corporation

Scanners capture photographs, drawings, handwritten signatures, and other visual images. Some systems such as Koala's MacVision can even capture video images from a video camera or video tape player. The quality and resolution of scanner-captured images, which you use with your Works word-processing documents as you would any other pictures, varies widely. Figure 12.8 shows an example of a scanned image.

Spelling and Grammar Checkers

Until (and unless) Microsoft decides to offer its own spell-checking feature for Works, you must either check the spelling of your word-processing documents yourself or purchase a spelling checker from a third-party software house. Lundeen & Associates, for example, offers a product called WorksPlus Spell, which was used to check this manuscript. WorksPlus Spell installs itself "alongside" Works and adds several choices to your Works menus, as shown in figure 12.9.

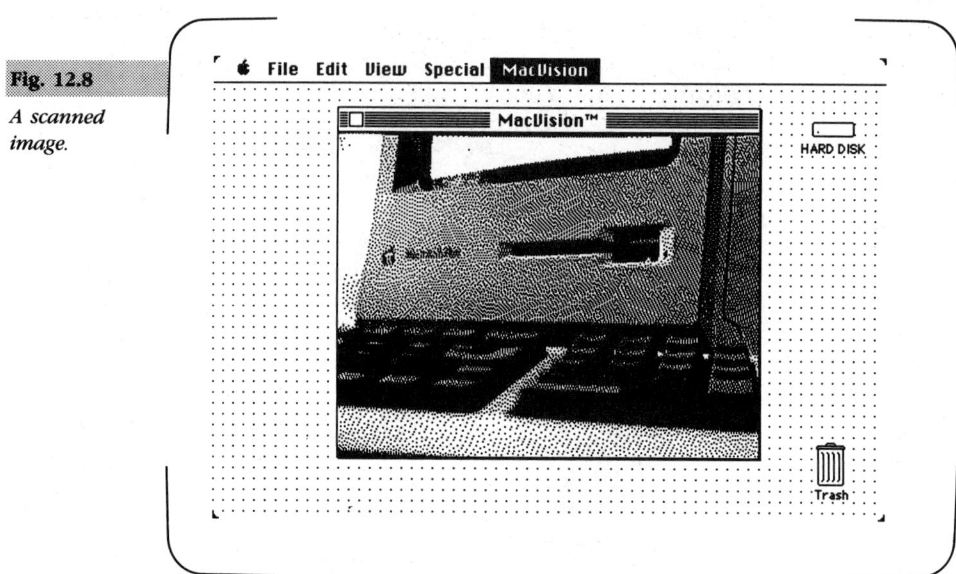

Fig. 12.8

A scanned image.

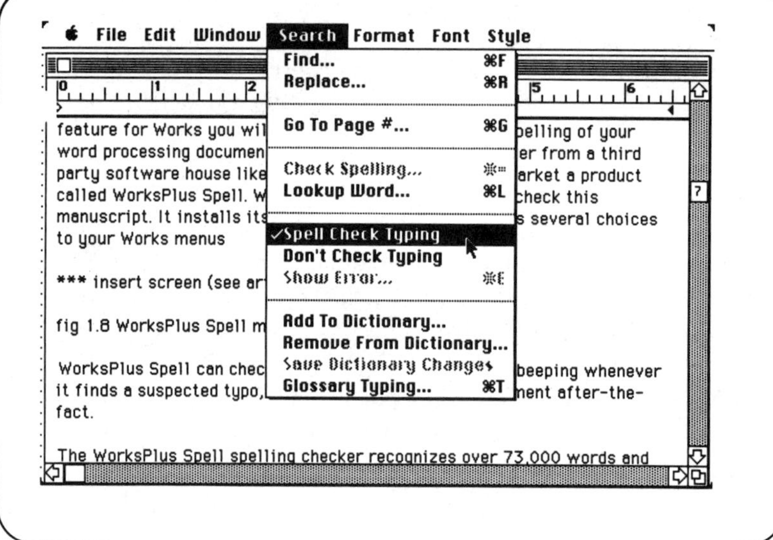

Fig. 12.9

WorksPlus Spell options on the Works Search menu.

You can use WorksPlus Spell to check your typing as you go (the program beeps whenever it finds a suspected typo). Or you can use WorksPlus Spell to check an entire finished document. The Lookup Word option can help you find the spelling of a particular (highlighted) word.

Add To Dictionary and Remove From Dictionary enable you to maintain the dictionary, which is particularly helpful if you use a lot of technical jargon or proper names not found in "normal" dictionaries.

WorksPlus Spell recognizes more than 73,000 words and can check up to 24,000 words per minute. When the program finds a word it doesn't recognize, it highlights the word and displays one or more guesses about the correct spelling, as shown in figure 12.10. If the guess is correct, press *return*. If one of the alternatives is correct, double-click on it.

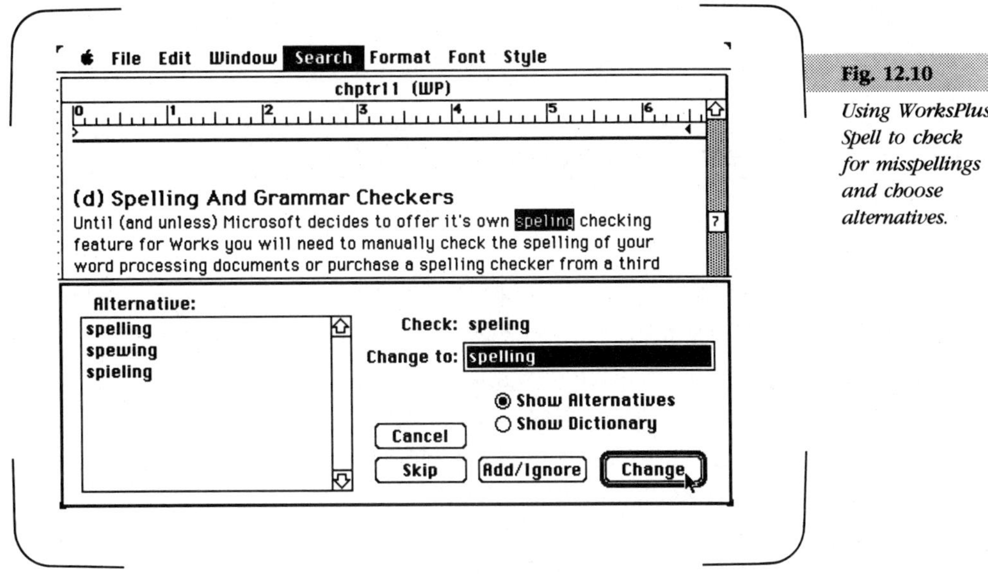

Fig. 12.10

Using WorksPlus Spell to check for misspellings and choose alternatives.

You can build your own custom list of words so that WorksPlus Spell recognizes your name, street address, technical jargon, and so on. You can build one list for all your documents, or you can create specific lists for particular word-processing documents. And you can tell WorksPlus Spell either to check upper- and lowercase or ignore the case.

The WorksPlus Spell glossary feature lets you define shorthand for frequently typed phrases. For example, when this book was being written, I typed *wk* and had WorksPlus Spell replace those letters automatically with the word *Works*, as illustrated in figure 12.11.

WorksPlus Spell also provides automatic hyphenation features, which you'll find useful (see fig. 12.12). You can have WorksPlus Spell make hyphenation decisions for you, or you can make each decision for yourself. Entire documents or selected portions of your work can be hy-

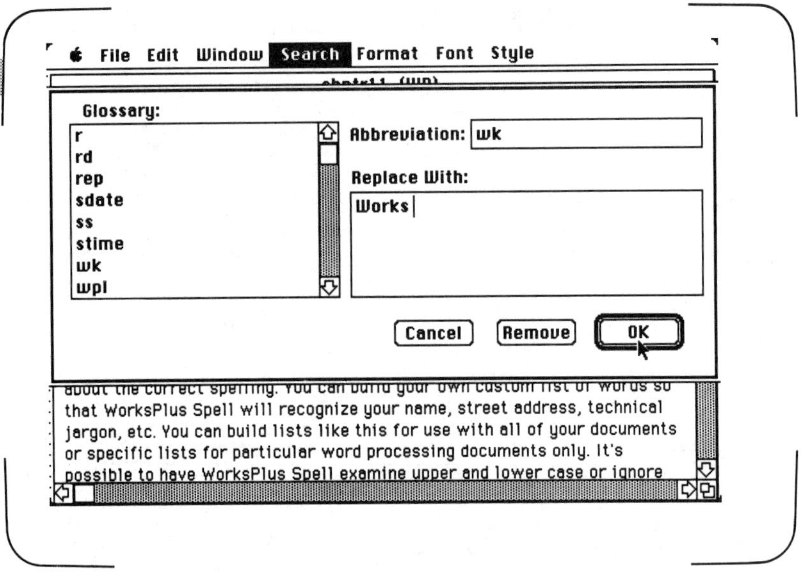

Fig. 12.11

Using a glossary of shorthand terms that WorksPlus Spell converts as you type.

phenated. You also can choose to justify your text. Notice the different appearances of the three examples in the figure.

WorksPlus Spell even spots spacing errors, which occur frequently in the small typefaces used on the Macintosh screen (see fig. 12.13).

If you do a great deal of writing, WorksPlus Spell may be the most helpful add-on you can purchase for Works. I couldn't test WorksPlus Spell with Version 1.1 of Works, but Lundeen & Associates claims that the latest versions of their programs are compatible.

Fonts

Works comes with five fonts: Boston, Athens, Monaco, Geneva, and Chicago. Examples are provided in figure 12.14. Below them are laser output. Notice how jagged Chicago and Venice are. They are not laser fonts; the rest (Courier, Geneva, and so on) are. Fonts usually consist of letters, numbers, and punctuation marks, but also can include other symbols.

Fig. 12.12.

Text before and after hyphenation.

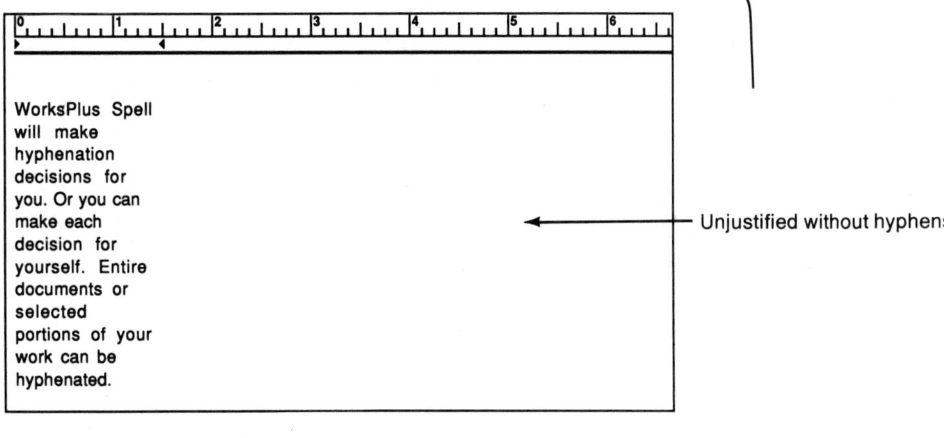

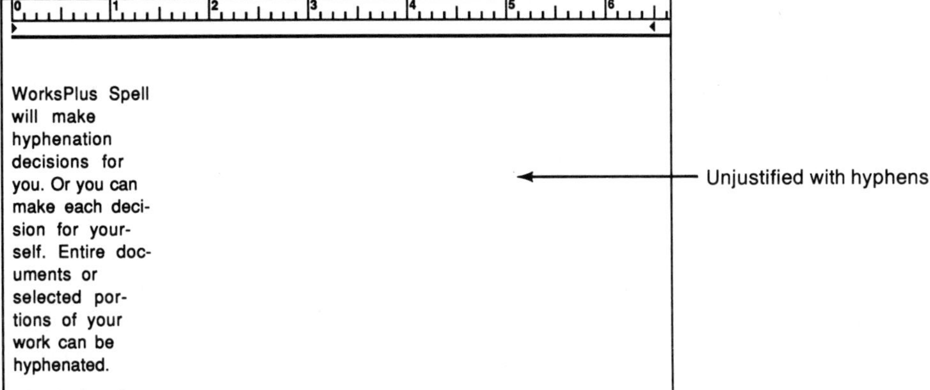

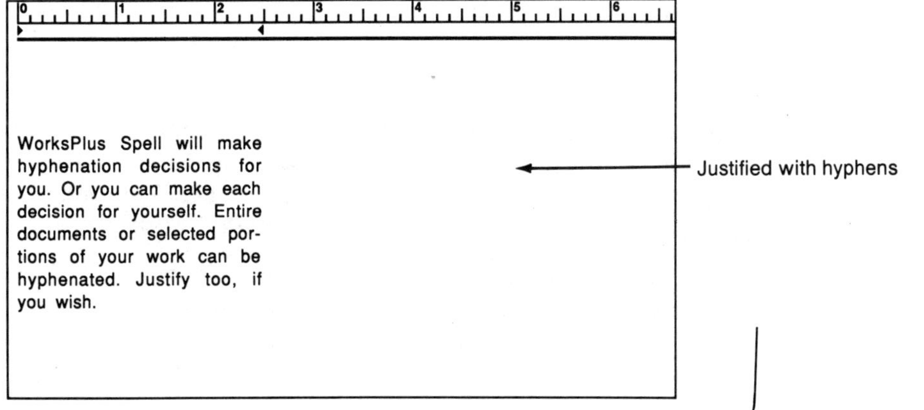

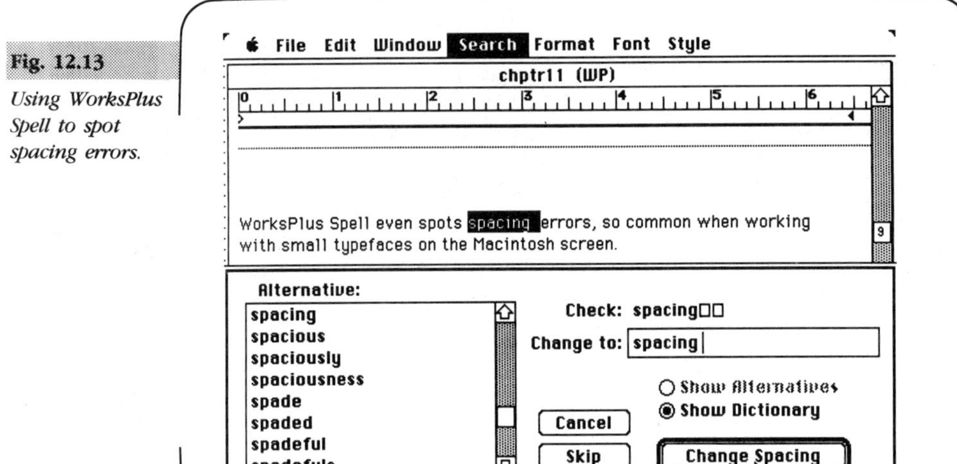

Fig. 12.13
Using WorksPlus Spell to spot spacing errors.

Table 12.4
Examples of Font Sources

Product	*Notes*	*Sold by*
Fluent Fonts™		Casadyware Inc.
Various	Shareware	Educomp
Various	Laser	Allotype Typographics
FONTagenix™	ImageWriter	Devonian International Software Company
LASERgenix™	LaserWriter	Devonian International Software Company

You can add additional fonts or eliminate the standard ones by using the Font/DA Mover program provided in your Apple System Folder. The process is described in your Macintosh manual. Many font manufacturers provide copies of the Font Mover and instructions with their products.

A wide variety of additional fonts are available from font vendors as well as from the public domain. For a list of some sources, see table 12.4.

This is a sample of the Chicago font printed on the laser printer

This is a sample of the Courier font printed on the laser printer

This is a sample of the Geneva font printed on the laser printer

This is a sample of the Helvetica font printed on the laser printer

This is a sample of the New York font printed on the laser printer

This is a sample of the Times font printed on the laser printer

This is a sample of the Venice font printed on the laser printer

This is a sample of the Boston font printed on the ImageWriter

This is a sample of the Athens font printed on the ImageWriter

This is a sample of the Chicago font printed on the ImageWriter

This is a sample of the Geneva font printed on the ImageWriter

This is a sample of the Monaco font printed on the ImageWriter

Fig. 12.14 *ImageWriter and laser printer copies of five standard fonts.*

Remember that additional fonts take up memory and that not all fonts are compatible with all printers. If you have a laser printer, you have to install both screen and printer versions of your fonts. Laser printer owners probably should replace the Boston font with the Helvetica or Times font, which came with your printer. Helvetica and Times are laser fonts and will give you smooth, nice-looking type like that shown in many of the examples in this book. Nonlaser fonts (like the Boston font supplied with Works) can be used on your laser printer, but the characters will be jagged and resemble those you see on your screen. Compare the ImageWriter and laser printer output in figure 12.14. For additional information on this subject, refer to your laser printer manual.

Productivity Tools

Works is a productivity enhancer in its own right, but software vendors have created complementary programs that can speed operations even more. For instance, print spoolers can free Works for other tasks while your printer prints. The Switcher and new MultiFinder utilities, which have been mentioned, let you keep other programs in memory along with Works, thereby speeding the process of moving from one program to another and back.

With other products—Tempo, for example—you can capture long sequences of mouse moves, keystrokes, menu choices, and so on, and then "play them back" at will. At least one company now offers disk-based tutorials that help you learn Works, and still other vendors offer spreadsheet templates that eliminate the need to set up your own spreadsheet equations and formats before performing "what if" analyses. Let's examine a few of these productivity enhancements in more detail.

Spoolers

Works and most other programs usually force you to wait until your printer finishes printing before you can do anything else. If you have a slow printer and a long document containing graphics and fancy fonts, the wait can seem eternal.

Spoolers can solve this problem. When installed on the Mac System disk, a spooler captures the output destined for the printer (see fig. 12.15). The printer then prints ***in the background***, allowing you to do other things with Works or other applications programs.

The better spoolers can keep you informed of printer progress and let you prioritize the printing queue, that is, set the order of items waiting to be printed (see fig. 12.16).

When purchasing a spooler, be sure that it's compatible with Works, your printer(s), your hard disk (if you have one), and any other software you intend to use regularly. And be certain that your computer has enough memory to run the spooler and your other software together.

Table 12.5 lists some of the spoolers available. In the preparation of this book, SuperLaserSpool, by SuperMace Software, Inc., was used with Works, an Apple hard disk, and a PS Jet Laser Printer.

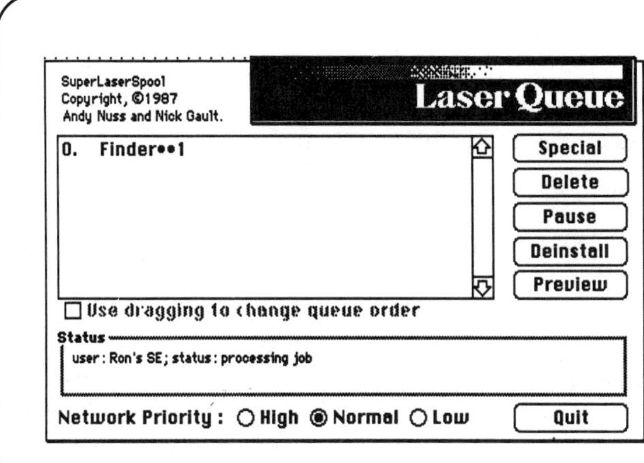

Fig. 12.15 *Using a spooler so that you can work on the Mac while your printer prints.*

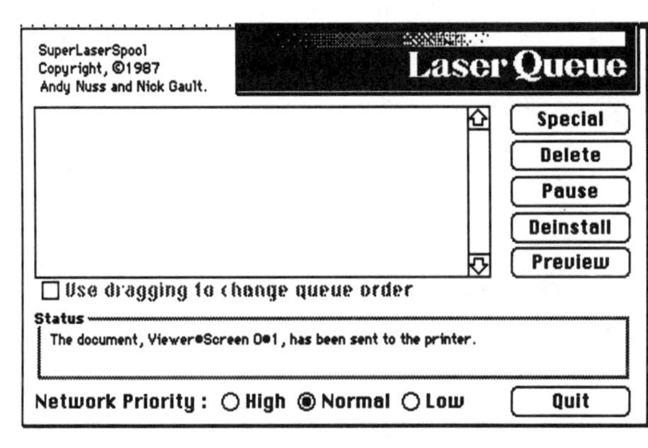

Fig. 12.16 *Printing-in-progress message from spooler.*

Table 12.5
Print Spoolers

Product	*Notes*	*Sold By*
SuperLaserSpool		SuperMac Software, Inc.
LaserServe™		Infosphere, Inc.

Switcher

Apple's Switcher program, which is available from your Apple dealer, assigns portions of your computer's memory to different programs. A program itself, Switcher should be loaded before Works.

As mentioned, Switcher enables you to have Works and something else—like MacPaint or GLUE's Viewer—in memory at the same time. You then can flip quickly back and forth between the applications without having to leave one application to run another.

Theoretically, Switcher can handle up to four applications (see fig. 12.17). Your ability to make full use of Switcher depends on how much memory your Macintosh has and what other package(s) you plan to use with Works. Because Works uses quite a bit of memory, you may find that not enough is left for other big applications like SuperPaint. Switcher tells you when your computer has run out of memory, as shown in figure 12.18.

Switcher also transfers Clipboard contents from one application to another. This is a great way to move MacPaint images to Works with only a few keystrokes or clicks.

Fig. 12.17

The Switcher screen.

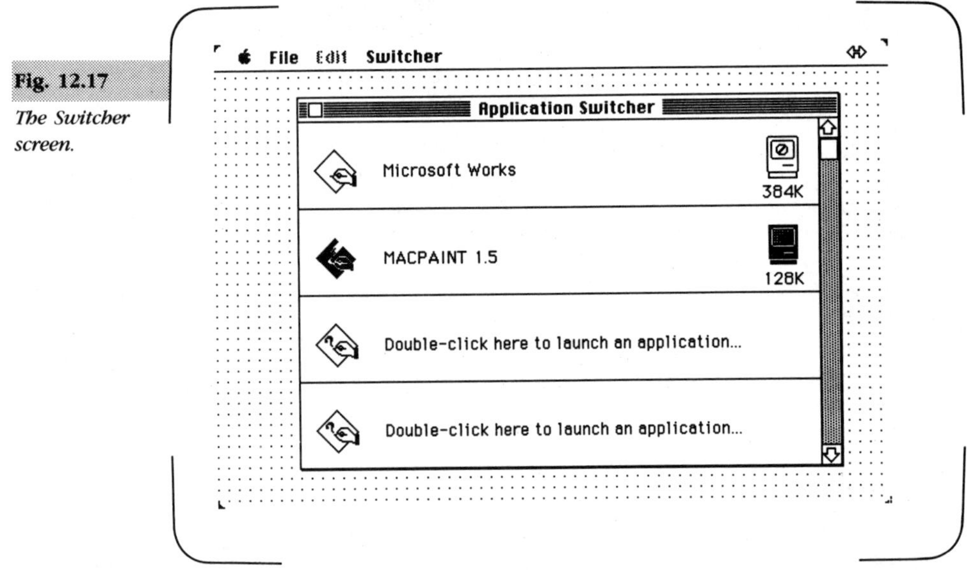

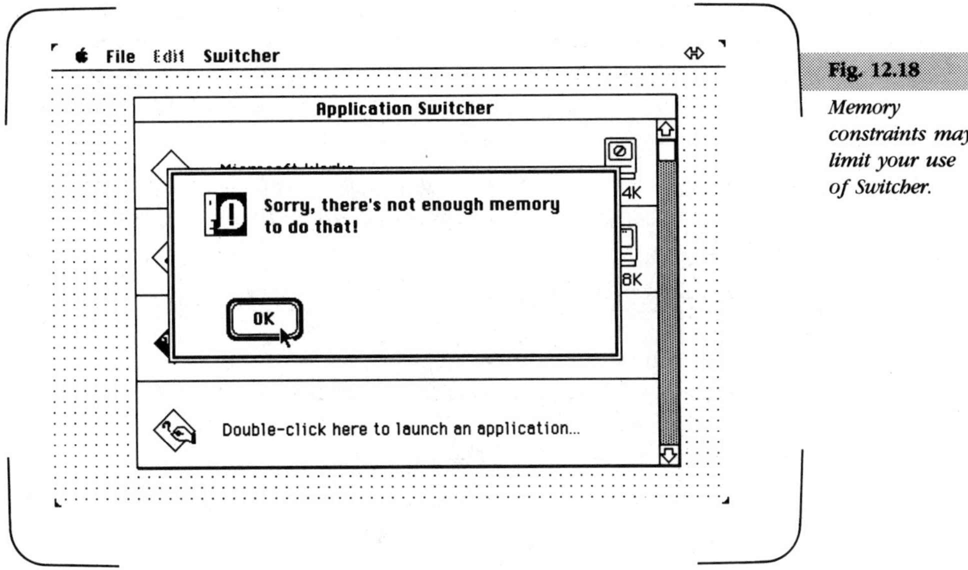

Fig. 12.18
Memory constraints may limit your use of Switcher.

NOTE: Use the latest version of Switcher (5.1 or greater). You may find that the system "locks up" from time to time when switching. Apple says that this problem is the fault of the applications software vendors (like the makers of Works), and the vendors blame the Switcher program. As this book goes to press, Apple is about to release MultiFinder, a program to replace Switcher. I have successfully tested a prerelease version of MultiFinder with Works Version 1.1. Works 1.0 does not work with MultiFinder. For more information, contact your dealer or a users' group.

Macro Makers

Do you find yourself performing the same long sequence of actions over and over again? For example, do you frequently open the same Works database, select the same report, choose the correct printer, and print the report? Do you wish you could make Works have your modem dial a remote computer in the middle of the night (when telephone rates are low), collect your mail, and hang up? If you answered yes to either of these questions, you may want to investigate programs that record and playback macros. These programs, Tempo, for example, can simplify almost any repetitive task.

Essentially, you go through the steps required to accomplish something while the macro maker "watches." Your actions are recorded on disk so that they can be "played back" later with or without your intervention. The better macro programs can even make decisions based on rules you've provided.

Macro programs like Tempo enable you to speed up the creation of Works spreadsheets, databases, reports, word processing, and so on.

Templates and Canned Databases

Setting up a new spreadsheet or database takes time; and entering the data, proofing it, and perfecting the spreadsheet can take even longer. Not surprisingly, some people decide not to undertake major new projects because of these time constraints.

If you're one of these people, consider purchasing the time and talents of others. A number of Works owners have spent time creating spreadsheets and databases in order to balance checkbooks, keep auto expense logs, perform mortgage calculations, do business planning, do engineering tasks, and so forth. For a small fee, these users will share their work with others. They've created spreadsheets called *templates* and collections of data called *canned databases*.

Firms like Heizer Software act as commercial clearinghouses for templates and databases. These companies offer programs of general interest—such as loan-calculation spreadsheets and telephone-area-code databases—as well as software specifically for engineers, pilots, and so on. Write or telephone these companies for their catalogs.

Local Macintosh users' groups and bulletin board services are also excellent sources of templates and databases. Check with your Macintosh dealer for names of users' groups and bulletin board services.

Information Exchange Devices

In an ideal world, you could take any word-processing document, database, or spreadsheet created on your computer, and use that file on any other machine, regardless of its make or model. But the world is far from ideal. As the number of computer brands and models increases, system compatibility becomes a major stumbling block to the exchange of information.

Manufacturers routinely select incompatible disk drives, file storage techniques, graphics standards, operating systems, and other design approaches that are beyond the scope of this book. The result is an almost numbing array of compatibility problems. Sometimes, the manufacturers do this on purpose.

Recently, computer hardware manufactures, software developers, and conversion specialists have started addressing this problem. They're doing so for two reasons. First, they're eager to have their new products coexist with today's massive "installed base" of computer hardware and software. And, second, users are demanding a simple way to upgrade to fewer products and share information among themselves. Works provides some powerful features to facilitate such exchanges.

Hardware Issues

Exchanging Works information with another Macintosh user usually is easier than exchanging information with another brand of machine. Although two Macintosh disk formats exist, they're more or less compatible, at least from an information exchange standpoint. Basically, all you need to do is take a disk to the other user's machine and copy files as needed. Users also can exchange files through modems.

If you need to exchange Works data with dissimilar machines (IBM PCs, for example), things are a bit trickier because the disk drives most likely are incompatible. Modems can help in these situations. If the dissimilar machines are in close proximity, you may be able to "hard wire" them by using a simple cable, thereby eliminating the need for modems and telephone lines. Another way to accomplish the exchange is to use a local area network that can accommodate both types of machines.

Compatibility Issues

Getting information from one machine's disk to another's does not solve the more serious software compatibility problems. Program files rarely run on dissimilar systems. For instance, you can't copy Microsoft Works to an IBM PC disk and then use the IBM PC to run the Works program. Files containing data—for example, word-processing text and database records—however, can frequently be used by different machines. But the files must first be "converted" or cleaned up (usually, but not always).

Some types of files that were designed to be exchanged work with little or no modification. The rest of this chapter deals with specific exchange and conversion procedures.

Data Exchange Standards

When two products (such as Works and Excel) create files that use the same standard, exchanging accurate data is much easier. A number of data exchange standards have evolved over time. Works supports several standards, including the following:

SYLK (short for Symbolic Link)

ASCII (also sometimes called text files)

Tab-separated fields within Return-separated records

Multiple-space-separated fields within Return-separated records

Standards are loose definitions at best. Most vendors, for example, have their own "dialect" of ASCII. They usually can agree on how to represent letters and numbers electronically; but exchanges of special symbols, underscore instructions, commands for boldface printing, and so on, are more complicated. Because of these problems, more and more companies are offering conversion programs, which act as intermediaries in the exchange process.

Built-In Works Conversion Features

Microsoft Works has some specific features that enable you to import information from selected non-Works programs. These features let you upgrade from a word-processing package like MacWrite to the power of Works without retyping all your frequently used MacWrite documents. You also can export items created by Works to programs like Aldus' PageMaker and similar desktop publishers. Moreover, you can exchange Works spreadsheets with many of today's popular stand-alone spreadsheet programs, such as Excel and Multiplan.

Although compatibility issues sometimes arise, the exchanges listed in table 12.6 are relatively easy to make.

Importing Word-Processing Text

You can easily import non-Works text files for use in a word-processing window.

Table 12.6
Ways Works Information Can Be Converted

From	*To*
Microsoft Word	Works word processing
MacWrite	Works word processing
Most ASCII word-processing files	Works word processing
Works word processing	Most desktop publishers
Works word processing	Most ASCII word processors
Works word processing	Most SYLK word processors
Excel spreadsheets	Works spreadsheets
Multiplan spreadsheets	Works spreadsheets
Works spreadsheets	Excel spreadsheets
Works spreadsheets	Multiplan spreadsheets
Most ASCII databases	Works databases
Works databases	Most ASCII databases

Before you begin, print a copy of the document you intend to convert, using the original word-processing software (Word, MacWrite, and so on). Then, you can refer to that hard copy to see what the finished conversion should look like. Use the following procedure to import Microsoft Word, MacWrite, and other ASCII files; but don't use it to import SYLK files.

1. Choose the Open option on the File menu.
2. Click on the Word Processor icon.
3. Click the Import File box. You'll see lists of ASCII files and folders containing ASCII files (see fig. 12.19).
4. Double-click on the desired file.

If all goes well, the resulting text file is usable, more or less. You may need to reformat it, change margins, add tabs, adjust page endings, and so on. Figure 12.20 shows a file immediately after it is imported. Figure 12.21 shows the "fixed" file. You also may need to change fonts, add underscoring, and make other stylistic adjustments.

Sometimes imported documents are a mess. Take figure 12.22, for example. Either this file wasn't really an ASCII document to begin with, or it's a nearly unusable dialect of ASCII. In such cases, you can delete the unwanted characters; however, if the document is large, that process may be more trouble than it's worth.

Fig. 12.19

Importing by highlighting the Word Processor icon and clicking Import File on the Open File screen.

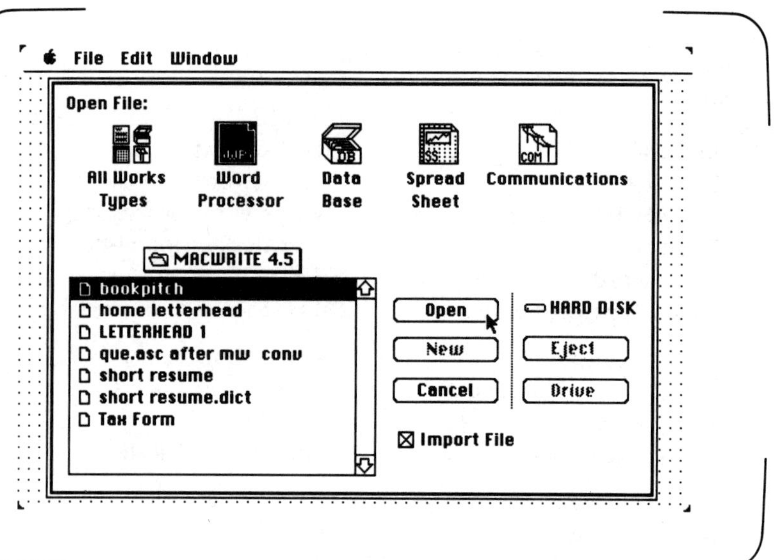

Fig. 12.20

Part of an imported file with a few problems.

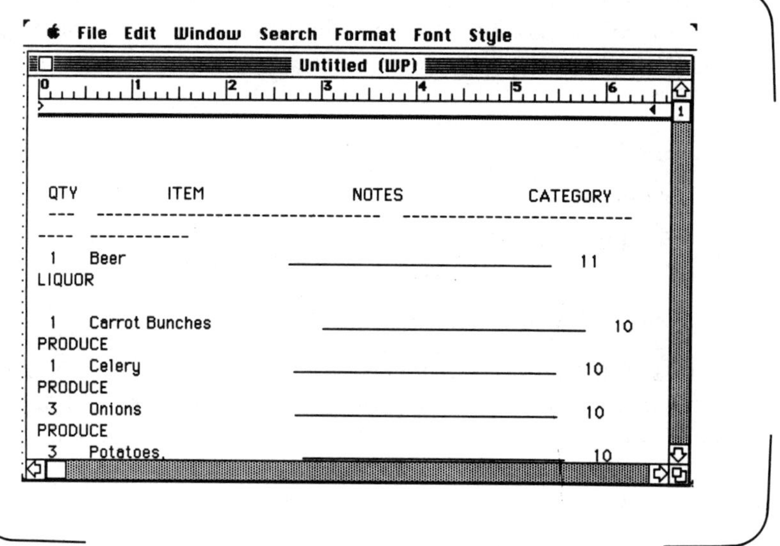

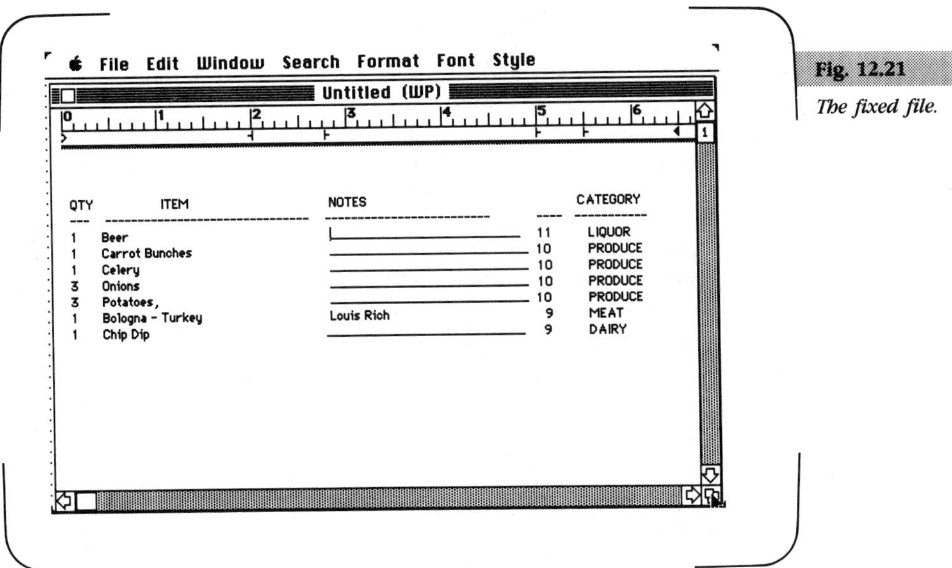

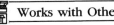

Fig. 12.21

The fixed file.

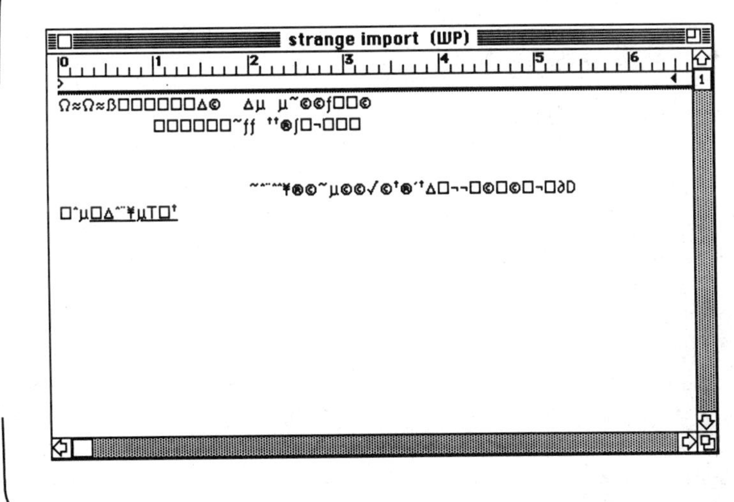

Fig. 12.22

An imported file with big problems.

Exporting Word-Processing Text

Many word-processing software packages, such as MacWrite, Microsoft Word, and WriteNow, can import ASCII (or text only) documents. And many desktop publishing packages—for example, PageMaker—also accept ASCII text.

For these reasons, you may want to save a Works word-processing file without pictures or formatting information. Then, other programs —word processors and desktop publishers, for instance—can use the text more easily. The process is an extension of the Save As technique you've already used. You tell Works that you want to export the file by clicking the Export File box in the Save Document As dialog box, as illustrated in figure 12.23.

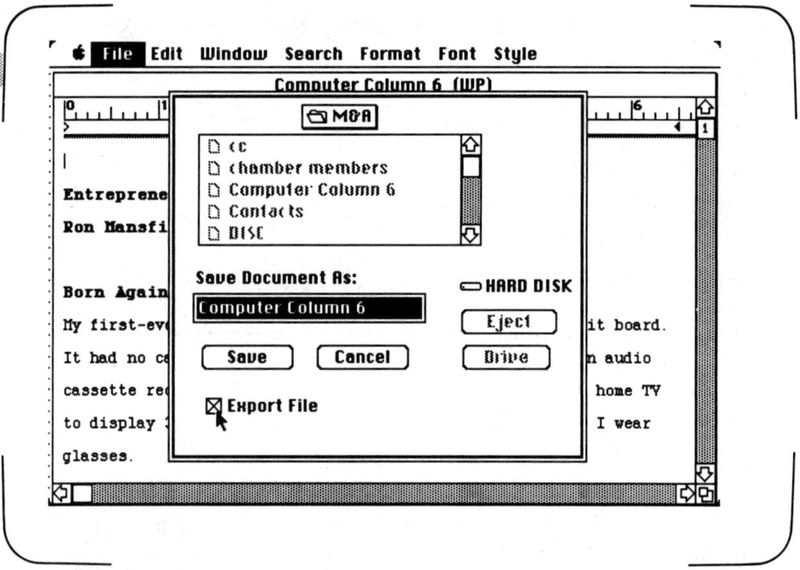

Fig. 12.23

Checking the Export File box in the Save Document As dialog box.

When you choose this option, Works strips the Works files of formatting characters and attributes. The resulting file contains only "vanilla" text—without boldface, underscores, tabs, pictures, font information, and so on. The file can be read by most programs that accept ASCII characters.

NOTE: Some of Apple's special characters—foreign accents, *option* and *command* characters, and so forth—may not be compatible with those of the importing system—if these characters are saved in your ASCII file at all. Be sure to proofread the results of your exports and imports carefully.

Each importing program (MacWrite, PageMaker, and so on) uses a slightly different technique to load and use ASCII files. MacWrite, for instance, requires you to open ASCII files only from the Finder by first selecting the ASCII document icon, then shift-clicking the MacWrite icon. You need to ferret out the details for your particular application or ask for experienced help.

Most desktop publishing packages accept ASCII text from Works. Increasingly, desktop publishing software such as PageMaker Version 2 can import Works files without converting them to ASCII. PageMaker Version 2 can even import pictures that have been pasted into your documents.

Converting Spreadsheets

Plenty of good reasons for converting spreadsheets exist. For example, a friend or associate may have developed (on a dissimilar computer system) a template that you want to use. Or you may want to buy a template that's available for only Excel or Multiplan. Or you may use a stand-alone spreadsheet program at home and use Works in the office. Whatever the motivation, you need to keep in mind several points.

First, no two spreadsheet packages are identical, even if they're sold by the same company. For example, Works and Excel both come from Microsoft, but they offer different features. If the spreadsheet you plan to convert uses features not supported by both the source and the destination products, problems arise. Sometimes you can work around them by redesigning the source spreadsheet or by using one technique on the source spreadsheet and a different approach on the destination spreadsheet.

Obviously, this process can be confusing and time-consuming. Developing a new spreadsheet from scratch may be quicker than converting and testing one. This factor is particularly true if you want to convert a complex spreadsheet created on a feature-rich product like Excel for use with Works.

Second, Works represents numeric values differently than many other spreadsheet programs do. For example, Works ignores the formatting of values contained in SYLK files and treats all numeric values as if they were in General format. Works also treats as text Date and Time formats sent by source files.

Third, Works, Excel, and Multiplan all treat error values differently; and Works supports fewer operators than Excel or Multiplan. Specifically, Works doesn't support union, concatenation, or intersection operators.

Finally, computations containing or resulting in extremely small and extremely large numbers may produce slightly different results from package to package. The three programs also handle logical values (And, Or, True, False, and Not) differently. As for special functions, Works sometimes treats them differently or doesn't support them at all. Table 12.7 compares the three programs.

Table 12.7
Different Functions in Microsoft Works, Excel, and Multiplan

Function	*Works*	*Excel 1.04*	*Multiplan*
ACOS	X	X	
AREAS		X	
ASIN	X	X	
ATAN2	X	X	
CHOOSE	X	X	
COLUMN		X	X
COLUMNS		X	
DATE		X	
DAVERAGE		X	
DAY		X	
DCOUNT		X	
DEGREES	X		
DELTA			X
DMAX		X	
DMIN		X	
DOLLAR		X	X
DSTDEV		X	
DSUM		X	

Function	*Works*	*Excel 1.04*	*Multiplan*
DVAR		X	
ERROR	X		
FIXED		X	X
GROWTH		X	
HLOOKUP*	X	X	
HOUR		X	
INDEX (Form 2)		X	
ISBLANK	X		
ISREF		X	
ITERCNT			X
LEN		X	X
LINEST		X	
LOGEST		X	
LOOKUP (Form 2)		X	
MATCH*	X	X	
MID		X	X
MINUTE		X	
MONTH		X	
NOW		X	
RADIANS	X		
RAND	X	X	
REPT		X	X
ROW		X	X
ROWS		X	
SEARCH		X	
SECOND		X	

Continued on next page

Table 12.7—*continued*

Function	*Works*	*Excel 1.04*	*Multiplan*
SSUM	X		
TEXT		X	
TIME		X	
TRANSPOSE**		X	
TREND		X	
TYPE*	X	X	
VALUE		X	X
VAR	X	X	
VLOOKUP*	X	X	
WEEKDAY		X	
YEAR		X	

* The Works implementation of this function is more general than that of the others. If you use the function in a form acceptable to Excel, Works gives the same result that Excel does. Works also allows some inputs that Excel does not.

** In Works, the TRANSPOSE operation is available as an option in the Paste with Options command.

Importing and Exporting Spreadsheets

You can import non-Works spreadsheets to Works by using one of two standards: SYLK or Text with Values/Formulas. If the source spreadsheet supports SYLK file formats, use that method of exchange. Microsoft Excel and Multiplan both create SYLK files for export to Works. SYLK files contain the labels, values, equations, formats, type attributes, and so forth.

The second spreadsheet importing option, Text with Values/Formulas, is useful when the source spreadsheet program creates files with cell contents separated by tabs and row endings indicated by Return characters. Works always loads these files beginning in cell A1.

Regardless of which importing standard you use, you must perform one extra step to open a new spreadsheet: Click the Import File box, as shown in figure 12.24. You do so before you click the Open button or double-click on the file desired.

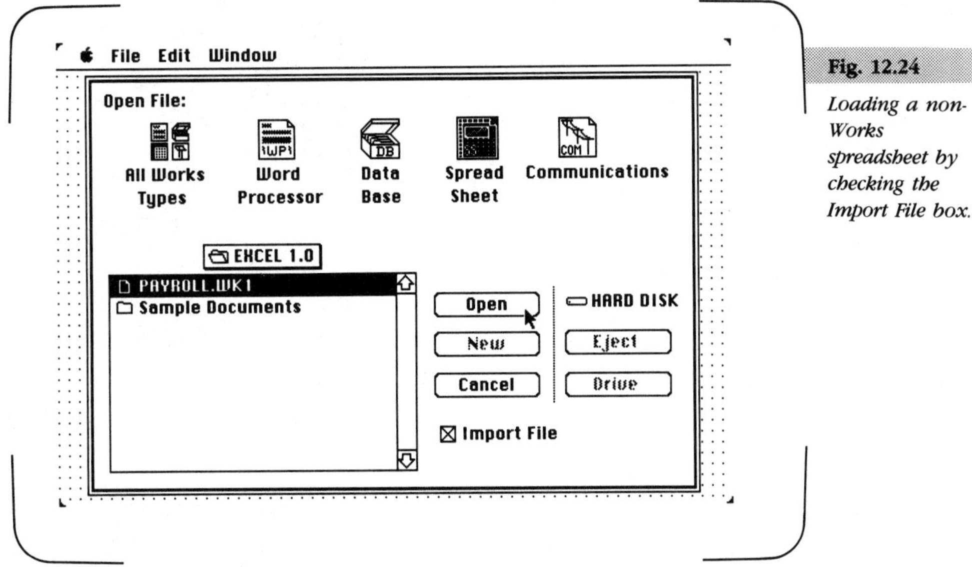

Fig. 12.24

Loading a non-Works spreadsheet by checking the Import File box.

You may then be presented with a list of files to import. Simply because a file name appears in the list, however, does not guarantee that the file contains a spreadsheet or that the file can be imported accurately. If no list is displayed, the disk may contain "foreign" files—or files that Works can't reorganize.

Pick a file by double-clicking, or highlight a name and click the OK button. Because you clicked the Import File box when you started to load a spreadsheet, you're given another choice at this point. Works asks you whether you want it to load the file by using the SYLK standard or to treat the file as Text with Values/Formulas (see fig. 12.25). Click the appropriate choice.

A blank spreadsheet appears, and Works begins to import and convert the spreadsheet. In the upper right corner of the spreadsheet, Works tells you what percentage of the spreadsheet has been converted. Eventually, the converted spreadsheet appears. As illustrated in figure 12.26, sometimes the spreadsheet does not convert. Works advises you of conversion problems with a warning message (see fig. 12.27).

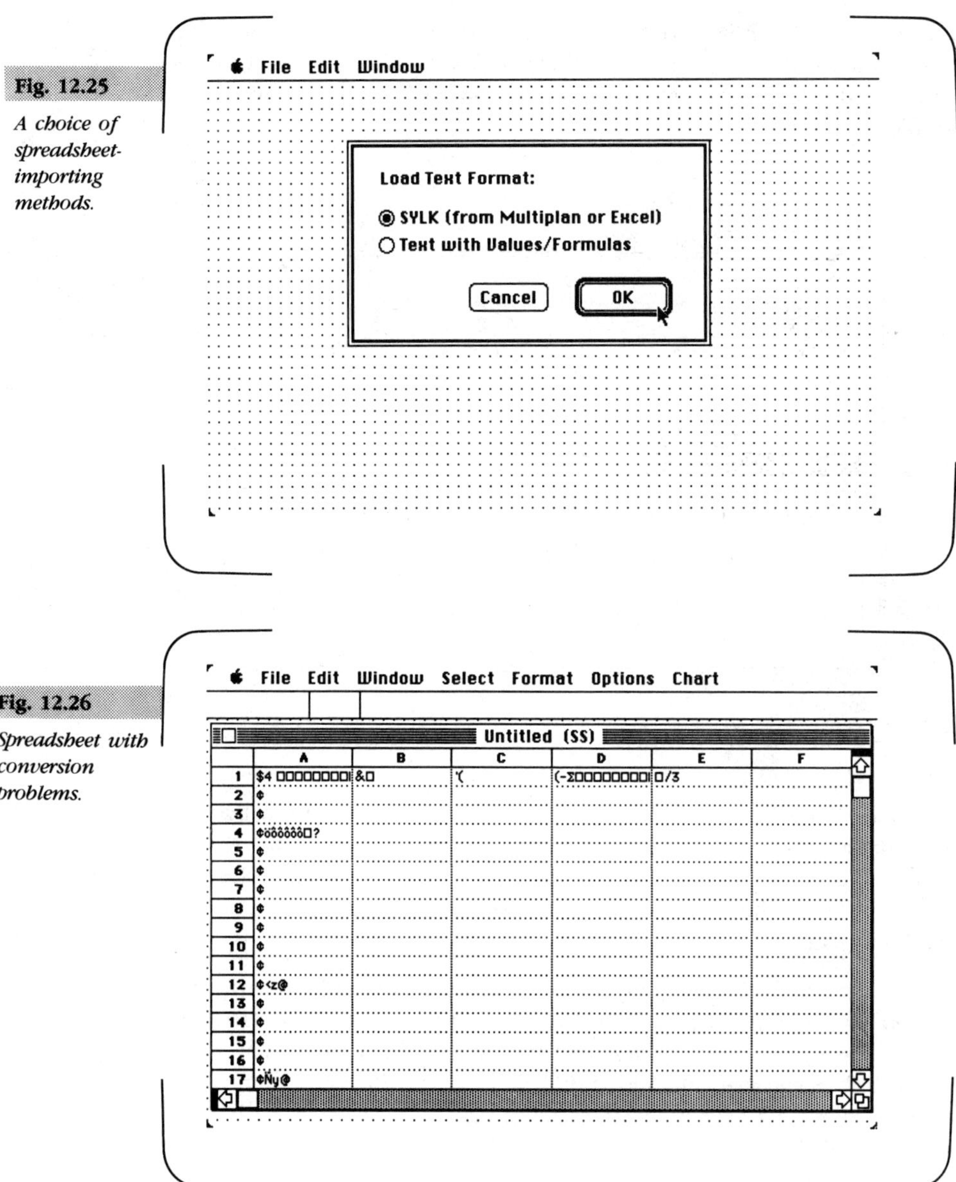

Fig. 12.25

A choice of spreadsheet-importing methods.

Fig. 12.26

Spreadsheet with conversion problems.

CAUTION: A spreadsheet may convert without any warning message from Works or may look all right after conversion takes place, but still not perform properly. You should subject the imported spreadsheet to all the testing you perform on any new design.

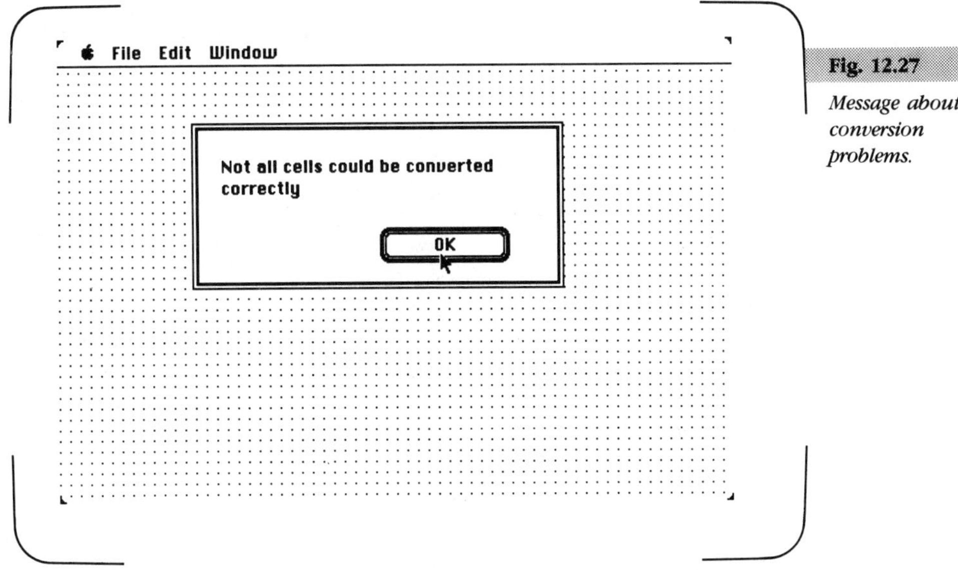

Fig. 12.27
Message about conversion problems.

You can export Works spreadsheets for use by Excel, Multiplan, and other spreadsheet packages. And you can export text versions of spreadsheets for use in word-processing packages. To access the SYLK, Text Only, and Text with Values/Formulas options, you click the Export File box in the Save Document As dialog box. Your choice will vary according to how you plan to use the exported file. If you plan to load the file into Excel or Multiplan, you should use SYLK to obtain the best results. If you choose the Text with Values Only option in the Save Text As dialog box, Works creates an ASCII file that most text editors and desktop publishing systems can use.

Exchanging Databases

On the surface, database conversion looks pretty straightforward when compared to spreadsheet conversion. Either the source data arrives properly or it doesn't. But data must be used after it's converted, and for this reason database conversion requires some forethought.

Think about how you plan to use the imported data. If you need a feature like date math, which is not provided by Works 1.0 or 1.1, you may not be wise to spend a great deal of time converting your Omnis® data into a Works database format. On the other hand, such Works database features as the list view make Works a powerful tool for many applications that other systems can't handle.

Before you convert big database files, do some quick testing. Enter a few records manually, and see whether Works (or any other destination database package) can handle your application. Large data conversions take time, and working for hours only to find that you need a feature not provided by the destination database is frustrating. Think before you click.

You also need to consider available memory. Remember that Works stores databases entirely in memory when using them. Some (but not all) other database programs use the disk for working storage and can frequently hold more records than Works. A big database may need to be divided into several smaller ones if Works is to use it, and this procedure is not always practical. You also need to understand something about the way the source database exports or imports information. So many variations exist that an entire book could be devoted to the subject of database conversion. The following information is enough to get you started with experiments of your own.

Using Popular Database Exchange Formats

For a database to import records from another database, the receiving database needs to "know" something about how the sender's fields and records are separated. This information is necessary to keep all items from a record together. Many different methods are available; Works supports three of the most popular:

- Tab-separated fields in records separated by Return characters
- Fields separated by multiple spaces
- Field count

Tab-Separated Fields

Many Macintosh database packages use fields separated by tabs and contained in records separated by Returns. As you may recall, this method is used to a prepare word-processing document for conversion to a database.

Fields Separated by Multiple Spaces

Using fields separated by multiple spaces is a risky way to import data: A simple typo anywhere in a field can ruin the rest of the conversion. Works simply looks for any occurrence of two contiguous spaces anywhere in the database and starts a new field. If the spaces are accidental (or intentionally typed within the contents of the field), the conversion is flawed. Use other conversion methods whenever possible.

Fixed-Field Formats

Some databases can export a specific number of fields per record, regardless of whether the fields are empty or not; these databases are sometimes called *fixed-field formats.* You simply tell Works how many fields to expect from each record. The rest is automatic—providing, of course, that the source file always contains a fixed number of fields per record.

Importing Databases

Before importing a database, you may want to print it. You can then use this hard copy to see what the finished conversion should look like.

In figure 12.28, data is being imported from a non-Works database.

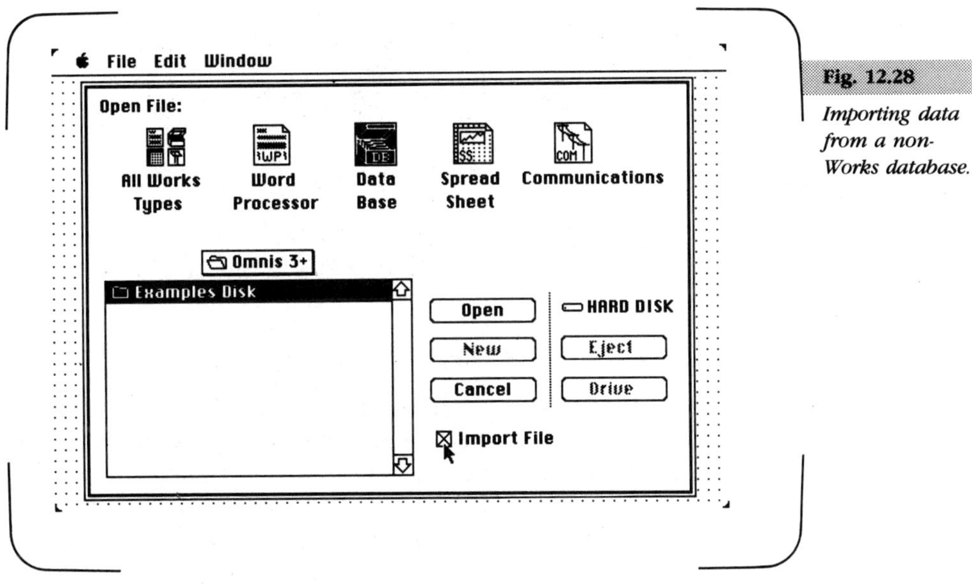

Fig. 12.28

Importing data from a non-Works database.

To import a database, you do the following:

1. Invoke the Open option on the File menu.
2. Click the Data Base icon.
3. Click the Import File box, as shown in figure 12.28. Works then displays ASCII files and folders containing ASCII files.
4. Double-click or highlight the appropriate file and click OK.

5. A new dialog box appears, as shown in figure 12.29. Select the appropriate import method—tabs, spaces, and so on. Works then imports the data.

6. Rename, rearrange, and resize the fields, if necessary.

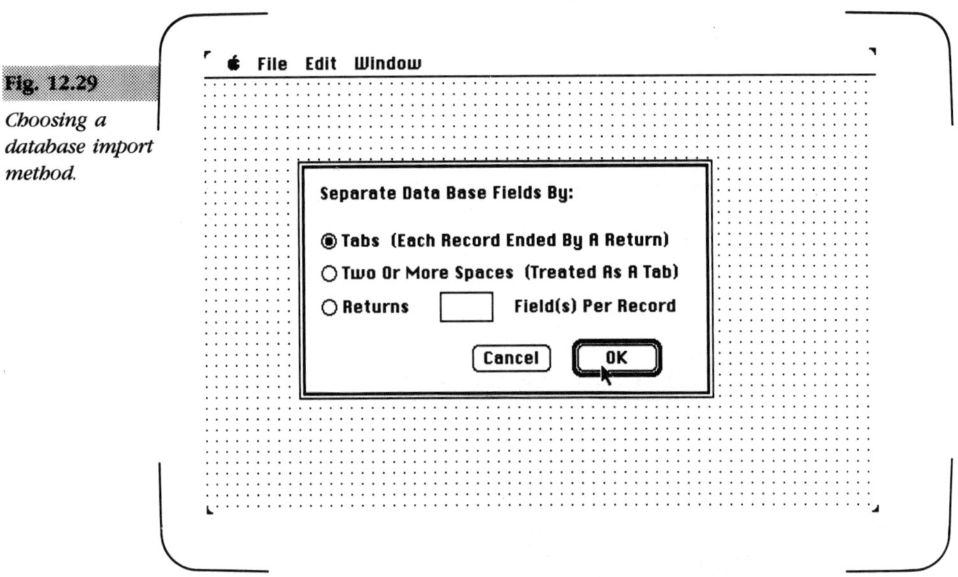

Fig. 12.29

Choosing a database import method.

Exporting Databases

You can export entire Works databases for use by other database packages, or you can export only selected records. To access these options, click the Export File box in the Save Document As dialog box (see fig. 12.30). Works exports records separated by Return characters; the fields within those records are separated by tabs.

Here's what you do:

1. Rearrange the order of the fields if necessary.

2. Choose Save As from the Edit menu.

3. Click the Export File box.

4. Click the Save Selected Records Only box, if appropriate.

5. Define selection criteria, if appropriate, using the selection methods explained in Chapter 8.

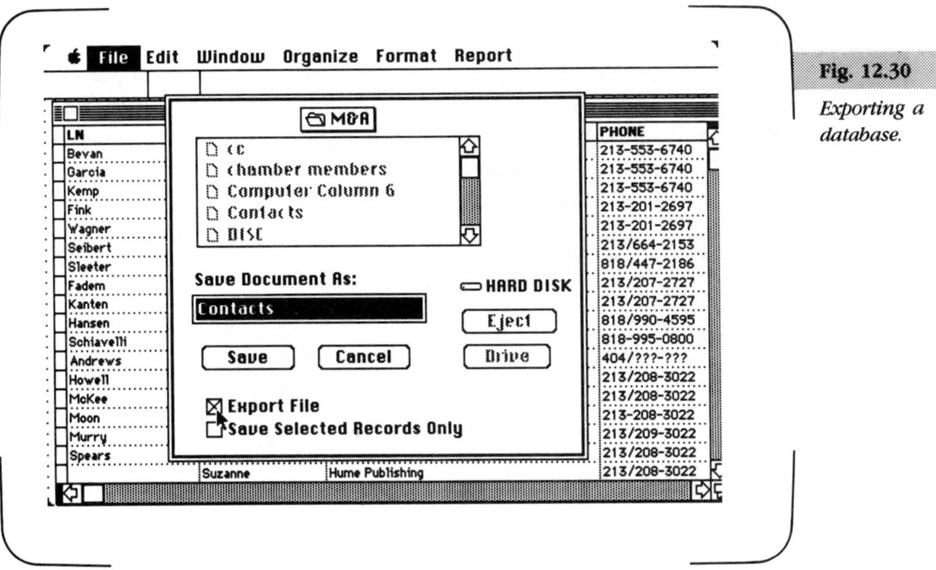

Fig. 12.30

Exporting a database.

6. Name the destination file.
7. Click the OK button.

Each importing database package uses a slightly different technique to load and use imported files. You need to find out the details for your particular application or ask for experienced help.

Networks

Networks enable groups of users to share information quickly without a great deal of disk swapping. Macintosh network examples include AppleShare and TOPS. Works Version 1.1 permits one (and only one) Works user to launch a single copy of Works. Each network user is expected to purchase his or her own copy of Works. Multiple users can "look at" the same Works file, but only the first person to open a file can change it.

Increasingly, networks are capable of supporting mixed computer types. TOPS, for instance, was designed to integrate Macintosh and IBM systems. Obviously, networks like these can be used in the conversion and data exchange processes described in this chapter. For instance, the TOPS network was used to convert the original Macintosh version of the text in this book manuscript into the IBM format required by the publisher.

Conclusion

That's it! If you've read this entire book, you've learned about a fascinating and powerful tool that enables you to organize your professional and personal life while adding some fun and style to even the most boring tasks. No doubt you'll discover new applications, techniques, and shortcuts as you use Works.

Resources

AD-Techs
7220 Old Kent Road
Amarillo, TX 79109
806/353-7063

Alternative Enterprises
3300 Jarrettsville Pike
Monkton, MD 21111
301/557-9670

Ann Arbor Softworks, Inc.
308-1/2 South State Street
Ann Arbor, MI 48104
313/996-3838

Apple Computer, Inc.
20525 Mariani Avenue
Cupertino, CA 95014
408/996-1010

Cassady Company
P.O. Box 223779
Carmel, CA 93922
408/646-4660

CompuServe
Information Services
P.O. Box 20212
5000 Arlington Centre Blvd.
Columbus, OH 43220
614/457-0802
(Time-sharing services)

Devonian International Software
P.O. Box 2351
Montclair, CA 91763
714/621-0973

Challenger Software
Corporation
18350 Kedzie Avenue
Homewood, IL 60430
312/957-3475

CompuCraft
P.O. Box 3155
Englewood, CO 80155
303/850-7472

Decision Science Software
P.O. Box 1483
Sugar Land, TX 77487
713/491-0073

EDUCOMP Computer Services
742 Genevive, Suite D
Solana Beach, CA 92075
619/259-0255
(Public domain and shareware, fonts, desk accessories, and more)

Dynamic Graphics
6000 North Forest Park Drive
Peoria, IL 61614
309/668-8800

Enabling Technologies
600 South Dearborne Street, #1304
Chicago, IL 60605
312/427-0408

Heizer Software
1941 Oak Park Blvd., Suite 30
Pleasant Hill, CA 94523
415/943-7667
(Templates, tutorials, and databases for Works and Excel)

Image Club Graphics
2828 19th Street, NE
Calgary, Alberta
Canada T2E 6Y9
403/250-1969

ImageWorld, Inc.
P.O. Box 10415
Eugene, OR 97440
503/485-0395

Infosphere, Inc.
4730 SW Macadam Avenue
Portland, OR 97201
503/226-3620

Kensington Microware
251 Park Avenue
New York, NY 10010
212/475-5200

Lundeen & Associates
P.O. Box 30083
Oakland, CA 94604
415/893-7587

Magnum Software
21115 Devonshire Street, #337
Chatsworth, CA 91311
818/700-0510

MicroMaps
P.O. Box 757
Lambertville, NJ 08530
212/850-6788

NewsNet
945 Haverford Road
Bryn Mawer, PA 19010
800/345-1301
(Time-sharing service)

Pleasant Graphic Ware
P.O. Box 506
Pleasant Hill, OR 97455
503/741-1401

Silicon Beach Software, Inc.
9580 Black Mountain Road,
Suite E
P.O. Box 261430
San Diego, CA 92126
619/695-6956

Simon and Schuster Software
One Gulf and Western Plaza
New York, NY 10023
212/333-2882

Solutions, Inc.
29 Main Street
P.O. Box 989
Montpelier, VT 05602
802/229-9146

The Source
Source Telecomputing
Corporation
1616 Anderson Road
McLean, VA 22102
703/821-6666
(Time-sharing services)

Springboard Software, Inc.
7808 Creekridge Circle
Minneapolis, MN 55435
612/944-3912

Sunshine
P.O. Box 4351
Austin, TX 78765
512/453-2334

SuperMac Software
950 N Rengstorff Avenue
Mountain View, CA 94043
415/964-8884

T/Maker Graphics
T/Maker Company
2115 Landings Drive
Mountain View, CA 94043
415/962-0195

Thunderware
21 Orinda Way
Orinda, CA 94563
415/254-6581

Wiley Professional Software
605 Third Avenue
New York, NY 10158
212/850-6788

B

Macintosh-Related Bulletin Boards

Commercial vendors provide access to information on a variety of subjects, from health and economics to trivia about the coffee industry. Moreover, many of the service vendors, CompuServe and The Source, for example, offer entertainment and electronic mail features, as well. The electronic mail (E-Mail) service provides computer users with the opportunity to communicate with other users through a central computer that acts like an electronic post office, with each subscriber getting a "post office box." You also can connect with free or lowcost bulletin board systems (BBS) run by hobbyists. See Appendix A for phone numbers and addresses of commercial services.

Following are two Macintosh-oriented bulletin board lists, directly from the actual bulletin board services. Because the services are free or charge a minimal fee, the bulletin boards appear and disappear regularly. Telephone numbers are accurate at the time of printing, but the numbers can change or be disconnected altogether.

EMACINTOSH BBS LIST (by Dennis Runkle)

— Dates refer to most recent mention I've seen on some other board
— Sysop names listed when known, with [CompuServe]/<DELPHI ID> if known
Please contact me via CompuServe [76174,374] or Delphi <CLEVEBURG> E-Mail for corrections/updates/deletions/etc. — Dennis Runkle
— PLEASE leave additions or deletions to this file ONLINE HERE on The HOTLINE Databoard (818) 766-6442.

===

THE ACTIVE WINDOW	201-384-8409	3/31/86 Brian ODowd [71236,455]
Super 68 BBS	212-927-6919	4/16/86
St. Elsewhere................	213-273-8489	
LA MUG BBS................	213-397-8966	11/11/85
Byte BBS	213-536-2651	8/4/85 RBBS
Ye Olde Pawn Shoppe........	213-659-2142	10/6/86 12/2400 baud
MacBBS	213-732-9131	10/21/85
Winter Springs BBS	305-699-1741	4/9/86 RR Host
The Rest of Us (TRoU) BBS ..	312-729-8768	4/5/86 Steve Levinthal <FAILSAFE>
		3/12/2400; TRoU MUG;
		voice validation reqd
Salt City BBS	315-451-7790	9/29/86 IBM Sysop: Mark Manning
		Mac Sysop: Eric Larson [73547,2716]
		Genie: EHLARSON; 300/1200; 24 hr
Mac BBS....................	319-381-4761	4/2/86 Mike Petersen <SKYGOD>
		SYNAPSE (Quebec Mac Club). 418-658-6955
		10/4/86 Martin Durand [76064,224]
		French version of RR Host; French
		only
Fido HOST 122..............	503-269-5202	4/4/86 Randy Bush — Modula2 group
UCSD Pascal Programmer BB..	503-581-1791	9/5/86 Henry Carstens [74166,3135]
		10pm-5am Sun-Thur
The Lifeboat	512-926-9582	Micro Analyst Mac Zap patch files
MIES BBS..................	609-228-1149	5/8/86 Tom Dolby [75226,1223] RR Host
		3/12/2400 baud, formerly TIES BBS?
N.I.C.E	614-890-7944	4/11/86 Frank Nichols, RR Host BBS
RRHost BBS.................	617-577-1652	4/8/86 until 6/1/86
Macro Ex...................	617-667-7388	5/6/86 Mac section
Sears BBS..................	617-843-6743	5/6/86 IBM/Mac software
Termexec...................	617-863-0282	5/6/86 300 baud
San Diego MUG	619-462-6236	8/3/85 MEBBS aka TeleMac
Cabbie BBS	619-565-1634	11/11/85
Tele-Mac BBS (SDMUG)......	619-582-7572	12/17/85 $12/yr/MEBBS-Delphi-SDMUG
Computer Merchant..........	619-582-9557	10/21/85
The Desktop	714-491-1003	8/3/85 — introduce yourself to the
		Sysops for access to up/download area
Dana Point BBS..............	714-493-0256	10/21/85 Weekends
MAC-UCI	714-494-6629	7/2/85
Hitchhiker's Guide to Mac	714-495-7281	11/5/85
The Roadhouse..............	714-533-6967{	
The Fireworks Co	714-537-1693	
Tavern (Mac Section)........	714-538-3103	2nd LINE ..714-541-6225

Chemical Energy	714-557-6483	
High Society/ Mouse Tracks	714-557-8467	evenings & weekends
Sunrise Express	714-558-7979	10/21/85
The Thieves Guild	714-671-0467	
IF Magazine PMS	714-772-8868	
Electric Warehouse	714-775-2560	
The Secret Service	714-776-7223	
Ancient Rome II	714-830-0400	
Computrends Fido BBS	714-856-1029	7/2/85 Dave Broudy/6-9P M-F/all wknd
		— 6pm - 9am M-F, all weekend
Ancient Rome	714-859-5857	
Mac Orange BBS	714-895-6041	
THE Mousehole	714-921-2252	8/19/85 Rusty Hodge
		— occasionally open for NEW members
		connections to MacTutor magazine
BBS FreedomLine 86	714-924-1189	9/6/86 Eric Dorn
Riverside, CA Mac BBS	714-924-8114	8/2/85
Graphic Violence	714-974-1650	
Computique BBS	714-990-2756	(300 BAUD)
Fido BBS	805-522-4211	7/8/85
J.C.International	805-688-6276	10/21/85
Midnight Magic	808-623-1085	4/6/86 Mike Clary [70366,774]
		3/12/2400
		RR Host BBS — Mililani, Hawaii
San Gabriel MUG	818-355-7641	10/21/85
San Gabriel Valley MUG	818-796-5042	10/28/85 Bryan Menell
Programmer's Haven	818-798-6819	9/29/85 Chuck Wannall — 20 hrs/day
Computer Connexion	818-810-7464	12/28/85
The Apple Bus	818-919-5459	8/24/85 Solely Mac User Grp (SMUG)
Magic Slate	818-967-5534	10/21/85
MacASM BBS	818-991-5037	6/20/85 Yves Lempereur

Press <SPACE-BAR>_

Hello! Here are some more computer-accessible Bulletin Board Systems that are unique! That is, they cater to a unique or specific service. The boards listed are supposedly available 24 hours and, hopefully, have at least 50% of their messages and bulletins related to the boards' unique topic. There are vast numbers of excellent dating/matching boards, multiline chat, game/fantasy, role-playing, and general-topic uploading/downloading type boards across the country; however, to include them here would defeat the purpose of this list.

Because of the volatile nature of BBS's, the user of this list will assume all responsibility for use of its data. Be considerate when using a silent modem; that "NO CARRIER" you may have detected may have just awakened somebody's Aunt Mildred. Final versions of this list are permitted to be distributed in any manner, provided it is in its original and unaltered form.

Updates to this list are more than welcome and very much appreciated!

Please forward as much information about the BBS as possible in either of the following manners:

by E-mail,
leave a COMMENT TO SYSOP on
International Collectors Network RBBS
(213) 204-0646 2400/1200/300
- or -
by U.S.P.S.-mail,

Pro-Fun Nterprises
c/o Harry Rosenfeld
Post Office Box 88703
Los Angeles, CA 90009-8703

P.S. This list will be known as
Final Version "13" 04/25/87

3 = 300 baud ONLY / $ = Fees requested / # = Source of this list

201 332-6098	Jersey City, NJ	EDGELIGHT ON-LINE BBS Sailing & Skiing
201 641-6265	Hackensack, NJ	SEARS BUSINESS CENTER
201 963-3115	Hoboken, NJ	THE POLICE STATION TBBS
201 988-0706	Bradley Beach, NJ	THE MOUSE'S ELECTRONIC COTTAGE Books, Film & TV
202 377-3870	Washington, DC	THE ECONOMIC BULLETIN BOARD Office of Business Analysis, U.S. DC
202 537-7475	Washington, DC	FEDERAL NATIONAL MORTGAGE ASSOC. Real Estate, taxes section
202 547-4418	Arlington, VA	ASTRO RBBS Astronomy
202 586-9359	Washington, DC	INFOLINK Nuclear Waste Info

202 653-1079		Washington, DC	U.S. NAVAL OBSERVATORY
203 698-0588		Old Greenwich, CT	STARPORT - PARANET Paranormal, UFO's
203 954-0271		Hartford, CT	LIFE CONTROL NETWORK BBS Money, Health, Job, News
206 328-7876		Seattle, WA	CARDIOBOARD Medical
212 254-3190		New York, NY	NYU MEDICAL FIDO
212 333-3285		New York, NY	BILLBOARD Genealogy
212 409-4194		New York, NY	SOFTLAW RBBS For Lawyers
212 432-7288		New York, NY	MANHATTAN SOUTH Investments
213 204-0646	#	Los Angeles, CA	INTERNATIONAL COLLECTORS NETWORK Antiq/Comics/Coin/Cards/Stamp/etc & Shows
213 325-7269		Lomita, CA	FIND-A-HOME Roommate/Rent/Property Finder in So. CALIF
213 372-4050		Redondo Beach, CA	TELEWEB BBS Real Estate & Misc.
213 465-0676		Los Angeles, CA	HOLLYWOOD MIDNIGHT EXPRESS Indep. Writers of So. Calif. (IWOSC)
213 467-1650		Los Angeles, CA	CHRIST'S CORNER Religious
213 470-4678		Los Angeles, CA	BUY-PHONE L.A. Directory, Movie & Restaurant Guide
213 479-4074	$	Los Angeles, CA	COMPUTER CONSULTANT'S NETWORK
213 545-6528		Manhattan Bch, CA	LA SPORTS BOOK Horse Racing & Sports
213 553-1473		Beverly Hills, CA	LEGACY - THE LAW NETWORK
213 559-7306		Los Angeles, CA	TELECOM & SPORTS LINE
213 666-8588		Hollywood, CA	VIDEOMAN Hollywood Industry & Restaurants Guide

213 732-6935	$	Los Angeles, CA	DIGITAL VISION Digitized Graphics
213 734-4800		Los Angeles, CA	SAFESPACE NETWORK Exploration of Paranormal, Futurism
213 826-4288		Los Angeles, CA	MIDI WORLD NETWORK BBS Music & Computers
213 836-6439		Los Angeles, CA	THE <PG> BOARD Personal Growth, Controversial
213 851-0780	3	W. Hollywood, CA	AWARE II SPORTS EFX
213 869-1351		South Gate, CA	CAP DATA REPOSITORY Civil Air Patrol, Aviation
213 934-2567		Los Angeles, CA	ALGONQUIN ROUND TABLE Professional Writers
213 938-5532		Los Angeles, CA	NORTHROP ADVANCED SYSTEMS DIVISION Job Employment Openings
214 245-5633		Dallas, TX	AVIATION CONNECTION
214 331-8813		Dallas, TX	H.A. BURDEN & ASSOC. Real Estate
214 463-6581		Denison, TX	DOC'S OFFICE Dental
214 522-1963		Dallas, TX	LAWSIG Legal
214 578-1311		Plano, TX	CRIME PREVENTION BBS
214 578-8640		Plano, TX	TEXAS WING Aviation, CAP
216 368-3888		Cleveland, OH	DOC-IN-THE-BOX Medical
216 883-6298		Cuyahoga Hts, OH	RAILNET Railroad Hobbyists
301 261-1423		Annapolis, MD	FAMILY RADIO FORUM Christian
301 588-9079		Washington, DC	PBB Digitized Pictures

301 596-0123	Washington, DC	COMPUTERS FOR CHRIST Religious
301 995-0032	Columbia, MD	COMPUTERS FOR CHRIST Religious
303 223-1297	Fort Collins, CO	AMNET Animal Rights, Pet Care
303 426-4052	Denver, CO	CHRISTIAN PROTOCOL Religious
303 449-3306	Boulder, CO	BAHA'I BBS Religious
303 473-3837	Colorado Sprgs, CO	PIKE'S PEAK GS Genealogy
303 497-6968	Boulder, CO	FIDO Geophysics, Weather
303 673-7743	Louisville, CO	GRIZZLY KING BBS Outdoor Recreation
303 674-1859	Evergreen, CO	FIDO Music, Horses
303 963-3688	Roar'g Fork Vy, CO	TOP OF THE ROCKIES BBS Ski Info, Solar Energy
303 987-7388	Lakewood, CO	COMPUTER CRIME Police
305 260-6397	Longwood, FL	BLACK HOLE Astronomy
305 276-6263	Boca Raton, FL	BOCA BYTES Genealogy
305 395-1267	Boca Raton, FL	ORIGINAL H^VESTORS Investments
305 842-1861	Palm Beach, FL	MENSABBS MENSA Club
312 280-8764	Chicago, IL	AMERICAN ASSOC. OF INDIVIDUAL INVESTORS Investment Related
312 436-3062	Chicago, IL	AMNET Civil Liberties

312 532-8209	Chicago, IL	GREAT LAKES REGION CAP Aviation
312 598-0525	Chicago, IL	SPORTFIDO Sports
312 752-7412	Chicago, IL	CHICAGO NEWS
312 922-3626	Chicago, IL	EXCHANGE-NEWS-EX Financial, Stock & Future Traders
313 545-1931	Detroit, MI	P-1 FIDO Real Estate
313 675-7459	Detroit, MI	SO. WAYNE CO. Aviation, CAP
313 774-7258	Detroit, MI	FREEFORM Legal
314 442-6023	Columbia, MO	CHARLIE'S BBS Food, Wine, Dining
316 688-5329	Wichita, KS	MEDNET BBS Healthcare Professionals
317 452-1535	Kokomo, IN	BIBLE BOARD
317 494-6643	Lafayette, IN	FAST AGRIC. COMM. TERMINAL (FACTS) Farming information
319 377-2547	Dubuque, IA	THE BOARD Aviation
401 849-0529	Portsmouth, RI	PROVIDENCE RI IEEE BBS Electrical Engineering & Computer Science
404 351-9757	Atlanta, GA	MEDICAL FORUM
404 377-1141	Decatur, GA	ILLUMI-NET Paranormal & Conspiracy Theories
404 476-2607	Duluth, GA	THE RIGHT PLACE UPI News Bulletins
408 225-2303	San Jose, CA	CALIFORNIA WING, TTH Aviation, CAP
408 268-5157	San Jose, CA	NORAD Science (Not accepting NEW USERS)
408 293-7894	San Jose, CA	VIETNAM VETS - THE LOONEY BIN

408 659-3078		Monterey, CA	PHANTOM Genealogy
408 732-4126		Sunnyvale, CA	CONSUMERS BBS AND INSURANCE CENTER Information for car owners
408 778-3531		Morgan Hill, CA	THE SDI CLEARINGHOUSE Space Exploration & Development
408 946-4933		San Jose, CA	QUEST Genealogy
408 997-2790		San Jose, CA	COMPUTERS FOR CHRIST Religious
412 225-8682		Washington, PA	WASHINGTON PA PCB Legal Forum
412 571-0472		Pittsburgh, PA	ASTRAL BOARD Deja vu, Out of Body, Martial Arts
415 332-6106	$	San Francisco, CA	THE WELL Good Conferences & Variety
415 337-8693		San Francisco, CA	VAUDEVILLE LOCAL Vaudeville & Circus Acts
415 339-8457		Oakland, CA	GOURMET BBS Food, Wine, Dining Out
415 364-4339		Redwood City, CA	TRULY TASTELESS BBS Humor
415 366-9033		Redwood City, CA	SPIRITUAL WORLD Spiritual Development
415 439-2515	3	Pittsburg, CA	PHOTOBYTES Photography
415 487-0310		Hayward, CA	COMPUCHEM RBBS Scientific & Mathematical
415 540-0529		Oakland, CA	THE LIVE WIRE Graphic Artists
415 546-0119		San Francisco, CA	SUPER RESUME Free resume compositions for MIS pros.
415 552-9070		San Francisco, CA	ENTREPRENEURS BBS Community Entrepreneurs Organization

415 562-5483		Oakland, CA	FAMILY RADIO FORUM Christian
415 571-6160	$	San Mateo, CA	PRODUCTION WORLD Prof. Broadcast TV, Video, Film...
415 584-0697		San Francisco, CA	ROOTS BBS Geneaology
415 621-5206		San Francisco, CA	RECOVERY BBS Rehabilitation Help & Info.
415 626-1246		San Francisco, CA	AIDS INFORMATION BBS
415 651-9496		Fremont, CA	EARTH-RITE RBBS Earth religion
415 672-2504		Concord, CA	BANKER'S LIFE FIDO Real Estate
415 771-2051		San Francisco, CA	THE PLAYERS CLUB NETWORK Performing Arts
415 790-6311		Fremont, CA	RISK & INSURANCE MANAGEMENT BBS
415 824-8767		San Francisco, CA	NEWSBASE News & Information
415 837-4610		Danville, CA	TRANSFER STATION Real Estate
415 843-6853		Berkeley, CA	TAX HAVENS - OFFSHORE BBS Tax information
415 864-3858		San Francisco, CA	THE GUIDEBOARD Cabbie's guide to San Francisco
415 885-1973		San Francisco, CA	DR. DON'S TBBS Sportscar, sports players & fans
415 964-9039		Mountain View, CA	SPACE Astronomy
415 967-6730		Mountain View, CA	COMMSOFT Genealogy
501 864-0699		El Dorado, AR	COMPUTERS FOR CHRIST Religious
513 398-0928		Mason, OH	THE TRAIN BOARD Train Collectors

515 673-3763		Oskaloosa, IA	SKUNK RIVER BBS Paranormal, UFO's
516 741-6914		Long Island, NY	RAILROAD BBS
517 339-3783		Lansing, MI	POLITICAL FORUM Senator
518 283-4855		Albany, NY	EMPIRE STATE NETWORK Railroad Historical Societies
602 235-9653		Phoenix, AZ	HEALTH-NET St. Joesph Medical Center
602 275-6644		Phoenix, AZ	CALL-A-LAWYER
602 584-7395		Sun City West, AZ	SUNWISE Original Writing, Investment
602 837-0062		Fountain Hills, AZ	PARANET Exploration of the Paranormal
602 941-3747		Scottsdale, AZ	EYENET FIDO Bores Eye Institute
603 964-7912		Rye, NH	DOWNEAST ROOTS Genealogy
604 682-1991	3	Vancouver, B.C., CANADA	BUY-PHONE Electronic Yellow Pages
606 269-1565		Richmond, KY	PROF BBS Financial Analysis, Real Estate
606 886-9494		Prestonsburg, NY	THE SECURITY CONNECTION BBS Security Store
608 255-5227		Madison, WI	INDRANET BBS Buddhist
609 358-3965		Franklinville, NJ	TRI-STATE INFORMATION SYSTEMS Variety
609 652-6030	$	Atlantic City, NJ	THE CASINO BBS Casino Information
612 681-9520		Eagan, MN	ASTRONOMERS RBBS Astronomy
614 488-4736	$	Columbus, OH	GENEALOG Genealogy

617 489-4930		Boston, MA	YELLOWDATA Variety
617 641-1080	3	Lexington, MA	QUINSEPT Genealogy
619 224-2636		San Diego, CA	ADVENTURE BOARD Whitewater Rafting, Bicycling & Skiing
619 462-4607		Imperial Beach, CA	OFF THE WALL Aviation
619 486-1014		San Diego, CA	FAMILY HEIRLOOMS Genealogy
703 237-4322		McLean, WV	CRYPTOLOGIC RESEARCH
703 665-3066		Winchester, VA	PARANET Paranormal
703 971-4491		Silver Spring, VA	BULLET 'N BOARD Second Amendment Rights
704 554-1102		Charlotte, NC	THE JOB LIST BBS EDP Corp's DP Employment Board
707 545-0746		Napa Valley, CA	SURVIVAL COMMUNICATION FORUM FIDO
712 246-2115		Shenandoah, IA	FAMILY RADIO FORUM Christian
713 460-0806		Houston, TX	INTERSTELLAR BBS Galaxy Explorations
713 664-8425		Houston, TX	HOUSTON INLINE Sports, Movies, Online Leagues
713 847-2121		Houston, TX	THE SPORTSMACHINE Sports Enthusiast
714 359-3290		Riverside, CA	WORD OF LIFE Christian Bible & Church History
714 524-9326		Placentia, CA	PARANET FIDO Paranormal, UFO's
714 653-0494		Sunnymead, CA	F&W GUNS
714 884-4922		San Bernardino, CA	MICROLINK BBS Public Library

714 982-2200		Upland, CA	NATIONAL COUNCIL OF EXCHANGERS Real Estate
716 377-3985		Fairport, NY	5TH GENERATION SYSTEMS Paranormal, UFO's
717 253-4354		Honesdale, PA	DENTAL CONNECTION
717 677-9573		Gettysburg, PA	THE DEAD BOARD Grateful Dead music information
718 217-0898		Bayside, NY	PHARMSTAT Pharmacy Related
718 499-1633	3	Brooklyn, NY	ELECTRONIC CALL BOARD Performing Arts, Stage Shows
800 634-4433		Los Angeles, CA	REAL COMM BBS California Association of Realtors
800 835-3001		Reston, VA	PC PURSUIT Info on saving $ using your modem
801 321-5030		Salt Lake City, UT	LDS HOSPITAL
801 374-8080	$	Salt Lake City, UT	FAMILY TIES Genealogy
801 521-5966		Salt Lake City, UT	OUTER CHAOS 5 Genealogy
803 585-8575		Spartanburg, SC	ALLIANCE FRANCAISE Parlez vous Francaise?
804 445-1627		Norfolk, VA	NARDAC U.S. Navy
805 273-8476		Palmdale, CA	LAWBOARD
805 522-4211		Simi Valley, CA	COM-TRICKS Compact Disks
813 531-7340	$	Clearwater, FL	THE FABULOUS BBS Food & Beverage Industry
818 247-6343		Glendale, CA	COMPUCAST Talent Agency
818 363-3192		San Fernando, CA	CALL SHEET Entertainment Industry

818 368-3068	Northridge, CA	WORLD OF TOMORROW Physics
818 766-6442	N Hollywood, CA	THE HOTLINE/COMPUTER ENTERTAINER ONLINE Online Computer Info/Gen'l Interest
818 796-1519	Pasadena, CA	WORDS & MUSIC BBS Musicians, Writers, Music Related
818 988-0452	Van Nuys, CA	AUDIOPHILE NETWORK Music Lovers
914 221-0774	Hopewell Jctn, NY	SPORTS NETWORK
914 482-3693	Yonkers, NY	QUARK, THE ELECTRONIC FANZINE Science Fiction
915 592-5424	El Paso, TX	DISABILITY INTEREST GROUP
915 697-4561	Midland, TX	JERICHO ROAD BBS Christian
915 481-6320	Sacramento, CA	FAMILY RADIO FORUM Christian
916 685-8690	Elk Grove, CA	DYNASTY Genealogy
916 725-5510	Sacramento, CA	BIZ_NET Business & CEO's
919 235-3656	Bailey, NC	DOCTOR'S OFFICE Medical
919 737-3990	Raleigh, NC	SESAME Wildlife & Fisheries
919 893-5206 $	Buies Creek, NC	FROLIC & DETOUR BBS Lawyers Only

INDEX

C

D

E

F

G

N

O

P

Q

R

S

T

U

V

W

X

Z

More Computer Knowledge from Que

LOTUS SOFTWARE TITLES

Title	Price
1-2-3 QueCards	21.95
1-2-3 for Business, 2nd Edition	19.95
1-2-3 Business Formula Handbook	19.95
1-2-3 Command Language	21.95
1-2-3 Macro Library, 2nd Edition	21.95
1-2-3 Tips, Tricks, and Traps, 2nd Edition	19.95
Using 1-2-3, Special Edition	24.95
Using 1-2-3 Workbook and Disk, 2nd Edition	29.95
Using Lotus HAL	19.95
Using Symphony, 2nd Edition	24.95

DATABASE TITLES

Title	Price
dBASE III Plus Applications Library	21.95
dBASE III Plus Handbook, 2nd Edition	21.95
dBASE III Plus Advanced Programming, 2nd Edition	22.95
dBASE III Plus Tips, Tricks, and Traps	19.95
R:BASE Solutions: Applications and Resources	19.95
R:BASE System V Techniques and Applications	21.95
R:BASE System V User's Guide, 2nd Edition	19.95
Using Reflex	19.95
Using Paradox	21.95
Using Q & A	19.95

MACINTOSH AND APPLE II TITLES

Title	Price
HyperCard QuickStart: A Graphics Approach	21.95
Using AppleWorks, 2nd Edition	19.95
Using dBASE Mac	19.95
Using Dollars and Sense	18.95
Using Excel	19.95
Using Microsoft Word: Macintosh Version	19.95
Using Microsoft Works	18.95
Using WordPerfect: Macintosh Version	19.95

APPLICATIONS SOFTWARE TITLES

Title	Price
Smart Tips, Tricks, and Traps	23.95
Using Dollars and Sense on the IBM	18.95
Using Enable, 2nd Edition	22.95
Using Excel: IBM Version	19.95
Using Managing Your Money	18.95
Using Quattro	21.95
Using Smart	22.95
Using SuperCalc4	19.95

WORD-PROCESSING AND DESKTOP PUBLISHING TITLES

Title	Price
Microsoft Word Tips, Tricks, and Traps	19.95
Using DisplayWrite 4	19.95
Using Microsoft Word, 2nd Edition	19.95
Using MultiMate Advantage, 2nd Edition	19.95
Using PageMaker on the IBM	24.95
Using WordPerfect, 3rd Edition	19.95
Using WordPerfect 5	19.95
Using WordPerfect Workbook and Disk	29.95
Using WordStar	18.95
WordPerfect Tips, Tricks, and Traps	19.95
WordPerfect Advanced Techniques	19.95

HARDWARE AND SYSTEMS TITLES

Title	Price
DOS Programmer's Reference	22.95
DOS QueCards	21.95
DOS Workbook and Disk	29.95
IBM PS/2 Handbook	19.95
Managing Your Hard Disk	19.95
MS-DOS User's Guide, 2nd Edition	21.95
Networking IBM PCs, 2nd Edition	19.95
Programming with Windows	22.95
Understanding UNIX: A Conceptual Guide, 2nd Edition	21.95
Using Microsoft Windows	19.95
Using PC DOS, 2nd Edition	22.95

PROGRAMMING AND TECHNICAL TITLES

Title	Price
Advanced C: Techniques and Applications	21.95
C Programmer's Library	21.95
C Programming Guide, 2nd Edition	19.95
C Self-Study Guide	16.95
C Standard Library	21.95
Debugging C	19.95
Turbo Pascal for BASIC Programmers	18.95
Turbo Pascal Program Library	19.95
Turbo Pascal Tips, Tricks, and Traps	19.95
Using Assembly Language	22.95
Using Turbo Prolog	19.95

Que Order Line: **1-800-428-5331**

All prices subject to change without notice. Prices and charges are for domestic orders only.
Non-U.S. prices might be higher.

MORE COMPUTER KNOWLEDGE FROM QUE

Using Dollars and Sense

by John Hannah

Written for users of Apple II and Macintosh computers, this applications-oriented book from Que addresses the questions most commonly asked of Monogram's support line for business applications. In the home and small business, *Using Dollars and Sense* will teach you how to track your accounts, determine your net worth, and estimate your tax liability at any time of the year. Additional features include "hands-on hints" and actual examples of business applications representing different business styles.

HyperCard QuickStart: A Graphics Approach

by Richard Maran

Learn HyperCard quickly with Que's unique *HyperCard QuickStart: A Graphics Approach.* Over 100 full-page illustrations provide a detailed view of the HyperCard environment and help you rapidly become productive with the program. These graphics are designed for quick reference and reinforce all topics covered in the text. This fast-paced book shows you how to browse through and modify HyperCard stacks, enter text, and create graphics. If you're a HyperCard beginner, get on the HyperCard fast track with Que's *HyperCard QuickStart*!

Using Excel

by Mary Campbell

A comprehensive reference, *Using Excel* offers a thorough examination of Microsoft's powerful spreadsheet for the Macintosh 512K. The author provides plenty of examples and screen shots to help you understand and use all of Excel's capabilities, including advanced features such as data management, graphics, macros, and arrays. This book's practical, hands-on approach will have you using Excel productively sooner than you ever expected.

Mail to: Que Corporation • P. O. Box 90 • Carmel, IN 46032

Item	Title	Price	Quantity	Extension
182	Using Dollars and Sense	$18.95		
198	Using Excel	$19.95		
841	HyperCard QuickStart: A Graphics Approach	$21.95		

Book Subtotal ______

Shipping & Handling ($2.50 per item) ______

Indiana Residents Add 5% Sales Tax ______

GRAND TOTAL ______

Method of Payment:

☐ Check ☐ VISA ☐ MasterCard ☐ American Express

Card Number ______________________ Exp. Date ______________________

Cardholder's Name ______________________

Ship to ______________________

Address ______________________

City ______________________ State ______________ ZIP ______________

If you can't wait, call **1-800-428-5331** and order TODAY.

All prices subject to change without notice.

FOLD HERE

Place
Stamp
Here

Que Corporation
P.O. Box 90
Carmel, IN 46032

R106

REGISTRATION CARD

Register your copy of *Using Microsoft Works* and receive information about Que's newest products. Complete this registration card and return it to Que Corporation, P.O. Box 90, Carmel, IN 46032.

Name ____________________ Phone ____________

Company ________________ Title ____________

Address ________________________________

City ____________________ ST ______ ZIP ______

Please check the appropriate answers:

Where did you buy *Using Microsoft Works?*

- ☐ Bookstore (name: ____________________)
- ☐ Computer store (name: ________________)
- ☐ Catalog (name: ______________________)
- ☐ Direct from Que
- ☐ Other: ____________________________

How many computer books do you buy a year?

- ☐ 1 or less ☐ 6-10
- ☐ 2-5 ☐ More than 10

How many Que books do you own?

- ☐ 1 ☐ 6-10
- ☐ 2-5 ☐ More than 10

How long have you been using Microsoft Works?

- ☐ Less than six months
- ☐ Six months to one year
- ☐ More than one year

What influenced your purchase of this book? (More than one answer is OK.)

- ☐ Personal recommendation
- ☐ Advertisement ☐ Que catalog
- ☐ In-store display ☐ Que postcard
- ☐ Price ☐ Que's reputation

How would you rate the overall content of *Using Microsoft Works?*

- ☐ Very good ☐ Not useful
- ☐ Good ☐ Poor

How would you rate the *Quick Start tutorials?*

- ☐ Very good ☐ Not useful
- ☐ Good ☐ Poor

COMMENTS: ______________________

How would you rate the special information *notes?*

- ☐ Very good ☐ Not useful
- ☐ Good ☐ Poor

COMMENTS: ______________________

How would you rate the *shortcuts* sections?

- ☐ Very good ☐ Not useful
- ☐ Good ☐ Poor

COMMENTS: ______________________

What do you like *best* about *Using Microsoft Works?*

What do you like *least* about *Using Microsoft Works?*

How do you use this book?

What other Que products do you own?

What other software do you own?

Please feel free to list any other comments you may have about *Using Microsoft Works.*

____

____

____

____

FOLD HERE

Place
Stamp
Here

Que Corporation
P.O. Box 90
Carmel, IN 46032

*Registration Card